THE MARK TWAIN PAPERS

Mark Twain's Letters
Volume 2: 1867–1868

THE MARK TWAIN PAPERS AND WORKS OF MARK TWAIN
is a comprehensive edition for scholars of the private papers and published works of Mark Twain (Samuel L. Clemens).

THE MARK TWAIN LIBRARY
is a selected edition reprinted from the Papers and Works for students and the general reader. Both series of books are published by the University of California Press and edited by members of the

MARK TWAIN PROJECT
with headquarters in The Bancroft Library, University of California, Berkeley.

Editorial work for all volumes is jointly supported by grants from the

NATIONAL ENDOWMENT FOR THE HUMANITIES,
an independent federal agency,
and by public and private donations,
matched equally by the Endowment, to

THE FRIENDS OF THE BANCROFT LIBRARY

The following volumes have been published to date by the members of the Mark Twain Project:

THE MARK TWAIN PAPERS

Letters to His Publishers, 1867–1894
Edited with an Introduction by Hamlin Hill
1967

Satires & Burlesques
Edited with an Introduction by Franklin R. Rogers
1967

Which Was the Dream? and Other Symbolic Writings of the Later Years
Edited with an Introduction by John S. Tuckey
1967

Hannibal, Huck & Tom
Edited with an Introduction by Walter Blair
1969

Mysterious Stranger Manuscripts
Edited with an Introduction by William M. Gibson
1969

Correspondence with Henry Huttleston Rogers, 1893–1909
Edited with an Introduction by Lewis Leary
1969

Fables of Man
Edited with an Introduction by John S. Tuckey
Text established by Kenneth M. Sanderson and Bernard L. Stein
Series Editor, Frederick Anderson
1972

Notebooks & Journals, Volume I (1855–1873)
Edited by Frederick Anderson, Michael B. Frank, and Kenneth M. Sanderson
1975

Notebooks & Journals, Volume II (1877–1883)
Edited by Frederick Anderson, Lin Salamo, and Bernard L. Stein
1975

Notebooks & Journals, Volume III (1883–1891)
Edited by Robert Pack Browning, Michael B. Frank, and Lin Salamo
General Editor, Frederick Anderson
1979

Letters, Volume 1: 1853–1866
Editors: Edgar Marquess Branch, Michael B. Frank, and Kenneth M. Sanderson
Associate Editors: Harriet Elinor Smith, Lin Salamo, and Richard Bucci
1988

Letters, Volume 2: 1867–1868
Editors: Harriet Elinor Smith and Richard Bucci
Associate Editor: Lin Salamo
1990

THE WORKS OF MARK TWAIN

Roughing It
Edited by Franklin R. Rogers and Paul Baender
1972

What Is Man? and Other Philosophical Writings
Edited by Paul Baender
1973

A Connecticut Yankee in King Arthur's Court
Edited by Bernard L. Stein, with an Introduction by Henry Nash Smith
1979

The Prince and the Pauper
Edited by Victor Fischer and Lin Salamo, with the assistance of Mary Jane Jones
1979

Early Tales & Sketches, Volume 1 (1851–1864)
Edited by Edgar Marquess Branch and Robert H. Hirst, with the assistance of Harriet Elinor Smith
1979

The Adventures of Tom Sawyer · Tom Sawyer Abroad
Tom Sawyer, Detective
Edited by John C. Gerber, Paul Baender, and Terry Firkins
1980

Early Tales & Sketches, Volume 2 (1864–1865)
Edited by Edgar Marquess Branch and Robert H. Hirst, with the assistance of Harriet Elinor Smith
1981

Adventures of Huckleberry Finn
Edited by Walter Blair and Victor Fischer,
with the assistance of Dahlia Armon and Harriet Elinor Smith
1988

THE MARK TWAIN LIBRARY

No. 44, The Mysterious Stranger
Edited by John S. Tuckey and William M. Gibson
1982

The Adventures of Tom Sawyer
Edited by John C. Gerber and Paul Baender
1982

Tom Sawyer Abroad · Tom Sawyer, Detective
Edited by John C. Gerber and Terry Firkins
1982

The Prince and the Pauper
Edited by Victor Fischer and Michael B. Frank
1983

A Connecticut Yankee in King Arthur's Court
Edited by Bernard L. Stein
1983

Adventures of Huckleberry Finn
Edited by Walter Blair and Victor Fischer
1985

Huck Finn and Tom Sawyer among the Indians, and Other Unfinished Stories
Foreword and Notes by Dahlia Armon and Walter Blair
Texts established by Dahlia Armon, Paul Baender, Walter Blair, William M. Gibson, and Franklin R. Rogers
1989

OTHER MARK TWAIN PROJECT PUBLICATIONS

The Devil's Race-Track: Mark Twain's Great Dark Writings
The Best from Which Was the Dream? *and* Fables of Man
Edited by John S. Tuckey
1980

Union Catalog of Clemens Letters
Edited by Paul Machlis
1986

Samuel L. Clemens, 1868.
Mark Twain Papers, The Bancroft Library (CU-MARK).

THE MARK TWAIN PAPERS

General Editor, ROBERT H. HIRST

Contributing Editors for this Volume

DAHLIA ARMON
BETH BERNSTEIN
JANICE E. BRAUN
ROBERT PACK BROWNING
VICTOR FISCHER
MICHAEL B. FRANK
KENNETH M. SANDERSON
CRAIG STEIN

A Publication of the Mark Twain Project
of The Bancroft Library

MARK TWAIN'S
LETTERS
VOLUME 2 ❦ 1867–1868

Editors
HARRIET ELINOR SMITH
RICHARD BUCCI

Associate Editor
LIN SALAMO

UNIVERSITY OF CALIFORNIA PRESS
Berkeley · Los Angeles · London
1990

CENTER FOR
SCHOLARLY EDITIONS
AN APPROVED EDITION
MODERN LANGUAGE
ASSOCIATION OF AMERICA

Publication of this volume was assisted by
a grant from the

PUBLICATION SUBVENTION PROGRAM,
DIVISION OF RESEARCH PROGRAMS,
NATIONAL ENDOWMENT FOR THE HUMANITIES,
an independent federal agency.

University of California Press
Berkeley and Los Angeles, California

University of California Press, Ltd.
London, England

Manufactured in the United States of America

Library of Congress Cataloging-in-Publication Data

(Revised for vol. 2)

Twain, Mark, 1835–1910
Mark Twain's letters.
(The Mark Twain papers)
Includes bibliographical references and index.
Contents: v. 1. 1853–1866 — v. 2. 1867–1868.
1. Twain, Mark, 1835–1910—Correspondence.
2. Authors, American—19th century—Correspondence.
3. Humorists, American—19th century—Correspondence.
I. Branch, Edgar Marquess, 1913– . II. Frank, Michael B.
III. Sanderson, Kenneth M. IV. Title.
V. Series: Twain, Mark, 1835–1910. Selections. 1990.
PS1331.A4 1987 818'.409 87-5963
ISBN 0-520-03668-9 (v. 1 : alk. paper)
ISBN 0-520-03669-7 (v. 2 : alk. paper)

Editorial work for this volume has been supported by a gift to
The Friends of The Bancroft Library from

JANE NEWHALL

and by matching and outright funds from the

NATIONAL ENDOWMENT FOR THE HUMANITIES,
an independent federal agency.

Without such generous support, this volume could
not have been produced.

Contents

Acknowledgments

THE SUSTAINED and intensive editorial labor necessary for this volume was made possible by the generous support of the American taxpayer, and by the professional encouragement of scholars who recommended funding for successive grants to the Mark Twain Project from the National Endowment for the Humanities, an independent federal agency. The University of California Press was likewise assisted in meeting production costs by a grant from the Endowment. We are grateful for this intellectual and material support, part of which the Endowment was able to grant by matching, dollar for dollar, a major contribution to The Friends of The Bancroft Library from Jane Newhall.

In addition, many individual and institutional donors contributed funds that have been matched by the Endowment in its continuing support of the Mark Twain Project, especially during the last ten years. We are grateful to the Alcoa Foundation; Mrs. Kurt E. Appert; the Belvedere Scientific Fund; Stanley J. Bernhard; The House of Bernstein, Inc.; the Edmund G. and Bernice Brown Fund; the Louise M. Davies Foundation; Frances K. and Theodore H. Geballe; Richard and Rhoda Goldman; the Estate of Helen R. Goss; the Evelyn and Walter Haas, Jr., Fund; the Crescent Porter Hale Foundation; Constance Crowley Hart; the William Randolph Hearst Foundation; the Hedco Foundation; the Heller Charitable and Educational Fund; Clarence E. Heller; Mrs. Edward H. Heller; the Flora Lamson Hewlett Memorial Fund; Dr. Myra Karstadt; the Koret Foundation; Daniel E. Koshland, Jr.; Theodore H. Koundakjian; the Mark Twain Foundation; the Charles E. Merrill Trust; the New York Community Trust; the Pareto Fund; the Estate of Helen F. Pierce; William M. Roth; the San Francisco Foundation; the L. J. Skaggs and Mary C. Skaggs Foundation; Marion B. and Willis S. Slusser; the Henry Nash Smith Memorial Fund; the Marshall Steel, Sr., Foundation; the Thomas More Storke Fund; Mrs. Calvin K. Townsend; Tomas S. Vanasek; and the Wells Fargo Foundation.

The Mark Twain Committee of the Council of The Friends of The Bancroft Library is chiefly responsible for encouraging these and other private donors to lend their support to the ongoing editorial work of the Project. Our thanks go to the present and former members of this committee: John W. Rosston and Willis S. Slusser, co-chairmen; Henry K. Evers, Stephen G. Herrick, and David J. McDaniel, former chairmen; William P. Barlow, Jr., Henry M. Bowles, Launce E. Gamble, Marion S. Goodin, James C. Greene, Constance Crowley Hart, James D. Hart, Roger W. Heyns, Kenneth E. Hill, James E. O'Brien, Joseph A. Rosenthal, Herbert E. Stansbury, Jr., and Norman H. Strouse, as well as Kimberley L. Massingale, secretary to the Council.

Several generations of scholars have done pioneering work in locating, collecting, and publishing Mark Twain's letters. We are indebted to all of them, particularly to Albert Bigelow Paine and his successors as Editor of the Mark Twain Papers: Bernard DeVoto, Dixon Wecter, Henry Nash Smith, and Frederick Anderson. Paine's *Mark Twain: A Biography* (1912) and *Mark Twain's Letters* (1917) are indispensable to the present undertaking, and are the sole source now known for some letters collected here. Wecter's *Mark Twain to Mrs. Fairbanks* (1949) and *The Love Letters of Mark Twain* (1949) were the first to publish Mark Twain's letters in accord with contemporary scholarly standards, in both their annotation and their transcriptions of the letters themselves. Henry Nash Smith and William M. Gibson's *Mark Twain–Howells Letters* (1960) likewise established a new and higher standard for publication of letters. Anderson assisted Smith and Gibson on that publication and, until his death in 1979, was responsible for the Mark Twain Papers series, which included among its first volumes Hamlin Hill's *Mark Twain's Letters to His Publishers: 1867–1894*. We have profited from these pioneering efforts in ways too numerous to bear mention in the notes.

Editing Mark Twain's letters has required continuing and demanding assistance with the ongoing research. For valuable aid over many years we are grateful to the staff of The Bancroft Library, especially Brenda J. Bailey, Anthony S. Bliss, Peter E. Hanff, Irene M. Moran, and William M. Roberts. Special thanks go to Rhio Barnhart and his colleagues at the Interlibrary Borrowing Service in the Main Library: Robert Heyer, Leon Megrian, Jo Lynn Milardovich, Kathleen Messer, and Helen Ram. Their enthusiastic and untiring efforts located many rare and valuable resources that have notably enriched the annotation. We are similarly indebted to Philip Hoehn of the Map Room and Daniel L. Johnston of the Photographic Service in the Main Library for patient assistance with their special expertise.

The Mark Twain Papers in The Bancroft Library is the largest archive of the original letters published in this volume; this collection of Mark Twain's own private papers was brought to the University of California in 1949 through the persuasive powers of Dixon Wecter and the generosity of Clara Clemens Samossoud. Two additional archives are the primary sources of manuscript letters in this volume: the Jean Webster McKinney Family Papers in the Vassar College Library, Poughkeepsie, New York; and The Henry E. Huntington Library, San Marino, California. We would like to thank the staff at the Vassar College Library, who since 1977 have generously provided us with access to their Mark Twain materials and graciously answered our repeated requests for supporting documentation: Frances Goudy, Barbara LaMont, Nancy S. MacKechnie, Eleanor Rogers, and, above all, Lisa Browar (now Assistant Director for Rare Books and Manuscripts at the New York Public Library). At the Huntington, we received timely and expert assistance from Sara S. Hodson and David Michael Hamilton. We are grateful for the unfailing cooperation of all the other libraries that own letters published in this volume. In particular, we have benefited from the generous assistance of Julius P. Barclay, Joan Crane, and Michael Plunkett of the University of Virginia Library; Rosanne M. Barker and Elizabeth Witherell of the University of California Library in Santa Barbara; Carol Beales and Richard Reilly of The James S. Copley Library in La Jolla, California; and Radley H. Daly of the Scroll and Key Society, as well as Daria Ague, Donald Gallup, and Patricia C. Willis of the Beinecke Rare Book and Manuscript Library, at Yale University. We are likewise grateful to Todd M. Axelrod, Mrs. Robin Craven, Robert Daley, and Victor and Irene Murr Jacobs, who generously made accessible to us the letters in their collections. Special thanks are due to Mrs. Theodore Whitfield for permission to reproduce some of the photographs collected on the *Quaker City* excursion by her ancestor and Mark Twain's traveling companion, Colonel William R. Denny. Special thanks go likewise to William P. Barlow, Jr., whose uniquely comprehensive collection of auction catalogs afforded us the opportunity for an unusually thorough search for letters not known to survive elsewhere.

In the course of transcribing, annotating, and tracing the provenance of these letters we received invaluable assistance from the following, who have our thanks: Donald Anderle, Lisa Browar, and Valerie Wingfield of the New York Public Library, which kindly granted us permission to reproduce a Tribune Association check from "Personal Miscellaneous. Samuel Clemens"; Pat Akre of the San Francisco Public Library; Frank J. Carroll and James H. Hutson of the Library of Congress; Sandra Cronkhite, Historian of the Village of Fort Plain, New York; Marianne J. Curling, Diana Royce, and Laura Vassell of the Mark Twain Memorial in Hartford; Mrs. H. Dale Green of the Chenango County (New York) Historical Society; Jean Montgomery Johnson and Philip A. Metzger of Lehigh University Libraries; Jean Rainwater of Brown University Library; Ann K. Sindelar of the Western Reserve Historical Society in Cleveland; Lola Szladits of the Henry W. and Albert A. Berg Collection in the New York Public Library; Joan L. Sorger of the Cleveland Public Library; Gordon Struble of the Patten Free Library in Bath, Maine; and Herbert A. Wisbey, Jr., of the Elmira College Center for Mark Twain Studies at Quarry Farm. We also thank the following for their assistance with specific problems of transcription and annotation: Guido Carboni of Turin, Italy; Leon T. Dickinson; John E. Duncan; Michael Fahy; Wilson H. Faude; Alan Gribben; Hamlin Hill; Holger Kersten of Kiel, West Germany; M. A. Khouri and Muhammad Siddiq; Jervis Langdon, Jr.; Horace Levy; Coralee Paull; and Mary N. Shelnutt.

Throughout the process of design and typesetting for this volume we have had expert assistance from several people at the University of California Press: Fran Mitchell, who patiently guided the book through the production process; Albert Burkhardt, who developed the design of the book; and Sandy Drooker, who created the dust jacket and acted as a consultant in other design matters. Our typesetters, Wilsted & Taylor Publishing Services, Oakland, California, provided patient, knowledgeable help in developing the typographical aspect of the transcription system used to represent the texts of Mark Twain's letters. In addition to Christine Taylor and LeRoy Wilsted, we are indebted to Burwell Davis for his meticulous care and remarkable accuracy in setting the book into type. He was ably assisted by Michelle Elkin, Nancy Evans, Mark LaFlaur, Matthew Lasar, Rosemary Northcraft, Vivian Scholl, Jan Seymour-Ford, Fronia Simpson, Mary VanClay, and Sherwood Williams. Paul DeFrates and Allen McKinney of Graphic Impressions, Emeryville, California, provided excellent photographs for the illustrations and manuscript reproductions. Don L. Cook provided a perceptive and helpful inspection of the volume for the Modern Language Association's Committee on Scholarly Editions, which granted the volume its seal of approval in 1989.

Finally, we wish to thank our colleagues at the Mark Twain Project for generous, enthusiastic, and always expert assistance. We have profited from their advice in the several areas of special knowledge about everything from Mark Twain to the details of bookmaking. In a tradition that now stretches back twenty years into the past, they willingly shared the burdens of checking, collating, and proofreading. Dahlia Armon prepared the genealogies of the Clemens and Langdon families—the most complete now available—and shared her research on Mark Twain's 1868–69 lecture tour. Robert Pack Browning provided careful readings of transcriptions for letters now owned by individuals or libraries in Indiana, Ohio, New York, and several other states. Victor Fischer offered patient and exceptionally helpful advice about every stage of the editorial work, as well as his special knowledge of typography and design during the production process. Michael B. Frank's informed and judicious criticism of the annotation was invaluable. Kenneth M. Sanderson substantially improved the accuracy and clarity of the notes, and freely lent his special expertise with Mark Twain's handwriting to establishment of the letter texts. The *Union Catalog of Clemens Letters* (1986), edited by our former colleague Paul Machlis, was indispensable to the orderly preparation of this volume, as it will be for all subsequent volumes. Beth Bernstein performed essential research on the illustrations and contributed significantly to the discussion and resolution of textual problems. We offer our special thanks to Janice Braun for her expertise in locating rare research materials. Several other students—Scott Bean, Michele Hammond, Amy Michiko Horlings, Patrick Kingsbury, Esther Ma, Craig Stein, Deborah Ann Turner, and William R. Winn—gave generous support and aid in a variety of clerical and editorial tasks, greatly facilitating our work. We wish to thank our administrative assistant, Sunny Gottberg, who takes care of office business with persistence, resourcefulness, and patience. These colleagues and friends have made the task of editing Mark Twain's letters a congenial and rewarding experience.

H. E. S. R. B. L. S.

Introduction

THIS VOLUME opens with Samuel Clemens's first extant letter of 1867, an informal business proposal to Edward P. Hingston (Artemus Ward's manager), written just three days after his arrival in New York from San Francisco, and concludes with a very personal letter to Olivia L. Langdon (soon to be his fiancée), written on the last day of 1868, in which Clemens looked back on a period of enormous personal change:

> The Old Year is passing. . . . it found me a waif, floating at random upon the sea of life, & it leaves me freighted with a good purpose, & blessed with a fair wind, a chart to follow, a port to reach. It found me listless, useless, aimless—it leaves me knighted with noble ambition. It found me well-nigh a skeptic—it leaves me a believer. It found me dead—it leaves me alive. It found me ready to welcome any wind that would blow my vagrant bark abroad, no matter where—it leaves me seeking home & an anchorage, & longing for them. It found me careless of the here & the hereafter—it leaves me with faith in the one & hope for the other.

In the intervening two years, Clemens had taken the several decisive steps that would transform him from an itinerant journalist and lecturer, savoring his first fame, into an author on the threshold of achieving national celebrity, as well as acceptance into eastern affluent society. In the more than one hundred and fifty letters collected for the first time here—all that are known to survive from this period—Clemens set down the most detailed and candid account of this transformation that we are ever likely to have.

In December 1866 Clemens had sailed from San Francisco as an official traveling correspondent for the San Francisco *Alta California*, planning to proceed from New York eventually on a trip around the world. In the meantime he intended to lecture in several eastern cities, and also to publish a book about the Sandwich Islands, cobbled together from his recent dispatches to the Sacramento *Union*. Once in New York, he promptly fell in with members of its Bohemian community, chief among them his San Francisco friend Charles Henry Webb, who was well connected with eastern journals and a fledgling publisher himself. Webb in turn introduced Clemens to several other New York journalists, and to at least one New York publisher, George W. Carleton, who in the previous decade had published books by virtually every rising young American humorist. Early in February 1867 Carleton declined to publish a small collection of Mark Twain's western journalism, and so the author turned to Webb, who agreed to edit and to publish what became his first book, *The Celebrated Jumping Frog of Calaveras County, And other Sketches*, which made its appearance on about the first of May. Clemens also enlisted the support of another western friend, Frank Fuller, who volunteered to manage his New York lecture debut—a crucial event that was eventually planned to coincide with the publication of his book.

By the end of February Clemens had made another decision that would prove momentous. He recalled in 1910 that he "had long had a desire to travel and see the world, and now the platform had furnished me the means. So I joined the 'Quaker City Excursion'" (*WIM*, 462). This five-and-a-half-month chartered voyage to Europe and the Holy Land was organized by (and largely for) members of Henry Ward Beecher's Plymouth Church in Brooklyn—and widely supposed to include Beecher himself. Clemens agreed with his employers to double his production of travel letters to two per week while the trip lasted, in return for the cost of his passage and some of his other expenses. The *Quaker City* set sail in June and returned to New York in late November 1867, but not before hostilities just short of open warfare had developed between Clemens and some of the more "respectable" passengers. "They will blow their horns about the thousand places they have visited and get the lockjaw three times a day trying to pronounce the names of them," Clemens jeered in the *Alta*, "but never, never in the world, will they open the sealed book of the secret history of their memorable pilgrimage. And I won't—for the present, at any rate" (SLC 1868c).

Instead, Clemens rejoined the world of professional journalism, this time in Washington, D.C., where he also served (nominally) as private secretary to Senator William M. Stewart of Nevada. Before even half of the *Alta* letters could be published, however, Clemens was approached by Elisha Bliss, Jr. (of the American Publishing Company, a subscription house in Hartford, Connecticut), who offered to publish a book based upon them. The result, published in mid-1869, was *The Innocents Abroad:* "being some account of the steamship Quaker City's pleasure excursion to Europe and the Holy Land; with descriptions of countries, nations, incidents and adventures, as they appeared to the author"—or, in other words, a somewhat attenuated version of the "secret history" to which Mark Twain had provocatively alluded in the *Alta*. Its enormous success would secure for Elisha Bliss the role of Mark Twain's publisher for the next ten years.

While some members of the *Quaker City* excursion unwittingly provided Mark Twain with a subject worthy of his powers, several others became his friends. Particularly important was Mary Mason Fairbanks, a well-educated and socially respectable matron from Cleveland, who clearly recognized Clemens's talent. With his eager cooperation she became a literary and social mentor, encouraging him to be "funny without being vulgar" (p. 188). She also took in hand Charles J. Langdon, a youth of nineteen whom Clemens likewise befriended, and who introduced Clemens to his family—including his older sister Olivia—when they visited New York City later that year. More than seven months elapsed, however, before Clemens could take advantage of Charles's invitation to visit the Langdons at their home in Elmira. During that time he became embroiled in a dispute with his *Alta* employers over the right to reuse his newspaper letters in the book. To secure their permission, he made a sudden business trip to California, where he also lectured again. Having reached a satisfactory agreement with the *Alta*, he remained briefly in California to finish the manuscript for his book, with the editorial help of his old friend Bret Harte. In July 1868 he departed San Francisco—for what would prove to be the last time—and was soon in Hartford, where he delivered his manuscript to Bliss.

In late August Clemens took the train to Elmira, where he fell precipitously in love with Olivia Langdon. He now began a long campaign, first to win her affection, then to prove himself worthy of it—which is to say, to earn the approval of her devoted and protective parents. The letters Clemens wrote almost daily to Olivia, beginning in September, mark an unmistakable change of voice. They are among the longest letters he ever wrote, much more intimate and self-examining than any that preceded them. In the end, however, they are perhaps best regarded simply as typical love letters. "Courtship lifts a young fellow far and away above his common earthly self," Clemens wrote in 1899, "and by an impulse natural to those lofty regions he puts on his halo and his heavenly war-paint and plays archangel as if he were born to it. He is working a deception, but is not aware of it" (*WWD*, 170). Clemens's letters to Olivia in these initial months of their courtship document his efforts to rise to her level—to reform his rough habits, overcome his religious skepticism, and adopt a more conventional, self-consciously Christian way of life. He may well have been working a deception about his own character and beliefs—but it is impossible to read these letters without realizing that if he was, he was not aware of it at the time.

With the counsel of a new friend, the Reverend Joseph Twichell of Hartford, and the continuing support and guidance of Mrs. Fairbanks, Clemens soon prevailed with Olivia—but satisfying her family would take longer. The end of 1868 found the former "Wild Humorist of the Pacific Slope" touring eastern and midwestern towns and cities to lecture on "The American Vandal Abroad," anticipating publication of his first major book, and longing for marriage and domesticity.

H. E. S. R. B.

Editorial Signs

THE EDITORIAL conventions used to transcribe Mark Twain's letters were designed, in part, to enable anyone to read the letters without having to memorize a list. The following is therefore offered less as a necessary preliminary than as a convenient way to look up the meaning of any convention which, in spite of this design, turns out to be less than self-explanatory. Only the editorial conventions used in this volume are given here, since each new volume will require a slightly different list. New or newly modified conventions are identified by an asterisk (*). Not included are the typographical equivalents used to transcribe Mark Twain's own signs and symbols in manuscript. For those equivalents, and for a more discursive explanation of editorial principles, see the Guide to Editorial Practice on pp. 479–506.

EDITORIAL HEADING

From . . .	Clemens is named in the heading only when he wrote jointly with someone else.
. . . with a note to . . .	Used when two persons are addressed in the same letter, but Clemens intended the second to read *only* the briefer part, or "note."*
per . . .	Precedes the name or identity of the amanuensis or agent who inscribed the document sent or received.
2? May	On this day—give or take a day.
1–3 May	On any day (or days) within this span.
1 and 2 May	On both days.

(MS) — The source document is the original letter, almost invariably Clemens's holograph manuscript.

(*damage emended*) — The source document has sustained significant damage, and the transcription therefore includes, without brackets, emendation to restore the affected text.

(MS facsimile) — The source document is a photographic facsimile of the MS, not the MS itself.

(*Paraphrase*) — The source document preserves some of the *words* of the original letter, but is manifestly not a deliberate transcription of it.

(Transcript) — The source document is a printed, handwritten, or typed (TS) transcription of the letter, not necessarily made at first hand.

Letter Text

NEW-YORK — Extra-small small capitals with no initial capitals signify printed text *not* originated by Clemens, such as letterhead or the postmark.

Feb. 13, — Text above a dotted underscore was inscribed in a printed blank in the original document.

. . . . — Editorial ellipsis points (always centered in an otherwise blank line) signify that an unknown amount of the original letter is judged to be missing.

[ruled border] — Ruled borders are an editorial device to represent the edge of a document, usually printed or partly printed, such as a telegram blank or newspaper clipping.

a two cance- deletions, — Cancellation is signified by slashes for single characters (and underscores), rules for two or more characters.

Well, *I* pass. — A hairline rule signifies a mock, or pretended, cancellation: words lightly and distinctively crossed out, easily read, and often still necessary to the sense.*

marking it ^up^	Insertion is signified by a single caret for single characters, two carets for two or more characters.
shaded words	Gray background identifies parts of a letter originated and inscribed by someone other than Clemens.
{ }	Author's square brackets are transcribed this way to avoid any confusion with editorial brackets.
[ ]	Editorial square brackets enclose [*editorial description*]; words or characters omitted by the writer an[d] now interpolated by [the] editors; and text modified by description, such as [*in margin:* All well].
◇iamond	The diamond stands for a character, numeral, or punctuation mark the editors cannot read because it is physically obscured or entirely missing.
double=hyphen	The hyphen is to be retained. Single hyphens at the ends of lines therefore signify division only.*
Sam*l*	Superscript ell is always italicized to prevent confusion between one (^{1}) and ell (^{l}). The sign ⁓ transcribes the author's paraph.
✉———	The envelope and full-measure rule signal that everything transcribed below them was written, stamped, or printed on the envelope or on the letter itself at the time of transmission or receipt.
|	Signifies the end of a line in the source document.

Letters: 1867–1868

NO LETTERS have been found for the month between 15 December 1866, when Clemens departed San Francisco for New York (by way of Nicaragua), and 15 January 1867, three days after his arrival, when he wrote the first letter in this volume. Most of what is known about that voyage, therefore, comes from one of Clemens's notebooks and from eight dispatches about the trip published by his employer, the San Francisco *Alta California:* one letter from Nicaragua, plus one telegram and six additional letters from New York (*N&J1*, 238–99; SLC 1867b–e, 1867h–i, 1867k–*l*).

It was a memorable trip. The first night out from San Francisco a violent storm nearly swamped the *America*, terrifying the passengers in steerage and making virtually everyone seasick. "Happily I escaped," Clemens observed, "had something worse." This unnamed illness kept him confined, though not completely solitary, both before and during the voyage. On 28 December he reached San Juan del Sur and, after a two-day trek overland, arrived at Greytown, where he boarded the *San Francisco*, bound for New York. On 2 January, one day out of Greytown, cholera struck. By 5 January three were dead and a fourth mortally ill. Thinking of the most recent victims—"both so well when I saw them yesterday evening"—Clemens wrote in his notebook, "I ~~almost~~ realize that I myself may be dead to-morrow" (*N&J1*, 245, 277).

Seven nerve-racking days later, on 12 January, the *San Francisco* steamed into New York harbor; by then seven had died (four from cholera), and there had probably been more deaths among the twenty-one passengers who fled the ship at Key West. Mark Twain described his arrival for the *Alta:*

> We swore the ship through at quarantine, which was right—she hadn't had any real cholera on board since we left Greytown—and at 8 o'clock this morning we stood in the biting air of the upper deck and sailed by the snow-covered,

wintry looking residences on Staten Island—recognized Castle Garden [in the Battery]—beheld the vast city spread out beyond, encircled with its palisade of masts, and adorned with its hundred steeples—saw the steam-tug and ferry-boats swarming through the floating ice, instinct with a frenzied energy, as we passed the [East] river—and in a little while we were ashore and safe housed at the Metropolitan. (SLC 1867*l*)

He stayed for nearly three weeks at the Metropolitan Hotel, well known as the "resort of Californians and people from the new States and Territories." It was a large, six-story brownstone building on the northeast corner of Broadway and Prince Street, capable of housing six hundred guests and "furnished throughout in the most splendid and costly style." Mark Twain classed it among the "great caravan hotels" that did "an immense transient business (try to get a room at one of them if you doubt it)." Since 1852 it had contributed to the fortunes of the Leland brothers (Charles, Simeon, Warren, and William), whom Clemens did not know, although he knew and liked two members of the second generation—Jerome B. and Lewis Leland, proprietors since 1863 of the Occidental Hotel—"Heaven on the half shell"—in San Francisco (Browne, 394; Morris, 5–6; James Miller, 66–67; SLC 1867aa; "Obituary. Charles Leland," New York *Times*, 20 Oct 85, 2; *ET&S1*, 474; *ET&S2*, 10, 367, 564).

New York itself had greatly changed since the first time Clemens saw it, in the summer of 1853, "when I was a pure and sinless sprout." For one thing, it was more expensive: you could pay as much as "$30 a week for the same sort of private board and lodging you got for $8 and $10 when I was here thirteen years ago." It was also more spread out, more populous—and, of course, colder. From the time of his arrival the temperature hovered around 25°F, and a heavy snowfall snarled the city on 17 January (SLC 1867n, 1867p; New York *Tribune:* "The Snow Storm," 18 Jan 67, 4; "The Weather," 31 Jan 67, 5). A New York correspondent of the San Francisco *Evening Bulletin* said on 24 January that he had met Mark Twain "a few days after his arrival" and

found him shivering and chattering his teeth at the "damnation cold weather," and complaining of the "infernal long distances" he had to travel in getting about the city from one place to another. He said he had already frozen two of his teeth, had corns on all his fingers, and a gum-bolt on each heel, and he almost regretted that he had ever wandered away from the clear skies, the balmy atmosphere, and the umbrageous shades of the Washoe country. . . . but it will, doubtless, be gratifying intelligence to his numerous friends on the Pacific Coast to learn that he bears up nobly under these trials and smiles unconcernedly at them as a true humorist should. In proof of this I need only state, that as I was about parting with him I said: "Marcus, will you smile?" whereat, without the least hesitation, he replied: "W-a-l, it[']s s-o d-a-r-n-a-t-i-o-n c-o-l-d I d-o-n-t c-a-r-e if I do." ("Gossip from New York," letter dated 24 Jan, San Francisco *Evening Bulletin*, 19 Feb 67, 1)

Clemens had at least three separate projects that required his walking such "infernal long distances." He was trying to publish a book based on his 1866 dispatches from the Sandwich Islands. He was intending to lecture in New York, and perhaps in other eastern cities. And he was bent on finding a New York (or at least an eastern) journal with a large circulation, willing to pay him well for regular contributions.

Between 1864 and 1866 he had published some work in the New York *Sunday Mercury*, the New York *Saturday Press* (now defunct), and (most recently) the New York *Weekly Review* and *Harper's New Monthly Magazine*. He now returned to some of these journals, while also exploring the New York *Evening Express*, the *Tribune*, the *Herald*, and Street and Smith's *New York Weekly*, among others. What he wanted, as he told a friend a year later, was "a paper that will give me room according to my strength—& pay me double price" (*ET&S1*, 347–56; SLC 1866d, 1866f–g; 25 Jan 68 to Bowen).

The Sandwich Islands book had been publicly urged upon Mark Twain (no doubt with his collusion) less than two weeks after he returned to San Francisco from Honolulu on 13 August 1866. It was probably his friend James F. Bowman—poet, journalist, and editor pro tem of the *Californian*—who wrote:

THERE SEEMS TO BE a very general impression that Mark Twain's Sandwich Island letters to the Sacramento *Union* possess sufficient intrinsic interest and value to justify their publication in book form. If the writer could be persuaded to collect and revise them, he would have no difficulty in finding a publisher; and we are satisfied that the book would prove both a literary and a pecuniary success. (*Californian* 5 [25 Aug 66]: 1)

On 2 October Clemens told his San Francisco lecture audience that "his object in delivering this lecture was to obtain funds which would enable him to publish an account of the Sandwich Islands in the form of a volume, with illustrations by [Edward] Jump," a French-born caricaturist with a modest local reputation. Probably by the time he reached New York, Clemens had arranged and presumably edited clippings of his *Union* letters, turning them into at least the rough manuscript for a book. His search for a publisher, however, would be harder than Bowman predicted: no sign until May has been found that anyone even agreed to consider the manuscript, which never was published (SLC 1866e; "Academy of Music," San Francisco *Dramatic Chronicle*, 3 Oct 66, 3; Hart, 216; *N&J1*, 109).

Clemens's expectations about lecturing in the East, and especially in New York, rested on the general encouragement (and caution) of his San Francisco colleagues, and on a few invitations from eastern cities which he received before departing. Bret Harte wrote the Springfield (Mass.) *Republican* after Mark Twain's first San Francisco lecture that he was "urged by his friends to extend his tour even to the East" (Stewart, 263). And the *Evening Bulletin* noted that Mark Twain was going East

> to attend to the publication of a book on the Sandwich Islands, and probably to try lecturing in a wider field. He will have the good wishes of a host of friends and admirers in California and Nevada, and if considerate enough for the social and aesthetic differences between this side of the continent and the other the author will achieve a gratifying success. ("Mark Twain's Lecture," San Francisco *Evening Bulletin*, 17 Nov 66, 5)

On 4 December, Clemens himself mentioned an invitation to lecture in Philadelphia, and he reportedly had offers from the "Mercantile Library Associations" of Cincinnati and St. Louis. A rudimentary scheme for an eastern lecture tour may even be detectable in what the *Alta* said in December about his travel plans: after arriving in New York, Clemens intended first to "visit the home of his youth—St. Louis," then to go "through the principal cities to the Atlantic seaboard again," and thence to Europe (SLC to JLC and family, 4 Dec 66, *L1*, 369; "Pen and Scissors," Virginia City *Territorial Enterprise*, 8 Dec 66, 2; "'Mark Twain's' Farewell," San Francisco *Alta California*, 15 Dec 66, 2).

No such royal progress would occur. In fact, Clemens needed to find a manager before he could undertake even a brief lecture tour. He also needed to decide exactly when to lecture in New York, and how (if at all) to change the lecture itself, in view of "the social and aesthetic differences" between western and eastern audiences. He soon discovered, however, that these differences were not necessarily what he or his friends supposed. On 2 February, he recorded his new perspective in an *Alta* dispatch written after seeing a performance of the *Black Crook*—notorious for its nearly naked "clipper-built girls": "Don't you suppose those friends of mine in San Francisco were jesting, when they warned me to be very choice in my language, if I ever lectured here, lest I might offend?" (SLC 1867n).

In choosing a manager, Clemens ultimately relied on the loyalty and enthusiasm of a friend—Frank Fuller (1827–1915). Born in Boston, Fuller studied to be a physician, then a dentist, before taking work as a newspaperman. In 1861 Lincoln appointed him secretary of Utah Territory under Acting Governor Francis H. Wootton, but he very soon became acting governor himself when Wootton left the territory. In 1906 Clemens mistakenly recalled meeting Fuller for the first time in Salt Lake City, in 1861, while he and Orion were en route to Nevada. (In fact, the Clemens brothers had departed Salt Lake on 7 August, a month before Fuller arrived there on 10 September.) Fuller himself remembered that they first met in Virginia City in 1862, sometime after Clemens joined the *Enterprise* staff in early October. Fuller also recalled that he later visited California, "found Mark Twain there," and they "became quite intimate. That was in 1863. He was writing chiefly for the Morning Call." But this greater intimacy may well have developed as late as 1864: even though Clemens was in San Francisco in May and June 1863, when he arranged to correspond from Virginia City for the *Call*, he did not become the *Call*'s local reporter until May 1864. Soon thereafter Fuller returned East, for by November 1865, along with Herman Camp and one other partner, he had opened a "Mining Bureau for all parts of the Continent" in New York City. In January 1867 he was still in New York but otherwise employed, "ensconced in a fine suite of offices at 57 Broadway . . . as Vice President of the Northern Pacific Railroad Company" ("Frank Fuller Dead; Utah War Governor," New York *Times*, 20 Feb 1915, 5; *Portsmouth Census*, 740; Whitney, 2:25, 104; AD, 11 Apr 1906, CU-MARK, in *MTA*, 2:350; "Matters at Salt Lake City," San Francisco *Evening Bulletin*, 16 Sept 61, 3; Rogers, 49; Fuller to A. B. Paine, 11 Jan 1912, Davis 1956, 1–2; Fuller, 5:10; "Letter from New York," San Francisco *Evening Bulletin*, 2 Dec 65, 1).

Paine reported that "Clemens had hunted up Fuller on landing in New York in January, and Fuller had encouraged the lecture then; but Clemens was doubtful," saying, "I have no reputation with the general public here. . . . We couldn't get a baker's dozen to hear me" (*MTB*, 1:312). The time of this exchange is confirmed by the *Evening Bulletin* correspondent who met Clemens "a few days after his arrival" in January, for Clemens told him then that a "committee of the most distinguished D.D.'s and L.L. D.'s had already waited on him in the sixth story of the Metropolitan Hotel . . . to request him to deliver the aforesaid lectures [on the Sandwich Islands] at Keeter Pooper's [that is, Peter Cooper's] Institute" ("Gossip from New York," letter dated 24 Jan, San Francisco *Evening Bulletin*, 19 Feb 67, 1). The identities of these "distinguished" persons are not known, but Fuller was probably one of them, for in April, when he was acting as Clemens's lecture manager, he summoned Californians to a meeting in support of Mark Twain "By order of the Committee" ("Special Notices," New York *Herald*, 28 and 29 Apr 67, 1).

Also in January, Clemens's plan to publish a Sandwich Islands book was preempted by a suggestion from yet another longtime friend, who urged him to publish a collection of his California and Nevada newspaper sketches. "I had but a slender reputation to publish it on," he recalled in 1906, "but I was charmed and excited by the suggestion and quite willing to venture it if some industrious person would save me the trouble of gathering the sketches together" (AD, 21 May 1906, CU-MARK, in *MTE*, 143). That "industrious person" was Charles Henry Webb (1834–1905), founder and editor (alternating with Bret Harte) of the *Californian* (1864–66).

Webb had preceded Clemens to New York by several months. On 30 May 1866 he reported that both Mark Twain and Bret Harte were even then much "appreciated" in the city, and he predicted "a warm welcome and open field" for both whenever they came East. When Clemens arrived at the Metropolitan on 12 January, Webb was already installed in rooms at 643 Broadway, just two blocks further uptown (*L1*, 314 n. 5, 374 n. 3; Webb 1866, 1867). Their first New York meeting occurred within days and was fondly remembered: "My, how that January day in your rooms in Broadway comes back!" Clemens reminisced to Webb in 1896; "there was a 'reporter's cobbler' there, & much cheer, & some young men who are old men now or dead—& all this was twenty-nine years ago. It was there that I first saw Ned House." He recalled elsewhere that he "saw House frequently during 3 or 4 months—from Jan. 15, 1867 onward—but the intercourse was not close enough to be called a friendship" (SLC to Webb, 16 Feb 96, CtY-BR†; SLC to Dean Sage, 5 Feb 90, ODaU†).

Edward Howard (Ned) House (1836–1901) was then a music and drama critic for the New York *Tribune*. He had been among the so-called

Bohemians associated with Henry Clapp, Jr. (1814–75), and he had contributed to Clapp's *Saturday Press* along with writers like William Winter (1836–1917) and Artemus Ward (Charles Farrar Browne, 1834–67), among others. As House himself said in May, the name "Mark Twain" was not utterly unknown to him even at their first meeting. He could easily remember the time in 1865 when "a communication entitled 'Joe Smiley and his Jumping Frog,' with the hitherto unknown signature of 'Mark Twain,' appeared in *The Saturday Press*. . . . the style of the letter was so singularly fresh, original, and full of character as to attract prompt and universal attention among the readers of light humorous literature" (Browne, 153–57; House, 2).

Clemens said in 1906 not only that Webb suggested he publish a "volume of sketches," but also that he "undertook to collate the sketches" for him (in *MTE*, 144). It is by now clear, however, that Clemens did much of this work himself. He had brought with him a scrapbook of his clippings from the *Californian* and the Virginia City *Territorial Enterprise*, from which most of the printer's copy for *The Celebrated Jumping Frog of Calaveras County, And other Sketches* would soon be drawn. He had probably compiled this scrapbook a year earlier, while still in San Francisco, shortly after Harte suggested that he "club a lot of old sketches together with a lot of his, & publish a book together" through a "New York publisher" (SLC to JLC and PAM, 20 Jan 66, *L1*, 328). This collaboration with Harte did not materialize, and by early 1867 Harte had decided to publish a volume, largely made up from his own *Californian* sketches, through George W. Carleton (1832–1901). For his part, Clemens soon began to follow Webb's suggestion for a book, making a tentative selection from his scrapbook, crossing out or revising every clipping in it—adjusting the diction and removing allusions to death, damnation, and drink—in order to avoid offending the supposedly more refined taste of his eastern audience (*ET&S1*, 503–46).

To Edward P. Hingston
15 January 1867 • New York, N.Y.
(MS: PBL)

Metropolitan Hotel,
New York, Jan. ~~16.~~15.

Friend Hingston—

I have been lecturing to crowded houses at Platt's Hall, the Academy of Music and Congress ~~$~~ Hall, in San Francisco, & as soon as I get my illustrated book on the Sandwich Islands in the hands of the printers, I am going to lecture here on California & perhaps on other subjects. ~~That~~

I want you to come and engineer me. Ward is so well established in London, now, that he can easily spare you till you have given me a start. You & Artemus both owe me a good turn for old acquaintance sake.[1]

I have several invitations to lecture—in Cincinnati, Boston & St Louis, but I don't want to start till I can start on a sure basis & not crucify myself through managerial inefficiency.

If you will come & get the ~~houses~~ audiences for me, I will engage to send them home d—d well satisfied—which is a great deal for a modest man to say.

State your terms & come along. Don't throw off on a fellow.

Give Artemus my love & tell him I am glad of his success & feel grateful to old England for her generous appreciation & kindly treatment of one of our boys.[2]

Yrs with great affection & distinguished consideration,, God be with us all, amen,

Mark Twain.

~~Room~~ Metropolitan ‸Hotel‸
New York

[*letter docketed in ink:*] Mark Twain

[1]Edward Peron Hingston (1823?–76), an Englishman, was an experienced theatrical agent and manager. Between 1856 and 1863 he had worked for the

"Wizard of the North" (John Henry Anderson, a popular magician) on tours of Australia and the United States. From 1863 to 1865 he had been the agent and friend of Artemus Ward on his American tour, as well as, since June 1866, in England. Hingston also helped John Camden Hotten become Ward's English publisher, even providing prefaces for Hotten's editions. Clemens had enjoyed several days of revelry with Hingston and Ward in December 1863, when Ward's American tour brought them to Virginia City (*L1*, 269–70 n. 5). In this letter to Hingston, he mentioned his own recent lectures not in chronological order, but in the descending order of their paid attendance. Hingston knew what it meant to command a "crowded house" at Platt's Music Hall (as Mark Twain had on 16 November) because three years before, Ward had done the same thing: Hingston recalled in *The Genial Showman* that the price of admission was "one dollar, and the receipts exceeded one thousand six hundred dollars." Clemens estimated his own paid attendance in Platt's Hall at fourteen hundred, while both Maguire's Academy of Music (which he filled on 2 October) and Congress Hall (which he filled on 10 December) were smaller, with crowds estimated at twelve to thirteen hundred and seven to eight hundred, respectively. He also recalled that from these lectures he "amassed twelve or fifteen hundred dollars," which "was about half—the doorkeeper got the rest," an allusion to Denis McCarthy, his manager at the time (Boase, 1:63, 1482–83; Seitz, 121–29, 170, 176, 184; Hingston, 299–300; SLC to James Redpath, 22 Jan 71, NN-B†; " 'Mark Twain's' Lecture," *Californian* 5 [6 Oct 66]: 5; "Mark Twain's Lecture," San Francisco *Morning Call*, 11 Dec 66, 1; AD, 11 Apr 1906, CU-MARK, in *MTA*, 2:351).

[2]In June 1866 Edward House escorted his ailing fellow Bohemian Artemus Ward to England, where he was met by Hingston. Ward found a warm welcome among the artists, writers, and wits of the Savage Club. His contributions to *Punch* brought him to the attention of a more general public, and when he opened his lecture on the Mormons at the Egyptian Hall in Piccadilly, on 13 November, his success was instantaneous, as well as highly profitable—probably at least $1,000 (in gold) each week. Despite his worsening tuberculosis, Ward continued to lecture through 23 January, when he was at last persuaded to rest, leaving London for the island of Jersey and ultimately for Southampton (Hingston, 515–19; Seitz, 184–222; "The Last Days of Artemus Ward," San Francisco *Alta California* supplement, 23 Apr 67, 3). In a letter that Clemens said he had "just received" from London on 23 February, Hingston presumably declined the request to become Mark Twain's manager, even as he reported that

> poor Artemus has caved in, through desperate ill health, and caved, too, just as the London "season" is on the point of commencement and all shows about to become Gould and Curry mines. He is rusticating at the seaside. The hope is that he will be well in a week or two and able to reappear. (SLC 1867p)

But Ward did not resume performing in London: on 6 March he died at Southampton.

To Mary E. (Mollie) Clemens
2? February 1867 • New York, N.Y.

(MS: NPV)

New York, Feb.

Dear Mollie—

I have tried several times to see your man here, but have not caught him in. His place is three miles from my rooms, & it is like Orion's thoughtlessness to put business in my hands when he knows I abhor everything in the nature of business & don't even attend to my own. I will have to get even with him for this, somehow. He could have this all attended to by writing to the man instead of to me. Time presses me mighty hard, here, & you know it destroys a whole day to make only a single visit in New York. However, Judge Dixson stays within 3 blocks of the Bowling-green, & he is going to attend to it for you. He will do it right, too, & I would be apt to do it wrong.[1]

I am going down to Washington next week, I think, & shall be there a month, no doubt.[2]

Several newspaper men have called on me & made me good offers—a little above what they pay anybody else~~,~~ ‸in my line‸—but I have not closed with any of them yet.[3] The Californians in town have almost ~~p~~ induced me to lecture, but I'll not do it yet. I won't until I have got my cards stocked to suit me. It is too hazardous a business for a stranger. I am not going to rush headlong in & make a fiasco of the thing when I may possibly make a success of it by going a little slow.

Give a "God bless you" to all my old friends if any still abide in Keokuk, & receive thou my blessing also, my sister.

Yr Bro

Sam

[1] Clemens's "rooms" at the Metropolitan Hotel during January were not "three miles," but only one and a half miles north of Bowling Green. By 2 February, however, Clemens had moved further uptown, for he mentioned in an *Alta* dispatch of that date that he was living "in East Sixteenth street," an address that would put him easily two and a half miles from Bowling Green. In the same dispatch, he also said that "Judge Dixson . . . of Carson" was then in the city, and he groused that in New York you could not "accomplish anything in the way of business, you cannot even pay a friendly call, without devoting a whole day

to it. . . . Many business men only give audience from eleven to one; therefore, if you miss those hours your affair must go over till next day" (SLC 1867n). The contents of the dispatch and of this letter are so similar that it seems likely Clemens wrote both on about the same date. Orion's "business" presumably concerned his stock in the Mount Blanc Gold and Silver Consolidated Mining Company, which operated its mine at American Flat, near Virginia City, and maintained a secretary (or agent) in New York—Edmund G. Sheppard, whose office was at 2 Bowling Green. In July of the previous year, while still in California, Orion had asked for an "advance" against what the trustees expected to receive for one-half of his stock in the mine, in order to pay for the trip home and for whatever arrangements he was attempting to make concerning the Clemens family's Tennessee land (Wilson 1866, 923; OC to Joseph A. Byers, 12 July 66, author's copy, CU-MARK). He and Mollie arrived in New York on 19 September, where they had a "wandering, sight-seeing stay of a few days." Orion may then have visited Sheppard (as he had promised trustee Joseph A. Byers he would) in order to reassure Sheppard that his motive for selling was not skepticism about the mine itself—a necessary step, since that had been his reason in 1864 for resigning as president of the company ("Passengers Arrived," New York *Tribune*, 20 Sept 66, 3; OC 1866a; OC to L. G. A. Coursolles, 26 Aug 64, author's copy, CU-MARK). Orion spent all of January and February in Tennessee, attending to the family property there (OC 1867c–e). Presumably his expenses now obliged him to ask for another advance against part or all of his remaining stock. He may have asked for Clemens's help through Mollie, who was staying with her parents in Keokuk. Clemens, in turn, entrusted this delicate matter to a friend: Judge Edward C. Dixon of Carson City. Orion had known Dixon well since at least August 1862, when they were both elected trustees of Carson's First Presbyterian Church. Dixon had served as probate judge of Ormsby County from December 1861 until July 1863, when he resigned on being appointed county commissioner; and in 1864 he represented Lander County in the territorial House of Representatives (Angel, 215, 529; "The Territorial Legislature," Virginia City *Evening Bulletin*, 8 Jan 64, 3).

2Clemens did not go to Washington, but remained in New York until his departure for St. Louis on 3 March (SLC 1867t). He implied in a later letter that one aim of this February plan was to "gouge" a government office for Orion out of Senator William M. Stewart (7 June 67 to JLC and family).

3Within a month, however, Clemens had "closed" with at least three such offers. On 3 March the *Sunday Mercury* published "The Winner of the Medal" by "that prince of humorous sightseers, Mark Twain, whose contributions to California light-literature have gained him a front-rank position among the sparkling wits of the Land of Gold" (SLC 1867f). It was to be the first of seven sketches Mark Twain published in the *Mercury* that year, the last being "Jim Wolf and the Tom-Cats," published on 14 July. Clemens recalled in 1900 that "early in 1867" he was "offered a large sum to write something for the *Sunday Mercury*, & I answered with the tale of 'Jim Wolf & the Cats'"—evidently forgetting the other six sketches, which show the strain of adjusting to an eastern audience. He also remembered that he "collected the money for it—twenty-five dollars," which "seemed over-pay." It seems a fair surmise that publishers William Cauldwell and Horace P. Whitney paid Mark Twain twenty-five dollars for each of the seven sketches in their *Sunday Mercury*, which had a circulation of about 65,000 at this time (Wilson 1866, 173, 750, 1082; Rowell, 177; SLC 1900, 30; see also SLC 1867j, 1867m, 1867q, 1867s, 1867cc–dd). On 5 March the sturdy and profitable *Evening Express* published "Barnum's First Speech in Congress" on page one. Nothing is known of Mark Twain's arrangements, if any, with editor and publisher James and Erastus Brooks, and nothing else by Mark Twain has been found in the *Express*, which had a circulation of under 5,000 (SLC 1867g; Wilson 1866, 127, 750; Rowell, 172). On 7 March the *New York Weekly* announced that it had "made an engagement with the celebrated 'Mark Twain,' the California wit and humorist, who will furnish us with a series of his inimitable papers." Beginning with the following issue it published five of Mark Twain's letters from the Sandwich Islands (the last on 27 June), without mentioning that they had already been published in the Sacramento *Union*. Clemens classed the *New York Weekly* among the papers that paid "splendidly," but nothing more precise is known about what proprietors Francis S. Street and Francis S. Smith offered him for the opportunity to reprint some of his work. Street and Smith, however, made no secret about their "liberal use of money in securing the best literary talent," or about the *Weekly*'s circulation, which was, for example, publicly attested at 92,695 copies for the 16 May issue (1 June 67 to JLC and family; Street and Smith's *New York Weekly:* "Another New Engagement," 7 Mar 67, 4; "A Galaxy of Talent," 6 June 67, 4; "Our Circulation!" 13 June 67, 4).

To John McComb
2?–7 February 1867 • New York, N.Y.

(*Paraphrase:* San Francisco *Alta California*, 15 Mar 67)

CALIFORNIAN AUTHORS.—In a private letter to the ALTA, "Mark Twain" says he has compiled a volume of his sketches for publication, but will get some literary friend to look it over before giving it to Carleton, the publisher. "Mark" says Carleton has in press a volume of Bret Harte's "Condensed Novels," which will be issued shortly.[1]

[1] The "private letter to the ALTA" was surely to John McComb (1829–96), who, after working as foreman on the *Alta* for many years, had recently become its "supervising editor" as well as one of its four owners. He was largely responsible for getting Mark Twain his current assignment as the newspaper's "SPECIAL TRAVELLING CORRESPONDENT," and for some time had been a consistent champion of Mark Twain's literary ambitions, specifically his ambition to publish a book. "If you don't like the treadmill work of a newspaper man," he reportedly said in 1864, "strike up higher; write sketches, write a book; you'll find a market for your stuff" (Langley 1862, 263; Langley 1867, 329; "The Alta California," Virginia City *Territorial Enterprise*, 4 Nov 66, 2; Brooks 1902, 225; SLC 1867h;

ET&S1, 28). In the *Alta*'s review of Mark Twain's second San Francisco lecture, it was probably McComb who wrote, in part:

If he would only commit to paper, for publication, the passage descriptive of the scene from the peak overlooking the crater his reputation as a "fine writer" would jostle his eminent renown as a humorist. In his promised book on the Sandwich Islands we shall eagerly look for these and other bursts of eloquence. ("Mark Twain's Lecture," 17 Nov 66, 1)

This letter (like the previous one) repeated news also found in Mark Twain's *Alta* dispatch of 2 February, namely that "Bret Harte's capital Condensed Novels are in press here." Although probably written on or about that date, it might have been written as late as 7 February, which would have left Clemens just enough time to show his compilation to "some literary friend" and to meet with George Carleton about publishing it, since Carleton himself left New York for Havana on 9 February (SLC 1867n; "Passengers Sailed," New York *Times*, 10 Feb 67, 8). Clemens's statement that he had "compiled a volume" of sketches refers to the rough printer's copy for what soon became the *Jumping Frog* book. It is his only known admission that he himself played a part in producing that book, which he elsewhere said or implied was compiled and edited exclusively by Webb: "I have made no suggestions" (SLC 1867w; see also SLC 1867x). The "literary friend" alluded to here might be Edward House, but is much more likely to be Webb. According to Clemens, it was Webb who made "an appointment for me with Carleton," his own publisher. In 1876 Clemens told a friend that "Carleton insulted me in Feb, 1867" when he rejected the *Jumping Frog* book (AD, 21 May 1906, CU-MARK, in *MTE*, 144; SLC to William D. Howells, 26 Apr 76, NN-B, in *MTHL*, 1:132). Many years later still, in 1906, he described, with undiminished bitterness, the encounter in Carleton's offices at 499 Broadway. He recalled that he "meekly asked [the clerk] the privilege of a word with Mr. Carleton, and was coldly informed that he was in his private office." When Clemens was finally allowed to enter this inner sanctum, Carleton "rose and said brusquely and aggressively, 'Well, what can I do for you?' "

I reminded him that I was there by appointment to offer him my book for publication. He began to swell, and went on swelling and swelling and swelling until he had reached the dimensions of a god of about the second or third degree. Then the fountains of his great deep were broken up, and for two or three minutes I couldn't see him for the rain. It was words, only words, but they fell so densely that they darkened the atmosphere. Finally he made an imposing sweep with his right hand which comprehended the whole room and said, "Books—look at those shelves. Every one of them is loaded with books that are waiting for publication. Do I want any more? Excuse me, I don't. Good morning." (AD, 21 May 1906, CU-MARK, in *MTE*, 144–45)

Carleton's memory of this exchange was less detailed, for obvious reasons, but just as lasting. William W. Ellsworth reported in 1919 that one of Carleton's "stories was that Mark Twain came into his store and offered him the manuscript of 'The Jumping Frog' and that he declined it 'because the author looked so disreputable' " (Ellsworth, 222). But in 1906 Mark Twain recalled that some years after his original offense, Carleton called on him,

shook hands cordially, and said at once, without any preliminaries, "I am substantially an obscure person, but I have a couple of such colossal distinctions to my credit that I am entitled to immortality—to wit: I refused a book of yours, and for this I stand without competitor as the prize ass of the nineteenth century."

Calling it "a most handsome apology," Mark Twain acknowledged that as "a long delayed revenge" it was still "sweeter to me than any other that could be devised"

(AD, 21 May 1906, CU-MARK, in *MTE*, 145). Bret Harte's *Condensed Novels. And Other Papers*, although "in press" as early as February, was not announced by Carleton until June, and not published until October (advertisement, *American Literary Gazette and Publishers' Circular* 9 [1 June 67]: 87; "New Publications," Boston *Evening Transcript*, 4 Oct 67, 2).

No letters have been found between the previous letter to John McComb and the following telegram, probably sent on 2 March to the proprietors of the San Francisco *Alta California*. When Clemens's early February interview with Carleton was not successful, Webb "bravely said that not all the Carletons in the universe should defeat that book; he would publish it himself on a ten per cent. royalty. And so he did" (AD, 21 May 1906, CU-MARK, in *MTE*, 145).

Before taking this step, however, Webb or Mark Twain evidently offered the manuscript to other publishers, for on 20 July the editor of the New York *Citizen*, Charles Graham Halpine (1829–68), better known as Private Miles O'Reilly, asserted that Mark Twain's " 'book,' in the form in which he had prepared it, was refused on all sides." And in 1889 Webb himself boasted of publishing the *Jumping Frog* book, "which the regular publishers to whom it was offered one and all refused" ("The San Francisco *Californian* . . . ," New York *Citizen*, 20 July 67, 3; Webb to Edmund Clarence Stedman, ca. 1889, AAA, lot 71). Despite Mark Twain's various statements to the contrary, he probably worked closely with Webb on the final selection and revision of his sketches, but he left New York for St. Louis on 3 March, well before either man had seen the proofs. The events that precipitated this abrupt departure occurred toward the end of February.

At the end of January, it had been announced in the New York press and widely repeated in newspapers across the country that (as the *Alta* noted on 30 January) the "members of Beecher's congregation are organizing an excursion to the Holy Land, Crimea and Greece. They propose to charter a steamer, and leave in June. Rev. Mr. Beecher and family go with them." Henry Ward Beecher (1813–87) was arguably the most famous minister in the country—a prominent figure among the liberal clergy whom Clemens had recently referred to as "the fast nags of the cloth" ("By Telegraph," San Francisco *Alta California*, 30 Jan 67, 1; SLC to JLC and family, 4 Dec 66, *L1*, 368).

In the *Atlantic Monthly* for January 1867, James Parton identified Beecher's Plymouth Church in Brooklyn as "simply the most characteristic thing of America."

If we had a foreigner in charge to whom we wished to reveal this country, we should like to push him in, hand him over to one of the brethren who perform the arduous duty of providing seats for visitors, and say to him: "There, stranger, you have arrived; *this* is the United States, the New Testament, Plymouth Rock, and the Fourth of July,—*this* is what they have brought us to. What the next issue will be, no one can tell; but this is about what we are at present." (Parton, 41)

Clemens, in fact, had a letter of introduction to Beecher. It is not known whether he used the letter at this time, but clearly he did submit himself to one of the "brethren" Parton describes. On 3 February he took the ferry across the ice-choked East River (when "the thermometer was at 180 degrees below zero"), apparently at the invitation of "a New York editor" who had authorized his use of "pew No. 46." The editor was probably Moses Sperry Beach (1822–92) of the New York *Sun*, a long-time member and former trustee of Plymouth Church who, with his daughter Emeline (1850–1924), would soon be among the "most prominent Brooklynites" to make the Holy Land trip (SLC to JLC and family, 4 Dec 66, *L1*, 368; SLC 1867o; "Obituary Notes," New York *Times*, 4 Mar 1924, 19; Hirst and Rowles, 15–17).

By the end of February, Mark Twain had been "bitten by the prospectus" that outlined the plans for this novel undertaking (SLC 1904, 75; see Appendix B). In a letter written on 2 March, he described these plans for his *Alta* readers:

Prominent Brooklynites are getting up a great European pleasure excursion for the coming summer, which promises a vast amount of enjoyment for a very reasonable outlay. The passenger list is filling up pretty fast.

The steamer to be used will be fitted up comfortably and supplied with a library, musical instruments and a printing-press—for a small daily paper is to be printed on board. The ship is to have ample accommodations for 150 cabin passengers, but in order that there may be no crowding, she will only carry 110. The steamer fare is fixed at $1,250, currency. The vessel will stop every day or two, to let the passengers visit places of interest in the interior of the various countries, and this will involve an additional expense of about $500 in gold. The voyage will begin the 1st of June and end near the beginning of November—five months—but may be extended by unanimous vote of the passengers. . . . Isn't it a most attractive scheme? Five months of utter freedom from care and anxiety of every kind, and in company with a set of people who will go only to enjoy themselves, and will never mention a word about business during the whole voyage. It is very pleasant to contemplate.

Several details in this summary show that Mark Twain was not relying solely on the published prospectus, but had learned of such things as the printing press and daily newspaper on board from some more current source. He explained that he had visited the excursion office sometime in late February, accompanied by "a *Tribune* man," for the purpose of making "some inquiries" about the trip. The *Tribune* man was Edward House, and Mark Twain reported that they "were received at the office of the concern with that distant politeness proper toward men who travel muddy streets on foot" and "go unshaven." Without warning, House introduced his companion as "the Rev. Mark Twain, who is a clergyman of some distinction, lately arrived from San Francisco," and went on to say that because he was "a Baptist," they were concerned that he might not be welcome, "inasmuch as Mr. Beecher is a Universalist"—an exaggeration of Beecher's liberal views (SLC 1867r).

The butt of this crude hoax was Captain Charles C. Duncan, the excursion manager and later the captain of the *Quaker City*. Paine said that this story, "though often repeated by Mark Twain himself," was "mainly apocryphal" (*MTB*, 1:311). But Duncan's daughter recalled,

> When Mr. Clemens came . . . to enquire about the cruise, he was with a friend. Both had had drinks, and . . . he announced himself as a Baptist minister.
>
> Said Captain Duncan, "You don't look like a Baptist minister and really, Mr. Clemens, you don't smell like one either!" (Gingrich, 6)

And, sometime in February 1877, Duncan himself was rash enough to speak publicly about it, thereby drawing Mark Twain's fire in the New York *World:*

> The "captain" says that when I came to engage passage in the Quaker City I "seemed to be full of whiskey, or something," and filled his office with the "fumes of bad whiskey." I hope this is true, but I cannot say, because it is so long ago; at the same time I am not depraved enough to deny that for a ceaseless, tireless, forty-year public advocate of total abstinence the "captain" is a mighty good judge of whiskey at second-hand.

Claiming indifference to Duncan's charges, Clemens added: "Why should I worry over the 'bad whiskey?' I was poor—*I* couldn't afford good whiskey. How could I know that the 'captain' was so particular about the quality of a man's liquor?" (SLC 1877).

In his 2 March letter to the *Alta* Mark Twain reported: "I went back yesterday with another friend, acknowledged my true occupation, entered my name for the voyage and paid the forfeit money required to secure a berth—the remainder of the $1,250 is not to be paid till the 15th of April, when all such accounts have to be squared" (SLC 1867r). The "forfeit money" was $125, according to the prospectus, which indicated that "no passage [was] considered engaged until ten per cent. of the passage money is deposited with the treasurer," Rufus R. Graves (Charles C. Duncan 1867a). Presumably on the same day Clemens announced the payment of his deposit, he also sent his telegram to the *Alta* proprietors.

To the Proprietors of the San Francisco *Alta California*
2? March 1867 • New York, N.Y.

(*Paraphrase:* Wallace et al., 333)

One day the proprietors of that journal were astonished to receive from him this curt message: "Send me $1,200 at once. I want to go abroad."[1]

[1]The proprietors of the *Alta* at this time were Frederick MacCrellish, William Augustus Woodward, Orlando M. Clayes, and John McComb. MacCrellish (1828–82) went to California from Pennsylvania in 1852 and was first associated with the San Francisco *Ledger* and *Herald*. In late 1854 he became the commercial editor of the *Alta* and, two years later, part owner. Woodward (1829?–85), also originally from Pennsylvania, went to San Francisco in 1856 and two years later became MacCrellish's partner. The two men were also brothers-in-law, having married sisters. Woodward remained a part owner of the *Alta* until it was sold in 1884. Clayes (1837–92) was a native of Illinois who moved to California in 1855 and was for many years associated with the *Independent*, a paper published first in San Andreas and later in Stockton; in 1864 he was elected state printer (Langley 1867, 132, 313, 508; masthead, San Francisco *Alta California*, 2 Mar 67, 1; "Death of Frederick MacCrellish," San Francisco *Morning Call*, 1 Nov 82, 1; San Francisco City and County 1867, s.v. "Woodward, William Augustus"; "Death of a Former Proprietor of the Alta California," Sacramento *Union*, 18 Apr 85, 1; Kemble, 190, 331; "Orlando M. Clayes," San Francisco *Morning Call*, 24 June 92, 8). Noah Brooks (1830–1903), then "managing editor" of the *Alta*, recalled the perplexity caused by this telegram, the surviving text of which may be incomplete. When the owners came to Brooks

> with a proposition that the office should advance to Clemens the sum needed to pay his expenses on a trip into the Mediterranean, on condition that he should write letters to the paper, I was not surprised that they should regard the scheme with grave doubt of its pay-

ing them for their outlay. But the persuasiveness of Clemens's fast friend and admirer, Colonel John McComb (then a member of our editorial staff), turned the scale, and Mark Twain was sent away happy on his voyage. (Brooks 1898, 98)

The first extant sign that the owners had taken this decision occurred on 9 April, when they published the *Alta* letter written on 2 March, which concluded its report of the trip as follows: "I expect to go on this excursion to the Holy Land and the chief countries of Europe, provided I receive no vetoing orders from the ALTA—and against all such I fervently protest beforehand.—[No veto. He has been telegraphed to 'go ahead.'—EDS. ALTA.]" (SLC 1867r). Although written on 2 March, this letter must not have left New York until the steamer of 11 March; it therefore arrived in San Francisco on 2 April aboard the *Montana* ("From Panama," San Francisco *Alta California*, 3 Apr 67, 1). Clemens clearly had time to write a longer letter of explanation, but no sign that he did so has been found.

To Charles Henry Webb
19 March 1867 • St. Louis, Mo.

(MS: ViU)

St Louis, M[ch] 19.

Friend Webb—

Everything is going well here, with the pilots, & I shall see that the same is the case with the New Orleans river men.[1]

Telegraph me ~~the~~ what date you expect to publish, & if it is to be more than ten days hence, I had better lecture here. I have been invited, & I have promised to give the committee an answer just as soon as you can telegraph me from N. Y. about the book. If you ‸are to‸ publish before March is out, though, I will preach in N. Y. first.[2]

Yrs Truly
Mark
1312 Chesnut street
St Louis.[3]

[1] Clemens left New York on "the New Jersey Central at 8 P.M." of 3 March and arrived in St. Louis at midnight on the night of 5 March: "I went straight home and sat up till breakfast time, talking and telling other lies" (SLC 1867t). Clemens's remark that things were "going well here, with the pilots" may indicate that he was publicizing his forthcoming *Jumping Frog* book among his friends on the river; no mention of the book has been found, however, in the river columns of St. Louis or New Orleans newspapers at this time.

[2]When Clemens departed New York, both he and Webb expected to publish in a matter of weeks. On 8 March the New York *Evening Post* reported that Webb was "about to publish" the book ("New Books," 1). In reply to Clemens's letter, however, Webb must have telegraphed that it could not be published until sometime in April. He probably named no exact date, for he did not register the book for copyright (as "The Jumping Frog of Calaveras County") until a month later, on 15 April, and Clemens did not specify a publication date until he wrote the *Alta* from New York on 19 April, naming 25 April, which would prove optimistic by five or six days (*ET&S1*, 542–43; SLC 1867w). Mark Twain explained, in another *Alta* dispatch, that on 17 March he had been asked to "make a few remarks" to a Sunday school, and that he "told that admiring multitude all about Jim Smiley's Jumping Frog," which in turn led to a more formal invitation. "I did not intend to lecture in St. Louis, but I got a call to do something of that kind for the benefit of a Sunday School." On 25 March he delivered his Sandwich Islands lecture before an overflow crowd of about one thousand at Mercantile Library Hall, for the benefit of the South St. Louis Mission Sunday School. The St. Louis *Republican* registered a typical reaction, which Mark Twain quoted for his California readers: "The audience was large and appreciative. . . . He succeeded in doing what we have seen Emerson and other literary magnates fail in attempting. He interested and amused a large and promiscuous audience" ("Mark Twain's Lecture on the Sandwich Islands," St. Louis *Missouri Republican*, 26 Mar 67, 3; SLC 1867u). Clemens repeated the lecture in the same hall on 26 March but, evidently because of bad weather, to an audience he later estimated at about eighty. Publicity both for and from these two lectures soon prompted at least three further invitations to lecture in towns along the river, which he accepted, starting with Hannibal, where on 2 April he lectured in Brittingham Hall "to the largest and most delighted crowd ever gathered in a public hall in that city." He then spoke at Keokuk, Iowa, on 8 April and at Quincy, Illinois, on 9 April (Emerson had spoken in both towns during February) (Fatout, 71–73; "The Veritable Individual Himself," Quincy *Herald*, 4 Apr 67, in Davis 1979, 1; Quincy *Herald:* "Mark Twain," 5 Apr 67, 4, and "Lecture Report," 17 Apr 67, 4; Bower, 4).

[3]The three-story brick house at this address was the residence of Clemens's widowed sister, Pamela Ann Moffett. The Moffetts had first rented the house in 1860; although forced to move when the owner briefly took possession during the war, they soon returned. The household at this time included (in addition to Pamela) Clemens's niece, Annie (aged fourteen), and nephew, Sammy (aged six); his mother, Jane Lampton Clemens; a German maid, Margaret; and possibly his brother Orion, who was back from work on the Tennessee land by 11 March, but may have left for Keokuk to see his wife by the date of this letter (*MTBus*, 47; Webster, 1; OC 1867e).

To Howard Tucker
11 April 1867 • St. Louis, Mo.
(MS: IaK)

St Louis, Ap^l 11,/67.

Howard Tucker Esq

Dr Sir—

I hasten to acknowledge the receipt of $35 from the Library Association, in full of all moneys due me from the proceeds of the lecture delivered by me on the 8th ins't.[1]

The "Mark Twain's" referred to are all right, now—I forgot them when I left Keokuk. Notwithstanding your damaging surmises, they are all the family I have got—or am aware of, at any rate.[2]

Remember me kindly to Mr Bower[3] & believe me

Yrs Truly
Sam Clemens

[1] Howard Tucker (b. 1829 or 1830), a hardware dealer in Keokuk, was the treasurer of the Keokuk Library Association, which sponsored Mark Twain's lecture at the Chatham Square Methodist Episcopal Church on 8 April. Admission was $.50, and since the association cleared $34.75 to Mark Twain's $35.00, attendance was about one hundred and forty (*Keokuk Census*, 22; OC 1857, 71; *History of Lee County*, 654; "Mark Twain's Lecture," Keokuk *Gate City*, 7 Apr 67, 4; Keokuk *Constitution*, 7 Apr 67, cited in Lorch 1929, 510; Bower, 4).

[2] It is not known what "Mark Twain's" Clemens "forgot" when he left Keokuk after a five-day stay. He had arrived at the Deming House in Keokuk four days before his lecture on 8 April; dissatisfied with the service there, he moved the next day to the Tepfer House ("Mark Twain," Quincy *Herald*, 5 Apr 67, 4; "Arrivals at the Tepfer House—April 5th.," Keokuk *Gate City*, 6 Apr 67, 4; SLC 1867w). It seems likely that Orion was also in Keokuk at this time, in order to visit Mollie, but his presence has not been demonstrated. Surely Clemens saw Mollie and her parents, William and Mary Stotts, as well as his "favorite companions" of old—Eleanor J. (Ella) Patterson and his second cousin Mary E. (Ella) Creel—both aged twenty-six or twenty-seven. In 1910, Margaret W. Patterson recalled for Clemens the time he "came to see us with the two Ellis, Creel and Patterson. Well it was evening and we had good Apples in the celler . . . you offerd to go with me to open a barall which we did, and had a good sociel time. . . . you were full of your expected trip to the Holy land" (*L1*, 101–2 n. 4; Margaret W. Patterson to SLC, 9 Jan 1910, CU-MARK).

[3] Robert F. Bower (b. 1824), a wholesale grocer in Keokuk since 1856, had been an important founding member of the Keokuk Library Association in

1863. As its current president, he introduced Clemens to his audience on 8 April. Bower recalled in 1882 that Clemens began by saying, "If I were as grand a specimen of manhood as the gentleman who has just introduced me, you might expect a magnificent lecture" (*Keokuk Census*, 35; *History of Lee County*, 654, 685; Keokuk *Constitution*, 18 May 82, quoted in Lorch 1929, 509).

To Alice J. Hyde
11 April 1867 • St. Louis, Mo.

(MS: CU-SB)

In my old home,
St Louis, Mo, Apl 11.

Dear Miss Alice[1]—

You remember I promised you, a long time ago in the Sandwich Islands, that I would ~~asc~~ be sure to get you a silver sword when I ascended Haleakala.[2] I got it *away down in the old crater*, & used to try to think to send it to you, but always recollected it at some unseasonable hour.

Packing my trunk to-night (for I leave to-morrow for New York, &, I suppose, for Europe a month later,) I came across the old swords, & hasten to send them, begging at the same time that you will excuse my characteristic negligence. I *had* to send them—I wouldn't consider the Island trip complete with so chivalrous a promise, so knightly a deed as the disarming of a crater many times larger than myself & the laying of his weapons at the feet of a lady, unaccomplished. How's that? I think I'll put that in my lecture.

Remember me kindly, & many, many times, to Mrs. Hyde,[3] & believe me

Your Obliged serv't
Upon many pleasant Occasions,
Sam. L. Clemens

[1] Alice (1844?–78) and her mother (see note 3), of San Francisco, were fellow passengers with Clemens on the *Ajax* when he sailed to the Hawaiian Islands in

March 1866. Alice was still unmarried when she was killed in an accident in 1878 (*New York Census* 1850, 244–45; "Passengers," Honolulu *Pacific Commercial Advertiser*, 24 Mar 66, 2; Langley 1867, 263; "Terrible Runaway Accident" and "Died," San Francisco *Alta California*, 12 Mar 78, 1, 4).

[2]The silversword plant (*Argyroxiphium sandwichense*) is found only in the high-altitude areas of the islands of Maui and Hawaii. The base of its tall central flower stem is surrounded by a dense head of slender, rigid, daggerlike leaves, eight to sixteen inches long, which are covered with silvery hairs. "In Hawaii the gathering of a silversword corresponds with the gathering of the edelweiss in the Alps, and furnishes the adventurous climber a prize well worth keeping as a memento of a trip that invariably costs much in exertion if not in actual peril" (William Alanson Bryan, 229). Clemens hiked up to the summit of Haleakala, a 10,023-foot-high dormant volcano with a crater 2,720 feet deep, during his visit to Maui from mid-April to 22 May 1866; his description of the trip may be found in chapter 76 of *Roughing It* (*N&J1*, 100).

[3]Jane V. B. Hyde (1811?–85) and her husband, William F. Hyde (1799?–?1858), a merchant, had five children, of whom Alice was the second youngest. They moved from New York City to San Francisco in December 1851. Alice's oldest brother, Henry Clay Hyde (b. 1835), became a prominent San Francisco attorney (*New York Census* 1850, 244–45; "Will of Jane V. B. Hyde," San Francisco *Morning Call*, 30 Dec 85, 1; Langley 1858, 162; Langley 1859, 157; Langley 1860, 174; Langley 1867, 263; Rasmussen, 2:131–32, 3:32–33; San Francisco City and County 1867, s.v. "Hyde, Henry Clay").

To Jane Lampton Clemens and Family
15 April 1867 • New York, N.Y.

(MS: ViU)

New York, Apl. 15.

Dear Folks—

I need not have hurried here so fast, but I didn't know *that*. ~~I~~ All passages had to be secured & the Twelve hundred & fifty dollars fare paid in to-day the 15th, for the Holy Land Excursion, & so I *had* to be here I thought—but the first man I met this morning was the chief of the Alta bureau with a check for $1,250 in his hand & a telegraphic dispatch from the proprietors of the Alta saying "Ship Mark Twain in the Holy Land Pleasure Excursion & pay his passage."[1] So we just went down & attended ~~th~~ to the matter. We had to wait awhile, because the chief manager was not in & we did not make ourselves known.[2] A newspaper man came in ~~to get~~ & asked how many names were booked & what notabilities were going, & a fellow—(I don't know who he was, but he seemed to be connected with the concern,) said, "Lt. Gen. Sherman, Henry Ward Beecher & Mark Twain are going, & probably Gen. Banks!"[3] I thought that was very good—an exceedingly good joke, [*in brown ink instead of black:* for a poor ignorant clerk.]

When my jolly old Captain came in, we squared accounts & then went down to look at the ship (steamer Quaker City.) She is a right stately-looking vessel.[4]

My book will probably be in the booksellers' hands in about two weeks. After that I shall lecture. Since I have been gone, the boys have gotten up a "call" on me, signed by about 200 Californians.[5]

Don't forget to remember me to Essie, & "Lou," & all the folks at 1312,—& tell my pet, Annie, that I will write her just as soon as the press of business is over. I will write Katie Lampton, too.[6]

Send letters to Metropolitan Hotel till further instructions.

Yrs affctin

Sam.

Scrap-book my letters in Alta.[7]

[1] Clemens returned to New York "in an express train . . . a distance of nearly twelve hundred miles by the route I came," probably arriving on the day before he wrote this letter. John J. Murphy, who was the "New York business agent" for the *Alta*, was probably "the chief of the Alta bureau" referred to here (SLC 1867aa, 1867w). The "telegraphic dispatch from the proprietors of the Alta" in Murphy's hands was presumably sent to him on or shortly after 9 April, when the *Alta* published Mark Twain's 2 March dispatch (SLC 1867r). The owners may have sent Clemens a separate telegram, or he could have been referring to the one Murphy received when he said on 19 April that he had "taken passage" on the excursion, "As per order of the ALTA, just received by telegraph. . . . You could not have suited me better" (SLC 1867w). Murphy subsequently gave Mark Twain the following undated letter of agreement (NPV):

Alta California Office
42 John St
New York

Sam*l* Clemens Esq
New York Dear Sir

I have the honor to inform you that Fredk MacCrellish & Co. Proprietors of "Alta California" San Francisco Cal. desires to engage your services as special correspondent on the pleasure excursion now about to proceed from this City to the Holy Land. In obedience to their instructions I have secured a passage for you on the vessel about to convey the excursion party referred to and made such arrangements as I hope will secure your comfort and convenience. Your only instructions are that you will continue to write at such times and from such places as you deem proper and in the same style that heretofore secured you the favor of the readers of the Alta California. I have the honor to remain with high respect and esteem

your obdt Servant
John J. Murphy

The $1,250 passage money was part of an advance against fifty letters to be written about the excursion, the number of letters being determined by doubling Mark Twain's usual rate of one per week over an estimated twenty-five weeks, or five months, needed to complete the voyage between "the 1st of June" and "near the beginning of November." Murphy's letter of agreement implies that what Mark Twain described in his 2 March *Alta* letter as an "additional expense of $500 in gold" for travel ashore was also part of the advance (SLC 1867r). If the cost of the ticket, which was specified as $1,250 in currency, or "greenbacks," is converted to gold ($900 at the current exchange rate of 72 percent) and added to the $500 in gold, the total is $1,400, or $28 per letter, even though Clemens's later memory was that the rate was $20 per letter (Barrett, 96; SLC 1904, 74–75). As a check on this calculation, if we convert $1,400 gold into greenbacks, the total is $1,944, which closely approximates Clemens's statement to Mollie Clemens in February 1868 that he had "only charged them for 50 letters what (even in) greenbacks would amount to less than two thousand dollars" (22? Feb 68 to MEC).

2Captain Charles C. Duncan (1821–98) was the "chief manager" and organizer of the excursion. Born in Bath, Maine, he went to sea as a boy and took his first command while still in his twenties. In 1853 he settled in Brooklyn and established himself as a shipping and commission merchant in South Street, New York, moving in 1855 to the 117 Wall Street office from which he now ran the excursion, and where Clemens and House had encountered him in late February. He soon became closely associated with Plymouth Church and friendly with Beecher himself, although he did not join the church formally until 1866. Shortly before the war he moved to England, where he continued his shipping business, leaving his New York office under the management of George W. Kendall. Duncan claimed that when he returned to New York in 1865, he found that Kendall had absconded with all the company funds, precipitating the bankruptcy of Charles C. Duncan and Company in 1866. Duncan nevertheless resumed his business at the same address. A desire to recover from bankruptcy played a part in Duncan's eagerness to undertake the excursion in the first place, although the basic conception of the trip had evidently come from Beecher (John E. Duncan, 2, 14, 23, 30–33, 39, 125–27; "Charles C. Duncan's Death," New York *Times*, 31 Mar 98, 12; Rode, 201; Wilson 1855, 266; Thompson, 241; Wilson 1867, 552; Gingrich, 6; "What an Old Shipmaster Thinks of the 'Head-Waiter,'" editorial addendum to SLC 1877; "Letters from New York," letter dated 7 June, San Francisco *Evening Bulletin*, 3 July 67, 1).

3On 23 March, Lieutenant General William Tecumseh Sherman (1820–91), then stationed in St. Louis, wrote to Captain Duncan: "I am now fully authorized to act, both General Grant and the President having committed themselves to my leave for the summer. You may therefore register my name and that of my daughter Minnie for your excursion. I have much to do in April and May, but can be in New York punctually in any day you may appoint in June" ("General

Sherman Going to Europe," New York *Evening Post*, 1 Apr 67, 3). The excursion managers soon began exploiting Sherman's commitment, which was announced in most New York newspapers by 5 April. General Nathaniel Prentiss Banks (1816–94), then serving as a congressman from Massachusetts, was also reportedly "added to the party, which, with the Rev. Henry Ward Beecher, at its head, is going to make the tour of the Holy Land" ("Gen. Banks," Keokuk *Gate City*, 11 Apr 67, 3). Henry Ward Beecher, unlike Sherman, was not—and evidently could not be—quoted as affirming his intention to accompany the excursion. But this did not prevent the New York *Times*, among others, from reporting as early as 29 January that "Mr. BEECHER and his family will be of the party—a party which will be select, and composed of friends, neighbors and acquaintances" ("Ocean Enterprise—A Grand Pilgrimage to the East," 29 Jan 67, 4). On 2 April, however, the Brooklyn *Eagle* reported that

> a rumor has reached us, and it appears to have some foundation, that Mr. Beecher is not going. This will be sad news for the Captain and may be fatal to his expedition. Mr. Beecher is the bell-wether of his flock,—where he goes they will go, where he don't go they will stay away from. Only seventy berths have been engaged so far, and if Mr. Beecher backs out, a dozen or two of his flock who have promised to go will withdraw, and the Captain will be left in the lurch. ("Is Mr. Beecher Going to Palestine?" 2 Apr 67, 2)

On 13 April the *Eagle* confirmed the rumor: Beecher would not go. Two reasons for his withdrawal seem plausible. First, he did not have the time to complete (let alone finish proofreading) his novel, *Norwood*, which would begin to appear in the New York *Ledger* on 18 May and would not conclude until November 1867. Second, he was responding to pressure from some "pew-holders who are not going to Palestine," who had objected to his planned absence for five months, saying "they paid high prices for seats to hear first class preaching, and they are not going to be put off with any second rate article from a substitute for the regular pastor" (Brooklyn *Eagle:* "Amusements," 13 Apr 67, 2; "Is Mr. Beecher Going to Palestine?" 2 Apr 67, 2). As the present letter implies, Clemens himself was soon reported among the celebrities joining the excursion. On 20 April, for instance, the New York *Times* ran a brief squib: "SAML. CLEMENS, Esq., (Mark Twain,) has taken passage in the *Quaker City* for the Mediterranean excursion. He is to furnish letters while absent for a San Francisco paper." And the New York *World* reporter soon included his name, among those "booked and berthed," as one "Samuel F. Clemens (Mark Twain)" ("Personal," New York *Times*, 20 Apr 67, 2; "The Mediterranean Excursion," New York *World*, 10 May 67, 2).

[4]Duncan leased the *Quaker City* around 1 April and promptly began to have her refitted. The ship was a 1,428-ton sidewheeler with a white-oak hull, built in Philadelphia in 1854. Converted to a gunboat during the war, at war's end it was purchased and reconverted to a passenger ship by Charles C. Leary, who ran it between New York and Charleston under the command of William H. West until Duncan's lease took effect ("The Mediterranean Excursion," Brooklyn *Eagle*, 5 Apr 67, 2; Lytle, 157; advertisement, New York *Herald*, 14 Mar 67, 12; Heyl, 355–56; "The Steamship Quaker City—Order to Stay Proceedings in Court," New York *Herald*, 19 Feb 68, 5). On about 1 May the ship was "taken up to Delamater's iron-works, at the foot of Thirteenth street," to be

> thoroughly repainted, refurnished, and refitted generally, together with having put in her four new tubular boilers. . . . Since Captain Duncan chartered her, her upper saloons

have been added to the general dining and sitting hall to enlarge it, and the berths run now entirely underneath the main decks, and are fifty-three in number. Though their capacity is for three, only two are to be placed in each, with one or two exceptions, as the complement of passengers, 110, will not require more. ("The Mediterranean Excursion," New York *World*, 10 May 67, 2)

Clemens's "look at the ship" occurred before it was moved from pier 14 on the East River, within a few yards of Duncan's Wall Street office. The ship was completely refitted and back at pier 14 by 3 June ("The Mediterranean Excursion," New York *World*, 2 May 67, 5; "Ocean Steamers," New York *Tribune*, 3 June 67, 7).

[5] Clemens's estimated date of publication is accurate. The "call" from his fellow Californians had been in evidence during January and February, and a version of the document mentioned here (albeit with about half this number of names) would soon be published to help advertise his lecture. The earliest public indication that Clemens had tentatively decided to lecture appeared on 21 April, a week after his return from St. Louis: "Many resident Californians and others, friends of Mr. SAMUEL CLEMMENS, better known as Mark Twain, have invited him to deliver in this City his lecture on the Sandwich Islands, which was received with considerable favor in California" ("Mark Twain," New York *Times*, 21 Apr 67, 5; see also "Lecture by 'Mark Twain,'" New York *Dispatch*, 21 Apr 67, 5).

[6] Esther (Essie) Pepper and Louisa (Lou) Conrad were friends and neighbors of Clemens's niece, Annie Moffett. Essie, aged eighteen, was the daughter of Samuel Pepper (1820–93) and Helen Leavenworth Pepper (b. 1829 or 1830) (see 23 Apr 67 to Stoddard, n. 2). The Peppers lived next door to the Leavenworths on Chesnut Street, one block from the Moffetts. Samuel Webster indicated that Lou Conrad was "generally adored, especially by Annie, who was some years younger," and Annie testified that "Uncle Sam admired Lou Conrad." Clemens may have known Conrad by sight when he lived in St. Louis, but he first became genuinely acquainted with her during his recent trip home, for on 7 January 1869 he referred to her as "a most estimable young lady whose friendship I acquired in St. Louis two years ago." Catherine C. (Kate) Lampton (b. 1856) was Clemens's first cousin, the daughter of his mother's half-brother, James A. H. Lampton, and Ella Hunter Lampton (*L1*, 280 n. 12; Webster, 1; TS for *MTBus*, CU-MARK, 136; *St. Louis Census* 1860, 180; Edwards 1867, 511, 582, 632; SLC to OLL, 7 Jan 69 [2nd of 2], CU-MARK†; SLC to PAM, 14 Jan 69, NPV; *L1*, 367 n. 1; see also SLC to JLC, 2 Apr 62, *L1*, 181).

[7] Annie Moffett recalled that Clemens "bought a scrapbook and asked my mother to paste the articles in it as we received them. She was very conscientious and careful about it" (*MTBus*, 92). This document survives: Scrapbook 7 in the Moffett Collection (CU-MARK). Mark Twain subsequently revised and removed clippings from it to make up the printer's copy for *The Innocents Abroad* (SLC 1869a).

To Jane Lampton Clemens and Family
19 April 1867 • New York, N.Y.

(MS: CU-MARK and ViU)

WESTMINSTER HOTEL, COR. OF IRVING PLACE AND
16TH ST. NEW YORK ROBERTS & PALMER PROPRS

April 19.

Dear Folks—

Direct my letters to ~~the~~ this hotel in future. I am just fixed, now. It is the gem of all hotels. I have never come across one so perfectly elegant in all its appointments & so sumptuously & tastefully furnished.[1] Full of "bloated aristocrats" too, & I'm just one of *them* kind myself—& so is Beck Jolly.[2]

The book will issue the 25th. James Russell Lowell ("Hosea Biglow,") says the Jumping Frog is the finest piece of humorous writing ever produced in America.[3]

Give my love to all my sweethearts.

Good bye

Sam

Dorsey[4] goes west in a day or two.

Orion Clemens Esq | 1312 Chesnut street | St Louis | Mo [*postmarked:*] NEW-YORK APR 19 [*postage stamp removed*][5]

[1] On returning from St. Louis, Clemens spent four or five days at the Metropolitan before moving on 19 April to the Westminster ("Arrivals in the City," New York *Times*, 20 Apr 67, 8). It is possible that he had roomed at the Westminster before going to St. Louis, since his *Alta* letters written on 2 and 18 February allude to his rooming in East Sixteenth Street (SLC 1867n–o). In a later letter to the *Alta*, he summarized his reasons for preferring "the European system" recently adopted by hotels like the Westminster, where everything was "quiet, and genteel and orderly." He noted that "it is costly, but it is comfortable—prodigiously comfortable," especially in comparison with the "great caravan hotels" like the Metropolitan (SLC 1867aa).

[2] Sobieski (Beck) Jolly (1831–1905) was a well-respected river pilot and a friend of Clemens's since they met in the fall of 1857, when Clemens served as a cub pilot under Jolly on the *John J. Roe* (*L1*, 74). He was currently piloting the *Virginia* between New Orleans and St. Louis, where he almost certainly saw

Clemens in mid-March ("River News," St. Louis *Missouri Democrat*, 16 Mar 67, 4).

[3] If James Russell Lowell (1819–91) made such a statement about Mark Twain's "Jim Smiley and His Jumping Frog," it has not been independently documented. The attribution is suspect because a New York correspondent for the San Francisco *Evening Bulletin* reported on 24 January that according to Webb, Lowell had called Webb's just-published *Liffith Lank* "the best thing of the kind ever written in America" ("Gossip from New York," letter dated 24 Jan, San Francisco *Evening Bulletin*, 19 Feb 67, 1).

[4] Dorsey is unidentified, although he was probably the same man Clemens mentioned in an 1861 Nevada letter (George Turner and SLC to OC, 18–30 Sept 61, *L1*, 128).

[5] Clemens seems routinely to have used Orion's name, rather than his mother's, in addressing envelopes for letters written to her and the family. Jane Clemens was not listed in the 1867 St. Louis directory, although both Pamela Moffett and Orion Clemens were (Edwards 1867, 257, 582).

To Malcolm Townsend
22 April 1867 • New York, N.Y.

(MS: NN-B)

WESTMINSTER HOTEL, COR. OF IRVING PLACE AND 16TH ST. NEW YORK ROBERTS & PALMER PROP^{RS}

April 22./67.

Malcolm~~b~~ Townsend Esq

Dear Sir—

I don't know what use you can make of my autograph, but as far as it will go you are welcome to it, cheerfully~~,~~—~~& if you are anythin~~ and a sentiment also:

THIRTY DAYS AFTER DATE I PROMISE TO PAY—

It was a slip of the pen—but you will excuse it—it comes of long habit—I so often put my autograph to ~~lit~~ that sort of sentiment.

We will change it to my favorite, which is homely but good:

"HERE'S LUCK!"

Yrs Respectfully

Mark Twain

P.S. Excuse all blots & blemishes, as the school-girls say.[1]

[1]The identity of this autograph seeker remains uncertain, but he may be nineteen-year-old Malcolm Townsend, born on 18 December 1847 in New York City and alive as late as 1917. He was the son of Cyrus Townsend, a carriage manufacturer and flatboat trader on the Mississippi and Ohio rivers. Almost three years after this letter, on 29 January 1870, he was married in Plymouth Church, by Henry Ward Beecher, to Emma Virginia Cox, born in Brooklyn in 1849 and a member of Plymouth Church since 1863. In 1891 Townsend was living in New York and reported that he had "been connected for many years with the Pennsylvania Railroad Company and its interests, as Foreign Freight Agent and in other official capacities." In addition to a genealogy of his family, Townsend compiled three books, apparently published privately: *"U.S."—An Index to Curious Facts in United States History. Historical, Geographical and Political; "Candle and Lamp Lore." Historical, Ecclesiastical and Legendary;* and *"Numbers, 1, 2, 3, 4, 5, 6, 7, 8, 9." Mystical, Historical, Ecclesiastical, Mathematical, Including Proverbs and Maxims* (Townsend, title page and s.v. "Cyrus Townsend" and "Malcolm Townsend"; Thompson, 240; "Freight Handling by Machines Now," New York *Times*, 16 Dec 1917, 11).

To Charles Warren Stoddard
23 April 1867 • New York, N.Y.

(MS: CU-MARK)

WESTMINSTER HOTEL, COR. OF IRVING PLACE AND 16TH ST. NEW YORK ROBERTS & PALMER PROP^{RS}

April 23, 1867.

My Dear Old Boy—

You see I have quit the Metropolitan, but I have got a hundred times better hotel.

I got your most welcome letter, to-day, & am so glad to hear you are going to publish.[1] Send a copy, with your Ortograft in it, to me, *care of Samuel Pepper of Gaylord & Leavenworth, Bankers, St Louis, Mo.*, & I will send you my book, which will be published day after to-morrow.[2] I suppose I shall sail for Palestine just about the time you receive this—June 8.

I want to endorse your book, because I~~n~~ know all about poetry & I know you can write the genuine article. Your book will be a success—your book *shall* be a success—& I will destroy any man that says the contrary. How's that? There is nothing mean about *me*. I wrote a sublime poem—"He Done His Level Best"—& what credit did I ever get for it?—None. Bret left it out of the Outcroppings. I never will write another poem. I am not appreciated.[3] But that don't set me against other poets,, Charley, like it might have done with other men, & so I will back up your book just as strong as I know how. Count on me to-day, to-morrow & *all the time*. And I don't say it in a whisper, but I say it strong.

[Signed & sworn to]—
Mark Twain

I haven't seen Miss Carmichael, but I hope I shall, soon.[4]

I was talking with Willie Winter, the talented reviewer of the Tribune & the Saturday Review, yesterday, & he said a lady had given him some of your poems, in MSS., & he, supposing they had not been published (I think she *told* him they had not,) printed them as original & got scissors for it in the San F. papers. Then he apologised in print, or explained, & the San F. papers scouted his explanation as a shabby falsehood. He is one of the finest young men on the press anywhere, & it is a pity to throw away his good will & his really great influence. The Cal. papers ought to let these papers here borrow from us occasionally,—it wouldn't actually help the Cal. paper to receive credit, & it *does* help us to be copied, with signature attached.[5]

How is Bret? He is publishing with a Son of a Bitch who will swindle him, & he may print that opinion if he chooses, with my name signed to it. I don't know how his book is coming on—we of Bohemia keep away from Carleton's.[6]

~~I~~ The papers here say I am going to lecture shortly, & I may. I don't know yet.[7]

Write to me, *sure*, care of Mr Pepper, St Louis (I mean to have my letters forwarded to Europe.)

Good-bye, & God bless you,
my boy,
Mark Twain

[1] Stoddard (1843–1909) and Clemens probably met in San Francisco in 1864 or 1865, when both were writing for the *Californian*. Stoddard first published his poems in 1861, at the age of seventeen, by submitting them anonymously (as "Pip Pepperpod") to the *Golden Era*. On their strength, Thomas Starr King encouraged him to pursue a literary career, and all the editors of the *Californian*, particularly Bret Harte and James F. Bowman, published his work frequently. Harte had, in fact, selected and edited the contents of the volume referred to

here—Stoddard's first book—a slim, elegantly printed octavo, illustrated by William Keith, called simply *Poems*. As early as 12 January the *Californian* reported that Stoddard, "the most richly gifted of our rising California poets, is about to publish in a handsome volume, a selection from the pieces which, during several years past he has contributed to literary papers of the State, together with others that have never been published." The book was supposed to issue "about the first of May"; A. Roman and Company did not publish it, however, until August. The *Californian* gave the book unqualified praise, but several other journals called Stoddard's verse imitative and superficial (Walker, 76–77, 228–32; *Californian* 6: "Stoddard's Poems," 12 Jan 67, 8; "Charles Warren Stoddard's Poems," 9 Mar 67, 4; *Californian* 7: "Charles Warren Stoddard's Poems," 24 Aug 67, 8; "A Californian Poet," 31 Aug 67, 8).

[2] Samuel Pepper and his brother-in-law, Mark Leavenworth (b. 1827 or 1828), were clerk and captain, respectively, of the *John J. Roe* when Clemens was its cub pilot. They left the river in June 1864 to form the St. Louis banking firm of Gaylord, Leavenworth, and Company with Samuel A. Gaylord, formerly of Erastus Gaylord and Sons. The *Missouri Democrat* characterized them as "well and favorably known steamboatmen," noting that Leavenworth had for "a long time commanded the steamer John J. Roe, and later, the steamer Champion." Pepper (and a fourth partner, James E. Kelso) had "both occupied positions which have given them a very extensive business acquaintance, not only in our city, but in every city of the Mississippi Valley" (*St. Louis Census* 1860, 180; "A New Banking House," St. Louis *Missouri Democrat*, 21 June 64, 1; Edwards 1867, 363). Stoddard did send Clemens a copy of *Poems*, autographed "Mark Twain | with the love of his | faithful friend— | Chas. Warren Stoddard" (ViU, quoted in Gribben, 2:667). The *Jumping Frog*, although announced for the trade on 25 April, was not in bookstores until 1 May. No copy inscribed to Stoddard has been found.

[3] On 17 June 1865 Mark Twain published "He Done His Level Best" in his third *Californian* "Answers to Correspondents" column, where it appeared as a contribution from Simon Wheeler of Sonora, written in praise of a certain parson who had "busted and gone home to the States":

Was he a mining on the flat—
He done it with a zest;
Was he a leading of the choir—
He done his level best. . . .

The object of ridicule here becomes clearer from what Mark Twain said as the avuncular editor of the column: he would encourage Wheeler to "continue writing" were it not that "the poet crop is unusually large and rank in California this year" (*ET&S2*, 187–96). Bret Harte's *Outcroppings: Being Selections of California Verse* (1865) had drawn venomous reviews from some of those whose work had been omitted from it, and was indirectly responsible for May Wentworth's *Poetry of the Pacific* (1867), originally conceived as containing at least one poem by every poet in California. Harte answered critics of *Outcroppings* in several ways, one of which was an editorial acknowledging that some poems of merit, including "He Done His Level Best," had been "wrongfully overlooked in the volume" (*L1*, 330–31 n. 7; Harte, 8). In fact, early in 1866 Clemens and Harte were itching for a chance to burlesque *Poetry of the Pacific*, plans for which were already being discussed in the press, long before it actually issued: "We know all the tribe of California poets, & understand their different styles, & I think we can just make them get up & howl" (SLC to JLC and PAM, 20 Jan 66, *L1*, 328–29; "More 'Outcroppings,'" San Francisco *Examiner*, 12 Jan 66, 3).

[4] Sarah Elizabeth Carmichael (1838–1901), a poet, was the daughter of Mormon parents, who in 1850 had settled in Salt Lake City. Although she had been publishing poems since 1858, Clemens doubtless knew her work from a small volume issued "for private circulation," which announced itself as "published with the consent—somewhat reluctantly given—of the authoress, by a devoted circle of her friends and admirers," who intended to "secure for her poems a more extended acquaintance and recognition." It was probably Bret Harte who reviewed *Poems* in the 14 July 1866 *Californian*, shortly before Clemens returned from the Sandwich Islands, describing it as worthy of "a broader and more public approbation than is modestly asked" and as having been "prettily gotten up by Towne & Bacon, somewhat in the style of Whittier's *Snow-Bound*." "Miss Carmichael" (as Clemens calls her) had in fact married Dr. Jonathan M. Williamson, a former army surgeon, on 4 November 1866 at Fort Bridger, Utah Territory. Shortly thereafter the couple traveled overland to New York, where she reportedly intended "to make arrangements for the publication of her new work on Mormonism," a project her husband urged upon her. On 23 March the New York *Round Table* announced that "Miss Carmichael, the Mormon poetess, who apostatized in favor of a husband exclusively hers, is about to publish a book on her life in Salt Lake City." But the book on Mormonism was evidently never published; within a year the poet's health deteriorated and her literary career came to a premature end (Carmichael, v; "Poems by Sarah E. Carmichael," *Californian* 5 [14 July 66]: 12; Murphy, 53–54, 60, 62–66; Salt Lake City *Union Vedette:* "Gone East," 3 Nov 66, 3; "Married," 6 Nov 66, 2; "On Dit," 21 Jan 67, 3; "Literariana," *Round Table* 5 [23 Mar 67]: 189).

[5] Since moving to New York from Boston in 1859, Winter had contributed to, and held various editorial positions with, such journals as Artemus Ward's *Vanity Fair*, Henry Clapp's New York *Saturday Press*, the New York *Weekly Review*, and the New York *Round Table* (subtitled *A Saturday Review of Literature, Society, and Art*—possibly the journal Clemens here calls the "Saturday Review"). From 1861 until 1867, Winter served as dramatic and literary critic on the New York *Albion*, signing himself "Mercutio." In July 1865 he also became the theater critic for the New York *Tribune*, a position he held for most of his professional life. More recently he had become the "dramatic editor" of the New York *Weekly Review*, to which he was already a frequent contributor ("Personal," New York *World*, 15 Feb 67, 4). The squabble over Stoddard's poems began on 20 October 1866, and seems to have been entirely between the *Weekly Review* and the *Californian*, not San Francisco newspapers generally. The *Californian* objected to the *Review*'s publishing Stoddard's "My Friend" in its 15 September issue under the heading "For the New York Weekly Review," since the *Californian* had itself paid for and published the poem on 28 October 1865: "This is not the first instance in which poems of Mr. Stoddard, which first appeared in THE CALIFORNIAN, have been republished as 'original' in the *Review*. We are quite at a loss as to the explanation of so singular a proceeding." On 8 December, the *Review* published a "simple" explanation: "The two or three of Mr. Charles Warren Stoddard's poems that have appeared in the REVIEW were sent to us, in their author's manuscript, by one of his friends in this city, with the intimation that

Mr. Stoddard would like to have them published. We printed them, therefore, as contributions, not knowing that they had ever been published elsewhere. No person is in fault for a natural misunderstanding." But on 5 January, the *Californian* still professed itself not satisfied: "Inasmuch as Mr. Stoddard never sent the manuscript of these poems to New York, or entrusted it to any person for that purpose, or intimated to any person his wish to have the poems published in the *Review*, the 'explanation' however 'simple,' still leaves a little mystery behind it." On 30 June, some two months after his conversation with Clemens, Winter wrote (or replied, possibly) to Stoddard himself: "My sentiments towards you have ever been those of good-will and respect. Your poetry I have read—here and there in the papers—with much interest and gratification. Of you, personally, I have heard, from Mrs. [Ada] Clare, from Mark Twain, and from Mr. Webb, none but the kindest reports. . . . For my part, Mr. F. B. Harte and you are my peculiar favorites among the writers of the 'Western Slope.'" Stoddard and Winter may both have been eager to indicate publicly that the misunderstanding had been resolved: when Stoddard's *Poems* was published in August, the *Californian* was quick to note that the *Weekly Review* "declares its intention to 'improve an early opportunity to review the book,' and adds: 'In Mr. Stoddard and in Mr. Frank Bret Harte, California has two writers of whom she ought to be proud;' a proposition which will be very generally and cordially endorsed in literary circles." And it soon quoted the 14 September issue of the *Weekly Review*, which alluded to Stoddard as "a young Californian, manifestly gifted with a pure spirit and a lively fancy, who has entered upon a career that is full of promise" ("'My Friend,'" *Californian* 5 [20 Oct 66]: 8; "My Friend," *Weekly Review* 17 [15 Sept 66]: 1; "My Friend," *Californian* 3 [28 Oct 65]: 1; "An Explanation," *Weekly Review* 17 [8 Dec 66]: 5; "An Explanation," *Californian* 6 [5 Jan 67]: 8; Winter to [Stoddard], 30 June 67, Walpole Galleries, lot 287; "The New York *Weekly Review* . . . ," *Californian* 7 [17 Aug 67]: 9; 7 [19 Oct 67]: 8). When reviewers in San Francisco, Sacramento, and Virginia City were more critical of *Poems*, the *Californian* replied:

> A LITERARY gentleman of New York, who holds a high position in the republic of letters, writes us, that Mr. Stoddard's volume of poems is highly spoken of in literary circles. In the New York *Weekly Review* of September 28th, a critical journal of considerable authority, over half a column is devoted to a notice of the volume . . . . Such appreciation as this, on the part of a recognized critical authority, may well console Mr. Stoddard for the ungracious and unintelligent criticism of the *Territorial Enterprise*, and other provincial reviewers. ("Mr. Stoddard's Poems," *Californian* 7 [9 Nov 67]: 8)

[6] Carleton did not issue Harte's *Condensed Novels* until October. No evidence has been found that "Bohemia" avoided Carleton, but the meaning of the term itself was changing at this time. In 1869, Junius Henri Browne said that New York's Bohemia had consisted of "fifteen or twenty journalists, the greater part of them young men of ability and culture," who "had their rise and association about twelve years ago, and flourished up to the commencement of the War, which broke up the Bohemian fraternity, not only here, but in other cities." And he suggested that the designation now meant "journalists generally, especially since the War correspondents during the Rebellion received the title. . . . Bohemian, particularly in New-York, has indeed come to be a sort of synonym for a newspaper writer" (Browne, 151–52).

[7] Although Clemens had discussed his New York lecture debut with Fuller in

January (see pp. 5–6), he did not decide exactly when to lecture until shortly after writing this letter. In 1906 he recalled:

When I arrived in New York I found Fuller there in some kind of business. . . . He said I must take the biggest hall in New York and deliver that lecture of mine on the Sandwich Islands—said that people would be wild to hear me. . . . I knew better. I was well aware that New York had never heard of me . . . yet that man almost persuaded me. (AD, 11 Apr 1906, CU-MARK, in *MTA*, 2:351–52)

In 1911 Fuller attributed the enthusiasm more to Clemens than to himself, and he reported a conversation that probably took place at least in part after Clemens's return from St. Louis:

I was sitting in my private office at 57 Broadway one day when Mark Twain arrived in New York after his successful lectures in San Francisco, Sacramento, Virginia City, and St. Louis. He walked into my office and drawled out:

"Frank, I want to preach right here in New York, and it must be in the biggest hall to be found. I find it is the Cooper Union, and that it costs $70 for one evening, and I have got just $7."

I told him he should have that big hall. . . . We started right away to interest the public in his lecture on the Sandwich Islands. We put advertisements in the papers calling on all citizens of the Pacific Coast to meet in the evening at the Metropolitan Hotel to take measures for stimulating interest in the lecture and to give him a big send-off. (Fuller, 5:10)

Clemens was probably not so urgent or decisive as Fuller remembered: the earliest notice of the lecture so far discovered appeared a week after Clemens's return ("Mark Twain," New York *Times*, 21 Apr 67, 5). In 1910 Fuller told Paine that Clemens had wanted Senator (formerly Governor) James W. Nye of Nevada "to accompany him to the platform and introduce him to the audience," and that Clemens wrote Nye with this request. Having received no reply, on 21 April Clemens sent Fuller—by then officially his manager—to make the request in person:

I took a night train to Washington and saw Gov. Nye in his rooms at Willards. I made known my errand and he assented and invited me to sit right down and write a polite affirmative assent to an invitation which I could write after I returned to New York. I got his signature and rushed back to New York. (Fuller to A. B. Paine, 7 Dec 1910, Davis 1956, 1)

The promise Nye signed was dated 22 April. On 23 April, the Cooper Institute and the sixth of May were first mentioned publicly as the place and date of the lecture ("Personal," New York *World*, 23 Apr 67, 4). And on 25 April, the New York *Evening Post* reported:

A large number of Californians now in this city have invited Mr. Samuel Clemmens, better known as "Mark Twain," to deliver his lecture upon the Sandwich Islands prior to his departure for Europe. The invitation has been accepted, and the lecture will be given at Cooper Institute on Monday evening, May 6. ("Lecture by 'Mark Twain,'" 25 Apr 67, 4)

On 27, 28, and 29 April, Fuller issued a summons in the advertising columns of (at least) the *Evening Post*, *Tribune*, *Times*, and *Herald*, designed to convene all Californians and to formalize their "call," or invitation to Mark Twain:

Californians and all others interested in the success of the Lecture which MARK TWAIN has been invited to deliver at Cooper Institute, on Monday, May 6, are requested to meet at the Metropolitan Hotel, on Monday evening, April 29, at 7½ o'clock, to adopt measures for a united effort in the premises. By order of the Committee. ("Mark Twain's Lecture," New York *Herald*, 29 Apr 67, 1)

This was probably the same "committee" of dignitaries which had waited on Clemens shortly after his arrival in January. Clemens opened the 29 April meeting "with a brief address" described as "both witty and clever. . . . His manner has all of the freedom and independence of a true Californian, and he is irresistibly droll in his delivery." A letter calling upon him to lecture "was signed by all present," but the meeting itself was not widely or fully reported, except in the *Tribune* ("'Mark Twain,'" New York *Tribune*, 30 Apr 67, 8).

To Charles Warren Stoddard with a note to the Postmaster 27 April 1867 • New York, N.Y.

(MS: CSmH and CU-BANC)

.—[**Confucius.**

Friend Charles—Every now and then, since, I received your Album, four or five days ago, I have tried to think of some subject proper to be treated in its pages[1]—one, I mean, which should be so simple that I might talk about it easily and comfortably, and not get myself stiffened out in the confounded straight-jacket language common to Album composition—one which should be learned without being pedantic, dignified without being overpowering, and unpretending without being entirely insignificant. If you have ever exercised your mind in the same direction, you know what the result was, without my telling you. I tried and rejected "The Decline and Fall of the Roman Empire," "The Decline and Fall of Adam and Eve," and "The Decline and Fall of Gould & Curry," and then declined to pursue that style of subject any further, and fell to meditating the perpetration of a Poem.[2] I dashed off the following felicitous line:

"How dear to my heart are the scenes of my childhood."

I rather liked that, but I could not get rid of the impression that I had seen it before, somewhere.[3] I have been too strictly raised by my parents to ever think of taking anything that does not belong to me, unless it is something I can eat, or trade off, or something of that kind, and so I scorned to use that line while there was a shadow of doubt in my mind as to whose property it was. Still, it occurred to me that I might borrow it for a model to build a great Poem on without wounding my morbid conscientiousness, and here follows the result:

> How sick to my soul are the scenes of my beer-hood,
> When sad retrospection presents them to view:—
> The station-house, gin-mill and deep-tangled railroad,
> (Which **never** was straight when I walked it at 2—A.M.),
> With the old soaken bummer, the iron-lined bummer,
> The moss-covered bummer¶ that hung to the Swell.*

After I had discharged this fine production from my system, I felt relieved, but not satisfied. I had to confess that I had seen better poems in my time. A conviction of this kind is death to flickering inspiration, and the light of my genius went out. I then went out myself, and took a drink. This latter species of inspiration is the safest to depend upon, after all. By its aid I saw (what I might have seen before, had I not been blinded by ambition,) that no profound essay, full of clattering syllables and sounding rhetoric—no venerable platitudes irreverently tricked out in the gew-gaws and flowers of fancy—no noble Song, fragrant with incense of the Eden-land of Poesy—were required of me, but only to stand up and answer "Here!" when my name was called. I do it with pleasure. I write no essay, no poem, no sermon, but instead, I heartily extend the right hand of fellowship, and say, with simple eloquence, "Here's luck!"

My young friend—(this is only for form's sake, you know—I merely introduce it because an Album contribution is necessarily incomplete without a word of fatherly admonition)—My Young Friend, you stand now upon the threshold of the grand, mysterious Future, and you are about to take the most momentous step in the march of your life—let me hope that you will cast from you the vanities and follies and petty ambitions of the world, and endeavor so to conduct yourself as to merit the continued esteem and approbation of

Your cordial friend,
Mark Twain

¶Refers to Emperor Norton.[4]
*Refers to me.

Charles Warren Stoddard, Esq | "Californian" Office | San Francisco | Cal. [*postmarked:*] NEW-YORK APR 27 [*written above address:*]
To Postmaster—D^r. Sir:
Per Steamer—d—n the Overland—
too many Injuns.[5]

Yrs Resp'y
Mark Twain

[1] Clemens probably received Stoddard's autograph album and a covering letter on the same day (23 April). He answered the letter on the day he received it (see the previous letter), but waited "four or five days" before inscribing the album and returning it to Stoddard in San Francisco—probably on 27 April, the date of the postmark on the mailing label, which has been separately preserved. Stoddard was an incurable and unabashed autograph collector, having kept this album since at least 1863, the "earliest date in it" (Pourquoi 1880a, 355).

[2] It is not known whether Clemens had read Gibbon's masterpiece this early; the only copy he is known to have owned was published in 1880. He had long been familiar with the Gould and Curry Silver Mining Company, which since 1860 had owned one of the most productive mines on the Comstock lode. For a variety of reasons, however, its value notably declined between 1862 and 1866. When Clemens returned to Virginia City in 1868 he noted, "The Gould & Curry, that . . . sold at six thousand three hundred dollars a foot, is worth fifty less than six hundred now" (Angel, 613; Lord, 124–29, 226; SLC 1868ccc).

[3] The "felicitous line" is from "The Bucket" by Samuel Woodworth (1784–1842), originally published on 3 June 1818 in the New York *Republican Chronicle:*

> How dear to this heart are the scenes of my childhood,
> When fond recollection presents them to view!
> The orchard, the meadow, the deep-tangled wild-wood,
> And every loved spot which my infancy knew!
> The wide-spreading pond, and the mill that stood by it,
> The bridge, and the rock where the cataract fell,
> The cot of my father, the dairy-house nigh it,
> And e'en the rude bucket that hung in the well—
> The old oaken bucket, the iron-bound bucket,
> The moss-covered bucket which hung in the well.
> (Woodworth, 12)

Clemens very likely knew the poem as set to music composed by George Kiallmark (1781–1835); words and music were probably first published together in 1843. By the time of this letter, the song had long been popular; since the early 1850s it had often been included in temperance songbooks "as a tribute to the potable properties of cold water" (Fuld, 413–14; Hughes and Wolfe, 555–57, 562, 566–68; Spaeth, 60).

[4] Joshua A. Norton (1818–80) of San Francisco declared himself "Norton I, Emperor of the United States" in 1857, and was henceforth a familiar and well-loved public figure who lived on the charity of that city (*L1*, 324–25 n. 2).

[5] Disruptive and sometimes violent clashes between settlers and troops posted to protect them (on the one hand) and various tribes of Cheyennes, Sioux, and Crows (on the other) had threatened overland travel increasingly since mid-1866, but on 25 April the New York *Tribune* reported that a "general war" was "imminent." On the day of this letter, the newspaper reported that military orders had "been sent to each post on the Santa Fe and Smoky Hill routes . . . informing them that the Indian war had broken out at last, and that the savages intended to be true to the threats they issued during the Winter." The immediate crisis was caused at least in part by General W. S. Hancock's decision on 20 April to burn a village of about three hundred lodges of Cheyennes and Sioux near Fort Dodge, Kansas, after the occupants had fled in terror at the approach of his troops (New York *Tribune:* "The Indian War," 25 Apr 67, 1; "The Indian War," 27 Apr 67, 4; "The Indians," 4 May 67, 1; *Annual Cyclopaedia 1868*, 399–401).

To Jane Lampton Clemens and Family
1 May 1867 • New York, N.Y.

(MS: NPV)

Westminster Hotel
May 1. 1867

Dear Folks—

Don't expect me to write for a while. My hands are full of business, on account of my lecture for the 6th inst., & everything looks shady, at least, if not dark. I have got a good agent—but now ~~that~~ after we have hired the Cooper Institute & gone to an expense in one way or another of $500, it comes out that I have got to play against Speaker Colfax at Irving Hall, Ristori, & also the double troupe of Japanese Jugglers—the latter opening at the great Academy of Music—& with all this against me I have taken the largest house in New York & cannot back water. Let her slide! If nobody else cares, I don't.[1]

I'll send the book soon.[2] I am awfully hurried, now, but not worried.

Yrs

Sam.

[1] Since 24 April it had been clear to anyone reading the theater advertisements in the New York newspapers that the "Imperial Troupe" of Japanese jugglers and acrobats, managed by San Francisco's Thomas Maguire, would open in New York at the Academy of Music on 6 May. Likewise, since 22 April it had been announced daily that Italian actress Adelaide Ristori would appear in a series of

six farewell performances at the French Theatre; on 6 May she was to portray Thisbe in Victor Hugo's *Angelo, Tyrant of Padua*. But the announcement that Speaker of the House Schuyler Colfax (1823–85) would deliver his "Across the Continent" lecture at Irving Hall to benefit the Southern Famine Relief Commission, also on 6 May, could not have been seen by Fuller or Clemens before the afternoon of 1 May, when it first appeared in a late edition of the *Evening Post*, presumably following the arrival in the city of Colfax himself ("Amusements," New York *Tribune*, 22 and 24 Apr 67, 6 May 67, 7; advertisement, New York *Evening Post*, 1 May 67, 4).

[2]Clemens inscribed a copy of the *Jumping Frog* "To | My Mother— | The dearest Friend I ever | had, & the truest. | Mark Twain | New York, May 1, 1867" (ViU†).

To Francis Bret Harte
1 May 1867 • New York, N.Y.

(MS: CtY-BR)

Westminster Hotel
May 1, 1867.

Dear Bret—

I take my pen in hand to inform you that I am well & hope these few line[s] will find you enjoying the same God's blessing.

The book is out, & is handsome. It is full of damnable errors of grammar & deadly inconsistencies of spelling in the Frog sketch because I was away & did not read the proofs—but be a friend & say nothing about these things.[1] When my hurry is over I will send you an autograph copy to pisen the children with.

I am to lecture in Cooper Institute next Monday night. Pray for me.

We sail for the Holy Land June 8. Try & write me (to this hotel,) & it will be forwarded to Paris, where we remain 10 to 15 days.

Regards & best wishes to Mrs Bret & the family.[2]

Truly Yr Friend
Mark

[1]Clemens was rightly dissatisfied with Webb's text, especially of the title sketch. In 1869, for instance, he marked one copy of the book in order (among other things) to correct, presumably from memory, sixteen unauthorized changes in the "Jumping Frog" story alone. Some of these corrections were for

"inconsistencies of spelling": for example, he corrected "risk" to "resk" (twice); "wan't" to "warn't"; and "cal'klated" and "edercate" to "cal'lated" and "educate" (*ET&S2*, 670; *ET&S1*, 534–35). Bret Harte (born Francis Brett Harte, 1836–1902) moved to California from the East in 1854, pursuing a variety of occupations as tutor, apothecary's assistant, expressman, and newspaperman before moving in 1860 to San Francisco. There he set type for the *Golden Era*, in which he soon began to publish his own verse and prose sketches. When Charles Henry Webb established the *Californian* in 1864, Harte became a major contributor and periodically replaced Webb as the editor, first soliciting Clemens's work for it in 1864. He had urged Clemens to collect his newspaper sketches as early as 1866 (*ET&S2*, 66–67; SLC to JLC and PAM, 20 Jan 66, *L1*, 328). At this stage of their literary careers, Mark Twain still looked upon Harte as something of a mentor.

[2]In August 1862 Harte married Anna Griswold of New York (b. 1832). By 1867 they had two sons: Griswold (1863–1901) and Francis King (1865–1917). Harte was an indulgent father, but a sullen if submissive husband. Dissatisfied with his modest income, Anna earned a reputation among Harte's intimates as demanding, tyrannical, and self-centered (O'Connor, 63–65, 68, 83–84, 300; "Obituary Notes," New York *Times*, 28 Apr 1917, 13).

NO LETTERS have been found for the next two weeks—a period during which Clemens neglected his *Alta* correspondence and may well have written very few personal letters, while he took the crucial step of lecturing for the first time before a New York audience. His debut at Cooper Institute occurred on 6 May; he repeated the lecture at the Athenaeum, in Brooklyn, the following Friday (10 May). Shortly after the next letter, he repeated it a third time (15 May), at Irving Hall in New York; and he planned (but canceled) a fourth appearance, in Brooklyn, at the Academy of Music.

In 1906 Clemens recalled his fears that the advertising for his lecture—which he had delegated to his manager, Frank Fuller—was not sufficiently vigorous:

> He hired Cooper Institute, and he began to advertise this lecture in the usual way—a small paragraph in the advertising columns of the newspapers. When this had continued about three days I had not yet heard anybody or any newspaper say anything about that lecture, and I got nervous. "Oh," he said, "it's working around underneath. You don't see it on the surface." He said, "Let it alone, now, let it work."

But Clemens was not entirely reassured: some "three or four days" before his first appearance he told Fuller to "advertise more energetically"

(AD, 11 Apr 1906, CU-MARK, in *MTA*, 2:353). Fuller did advertise in (at least) the *Times*, the *Evening Express*, the *Citizen*, the *Evening Post*, and the *Tribune* on 4, 5, or 6 May. In each of the last two newspapers (on 4 and 6 May, respectively) he reproduced both Senator Nye's endorsement and the "call," with some ninety names signed in support: Senator William M. Stewart, M. G. Upton (chief editor of the *Alta*, who must have signed before he sailed for France on 16 April), Clement T. Rice, Marcus D. Larrowe, Charles Henry Webb, John J. Murphy, Robert M. Howland, Edward C. Dixon, Frank Fuller, and Thomas Maguire—to mention only the more familiar names ("Amusements," New York *Times*, 4 and 6 May 67, 7; "Lectures," New York *Evening Express*, 4 May 67, 3; "Cooper Institute," New York *Citizen*, 4 May 67, 8; "Lectures and Meetings," New York *Tribune*, 4 and 6 May 67, 7; "Amusements," New York *Evening Post*, 4 May 67, 4; SLC 1867w). Clemens's lecture also received various brief advance notices from his many newspaper friends. On 3, 4, and 6 May, James and Erastus Brooks's New York *Evening Express* devoted several lines to it ("Amusements," 3 May, 1; "The Drama and Music," 4 and 6 May, 2). It was probably Charles Halpine who said, anonymously, in the weekly New York *Citizen* of 4 May:

> MARK TWAIN, the gifted humorist from California, will lecture on Monday evening, at the Cooper Institute. The subject is "Kanakadom, or the Sandwich Islands," and a rarer combination of useful information and brilliant wit was never listened to. We certainly hope he will meet with the reception his talents and sterling qualities as a gentleman and a journalist have entitled him to, at the hands of all cultivated and appreciative people. (4 May 67, 5)

Also on 4 May Halpine's associate on the *Citizen*, James Copper Bayles, devoted some thirty lines to "the long expected and much hoped for event." He praised "the great ability of this young man as a humorist" and urged his readers to buy the *Jumping Frog* book as well as attend the lecture, noting that "his already extensive reputation is prophetic of still greater successes in the future" (Bayles, 8). And Clemens himself preserved (and identified) a clipping from the 4 May issue of *Stage*, "a theatrical advertising medium, used as a programme," with a daily circulation of 10,000 (Rowell, 71):

> MARK TWAIN, otherwise known as "The Wild Humorist of the Pacific," whose funny writings have convulsed half a continent, and whose book—"The Jumping Frog,"—just issued from the press of Webb, is now introducing the accomplished and talented author into new fields, new harvests, and new

triumphs, appears before the New York public on Monday evening next, at Cooper Institute, to relate his last year's "Experiences in the Sandwich Islands." There could be no doubt of Mark's ability to be intensely funny, nor of the impossibility of his being anything else, if we were to judge of his quality solely by his humorous publications; but we have the assurance of the San Francisco press that the address contains an immense amount of valuable descriptive matter, not to be found elsewhere, while the quaint similes and expressions are lavished upon the audience in quantity sufficient for an entire course of lectures by any other orator in America. Seth Twain is young, handsome, single and rich, and his future is altogether fair and promising. He sails for the Holy Land with General Sherman's party, June 8th, and this lecture is delivered now on the invitation of many friends, who have determined to give him a right, royal benefit at parting. Senator Nye, of Nevada, takes much interest in Mr. Twain, and will introduce him to the audience in a speech. The Senator is a good deal of a humorist, and if he "does his level best," Mark must look to his laurels. (Clipping identified by SLC as "Stage | May 4," CU-MARK†)

A similar notice appeared in the weekly New York *Dispatch*, and the *Times* published a much briefer one, both on the day before the lecture ("Mark Twain's Lecture on 'Kanakadom,'" New York *Dispatch*, 5 May 67, 5; "Mark Twain's Lecture," New York *Times*, 5 May 67, 5). Moreover, at least five New York newspapers—the *Times*, *Evening Express*, *Citizen*, *Tribune*, and *Dispatch*—favorably noticed the *Jumping Frog* book before 6 May ("New Publications," New York *Times*, 1 May 67, 2; "Literary," New York *Evening Express*, 1 May 67, 2; "The Citizen's Book Table," New York *Citizen*, 4 May 67, 4; "New Publications," New York *Tribune*, 4 May 67, 6; "New Publications," New York *Dispatch*, 5 May 67, 7).

In short, the anxiety Clemens felt about publicity for his lecture was unnecessary. Nevertheless, shortly before his initial performance he instructed Fuller to "paper the house" with "thousands of complimentary tickets." Fuller agreed, and sent tickets "to every public-school teacher within a radius of thirty miles of New York." The result, as Clemens later recalled, was that "on the appointed night they all came. There wasn't room in Cooper Institute for a third of them" (AD, 11 Apr 1906, CU-MARK, in *MTA*, 2:353–54). At least one New York newspaper noted at the time that a "large number of persons were unable to hear this lecture at Cooper Institute last week, and it is repeated by request" ("'Mark Twain' will repeat . . . ," New York *Evening Post*, 13 May 67, 3).

The lecture performance was clearly a success, even though Senator Nye inexplicably failed to appear. Newspaper estimates of attendance ranged from two to three thousand ("'Mark Twain' delivered . . . ," New York *Times*, 7 May 67, 4; "Mark Twain's Lectures," Brooklyn *Union*, 9 May 67, 4). And those who noticed or reviewed the performance were favorable. The critic for the *Times* reported that "seldom has so large an audience been so uniformly pleased as the one that listened to Mark Twain's quaint remarks last evening" ("Mark Twain's Lecture," New York *Times*, 7 May 67, 5). The *Herald*, which would be the only newspaper to notice all three performances, shared this enthusiasm:

> The lecture is descriptive of the life, manners and customs of the natives of the islands of the Pacific, and is embellished with sparkling wit, happy hits and a genial humor wholly peculiar and unexcelled. In its entirety it is unreportable, but the manner of the gentleman and his style of delivery is so pleasing and acceptable that he, in a moment's acquaintance with his audience, makes them his friends, and with constant laughter and genuine enthusiasm carries them along with him to the end, dismissing them in the happiest possible frame of mind. The mantle of the lamented Artemus Ward seems to have fallen on the shoulders of Mark Twain, and worthily does he wear it. ("Mark Twain at the Cooper Institute," New York *Herald*, 7 May 67, 4)

"Ajax," the New York correspondent of the Sacramento *Union*, commented on the eastern response to western humor—a matter that had concerned Clemens since January:

> "Twain's" debut took place at Cooper Institute before at least 2,300 people. . . . I have seldom seen a more intelligent audience anywhere. . . . Some of his wit was a little coarser than our lecture-room audiences were accustomed to, and many quiet lovers of a good joke were amazed and confounded at the impudence and freedom of this wild Californian. (Ajax, 1)

Reporting the "first rate notices" of the major New York newspapers, Ajax observed that "the *Tribune*, through some blunder, failed to get its report in due season and appears without any comments on the lecture."

> Mark says the *Tribune* sent their highest art critic to review his lecture; that the critic went off to his hotel (the Axminster) to write up his notes, and the "darned pelican of a reporter" sent to get his copy went to the wrong hotel, and so he failed to get a hearing in the *Tribune*. (Ajax, 1)

The *Tribune*'s "art critic" was none other than Clemens's recent acquaintance Edward House, evidently also then living at the Westminster (slightly garbled by the Sacramento typesetter). House's perceptive review, which obviously benefited from his personal familiarity with

Clemens, appeared on 11 May, following the second performance. (Clemens himself identified House as the reviewer: see 28 Nov 68 to OLL, and Appendix E, which reproduces the House review in full.)

Clemens's 10 May lecture in Brooklyn was praised by the New York *Herald* and the Brooklyn *Union* ("Mark Twain in Brooklyn," New York *Herald*, 11 May 67, 4; "Mark Twain at the Athenaeum," Brooklyn *Union*, 11 May 67, 4), as well as by the Brooklyn *Eagle*, whose reviewer wrote:

> It would be manifestly unfair to report this most acceptable lecture, and no type could do justice to the cool, self-possession of the lecturer. His style is quaint and taking, and commends itself to an audience before they are aware of it, and is entirely original. To those who may think that the moderate style of manner is put on, it is only necessary to say that Mr Twain in everyday life is as staid and circumspect as he is before the public. . . . It is a pleasure to know that he will visit Brooklyn again before leaving in June on the grand excursion trip to the Holy Land. ("Mark Twain on the Sandwich Islands," Brooklyn *Eagle*, 11 May 67, 3)

Three days after this notice appeared, Clemens wrote the next letter to John Stanton, who may have been the *Eagle* reviewer.

To John Stanton (Corry O'Lanus)
14 May 1867 • New York, N.Y.

(MS: CU-MARK)

Westminster Hotel,
New York, May 14.

Corry O'Lanus, Esq

DEAR SIR—I am to deliver a lecture in Brooklyn, shortly, at the Academy of Music, & if you will be so obliging to a brother member of the press as to appear on the stage on the evening in question & introduce me to your fellow citizens, I shall be very grateful indeed.

Hoping that this request may meet with a favorable consideration at your hands,[1]

I remain
Very Truly yours,
Mark Twain

[1] John Stanton (1826–71) began his newspaper career in Brooklyn, serving as a reporter for the *Williamsburg Times* and then as city editor of the *City News*. He was now on the staff of the *Eagle*, where he had "acquired some local celebrity by the fresh and original mode of his police reporting" before becoming city editor, a position he still held. Under the pen name "Corry O'Lanus" he also wrote a humorous weekly "epistle," which enjoyed great local popularity. A writer for the Brooklyn *Programme* commented:

> As a writer Mr. Stanton is forcible, rather than elegant, and in those of his contributions to newspapers which do not profess to be humorous, there is a sameness which sufficiently stamps their authorship. But as a humorous writer he has no equal in New York or Brooklyn. While his fun is not so boisterous as Artemus Ward's, or so cutting and sarcastic as Orpheus C. Kerr's, or so wildly burlesque as John Phoenix's, there is a gentle ripple of pure fun about it—humor, in fact—which makes one hug himself with pleasure to read. Outside the reading circle of the EAGLE many of his good points would be necessarily lost, for it is in the local application of his genius at nickname that most of his power resides. We hope, therefore, to see Mr. Stanton address his humorous powers to some matter of more than local importance, and to greater extent than a simple "epistle," and we feel sure that his effort must be successful in placing his name by the side of the best of the latter-day American wits. ("Brooklyn Newspaper People," Brooklyn *Eagle*, 11 July 67, 2, reprinting the Brooklyn *Programme*)

Toward the end of 1867, Stanton published *Corry O'Lanus: His Views and Experiences* through George W. Carleton. The *Nation* said: "The author, whoever he is, hardly deserves a place in Mr. Carleton's humorous library with Josh Billings, Artemus Ward, John Phoenix, and Orpheus C. Kerr. He now and then says a sharp thing. . . . But most of the book is a thing to be delivered from" ("Corry O'Lanus . . . ," *Nation* 5 [12 Dec 67]: 479). The lecture for which Clemens solicited (and received) Stanton's agreement to introduce him would have been his fourth, but did not occur.

To John Stanton (Corry O'Lanus)
20 May 1867 • New York, N.Y.

(MS: CU-MARK)

WESTMINSTER HOTEL, COR. OF IRVING PLACE AND 16TH ST. NEW YORK ROBERTS & PALMER PROPRS

May ~~19~~ 20th 1867.

Friend Corry O'Lanus

I am one magazine article & eighteen letters behindhand (18 days to do them in, before sailing,) & so I am obliged to give up the idea of lecturing any more. Confound me if I won't have a hard time catching up anyhow. I shall stick in the house day & night for 2 weeks & try, though, anyhow.[1]

I got Mallison's note, & went over the river ~~s~~ Sunday, backwards & forwards 6 times, & then visited the closed *Eagle* & stood around till a quarter past 11 A.M, but found nobody; & returned to New York.[2]

I wanted to tell you I had given up my Brooklyn lecture, but it will do just as well now, perhaps.

I am glad to hear your tickets are going off so fast, & hope you will sell a thousand more than the house will hold.[3]

Remember me to Mallison & the boys, & say I will be over as soon as I have got half of my letters written.

And so, with a thousand thanks for the valuable favor you were so willing to do me,[4]

I remain,
Yours Sincerely
Mark Twain

[1] All but two of Mark Twain's seven contributions to the New York *Sunday Mercury* had been published by this time: the exceptions were "A Reminiscence of Artemus Ward" and "Jim Wolf and the Tom-Cats," which appeared on 7 and 14 July, and are probably the "magazine" articles referred to here and in the next letter (SLC 1867cc–dd). Clemens seems to have exaggerated the number of dispatches to the *Alta* which he had yet to write before departure on 8 June. Prior to the *Quaker City* trip, he was supposed to write "weekly." By the end of April, twenty weeks into his commission, he had completed sixteen dispatches. In early May he fell somewhat further behind, probably because of his lectures, but was at most seven behind at the time of this letter. On 17 May he began catching up, writing one a day for the next four days. By 6 June he had written a total of twenty-six dispatches in as many weeks.

[2] The subject of the note from Francis Avery Mallison (1828?–77), a colleague of Stanton's on the Brooklyn *Eagle*, remains unknown. Mallison had begun his career on the Rome (N.Y.) *Sentinel*, joined the staff of the Brooklyn *City News* in 1859, and soon thereafter moved to the *Eagle*, where he served for many years as city editor. In 1864, he and Joseph Howard, Jr., then also on the *Eagle*, devised a hoax document "purportedly from Lincoln," which announced that "Grant's Va. campaign had come to an unsuccessful end, set aside 'a day of fasting, humiliation, and prayer,' and called for a draft of 400,000 men." He and Howard were "confined in Fort Lafayette six months for participation in the forgery." Later in 1867 he was elected to the New York Assembly but continued to serve as the *Eagle*'s Albany reporter during and after his term of office (Boatner, 412–13; "Death of F. A. Mallison," New York *Times*, 23 June 77, 2).

[3] Stanton delivered his own first lecture—"Who Killed Cock Robin?"—at the Brooklyn Institute on 27 May. His newspaper described his performance as "a humoristic success, displaying that pungent, epigrammatic wit in which the lec-

turer is so conspicuous. . . . Meantime the community are just as wise as to 'Who Killed Cock Robin' as they were before the lecture." A writer for the Brooklyn *Programme*, however, later termed the lecture a "failure": it was "bewilderingly various, and the house was crowded, but Corry O'Lanus has not a voice to deliver it effectively. Hundreds went away disappointed at not being able to hear the man whose writings have made him so familiar to them" ("'Who Killed Cock Robin?'—Solution by Corry O'Lanus—A Fine Audience," Brooklyn *Eagle*, 28 May 67, 2; "Brooklyn Newspaper People," Brooklyn *Eagle*, 11 July 67, 2, reprinting the Brooklyn *Programme*).

[4] See the previous letter.

To Henry M. Crane
20 May 1867 • New York, N.Y.

(MS: WU)

WESTMINSTER HOTEL, COR. OF IRVING PLACE AND
16TH ST. NEW YORK ROBERTS & PALMER PROP^{RS}

May 20, 1867.

Henry W. Creal, Esq

I have received your kind note, & would gladly accept your invitation but that I ~~am~~ find myself so pressed for time, now, that I dare not do it.[1] My newspaper correspondence has fallen so behindhand in these last few weeks that if I lose a single day I shall not catch up before I leave. A magazine article or two, still unfinished, must be attended to.

I was to have lectured in Brooklyn again, & even hired the Academy of Music, but inexorable duty to my employers in San Francisco compelled me to give the lecture up.

I know Rondout pretty well, through my old shipmate, Kingman,[2] & I assure ~~th~~ you that I am sincerely sorry I cannot get up there this trip.

With many thanks,
I remain
Yrs Truly
Sam. L. Clemens

✉ ———

Henry W. Creal Esq | Sec'y Lincoln Literary Association | Rondout |

N. Y. [*postmarked:*] NEW-YORK MAY 21 [*postage stamp removed*] [*docketed:*] "Mark Twain" | May 1867

1 "Creal" is Clemens's misreading of Crane's signature. Crane was a resident of Rondout (now Kingston), New York, and, according to Clemens's envelope, secretary of the Lincoln Literary Association there. Crane later repeated his invitation, and Clemens eventually lectured in Rondout in 1868, 1870, and 1871 (Fatout, 136, 161).

2 Hector J. Kingman, late of Reese River, Nevada, was one of Clemens's fellow passengers on the 1866–67 trip from San Francisco to New York. His connection with Rondout has not been further documented ("Eastward Bound," San Francisco *Alta California*, 15 Dec 66, 1; SLC 1867n).

To Jane Lampton Clemens and Family
20 May 1867 • New York, N.Y.

(MS: CU-MARK)

WESTMINSTER HOTEL, COR. OF IRVING PLACE AND 16TH ST. NEW YORK ROBERTS & PALMER PROPRS

May 20, 1867.

Dear Folks—

Don't,—*don't* ask me to write. I for a week or two. I am 18 ~~letters~~ *Alta* letters behindhand, & I *must* catch up or bust. I have refused all invitations to lecture in the interior towns of this & neighboring States, & have settled down to work. Don't know how my book is coming on, —shall leave instructions here to send such money as may accrue from it to Ma every few weeks. I It may make her rich, or it ~~po~~ may reduce her to abject poverty, possibly.[1]

I hardly think Dick & Fitzgerald will accept the Sandwich Island book, but if they should, I shall leave the same instructions with them.[2]

Love to all. In haste,

Yrs Affty

Sam

1 Bindery records show that the first 1,000 copies of the *Jumping Frog* book were bound (or ordered bound) on 30 April; on 20 May a second batch of 552 copies was bound. Clemens's contract with Webb was oral, and its terms are

therefore uncertain, but it probably specified a 10 percent royalty on the list price of all copies sold, whether in paper covers ($1.00) or cloth ($1.50). No evidence has been found that Webb ever made any royalty payments to Clemens or his mother (*ET&S1*, 545 nn. 43–44; advertisement, New York *Tribune*, 4 May 67, 6).

[2]Clemens could have offered his book manuscript to Dick and Fitzgerald at 18 Ann Street anytime since arriving in New York on 12 January. Dick and Fitzgerald specialized in mail-order sales of inexpensive books for self-instruction and home entertainment, including works of at least two humorists: Benjamin P. Shillaber's *Mrs. Partington's Carpet-Bag of Fun* (1863?) and George Washington Harris's *Sut Lovingood. "Yarns Spun by a Nat'ral Born Durn'd Fool,"* published in April 1867, a copy of which the publishers sent Clemens by 23 May (Stern, 101–14; "New Publications," New York *Tribune*, 13 Apr 67, 6; SLC 1867ee). The firm did not publish the Sandwich Islands book, but over the years it reprinted numerous Mark Twain pieces, beginning with his January 1868 speech on "Woman," printed later that year in *Brudder Bones' Book of Stump Speeches, and Burlesque Orators*.

To Jane Lampton Clemens and Family
1 June 1867 • New York, N.Y.

(MS: NPV)

Westminster Hotel,
New York, June 1.

Dear Folks—

I know I ought to write oftener (just got your last,) & more fully, but I can *not* overcome my repugnance to telling what I am doing or what I expect to do or propose to do. Then, what have I left to write about? Manifestly nothing.

It isn't any use for me to talk about the voyage, because I can have no faith in that voyage or any other voyage till the ship ~~un~~ is under way. How do I know she will ever sail? ~~I~~ My passage is paid, & if the ship sails, I sail in her—but I make no calculations, have bought no cigars, no sea-going clothing,—have made no preparation whatever—shall not pack my trunk till the morning we sail. Yet my hands are full of what I am *going* to do the day *before* we sail—& what isn't done that day will go undone.[1]

All I do know or feel, is, that I am wild with impatience to move—

move—*Move!* Half a dozen times I have wished I had sailed long ago in some ship that wasn't going to keep me chained here to chafe for lagging ages while she got ready to go. Curse the endless delays! They always kill me—they make me neglect every duty & then I have a conscience that tears me like a wild beast. I wish I never had to stop *any*where a month. I do more mean things, the moment I get a chance to fold my hands & sit down than ever I can get forgiveness for.

Yes, we are to meet at Mr Beach's next Thursday night, & I suppose we shall have to be gotten up regardless of expense, in swallow-tails, white kids & everything *en régle*.[2]

I am resigned to Rev. Mr. Hutchinson's or anybody's else's supervision. I don't mind it.[3] I am *fixed*. I have got a splendid, immoral, tobacco-smoking, wine-drinking, godless room-mate who is as good & true & right-minded a man as ever lived—a man ~~whole~~ whose blameless conduct & example will always be an eloquent sermon to all who shall come within their influence.[4] But send on the professional preachers—there are none I like better to converse with—if they ain't narrow minded & bigoted they make good companions.

I asked them to send the N. Y. Weekly to you—no charge. I am not going to write for it—like all other papers that pay one splendidly, it circulates among stupid people & the *canaille*. I have made no arrangement with any New York paper—I will see about that Monday or Tuesday.[5]

Love to all.
Good bye
Yrs affy
Sam

1 Clemens's doubt whether the *Quaker City* would ever sail was prompted at least in part by General Sherman's decision to withdraw. On 27 May, the Brooklyn *Eagle* reminded readers of Captain Duncan's recent difficulties over Beecher's withdrawal in April, and pointed out that Duncan had resolved this earlier problem

> by securing another lion,—General Sherman. . . . The advantage[s] of having the great military hero with the party were duly expatiated upon; the honors and attention he would receive at every place the party visited, and which of course the company at large would come in for a share of, were set forth, and the tickets began to go off again. Now comes a rumor that General Sherman is going to desert—that he cannot arrange his private affairs so as to leave the country for so long a time as the trip will take. Here is a bombshell on Captain Duncan's quarter-deck? Can the rumor be true? We must demand of the General,

as we did of Mr. Beecher, a categorical answer forthwith, whether or not he goes to Jerusalem with the Duncan party. Meantime we are assured that Mark Twain will not back out, and that Maggie Mitchell is going along, so that if the party loses in clerical and military distinction it will make up in the material for social enjoyment. ("Is General Sherman Going to Palestine?" 27 May 67, 2)

In a letter dated 25 May and published in the principal New York newspapers on 31 May, Sherman made it clear that "circumstances have occurred to prevent the fulfillment" of his intention to go to Europe with the Duncan party. Sherman's command covered vast areas of Indian territory, and because "various tribes of Indians . . . being pressed from every quarter, have become nervous, excited, and, in some cases, positively hostile," he could not leave his post for so long a period ("Major-General Sherman," New York *Tribune*, 31 May 67, 5). Shortly after the *Quaker City* departed in June, the *Times* described the effect that the withdrawals of Beecher and Sherman seemed to have had on the passenger list:

This excursion was set on foot some four months ago by Capt. DUNCAN, and was originally designed to embrace a select and somewhat exclusive party, but before the steamer sailed it was found necessary to lower the standard a little, and ordinary persons with $1,200 to spend were enabled to purchase tickets. Rev. HENRY WARD BEECHER, who was early announced to be of the party, found it inconvenient to make the trip, and more recently Gen. SHERMAN was compelled to forego the pleasure; so that after the withdrawal of these two leading names from the bill of attractions, the passenger list gradually diminished until the steamer was obliged to sail with about half the complement of names provided for in the original programme [i.e., half of 110]. Nevertheless the party will doubtless be equally jolly, if not quite so select as at first contemplated. ("The Pleasure Excursion to Europe and Palestine—Sailing of the Quaker City," 9 June 67, 8)

[2] Moses Beach had postponed his own decision to go until mid-May, when he finally wrote Duncan a letter (widely reprinted) in which he praised the plans for the excursion and promised to be on board when "the Quaker City parts Company with that Steamboat escort down the bay, which you propose to provide for the friends of her passengers" ("The Mediterranean Excursion," Brooklyn *Eagle*, 18 May 67, 2). Beach was accompanied by his seventeen-year-old daughter, Emeline (Emma), and in Paris they would meet his son Charles, who took another ship to Europe. A member of Plymouth Church since 1854, Beach lived next door to Beecher on Columbia Heights, Brooklyn, and seems to have assumed something of Beecher's role when Beecher himself could not go. He wrote a series of letters to the *Sun* about the excursion, and before departure he provided passage money for the unofficial photographer of the trip, William E. James (Hirst and Rowles, 15–17). On 6 June the passengers were to convene at his home "to consult concerning the voyage, and to get acquainted." The *Sun* reported that the seventy guests present enjoyed an "excellent repast," and that "Mark Twain . . . enlivened the company with ebul[l]itions of wit" (SLC 1867*ll*; "Brooklyn," New York *Sun*, 7 June 67, 4).

[3] The Reverend Eleazer Carter Hutchinson (1804–76), a fellow excursionist and evidently an acquaintance of Jane Clemens's, in 1855 founded the Trinity Protestant Episcopal Church in St. Louis, where he was currently rector. Educated at Brown University and Princeton Theological Seminary, he served as president of Kemper College in 1840–45, and in 1845–52 as pastor of St. George's Church, both in St. Louis (Conard, 3:337, 523; Scharf, 2:1724–26).

Carte de visite of the Reverend E. Carter Hutchinson, preserved and identified by Colonel William R. Denny. Collection of Mrs. Theodore Whitfield. See p. 51 n. 3.

[4]Clemens described Daniel Slote (1828?–82) in an *Alta* letter written on 28 May as "a nice moral room-mate" who "has got many shirts, and a History of the Holy Land, a cribbage-board and three thousand cigars. I will not have to carry any baggage at all." Fellow passenger (Confederate) Colonel William Ritenour Denny recorded in his journal that Slote was "a short, fat chubby fellow that has a portly face, a clean black eye, an open countenance, that loves good living and laughf's and grows fat over it, clever to a fault." Slote—who, like Clemens, was a Mason—was co-owner of Slote and Woodman, a blank-book and stationery manufacturer in New York (SLC 1867gg; Denny, entry for 11 Sept; "Daniel Slote," New York *Herald*, 14 Feb 82, 5; Wilson 1867, 957; "Business Notes," *Publishers' Weekly* 14 [27 July 78]: 124).

[5]Street and Smith's *New York Weekly* had been courting Clemens as a contributor since early 1867 and by 27 June had reprinted five of his Sandwich Islands

letters. Within a week, Clemens arranged to write letters during the trip for two other New York newspapers (see 2? Feb 67 to MEC, n. 3, and 7 June 67 to Bowen, n. 3).

To Frank Fuller
1 and 8 June 1867 • New York, N.Y.
(MS: CtHMTH)

WESTMINSTER HOTEL, COR. OF IRVING PLACE AND 16TH ST. NEW YORK ROBERTS & PALMER PROPRS

New York, June 1, 1867.

Gov. Frank Fuller—

Dear Sir: Please take charge of my affairs while I am gone to Europe, (as per previous understanding,) & in the absence of a better, let this note be full & sufficient authority. Collect the ten ~~per cent~~ cents a copy due me on all sales of my book ("The Jumping Frog & Other Sketches—by Mark Twain,") from my publisher, C.H. Webb, from time to time, & remit all such moneys to my mother, Mrs. Jane Clemens, 1312 Chesnut street St. Louis, Mo.[1]

& Oblige
Yrs Very Truly
Sam. L. Clemens

[*remainder in pencil:*]

P. S.—On board Quaker City, N.Y. harbor, June 8.—I forgot to forward this to you several days ago. I thought I had done so.

Sam L. Clemens

[1] The royalty due Clemens was probably 10 percent of the list price (ten or fifteen cents, depending on the binding)—the rate he crossed out, evidently in some doubt about the terms of his agreement with Webb. See 20 May 67 to JLC and family, n. 1.

To William Bowen
7 June 1867 • New York, N.Y.

(TS and MS, *damage emended:* CU-MARK and TxU)

Westminster Hotel,
New York, June 7, 1867

Dear Will:

We leave tomorrow at 3:00 P. M.[1] Everything is ready but my trunks. I will pack them first thing in the morning.

We have got a crowd of tiptop people, & shall have a jolly, sociable, homelike trip of it for the next five or six months. And then—if we all go to the bottom, I think we shall be fortunate. There is no unhappiness like the misery of sighting land (& work) again after a cheerful, careless voyage. They were lucky boys that went down in sight of home the other day when the Santiago de Cuba stranded on the New Jersey shore.[2] However I have a roving commission, anyhow, & if I don't like to land when we get back, I will just shift on to some other ship & go away again.

I am going on this trip for fun only. I have to keep up my San Francisco correspondence, of course, & must write two letters a month for the New York Tribune (they pay best & that is what I work for) till we reach Egypt, & then I have to write oftener.[3] Herbert of the *World* has just taken passage to-day, & he is a splendid ship-mate—knows everything it is possible for one man to know, & is almighty jolly—& is also the most brilliant writer in America, except, perhaps House.[4] I guess we shan't have any *very* bad time, my son. All the *World's* foreign correspondents will have to put him through, & all the *Tribune's* & the San Francisco *Alta's* will have to waltz me along, & so I do not see that we need care particularly whether school keeps or not.[5]

Remember me lovingly to Mrs Bowen, & say to Bart that if I can favor him by walking into a furnace, I will do it. I want to be remembered to all your mother's family & its branches except Sam Bowen. But the idea of that fellow's being in St Louis 3 days & never calling on me, & never being where I could find *him*, is infamous. I'll recollect the scoundrel.[6]

How is Miriam? Tell her I dream of her still. And I dream of Mrs. Robbins too, but not so much.[7] Good bye, my oldest friend.

Yrs Ever,
Sam Clemens

[1]This departure time had been fixed since at least the beginning of April, when the *Quaker City* was selected for the trip ("The Mediterranean Excursion," Brooklyn *Eagle*, 5 Apr 67, 2).

[2]In the early morning of 22 May, the *Santiago de Cuba*, bound for New York out of Greytown, ran aground within two hundred and fifty yards of the New Jersey shore, about six miles below Atlantic City. Two men and five women, out of about four hundred passengers and crew, drowned when their lifeboats capsized (New York *Times:* "Marine Disasters," 23 May 67, 1; "The Stranding of the Santiago de Cuba," 24 May 67, 1; "Marine Disasters," New York *Tribune*, 23 May 67, 1).

[3]Clemens agreed to correspond for the *Tribune* and, without signature, for the rival New York *Herald* (Ganzel 1964, 270–73). The *Tribune* probably paid him at the rate of forty dollars per column of type (1 Dec 67 to Young, n. 1), eventually publishing six letters that averaged slightly more than a column apiece. He published four letters in the *Herald*, three at an unknown but presumably lower rate (because they were unsigned) and, upon his return, one that was supposed to be signed, at a rate comparable or identical to the *Tribune*'s: fifty dollars for one and one-quarter columns, notably better than the thirty-nine dollars (in greenbacks) paid by the *Alta* (see 2 Dec 67 to Fairbanks, and 15 Apr 67 to JLC and family, n. 1).

[4]William Henry Hurlbert (1827–95) joined the staff of the New York *World* in 1862 and was its correspondent to the 1867 Paris exposition, but he was not finally one of the *Quaker City*'s passengers. He departed instead on the *Arago*, which sailed on the same day the *Quaker City* did, bound directly for Le Havre. On 13 February, Hurlbert had been elected second vice-president of the New York Press Club. He later served from 1876 to 1883 as editor-in-chief of the *World* ("Departures Yesterday," New York *Herald*, 9 June 67, 9; "Ocean Steamers," New York *Tribune*, 3 June 67, 7; "The New York Press Club," New York *Evening Post*, 14 Feb 67, 2).

[5]The *Alta*'s correspondent at the Paris exposition was M. G. Upton (SLC 1867w). On 5 June, John Russell Young (1840–99), the twenty-six-year-old managing editor of the New York *Tribune*, wrote at least three letters of introduction for Clemens: one to Lothar Bucher (1817–92) in Berlin, a high official in the Prussian government (NPV); one to W. D. Spalding in London (NPV); and one to William Henry Huntington (1820–85), the *Tribune*'s correspondent in Paris (CaQMMRB; Crankshaw, 232; Baehr, 33). Clemens carried the letters with him, but—since he did not visit either London or Berlin—presumably used only the letter to Huntington, which read as follows:

OFFICE OF THE TRIBUNE.

NEW YORK June 5th 186 7.

My Dear Mr Huntington:

This will introduce to you Mr Samuel Clements of San Francisco, whose fame as a writer has I have no doubt reached you under his *nom de plume* of "Mark Twain." He is a very nice gentleman, one whom I am certain you will be glad to know. Any courtesy you may extend to him will be appreciated by

Yrs
Jno. Russell Young

W. H. Huntington, Esq.
Paris, France

[6]William Bowen (1836–93) was still living in Hannibal, his birthplace, where he probably last saw Clemens when Clemens lectured there on 2 April. They

had been schoolmates, close boyhood friends, and fellow pilots (see *L1*, 15–16 n. 8). Bowen was president of the Western Boatman's Benevolent Association at this time, and he did not leave "the river" (piloting) until September 1868, soon thereafter joining the Hannibal insurance firm of Moses P. Green and Company, according to his son Royden Burwell Bowen (b. 1883). Evidently in anticipation of his retirement from piloting, however, Bowen was already a partner in a St. Louis restaurant: see note 7. Clemens asked to be remembered to Will's wife, Mary (Mollie) Cunningham Bowen (d. 1873), whom he had married in 1857; to his mother, Amanda Warren Stone Bowen (1802–81), also in Hannibal, a widow since 1853; to his older brother Barton Stone Bowen (1830?–68), a steamboat pilot and later captain with whom Clemens had served as a pilot, now possibly living in Hannibal too; and, somewhat more irascibly, to Samuel Adams Bowen, Jr. (1838?–78), Bart's and Will's younger brother, still a pilot and evidently boarding in St. Louis (Edwards 1867, 131, 211; *MTLBowen*, 5–7; *Inds*, 303–6; *L1*, 340–41 n. 4; "Death of a Steamboat Captain," San Francisco *Times*, 23 June 68, 1).

[7]Clemens was dreaming of Nancy Miriam Robbins (1848–81), also known as Myra, and of her mother, Susan L. Robbins (1819–73). Miriam was the only daughter of Susan and James Kenyon Robbins (1812–83) of St. Louis. Clemens's acquaintance with the family probably dated from his own piloting days, in 1858–61. It is likely he asked Bowen to pass along his message because he knew that Bowen was a partner with James Robbins and Oscar F. Summers in a restaurant located at 24 Olive Street in St. Louis. Bowen's granddaughter Agnes recalled "a family tradition that Miriam, the daughter of Mrs. Robbins, was one of Clemens's 'sweethearts,' and something of a beauty" (*MTLBowen*, 10, 30). Her memory is corroborated by June Ransburgh, a distant relative of Myra Robbins, who in 1960 related several plausible details of the Robbins-Clemens relationship, quite independently of the Bowen family's "tradition":

> During her young days in St. Louis . . . Miss Myra met a riverboat pilot by the name of Samuel L. Clemens (later, the famous Mark Twain). During the friendship which followed the riverboat pilot would bring fine foods and gifts to Miss Myra when he returned from New Orleans.
>
> At one time, when Miss Myra was visiting at the Robbins farm near Point Pleasant [near New Madrid, Missouri, an area Clemens knew well as a pilot], Clemens tied his boat up at the Point and sent a beautiful decorated cake which he had the chef make for Miss Myra.
>
> After Miss Myra returned to St. Louis, this friendship had gotten to the point that Clemens spoke to her father asking permission to pay court to his daughter. At this James Kenyon Robbins refused, telling Clemens that he did not approve of river men. ("Mark Twain Pays Court to Miss Myra Robbins at Point Pleasant," New Madrid *Weekly Record*, 20 or 21 Oct 1960, 3)

(Edwards 1866, 692, 780; *St. Louis Census* 1870, 345; St. Louis *Post-Dispatch:* "Died," 23 Nov 81, 5; "Died," 7 July 83, 5; "Deaths," St. Louis *Missouri Republican*, 24 Jan 73, 5; *New Madrid Census*, 707; Branch and Hirst, 33–61.)

To Jane Lampton Clemens and Family
7 June 1867 • New York, N.Y.

(MS: NPV)

New York, June 7.

Dear Folks—

I suppose we shall be many a league at sea tomorrow night, & goodness knows I shall be unspeakably glad of it.

I haven't got *any*thing to write, else I *would* write it. I have just written myself clear out in letters to the *Alta*, & I think they are the stupidest letters that were ever written from New York. Corresponding has been a perfect drag ever since I got to the States. If it continues, abroad, I don't know what the Tribune & Alta folks will think.

I have withdrawn the Sandwich Island book—it would be useless to publish it in these dull publishing times. As for the Frog book, I don't believe that will ever pay anything worth a cent. I published it simply to advertise myself & not with the hope of making anything out of it.[1]

Well, I haven't anything to write, except that I am so tired of staying in one place that I am in a fever to get away. Read ~~r~~ my Alta letters—they contain everything I could possibly write to you. Tell Zeb & John Leavenworth to write me—they can get plenty of gossip from Essie & Lou & the pilots.[2]

An importing house[3] sent ~~me~~ two cases of exquisite champaign aboard the ship for me to-day—Veuve Cliquot & ~~L'a~~ Lac d'Or. I & my room-mate have set apart every Saturday as a solemn fast-day, wherein we will entertain no light matters or frivolous conversation, but only get drunk. [That is a joke.] His mother & sisters are the best & most home=like people I have yet found in a brown-stone front. There is no style about them except in house & furniture.[4]

I wish Orion were going on this voyage, for I believe with so many months of freedom from business cares he could not help but be cheerful & jolly. I often wonder if his law business it going satisfactorily to him, but knowing that the dull season is setting in now (it looked like it had already set ~~it in~~ in before,) I have felt as if I could almost answer the question myself—which is to say in plain words, I was afraid to ask. I wish I had gone to Washington in the winter instead of going West. I could have gouged an office out of Bill Stewart for him, & that would have atoned for the loss of my home visit.[5] But I am so worthless that it seems to me I never do anything or accomplish anything that lingers in my mind as a pleasant memory. My mind is stored full of unworthy conduct toward Orion & toward you all, & an accusing conscience gives me peace only in excitement & restless moving from place to place. If I could say I had done one thing ~~that~~ ‸for‸ any of you that entitled me to your good opinions (I say nothing of your love, for I am sure of *that*, no matter how unworthy of it I may make myself,—from Orion down, you have always given me that, all the days of my life, when God Almighty knows I have seldom deserved it,) I believe I could go home & stay there—& I *know* I would care little for the world's praise or blame. There is no satisfaction in the world's praise, anyhow, & it has no worth to me save in the way of business. I tried to gather up its compliments to send to you, but the work was distasteful & I dropped it.[6]

You observe that under a cheerful exterior I have got a spirit that is angry with me & gives me freely its contempt. I can get away from that at sea, & be tranquil & satisfied—& so, with my parting love & benediction for Orion & all of you, I say good bye & God bless you all—& welcome the winds that wafts a weary soul to the sunny lands of the Mediterranean!

Yrs forever

Sam.

[1] Clemens admitted in December 1870 that when he published the *Jumping Frog* book in 1867, he "fully expected" it to "sell 50,000 copies & it only sold 4,000," the latter being an accurate approximation of its actual sale in the United States by that time (SLC to Francis S. Drake, 26 Dec 70, NN-B†; *ET&S1*, 544–46). Mark Twain was unaware until the spring or summer of 1868 that George Routledge and Sons had reprinted the volume in England, where it was not protected by British or American copyright law. By 1870 the book had also been reprinted in England by John Camden Hotten, and by the time of Hotten's death in 1873, these two publishers had printed some 43,000 copies of it (*ET&S1*, 547–48). Mark Twain's Sandwich Islands manuscript, on the other hand, seems not to have interested Dick and Fitzgerald—or any other publisher. On 15 June the *American Literary Gazette and Publishers' Circular* noted, "The Trade is reported quiet at present; some publishers intimating that they will now wait until fall before putting out any new books" ("Notes on Books and Booksellers," 9 [15 June 67]: 100). The book was never published, and the manuscript is not known to survive.

[2] Zebulon Leavenworth (1830–77), still an active pilot, and his brother John M. Leavenworth (b. 1835 or 1836), formerly a clerk in a wholesale grocery firm

but now a steamboat captain, were both old friends of Clemens's whom he had doubtless seen most recently in St. Louis where, on 27 March, his application for reinstatement in the Masons' Polar Star Lodge No. 79 was formally submitted, endorsed by "Brothers Leavenworth and W. P. Curtis" (*L1*, 107 n. 2; *St. Louis Census* 1860, 180; Edwards 1867, 511; Denslow, 57). For Essie Pepper and Lou Conrad, see 15 Apr 67 to JLC and family, n. 6.

[3] Unidentified.

[4] Ann J. Slote (b. 1801 or 1802), widow of Daniel Slote, Sr., lived with her son and his sisters—Josephine, aged about twenty-nine, and Ann, aged about twenty-six—at 44 East Twenty-sixth Street, just north of Madison Square (Wilson 1867, 957; *New York Census* 1860, 920–21).

[5] Although Orion had been in St. Louis or Keokuk, or both, during Clemens's visit, he spent most of his time in 1867 attending to the family property in Tennessee. From October 1866 until nearly the end of April 1867, he contributed nine letters to the San Francisco *Times*, for which he was presumably paid, but probably very little. When in St. Louis, he boarded (for an unknown but probably minimal fee) with his sister and mother, listing himself in the city directory as a lawyer and taking whatever work he could find. On 9 May, for instance, Orion reported to Mollie (still living with her parents in Keokuk) that "Ludington paid me twenty dollars yesterday for legal services. I send you five. I paid Pamela five on account" (OC 1866a–b, 1867a–g; Edwards 1867, 257; OC to MEC, 9 May 67, CU-MARK). But evidently he was also hoping for employment as a correspondent with a New York periodical. On 25 May Pamela reported to Orion:

> I wrote you that the article you sent the N.Y. Weekly had been published. I now send you the paper. You will not fail to observe the invitation to write as often as convenient. The natural inference is that they were pleased with the article. Now I want to advise you to write several contributions, and wait until they are published, before you say anything about pay. I think this is important.
>
> Mrs. Green says she has always liked your writings. She thinks your style is particularly pleasing. I believe it is Mrs. Ludington who says, if any thing, she likes your style better than Sam's. I think your style will be popular if you once become known to the public. We have rec'd no California paper since you left. (PAM to OC, 25 May 67, NPV)

Orion's last two letters to the San Francisco *Times* (the "California paper" Pamela mentioned) were published on 22 and 23 May, and had therefore not yet reached St. Louis. His letter to Street and Smith's *New York Weekly* (presumably the journal Pamela referred to) has not been found, and Orion seems not to have pursued the matter, at least not successfully. William M. Stewart (1827–1909), Republican senator from Nevada (1864–75 and 1887–1905), had been first among equals in signing the "call" for Clemens to lecture in New York. At the time of this letter, Stewart had just sent (or was about to send) Clemens himself an offer of a post as his private secretary (Effie Mona Mack, 55).

[6] Frank Fuller did, however, collect "a lot of notices" of Clemens's New York lecture debut, giving them to Clemens in November 1868 (28 Nov 68 to OLL).

To Frank Fuller
7 June 1867 • New York, N.Y.
(MS: ViU)

WESTMINSTER HOTEL, COR. OF IRVING PLACE AND
16TH ST. NEW YORK ROBERTS & PALMER PROP^{RS}

New York, June 7, 1867.

Frank Fuller Esq

You are hereby authorized to collect all moneys accruing to me from the publication of my book, "The Jumping Frog," & receipt for the same. Particulars will be found in my former note.[1]

My mothers address is 1312 Chesnut street, St Louis

Yrs Truly,
Mark Twain

[1] See 1 and 8 June 67 to Fuller.

To John McComb
8 June 1867 • New York, N.Y.
(MS facsimile: Daley)

New York June 8.
2 A.M.

Dear John—

D—n it I have intended all along to write you the night before sailing, but here it is within 12 hours of leaving & I have ‸not‸ been to bed or packed my trunk yet.[1] But I ~~di~~ went to dinner at 3 P.M with "Private Miles O'Riley" & Jno Russell Young, Managing Editor of the Tribune (I am going to write for that—I find the Weekly has 200,000 circulation)—drank wine;[2] dined from 6 to ~~n~~ 9 at Jno Murphy's (*God* made *him*, you know, & Mrs M. too,)—drank several breeds of wine there, naturally enough; dined again from 9 till 12 at Mr. Slote's, (my shipmate's,) whom the same God made that made Jno Murphy—& mind you

I say that such men as they are, are almighty scarce—you can shut your eyes & go forth at random in a strange land & pick out a son of a bitch a great deal ~~easily~~ easier;—drank much wine there, too. So I am only just getting over it now. Mr MacCrellish & I are to take Christmas dinner at Jno Murphy's.[3]

Now I feel good—I feel *d—d* good—& I could write a good correspondence—can, anyway, as soon as I get out of this most dismal town. *You'll see.* Got an offer to-day for 3-months course of lectures next winter—$100 a night & no bother & no expense.[4] How's that?

John, I'll write from Paris. God be with you

Yrs fraternaly[5]

Mark.

[1] Duncan began running an advertisement in the *Tribune* and other newspapers on Monday, 3 June, announcing that "all baggage should be on board on SATURDAY MORNING, and passengers are requested to be on board at 2 o'clock. The ship will positively sail at 3" ("Ocean Steamers," New York *Tribune*, 3 June 67, 7).

[2] "Private Miles O'Reilly" was Charles Graham Halpine, editor of the New York *Citizen*, the organ of the reform movement. He was an Irishman, educated at Trinity College, Dublin, who had worked on B. P. Shillaber's Boston *Carpet-Bag*, as well as on the New York *Times*, *Herald*, and *Leader* before he enlisted in the Union forces, where he distinguished himself both in battle and as an administrator, resigning ultimately with the brevet of brigadier general. Halpine's creation "Miles O'Reilly," an uneducated Irish private in the Forty-seventh New York Regiment, became popular through his wartime newspaper letters. In early 1864 these and other works by Halpine were published by Carleton as *The Life and Adventures, Songs, Services, and Speeches of Private Miles O'Reilly (47th Regiment, New York Volunteers)*, with comic illustrations by Edward F. Mullen. This volume sold well, and was followed promptly in 1866 by *Baked Meats of the Funeral. A Collection of Essays, Poems, Speeches, Histories, and Banquets. By Private Miles O'Reilly*, also published by Carleton. Charles Henry Webb had recently been contributing to the New York *Citizen* (as well as half a dozen other journals) and may have introduced Clemens to Halpine, whose journal had puffed his lecture and reviewed the *Jumping Frog* book favorably in early May ("The Citizen's Book Table," New York *Citizen*, 4 May 67, 4). Halpine and Clemens dined with John Russell Young, managing editor of the New York *Tribune*, the weekly edition of which had a circulation of 190,000, making it one of the most widely sold periodicals in the United States. Clemens's letters appeared first in the daily *Tribune*, which had a circulation of about 43,000, and then in the weekly. His New York *Herald* letters reached 65,000 in the daily form, more than 10,000 in the weekly. By contrast, the San Francisco *Alta California* (one of the largest western newspapers) had a circulation of 10,000 in its daily form, and at least 5,000 in its weekly (Rowell, 11, 71, 171).

[3] The New York business agent for the *Alta California*, John J. Murphy, and his wife (who is otherwise unidentified) lived at 36 East Thirty-first Street, just

five blocks uptown from Dan Slote's house (Wilson 1867, 752). Frederick MacCrellish, principal owner of the *Alta*, lived in San Francisco but, by this account, was planning to be in New York by Christmas.

[4]The likely source of this offer is suggested by the notebook Clemens kept between mid-May and 2 July 1867. On its endpaper he wrote: "Edwin Lee Brown | Lecture Man | Chicago." Brown represented the Young Men's Library Association in Chicago and, until recently, had served also as secretary of the Associated Western Literary Societies, whose chief task was to coordinate the requests of the member societies with the available time of individual lecturers. On 8 May, however, by a vote of the delegates at their annual meeting in Chicago, Brown was replaced by G. L. Torbert. Brown promptly "established a lecture agency of his own in direct opposition to the Associated Western Literary Societies," and he evidently declined to turn over even the membership records to Torbert (*N&J1*, 315; Hoeltje, 126–29; "Northwestern Literary Association," Chicago *Times*, 9 May 67, 4). Clemens must have replied favorably to Brown's initial inquiry, since he apparently received another, more specific, offer from Brown in August through his agent, Frank Fuller: see 7 Aug 67 to Fuller.

[5]Clemens and McComb were both Masons. At this time and until October 1867, McComb was serving as grand marshal of the Grand Lodge of Free and Accepted Masons of the State of California (Langley 1867, 673).

No letters have been found for the first two weeks of the trip. The *Quaker City* left her berth at 2:00 p.m. on 8 June (an hour earlier than had been previously announced) carrying some sixty-five passengers, only a handful of whom were from Brooklyn, let alone Plymouth Church. (A complete passenger list appears in Appendix C; a complete itinerary, based on a wide variety of contemporary letters and documents, appears in Appendix D, which serves as the source for the travel dates mentioned in the notes.)

Moses Beach described the *Quaker City*'s departure in one of his letters to the New York *Sun:*

> Promptly at the hour named—so promptly that some watches had not yet fully determined to indicate the hour fixed for sailing—the last hawser was cast off and the Quaker City steamed her way into the river. . . . Two excursion boats had been engaged—the "Fletcher" and "Pierce" and these with noisy demonstrations from throats of flesh and brass, gambolled and frisked about our huger "City." (Beach 1867a)

But the ship got only as far as Gravesend Bay, off Brooklyn, where the captain dropped anchor to wait out rough seas. For two days of stormy weather the ship remained at anchor while the passengers sang hymns and fought seasickness. "We are still anchored where you left us," wrote Daniel D. Leary, a passenger and one of the *Quaker City*'s owners:

> As far as I can see I am not very favorably impressed with the party on board taken as a whole, they are nothing but a common lot of western people, however I hope to find enough exceptions to the rule to make it pleasant for me. The organ has just struck up and they are singing a hymn, I hope they will not overdo this kind of thing, because if they do I shall feel as if an accident should happen to that organ. (Leary to Arthur Leary, 8 June 67, transcript, CU-MARK, in Leary, 197–98)

On Monday, 10 June, at 12:30 P.M., the *Quaker City* at last put out to sea. Dr. Benjamin B. Nesbit noted in his diary: "Raised anchor at 12 M, passed Sandy Hook at 2 P.M. Sea rough nearly all sick" (Charles C. Duncan 1867b, entries for 8–10 June; Nesbit, entry for 10 June).

Clemens discovered almost immediately that many of the passengers were not simply older than he, they were more staid, somewhat stiff, even solemn and sanctimonious—and they did not always appreciate his playful and sometimes irreverent humor. In the "Conclusion" to *The Innocents Abroad* he summarized his relationship with his fellow travelers: "I was on excellent terms with eight or nine of the excursionists (they are my staunch friends yet,) and was even on speaking terms with the rest of the sixty-five." These "eight or nine" compatible friends, whose company he frequently sought during the voyage, included Daniel Slote and Emma Beach (both identified earlier), as well as the following:

■ Charles Jervis Langdon (1849–1916) was a youth of seventeen from Elmira, New York—the only son of wealthy coal dealer Jervis Langdon and his wife, Olivia Lewis Langdon (see Appendix A for a full Langdon genealogy). They had sent Charles on the *Quaker City* excursion as a safe approximation of the more traditional grand tour. (The Langdons were founding members of Elmira's Park Church, where Thomas K. Beecher, Henry Ward Beecher's half-brother, presided.) Charles's friendship with Clemens seems to have become established chiefly toward the end of the voyage, although in letters home to Elmira, Charles mentioned him as early as mid-August: "Mr. Clemens and some others dared to break the laws of the country and go in the night to the Pantheon [i.e., Parthenon]." After the Holy Land journey, in early October, Charles wrote that Clemens "made the journey from Damascus through the country" and "says he has lost every bit of veneration he ever had for the Prophets and Men of Old. Says God has his hands full to take care of them and that they were just like these present scamps who infest the ground." Probably in October or early November he wrote that he had "been hearing Clemens' Holy Land letters [presumably read aloud by their author] . . . they are characteristic of him. I do not like them as a whole but he says some good things" (excerpts from Charles J. Langdon to Jervis and Olivia Lewis Langdon, various dates in Aug–Nov 67, Hamilton Galleries, lot 111).

■ John A. (Jack) Van Nostrand (1847?–79) of Greenville, New Jersey, and New York City, did not make a good first impression on Clemens, to judge from his notebook near the start of the trip:

> The long-legged, simple, green, wide-mouthed, horse-laughing young fellow, who once made a sea-voyage to fortress Monroe in the Oceanica, & now knows it all. . . . He says the most witless things & then laughs uproariously at them—& he has a vile notion that everything everybody else says is meant for a witticism, & so laughs loudly out when very often the speaker had spoken seriously, or even had meant to say something full of pathos. (*N&J1*, 330)

But Clemens eventually warmed toward the "good-hearted and always well-meaning" youngster, offering him brotherly advice: Van Nostrand later recalled Clemens's "great love of veracity" and "the many lectures you have in times past given me upon lying" (SLC 1870, 58; Van Nostrand to SLC, 29 June 75, CU-MARK). This more charitable view of Van Nostrand was confirmed by Colonel Denny, who described him in his journal as "a young man about twenty years old, hansom, slender, tall, [with] a good face, kind heart and amiable disposition." After the *Quaker City* voyage, Van Nostrand moved to the West—evidently to stave off the effects of tuberculosis—where he took up sheep farming, spending his last few years in Colorado and New Mexico, where he died at the age of about thirty-two (Denny, entry for 11 Sept; Alta California Bookstore, lot 90).

■ Julius Moulton (1843?–1916) was the elder son of the former Jane Emma Smith and Jonathan Benjamin Moulton (1810–97) of St. Louis, chief engineer of the North Missouri Railroad. Until recently he had been employed as an assistant engineer on his father's railroad. Denny described him as "a clever youth of about 22 Summers," who was "tall, slender and kind" and "belongs to Church." During the excursion

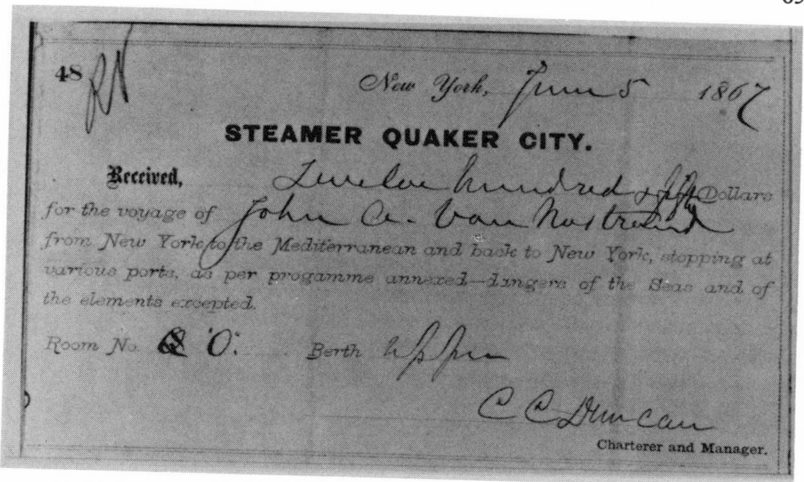

48 RN

New York, June 5 1867

STEAMER QUAKER CITY.

Received, Twelve hundred & fifty Dollars

for the voyage of John A. Van Nostrand

from New York to the Mediterranean and back to New York, stopping at various ports, as per programme annexed—dangers of the Seas and of the elements excepted.

Room No. 8 O. Berth upper

C C Duncan

Charterer and Manager.

Van Nostrand's receipt for the $1,250 fare. Its date (5 June) and number (**48**) show that he was among the late additions to the passenger list. Alta California Bookstore, lot 90. See p. 64.

Moulton wrote at least six travel letters to the St. Louis *Missouri Republican*. He accompanied Clemens both on the Holy Land trek and on the trip through Spain. In 1907, commenting on his reference to "Moult" in chapter 4 of *The Innocents Abroad*, Clemens explained that he "was a young fellow from Mo. quiet & rather diffident; he had not been away from home before. I have never heard of him since" ("Deaths," St. Louis *Post-Dispatch*, 17 Feb 1916, 18; *St. Louis Census* 1860, 357; Denny, entry for 11 Sept; Conard, 4:497–98; Edwards 1866, 616; Edwards 1867, 590; Isabel V. Lyon's notation on Robert P. Elmer to SLC, 4 Aug 1907, CU-MARK†).

■ Dr. Abraham Reeves Jackson (1827–92) was born in Philadelphia. In 1848 he received his medical degree from Pennsylvania Medical College and set up a general practice in Stroudsburg, Pennsylvania. During the Civil War he served as assistant medical director of the United States Army of Virginia. In 1869 Jackson's wife of nearly nineteen years died, and in 1871 he married Julia Newell, whom he had met on the *Quaker City* trip. The couple lived in Chicago, where Jackson became a prominent and highly respected gynecologist. Clemens enjoyed his witty manner, which he described in *The Innocents Abroad:* "The doctor asks the questions, generally, because he can keep his countenance, and look more like an inspired idiot, and throw more imbecility into the tone of his voice than any man that lives" (chapter 27). Jackson was engaged to write travel letters to the Monroe County (Pa.) *Democrat* during the *Quaker City* voyage.

■ Solon Long Severance (1834–1915) was a prominent Cleveland banker who began his career as a messenger, then worked for many years as a teller. In 1861 he joined with others in establishing the Euclid Avenue National Bank, serving in turn as its cashier, vice-president, and then president. After retiring from active business in 1867, he indulged his love for travel and prepared illustrated lectures about his journeys around the world.

■ Emily Charity Allen Severance (1840–1921), daughter of a noted physician, had married Solon in 1860. Mrs. Severance kept a journal during the voyage, which was privately published in 1938 by her daughter. She also helped Captain Duncan write several letters reporting on the excursion, which were published by the New York *Independent* during the voyage (Severance, 33).

■ Mary Mason Fairbanks (1828–98) was born in Perry, Ohio, but later lived in New York State, where she attended the Norwich Academy and the Troy Female Seminary. She taught school in South Carolina, Kentucky, and New York before marrying, in 1852, Abel Fairbanks, co-owner of the Cleveland *Herald*, who did not join the excursion (*MTMF*, xx; Lorenzo Sayles Fairbanks, 551–52; Mary Mason Fairbanks 1898, 352–54; "Mrs. Fairbanks Passes Away," Cleveland *Plain Dealer*, 9 Dec 98, 5; for more on Abel Fairbanks see 5 Oct 68 to Abel Fairbanks, n. 1). Mrs. Fairbanks was writing her own correspondence for her husband's newspaper. In her second letter, dated 9 June, she recorded her first impression of Mark Twain:

> There is one table from which is sure to come a peal of contagious laughter, and all eyes are turned toward "Mark Twain," whose face is perfectly mirth-provoking. Sitting lazily at the table, scarcely genteel in his appearance, there is nevertheless a something, I know not what, that interests and attracts. I saw to-day at dinner, venerable divines and sage looking men, convulsed with laughter at his drolleries and quaint original manners. To my mind, however, he can never win the laurels that were destined to deck the brow of our poor friend who sleeps at "Kensal Green." (Mary Mason Fairbanks 1867a)

The last sentence alluded to Artemus Ward, who first rose to prominence on the Cleveland *Plain Dealer* and had only recently been buried at Kensal Green in London. But she was quicker than this remark might imply to recognize Clemens's great talent. In a later reminiscence she wrote:

> Those who had the good fortune to share with him the adventures with which his remarkable and grotesque narratives have made the public familiar, recall with interest the gradual waking up of this man of genius. His keen eyes discerned the incongruities of character around him, into which his susceptibility to absurdities gave him quick insight. (Mary Mason Fairbanks 1892, 430)

Mrs. Fairbanks was the central figure in this whole group of *Quaker City* acquaintances. She and the Severances were already on familiar terms, since they knew each other from Cleveland, and Langdon, Van Nostrand, Moulton, and Clemens probably came to know her as well as each other in part through their mutual dependence on her sober, but not overbearing, advice.

To Jane Lampton Clemens and Family
21 and 29 June; 1, 3, and 5 July 1867
Island of Fayal, Azores; Gibraltar; Tangier, Morocco; SS *Quaker City* en route from Gibraltar to Marseilles; and Marseilles, France

(MS: NPV)

Fayal, (Azores,) June 20.

Dear Folks—

We are having a lively time here, after a stormy trip. We meant to go to Sau Miguel, but were driven in here by stress of weather. Beautiful climate.[1]

Yrs aff Sam.

Gibraltar, June ~~2~~ 30.

Dear Folks—

Arrived here this morning, & am clear worn out with riding &

climbing in & over & around & about this monstrous rock & its fortifications. Summer climate & very pleasant.[2]

Yrs Sam.

Tangier, Morocco, (Africa,)
July 1, 1867.

Dear Folks—

Half a dozen of us came here yesterday from Gibraltar, & some of the company ‸took the other direction‸ went up through Spain to Paris by rail. We decided that Gibraltar & San Roque were all of Spain that we wanted to see at present & are glad we came here among the Africans, Moors, Arabs & Bedouins of the desert. I would not give this experience for ~~the~~ all the balance of the trip combined. This is the infernalest hive of infernally costumed barbarians I have ever come across yet.[3]

Yrs Sam.

[*in top margin, in pencil:* I inclose Moorish coins of Tangier dated 1216 & 1268 of the Hegira.][4]

At Sea, July 2.

Dr Folks—

We are far up the intensely blue & ravishingly beautiful Mediterranean. And now we are just passing the island of Minorca. The climate is perfectly lovely, & it is hard to drive anybody to bed day or night. We run the whole night through, occasionally, & by this means enjoy the rare sensation of seeing the sun rise. But the sunsets are soft, rich, warm, superb!

We had a ball last night under the awnings of the quarter deck, & the share of it of 3 of ~~it~~ ‸us‸ was masquerade. We had full, flowing, picturesque Moorish costumes which we purchased in the bazaars of Tangier.[5]

Yrs Sam.

Marseilles, France, July 5.

We are here. Start for Paris to-morrow.[6] All well. [*insertion in pencil:*] ‸Had a gorgeous 4th of July jollification yesterday at sea.‸[7]

Yrs Sam.

[*enclosure:*]

[*on the back, in pencil:*]

Cape Spartel

---

below Tangier
African coast.
June 30/67[8]

[*photograph stamped on back:*] MRS. P. A. MOFFETT.

[1]The excursion program specified a stop of a "day or two" at St. Michael (São Miguel), the largest of the Azores, which was somewhat farther east than Fayal (Charles C. Duncan 1867a). But, as Clemens explained in his first letter to the New York *Tribune*,

> We had to change our notions about San Miguel, for a storm came up, toward noon, that so pitched and tossed the vessel that common sense dictated a run for shelter. Therefore we steered for the nearest island of the group—Fayal (the people there pronounce it Fy-all, and put the accent on the first syllable.) We anchored in the open roadstead of Horta, half a mile from the shore. (SLC 1867hh)

They reached Horta early on 21 (not 20) June. Like most of the other passengers, Clemens spent a busy day on shore and probably began this letter when he returned to the ship that evening. Continued rough seas delayed departure for Gibraltar until noon of 23 June.

[2]The ship anchored in Gibraltar Bay on the morning of 29 (not 30) June, and most of the passengers spent the planned "day" at Gibraltar as the excursion prospectus suggested, "looking over the wonderful subterraneous fortifications." Clemens, Slote, and Jackson, together with one other unidentified passenger, "rode on asses and mules up the steep, narrow streets and entered the subterranean galleries the English have blasted out in the rock," according to Clemens. They then went shopping in the town of Gibraltar, and concluded the day by listening to military bands playing operatic selections in the public park. Departure for Marseilles was rescheduled for the afternoon of 1 July in order to provide enough time to clean the *Quaker City*'s boilers and to resupply the ship with coal (Charles C. Duncan 1867a; Abraham Reeves Jackson 1867b; SLC 1867pp; Duncan and Severance).

[3]The travelers who "went up through Spain" were Moses and Emma Beach, Thomas S. Beckwith, the Reverend Henry Bullard, Charles Langdon, and Solomon N. Sanford. On the evening of 29 June they took a steamer to Cádiz, then went overland to Madrid and, after a thirty-six-hour train ride, arrived in Paris on 11 July. They returned to the ship at Leghorn in late July (Charles Jervis Langdon, entry for 28 July). Clemens contemplated going with them: "D—d glad when I *knew* it was too late & we couldn't go" he noted to himself. "Now as to Tangiers there shall be no pulling & hauling—we will *go*. I shall answer no questions, & *not listen* to any d—d fears, surmises, or anything else" (*N&J1*, 351). On 30 June Clemens boarded a small steamer that crossed the strait to the port of Tangier in about four hours. With him were six other passengers: Slote, Jackson, Major James G. Barry, Frederick H. Greer, Colonel James Heron Foster, and Colonel Denny. They were accompanied by an English merchant named Redman, who spoke Arabic. They spent the night at the Royal Victoria Hotel and returned to the *Quaker City* at Gibraltar by 6:00 P.M. on 1 July, when the ship got under way for Marseilles (Charles Jervis Langdon, entry for 11 July; Charles C. Duncan 1867b, entries for 30 June–1 July; Denny, entries for 30 June–1 July).

[4]Clemens wrote the *Alta California* on 1 July, "They don't coin much money nowadays, I think. I saw none but what was dated four or five hundred years back, and was badly worn and battered" (SLC 1867qq). Clemens was mistaken, however, about the age of the coins he enclosed (which have not been found): because the Hegira—or Muhammadan era—began with Muhammad's flight from Mecca to Medina in A.D. 622, and because the Muslim calendar uses a lunar year (354 or 355 days), year 1216 of the Hegira began in May of A.D. 1801, and year 1268 began in October of A.D. 1851.

[5]Clemens informed the New York *Herald* in November that "on three separate evenings" dances were held on board the *Quaker City* before the diversion (which he termed a "melancholy orgie") was "voted to be sinful and dancing was discontinued" (SLC 1867sss). The first two dances occurred on 17 and 24 June; the third—at which Jackson and Slote joined Clemens as masqueraders—took place on the evening of 2 (not 1) July. Evidence that Clemens wrote this part of

his letter on 3 (not 2) July is provided by Mrs. Severance, who on 3 July noted that "last evening," following a meeting "to appoint committees for making arrangements to celebrate July 4," the "lanterns were lighted, and there was a very funny dance. The party returning from Africa came out in Moorish costumes which they had purchased." Another passenger, Dr. Nesbit, recorded passing Majorca (and presumably Minorca) on 3 July (Charles C. Duncan 1867b, entries for 17 and 24 June; Cutter, 27–28; Severance, 51–52; Nesbit, entries for 2–3 July).

6 When the *Quaker City* arrived in Marseilles on the evening of 4 July, Clemens, Jackson, and Slote left the ship, taking rooms at the Grand Hôtel du Louvre et de la Paix, the largest hotel in the city, on Rue Noailles. Jackson quipped that it had "a very long and magnificent name for a very moderately good hotel." They left Marseilles on the evening of 5 July (not "tomorrow," 6 July), arriving in Paris the following evening (Baedeker 1886, 393, 396; Abraham Reeves Jackson 1867c).

7 Captain Duncan recorded the celebration as follows:

> Weather delightfull 13 guns fired at daylight, Bell rung, Steam whistle blown and a general row kicked up
> At 10[30] Passengers & officers and part of the crew assembled on the quarterdeck. Col Kinney the Pres[t] called the meeting to order Prayer by Rev Dr Hutchinson Reading Declaration of Independence by Mr Church of Cincinnatti Oration by Mr Crocker of Cleveland Ohio—"Music by the Band" Prayer & Benediction by Rev Mr Quereau
> Dinner at 2 after which champagne & toasts, 13 regular ones & replied to in order by Mr Leary, Dr Crane, Col Kinney Capt Hoel, Dr Crane, Dr Payne, Mr Nelson, Mark Twain Col Haldeman Col Foster the Captain & two others, names forgotten. (Charles C. Duncan 1867b, entry for 4 July)

In chapter 10 of *The Innocents Abroad* Mark Twain said that Captain Duncan made the only "good speech": "LADIES AND GENTLEMEN:—May we all live to a green old age, and be prosperous and happy. Steward, bring up another basket of champagne" (SLC 1869a, 93).

8 Clemens may have misdated the photograph, since he mistook the date of the *Quaker City*'s arrival in Gibraltar (see note 2). It is not known whether he purchased the picture, which shows Cape Spartel as it appears to someone looking west through the strait, in Gibraltar or in Tangier. And it is not entirely certain that he enclosed it with this letter.

~~To Eliza (Lillie) Hitchcock~~ (*not sent*)
To Jane Lampton Clemens and Family
12 July 1867 • Marseilles, France
(MS: NPV)

GRAND HÔTEL DU LOUVRE & DE LA PAIX. MARSEILLE.
ECHALLIER & FALQUET.

July 12, 1867.

My Dear Lily—

I should think you would feel mighty rascally now to let me go away without that picture. All right, my dear. I am coming back to Paris before long & when I do the Grand Hotel du Louvre will not be big enough to hold both of—

My Dear Folks—I started to write to Lily Hitchcock of San Francisco, ‸(she is in Paris)‸ but this hotel is out of paper & I shall have to let her go by till some other time.[1] I promised her & Etta Booth & Mrs ~~Fre~~ Ferris & Mrs John B Winters & I don't know how many more, to meet them at the Grand Hotel yesterday morning at 9 when I knew perfectly well I woould be on my way to Marseilles by that time.[2] How the world is given to lying![3]

We had a gorgeous time in Paris. It isn't any use to try to say anything about it—I am only writing to let you know I am well.

Oh, confound it, I can't write—I am full of excitement—have to make a trip in the harbor—haven't slept for 24 hours.

Love to all,
Yrs aff^{ty}
Sam

[1] Jackson, Slote, and Clemens again stayed at the Grand Hôtel du Louvre et de la Paix in Marseilles on the night of 12 July after returning from Paris, where they had been since 6 July. In Paris they had stayed at the Grand Hôtel du Louvre, a "huge, palatial edifice" of seven hundred rooms on the Rue de Rivoli between the Louvre and the Palais Royal (Baedeker 1872, 4). Eliza (Lillie) Wychie Hitchcock (1843–1929), a famous San Francisco belle, was in Paris with her mother, the former Martha Hunter of North Carolina (1818–99). Lillie was well known for her independent spirit and unconventional behavior. According to one contemporary, with her "brilliant accomplishments and personal graces"

she "would entertain at one time a circle of twenty gentlemen" (Ellet, 451). During the Civil War, Lillie's father insisted that she and her mother spend a large part of each year in Paris, fearing that their Southern sympathies might lead to accusations of treason—and perhaps even the confiscation of the family property in the South. In 1862 Lillie became the Paris correspondent of the San Francisco *Evening Bulletin*, and by 1867 her detailed and well-informed "Letter from Paris | [FROM OUR LADY CORRESPONDENT.]" appeared almost weekly. The firemen of San Francisco's Knickerbocker Engine Company Number Five made her an honorary member in 1863, because of her enthusiastic interest in fire fighting and her many kindnesses to them (Green, 1, 6, 19, 45; Holdredge, 12, 140–42, 156–58, 217–18). Clemens had known her since 1864, when he and the Hitchcocks were living at the Occidental Hotel. In January 1869, two months after Lillie had eloped with fellow San Franciscan Howard Coit, Clemens recalled that when he "saw the family in Paris, Lily had just delivered the mitten to a wealthy Italian Count, at her mother's request (Mrs. H. said Lily loved him,)" (Green, 26–27; SLC to OLL, 13 and 14 Jan 69, CU-MARK, in *LLMT*, 51).

[2] Etta Booth was probably the daughter of Lucius A. Booth of Virginia City, proprietor of the Winfield Mill and Mining Company (Kelly, 161, 175; Angel, 274). Replying to a letter from her in 1877, Clemens recalled, "I first saw you in Virginia City. It was at a ball . . . & you were a child then—8 years of age, I think" (SLC to Etta Booth, 10 Sept 77, CU-MARK†). In April 1906, having just encountered her by accident on the streets of New York City, Clemens recalled the Virginia City ball in more detail, placing the event at "the beginning of the winter of 1862" and estimating her age at the time as thirteen:

> There were two or three hundred stalwart men present and dancing with cordial energy. And in the midst of the turmoil Etta's crimson frock was swirling and flashing; and she was the only dancer of her sex on the floor. . . . Half of the men represented ladies, and they had a handkerchief tied around the left arm so that they could be told from the men. I did not dance with Etta, for I was a lady myself. I wore a revolver in my belt, and so did all the other ladies—likewise the gentlemen. (AD, 6 Apr 1906, CU-MARK, in *MTA*, 2:326–27)

Mrs. Leonard W. Ferris was another Nevada acquaintance. Her husband was probate judge of Storey County in 1861–64, and Clemens stayed with the Ferrises for a time in 1863 after his Virginia City hotel was destroyed by fire. On 18 February 1867 he wrote the *Alta* that Mrs. Ferris and her daughter were "sojourning" in New York before sailing for France in the *City of Paris* (SLC to JLC and PAM, 5 Aug 63, *L1*, 261–63; SLC 1867o). Mrs. John B. Winters, also visiting Paris without her husband, was another Nevada friend, whom Clemens described as "the very image of Pamela." Her husband was a prominent Nevada businessman, active in mining and milling (SLC to JLC and PAM, 4 June 63, *L1*, 257; Doten, 2:933; *ET&S1*, 488).

[3] Falstaff's lament in *King Henry IV, Part I*, act 5, scene 4: "Lord, Lord, how this world is given to lying!"

To Jane Lampton Clemens and Family
15 July 1867 • Genoa, Italy

(MS: NPV)

Genoa, Italy, July 14.

Dear Folks—

I am just on the eve of starting on a month's trip to Milan, Padua, Verona, Venice & Rome, & shall rejoin the ship at Naples on the 9th of August.[1]

I wrote you from Paris & Marseilles, but wrote little. It seems to me I have no time to do anything. We are rushing constantly. Since we touched dry land we have gone to bed after midnight & rose again at 7 to rush all day. I cannot even get a chance to write newspaper letters regularly—but such as they are you must take them as home letters.[2]

We tired ourselves out here in this curious old city of palaces yesterday & shall again to-day. We may possibly leave here at daylight to-morrow morning.[3] The city has 120,000 inhabitants & ⅔ of them are women & the most beautiful one can imagine[.] ~~We a~~ And they are the most tastefully dressed & the most graceful. We sat in a great gas-lit public grove or garden till 10 last night, where they were crowded together drinking wine & eating ices, & it seems to me that it would be goo[d] to die & go there.[4]

These people think a good deal [of] Columbus, now, but they didn't formerly[.][5]

Yrs aff.

Sam.

1 Over the next two and a half weeks, Clemens, Jackson, and Slote stopped a day or two each in Milan, Bellagio on Lake Como, Venice, Florence, and Rome. They passed through, but did not stop in, Padua and Verona. On or about the evening of 25 July, after traveling from Florence with a brief stop in Pisa, they rejoined the *Quaker City* at Leghorn. Because the ship was expected to be put in quarantine at Naples, its next stop, they left it again the following morning and sailed for Civitavecchia on a French steamer. From there they took a train to Rome. Upon their arrival in Naples about 1 August, the same day the *Quaker City* arrived there, they took rooms in the city while the ship waited out its quarantine. The *Quaker City* sailed from Naples on the morning of 11 August.

2 Although by 1 July Clemens had written four letters to the *Alta* and one to the *Tribune* (SLC 1867oo–rr, 1867hh), since then he had written only one addi-

tional *Alta* letter, on 12 July (SLC 1867ss). Since he intended to produce a total of fifty *Alta* letters (two per week during the twenty-five-week voyage), plus an unknown number of *Tribune* and *Herald* letters, he was indeed behind schedule, even though it was unrealistic to expect to write four letters during the first two weeks of the trip, which were spent entirely at sea.

[3] The *Quaker City* arrived in Genoa on the morning of 14 July. Clemens must therefore have written this letter on 15 July. He and his companions did leave Genoa by train on 16 July, arriving in Milan that evening.

[4] According to Jackson,

> On the evening of our arrival we strolled into the *Corso*, a handsome public garden, or park, in the centre of which is a fine fountain, and where every evening the walks are thronged with all classes of the community, who meet here for social intercourse, visiting at each others houses being almost unknown. The men are handsomely dressed—much more so, to my surprise, than the Parisians. The women are clean and neat, rather given to ornamentation (not peculiar, I believe to Genoa) and wear their beautiful black hair plainly divided in front, with the back part braided and confined with a large gold pin. A similar one attaches a scarf of white illusion to the top of the head, and this, falling down on each side nearly to the feet, gives them a peculiarly neat and graceful appearance. (Abraham Reeves Jackson 1867e)

[5] Jackson reported that at the "*Municipal Hall* we were shown three magnificent letters of Columbus preserved with great care. Near this place a handsome sculptured monument bearing his likeness has been erected to the memory of this pride of the Genoese. We were also shown the house where he formerly lived" (Abraham Reeves Jackson 1867e).

To Frank Fuller
7 August 1867 • Naples, Italy

(Transcript facsimile: CtY-BR)

Naples, Italy, Aug 7/67

Friend Fuller

Don't make any arrangements about lecturing for me. I have got a better thing, in Washington.

Shall spend the winter there.[1]

It will be well for both of us, I think—& surely must be for me—better than lecturing at $50. a night for a Literary Society in Chicago & paying my own expenses. I have calculated all that & there isn't any money in it. If I lectured 50 times during the season it would only pay each of us $750. Deduct traveling expenses & would there be "monthly wages" left? Hardly. Going about on our own hook would be worse if it snowed any. Winter after next will be early enough to dare that,—& I may be better known, then, after a winter spent in Washington.

I must not commit myself on paper, but will explain fully when I see you in October.[2]

I have had a good deal of fun on this trip, but it is costing like Sin. I will be a busted community some time before I see America again. The worst of it is, that a ship is a bad writing desk & I can't write on shore because I have too much to see there. So I neglect my correspondence half the time & botch it the balance.[3] Tell Webb I saw Lily Hitchcock in Paris & she was chief among the ten thousand American roses there & altogether lovely.[4] I did so yearn to kiss her for her mother but it was just my luck—her mother was there herself. But she is a splendid girl—both of them I mean. I long to have a talk with you, my old compound of miraculous suavity & gorgeous address,—& a smoke—& shall I hope before a great many weeks.

Good-bye & give my love to your brother[5]

Yours ever
Mark

[*in margin:* (over)]

Aug 7/67

PS Italy is a beautiful land, & its daughters are as fair as the moon[6] that holds her silvery course above their heads & its traditions are rich with the poetry & romance of the old crusading days,—happy days! glorious days but destined never to return! I like Italy.

Yrs
Mark

1 Clemens was about to accept Senator William M. Stewart's offer of a private secretaryship (see 9 Aug 67 to JLC and family).

2 Fuller seems to have relayed a lecture offer from Edwin Lee Brown of the Young Men's Library Association of Chicago, who in early June had expressed an interest in arranging a three-month tour, probably about fifty lectures. The $50 fee Clemens mentioned here, however, does not accord with the $100 fee previously offered (8 June 67 to McComb). And Clemens's calculation that the tour would pay them only $750 is correct only if we assume he was deducting $1,000 in travel expenses. Since this letter is preserved only in a modern transcript, these anomalies suggest that one or more of the figures in the text may misrepresent the manuscript. Despite his refusal, Clemens's name appeared in December on a list of "celebrities" scheduled to lecture for Brown's organization, indicating that it still hoped to book him. Clemens did not lecture in Chicago until 7 January 1869, during his 1868–69 midwestern lecture tour, which was sponsored by the Associated Western Literary Societies, to which the Young

Men's Library Association belonged ("Chicago," New York *Evening Post*, 11 Dec 67, 1; "The American Vandal Abroad," Chicago *Times*, 8 Jan 69, 3).

3 In the three weeks since 15 July, Clemens had probably written six *Alta* letters (SLC 1867uu–vv, 1867yy–zz, 1867aaa, 1867eee), one *Tribune* letter (SLC 1867tt), and two *Herald* letters (SLC 1867mm–nn), bringing his total to fifteen in the eight and a half weeks since the start of the trip. Over the next four days he apparently wrote three more to the *Alta* (SLC 1867bbb–ddd), although some of these may have been back dated.

4 Song of Solomon 5:10, 16: "My beloved is white and ruddy, the chiefest among ten thousand. . . . yea, he is altogether lovely."

5 Fuller had one younger and two older brothers as well as a sister, but the brother mentioned here has not been identified (Fuller to Mr. Brown, 27 June 1912, CLjC).

6 Song of Solomon 6:10, one of Clemens's favorite verses: "Who is she that looketh forth as the morning, fair as the moon, clear as the sun, and terrible as an army with banners?" Compare *L1*, 96 n. 8, and 169 n. 16.

To Daniel Slote
7 August 1867 • Naples, Italy
(MS, *not sent:* TxU)

Bier bot. 3,	1.20.
Au	20.
Chandel	1.
Deiuné[1]	1.20.
	3.60
	2.60
	fr 6.20
Paid	

7th Morning—I have paid this breakfast bill, Dan. Tell the Doctor, I am gone to The Island of Ischia—will return to Naples to-morrow—leave Herculaneum & Vesuvius alone till Thursday[2]—*we* don't want to go with those inf[3]

1 The bill lists the following items: three bottles of beer (correctly, bière, bouteilles 3); water (eau); candle (chandelle); and breakfast (déjeuné).

2 Since Clemens wrote this note on a Wednesday, he must have meant "Friday" here, instead of "Thursday": Friday was in fact the day he returned from Ischia and visited Vesuvius (see the next letter).

3 Clemens described the party that went to Ischia in an *Alta* dispatch as "two or three of us," but its other members have not been identified (SLC 1867bbb). Clemens stopped writing in the middle of a line and probably never gave or sent

this note to Slote, perhaps because he found he could tell him what he had written, or intended to write. The note itself apparently remained in Clemens's possession until his death: see the textual commentary for this letter.

To Jane Lampton Clemens and Family
9 August 1867 • Naples, Italy

(MS, *damage emended:* CU-MARK)

Naples, Aug. ~~7~~ 9.

Dear Folks—

I can't write but a word. I have been away a day or two—slept none last night & sailed ~~for~~ on return to Naples at daylight, thinking I would go to bed when I got here—got to talking—then went to see the king's palace—lost time in one way or another till now it is night & I learn for the first time that our own party have decided to start for Vesuvius at midnight.[1] I have some little preparation to make. Good-bye.

I wrote to Bill Stewart today accepting his private secretaryship in Washington next winter. When I come to think of it, I believe it ~~is~~ can be made one of the best paying berths in Washington. Say nothing of this. At least I can get an office for Orion, if he or the President will modify their politics.[2]

Yrs fdly

Sam.

Orion Clemens, Esq. | 1312 Chesnut street | St Louis Mo | United States of America. [*two postmarks:*] NAPOLI 9 AGO ◇◇ 12 ◇ [*and*] TORINO 11 AGO 67 12 M UF° SUCCURSALE N. 4[3] [*one or more postmarks and postage stamps torn away*]

[1] Clemens's party, consisting of four men and four women, departed late in the evening of 9 August for Vesuvius. Only three of his companions have been identified: Dr. Jackson, Dr. Nesbit, and Julia Newell (Abraham Reeves Jackson 1867f; Nesbit, entry for 10 Aug; Newell 1867a).

[2] Orion Clemens openly sided with the Radical Republicans in Congress against President Andrew Johnson's pro-Southern Reconstruction policies. The passage of the First Reconstruction Act on 2 March 1867—over Johnson's veto—prompted Orion to write the San Francisco *Times:*

> Congress, by passing the Reconstruction law, has steered the Ship of State past two dangers: First—Rebel votes and corruption forcing the United States to pay the rebel debt.

Second—Rebel Governors and rebel Congressmen fomenting a foreign war, and then joining the enemy against their own country. . . . If any newspaper correspondent should write that the late rebels are friends of the whole country, put him down as a Copperhead, beslabbering his party with false praise. (OC 1867e)

At the time of the present letter Orion was evidently growing desperate for any sort of employment. By September he had begun approaching several friends and acquaintances in his original profession of typesetting:

I asked [William] McKee [of the *Missouri Democrat*] for a situation any where about his office—job office, newspaper, or reporter. He said he would let me know if there was a vacancy, but job printing was very dull. He had discharged half a dozen hands last week. I went to the [Missouri] Republican office, but there were only a few men in the job office, and half of them seemed to bridle. I went to Levisons. Two men were at work, but seemed to have little to do. I asked [Thomas Watt] Ustick for work in his job office. He said they were full. (OC to MEC, 6 Sept 67, CU-MARK)

[3]That is, "ufficio succursale n. 4," branch office number 4. Why the letter went to Turin has not been explained.

To Charles C. Duncan
14 August 1867 • Piraeus, Greece

(MS, *draft:* CU-MARK)

On Board Steamer
Quaker City, Aug 14.

Capt C C Duncan

Sir—Whereas—

First—There is nothing to see at Sebastopol but a bare & uninteresting battle-field where military fortifications *have been* but no longer exist[1]—and

Secondly—Several among us ~~have~~ ‸having‸ stood ~~am~~ in the midst of ~~such~~ scenes of this character of infinitely greater importance in our own Country in the smoke & carnage of battle—and—

Thirdly—The remainder of our company ~~have~~ ‸having‸ seen a sufficiency of such things after the battles were over—and

Fourthly—Since, by leaving Sebastopol out of the excursion we can gain a precious addition of time for travel in Palestine,—

Therefore, Satisfied that ~~the minority~~ if a short trip be taken through the Bosphorus & into the Black Sea, all parties will be willing to forego the extension of it to desolate Sebastopol with its notable ~~pyr~~ pile of porter bottles, we respectfully request that you will altar your programme in accordance with the suggestion contained in this last paragraph.

Respectfully[2]

[1] Before the Crimean War (1853–56), the fortified port of Sevastopol, on the Crimean peninsula, had a population of 43,000 and was Russia's chief Black Sea naval installation. Beginning in late September 1854, the combined armies of France, Britain, Turkey, and Sardinia laid siege to the city, subjecting it to fearsome bombardments. An estimated 173,000 men on both sides were killed in the year-long battle, and thousands more succumbed to disease. When the Russians evacuated in September 1855, only fourteen buildings in the entire city were relatively undamaged. The occupying allies immediately razed the remaining dockyards and fortifications, and the Paris treaty of 1856 forbade their reconstruction. In the early 1860s, only about 6,000 people lived in Sevastopol's ruins.

[2] It is not known who or what prompted Clemens to draft this petition in his notebook, nor whether any version of it was ever presented to Captain Duncan. The captain did, however, record in his log on 18 August, while in Constantinople, that "most of them [the passengers] had intended remaining here while the ship went to Russia but now all but six decide to remain by the ship" (in fact, eight stayed behind: Slote, the Beaches, Bullard, Foster, Severance, Van Nostrand, and the Honorable Jacob Samils Haldeman). The trip prospectus, which stated that any change in itinerary required a "*unanimous* vote of the passengers," stipulated a two-day stay at Sevastopol and nearby Balaklava, but the ship actually spent only one day, 21 August—an apparent compromise (Charles C. Duncan 1867a; Charles C. Duncan 1867b, entries for 18 Aug and 30 Aug; *N&J1*, 402 n. 41). Julia Newell, who was corresponding for her hometown newspaper in Janesville, Wisconsin, probably expressed the feelings of many others when she wrote about Sevastopol:

> Some of our party were greatly interested and pleased with the sight-seeing of the day, but as for myself, I don't like battle fields and camping grounds with all the sickening traces of hardships, conflict and bloodshed, nor yet the sad sight of battered walls and beautiful mansions shattered and in ruins. (Newell 1867b)

To Jane Lampton Clemens and Family
26 August 1867 • Yalta, Russia
(MS: NPV)

Yalta, Russia, Aug. 25.[1]

Dear Folks—

We have been representing the United States all we knew how, to=day. We went to Sebastopol, after we got tired of Constantinople (got your letter there, & one at Naples,) & there the Commandant & the whole town came aboard & were as jolly & sociable as old friends. They said the Emperor of Russia was at Yalta, 30 miles or 40 away, & urged us to go there with the ship & visit him—promised us a cordial welcome. They insisted on sending a telegram to the Emperor, & also a courier overland to announce our coming. But we knew that a great English excursion party, & also the Viceroy of Egypt, in his splendid yacht, had been refused an audience within the last fortnight, & so we thought it not safe to try it.[2] They said, no difference—the Emperor would hardly visit our ship, because that be a most extraordinary favor & one which he uniformly refuses to accord under any circumstances, but he would certainly receive us at his palace. We still declined. But we had to go to Odessa, 250 miles away, & there the Governor General urged us, & sent a telegram to the Emperor, which we hardly expected to be answered, but it was, & promptly.[3] So we sailed back to Yalta. ~~They had told us~~ We all ~~put~~ went to the palace at noon, to-day, (3 miles,) in carriages & on horses sent by the Emperor, & we had a jolly time. Instead of the usual formal audience of 15 minutes, we staid 4 hours & were made a good deal more at home than we could have been in a New York drawing-room. The whole tribe turned out to receive our party—Emperor, Empress, the eldest daughter (Grand-Duchess Marie, a pretty girl of 14,) a little ~~g~~ Grand Duke her brother, & a platoon of Admirals, Princes, Peers of the Empire, &c.,[4] & in a little while an aid-de camp arrived with a request from the Grand Duke Michael, the Emperor's brother, that we would visit his palace & breakfast with him.[5] The Emperor also invited us, on behalf of his absent eldest son & heir (aged 22,) to visit *his* palace & consider it a visit to him.[6] They all talk English & they were all very neatly but very plainly dressed. You all dress a good deal finer than they were dressed. The Emperor & his family threw off all reserve & showed us all over the palace themselves. It is very rich & very elegant, but in no way gaudy.

I had been appointed chairman of a committee to draught an address to the Emperor on behalf of the passengers, & as I fully expected, & as they fully intended, I had to write the address myself. I didn't mind it, because I have no modesty & would as soon write an Emperor as to anybody else—but considering that there were 5 on the committee I thought they might have contributed *one* paragraph among them, anyway.[7] They wanted me to *read* it to him, too, but I declined that honor—

not because I hadn't cheek enough (& some to spare,) but because our Consul at Odessa was along, & also the Secretary of our Legation at St Petersburgh, & of course one of those *ought* to read it. The Emperor [thanked us for] the address (it was his business to do it,) & so many others have praised it warmly that I begin to imagine it must be a wonderful sort of document & herewith send you the original draught of it, to be put into alcohol & preserved forever like a curious reptile.[8]

They live right well at the Grand Duke Michael's—~~ther~~ their breakfasts are not gorgeous but very excellent—& if Mike were to say the word I would go there & breakfast with him tomorrow.

Ys aff
Sam.

[*written across previous paragraphs:*]
They told us it would be polite to invite the Emperor to visit the ship, though he would not be likely to do it. But he dint give us a chance—he has requested permission to come on board with his family & all his relations to-morrow & take a sail, in case it is calm weather. I can entertain them. My hand is in, now, & if you want any more emperors feted in style, trot them out.

[*enclosure:*]
To His Imperial Majesty Alexander II, Emp of Russia.

We are ~~only~~ a handful of ~~unofficial~~ ‸private‸ citizens of ~~America~~ ‸the United Stats‸, ~~going about the world with no end in view~~ traveling simply for recreation, & unostentatiously, as becomes our unofficial state, ~~(~~& therefore we~~)~~ have no excuse ‸to tender‸ for presenting ourselves before your~~,~~ ‸Majesty‸ save ~~that~~ the desire of ~~seeing~~ offering our grateful acknowledgments to the lord of a ~~land~~ realm which, through good & through evil report, has been the steadfast friend of the land we love so well.

We could not presume to take a step like this, did we not know ~~full~~ well that the words we speak here & the sentiments wherewith they are freighted, are but the reflex of the thoughts & the feelings ~~that dwell in all~~ ~~the hearts~~ of all our countrymen, from the green hills of New England to the ~~snow clad peaks that girt the~~ ~~‸Sierras of the far‸~~ ‸snowy peaks of the far‸ far Pacific. ‸We are few in number, but‸ ~~Through our feeble lips speak~~ ‸we utter ~~th~~‸ the voice of a nation!

One of the brightest pages that has graced the world's history ~~for many generations~~ ‸since written history had its birth‸ was recorded by your

‸Majesty's‸ hand when ~~you~~ ‸it‸ loosed the bonds of twenty million serfs, & Americans can but esteem it a privile~~d~~ge to do honor to ~~one~~ a ~~monarch~~ ‸ruler‸ who has wrought so great a deed. ~~For this, in the name of our countrymen,~~ The lesson that was taught us then, we have profited by, & are free in truth to-day, even as we were before in name. America owes much to Russia,~~—~~ ~~We sincerely trust that~~ is indebted to her in many ways—~~& we sincere~~ ~~chief~~ & ~~more than all,~~ ‸chiefly‸ for her unwavering friendship in seasons of ~~deepes~~ ‸our‸ greatest need.~~; t~~That that friendship may still be hers in times to come, we ~~all~~ confidently pray; that she is & will be grateful to ~~her~~ ‸Russia‸ & to her sovereign for it, we know full well; that she ~~can~~ ‸~~will~~‸ ~~ever fail~~ will ever forfeit ~~it by any wilful act of her own~~ it by any ‸premeditated,‸ unjust act, ~~&~~ or unfair course, ~~we~~ it were treason to believe.

[*on back of page 2 of enclosure:*]

Pamela, *you* (not anybody else,) write to "Capt. Jno. McComb,~~,~~ care *Alta*," to send you the back numbers containing my letters, & to continue to send the paper.[9] He is a splendid fellow & will attend to your request, but he'll forget it if I write him. Tell him I told you. My love to Ma & Orion & Mollie, & to Annie, Sammy, Essie, Lou, all the family & all the friends, never by any means forgetting Margaret.[10]

Yrs

Sam.

1 Clemens mistook the date: the visit to the tsar described in this letter actually occurred on 26 August (*N&J1*, 402 n. 41; Charles C. Duncan 1867b, entry for 30 Aug).

2 The "great English excursion party" has not been identified. Ismail Pasha (1830–95), viceroy of Egypt from 1863 to 1879, was in the area on a visit to the sultan of Turkey. Ten days earlier, when the *Quaker City* was in the Sea of Marmara approaching Constantinople, Clemens recorded in his notebook, "The Viceroy of Egypt passed us in his lightning yacht, like we were standing still—waved his hand to us" (*N&J1*, 395–96). Denny likewise noted, "This evening there passed by us perhaps as fast a running steam ship as is in the world, that of the Viceroy of Egypt. It is a beauty and had the Viceroy and his suit on board on a visit to the Sultan" (Denny, entry for 16 Aug). It is not known whether the viceroy was refused an audience with the tsar.

3 From 1862 to 1874, Pavel E. Kotsebu served as governor general of Novorossiia—a large region in southern Russia encompassing several provinces—and was stationed in Odessa, its principal city (Herlihy, 157).

4 Aleksandr Nikolaevich Romanov (1818–81), Tsar Aleksandr II of Russia, seemed to Clemens "much nobler than the Emperor Napoleon." Considered moderate, for an autocrat, because in 1861 he ended the system of serf labor and had also begun various judicial and military reforms, he was nevertheless not a

popular ruler: at the time of Clemens's visit to Livadia, his summer home, he had already survived two attempts on his life (the most recent in Paris, a month before Clemens's stay there). In 1841 he married Maria Aleksandrovna (1824–80). Clemens described their only surviving daughter, Grand Duchess Maria Aleksandrovna (1853–1920), as "a pretty, blue-eyed, fair-haired girl." In 1874 she married Queen Victoria's second son—Prince Alfred, Duke of Edinburgh. The "little Grand Duke her brother" was Sergei (1857–1905), the tsar's fifth son. Tsar Aleksandr II was assassinated in 1881 by members of a revolutionary party called the People's Will (Louisa M. Griswold, 185; SLC 1867xx). The "platoon of Admirals, Princes, Peers of the Empire, &c." evidently included Prince Nikolai Dolgoruky, aide-de-camp to the tsar and, according to Clemens, "the Grand Chamberlain"; Count Festetics, a Polish officer on the staff of the tsar's youngest brother (see the next note); and Admiral Glasenapp, commander of the Russian Black Sea fleet (*N&J1*, 409 n. 53, 410).

[5] According to accounts from other passengers, the palace, named Orianda, actually belonged to Konstantin Nikolaevich Romanov (1827–92), the tsar's younger brother, who was absent in St. Petersburg. Grand Duke Mikhail Nikolaevich Romanov (1832–1909)—the tsar's youngest brother and, since 1865, commander of the Caucasus Military District—acted as host for the luncheon (called breakfast, since in Russian the same word is used for both meals). Clemens described "Grand Duke Michael" in his notebook as "a rare brick" (Moulton 1867b; Severance, 143; James, 2; *N&J1*, 409).

[6] Aleksandr Aleksandrovich Romanov (1845–94), the tsar's second son, had become the heir upon the death of his older brother, Nikolai (1843–65). (After the assassination of his father in 1881, he would become Tsar Aleksandr III.) In 1866 he married Nikolai's fiancée, Maria Feodorovna, whose sister was the wife of Albert Edward, Prince of Wales, later Edward VII. His palace had originally belonged to Nikolai. At the time of the *Quaker City* visit, he was in Denmark, his wife's native land (Severance, 143; Nesbit, entry for 26 Aug).

[7] In addition to Clemens, the committee included Solomon N. Sanford, Timothy D. Crocker, Colonel Kinney, and Dr. William Gibson. After drafting the speech, Clemens made a copy in his notebook, adding:

> That job is over. Writing addresses to Emperors is not my strong suit. However, if it is not as good as it might be, it don't signify—the other committeemen ought to have helped write it—they had nothing else to do, & I had my hands full. But for bothering with this matter, I would have caught up entirely with my N.Y. Tribune correspondence, & nearly up with the San Francisco cor[r]. (*N&J1*, 407–8)

[8] The address was read to the tsar by the United States consul at Odessa, Timothy C. Smith. The secretary of the legation at St. Petersburg was Jeremiah Curtin. Clemens included the text in his letters of 26 August to the *Tribune*, and 27 August to the *Herald* and to the *Alta*. Before the speech was printed as a broadside on the *Quaker City*'s printing press (see the illustration below), Clemens further revised and simplified it (Interior Department, 4; SLC 1867ww–xx, 1867ooo; *N&J1*, 408 n. 48). The speech was also translated into Russian and published in the Odessa *Vestnik* on 24 August—i.e., 5 September on the modern Gregorian calendar (Startsev, 119).

[9] See 15 Apr 67 to JLC and family, n. 7.

[10] Annie and Sammy Moffett, Essie Pepper, Lou Conrad, and the Moffetts' German maid, Margaret.

ADDRESS.

To His Imperial Majesty;--
ALEXANDER II. Emperor of Russia.

We, a handful of citizens of the United States, travelling for recreation—and unostentatiously, as becomes our unofficial state,—have no excuse for presenting ourselves before your Majesty, save a desire to offer our grateful acknowledgments to the Lord of a Realm which, through good and through evil report, has been the steadfast friend of our Native Land.

We could not presume thus to present ourselves did we not know that the words we speak and the sentiments we utter, reflect the thoughts and feelings of all our countrymen; from the green hills of New England to the snowy peaks of the far Pacific. Though few in number, we utter the voice of a Nation.

One of the brightest pages that has graced the worlds" history; since written history had its birth, was recorded by your Majesty's hand when it loosed the bonds of twenty millions of men, and Americans can but esteem it a privilege to do honour to a ruler who has wrought so great a deed; The lesson then taught us we have profited by, and our Country is as free in fact today, as before it was in name.

America owes much to Russia: is indebted to her in many ways; and chiefly for her unwavering friendship in the season of her greatest need. That the same friendship may be hers in time to come, we confidently pray; that she is, and will be gratefull to Russia, and to her Sovereign for it, we know full well; that she will ever forfeit it by any premeditated, unjust act, or unfair course; it would be treason to believe.

Samuel Clemens, Wm Gibson, T D Crocker, S N Sanford, P Kinney, Committee

Respectfully tendered on behalf of the excursionists of the A-merican Steam Yacht Quaker City.

Yalta August 26th 1867.

Clemens's address to Tsar Aleksandr II. Mark Twain Memorial, Hartford, Connecticut (CtHMTH). See p. 84 n. 8.

From Samuel L. Clemens and Others to Daniel D. Leary 26 August 1867 • Yalta, Russia

(Transcript: CU-MARK)

Yalta Aug 26 '67

D.D. Leary Esqr.

Dear Sir

Whereas we the undersigned fellow passengers of the Steamer Quaker City, appreciating your kindness in affording us an opportunity to visit the Emperor of Russia at Yalta—

Resolved, That we thereby acknowledge the great favour and tender you our sincere thanks.[1]

W. E. James — T. D. Crocker
Mrs. T. D. Crocker — Wm. Gibson
Mary M. Fairbanks — Mr. P. Kinney
Susan Gibson — S. N. Sanford
E. A. Severance — James H. Payne
Mrs. J. H. Payne — J. W. Davis
Mrs. S. M. Griswold — Wm. F. Church
Sam L. Clemens — C. J. Langdon
C. D. Chadeyne — Stephen M. Griswold
James G. Barry — R. Bell
Julius Moulton — Thomas B. Nesbit
Wm. R. Denny — Lucius Moody
Fred P. Jenkins — B. B. Nesbit[2]
Nina Larrowe

[1] Daniel Leary joined the excursion in part because he hoped it would bring him an opportunity to sell the ship (his asking price was £50,000, or $250,000, although he was willing to accept "something less") (Leary to Arthur Leary, 1 July 67, transcript, CU-MARK, in Leary, 200). By his own account, Leary was instrumental in arranging the visit to the tsar:

> We arrived this morning from Yalta, the summer residence of the Emperor of Russia, and a fashionable watering place for the Russian nobility. I was induced to go there in the hope that the steamer might tempt the Emperor to purchase as I understood that he had no extra vessel to carry his suits when he travels, and the Quaker would suit very well for this. I had telegraphed from Odessa at the suggestion of the Governor there to the Governor at Yalta, announcing my intention to visit the Emperor, so when we arrived an aide

of the Governor came out to receive us, and invited me ashore to call on the Governor General, who said the Emperor would receive us the next day at the palace, which he did in a most cordial manner. (Leary to Arthur Leary, 30 Aug 67 [misdated 29 Aug], transcript, CU-MARK, in Leary, 200–201)

According to William E. James's letter to the Brooklyn *Eagle*, during the reception of 26 August Leary tried to persuade the tsar to visit the ship:

[The tsar] stood there awhile, looking ill at ease and nervous, and finally turned to get to the rest of the party to speak to them, but was headed off by Leary, who would post himself directly in front of him, with his mouth wide open, showing his teeth, and putting his hand on his shoulder, urging him to come on board; three times was this repeated. (James, no page)

The tactic failed: although the tsar agreed to visit the ship on 27 August provided the weather was calm, he did not appear. In his stead, however, several Russian dignitaries did, and Leary pursued his goal with them:

Prince Dolgozonxy [i.e., Dolgoruky] with whom I dined just before told me the truth about the matter that it was contrary to established custom for the Emperor to visit vessels. Of course I could not talk with the Emperor about the sale of the ship, as he would at once have thought that was my object in visiting him, but I sounded Admiral Glassenapp on the subject who visited on board. He said the Emperor was having two yachts built at St. Petersburg and that I could do nothing as they were in favor of iron vessels. . . . The time taken at Yalta will be deducted from the Holy Land, 3 days. Still these outside excursions cost considerable money, but there seemed a good chance of doing something and I did not wish to omit anything that might result in a sale. (Leary to Arthur Leary, 30 Aug 67, transcript, CU-MARK, in Leary, 201)

Leary also tried, unsuccessfully, to sell the ship to Ismail Pasha, viceroy of Egypt (Solon L. Severance to A. B. Paine, 13 Mar 1912, Davis 1967a, 3). See also 12 Dec 67 to Fairbanks, n. 4.

[2] The full names of the twenty-seven passengers who signed this letter are given in the complete passenger list in Appendix C.

To Jane Lampton Clemens and Family
1–2 September 1867 • Constantinople, Turkey

(MS: NPV)

Constantinople, Sept. 1.[1]

Dear Folks—

All well. Do the *Alta's* come regularly? I wish I knew whether my letters reach them or not. Look over the back papers & see. I wrote them as follows:[2]

1—Letter from Fayal, in the Azores Islands.

1 from Gibraltar, in Spain.

1 from Tangier, in Africa.

2 from Paris & Marseilles, in France.[3]

1 from Genoa, in Italy.

1 from Milan ——

1 from Lake Como ——

1 from some little place in Switzerland—have forgotten the name.

4 concerning Lecco, Bergamo, Padua, Verona, Battle-field of Marengo, Pastachio, & some other cities in Northern Italy.[4] (over)

2 from Venice.

1 about Bologna

1 from Florence.

1 from Pisa.

1 from Leghorn.

‸1 from Rome & Civita Vecchia.‸

2 from Naples.

1 about Pozzuoli, where St Paul landed, the Baths of Nero, & the ruins of Baia, ~~&~~ Virgil's tomb, the Elysian Fields, the Sunken Cities & the spot where Ulysses landed.

1 from Herculaneum & Vesuvius.

1 from Pompeii.

1 from the island of Ischia.

1 concerning the Volcano of Stromboli, the city & Straits of Messina, the island of Sicily, Scylla & Charybdis &c.

1 about the Grecian Archipelago.

1 about a midnight visit to Athens, the Piraeus & the ruins of the Acropolis.

1 about the Hellespont, the site of ancient Troy, the Sea of Marmora, &c.

~~1~~ 2 about Constantinople, the Golden Horn & the beauties of the Bosphorus.

1 ~~about~~ from Odessa & Sebastopol in Russia, the Black Sea, &c.

2 from Yalta, Russia, concerning a visit to the Czar.

And yesterday ~~& ◇~~ I wrote another letter from Constantinople and 1 to-day about its neighbor in Asia, Scutari. I am not done with Turkey yet. Shall write 2 or 3 more.

I have written to the New York Herald 2 letters from Naples, (no name signed,) & 1 from ~~Yalta.~~ Constantinople [*in margin:* ~~ov~~ (over)]

To the New York Tribune I have written

1 from Fayal.

1 from Civita Vecchia in the Roman States.

~~And~~ 2 from Yalta, Russia.

And 1 from Constantinople.

I have never seen any of these letters in print except the one to the Tribune from Fayal, & that was not worth printing.

We sail hence to-morrow, perhaps, & my next letters will be mailed at Smyrna, in Syria; ~~, the~~ I hope to write from the Sea of Tiberius, Damascus, Jerusalem, Joppa, & possibly other points in the ~~h~~Holy Land. The letters from Egypt, the Nile & Algiers ~~(Africa,)~~ I will look out for, myself. I will bring them in my pocket.

They take the finest photographs in the world here. I have ordered some. They will be sent to Alexandria, Egypt.[5]

You cannot conceive of anything so beautiful as Constantinople, viewed from the Golden Horn or the Bosphorus. I think it must be the handsomest city in the world. I will go on deck & look at it for you, directly. I am staying on the ship, to-night. I generally stay on shore when we are in port. But yesterday I just ran myself down. Dan Slote, my room-mate, is on shore. He remained here while we went up the Black Sea, but it seems he has not got enough of it yet. I thought Dan had got the stateroom pretty full of rubbish at last, but a while ago his dragoman arrived with a bran new, ghastly tomb-stone of the Oriental pattern, with ~~him~~ his name handsomely carved & gilded on it in Turkish characters. That fellow will buy a Circassian slave, next.

I am tired. We are going on a trip, tomorrow.[6] I must to bed. Love to all.

I don't prepay postage. Letters are too uncertain.

Yrs

Sam.

[1]The dates of Clemens's notebook entries for 28–31 August and 1–2 September are behind by one day, indicating that he was confused about the date while in Constantinople (*N&J1*, 410–13). His comment below that the ship would "sail hence to-morrow, perhaps," together with his mention that he was also planning a trip "tomorrow," imply that the letter may have been written on 2, rather than 1, September: the *Quaker City* departed Constantinople on the evening of 3 September, the same day that a party of excursionists, which probably included Clemens, took a trip to Scutari (see note 6; Nesbit, entries for 30–31 Aug, 1–3 Sept).

[2]Out of the thirty-seven letters to the *Alta* listed below, only twenty-three

were published. Dewey Ganzel has speculated that the fourteen missing letters were lost in the mails, and that Clemens discovered their loss when he reached Egypt (Ganzel 1968, 102, 139, 147–48, 157, 167, 178). But it is unlikely that mail losses account for even half the missing letters, or that Clemens knew how many had been lost before he arrived in New York, if then. By February 1868 he seemed only vaguely aware that some had not reached San Francisco: see 21 Feb 68 to JLC and family. In 1904, however, he remembered that "six of them miscarried, and I wrote six new ones to complete my contract" (SLC 1904, 75). It therefore seems more likely that in listing letters here he was reconstructing rather than remembering exactly what he had done, perhaps because he had lost his own written records, and that in fact he never wrote any dispatch from some of the places on his list. Clemens's notebook for the period 3 July through 10 August has long been missing and may well have been lost even before he wrote this letter. Certainly it is suspicious that many of the cities for which no letter was published are places Clemens did not visit for any significant length of time. For instance, he passed through the cities of northern Italy between Lecco and Venice in a single day, stopping only occasionally for a meal or a short walk. It seems unlikely that he would have written as many as four letters in close succession, describing places he had not seen; certainly none of the *surviving* letters is about such a place. Moreover, at the rate of two letters per week (his agreed-upon rate for the *Alta*), the letters he claimed here to have written would have put him thirteen ahead of schedule only one week after he complained in his notebook about being behind schedule for both the *Alta* and the *Tribune* (26 Aug 67 to JLC and family, n. 7). The notes below give detailed information about Clemens's list, which is summarized in the following chart:

Location	**No. listed**	**No. published**	**SLC citation**
Fayal	1	1	1867oo
Gibraltar	1	1	1867pp
Tangier	1	2	1867qq–rr
Paris etc.	2	1	1867ss
Genoa	1	1	1867uu
Milan	1	1	1867vv
Lake Como	1	1	1867yy
Switzerland	1	0	
Lecco etc.	4	0	
Venice	2	1	1867eee
Bologna	1	0	
Florence	1	1	1867zz
Pisa	1	0	
Leghorn	1	0	
Rome etc.	1	0	
Naples	2	1	1867bbb
Pozzuoli etc.	1	1	1867ccc
Herculaneum etc.	1	1	1867ddd
Pompeii	1	1	1867aaa
Ischia	1	0	
Stromboli etc.	1	0	
Grecian Archipelago	1	0	
Athens etc.	1	1	1867fff
Hellespont etc.	1	1	1867ggg

Location	No. listed	No. published	SLC citation
Constantinople etc.	2	2	1867hhh, 1867jjj
Odessa etc.	1	2	1867*lll*, 1867nnn
Yalta	2	2	1867ooo, 1867qqq
Constantinople	1	1	1867kkk
Scutari	1	0	
ALTA SUBTOTAL	37	23	
Naples (*Herald*)	2	2	1867mm–nn
Constantinople (*Herald*)	1	1	1867ww
Fayal (*Tribune*)	1	1	1867hh
Civitavecchia (*Tribune*)	1	1	1867tt
Yalta (*Tribune*)	2	1	1867xx
Constantinople (*Tribune*)	1	1	1867iii
TOTAL	45	30	

[3]Clemens forgot to list a second letter from Tangier, even though he correctly recorded both in the notebook he kept from the start of the trip through 2 July (*N&J1*, 328). The *Alta* published only one letter from Paris (none from Marseilles), and it is possible that he simply transposed the correct numbers for this and the previous entry.

[4]The *Alta* never published a letter from the "little place in Switzerland" (possibly Chiasso, just across the border from Como), nor from Lecco, Bergamo, Padua, or Verona. No town in Italy was named "Pastachio." Clemens may have meant Peschiera (on the railway line he traveled between Bergamo and Venice) or, more likely, Piteccio or Pistoia (both of which were on the railway line he traveled from Venice to Florence) (Baedeker 1879, 147, 171, 312–13). When Clemens wrote up this part of the trip in *The Innocents Abroad*, he reported traveling by steamer from Como to Bellagio and from Bellagio to Lecco, then by carriage from Lecco to the train station at Bergamo, and by train from there to Venice, passing through Verona and Padua along the way. (Marengo is not in this area, but farther west.) He dismissed this day's journey, saying he would "not tarry to speak of the handsome Lago di Gardi [i.e., Garda] . . . nor yet of ancient Padua or haughty Verona" but would "hurry straight to the ancient city of the sea," Venice. And when he described the trip from Venice to Florence, he reported that "we rattled through a good deal of country by rail without caring to stop. I took few notes. I find no mention of Bologna in my memorandum book. . . . Pistoia awoke but a passing interest" (SLC 1869a, 199, 207, 215–16, 244).

[5]Clemens and at least seven other excursionists—two of whom have been certainly identified, Van Nostrand and Slote—had their photographs taken in Constantinople by Abdullah Frères, official photographers to his imperial majesty the sultan of Turkey, Abdul-Aziz (1830–76). Clemens's photograph is reproduced below; for his comments on it see 8 Jan 68 to Beach. (The location of Van Nostrand's is not known, but its existence is established by Alta California Bookstore, description of lot 90; Slote's photograph is privately owned, but is reproduced in Ganzel 1968, following page 66; L. H. S. Robson to Cyril Clemens, 12 Mar 1935, PH in CU-MARK, mentions the existence of eight photographs of *Quaker City* passengers taken in Constantinople, possibly by Abdullah Frères, among Jackson's effects.) Clemens also purchased photographs of public figures which he later used to illustrate *The Innocents Abroad*. Four of these survive (the

Carte de visite photograph of Clemens taken at the studio of Abdullah Frères, Constantinople. Mark Twain Papers, The Bancroft Library (CU-MARK). See p. 91 n. 5.

first three at CtY-BR, and the last at NN-B): Abdul-Aziz (chapter 13); Aleksandr II (chapter 37); Ismail Pasha (chapter 57); and Abd-el-Kader (1807?–83), an Arab leader imprisoned by the French in 1847 and freed in 1852 by Napoleon III (chapter 57).

[6]The planned trip was probably to Scutari on 3 September, the morning of the same day the *Quaker City* departed Constantinople at 10:00 P.M. If an *Alta* letter about Scutari was indeed already written and not simply anticipated, Clemens must have made an earlier visit there, either during his first sojourn in Constantinople on 17–19 August or sometime after his return there on 30 August.

To Jane Lampton Clemens and Family
10 September 1867 • Beirut, Syria
(MS: NPV)

U.S. Consul's Office,
Beirut, Syria, Sept. 11.

Dear Folks—

We are here, eight of us, making a contract with a dragoman ~~for~~ to take us to Baalbek, then to Damascus, Nazareth, &c, then to Lake Genassareth (Sea of Tiberias,) then south through all the celebrated Scriptural localities, to Jerusalem—then to the Dead Sea, the Cave of Macpelah & up to Joppa where the ship will be. We shall be in the saddle three weeks—we have horses, tents, provisions, arms, a dragoman & 2 other servants, & we pay five dollars a day apiece in gold.[1]

Love to all.
Yrs
Sam.

We leave ~~tomorrow~~ tonight at 2 oclock in the morning.[2]

[*letter docketed:*] Rec'd in St. Louis Oct. 11. P.A.M.

[1] The eight were Clemens, Slote, Van Nostrand, Moulton, Davis, Birch, Church, and Denny. Clemens must have written this letter on 10 (not 11) September, for he implies that the contract had not yet been settled, and Denny's journal shows that negotiations for the trip were completed on 10 September, when a "committee" of three (Church, Birch, and Denny himself), acting for the party, paid the dragoman "in the presence of our Consul one half the cost." The total cost of the expedition was "one pound sterling each per. day for twenty days," or $800, the remaining half of which was due on arrival in Jaffa. On 11 September Clemens wrote in his notebook:

> Abraham, of Malta, is Chief Dragoman, & Mohamed ——— of Alexandria, Egypt is 1st Assistant.
>
> Camp Equipage: 3 sleeping tents; 1 kitchen tent, & 1 eating tent—all large, finely furnished & handsome.
>
> Our caravan numbers 24 mules & horses, & 14 serving men—28 men all told.

The United States consul general in Beirut was J. A. Johnson (*N&J1*, 416–17; Denny, entry for 10 Sept; Interior Department, 8).

[2] Clemens's notebook records, and Denny's journal confirms, that the party left Beirut on 11 September at 3:00 P.M. Denny noted that they mounted and

set out from in front of "the Hotel Belview in Beyrout a meray happy company eight in number" (*N&J1*, 416; Denny, entry for 11 Sept).

To Mr. Esais
24 September 1867 • Jerusalem, Syria
(MS: CU-MARK)

Mediterranean Hotel,
Jerusalem Sep. ~~21~~ 24[1]

Mr. Esais—Fix up the little Bible I selected (I don't want any other)—the one that has backs made of Balsam-wood from the Jordan, oak from Abraham's tree at Hebron, olive-wood from the Mount of Olives, & whatever the other stuff was—ebony, I think. Put on it this inscription: "Mrs. Jane Clemens—from her son—Mount Calvary, Sept 24, 1867." Put "Jerusalem" around on it loose, somewhere, in Hebrew, just for a flyer.[2] Send it to our camp, near head of the valley of Hinnom—the third tents you come to if you leave the city by the Jaffa Gate—the first if you go out by the Damascus Gate.[3]

Yrs
Sam L. Clemens

[*on back of letter as folded:*]

Forward[d] per politeness of Mr.
Weintraub.

Mr. Esais
Bookstore
Near church of Holy Sepulchre[4]

[1]Clemens and his party arrived in Jerusalem at noon on 23 September after departing the village of Lubban at 2:30 that morning. Riding ahead of their tents and equipment, they took rooms at the Mediterranean Hotel, "a large and commodious house, well situated near the British Consulate, and not far from the Damascus gate," according to a contemporary guidebook. Clemens noted to himself: "Loafed all the afternoon in the Mediterranean Hotel." But judging from the entries in his notebook, Clemens spent all of the following day inspecting the landmarks of the city (Murray, 1:73; *N&J1*, 432–35).

[2]This small (diamond type, 16mo) King James Bible, now in the Mark Twain Papers, was printed at Oxford University Press for the British and Foreign Bible Society in 1863, and was later bound or rebound as Clemens describes. The inscription Clemens ordered appears verbatim in gothic lettering on the front and back panels, with "Jerusalem" in Hebrew characters between "Mount Calvary" and "Sept. 24, 1867" on the back panel. Clemens himself inscribed the front flyleaf in pencil: "Mrs. Jane Clemens | From her Son— | Jerusalem, Sep. 24, 1867." (Orion Clemens later traced over the inscription in purple ink and added, "The above, in pencil, but traced in ink May 15, 1874 by O. C.")

[3]On the morning of 25 September, Clemens's party set off for Jericho and Bethlehem, returning to Jerusalem and the Mediterranean Hotel on 27 September. After two more nights at the Mediterranean Hotel, they left Jerusalem on 29 September to rejoin the *Quaker City* at Jaffa the following day (*N&J1*, 432–43; Clemens's notebook entries for 22–28 September are misdated: see Denny, entries for 22–30 Sept).

[4]Neither Mr. Weintraub, to whom Clemens entrusted delivery of his note, nor Mr. Esais, from whose bookstore he purchased the Bible, has been further identified.

To Samuel E. Moffett
1–2 October 1867 • SS *Quaker City* en route from Jaffa, Syria, to Alexandria, Egypt

(MS book inscription, *damage emended:* CtHMTH)

[*on back flyleaf and facing page:*]

This rose has a history.[1]

[*pressed rose, now lost*]

At Sea, October, 1867.[2]

To Sammy Moffett—
From his Uncle Sam*l.*

Read this book carefully, Sammy, & study its precepts well. In urging this, I am inspired by the hope that you will derive as much satisfaction from its perusal as I have done. No words can express the comfort this little book has been to me. Often, in lonely nights at sea, I have taken her down & tackled her, first at one end & then at the other, & finally sailed in at the middle & waltzed out at both ends,, while tears of gratitude suffused my eyes for the blessed missionary brick that[3]

[*on a sheet affixed to the front flyleaf:*]

[*up to four lines of inscription (about 20 words) lost*][4]

ARABIC NEW TESTAMENT
PRINTED AT THE
AMERICAN MISSION PRESS.

PRESENTED BY THE AMERICAN MISSION
TO

صموئيل كليمنس ‸(Sam. L. Clemens)‸

PASSENGER BY THE STEAMER
QUAKER CITY, ‸the ship.‸

BEIRUT, SYRIA, SEPTEMBER 1867.

[*written in pencil by Moffett on the page facing the title page:*] To Sammy Moffett | From his uncle

[1]Probably Clemens's caption for a rose pressed between the back flyleaf and facing page of this Arabic book (see note 3). The history to which it alludes has not been explained. Clemens's decision to begin his inscription at the back (which to Western readers would appear to be the front) was deliberate.

[2]Clemens was at sea for three different periods during October: in addition to 1–2 October (the one that seems the most likely for this letter), from 7 through 17 October (en route from Alexandria to Gibraltar), and from 25 through 31 October (en route from Gibraltar to Bermuda, where he arrived on 11 November). If, as also seems likely, he intended the book as an amusing gift for his nephew's seventh birthday on 5 November, he could expect timely delivery in St. Louis by that date only if he sent it on or shortly after his arrival at Alexandria (2 October). But no evidence has been found which would positively exclude a letter date within the second or third October periods at sea.

[3]This word falls at the end of the page facing the back flyleaf (originally blank)

of the book, an Arabic translation of the New Testament printed in 1866 by the American Mission in Beirut and bound by F. Rosenzweig in maroon leather with gold tooling and brass corner pieces. It was the first such translation ever made: begun in 1847 by missionary Eli Smith, it was completed in 1865 by Cornelius Van Alen Van Dyck. Seventy copies of this New Testament in Arabic were evidently prepared as gifts for the *Quaker City* passengers, presumably from a passenger list sent in advance of the ship's arrival at Beirut. Each contained a printed presentation sheet pasted onto the front flyleaf (i.e., at what would seem to be the back of the book), with the passenger's name inscribed in Arabic. Captain Duncan recorded that on the morning of 10 September, the day the *Quaker City* arrived in Beirut, the Reverend Henry Harris Jessup (1832–1910) came aboard and "invited all our party" to visit the boarding school for girls maintained by the mission at 5:00 that afternoon. Although a party of thirty or forty excursionists accepted the invitation and were presented with their Arabic testaments at the school, Clemens was probably not among them, and must therefore have received his copy later, aboard the ship, possibly that same evening or the next morning (Isham, 1; Severance, 152–53; Charles C. Duncan 1867b, entry for 10 Sept).

[4]This estimate of missing text is highly conjectural. It assumes that Clemens continued his remarks about beginning "first at one end & then at the other" by completing his last sentence and signing the letter in about an inch of space at the top of the printed presentation sheet. He clearly did write on this sheet, only a fragment of which survives, containing several of the printed words and two insertions in his hand. The printed text here has been supplied from the presumably identical printed sheet pasted onto the front flyleaf in the copy given to Charles Langdon; Clemens's name in Arabic has been redrawn. (Four of these gift copies are known to have survived: Clemens's and Langdon's copies are now at CtHMTH, and are the only ones that have been examined; the existence of Gibson's is established by Leamington Book Shop, description of lot 131; and Jackson's copy is described in L. H. S. Robson to Cyril Clemens, 12 Mar 1935, PH in CU-MARK.) Both the text of the printed statement and Clemens's glosses on it may be incompletely recovered.

To Jane Lampton Clemens and Family 13, 15, and 17 October 1867 • SS *Quaker City* at Cagliari, Sardinia; Algiers, Algeria; Málaga, Spain; and Gibraltar

(MS: NPV)

‸P.S. I wrote you from Jerusalem & Egypt,—notes to say all well.‸

Cagliari, Sardinia, Oct. 12.

Dear Folks—

We have just dropped anchor before this handsome city and

Algiers, Africa, Oct. 15.

They would not ~~land~~ let us land at Cagliari, on account of cholera. Nothing to write.[1]

Malaga, Spain, Oct. 17.

The Captain & I are ashore here under guard, waiting to know whether they will let the ship anchor or not. Quarantine regulations are very strict, here, on all vessels coming from Egypt. I am a little anxious, because I want to go inland to Granada & see the Alhambra. I can go on down, by Seville & Cordova & be picked up at Cadiz. Later—We cannot anchor—must go on. We shall be at Gibraltar before midnight, & I think I will go horseback (2 long days) & thence by rail & diligence to Cadiz. I will not mail this till I see the Gibraltar lights—I begin to think they won't let us in anywhere.[2]

11.30 PM—Gibraltar.

At anchor & all right, but they won't let us land till morning—it is a waste of valuable time. We shall reach New York middle November.

Yrs
Sam

[1] The *Quaker City* dropped anchor in the Gulf of Cagliari, some two miles from the town, at 9:00 P.M. on 13 (not 12) October. Captain Duncan wrote, "An official informed us that cholera existed at Cagliara and that foul bills of health were issued to every vessel leaving— We had heard enough and hastily leaving returned to the ship" (Charles C. Duncan 1867b, entry for 13 Oct). The excursionists were eager to maintain the ship's clean bill of health, having already suffered great inconvenience and disappointment as a result of quarantine restrictions.

[2] The Spanish port officials at Málaga required a seven-day quarantine for any ship—regardless of its bill of health—arriving from another Mediterranean port (Charles C. Duncan 1867b, entry for 17 Oct). Julia Newell, in a letter to the Janesville (Wis.) *Gazette*, remarked on "the absurdity of quarantining a ship with a perfectly 'clean bill of health,' and on board of which for five months there had been no disease more serious than seasickness," adding that since Gibraltar was "regulated in its affairs by English good sense," the passengers *were* allowed to land there (Newell 1867c). Since Málaga was the only Spanish port from which Granada could be easily reached, passengers who were intent on seeing the Alhambra, but unwilling or unable to pursue the alternative Clemens mentioned here, were thereby prevented from seeing it at all.

To Jane Lampton Clemens and Family
24 October 1867 • Cádiz, Spain
(MS: NPV)

. . . .

Cadiz, Oct. 24.

We ~~g~~ ~~w~~ left Gibraltar at noon & rode to Algeciras, (4 hours) thus dodging the quarantine,)—took dinner, & then rode horseback all night in a swinging trot, & at daylight took a caleche (2-wheeled vehicle) & rode 5 hours—then took cars & traveled till ~~ten~~ ‸twelve‸ at night. That landed us at Seville & we were over the hard part of our trip & somewhat tired. Since then we have taken things comparatively easy, drifting around from one town to another & attracting a good deal of attention—for I guess strangers do not wander through Andalusia & the other Southern provinces of Spain often. The country is precisely as it was when Don Quixotte & Sancho Panza were possible characters.[1]

But I see now that the glory of Spain must have been when it was under Moorish domination. No, I will not say that—but then when one ~~becomes~~ is carri‸ed‸~~age~~ away, infatuated, entranced, with the wonders of the Alhambra & the supernatural beauty of the Alcazar, he is apt to overflow with admiration for the splendid intellects that created them.[2]

[*remainder in ink:*]

I cannot write now. I am only dropping a line to let you know I am well. The ship will call ~~f~~ here for us tomorrow. We may stop at Lisbon, & shall at the Bermudas, & will arrive in New York ten days after this letter gets there.

Yrs

Sam.

[1] On 18 October Clemens, Denny, Jackson, Moulton, and Newell (and possibly an additional few of their fellow passengers) hired a Spanish guide, Michael Beñunes, and rode around Gibraltar Bay to Algeciras, intending to take a steamer from there to Málaga, and to reach Granada from Málaga by an eleven-hour carriage and railway trip. Discovering that the next steamer for Málaga would not leave for three days, Denny (and any unidentified companions) returned to the ship that night, but the other four passengers and their guide undertook the trip described here. They rode all night, more than thirty miles, to

Vejer (or Bekkeh), where on the morning of 19 October they hired calèches, which conveyed them to San Fernando. At 4:00 P.M., having abandoned the plan to visit Granada, they boarded a train for Seville, arriving about midnight. After a day and a second night in Seville they took the train to Córdoba on 22 October, returning to Seville the next day and, with a stop at Jerez, finally reaching Cádiz on 24 October (Ford 1869, 1:390; Denny, entry for 18 Oct; Newell 1867c; SLC 1903–4, entry for 3 Nov 1903; Ford 1845, 1:223; SLC 1868hhh). In a chapter written for *The Innocents Abroad* in June 1868, but ultimately omitted from that book, Clemens recapitulated the itinerary of his "flying trip" through Spain:

> [We] hired a guide, took a carriage, crossed the neutral ground & drove around the seashore to Algeciras, where we arrived about three in the afternoon. . . .
>
> At five, the guide brought some immense, high-trotting horses, ~~with~~ furnished with unimaginable & indescribable saddles, & we mounted & left. . . . [We went] flying~~, un~~ through Spain, unencumbered, over a faultless road. . . .
>
> We seldom galloped. We went in a swinging trot all night. . . .
>
> Just as it ~~came~~ ‸turned‸ broad daylight we ~~came~~ ‸~~went,~~‸ ‸came‸ clattering up to a diligence station called Bekjes, or some such barbarous name. ~~We lay down till~~ We took breakfast, hired a couple of ‸covered‸ one-horse go-carts called *caleches*, and ~~s~~ drove off through ~~An~~ sunny Andalusia, among picturesque villages, scenes of rural beauty & mild mountainous grandeur, stopping now & then to look & admire, or halting a moment at a peasant's house to eat pomegranates & ~~gra~~ luscious grapes. Away again, meeting quaintly-costumed Sancho Panzas riding sedate~~, contented~~ little asses, & wondering ~~where in~~ why ~~in~~ the mischief the redoubtable Don Quixotte, ~~did~~ solemn & extravagant, did not emerge from the wayside trees or from some grim stone dungeon of a Spanish inn. . . .
>
> We reached the fine city of San Leandro, or San Lorenzo, or some such name, after a while, rather jaded & sleepy. The diligence was ~~crowd~~ ready to start, it was ~~cr~~ full, we were tired ~~& jaded & sleepy~~, the weather was hot, it was sixteen awful hours to Granada & the Alhambra—we sighed, said it was too much, & ~~gave~~ sorrowfully gave it up. . . . The Alcazar was said to be a Moorish palace a thousand years old—it was the Alhambra in miniature—its rich architecture had been perfectly restored, its gardens ~~l~~ & fountains likewise;—enough—let argument cease—we would fly to Seville.
>
> We took the cars at once. . . . At midnight we started from a doze & . . . ‸in another moment‸ we were in charming Seville. . . .
>
> We took the cars & went to ancient Cordova. . . . We were lions in Cordova~~,~~—especially our lady with her short traveling dress. Those curious interior people seldom see foreigners ~~I think.~~ ‸no doubt.‸ Dressed in the quaint costumes of five hundred years ago, they flocked after us & gazed upon us ~~as though~~ somewhat as if we had dropped out of heaven, but more as if we had come up from the other place. . . . We staid all night at the ~~funniest,~~ ‸strangest‸ old-fashioned Spanish hotel. . . .
>
> At 9 A.M. we hurried to the depot. . . . We got in the car—we moved—flew— ‸toward Cadiz.‸ (SLC 1868hhh, 1289–90, 1299, 1301–3, 1306–8, 1314–15, 1317, 1321†)

[2] The Alhambra was "the Acropolis, the Windsor Castle, of Granada," according to one guidebook—but as Clemens's 1868 chapter shows, he never visited Granada, having decided to settle for the Alcazar, palace of the Moorish kings, which he saw on his first morning in Seville: "I cannot describe it. In my memory its courts & gardens will always be a hasheesh delusion, its Hall of Ambassadors a marvelous dream" (Ford 1869, 1:347; SLC 1868hhh, 1309†).

To Joseph T. Goodman
24 October 1867 • Cádiz, Spain

(*Paraphrase:* Virginia City
Territorial Enterprise, 1 Dec 67)

MARK TWAIN.—It seems that the Holy Land excursion, about which so much has been written, has not been a perfect success in every respect. In a private letter to the editor of this paper,[1] dated "Cadiz, Spain, October 24, 1867," "Mark Twain" says: "Between you and I, (I haven't let it out yet, but am going to,) this pleasure party of ours is composed of the d——dest, rustiest, ignorant, vulgar, slimy, psalm-singing cattle that could be scraped up in seventeen States. They wanted Holy Land, and they got it. It was a stunner. It is an awful trial to a man's religion to waltz it through the Holy Land."[2] The most of the excursionists were probably a little too straight-laced for "Mark"—hence, the rough manner in which he sums up the general characteristics of the crowd. It is evident from his letters that he has not been especially pleased with his fellow-travelers as a body, and has found it difficult to refrain from giving them a taste of his vengeance in his correspondence. He seems to have been in a state of exasperation the most of the time, and, with the exception of the Emperor of Russia and family, has scarcely written a pleasant word of any one. He is strangely intolerant and irritable, and it is under the inspiration of some real or imaginary grievance of a trifling character that he gives vent to his most comical conceits. "Europe in a hurry" and "Europe on foot" have been contributed to our literature.[3] It remains for "Mark Twain" to furnish us with a volume or two of "Europe in a rage."[4] While in Cadiz, he informs us, he visited a four-story billiard saloon and amused himself by playing for three or four hours. He says the place "was filled with gold-laced bilks with crowns on their hat bands—because, you know, five men out of every six in Spain wear gorgeous uniforms." For some reason the display of gold lace rendered him as furious as an Andalusian bull with a streamer of red flannel flaunted in his face, and he prayed for two or three Virginia "roughs" to "clean out" the crowd. As it was, he was compelled to content himself by safely blackguarding the most ostentatious of the Spaniards in a language they could not understand. He will soon be in

New York, if he has not reached there already, and has been engaged as a Washington correspondent of the ENTERPRISE.[5]

[1] Goodman (1838–1917) was a longtime friend as well as a shrewd literary adviser of Clemens's. Since 1865 he had been sole proprietor as well as chief editor of the Virginia City *Territorial Enterprise*, for which Clemens had worked as a local and a political reporter (late September 1862 through May 1864) and as its San Francisco correspondent (mid-1865 to early March 1866) (*ET&S1*, 12–38; *L1*, 242 n. 2).

[2] Clemens's relationship with most of the excursionists had been growing more fractious as the trip wore on, but this tendency received a special impetus between 18 October, the morning after the ship arrived at Gibraltar on the way home, and 25 October, when Clemens and his party returned to the ship at Cádiz. According to Captain Duncan, "at daylight" on 18 October they received "an immense mail—letters and papers from home! How eagerly they were caught up, opened and read!" (Charles C. Duncan 1867b, entry for 18 Oct). Presumably among those papers was a copy of the New York *Tribune* for 19 September, including Mark Twain's letter about the visit to the tsar in which he said, in part, that the Russians

> are able to make themselves pleasant company, whether they speak one's language or not, but our tribe can't think of anything to do or say when they get hold of a subject of the Czar who knows only his own language. However, one of our ladies, from Cleveland, Ohio, is a notable exception to this rule. She escorts Russian ladies about the ship, and talks and laughs with them, and makes them feel at home. . . . I wish we had more like her. They all try, but none succeed so well as she. (SLC 1867xx)

This praise of Mrs. Fairbanks doubtless made Clemens's low opinion of the rest of the ladies seem a deliberate, public insult, and Moses Beach promptly rose to their defense. Although he himself had missed the visit to the tsar, he nevertheless described it in a letter to the *Sun* dated 21 October from Gibraltar:

> And let me add here—the *Tribune* correspondent to the contrary notwithstanding—that our Quaker City company acquitted themselves well. As representatives not only of every part of their country, but of almost every shade of society in every part, they so appeared as that the most fastidious need not blush for word or act. (Beach 1867c)

Charles Langdon long recalled the same incident for another reason. According to his son's version of the story, Langdon had been rebuffed earlier by Clemens for offering him advice about a card game: "Young man, there's a prayer-meeting forward in the dining saloon and they need you there." He was therefore gratified when the *Tribune* letter

> found its way back to the ship just before Mr. Clemens returned from a side trip, and it was the pleasure of the youthful card coach to espy the discredited man of letters coming on board and to give him in detail just the temper of Mrs. This and Mrs. That, with the sound advice that he keep pretty closely to his cabin for a few days, and give the weather a chance to clear. (Jervis Langdon, 4)

The side trip was certainly Clemens's excursion through Spain. While Clemens was away, the *Quaker City* spent nearly a week at Gibraltar, recoaling and reprovisioning for the Atlantic crossing, so that the passengers' displeasure had time to become quite general. Clemens himself later alluded with some bitterness to "what they said about me at Gibraltar when I was absent" (17 June 68 to Fairbanks). The superheated remarks about the passengers in this letter to Goodman may indicate that Clemens had caught some inkling of their resentment even before he left Gibraltar at noon on 18 October.

[3]*Europe in a Hurry*, by George Wilkes (New York: H. Long and Brother, 1853) and, possibly, *Views a-Foot; or, Europe Seen with Knapsack and Staff*, by J. Bayard Taylor (New York: Wiley and Putnam, 1847). The latter, which issued in twenty "editions" during its first ten years in print, was for many years one of the most popular among a number of books on the subject of European pedestrian travel.

[4]Clemens's anger at some of his fellow passengers was stimulated further during the voyage home by their complaints to the captain about the "sinful" pastimes of the party of fast young men on board. In a play fragment Clemens probably wrote soon after returning to New York, he created a stodgy character named "Elder Homily," who makes the following speech:

> They drink & drink & drink, in that No. 10 till it is horrible—perfectly *hor*rible! And they smoke there—which is against the ship's rules—& they have bribed the cabin crew & the porter & they burn safety lanterns there all night ‸(which is against the rule, too)‸ & say they are writing to the newspapers—which is a *lie*, brethren & sisters—they're playing sinful 7-up.+That's what they're doing. (SLC 1867vvv, act 2, 8–9; fully transcribed in Appendix E)

There must have been some truth in these grievances against Clemens and his friends, for Captain Duncan noted in his journal soon after departing Cádiz that he had "issued notices touching the better observance of the regulations touching Lights complaints having been made that open lights and lighted pipes & segars were used in State rooms" (Charles C. Duncan 1867b, entry for 26 Oct).

[5]Clemens was addressing the problem of maintaining his income after the excursion returned. He eventually wrote ten letters from Washington and one from New York for the *Enterprise* between 4 December 1867 and 2 March 1868. He reached New York on 19 November, twelve days before Goodman published this letter in Nevada.

To Jane Lampton Clemens and Family
20 November 1867 • (1st of 2) • New York, N.Y.

(MS: NPV)

New York, Tuesday,
Nov. 19.

Dear Folks—

W The Quaker City arrived at 10 this morning—I suppose the passengers have been worrying all day, but I got off at once—got introduced to the head Customs Inspector & he passed my trunks without opening them.[1] I have been bumming around the newspaper offices all day—the Herald folks got me at 6 o'clock, & notwithstanding I had an engagement to dine at the ~~s~~ St Nicholas with some ladies & take them to the theatre, I sat down in one of the editorial rooms & wrote a long article that will make the Quakers get up & howl in the morning. I did not get through till 10 PM—didn't go to the theatre, of course.[2] I have been trying to get home to the Westminster ever since—just accomplished now, after midnight,—have seen a good many friends, you bet you. When Charles Dickens sleeps in this room next week, it will be a gratification to him to know that I have slept in it also.[3]

I sent a package to you by Julius Moulton, but have forgotten to give him your address.[4] I leave for Washington to-morrow.

Yrs aff

Sam.

[*written across previous paragraphs:*]
We were in the Bermudas during the whole of the late awful storm—fortunate, wasn't it?[5]

Send the enclosed article to the Republican[6]—

[1] John L. Von Buskirk had been supervisor since 1831 of the two hundred inspectors at the New York Custom House. Although he was nearly eighty years old, his "extraordinary physical health" enabled him to attend to his duties from "sunrise to sunset, all the year round, seven days in the week." Since he visited "*every ship* under his charge in the harbor of New York," he probably met Clemens on board the *Quaker City* (Wilson 1867, 1049, and "City Register," 5; Thorpe, 20).

[2] Clemens mentioned elsewhere that he planned to dine at the St. Nicholas Hotel—on Broadway at Spring Street—with Mary Mason Fairbanks and Charles Langdon; his other companions have not been identified. The article he spent the evening writing for the New York *Herald*, "The Cruise of the Quaker City," was published on the morning of 20 November. It incorporated an earlier draft, an "old article" he happened to have in his pocket, which Mrs. Fairbanks had evidently read (2 Dec 67 to Fairbanks; 22 Nov 67 to Young; James Miller, 67; SLC 1867sss).

[3] On the evening of 19 November, just a few hours before Clemens wrote this letter, Dickens arrived in Boston to begin a five-month lecture tour of the eastern United States. George Dolby, his agent, had stayed at the Westminster the previous week and presumably arranged for Dickens's stay there during his New York performances. The New York *Herald* reported him enjoying the "quiet, elegant and comfortable appointments of the Westminster Hotel" upon his arrival on 7 December (Moss, 331–33; New York *Times:* "Arrivals in the City," 14 Nov 67, 8; "Arrival of the Steamship Cuba and of Charles Dickens," 20 Nov 67, 1; "Arrival of Mr. Dickens," 8 Dec 67, 5; "Dickens," New York *Herald*, 10 Dec 67, 8).

[4]It is not known whether Moulton delivered this package, or what it contained, but Clemens may well have entrusted to him the Bible he purchased for his mother in Jerusalem (see 24 Sept 67 to Esais).

[5]The excursionists arrived at St. George, Bermuda, on the morning of 11 November, planning to depart for New York on 14 November. They had fair weather for most of the Atlantic crossing, including their first two days in Bermuda, but according to Captain Duncan, on 13 November a "hard gale from SW to North West" momentarily imperiled the ship and postponed departure until 15 November. Clemens evidently assumed that this gale represented the passage northward of an unusually severe hurricane which had caused extensive damage in the West Indies on 29 October, more than two weeks before, and which his family had presumably read about in the St. Louis newspapers (Denny, entries for 25 Oct–15 Nov; Charles C. Duncan 1867b, entries for 25 Oct–13 Nov; New York *Times:* "The West Indies," 16 Nov 67, 1; "Tortola" and "St. Domingo," 19 Nov 67, 1; "West Indies," 21 Nov 67, 5).

[6]The original enclosure has not been found, but it was almost certainly a clipping of the article in the New York *Herald* mentioned in the first paragraph, comprising Clemens's letter to the editor introduced by the newspaper's additions: descriptive subtitles, an explanatory paragraph, and an incomplete passenger list. Clemens's letter, with the *Herald*'s subtitles but without its added paragraph and passenger list, appeared in the St. Louis *Missouri Republican*—with the title "Mark Twain on the Quaker City Pilgrimage"—on 24 November (page 4), and again the next day (page 2). Unlike the *Herald* printing, which carried no by-line or signature, the *Republican* letter was signed "Mark Twain," perhaps because Clemens supplied the name on the clipping he enclosed in this letter (see the next letter). The text of the *Herald* article is given in full in Appendix E.

To Jane Lampton Clemens and Family
20 November 1867 • (2nd of 2) • New York, N.Y.

(MS: NPV)

New York Nov. 20.

Dear Folks—

I am ashamed to go to the Tribune office, almost—they have treated me so well & I have not written them a third of the letters I promised.[1]

I had a fine row with the Herald people this morning because they left out my signature—however, I went to dinner with the whole editorial corps & they explained & we settled it without bloodshed. It looked shabby to me, but the foreman was innocently to blame in the matter, not the editors.[2]

In consequence of that dinner & meeting a lot of old friends & new acquaintances, I did not get off for Washington today, but I think I shall to-morrow.

~~I went up~~ My old room-mate's mother (Dan Slote, who left the ship in Egypt,) sent her carriage this morning, & I went up & kissed the whole family for Dan, from his mother straight through aunts, cousins, sisters-in-law & everything, down to his youngest sister. I guess they think I am a ~~sociable~~ sociable cuss.[3]

The Quakers are all howling, to-day, on account of the article in the Herald. They can go to the devil, for all I care.[4]

Drop a note in the Postoffice directed to Julius Moulton, St. Louis, & ask him to call on you. He & I traveled together in Palestine. He is a splendid fellow—just as good a boy as ever lived. I know it because I always called him a nigger & told him niggers were not allowed in the ‸after‸ cabin after eight bells—& he never got mad.

I will move Heaven & earth for Orion.[5]

The reason I brought nothing from any of these was because it was a bore, & when I did, I lost it, which were it not considering to inefficiency of things, notwith[stand]ing in Europe they do & sometimes even in Asia, withal.

[*no signature*][6]

[1] By his own account, Clemens agreed to write the New York *Tribune* "two letters a month . . . till we reach Egypt" (June–October), at which point he expected to write "oftener" (7 June 67 to Bowen). But by the time the *Quaker City* set out across the Atlantic from Cádiz on 25 October, he had sent only six letters to the *Tribune*, the last of which was written in September and appeared on 9 November.

[2] Because Clemens signed his articles in the *Tribune*, he could not also sign those he published in the rival *Herald*—an arrangement he took care to confirm when the trip was over (see 25 Nov 67 to Young). "The Cruise of the Quaker City," his fourth and last *Quaker City* article in the *Herald* (SLC 1867sss), differed only in that he tried several times, without success, to give it to the *Tribune*, as the next letter shows, and therefore expected to sign it wherever it appeared. Evidently the distinction was not made clear to the *Herald*'s foreman (not further identified), who therefore made certain that it appeared as Clemens's three previous articles had—unsigned and unattributed (Ganzel 1964, 270–73). The next morning the *Herald* published an editorial identifying the previous day's article as "a most amusing letter from the pen of that most amusing American genius, Mark Twain." It continued:

We are not aware whether Mr. Twain intends giving us a book on this pilgrimage, but we do know that a book written from his own peculiar standpoint, giving an account of the characters and events on board ship and of the scenes which the pilgrims witnessed, would command an almost unprecedented sale. There are varieties of genius peculiar to America. Of one of these varieties Mark Twain is a striking specimen. For the development of his peculiar genius he has never had a more fitting opportunity. Besides, there are some things which he knows and which the world ought to know about this last edition of the May Flower. ("The Quaker City Pilgrimage," New York *Herald*, 21 Nov 67, 6)

The specific members of the "editorial corps" who were present at the reconciliation dinner have not been identified, but they may have included James Gordon Bennett, Jr. (1841–1918), managing editor; William H. Chase (1831?–81), who since 1866 had written the *Herald*'s art criticism, as well as some book reviews and dramatic notices; and Samuel R. Glen (1818?–80), foreign-correspondence editor, who had joined the *Herald* staff in 1845 ("Death of William H. Chase," New York *Times*, 24 June 81, 8; "Death of Samuel R. Glen," New York *Times*, 14 May 80, 3).

[3]Slote had left the ship in order to travel for several more months in Europe (*N&J1*, 446 n. 128). Clemens had met Slote's mother and sisters before the *Quaker City* departed (see 7 June 67 to JLC and family, n. 4). Dan's "sisters-in-law" were probably the wives of his two brothers, Alonzo (aged about thirty-five) and John (aged about twenty-four) (*New York Census* 1860, 920–21).

[4]These "howling" passengers are not known to have published their feelings, and they themselves remain unidentified. It is apparent, however, that Mrs. Fairbanks, Charles Langdon, and possibly Moses and Emma Beach were among those who felt injured by the *Herald* letter (see 5 Dec 67 to Beach). In her last letter to the Cleveland *Herald*, published on 14 December, Mrs. Fairbanks wrote:

There have been various comments upon "the Holy Land Expedition." There have been some criticisms. I shall attempt to answer none of them. . . . I have read all the "squibs" and the "flings" at the "Pilgrims" and the "Quaker City." I have listened to more, but notwithstanding all I still aver that the agreeable features of the voyage far outweigh the disagreeable. In every community there are some elements of discord. Seventy passengers have not always been of one mind. There have been some errors in the "administration of affairs," but they have been oftener errors of the head than the heart.

"Mark Twain" may have ridiculed our prayer-meetings and our psalm-singing—that is his profession—and his newspapers expected it of him; but the better man, Samuel L. Clemens, I believe in his heart reverences the sacred mission of prayer, and will, I am sure, often recall with satisfaction the evening hours when his voice blended with others in the hymns of the "Plymouth Collection." (Mary Mason Fairbanks 1867d)

[5]Clemens still hoped to secure a political appointment for his brother.

[6]Clemens wrote this and the previous letter on leaves subsequently torn from his notebook, now numbered 10 (*N&J1*, 453–95). The bibliographical evidence cannot exclude the possibility that the present letter, consisting of two leaves, originally had a third (now lost), on which Clemens completed and presumably signed his letter. But this physical evidence is nevertheless equally consistent with his concluding without a third leaf. The absence of a normal signature must be weighed against the evidence that, while he wrote on both sides of the first leaf, on the second he left blank the last (ruled) line of space as well as all of the verso. The letter has therefore been judged complete as it stands.

To John Russell Young
22 November 1867 • Washington, D.C.
(MS: DLC)

Washington, Nov. 22.

Dear Mr. Young—

I called at the Tribune several times but failed to find you in. I had an article partly written about the Quaker City humbug, which I thought you might possibly accept, although it was rather roughly written, & may ‸be‸ even a little coarse—but I did not like to consult with a stranger about it, & so I never told any one what I came for. When it grew late, I answered a call from the Herald, & finished & printed it there. I was at the Tribune office twice on succeeding days, but they always said you were out.[1] What I wished, was to leave you some Holy Land letters to accept or refuse. I don't know any way now but to send you two or three by mail, asking as a favor that if you do not approve them you will return them to me directed to 242 ~~F~~ F street Washington,[2] cor. 14th. I stopped writing for the Tribune, partly because I seemed to write so awkwardly, & partly because I was apt to betray the glaring disrespect for the Holy Land & the Primes and Thompson's who have glorified it which travel there had created in me.[3] But coming home I cramped myself down to at least something like *decency* of expression, & wrote some twenty letters, which have survived the examin~~ed~~ation of a most fastidious ~~censer~~ censor on shipboard and are consequently not incendiary documents. There are several among these that I think you would probably accept, after reading them.[4] I would so like to write some savage letters about Palestine, but it wouldn't do. ~~I~~ And I would so like to modernize the b‸i‸ographies of some of the patriarchs—but that would not do, either.[5]

I have some hope that the harmless squib in the Herald will bring out bitter replies from some of the Quaker City's strange menagerie of ignorance, imbecility, bigotry & dotage, & so give me an excuse to go into the secret history of the excursion & tell truthfully how that curious company conducted themselves in foreign lands and on board ship.

I have located here for the winter. Have called 3 times at the Tribune bureau, but always missed the staff by some five aggravating minutes. I know Mr. Foley.[6]

If I had know[n] the letters in the Tribune were being copied I would have continued them anyhow—for to copy a letter is to invest it with importance, at any rate, whether it has any ~~ac~~ actual *merit* or not.[7]

I wish I could have talked with you. The letters I have sent you heretofore have been—well, they have been worse, much worse, than those I am sending you now.

I am, with great esteem,
Yrs Truly
Sam. L. Clemens

[*letter docketed:*] *File* | Y.

[1]In 1868, Amos J. Cummings, then the *Tribune*'s "City and Political Editor," published a vivid, insider's description of Young at the *Tribune* offices:

> Our cards go in, and in ten seconds we are ushered into the presence of the Managing Editor of *The Tribune*. . . . What! this blue-eyed boy the Managing Editor of the most influential journal in America! You can hardly believe it. In personal appearance Mr. Young is the most insignificant person about the office. He is light-complexioned, has a large, sloping head, thatched with brown hair, a clear forehead, and a prominent nose, and is as quick of motion as a sparrowhawk. He is of medium height—say five feet eight. His words flow from his lips in rapid succession, as if each one was struggling to get out of his mouth ahead of the other. . . .
>
> Young is a strict disciplinarian. He runs the editorial department like a machine. Every cog strikes its groove with punctual regularity. When he is absent his duties fall on Mr. John R. G. Hassard. If Hassard is missing, Mr. Amos J. Cummings takes the manager's chair, and so perfect does everything jibe, that if all the editors were absent the oldest reporter, like the senior sergeant of a company destitute of commissioned officers, would take charge. (Cummings 1868b, 106–7)

[2]Probably Clemens took the night train of 21 November to Washington, D.C., arriving on the morning of 22 November. He roomed with his employer, Senator William M. Stewart, at 224 (not 242) F Street North. Forty years later, Stewart published the following description of their rooms and Clemens's arrival that morning:

> About the winter of 1867, I think, while my family was in Paris, I lived in a rather tumble-down building which at that time stood on the northwest corner of Fourteenth and F Streets, N. W., opposite the old Ebbitt House, where many of my Congressional cronies had quarters. The house was a weather-beaten old place, a relic of early Washington.
>
> Its proprietress was Miss Virginia Wells, an estimable lady about 70 years of age, prim, straight as a ramrod, and with smooth-plastered white hair. She belonged to one of the first families of Virginia, which were quite numerous in Washington, and was very aristocratic; but having lost everything in the war, she had come to Washington, and managed to make a precarious living as a lodging-house keeper.
>
> I had the second floor of her residence, one of the rooms, facing upon both streets, a spacious apartment about seventy-five feet long, which I had divided by a curtain drawn across it, making a little chamber at the rear, in which I slept. The front part was my sitting room. I had a desk there, and tables, with writing materials, and my books, and a sideboard upon which I kept at all times plenty of cigars and a supply of whiskey, for I occasionally smoked and took a drink of liquor.

I was seated at my window one morning when a very disreputable-looking person slouched into the room. He was arrayed in a seedy suit, which hung upon his lean frame in bunches with no style worth mentioning. A sheaf of scraggy black hair leaked out of a battered old slouch hat, like stuffing from an ancient Colonial sofa, and an evil-smelling cigar butt, very much frazzled, protruded from the corner of his mouth. He had a very sinister appearance. He was a man I had known around the Nevada mining camps several years before, and his name was Samuel L. Clemens. (William M. Stewart, 219–20)

[3] Circumstances since mid-October obliged Clemens to use the Holy Land for the subject of his letters, since the Mediterranean ports from Egypt onwards, about which he originally planned to write "oftener" than twice a month, went largely unvisited because of quarantine restrictions. William Cowper Prime (1825–1905) was the son of a Presbyterian minister and currently editor of the New York *Journal of Commerce* as well as president of the Associated Press. He published *Tent Life in the Holy Land* in 1857. William McClure Thomson (1806–94) was a Presbyterian minister and missionary in Syria for over forty years. (He visited the *Quaker City* when it arrived at Beirut in September.) Thomson published *The Land and the Book* in 1858, which, when republished in England, ostensibly sold more copies than "any previous American book except *Uncle Tom's Cabin*." Clemens was familiar with both books and did not hesitate to ridicule Prime's, at any rate, in his letters to the *Alta* (*DAB*, 18:490; Mary Mason Fairbanks 1867c; SLC 1868hh).

[4] This burst of writing between 25 October and 11 November produced at least twenty-one letters, including the one just published in the *Herald*, contrary to the advice of his "censor," Mrs. Fairbanks. Solon Severance informed Paine of an instance of her censorship that preceded the trip home:

One afternoon I saw him tearing up a bunch of the soft, white paper—copy paper, I guess the newspapers call it—on which he had written something, and throwing the fragments into the Mediterranean. I inquired of him why he cast away the fruits of his labors in that manner.

"Well," he drawled, "Mrs. Fairbanks thinks it oughtn't to be printed, and, like as not, she is right." (*MTB*, 1:328)

Emma (Beach) Thayer recalled Clemens's reading his work aloud "for the sake of Mrs. Fairbanks' criticism by which I think he abided, as he would declare that she had destroyed 'four hours of work' or such and such an amount. I think it was what seemed to her irreverence or too much profanity that she objected to" (Thayer to A. B. Paine, 22 June 1907, Davis 1967a, 2).

[5] In a 3 September 1867 notebook entry, Clemens wrote "Biography of Samson for N. Y. Tribune," but no text has been found (*N&J1*, 414).

[6] John P. Foley had recently left the New York editorial staff of the *Tribune* and taken on a new assignment as the paper's Washington correspondent, "until the first of April." In 1866, when John Russell Young became managing editor of the *Tribune*, he had appointed his brother—James Rankin Young (1847–1924), nearly seven years his junior—head of the Washington bureau. According to Cummings, this bureau was "the most important and expensive Bureau attached to the journal," employing five men ("Personal," New York *World*, 18 Nov 67, 4; Baehr, 31; Cummings 1868a, 89; Cummings 1868b, 109).

[7] Although newspapers as diverse as the Brooklyn *Eagle* and the Virginia City *Territorial Enterprise*—as well as the San Francisco *Evening Bulletin* and even the *Alta* itself—felt free to copy Clemens's occasional letters in the *Tribune*, some editors judged them unworthy of reprinting. The New York *Round Table*, for

instance, observed that "Mark Twain's [*Jumping Frog*] book contains better things than those who have read only his letters to *The Tribune* might believe possible." And the editors of the San Francisco *Californian* wrote only partly in jest when they declared Mark Twain "not the sort of man to be sent to the Holy Land. . . . We will not republish the wicked things that Mark Twain says—we are surprised that the *Tribune* did not cut out some of them" ("Library Table," *Round Table* 6 [7 Dec 67]: 376; "Wicked Mark Twain," *Californian* 7 [7 Dec 67]: 1).

To Frank Fuller
24 November 1867 • Washington, D.C.

(MS: Craven)

P.S.—Mum, my boy, about the contents. My address is 224 F, cor. 14th.

Washington, Nov. 24.

Dear Gov:

Dog-gone it, I wrote you from Naples, four years ago, that I wanted to go free of lecturing this season,—*you* know that, you old rip.[1] In the spring I mean to talk 3 nights in San Francisco, 1 in Sacramento & *maybe* 1 in Virginia—*there* is $2,000 to $3,000 in gold—*you* are safe—isn't that enough?

I am not playing my hand thoughtlessly. If I lecture *now*, I shall have to do it solely on the Quaker City's fame, & take many, *very many* chances—chances that might utterly damn me. If I stay here all winter & keep on hanging out my sign in the *Tribune* & getting well acquainted with great dignitaries to introduce ~~my~~ me, like Gov. Nye,[2] I can lecture next season on my *own* reputation, to 100 houses, & houses that will be readier to accept me without criticism than they are now.

I have to make a bran new start in the lecturing business, & I don't mean to do it in Tuttletown, Ark., or Baldwinsville, Michigan, either. I won't start in the provinces, Gov. I won't do it. You have been a bully good friend to me, & I don't intend you shall suffer for it *long*, but you *must* suffer for it a while. There is no question about that. I have solemnly yielded up my liberty for a whole session of ~~c~~Congress,—enrolled my name on the regular Tribune staff, made the Tribune bureau here my headquarters, taken correspondences for two other papers & one magazine,[3] & started resolutely in to make a lecturing reputation that shall stand fire & enable me to succeed without the kind assistance of the public schools.[4]

Tell those 18 Societies I am truly & sincerely obliged for the compliment they have paid me, but I am already clerk of a Senate Committee & proxy for a ~~Ch~~ member of it & must stand my ground & vote on acceptance or rejection of reports.[5] I don't have a devilish thing to do, & six dollars a day ~~for *that*~~ in the hand is better than eighteen hundred in "the bush."

It would take a month to do 18 lectures—board and traveling expenses $400~~,~~—$400 for you—total $800—profit $1,000—next six months, *nothing to do*.[6] Here, in the next six months I will make twice that, & a *reputation* that will not be as precarious a capital as it is now. See it? Write me, and *forgive me, & be not hard upon me, but good & charitable*.

Yrs. Ever,
Sam. Clemens.

[1]See 7 Aug 67 to Fuller.

[2]See 23 Apr 67 to Stoddard, n. 7.

[3]The two "correspondences" were for the San Francisco *Alta California* and the Virginia City *Territorial Enterprise*. Clemens wrote his first *Enterprise* letter on 4 December (SLC 1867eeee). His first *Alta* letter was dated 10 December and published on 15 January (SLC 1868h), a week after the *Alta* editors printed the following premature announcement:

> We publish to-day the first of a series of letters to be written to the ALTA by "Mark Twain," from the other side of the continent. Our readers will be glad to know that Mark's inimitable letters from the Holy Land are not yet exhausted, but a number are on the way, and will be published hereafter, from time to time, without any reference to the new series of letters, with which they have no necessary connection. "Mark Twain's" Letters from "The Holy Land" have attracted great attention throughout the country, and their termination will be regarded with real regret by many thousand readers. ("Editorial Notes," 8 Jan 68, 2)

In addition to these correspondences, Clemens is known to have sent a letter to the Washington *Evening Star* dated 14 December, and one to the New York *Citizen* dated 15 December (SLC 1867aaaa, 1867cccc). The "one magazine" commitment was to the *Galaxy*, which published "General Washington's Negro Body-Servant: A Biographical Sketch" in its February 1868 issue, and therefore must have received Clemens's manuscript in December (SLC 1868p). All of this work was in addition to at least three "occasional" contributions to the *Tribune* (SLC 1867ffff, 1868*l*, 1868x).

[4]See p. 42.

[5]No record has been found of Clemens's having officially clerked for a Senate committee. Senator Stewart served on four committees at this time—Judiciary,

Public Lands, Pacific Railroad, and Mines and Mining—and the possibility remains that Clemens served as a clerk for one of these without creating an official record of his service (Senate 1868, 2–3).

[6]The eighteen "Societies" from which Fuller had evidently forwarded a lecture-tour offer were presumably members of the Associated Western Literary Societies (the earlier offers from Edwin Lee Brown were for a three-month tour, roughly fifty lectures: see 8 June 67 to McComb and 7 Aug 67 to Fuller). The association, founded in 1864 as an alliance of more than one hundred lyceums in towns ranging from western Pennsylvania to Iowa, furnished its member societies, for annual dues of twenty dollars, the names of available speakers with their topics and fees (Eubank, 76–81; Hoeltje, 125–31). It was probably Fuller who passed on the news of this lecture offer to the New York *Evening Telegram*, which noted on 29 November, "'Mark Twain' has already received and declined, since his return from abroad, eighteen offers to lecture for the round sum of eighteen hundred dollars. He prefers the quiet life of private secretary to an United States Senator" ("Personalities," 2).

To John Russell Young
24 November 1867 • Washington, D.C.

(MS: DLC)

Washington, Nov. 24.

Mr. Young

Dear Sir: Out of a mass of letters not yet mailed I ~~have~~ send you three. The letters all seem to be about al^i^ke, but I take these because one blackguards Palestine scenery, another mentions Nazareth which is a town widely know^n^ in America, the third gently touches the stupid gang of scholastic asses who go browsing through the Holy Land reducing miracles to purely natural occurrences—& all three tickle my pilgrims on the raw.[1] Out of the three letters perhaps your foreign editor can cull one, at any rate.[2]

I send the things to you ~~in order that~~ so that you will recollect to order that they be returned to me if not printed.

Your obliged fellow=
servant in Christ,
Sam. L. Clemens

[*letter docketed:*] File JRY

[1]As Clemens later said explicitly (1 Feb 68 to Young), he took these letters (presumably enclosed) from the sequence of those he had written for, but not yet sent to, the *Alta*. The enclosures themselves have not been found and can be further identified only indirectly. They did not appear in the *Tribune*, which published no Holy Land letters later than 9 November. The *Alta*'s numbered sequence of letters, however, omitted numbers 40, 41, and 42—almost certainly because they were sent to Young, who did not immediately return them. One of the letters may have been published by the *Alta* on 5 April 1868: it is explicitly subtitled "Palestine Scenery," and was, according to the author's note at the end, "written in place of No. 51, which was mislaid for a time, but was found subsequently" (SLC 1868ss). Part or all of the other two letters may have found their way into the manuscript of *The Innocents Abroad*, which Clemens prepared in the spring of 1868 largely by revising clippings of the *Alta* letters, at least in the Holy Land portion of the narrative. In that portion an unusually long section of previously unpublished material appears between what was reprinted from letter 39 and what was reprinted from letter 43 (SLC 1868z, 1868ff): most of the latter half of chapter 50, containing a very full burlesque of William C. Prime, and the first half of chapter 51, which continues the description of Nazareth begun in letter 39 (SLC 1869a, 529–46). This new material may have been written anew for the book during the period of March–June 1868. But part or all of it may very well have originated as one of the letters sent to Young, though written for the *Alta* during October–November 1867.

[2]The foreign editor of the *Tribune* from 1860 to 1869 was Alexander Jacob Schem (1826–81), born in Westphalia, Germany. City editor Cummings described him as

> a large, smooth-faced German, with eyes of imperial blue, and a head broad and well balanced, somewhat resembling portraits of Bismarck. The absence of a good growth of hair gives it the appearance of a polished egg-plant, dead ripe. His eyes are full of language. He has frequently been mistaken for Mr. Greeley. He compiles the "Foreign News," and writes the editorials on European and other foreign matters of interest. The Professor is a great linguist, and translates thirteen different languages with ease and facility. He has a happy faculty of catching an unconscious nap during the composition of his editorials. . . . His slight accent betrays his Teutonic origin. (Cummings 1868b, 107)

To Charles Henry Webb
25 November 1867 • Washington, D.C.

(MS: InU-Li)

Washington, Nov. 25.

Dear ~~F~~ Webb—

I send the inclosed to show you that I had the *will* to do that thing—but I haven't the time.[1] I am enrolled as an "occasional" on the Tribune staff, have received a letter from the Herald offering me the same position in that paper, (shall accept if it don't interfere with the Tribune arrangement)[2] & must keep up a Pacific coast correspondence. If you were *here* ~~we cou~~ to stir me up, we could do the play, sure. As it is, I don't think I will accomplish anything but my correspondence.

Remember me to the Gov—& to Pauline. I hunted for her & couldn't find her. She was gone from Amity Place, Ben Bolt.[3]

Yrs Ever
Sam Clemens
224 F street cor. 14th.

[1] The enclosure was Clemens's penciled draft of the first two acts of a play about the *Quaker City* excursion. It is fully transcribed in Appendix E.

[2] See the next letter.

[3] The "Gov" was clearly Frank Fuller, but "Pauline" is more difficult to identify. Early in 1912, Fuller wrote Paine: "I verily believe that I could tell you things concerning which you have never heard one word. Did he ever mention his Cleveland, Ohio Sweetheart, Pauline?" Paine answered on 8 April, "Write me . . . about Mark's Ohio sweetheart, Pauline. I want so much to know all about these things, whether I can make much use of them or not." But Fuller thought better of his promised revelation and replied: "As to Pauline, we better maintain a profound silence. Mark was smitten with her good looks and qualities and talked with me about her and no one else" (Fuller to A. B. Paine, two undated letters, Davis 1956, 3, 2; A. B. Paine to Fuller, 8 Apr 1912, ViU). Pauline's last name has not been found, but Clemens clearly knew her in New York, not Cleveland (even if she came from Cleveland), during the period before sailing on the *Quaker City*. Amity Place in New York was on Laurens Street (now West Broadway), between Amity and Bleecker streets, four blocks west of Broadway. The name "Ben Bolt" comes from a popular song of that title, written by Thomas Dunn English in 1848 and well known to Clemens. The predominantly anapestic meter of its lines, many of which end with this name ("Oh, don't you remember sweet Alice, Ben Bolt?"), may have suggested Clemens's whimsical allusion (Spaeth, 123; Ogilvie, 99).

To John Russell Young
25 November 1867 • Washington, D.C.

(MS: DLC)

Tribune }
Nov. 25 }

Dear Mr Young

I have neglected until this last moment (5 PM) to write you that Mr Bennett Jr offers me an occasional correspondence ~~for~~ with the Herald—impersonal, of course, I suppose.[1] I spoke to your brother[2]—he said I had better write you. I wish to remain on the Tribune, with signature,—on the Herald without, will not make any difference will it?

I will not answer Mr. Bennett finally until I hear from you.

Very Truly
Sam Clemens

[*letter docketed:*] *File*

[1] Either Young did, in fact, object to this division of loyalties, or Clemens wrote nothing for the *Herald* which is still identifiable as his, at least not until February 1868, when James Gordon Bennett, Jr., offered him a more tempting assignment: see 24 Jan 68 to JLC and PAM, n. 1. Bennett had been managing editor of the *Herald* since 1866. His father, who founded the *Herald* in 1835, continued to exercise significant editorial control until his death in 1872.

[2] James Rankin Young, Washington bureau chief of the *Tribune*.

To Jane Lampton Clemens and Family
25 November 1867 • Washington, D.C.

(MS: NPV)

‸P. S.—I room with Bill Stewart & board at Willard's Hotel.‸[1]

Wash, Nov. 25

Dear Folks—

Tired & sleepy—been in Congress all day & making newspaper acquaintances. Stewart is to look up a clerkship in the Patent Office for Orion—things necessarily move slowly where there ~~are~~ ‸is‸ so much business & such armies of office-seekers to be attended to. I guess it will be all right. I *intend* it shall be all right.[2]

I have 18 invitations to lecture, at $100 each, in various parts of the Union—have declined them all.[3] I am for business, now.

Belong on the Tribune staff, & shall write occasionally. Am offered the same berth to-day on the Herald by letter. Shall write Mr. Bennett & accept, as soon as I hear from Tribune that it will not interfere.[4] Am pretty well known, now—intend to be better known. Am hob-nobbing with these old Generals & Senators & other humbugs for no good purpose.[5] Don't have any more trouble making friends than I did in California. All serene. Good-bye. ‸Shall continue on the "Alta."‸

Yrs aff'ly Sam.

224 F. cor. 14th.

[1] Willard's was on Pennsylvania Avenue at the northwest corner of Fourteenth Street West, less than a block from Stewart's and Clemens's rooms, and across the street from the Washington bureau of the *Tribune*, which was at 470 Fourteenth Street West. Refurbished and renamed in 1847 from the old City Hotel, it was a fashionable gathering place for Washington society (Wilhelmus Bogart Bryan, 2:445 n. 1; Marbut, 136; Poore, 97).

[2] In 1867 the Patent Office in Washington employed ninety-three clerks and temporary clerks at yearly salaries ranging from $1,000 to $1,600 (Interior Department, 151–52). See also 9 Jan 68 and 24 Jan 68, both to JLC and PAM.

[3] See 24 Nov 67 to Fuller.

[4] See 25 Nov 67 to Webb, n. 2.

[5] The surviving documents do not establish which "old Generals & Senators & other humbugs" Clemens encountered between 22 November and the date of this letter. On 21 November the Senate began to meet in a special extension of the first session, adjourning on 2 December, the same day the second regular session of the Fortieth Congress convened.

To John Russell Young
1 December 1867 • Washington, D.C.

(MS: DLC)

Washington, Dec. 1, 1867.

Mr. Young—

Dear Sir: This ‸is‸ to acknowledge a draft for $65, from the Tribune Association as payment in full for foreign correspondence to date.

I am by no means sure, but at the same time it is possible that there is a mistake. I wish ~~w~~ Mr. McEwen would look at the memorandum of terms again, & the number of columns printed, & *then*, if the mistake is in my favor, very well; but if it is in the *Tribune's* favor, why of course we won't say anything about it. The matter of whether a mistake is in one individual's favor or in a totally different individual's favor, makes all the difference in the world.[1]

I am going to send a squib in a day or two which I think will do for publication.[2]

Yours Very Truly
Sam. L. Clemens

[*letter docketed:*] Ans^{d} giving our record. M^{c}E. [*and*] *File*

[1] The check, dated 27 November, is reproduced in facsimile below. It is signed by the publisher Samuel Sinclair (the largest stockholder in the *Tribune*) and countersigned by the secretary of the Tribune Association and the *Tribune*'s financial editor, S. T. Clarke. Young did not publish the three letters sent to him on 24 November. In all likelihood, therefore, the sixty-five dollars was payment for two letters the *Tribune* had already published, on 2 and 9 November (SLC 1867mmm and 1867ppp). If it were payment for only one letter, the rate would be rather high: sixty-five dollars per column, at least 50 percent more than either the *Alta* or the *Herald* paid. Conversely, if it were payment for not two but three letters, including the one published on 25 October (SLC 1867iii), the rate would be too low: twenty-five dollars per column, scarcely what Clemens would have described as "best" (7 June 67 to Bowen). A reasonable inference, therefore, is that since the *Tribune* paid Clemens sixty-five dollars for two letters totaling one and three-fifths columns, his rate of pay was forty dollars per column. D. C. McEwen was private secretary to Young, who was himself known for paying "strict attention to the business details of the office. Every letter, every bill, every rejected communication is filed. He is able to furnish, at a moment's notice, a filed voucher for every cent of expenditure during his administration" (Cummings 1868a, 89; Cummings 1868b, 106–8).

[2] Possibly the "Biography of Samson" Clemens mentioned in his notebook: see 22 Nov 67 to Young, n. 5.

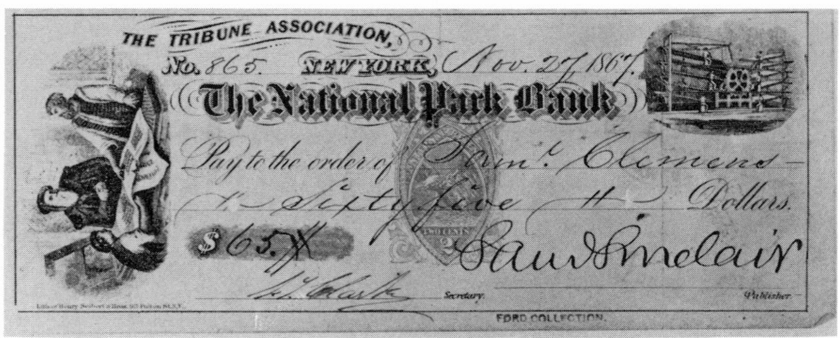
THE TRIBUNE ASSOCIATION,
No. 865. NEW YORK, Nov. 27 1867.
The National Park Bank
Pay to the order of Saml Clemens
Sixty five Dollars.
$65.xx
Saml Sinclair
Publisher
S. T. Clarke
Secretary
FORD COLLECTION.

New York Tribune Association check, dated 27 November 1867 and signed by Samuel Sinclair. Rare Books and Manuscripts Division, The New York Public Library, Astor, Lenox and Tilden Foundations (NN). See note 1.

To Elisha Bliss, Jr.
2 December 1867 • Washington, D.C.
(MS: CU-MARK)

Washington, Dec. 2, 1867.

E. Bliss, Jr. Esq.

Sec'y American Publishing Co.—

Dear Sir:

I only received your favor of Nov. 21st last night, at the rooms of the Tribune Bureau here. It was forwarded from the Tribune office, New York, where it had lain eight or ten days. This will be a sufficient apology for the seeming discourtesy of my silence.[1]

I ~~have written~~ ‸wrote‸ fifty-~~f~~two letters for the San Francisco "Alta California" during the Quaker City excursion, about half of which ‸number‸ have been printed, thus far.[2] The "Alta" has few exchanges in the east, and I suppose scarcely any of these letters have been copied on this side of the Rocky Mountains. I could weed them of their chief faults of con[s]truction & inelegancies of expression, & make a volume that would be more acceptable in many respects than any I could now write. When those letters were written my impressions were fresh, but now they have lost that freshness; they were warm then—they are cold, now. I could strike out certain letters, & write new ones wherewith to supply their places. If you think such a book would suit your purpose, please drop me a line, specifying the size & general style of the volume; ‸*when* the matter ought to be ready;‸ whether it should have pictures in it or not; & particularly what your terms with me would be, & what ~~I~~ amount of money I might possibly make out of it. The latter clause ‸has‸ ~~possess~~ a degree of importance for me which ~~I~~ is almost beyond my own comprehension. But you understand that, of course.

I have other propositions for a book, but have doubted the propriety of interfering with ~~excellent~~ ‸good‸ newspaper engagements except my way as an author could be demonstrated to be plain before me.[3] But I know Richardson, & learned from him, some months ago, something of an idea of the subscription plan of publishing. If that is your plan invariably, it looks safe.[4]

I am on the N. Y. Tribune staff here as an "occasional," ~~& am in~~

~~receipt of a proposition from Mr. Bennett to write an occasional letter to the Herald, also.~~ among other things, and a note from you addressed to

Very Truly &c
Sam. L. Clemens

New York Tribune Bureau, Washington, will find me, without fail.

[*letter docketed:*] ✓ [*and in pencil*] *authors* [*and in ink*] Samuel L Clemens | Dec 2/67

[1] The letter to which Clemens replied has not been found in its original form. It is here reproduced from the transcription published by Paine (*MTL*, 1:140):

OFFICE OF THE AMERICAN PUBLISHING COMPANY.
HARTFORD, CONN., *Nov. 21, 1867.*

SAMUEL L. CLEMENS Esq.
Tribune Office, New York.

DR. SIR,—We take the liberty to address you this, in place of a letter which we had recently written and was about to forward to you, not knowing your arrival home was expected so soon. We are desirous of obtaining from you a work of some kind, perhaps compiled from your letters from the East, &c., with such interesting additions as may be proper. We are the publishers of A. D. Richardson's works, and flatter ourselves that we can give an author as favorable terms and do as full justice to his productions as any other house in the country. We are perhaps the oldest subscription house in the country, and have never failed to give a book an immense circulation. We sold about 100,000 copies of Richardson's F. D. & E. (Field, Dungeon and Escape) and are now printing 41,000 of "Beyond the Mississippi," and large orders ahead. If you have any thought of writing a book, or could be induced to do so, we should be pleased to see you, and will do so. Will you do us the favor to reply at once, at your earliest convenience.

Very truly, &c.,
E. BLISS, Jr.
Secty.

Bliss (1821–80) was originally a dry-goods merchant in Springfield, Massachusetts, then in New York, and subsequently a lumber merchant in Hartford before becoming, in 1867, secretary of the American Publishing Company, a subscription-book house founded there in 1865. He became and remained Mark Twain's principal publisher until his death ("Death of Elisha Bliss, Jr.," Hartford *Courant*, 29 Sept 80, 2; biographical information on Bliss, CtHSD; Hill, 3).

[2] By 1 December, the *Alta* had published twenty-seven out of an eventual fifty letters.

[3] Although in 1908 Clemens recalled that he had "made a satisfactory arrangement with Harper Brothers" at this time, nothing more is known of his "other propositions for a book" (SLC 1977, 55).

[4] Albert Deane Richardson (1833–69), a journalist and western traveler, became chief war correspondent for the New York *Tribune* in 1860. Captured at Vicksburg while attempting to run past the Confederate batteries with two other reporters, he escaped from a Southern prison eighteen months later. After the war he compiled two books incorporating his *Tribune* dispatches: *The Secret Ser-*

vice, the Field, the Dungeon, and the Escape (1865), which had a sale of one hundred thousand copies, and *Beyond the Mississippi* (1867), which sold seventy-five thousand copies by late 1869. Both books were published and sold by the American Publishing Company ("Albert D. Richardson," New York *Tribune*, 3 Dec 69, 1). Clemens's conversation with Richardson "some months ago" probably occurred in January 1867, for on 2 February he said in his letter to the *Alta* that "Richardson is hard at work on his new book concerning the Far West," published in mid-1867 as *Beyond the Mississippi*. Richardson's current project for the American Publishing Company, which would bring him to Washington, was *A Personal History of Ulysses S. Grant* (1868) (SLC 1867n). The subscription method of publishing was safe for the publisher, because a book would not be printed until sales agents had taken enough orders to assure a profit. If the orders were insufficient, the book would not be issued at all. The author was no safer than he would be if his book were published in the normal way, but his profit was potentially much larger: aggressive agents frequently garnered large sales, especially in areas where there were no book shops or to people who did not normally visit such shops, and subscription books often cost more than normal trade books.

To Mary Mason Fairbanks
2 December 1867 • Washington, D.C.

(MS: ViU)

‸P.S—Oh, excuse haste, bad grammar & *everything*. I am in a fidget *all* the time. {I am getting to italicise, like a girl.}‸

N. Y. Tribune Bureau
Washington D.C. Dec. 2.

My Dear Forgiving Mother—

It all came of making a promise! I might have known it. I never keep a promise. I don't know how. They only taught about the wise virgins & the stupid ones, in our Sunday School—never anything about promises. The truth is, Mr. Bennett[1] sent for me two or three times before I ~~consented to~~ approach‸ed‸ the Herald. They found me, the last time, within 200 yards of the St Nicholas, whither I was going to dine with you & Charlie. Well, I was bitter on those passengers. You don't know *what* atrocious things women, & men too ~~old~~ gray-haired & old to have their noses pulled, said about me. And but for your protecting hand I would have given them a screed or two that would have penetrated even *their* muddy intellects & ~~given~~ ‸afforded‸ them something worth abusing me about.[2] Well, the last time I was sent for, ~~Mr~~ it was Mr. Glen, chief of the foreign correspondence department that came, & he just happened to touch this old bitterness ~~&~~ in the right place. I had had no time to go anywhere or get any money; I wanted fifty dollars; I thought, now, I can make that in two hours, & stir up those Quakers most ~~lusciously~~ ‸delightfully‸ at the very same time—& yet, say nothing that will sound malicious. I found part of that old article in my pocket, & ~~roped~~ ~~‸rung‸~~ ~~‸darted‸~~ it in.[3] It was well I didn't find it all—& well it was, also, that all real malice passed out of my heart while I wrote. Else I ~~would~~ ‸must‸ have said b~~e~~‸i‸tter things. And yet to this day I have a strong desire, whenever I think of some of the events of that trip with that ~~menagerie~~, to print the savagest kind of a history of the excursion. ~~I hear that~~ I have promised you that I wouldn't, & so I haven't the slightest doubt in the world *but that I will*. I can't keep a promise. When I get married I shall say: "I take this woman to be my lawfully wedded wife, & *propose* to look out for her in a sort of a general way, &c. &c." It would be dangerous to go beyond that.

But I didn't *promise* you that I wouldn't swear—yet *no* man is freer from the sin of swearing than is thy servant this day; & no man is freer from the *inclination* to swear, than he, whether ‸he is‸ in a passion or otherwise. I was the worst swearer, & the most reckless, that sailed out of New York in the Quaker City. I shamed Bursley; I shamed Harris;[4] I shamed the very fo'castle watches, I think. But I am as perfectly & as permanently cured of the habit as I am of chewing tobacco. Your doubts, Madam, cannot shake my faith in this reformation. I have *no* inclination to swear, albeit I boil over as often as ever; more ~~this~~ than this, I feel the same *uncomfortableness* in the hearing of oaths that I feel when I listen to things that have always been distasteful to me. Shall these signs pass for nothing? Have not they a deep meaning? Do not they show that it is not merely that the idle tongue has been taught a new trick which it may discard when the novelty is gone, but that the lesson has gone down, down, to the spirit that orders the tongue & commands its movements? Verily this is so, O thou of little faith![5] And while I remember you, my good, kind ~~wo~~ mother, (whom God preserve!) never believe that tongue or spirit shall forget this priceless lesson that you have taught them.

But as for those Quakers, I don't want their friendship, I don't want their good opinions, I wouldn't have their good offices. I don't want any commerce with people I don't like. They can hurt me. Let them. I would rather they should hurt me than help me. All the friends I wanted in that ship were: Yourself; Mr & Mrs. Severance; the cub;[6] Emma Beach; Dan; Moulton; Jack; I don't remember any others—I don't suppose there *were* any others.[7] My opinion of the rest of the ~~gang~~ is so mean, & so vicious, & so outrageous in every way, that I could not collect the terms to express it with out of any less than sixteen or seventeen different languages. Such another ~~drove of cattle~~ *never* went to sea before. Select party! Well, *I* ~~pass.~~

Those vapid, senseless letters I published in the Tribune had *one* good effect. They procured me several propositions from the book publishers. I like that of the American Publishing Co., of Hartford, much the~~y~~ best. They publish only by subscription, & by this means gave A. D. Richardson's first book 100,000 ~~circle~~ circulation & have already given his last one 41,000. I have written them to give me an explicit statement of what they want, *when* they want it, &c.

I am *Tribune* "occasional," *Alta* "special" & have propositions from the *Herald*. I have magazine engagements—but unhappily I have *promised*. I have had, & still receive, lecturing invitations, but cannot accept, of course.[8] I am full of work, &, as usual, am doing nothing. I give you these foolish details, believing they will interest you.

Give me another sermon!

Yr. Improving ~~p~~Prodigal,
Sam L. Clemens

1 James Gordon Bennett, Jr.

2 See 24 Oct 67 to Goodman, nn. 2, 4.

3 Clemens elaborately interlined and then deleted both "rung" and "darted"—in such a way, however, that they were visibly distinct from his normal deletions. Like several canceled words further on, they were clearly intended to be read, and are therefore shown lined-through with a thinner and higher rule.

4 Ira Bursley was the *Quaker City*'s sailing master and executive officer; John Harris was the ship's chief engineer.

5 Matthew 14:31: "O thou of little faith, wherefore didst thou doubt?"

6 Charles J. Langdon.

7 Emma (Beach) Thayer described Clemens's acquaintances on the *Quaker City* in a 1907 letter to Paine: "Mr. Clemens foregathered with two quite different sets of people on the 'Quaker City': the smoking-room set, and a little group in the cabin to whom in the late afternoon he read what he had written that day" (Thayer to A. B. Paine, 22 June 1907, Davis 1967a, 2). In 1911, Solon Severance recalled that

Mr. Clemens did "take on" about some of the "pilgrims." . . . There was a charmed circle on the steamer, Mr. Clemens, Mrs. Fairbanks, Mrs. Severance, Langdon and Yours Truly. It was very interesting to see the way Mrs. Fairbanks mothered him and how well he obeyed. . . . Reading this over I am sure that I should add a few more names to the "charmed circle", Emma Beach, Dan Slote, Jack Van Nostrand, and Moulton. (Severance to A. B. Paine, 23 Nov 1911, Davis 1967a, 2)

Clemens was also on good terms with Dr. Jackson and Julia Newell, whom he does not mention here.

[8] See 24 Nov 67 to Fuller.

To Frank Fuller
2 December 1867 • Washington, D.C.

(MS: PBL)

Washngton, Dec. 2.

Dear Gov—

I want you to ~~t~~ write my next lecture. You can do it better than I.

Keep California in your mind—2 lectures—both *repeated* in San Francisco—delivered once each in Sac. & Va. City—not elsewhere. I know. I have been there. The other places are not worth $20 apiece hardly, when you average them. Va. isn't *very* good, for the Alta copy=righted the letters & the Enterprise couldn't publish.[1] ~~Next~~

The American Publishing Co. of Hartford want a book. They published for Richardson. I have written them to state just what they want, when they want it, & *how much bucksheesh?* That was business, wasn't it? I thought so. Their house is a very live concern.

Yrs always,
Sam. L. Clemens
Address – – Tribune Bureau
Washington

If you know of any villainy here that has money in it, let me know.

[1] On 12 August 1867, Frederick MacCrellish and Company registered its copyright for "The Holy Land Excursion | Mark Twains Letters" (DLC). This unusual step was probably effective in discouraging the *Alta*'s exchanges from reprinting all of Clemens's letters, even though many reprinted selections from them: the Virginia City *Territorial Enterprise*, the San Rafael (Calif.) *Marin County Journal*, the San Francisco *California Weekly Mercury*, the San Francisco *Examiner*, and the Sacramento *Union*, to name only a few.

To John Russell Young
4 December 1867 • Washington, D.C.
(MS: DLC)

Tribune ~~T~~ Bureau }
Washington Dec. 4. }

[*two or three heavily canceled words*] Jno. Russell Young Esq

D[r] Sir:—I thought Swinton was going up today, but he has put it off. I wanted him to call & get those three Holy Land letters I sent up.[1] I was afraid, myself, that they would not pass muster. I did not suppose I would need them, but I may. I have a proposition from Richardson's Hartford publishers, & if I make a move toward getting up a book I can make some sort of use of those three letters. Wherefore, ~~I~~ if they have been condemned, ~~I~~ ~~I will~~ I wish you would order that they be re-mailed to me, else I fear they may be destroyed & the world come to grief in consequence.

That stupid burlesque I sent up has "gone up," too.[2] No matter. I will strike a serious vein yet, that will corral the Tribune.

I am sorry to trouble you so much, but behold the world is full of sorrows~~,~~, & grief is the heritage of man.

Yrs Truly
Sam. L. Clemens

P. S.—And at the same time, please have the crazy burlesque returned, also, if it is not destroyed. ~~I wish to deposit it~~ & oblige yrs Truly

[1] William Swinton (1833–92), described by the New York *Citizen* as "tall, red-whiskered, sedate," was a special correspondent for the New York *Times* during the war and became notorious for his overly revealing and critical reports on Union troop movements. In 1864, General Ambrose E. Burnside ordered Swinton shot for his activities, but General Grant intervened, merely banishing him from Union lines ("William Swinton," New York *Citizen*, 25 May 67, 3; Grant, 2:143–45). Clemens apparently knew Swinton rather well: later that winter the two men roomed together in Washington (see 21 Feb 68 to JLC and family, n. 1). In 1906 Clemens recalled that they also cooperated in a "Newspaper Correspondence Syndicate," for which they wrote "a letter apiece once a week and copied them and sent them to twelve newspapers, charging each of the newspapers a dollar apiece. And although we didn't get rich, it kept the jug going and partly fed the two of us" (AD, 15 Jan 1906, CU-MARK, in *MTA*, 1:323–24). Unfortunately, no evidence has been found to corroborate Clemens's memory.

So far as is known, Swinton was not now working for the *Tribune*, the *Times*, or any other newspaper, but he would certainly have been well known to Young. In April 1867 he published *The Twelve Decisive Battles of the War: A History of the Eastern and Western Campaigns, in Relation to the Actions That Decided Their Issue*, through Dick and Fitzgerald, who later declined Mark Twain's book about the Sandwich Islands. In his 17 December letter to the *Alta*, Clemens wrote that A. D. Richardson, with *Beyond the Mississippi*, "and Swinton ('Twelve Decisive Battles.') have published the most saleable books, I believe, that have issued from the press this year" (SLC 1868n). For a discussion of the "three Holy Land letters" see 24 Nov 67 to Young, n. 1.

[2] See 1 Dec 67 to Young, n. 2.

To Emeline B. Beach
5 December 1867 • Washington, D.C.

(MS: CCamarSJ)

St. Valentine's Day,
Washington, Dec. 5.

Dear Miss Emma—

I ~~ha~~ suppose I have made you, mad, too, maybe, but with all my heart I hope I haven't. You wasn't particularly civil to an old & defeated chess antagonist, the day you left the ship, but I declare to goodness (pardon the expression,) I cannot bear malice for *that*. Mr. Beach told me in New York, that even Mrs. Fairbanks felt hurts about that best-natured squib that ever was written (I refer to the one in the Herald,) & Charlie, Langdon has not dropped me a line.[1] Mrs. Fairbanks has, though, & scolds—scolds hard—but she can't deceive this Prodigal Son—I detect the good nature & the forgiveness under it all.

I lost the sermon at Mr. Beecher's, because I left for Washington long before Sunday came round.[2]

Nothing but the happy occurrence of St Valentine's Day at this unexpected season of the year could have given me an excuse to write to a young lady whom I have known so long, esteemed so well & met in so many continents, I suppose, though it seems absurd enough to me that one should be privileged only once a year to say a friendly word in cases like these.

But I wanted to know whether you are maliciously disposed or not—& moreover I wanted to know whether you have barred pew No. 54 against me or not.[3] Beware how you close the church against the ~~seeker a~~ sinner, old fellow—you wot not what mischief you may do.

I perceive by the almanac that St Valentine's Day will continue in force until just a week from to-day. That is ~~mighty~~ ‸particularly‸ fortunate for me, Miss Emma, because now you can sit down and dash off an answer to this, immediately. And I am perfectly well satisfied that you are kind enough & good enough to do it, too.

I am behaving myself, now, in a ~~whi~~ way which would entirely satisfy Mrs. Fairbanks.

Yours, with all respect & esteem,
Sam. L. Clemens,
224 F street, Washington

(over).

P. S. It was not I that wrote the critical article in the Herald signed "A Passenger." It was D[r] Jackson.[4] ~~I do~~

S. L. C.

[1] Emma (Beach) Thayer recalled in 1907 that at night on board the ship Clemens "used to play chess with me and I now think that he purposely let me win—I was only seventeen" (Thayer to A. B. Paine, 22 June 1907, Davis 1967a, 2). For the *Herald* letter, see 20 Nov 67 to JLC and family (2nd of 2).

[2] Clemens left New York for Washington on Thursday evening, 21 November. On the Sunday following his departure, the "ordinances of baptism and the Lord's Supper" were "to be administered in the Plymouth Church" by Henry Ward Beecher and "the water used will be from the River Jordan, and the wine from the city of Jerusalem. Captain Duncan, of the steamer Quaker City, brought these supplies." The topic of Beecher's sermon on that occasion is not known. The Beaches had been attending Plymouth Church since 1854, although Emma was not formally admitted until 1866, when she became of age ("Mr. Beecher's Church To-morrow," New York *Evening Post*, 23 Nov 67, 3; Thompson, 238).

[3] Pews in Plymouth Church were auctioned every January for a fixed valuation plus a premium. In 1867 the Beaches occupied pew number 56 (not 54), for which they paid $100 rent and a $280 premium ("Sale of Pews in Beecher's Church," New York *World*, 10 Jan 67, 2; Thompson, diagrams following 236, 240).

[4] "The Quaker City Pilgrimage. A Malcontent Passenger's Story of the Excursion—The Serio-Comic Features of the Enterprise" appeared as a letter to the editor in the New York *Herald* for 21 November (Abraham Reeves Jackson 1867g).

To Frank Fuller
5 December 1867 • Washington, D.C.
(MS: CtY-BR)

224 F street
Wash, Dec. 5.

Dear Gov—

You hit powerful hard, but Lord, I can forgive. We can't tell anything about business, till we talk face to face—because, you know, I don't know whether you will want ~~an eighth~~ a quarter, or a half, or *all* the money—because you got it all in New York, you remember. (That's *one*.)[1]

I dread the idea of appearing before those miners of Montana, or those Mormons of Salt Lake. I don't believe I can do it. Another devilish thing is that the Alta *copyrighted* the letters—that was rough—they know me less, everywhere west of the Missippi, now, than they did before—I have not been *copied*. I am good for 3 nights in San F., 1 in Sac., 2 in Va, & 1 in Carson—that is all *I* can swear to. It is all I would attempt, on the coast. Maybe we can make it pay two of us,—maybe we can't. But for your overweening pride, we *could*—for you could keep door & peddle photographs—but not of *yourself*, for God Almighty's sake. (That's *two*.) ~~[And on 2 I rest my rebuttal.]~~

I *do* write ~~two~~ ‸too‸ good a hand for a Senator, but I am practising hard & improving fast—I do it worse & worse every day. I can frank letters, now, very well, with that signature; yesterday I drew my first stationery, & did it without detection; in ten days more I hope to be able to ~~collct~~ collect little dabs of mileage on it, & such things.[2]

Come! hurry down here—I want to swap lies & business both, with you. I shan't swindle you if I can keep nature down. Perhaps you can make it appear that the children of the Plains are crying for me. I think so, because you can make a corn-sheller appear well that won't shell any corn. (That's *three* for you. I rest my case.)

Yrs ever
Mark.

[1] Fuller recalled of Clemens's 6 May debut at Cooper Union, "The expense of the lecture was a little over $600; the receipts were not quite $300" (Fuller, 5:10).

[2]The congressional privilege of franking mail with a member's signature was so widely abused that in 1873 it was abolished altogether and not fully restored until 1895 (Alexander W. Randall, 30–31; Cullinan, 59, 86, 258). See Clemens's letter of 9 January 1868 to his family for a reproduction of an envelope he franked with Stewart's name. On 20 December 1867 Clemens wrote in his *Enterprise* letter:

> I wrote an order for four reams of fancy foolscap and got a blind lunatic to sign Charles Sumner's name to it (no man can counterfeit the genuine signature unless there is something awful the matter with him), and went up to the Senate and presented it. They said it would not do. I asked if they meant to insinuate anything against the soundness of the signature. They said no; they could see by the general horribleness of it that some member of Congress wrote it. (SLC 1868e)

On 2 December he wrote "The Facts Concerning the Recent Resignation" for the *Tribune* (published on 27 December), satirizing—among other things—the practice among territorial delegates of charging for mileage "both ways, although they never go back when they get here once," and claiming to have submitted a bill to the government requesting $2,800 compensation for "Mileage to and from Jerusalem via Egypt, Algiers, Gibraltar, and Cadiz, 14,000 miles, at 20c. a mile" (SLC 1867ffff).

To Jane Lampton Clemens and Family
10 December 1867 • Washington, D.C.

(MS: NPV)

224 F street
Washington Dec. 10.

Dear Folks—

I called on the Secretary of the Interior, yesterday, but said nothing about a place for Orion, of course—must get better acquainted first—must see his wife—*she* is the power behind the throne.[1] If it were *myself*, I could get a place pretty easily, because I have friends in high places who offer me such things—but it is hard to get them interested in one's relatives. Judge Field ‸of the Supreme Bench‸ is a case in point.[2] He wanted to make me Post Master of San Francisco, & I suppose I *would* have been, without knowing it myself, but that the place ~~was~~ had just been filled when he spoke to the President.[3] I told him *I* didn't want any office. But he said, "You *must* have an office, with a good salary & nothing to do. ~~You have writt~~ *You* are no common scrub of a newspaperman. You have written the best letter about Pompeii that ever *was* written about it[4]—& if you had an easy berth you could write *more.*⁄ Say what office you want in San Francisco, & the President shall give it you." I

~~thou~~ didn't remember the Pompeii letter, but I thought I wouldn't say so. ~~But~~ I ~~*did* think~~ like compliments from people who take an interest in me—newspaper compliments I don't care anything about beyond their market value. But I *did* think that if I could only turn his good offices over to Orion, it would suit exactly. I had no chance to try it, & it is a delicate business anyhow. But I will call & see him privately in a few days.

I am writing a lecture—have half promised to deliver it ~~b~~ for the ~~Cor~~ Newspaper Correspondents' Club here after the holidays—~~may,~~ ‸maybe I may—‸& I may not.[5]

Dr Birch, of Hannibal, has got a bottle of water which he & I got out of the Pool of Bethesda, in Jerusalem one‸ Sunday morning when the angel wasn't around.[6] Part of it is mine. I'll give it to you & Mr. Schroter & Sallie Hawes, if you want it & will send for it.[7] You can get Essie,[8] or Lou Conrad, or some other angel to stir it, & you can start a hospital & cure all the cripples in your camp. I have got some Jordan & some Dead Sea water somewhere, too. I guess it must be in ~~Y~~ New York.

Inclosed is a letter to me from ~~the wife of the editor of the Cleveland Herald.~~ ‸one of our fellow-passengers.‸[9] She was the most refined, intelligent, ~~educated~~ &‸ cultivated lady in the ship, & altogether the kindest & best. She sewed my buttons on, kept my clothes in presentable trim, fed me on Egyptian jam, ~~& cured~~ ‸(when I behaved,)‸ lectured me awfully on the quarter-deck on moonlit promenading evenings, & cured me of several bad habits. I am under lasting obligations to her. She looks young, because she is so good—but she has a grown son & daughter at home.[10] I wrote her, the other day, that my buttons were all off, again. She had another pup under her charge, younger than myself, whom I ~~called~~ always called the "cub."[11] Hence her reference to cubs & bears. Lucius Moulton[12] was another cub of hers. We all called her "mother" & kept her in hot water all the time about her brood. I always abused the sea-sick people—I said nobody but almighty mean people ever ~~g~~ got sea=sick—& she thought I was in earnest. ‸She never got sick herself.‸ She always drummed us up for prayer meeting, with her monitory "Seven bells, my boys—you know what it is time for." We always went, but we liked ~~six~~ ‸four‸ bells best, because it meant hash—*dinner*, I *should* say.

Love to all the household, & amen.

Yrs a‸ffectionately
Sam.

[1]Orville Hickman Browning (1806–81) was secretary of the interior from 1866 to 1869. As a strong opponent of Radical Reconstruction he supported President Johnson throughout the effort to impeach him in 1867–68. He had been married to the former Eliza Caldwell since 1836.

[2]Associate Justice of the United States Supreme Court Stephen Johnson Field (1816–99), originally from Connecticut, went to California in 1849, where he was elected to the state legislature in 1850 and appointed to the state supreme court in 1857. In March 1863 Lincoln appointed him to the United States Supreme Court. Clemens had probably met him while working for the San Francisco *Morning Call* in 1864, when Field was presiding in San Francisco over the United States Circuit Court for the District of California (*CofC*, 189). In a letter dated 20 December 1867 to the *Enterprise* Clemens declared that "Associate Justice Field of the Supreme Bench is widely talked of, latterly, as the Democratic candidate for President of the United States—an able man, a just one, and one whose judicial and political garments are clean—a man well fitted for the place" (SLC 1868e).

[3]The four-year commission of the incumbent San Francisco postmaster would expire in January, but his successor was not in fact appointed for many months. From innumerable candidates only three were actually nominated by the president, and only the last gained the approval of the Senate. At the time of this letter, the candidate most recently said to be under consideration was Samuel Purdy, formerly (1852–56) lieutenant governor of California under John Bigler. In a letter to the *Enterprise* Clemens explained that as soon as a candidate "gets the President in his favor the Senate will be down on him for it, and . . . if he gains the Senate's affections first, the President will be down on him" (SLC 1868jj). The current assistant postmaster, Holland Smith, was finally confirmed as the new postmaster on 25 July 1868 (Rincon 1868a; Hittell, 4:81, 134–35; Senate 1887, 13:380, 386, 16:319, 322, 340, 341, 357, 370; Langley 1867, 652; Langley 1868, 458, 734). Before that date, however, the subject of the postmastership recurred several times in Clemens's personal letters as well as in his newspaper correspondence (see 4 and 6 Feb 68 to Bliss; 6 Feb 68 to JLC and PAM; 10 Feb 68 to Beach; 21 Feb 68 to JLC and family; 21 Feb 68 to OC; SLC 1868h, 1868tt).

[4]Field was praising Clemens's letter to the *Alta* dated "August" from Naples, which was published on 29 September (SLC 1867aaa).

[5]The Washington Correspondents' Club, an association of journalists writing about Washington news for newspapers elsewhere, was founded in February 1867. In an *Alta* letter dated 17 December, Clemens mentioned being "at a dinner in the early part of the week" (probably 8 or 9 December) "given . . . to the Newspaper Correspondents' Club, of Washington." And in the fall of 1868 he was still listed as an active member, without newspaper affiliation. His friend John Henry Riley, the regular Washington correspondent for the *Alta*, said in a newspaper letter dated 15 December 1867 that Mark Twain was "preparing a lecture to be delivered shortly before the Washington Press Club," evidently a misnomer for the Correspondents' Club. Clemens did speak at the club's first annual dinner on 11 January 1868, but his talk on that occasion was a response to the toast to "Woman," not the lecture called "The Frozen Truth," on which he was presently working (see 8 Jan 68 and 13 Jan 68, both to JLC and family). Even after his successful toast, however, he still planned to give a benefit lecture

for the club: on 22 January one Washington paper reported that a "loud call has been made upon him by the *Correspondents' Club* to 'speak his piece' in public, about his trip to the Sandwich Islands, preluded by his affecting story of the 'Miner and his Cat.'" And on 26 January, Riley again noted that "'Rev.' Mark Twain has promised to lecture before the Washington Correspondents' Club at an early date." No evidence has been found, however, that Clemens ever did lecture for it (SLC 1868n; Marbut, 243; Riley 1868a; "Washington News and Gossip," Washington *Evening Star*, 22 Jan 68, 1; Riley 1868b).

[6] Dr. George Bright Birch (1822?–?73) lived in Hannibal, Missouri. He was a member of Clemens's party on the Holy Land trek and, according to Colonel Denny (writing in September 1867), he was "rather heavy set a plain, old fashioned Gentleman that cares more for substance than show, and hartily despises meanness, parade and vanity. He is about forty five years old and does not belong to church." In 1874, on hearing of his death, Clemens wrote Emma Beach: "I have always held D[r.] Birch in grateful memory because he stood by me so stanchly when I was dangerously ill in Damascus." In chapter 47 of *The Innocents Abroad*, Clemens attributed this steadfastness to William F. Church, whom he overheard say "he did not care who went or who staid, *he* would stand by me till I walked out of Damascus on my own feet or was carried out in a coffin" (Denny, entry for 11 Sept; SLC to Beach, 4 Feb 74, CCamarSJ, in Booth, 230; SLC 1869a, 499). The pool of Bethesda was traditionally identified with a large reservoir called Birket Israîl, near St. Stephen's gate in Jerusalem. According to John 5:4, its water had miraculous healing powers: "For an angel went down at a certain season into the pool, and troubled the water: whosoever then first after the troubling of the water stepped in was made whole of whatsoever disease he had." Clemens called the pool a "slimy cesspool" in an *Alta* letter, but he and Dr. Birch returned to it on Sunday, 29 September, after their side trip to Bethlehem, specifically in order "to get a flask of the water" (Thomson, 2:524; Murray, map following 1:72, 107; Louisa M. Griswold, 251; SLC 1868uu; *N&J1*, 434, 442 [entry misdated 28 Sept], 485).

[7] George Schroter (b. 1813 or 1814) had been William A. Moffett's business partner, first in Hannibal, and then in St. Louis from about 1855 until Moffett's death in 1865. Although Schroter may not have been living in St. Louis at the time of this letter, he did have frequent contact with Clemens's family during 1867 and early 1868 (OC to MEC, 9 May 67 and 20 Feb 68; OC to JLC and PAM, 17 Nov 67; all in CU-MARK). Sarah (Sallie) Humphreys Hawes (b. 1828 or 1829) was the wife of George A. Hawes, a prominent Hannibal merchant and a nephew of Clemens's uncle John Quarles; Hawes had lived with William Moffett's family in Hannibal for a time before his marriage in 1851 (*MTBus*, 26, 38, 72; *Hannibal Census*, 306, 310, 323; PAM to MEC, 23 June 70, CU-MARK; Holcombe, 953; *Portrait*, 198).

[8] Essie Pepper.

[9] The letter from Mrs. Fairbanks is not known to survive, but some idea of its contents may be inferred from the next letter, evidently Clemens's response to it.

[10] Mrs. Fairbanks was thirty-nine. Her stepchildren, offspring of Abel Fairbanks and his first wife, Alice Holmes (d. 1849), were Frank Fairbanks (b. 1845) and Alice Holmes Fairbanks (b. 1847) (Lorenzo Sayles Fairbanks, 552).

[11] Charles J. Langdon.

[12] Julius Moulton.

To Mary Mason Fairbanks
12 December 1867 • Washington, D.C.
(MS: CSmH)

224 F street
Washington, Dec. 12.

Bless me, how curious it seems to hear ‸you talk of‸ your "little cub," & your "Red Riding Hood" & your & son & daughter that are so tall that you must look up to them!—you who seemed almost the youngest lady in the ship.[1]

But why mourn for Albert Crane? why sorrow for Dr Andrews?—why grieve that the ark hath rested upon Ararat & the animals departed two by two to be seen ~~m~~ no more of Noah & his sons? There are other kangaroos that you can scrape acquaintance with‸?‸ ~~? th~~ There be those that ~~be~~ ‸are‸ lovelier than Dimon—there be ripples of silvery laughter that issue from other lips than Lockwood's—Cutter is not, but behold we have Shakspeare ~~always~~ with us always. Cheer up—Duncan will drum the old menagerie together again some day.[2]

I ~~got~~[3] received a letter from Charlie Langdon this afternoon, the best cub you had in the ship, by long odds. He says the ~~l~~ Learys have ~~busted~~ gone to protest, & that the $1,100 loaned to Dan. Leary by Mr. Nesbit has not been paid.[4] I am sorry a little for Nesbit (not much, though,—he might have enjoyed that money in Europe, but he wouldn't,) & sorry a good deal for Dan Leary, for although he had unpleasant traits, he ‸had‸ more than sufficient generous instincts to make up for them. You don't believe it, but I do.[5]

"A good wife would be a perpetual incentive to progress"—& so she would—I never thought of that before—progress from house to house because ~~c~~ I couldn't pay the rent. The idea is good. I wish I had a chance to try it. But seriously, Madam, you are only just proposing luxuries to Lazarus. That is all. I want a good wife—I want a couple of them if they are particularly good—~~w~~ but where is the wherewithal? It costs ~~sixty dollars~~ ‸nearly two letters‸ a week to keep *me*.[6] If I doubled it, the firm would come to grief the first time anything happened to the senior partner. Manifestly you haven't looked into this thing. I am as good an economist as anybody, but I can't turn an inkstand into Aladdin's lamp.[7] You haven't examined into this thing at all, you see.

I was writing a lecture, to-day, to be delivered for the benefit of the widow's & orphans of the Correspondents' Club here a month hence, when I ~~got~~ received Charlie's letter‸,‸~~, to-day.~~ I stopped to answer that, but will finish the lecture to-morrow or next day, & then I will tell you whether I think it will do or not. But seriously again, if I were settled I would quit all nonsense & swindle some ~~poor~~ girl into marrying me. But I ~~don't~~ ‸wouldn't‸ expect to be "*worthy*" of her. I wouldn't *have* a girl that ~~I thought~~ *I* was worthy of. *She* wouldn't do. She wouldn't be respectable enough.

But at the same time, I am worthier of anybody than I was—because, as duly reported in my last, I *still* never think of swearing, now, & consequently never *do* it. ~~I~~ ‸Wherefore, I‸ receive your kind hand across the white page with no blush, with ‸no‸ shame, with no hesitation—for as yet I am worthy—I have ~~failed~~ kept the bond—I have failed not in the task you have set me to do.

I am not as lazy as I was—but I am lazy enough yet, for two people. But I am improving all the time. I always make it a point, now, every day, to resolve deliberately to do something the next day. It is a powerful incentive to industry—I wish I had adopted it sooner.

Good-bye. Be you happy, always, in your pleasant family; & when ye are gathered together, remember ye kindly the cubs that are far away. Amen.

Give me another Sermon—
Improvingly, yr friend
Sam L. Clemens.

[1] Mentioned are Charles Mason Fairbanks (1855–1924), Mary Paine Fairbanks (b. 1856), and two stepchildren (see the previous letter, n. 10) (Lorenzo Sayles Fairbanks, 552; "Charles M. Fairbanks, Newspaper Man, Dies," New York *Times*, 30 May 1924, 15).

[2] Clemens alludes to Genesis 8:4 ("And the ark rested . . . upon the mountains of Ararat") and mentions Captain Charles C. Duncan and the following *Quaker City* passengers: Dr. Albert Crane of New Orleans; Dr. Edward Andrews of Albany—dubbed the "Oracle" in his *Alta* letters; Frederick Dimon and E. K. Lockwood of Norwalk, Connecticut; and Bloodgood Haviland Cutter (1817–1906) of Little Neck, Long Island—the "Poet Lariat" in *The Innocents Abroad* (Winterich, no page). Andrews and Cutter became objects of Clemens's scorn at the very outset of the excursion. In late June he referred to Andrews in his notebook as an "old fool," and satirized him in an *Alta* letter (*N&J1*, 349; SLC 1867pp). Twenty years later he had not modified his opinion. In response to an

inquiry about Andrews's "reputation, if any, as an art critic," Clemens wrote: "He was a quack, not a doctor. I cannot conceive of his buying a picture of any kind; he had no taste, no brains, no education; he must have been born in a sty & reared in a sewer. I am well satisfied he never saw the day when he could tell an oil painting from a horse-blanket" (Frederick J. Collier to SLC, 11 Jan 88, CU-MARK; SLC to Collier, 16 Jan 88, Wiltshire†). Clemens described Cutter in his notebook soon after the voyage began:

> He is fifty years old, & small of his age. He dresses in homespun, & is a simple-minded, honest, old-fashioned farmer, with a strange proclivity for writing rhymes. He writes them on all possible subjects, & gets them printed on slips of paper, with his portrait at the head. These he will give to any man that comes along, whether he has anything against him or not. He has already written interminable poems on "The Good Ship Quaker City;" & an "Ode to the Ocean;" & "Recollections of the Pleasant Time on Deck Last night"—which Pleasant Time consisted in his reciting some 75 stanzas of his poetry to a large party of the passengers convened on the upper deck. (*N&J1*, 334)

And in 1880 Clemens also replied to a question about Cutter: "Yes, it is the same mildewed idiot. His friends call him a lunatic—but that is pretty fulsome flattery; one cannot become a lunatic without first having brains. Yes, he is the 'Poet Lariat' " (so named, according to Clemens, because Andrews "always distorted the phrase 'Poet Laureate' ") (SLC to Miss Perkins, 30 Apr 80, CtY-BR†; SLC to Mary Mason Fairbanks, 31 Mar and 1 Apr 69, CSmH, in *MTMF*, 89–90).

[3] See 2 Dec 67 to Fairbanks, n. 3.

[4] Daniel D. Leary and his brothers, Charles C. and Arthur, were business partners in New York. Charles had owned a share of the *Quaker City* since April 1865; Daniel apparently purchased his share in 1867, when he joined the excursion; and Arthur, although not listed explicitly as an owner, was the ship's "husband and agent" and "had the entire management of employing all the crew, furnishing all supplies and making all contracts, and receiving all the earnings of the said ship." Daniel's efforts during the trip failed to sell the vessel, evidently leaving them in financial difficulties. On 18 February 1868, a New York correspondent of the San Francisco *Evening Bulletin* reported that the "*Quaker City* steamship pleasure excursion . . . has come to a disreputable *finale*. It appears that neither the seamen, nor the parties who furnished the supplies, were paid by the enterprising manager of the excursion, and so the steamer was seized, and on Saturday was knocked off at auction by the U.S. Marshal. The seamen's claims for wages amount to $9,000." The 15 February auction brought a mere $18,000, part of which went to meet the $9,000 claim for wages, and part to cover two claims for supplies totaling $1,145. Nothing more is known about the "$1,100 loaned to Dan. Leary" by fellow passenger Thomas B. Nesbit from Fulton, Missouri. At the request of several other part owners of the ship, and after Arthur Leary assured a United States District Court judge that "all claims against said ship and owners were arranged for and would be duly paid," this sale was set aside. The ship was reauctioned on 11 April, bringing $40,000 this time—still a disappointment, since the Learys originally hoped to get $250,000 for it (Wilson 1867, 599; Heyl, 355–56; New York *Herald:* "Yesterday morning . . . ," 16 Feb 68, 6; "The Steamship Quaker City—Order to Stay Proceedings of Sale," 19 Feb 68, 5; "Letter from New York," San Francisco *Evening Bulletin*, 17 Mar 68, 1; "Home News," New York *Tribune*, 13 Apr 68, 8).

[5] At the start of the voyage, Daniel Leary wrote his brother Arthur in a way that suggests why Clemens found him possessed of "generous instincts." Leary complained that

the captain is a psalm singer and [so are] quite a number of others on board and they managed to get up quite a "revival" among themselves. They commenced with services once on Sunday, and finally we had it every evening and twice on Sunday, which did not suit myself or about a dozen other of the best people on board. (Leary to Arthur Leary, 1 July 67, transcript, CU-MARK, in Leary, 199)

[6] At this time Clemens was writing roughly two letters per week: one to the *Alta* and one to the *Enterprise*. The revision in this sentence suggests that he was paid about thirty dollars apiece for them.

[7] See 4 Dec 68 to OLL (2nd of 2), n. 7.

To Frank Fuller
13 December 1867 • Washington, D.C.

(MS: Craven)

224 F street }
Wash. Dec. 13 }

Dear Gov:

I believe I have made a mistake in not lecturing this winter. I did not suppose I was any better known when I got back than I was before I started—but every day I find additional reasons for thinking I was mistaken about that. I have prepared a new lecture which I think I shall like better than the old one, when I shall have finished amending it. The Correspondents' Club have threatened to call me out for a speech for the benefit of their widows & orphans, & if they do I shall respond,—say any time within the next 2 or 4 weeks.[1] If it made anything of a hit, I should be tempted to receive proposals from Young Men's Christian Ass.'s & such like. Because I am already dead tired of being in one place so long. I have received 2 or 3 calls lately from N. Y. & Indiana towns. When are you coming down? I might take a "disgust" any moment & sail for Cal.

Lovingly,
Sam Clemens.

[1] For the "new lecture," called "The Frozen Truth," see 8 Jan 68 to JLC and PAM, n. 7. For the Correspondents' Club, see 10 Dec 67 to JLC and family, n. 5.

To Emily A. Severance
24 December 1867 • Washington, D.C.

(MS: OClWHi)

224 F st
Washington, Dec. 24.

Mrs. Severance—
My Dear Friend—

Your letter came seven days ago. The news it contained, of Mrs. Fairbanks' bereavement,[1] stunned as well as saddened me—shocked me, & stunned me both—for the first thought that flitted through my brain was that my last foolish letter must have reached Cleveland ~~w~~ at a moment when it ought more properly to have fallen by the wayside & been seen no more. I cannot tell how sorry your sad tidings made me feel. But I can say that they made me stop & think~~s~~ of my own mother—& reflection taught me that my half-formed notion of sailing for California without going first to St Louis ‸to see her‸ would plainly be ungrateful, even criminal—for she is old & I might not see her again. I shall visit St Louis before I take shipping again.

Please remember me most kindly to Mrs. Fairbanks‸.‸~~, & th~~ It is needless for me or for any one with only human lips to try to comfort her at a time like this—for words are vain & little worth, save those a true Christian such as she is knows where to seek. “Come unto me all ye that labor & are heavy laden, & I will give you rest—*rest*.[2] No words my lips might frame, could be so freighted with compassion as are these—so fraught with sympathy, so filled with peace. Even to me, sinner that I am, this is the most beautiful sentence that graces any page—the tenderest, the most touching, the softest to the ear. To her, then, standing in the light, it has a world of significance that I can only dimly imagine—not appreciate.

I came near starting west this morning, & ‸if‸ I had I would have tarried a day or two in Cleveland, no doubt, but I was going with the U.S. Minister to the Sandwich Islands, on business, but found that troublesome delays ‸westward‸ might be anticipated. I have bothered so much with that treaty of his that I begin to feel a personal interest in its ratification.[3] I wish I were in the Islands now—or in California. This terrific weather takes all the life out of me. I look forward anxiously to my release from Washington. I could just as well have been at sea in the Pacific for China now as not, & visited home besides, but for making engagements that tie me here for a season.[4] I am in a fidget to move. It isn't a novel sensation, though—I never was any other way. What do you mean by poking your babies at me & telling me about your home happiness?—do you want to make a fellow feel any more mean & discontented than he *does* feel?[5]

It is 8 bells (midnight.) Ask Severance to look ‸in‸ at the ~~comp~~ 'midships gangway & see that the cabin lights are all out; report how she heads, & call the larboard watch.

Truly Yr friend,
Sam L. Clemens.

[1] The death of Mrs. Fairbanks's mother, Emma Harris Mason (b. 1803 or 1804). Her father, Isaac Newton Mason (b. 1800), had died in 1862, in Clinton, Ohio (*MTMF*, 9; Mary Mason Fairbanks 1898, 352; *Cleveland Census* 1850, 91; "James Mason Family," 2).

[2] Matthew 11:28. Clemens's repetition of the word "rest" gives the quotation a special emphasis that reflects his lifelong response to death, and that he echoed in a letter written less than a week after the death of his daughter Jean: "I am so glad she is out of it & safe—safe!" (SLC to Clara Clemens Gabrilowitsch, 29 Dec 1909, TS at CSmH, in *MTB*, 3:1554).

[3] Edward Moody McCook (1833–1909) arrived in the Hawaiian Islands as the newly appointed United States minister on 22 July 1866, three days after Clemens himself had sailed for San Francisco. McCook served in that post until 1869, when President Grant appointed him governor of Colorado Territory, which he had earlier helped to organize. During the Civil War he achieved a brilliant record in the Union cavalry, earning the brevet of major general, and he served briefly as military governor of Florida before taking his Hawaiian post. In May 1867, the newly proposed trade-reciprocity treaty between the Hawaiian government and the United States (the fourth such attempt since 1848) was signed in San Francisco. On 10 December, Clemens wrote the *Alta* that he had

> talked frequently with General McCook, United States Minister to the Sandwich Islands, since I have been here. As you are aware, his business in Washington is to get the reciprocity treaty between Hawaii and this country through the Senate. It has been slow work, and very troublesome, but a fair degree of progress is being made. . . . I do not see why they don't take to it instantly, and with enthusiasm. It has got more statistics and more constitutionality in it than any document in the world. That treaty has grown upon my reverence until, in my eyes, it has become a perfect monument of mathematics and virtue. (SLC 1868h)

Clemens had not been favorably disposed toward the treaty when he first mentioned it in May; his change in attitude may reflect Senator Stewart's as well as McCook's support for it. Ultimately the treaty was rejected by the Senate in June 1870, on the grounds that it would lose the United States too much revenue from duties on imported sugar. Not until March 1875 did the Senate finally ratify such a treaty, which became effective in September 1876 (*L1*, 346 n. 8; Senate 1887, 15[2]:792; Senate 1901, 17:465–66, 20:41–43; Kuykendall, 211–12, 225–27, 250–52; SLC 1867ff).

[4]Clemens's only commitments in Washington at this point were his several journalistic ones to the New York *Tribune* and *Herald*, the *Alta*, and the *Enterprise*, for on 16 December he had announced to his *Enterprise* readers that "E. A. Pretois, formerly of Virginia and Sacramento, is Senator Stewart's private secretary, now." In "My Late Senatorial Secretaryship," written for the *Galaxy* about this time, he said that he had held the secretarial position for "two months in security and in great cheerfulness of spirit," but that when the senator bellowed "Leave the house! Leave it forever and forever, too!" he "regarded that as a sort of covert intimation that my services could be dispensed with, and so I resigned." In "The Facts Concerning the Recent Resignation," written on 2 December, Clemens claimed he had been clerk of the "Senate Committee on Conchology" for "six days." Even though he evidently was not an official Senate clerk, he might have served in some capacity during the special session of the Senate which began on 21 November. His stint would have begun on Monday, 25 November, the first business day after his arrival in Washington, and ended at mid-day on Monday, 2 December, when the session adjourned (SLC 1868b, 1889, 1868ww, 1867ffff). Clemens might have been "at sea in the Pacific for China" at this time had he agreed to apply for the position of United States minister to China, as suggested by Senator Conness (see 6 Feb 68 to JLC and PAM, n. 4).

[5]The Severances, who were married in October 1860, had three young children: Julia, the oldest, and "twin babies in arms," Allen and Mary Helen (Severance, iii, 53).

To the Brooklyn *Eagle*
30 December 1867 • New York, N.Y.

(Brooklyn *Eagle*, 31 Dec 67)

NEW YORK, Monday 29.[1]

DEAR EAGLE:

In your issue of the 24th inst, you called upon me, as upon a sort of Fountain-Head of Facts (an intimation which touched the very marrow of my ambition, and sent a thrill of ecstacy throughout my being), to pour out some truth upon the Quaker City muddle, which Captain Duncan and Mr. Griswold have lately stirred up between them, and thus so rectify and clarify that muddle, that the public can tell at a glance whether the Pilgrims behaved themselves properly or not during the progress of the recent excursion around the world.[2]

Briefly, then, the muddle had this shape: Captain Duncan declares that he witnessed ten-tenths of drunkenness from the time he sailed from New York until he got back again, and that the large proportion of nine-tenths of it was in his own ship. Mr. Griswold denies the truth of this statement.[3] Of course the question simply is, which of the two gentlemen is right. I must decide that Mr. Griswold, in acknowledging that he saw one man intoxicated on board the Quaker City, more than proved Duncan to be right, as far as my own observations extended—for I was with the excursion throughout, and I do not just now remember having seen even one man intoxicated in Europe. So, Griswold's one man is sufficient to make up Captain Duncan's nine-tenths and something over, as far as my individual knowledge goes.

But it isn't the *dictionary* meaning of the words we speak that must be weighed, in order to get at the absolute correctness or incorrectness of the statement, but the *impression* they convey.

Captain Duncan's words were true, I think, but that prodigious nine-tenths business was bound to create the impression that there was a vast deal of drunkenness on board the Quaker City—and that was a very grave error. If Captain Duncan had simply said he saw ten men intoxicated in his ship in the course of five months, and one man intoxicated in Europe, it would have been a severer statement than the one he did make, but the impression left by the reading of it would have been infinitely more favorable to the ship's company. Captain Duncan, without ever intending to do it, made the set language of an unimpeachable fact convey to the public mind that which was not by any means a fact. If Mr. Griswold had attacked the Captain on this ground, victory would have perched upon his banner. {I use this expression figuratively, and without any intention of conveying to the public the impression that Mr. Griswold carries a banner. But, then, the best intentioned language is such an unreliable vehicle for thought—as is amply shown in Captain Duncan's case—that I prefer to take no chances, and therefore beg to withdraw that expression and say that if Mr. Griswold had followed the above line of argument, victory would have perched upon his umbrella. I am aware that Mr. Griswold carries an umbrella, at any rate.}

But do you know that even the baldest facts and figures, while stating a fact in every way creditable and complimentary to a man, can at the same time give him a most injurious reputation in the eyes of the public? For instance—imagine that I am taking the following extract from my note-book of the voyage:—

"At sea, August 14—Captain Duncan appeared at breakfast this morning entirely sober. Heaven be praised!

"At sea, August 18—Four days of forebodings and uneasiness. But at last Captain Duncan appeared at breakfast again, apparently entirely sober. Cheerfulness sat upon every countenance, and every heart was filled with thankfulness.

"At sea, August 24—The awful storm gradually abated, the thunder and the lightning ceased, and at midnight a great calm fell upon the sea. Throughout all these days of peril and distress, Capt Duncan has not once been in liquor. Oh, how grateful we ought to be! A movement is on foot to present him a silver dinner service when we shall have arrived in Rome.

"At sea, August 25—Nobody drunk to-day.

"At sea, August 26—Only one man drunk between seven bells and breakfast.

"At sea, September 10—It is said there was not a single case of absolute drunkenness in the whole ship yesterday. How much quieter and pleasanter the Sabbath is when all on board are sober."

I could have put those items in my note-book and stated nothing but the plain truth. Yet, with the very best intentions, I could print all those high compliments to Captain Duncan, with no explanation attached, and ruin his reputation forever! They do not state that he was ever in liquor at all—the dictionary meanings of the words convey a positive fact—but the impression they leave behind conveys a positive untruth. Anybody that read them would gather the idea that Captain Duncan had a pretty general fashion of appearing at breakfast in a state of blooming and gorgeous intoxication. Anybody would gather that idea as surely as the Captain's nine-tenths estimate would convey the idea that our dreadfully proper and patriarchal pilgrims were the victims of an elaborate system of intoxication, the like of which could not be found in all Europe! Yet Captain Duncan was never in liquor in his life, and intoxication among his passengers was very, very far from being general.

I merely reiterate that Capt. Duncan told the truth in words, but the words didn't convey it to the public. There are sixty-four more Quakers to be heard from, yet. I wish you would ask them to come forward and testify. Let us pour ink upon the troubled waters.

Yours,

MARK TWAIN.

P. S.—I am sorry, I am truly sorry to say that in Italy Capt. Duncan bought wine and drank it on board the ship——, and it almost breaks my heart when I reflect that in all human probability it was his example that seduced the innocent passengers into getting intoxicated, and I almost shudder to think that he may have done it in order to create telling illustrations for his intended lecture before the Temperance League in Brooklyn, of which he is President. Oh, the thought is more than I can bear! Capt. Duncan offered wine to me—he tried to make even *me* fall with his horrid Italian intoxicating bowl—but my virtue was proof against his wiles. I sternly refused to taste it. I preferred the French article. So did Griswold.[4]

M. T.

[1] Monday fell on 30 (not 29) December. Clemens had been in New York "ever since Christmas day"; he initially checked into the Westminster, but moved almost immediately to Dan Slote's house, where he stayed until his return to Washington (8 Jan 68 to JLC and PAM; "Hotel Arrivals," New York *Evening Express*, 26 Dec 67, 4).

[2] Clemens was responding to the invitation at the end of the following article, which appeared in the Brooklyn *Eagle* on 24 December (page 2); the *Eagle* published his reply on 31 December (page 3):

Trouble among the Pilgrims.

The select band of pilgrims who under the guidance of the gallant Captain Duncan made their way to the Holy Land and back, are agitated by a cruel reflection on their sobriety, coming from no less a person than the Captain himself. The pilgrimage was properly an enterprise of Plymouth Church, the pastor of which was to have been its spiritual leader and guide; but Mr. Beecher had his novel to write and could not go, and because he did not go many of the lambs of his fold who were prepared to follow the sheph[e]rd to the ends of the earth backed out also. Some three score of adventurous spirits however, stuck to Captain Duncan, and sailed with him in the good ship Quaker City. When the pilgrims came back there were many anxious friends ready to welcome them, and anxious to hear how they fared, and to gratify their curiosity Captain Duncan delivered a lecture at Plymouth Church. The captain, like all old salts, is blunt of speech, and did not give a very good account of the conduct of his fellow pilgrims. He said that some of them were under the influence of liquor from the time the vessel left New York until they returned. For a time the Captain remained unanswered, and the pilgrims were given up as a bad lot. But on Sunday last, Brother Griswold, a pilgrim and a Plymouth churchman, delivered a lecture on the pilgrimage, repelled the Captain's accusation, and bore testimony to the general sobriety of his fellow pilgrims; the only exception being a gentleman afflicted with consumption who drank under medical advice. Correspondents have taken the question up, and it is getting to be a very pretty quarrel as it stands. Captain Duncan is going to return to the charge in the lecture room, so is Griswold,—there is an indefinite prospect of lectures and correspondence on this momentous question. Mark Twain is the man to settle the point, let us hear from him. Mark has compared the excursion to a funeral, only wanting the corpse to complete the resemblance. This however, throws no light on the grave question, did the Pilgrims keep sober? It is the custom with some people, to hold wakes on funeral occasions and to drown their grief in mountain dew. Was it a funeral of this sort? Let us hear from Twain.

Stephen M. Griswold (1835–1916) was a prominent member of Plymouth Church. Raised on a farm in Connecticut, he moved to Brooklyn while still a young man and took a job in a grocery store, then in a jewelry business. In 1857 he opened his own jewelry store in Brooklyn, which he ran until his death. In 1885 he was elected to the state senate, and in later years served as the president of the Union Bank of Brooklyn ("Ex-Senator Stephen M. Griswold," New York *Times*, 3 June 1916, 13). In 1909, Clemens commented on a photograph of Griswold used as the frontispiece to his *Sixty Years with Plymouth Church:* "Here is the real old familiar Plymouth-Church self-complacency of 40 years ago. It is the way God looks when He has had a successful season" (SLC 1909).

[3] Within a week of returning to New York, Duncan had announced his 3 December lecture at Plymouth Church on the *Quaker City* excursion. No complete transcript of what Duncan said has been found, but the *Eagle* indicated that he claimed to have seen "more drunkenness on board the Quaker City, than he saw elsewhere during the entire trip" (advertisement, Brooklyn *Union*, 26 Nov 67, 3; "Griswold versus Duncan," Brooklyn *Eagle*, 24 Dec 67, 2). Griswold, who had joined the ship only at Constantinople and left it at Alexandria, returning home later than Duncan, finally responded to this allegation on 22 December. In the first of his own three lectures on the excursion, Griswold noted that the captain's statement "had hurt the feelings of quite a number of passengers, including some of the officers of the steamer." And he added that he "never saw but one of the passengers who appeared to be under the influence of intoxicating drinks, and that was a gentleman almost dying of consumption" ("The Quaker City Excursion," Brooklyn *Union*, 23 Dec 67, 4; "Jerusalem—Griswold's Second Discourse on the Holy Land," Brooklyn *Eagle*, 6 Jan 68, 2).

[4] In an article published on the same day as Clemens's letter, the editors of the Brooklyn *Eagle* wrote:

> It seems that the Pilgrims though temperance men were unable to subdue their Yankee curiosity and tasted the wines of the countries they visited. . . . Duncan's opinion of Italian wines will be interesting to connoisseurs, while Griswold can tell us why he preferred French wines. A discussion on the relative merits of French and Italian wines between two thorough-going temperance men, like Duncan and Griswold, would be very entertaining. . . . Some preferred Italian, some French wines, and some of them, perhaps, preferred their native Bourbon. But why quarrel about it? ("Did the Pilgrims Drink?" Brooklyn *Eagle*, 31 Dec 67, 2)

No doubt Duncan thought he would have the last word on this matter when, on 2 January 1868, the *Eagle* published this letter (Charles C. Duncan 1868):

> *To the Editor of the Brooklyn Eagle:*
>
> I have read Mark Twain's last in to-day's EAGLE, and am of opinion that when *that* letter was written Mark Twain was sober.
>
> Yours, truly, C. C. DUNCAN.
>
> Brooklyn, December 31, 1867.

But Mark Twain took his revenge in chapter 10 of *The Innocents Abroad* (see 21 and 29 June; 1, 3, and 5 July 67 to JLC and family, n. 7).

To Jane Lampton Clemens and Pamela A. Moffett
8 January 1868 • Washington, D.C.

(MS: NPV)

224 F. street,
Wash Jan. 8.

My Dear Mother & Sister:

And so the old Major has been there, has he? I would like mighty well to see him. I was a sort of a benefactor to him, once. I helped to snatch him out when he was about to ride into a Mohammedan Mosque in that queer old Moorish town of Tangier, in Africa. If he had got in, the Moors would have knocked his venerable old head off,, for his temerity.[1]

I have just arrived from New York—been there ever since Christmas day, staying at Dan Slote's house—my Quaker City roommate, & having a splendid time. Charlie Langdon, Jack Van Nostrand, & Dan & I, ~~had~~ (all Quaker City night-hawks,) had a blow-out at Dan's house & a lively talk over old times. We went through the Holy Land together, & I just laughed till my sides ached, at some of our reminiscences. It was the unholiest gang that ever cavorted through Palestine, but those are the best boys in the world. We needed Moulton badly.[2] I started to make calls, New Year's Day, but I anchored ‸for the day‸ at the first house I came to—Charlie Langdon's sister was there (beautiful girl,) & Miss Alice Hooker, another beautiful girl, a niece of Henry Ward Beecher's. We sent the old folks home early, with instructions not to send the carriage till midnight, & then I just staid there & deviled the life out of those girls.[3] I am going to spend a few days with the Langdon's, in Elmira, New York, as soon as I get time, & a few days at Mrs. Hooker's, in Hartford, Conn., shortly.[4]

Henry Ward Beecher sent for me last Sunday to come over & dine (he lives in Brooklyn, you know,) & I went. Harriet Beecher Stowe was there, & Mrs. & Miss Beecher, Mrs. Hooker & my old Quaker City favorite, Emma Beach.[5] We had a very gay time, if it *was* Sunday. I expect I told more lies than I have told before in a month. We had a tip-top dinner, but nothing to drink but cider. I told Mr. Beecher that no dinner could be perfect without champaign, or at least some kind of Burgundy,

& he said that privately he was a good deal of the same opinion, but it wouldn't do to say it loud. I went back, by invitation, after the evening service, & finished the blow-out, & then staid all night at Mr. ~~Beech~~ Beach's. Henry Ward is a brick.[6]

I found out at 10 oclock, last night, that I was to lecture to-morrow evening & the next, & so you must be aware that I have been working like sin all night to get a lecture written. I have finished it, but don't think a very great deal of it. I call it "Frozen Truth." It is a little top-heavy, though, because there is more truth in the title than there is in the lecture. But thunder, I mustn't sit here writing all day, with so much business before me.[7]

Good bye, & kind regards to all.

Yrs aff'ly
Sam L. Clemens

[1]Major James G. Barry (1800–1880) was born in Ireland and moved to St. Louis in the early 1830s, where he conducted a real-estate business and served in the municipal government—as an alderman in 1839–40, 1842, and 1845–46, and as mayor in 1849–50. Barry and his wife, Elizabeth, had one daughter, born in 1842. (His title of "Major" was evidently honorary, since no record of any military service has been found.) Barry was a member of Clemens's party on the trip to Tangier (see 21 and 29 June; 1, 3, and 5 July 67 to JLC and family); Clemens recorded the incident he mentions here in his notebook, in one of his *Alta* letters, and in chapter 9 of *The Innocents Abroad* (Jensen, 76–77; Scharf, 1:680, 720–21; *N&J1*, 358; SLC 1867rr).

[2]The date of this "blow-out" has not been determined. Clemens arrived in New York on Christmas day, whereas Charles Langdon had been there since about 20 December, when he was reported at the St. Nicholas Hotel with his father and sister ("Hotel Arrivals," New York *Evening Express*, 20 Dec 67, 4; "Personal," New York *Evening Telegram*, 20 Dec 67, 2). Although Charles attended the party, he had not in fact been a member of Clemens's "unholiest gang" on the trip through Palestine. Van Nostrand had two addresses—one in Greenville, New Jersey, and the other in New York City, at 19 Ferry Street (Denny, entry for 10 Sept). Julius Moulton apparently remained at home in St. Louis.

[3]The occasion was the second or third time Clemens had met Olivia Louise Langdon. He recalled that she originally came to his attention in early September, when he saw her photograph in "an ivory miniature in her brother Charley's stateroom in the steamer *Quaker City* in the Bay of Smyrna" (AD, 1 Feb 1906, CU-MARK, in *MTA*, 2:26). In 1906 he stated that their first meeting occurred when he accepted an invitation from the Langdons to dine with them at the St. Nicholas Hotel: "That first meeting was on the 27th of December, 1867, and the next one was at the house of Mrs. Berry, five days later. Miss Langdon had gone there to help Mrs. Berry receive New Year guests" (AD, 13 Feb 1906, CU-MARK, in *MTA*, 2:103). If Clemens first met Olivia on 27 December, his 1906

reminiscence failed to mention their second meeting, which demonstrably occurred on 31 December when he and the Langdons heard Charles Dickens read in Steinway Hall. In 1907 Clemens recalled that "on that day I called at the St. Nicholas Hotel to see my Quaker City Excursion shipmate, Charley Langdon, and was introduced to a sweet & timid & lovely young girl, his sister. The family went to the Dickens reading, and I accompanied them" (AD, 12 Oct 1907, CU-MARK, in *MTE*, 213). Clemens described this performance for his *Alta* readers, mentioning that Dickens read from *David Copperfield;* the only evening Dickens read from that book when Clemens was in New York City was 31 December (the performance he described began at 8:00 P.M., so the only other possibility, an afternoon matinee on 28 December, is ruled out). It remains possible that Clemens first met Olivia and dined with the Langdons on the same evening they heard Dickens ("Mr. Dickens' Readings," New York *Times*, 31 Dec 67, 4; Moss, 331). The very next day, 1 January, Clemens saw Olivia again at 115 West Forty-fourth Street, the home of Thomas S. and Anna E. Berry, friends of the Langdons'. There he found Olivia, her good friend Alice Hooker (visiting New York with the Langdons), and the "old folks" mentioned here (presumably one or more of Olivia's and Alice's parents). In 1906 he vividly recalled the day: "I had thirty-four calls on my list, and this was the first one. I continued it during thirteen hours, and put the other thirty-three off till next year" ("Langdon Guest Book," 1; Wilson 1867, 87; AD, 13 Feb 1906, CU-MARK, in *MTA*, 2:103; see also SLC to OLL, 7 Jan 69, CU-MARK, in *LLMT*, 42–46, and Anna E. Berry to SLC, 29 Nov 1905, CU-MARK).

4 Clemens did not visit the Langdons in Elmira until August, but he stayed at the Hookers' home for several days in late January. Alice B. Hooker (1847–1928) was the daughter of Isabella Beecher Hooker (1822–1907)—half-sister of Henry Ward Beecher—and John Hooker (1816–1901), a lawyer. The Hookers were original residents of the Nook Farm community in Hartford, Connecticut, and had become good friends of the Langdons' through Mrs. Hooker's full brother, Thomas K. Beecher, pastor of the Park Congregational Church in Elmira, to which the Langdons belonged (Andrews, 3, 16–18; "Nook Farm Genealogy," 6, 16; Jerome and Wisbey, 20).

5 Harriet Beecher Stowe (1811–96) lived with her husband at Nook Farm, where she also provided a home for her unmarried sister, Catharine Beecher (1800–1878), an educator and author; both women were sisters of Henry Ward Beecher. He had been married to the former Eunice White Bullard (1812–97) since 1837 ("Nook Farm Genealogy," Beecher Addenda, iii; Andrews, 16–18).

6 Beecher was a temperance reformer who advocated laws prohibiting the sale of liquor, which he claimed was a major cause of poverty, vice, and crime. As recently as 5 December he had delivered one of his "stirring speeches" against the evils of drink (Clark, 126; "A large and enthusiastic temperance meeting . . . ," New York *Times*, 6 Dec 67, 4). Clemens attended the evening service at Plymouth Church on 5 January 1868, presumably accompanying Emma Beach and her parents, Moses S. and Chloe Buckingham Beach.

7 Clemens made his Washington debut on 9 January at Metzerott Hall with a lecture entitled "The Frozen Truth," an account of the *Quaker City* voyage. According to Paine, "The arrangement for his [lecture] appearance had been made by a friend during his absence—'a friend,' Clemens declared afterward, 'not entirely sober at the time.'" In another account, Clemens said that he "had not

been in Washington more than a day or two before a friend of mine came to my room at the hotel early one morning, wakened me from a sound sleep, and nearly stunned me by asking if I was aware of the fact that I was to deliver a lecture at Lincoln Hall that evening." Clemens described his would-be agent as "an old theatrical friend of mine" who "thought he would do me a favor" by arranging and advertising the lecture, but who "started out by getting drunk." The friend has not been further identified (*MTB*, 1:356; Will M. Clemens, 26). The Washington *National Republican* reported that

> the lecture embraced a general review of the excursion. . . . The state-room accommodations on the steamer, the various sensations and stages of sea-sickness, the sociability of the passengers and their peculiarities, were inimitable, and elicited uncontrollable bursts of laughter from the audience, while his reminiscences of the noble cities of to-day and those of the past, visited by the voyagers, were given with all the genuine freshness of a traveler who has seen with observing eyes and a reflective mind all that he reproduces to his hearers. . . . Mark Twain possesses that rare but happy combination of talking as well as he writes; and if any of our readers may be laboring under a fit of the "blues," we recommend to them a speedy relief in the brief advice, "Go and hear Mark Twain." ("Amusements," 10 Jan 68, PH in CU-MARK)

Part of a manuscript draft of "The Frozen Truth" has survived, and a deleted passage in it suggests Clemens intended to repeat his lecture "on Saturday evening," 11 January, not on 10 January as he says in this letter (SLC 1868d, 75†). He was obliged to cancel the second engagement: see 9 Jan 68 to JLC and PAM, and 10 Jan 68 to the editors of the Washington *Morning Chronicle*.

To Emeline B. Beach
8 January 1868 • Washington, D.C.

(MS: CCamarSJ)

224 F street,
St Valentine's Day
Washington, Jan. 8. }

My Dear Miss Emma—

It is singular that the battle of New Orleans[1] & St Valentine's Day both come on the same day this year—singular is too tame a word—it is positively astounding. However, that isn't ~~wat~~ what I was going to write about.

I am a thousand times obliged to you for that most charmingly worded letter. You have not listened to Mr. Beecher & marked his felicity of expression for nothing. I am not saying these things because I think they will be news to you, for they will not, or because I was surprised that you should write an excellent letter, for I was not, but because it is easier to say what is in one's mind than to leave it unsaid.

And while I think of it, Miss Emma, I wish you would—well, never mind—it would be putting you to too much trouble. I am trying my best to write so that you can read the manuscript, but I am not succeeding very well. I have been up all night writing a lecture which I̸ is to be delivered to-morrow evening, & now my fire is out, & the gray dawn is chilly, & my hand is unsteady with cold & fatigue. But I shall be very busy to-morrow & the next day (when I ‸am to‸ lecture again,) & I **must** thank you for writing.[2] People don't like to have their self-complacency touched, you know, & I *did* feel so ridiculous in church last Sunday for writing a Valentine to a young lady, there present, who hadn't taken any notice of it! I am very grateful that that humiliation is removed, I do assure you.[3]

With enormous effrontery, I have entitled my lecture "The Frozen Truth,‸!" How will that strike Mrs. Beach?[4] It has got just about as much truth in it h̸ as it has poetry—& you may reprove me for that, now, & I won't get angry {but if that chambermaid don't quit hammering at that door, I'll make her jump out of the window—I wonder if she thinks I am the early bird that catches the worm.] Chambermaids are absurd people. I hate the whole tribe of them. I wouldn't want any better fun than writing obituaries for ‸chambermaids.‸ ~~them.~~ But I am wandering from my subject. I am going to send Mr. Beecher my book[5] as soon as I recover from this rush of business. I was going to hand it to Mr. Beach in New York, but I had so many things to do that I could not attend to it. I am going to send Mrs. Beach one, ‸also,‸ so that she can see that I can tell the truth in print when I brace myself up to it.

When you see Capt. Duncan I wish you would tell him how busy I am, getting ready to tell the truth to-morrow night; I told him I would be present at his lecture this evening, but now I shall not be able to do it. ‸Never mind—I WILL go & hear him to-night.‸[6] I did not know that I was to lecture, myself, until I was informed of it at 10 o'clock last night. If I were unoccupied, I would run about town & canvas for the Captain to-day. It wouldn't help his pocket any, but lecturers always like to have a crowded house.

You do say the *naivest* things that ever anybody said in the world, & hit the hardest possible hits, in the most comfortable way—but I like it. Your reproofs are so honest, & so pleasant, withal, that I really can't help feeling a strong desire to deserve more of them! But I will conquer it & try to behave myself. I won't make fun of the prayer-meetings any more. But the idea of my "reproving you in return" won't do at all. I don't know anything to reprove you about. I don't know anything except to reprove you for your curious notion of offending me with a long letter. Nothing is pleasanter to me than to be offended in that way, & I shall reprove you very severely if you don't do it again. I shall be ever so much obliged to you if you will sit down now & proceed to offend me awfully.

What was it I put on that envelop that suggested that Mrs. Beach was the principal of a boarding school? What in the world could it have been? What do you ask such conundrums for, & then not send the answer? I only wrote "Miss Emma Beach, 66 Columbia Street, Brooklyn, N. Y."—that was all. Now tell me what it was that put that notion in your head?

I have searched everywhere for my photographs, but I cannot find a single one. I must have put them away somewhere very carefully—& when I put anything away, I never can find it again. Still, I will institute another search, & will find a picture & send it to you. Those Constantinople pictures were very bad, though. I might almost as well send you a photograph of the Sphynx—it would look as much like me.[7]

I got a good long letter from Mrs. Fairbanks, yesterday,—just such a bright, pleasant letter as that most excellent woman always writes.

Come, Miss Emma, send me some more ~~ref~~ reproofs, & upon my word I will do all I can to profit by them—do you note my address?

Your friend, & always your well-wisher,
Sam L. Clemens.

[1] The final engagement of the War of 1812 occurred on this day in 1815.

[2] See the previous letter, n. 7.

[3] Beach evidently did not reply to Clemens's letter of 5 December until after they met at Henry Ward Beecher's on Sunday, 5 January: see the previous letter.

[4] Chloe Buckingham Beach, originally from Waterbury, Connecticut, married Moses S. Beach in 1845.

[5] *The Celebrated Jumping Frog of Calaveras County.*

[6] Captain Duncan repeated his *Quaker City* lecture (first given on 3 December in Brooklyn and again on 26 December in New York) for a Washington audience in Metzerott Hall on 8 January (advertisement, Brooklyn *Eagle*, 24 Dec 67, 1; advertisement, Washington *National Intelligencer*, 8 Jan 68, 3).

[7] The photograph of Clemens taken in Constantinople is reproduced on p. 92.

To Stephen J. Field
9 January 1868 • Washington, D.C.
(MS: CU-MARK)

Washington, Jan. 9, 1868.

Dear Judge—

I wish you would recommend the appointment of Harvey Beckwith to a Special Revenue Agency for San Francisco—by Special Revenue Agent I mean an officer who ferrets out illicit distilleries & other whisky frauds & brings the law upon them. Beckwith is a first-rate man in every way—steady, faithful, smart & particularly energetic. ~~He is honest, also, but he can't help that—he will do the best he can.~~ Beckwith was Superintendent of the great "Mexican" silver mine at Virginia City, Nevada for several years, & also held such a position in the "Gould~~"~~ & Curry" afterward.[1] These facts are certainly sufficient evidence of his *capacity*. In politics he was ~~a~~ for the war, while it lasted, & is a conservative Democrat, now.[2] You see yourself that his virtues are of no common order. God never made *two* such men. However, you know Harvey Beckwith yourself, I suppose, & better than I, for aught I know, though I have known him six years. He would like to have that office, *I* would be very glad if he could get it, & the nation generally would rejoice—at least they would if they knew Beckwith.

Your friend
Sam. L. Clemens.

Hon. Stephen J. Field.

✉———

[*letter docketed:*] From Sam L. Clemens | Jan 9th 1868 | [*flourish*]

[1]Clemens hoped that Field would recommend Beckwith to President Johnson, who at this time held the power to appoint special revenue agents without the approval of the Senate. The need for such agents was a result of widespread attempts to evade the extremely high whiskey tax, which had risen from twenty cents to two dollars per gallon since 1863. Twenty-four special agents were currently employed by the Treasury Department to uncover producers of illicit untaxed whiskey and to investigate "other whisky frauds," which often involved collusion between government officials, distillers, and politicians. Although Beckwith was not appointed to a special agency, in May 1868 the president did nominate him to be superintendent of the United States branch mint at San Francisco. The Senate, however, declined to confirm him ("Editorial Notes,"

San Francisco *Alta California*, 9 Feb 68, 2; Chommie, 143–44; McCulloch, 19; Senate 1887, 16:240, 288–89). Clemens had known Beckwith since at least October 1862, when he mentioned him as superintendent of the Spanish, or Mexican, mine in a news story for the Virginia City *Territorial Enterprise* (*ET&S1*, 166). Beckwith's connection with the Gould and Curry mine has not been documented.

[2] Associate Justice Field's politics were the same as Beckwith's: although pro-Union during the war, he returned to the Democratic party after it, supporting President Johnson's lenient policy toward the South. In a letter to the *Alta* dated 23 December Clemens wrote:

> On the Democratic side of the fence, Judge Field, of California, is talked of more and more every day in connection with the Presidency of the United States. . . . [The Democrats] must have a man whose record as a *Union* man is unblemished; whose record as a *war* man is spotless; and one whose *conservatism* cannot be gainsaid. Thus far, Judge Field is the only man they have found who fills this bill. (SLC 1868w)

To Jane Lampton Clemens and Pamela A. Moffett
9 January 1868 • Washington, D.C.

(MS: NPV and ViU)

‸P. S. The marked paper from one Geo. W. Elliott (I think that was the name) referred to by Pamela, had no marks or writing done by *me*—don't you know my handwriting yet? The request was to *me* to acknowledge the receipt of the paper—that was all.‸[1]

224 F street
Wash, Jan. 9.

My Dear Mother & Sister =

That infernal lecture is over, thank Heaven! It came near being a villainous failure. It was not advertised at all. The manager was taken sick yesterday, & the man who was sent to tell me, never got to me till after noon to-day. There was the dickens to pay. It was too late to do anything~~,~~—too late to stop the lecture‸.‸~~—~~I scared up ~~the~~ a door-keeper, & was ready at the proper time, & by pure good luck a tolerably good house assembled & I was saved! I hard~~y~~ly knew what I was going to talk about, but it went off in splendid style. I was to have preached again Saturday night, but I won't—I can't get along without a manager.[2]

I have been in New York ever since Christmas, you know, & now I shall have to work like sin to catch up on my correspondence.[3]

And I have to get up that confounded book, too. Cut my letters out of the Alta's & send them to me in an envelop. Some, here, that are not mailed yet, I shall have to copy, I suppose.[4]

A movement is on foot to keep the present Patent Office man in his place. If it succeeds, I think it will be very well for Orion.[5]

I have got a thousand things to do, & am not doing *any* of them. I feel perfectly savage.

Good bye—

Yrs affly

Sam

Mrs. Wm. A. Moffett, | 1312 Chesnut street | St Louis | Mo. [*postmarked:*] WASHINGTON D.C. '68 FREE [*and*] COLLECTED JAN 10 5 P.M. WASH'N, D.C. [*franked by Clemens:*] Wm M Stewart | USS

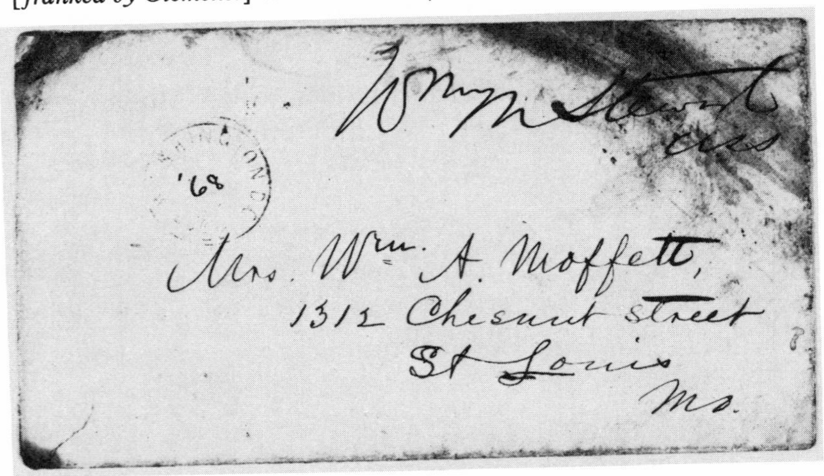

Envelope franked by Clemens with Senator Stewart's name. Special Collections Department (Clemens 6314-q), Clifton Waller Barrett Library, University of Virginia, Charlottesville (ViU).

1 The "marked paper" has not been found, but was presumably an issue of the weekly Fort Plain (N.Y.) *Mohawk Valley Register*. By the end of 1868 George W. Elliott was an associate editor of this newspaper, and was very likely already connected with it. Although nothing Clemens might have sent to his family has been found in the now-incomplete files of the newspaper, it is likely that the "marked" issue contained a sample of the grandiose praise Elliott later showered on Mark Twain (see 19 and 20 Dec 68 to OLL, n. 11). Elliott was probably behind one of the unexpected "calls" to lecture which Clemens told Fuller on 13 December 1867 had arrived "lately from N. Y. & Indiana towns." Clemens did eventually lecture in Fort Plain, in December 1868.

[2]Whatever problems were caused by this unidentified manager (see 8 Jan 68 to JLC and PAM, n. 7), Clemens also had a conflicting obligation, since he had agreed to respond to one of the toasts at the Washington Newspaper Correspondents' Club annual banquet on the evening of Saturday, 11 January. By the afternoon or evening of 10 January, he had received still another reason to cancel the second performance. As he explained to the *Alta* on 11 January, one of the newspapers (the *Evening Star*) "published a synopsis" of the lecture: "I was sorry for that, although it was so well meant, because one never feels comfortable, afterward, repeating a lecture that has been partly printed; and worse than that, people don't care about going to hear what they can buy in a newspaper for less money" (SLC 1868s).

[3]Clemens wrote two letters to the *Enterprise* on 10 and 11 January, and two letters to the *Alta* on 11 and 12 January (SLC 1868o, 1868aa, 1868s, 1868dd).

[4]Although evidently still without a firm commitment from Elisha Bliss (see 24 Jan 68 to JLC and PAM), Clemens had begun to write, and to collect his newspaper letters for, *The Innocents Abroad.*

[5]In December the commissioner of patents, Thomas C. Theaker (1812–83), had been urged to resign "in accordance with the invitation of the President through the Secretary of the Interior," Orville Browning, who wanted to appoint a "practical mechanic thoroughly acquainted with the various inventions." Theaker resigned on 13 December (effective 15 January). But shortly after Clemens left for New York, the *Star* reported, "Strong influence is being brought to bear upon the President to induce him not to accept the resignation." Clemens evidently thought Orion's politics would recommend him (for a Patent Office clerkship) more highly to Theaker, a Republican, than to any candidate supported by President Johnson. But one week after Clemens wrote this letter, on 16 January, the president accepted Theaker's resignation (Washington *Evening Star:* "Commissioner of Patents," 10 Dec 67, 1; "Resigned," 13 Dec 67, 1; "Commissioner of Patents," 28 Dec 67, 1; "Resignation Accepted," 16 Jan 68, 1).

To Charles Henry Webb
10 January 1868 • Washington, D.C.

(Transcripts: AAA 1927, lot 109;
Parke-Bernet Galleries 1940, lot 188)

Washington, Jan. 9

. . . .

Please send me 3 copies of the Jumping Frog—I never got but 6 of the lot you gave me an order for. I lost the order. Send them (the 3) through the mail. It is 2 A.M.—I will to bed.[1]

Yr. Friend
Saml. Clemens.

[1]That is, presumably, early in the morning of 10 January.

To the Editors of the Washington *Morning Chronicle* 10 January 1868 • Washington, D.C.

(Washington *Morning Chronicle*, 11 Jan 68)

EDS. CHRONICLE:[1] I am sorry to see that the papers announce another lecture from me for this evening.[2] I meant to be understood last night as postponing the second lecture, but I suppose I was not. The gentleman who engaged me to lecture was taken very sick twenty-four hours before I was to address the public. (I had been reading my lecture to him, but upon my sacred honor I did not think it would be so severe on him as all that.) He is sick yet. I cannot lecture without an agent to attend to business. Please print this for me, and let it stand as a postponement of my lecture—until what time the health of my unfortunate friend must determine. I will give him a chance, though—I will not read the lecture to him any more.

Very truly,
MARK TWAIN.

[1]The proprietor and chief editor of the Washington *Chronicle* was John W. Forney (1817–81), who began his career as an editor and then co-proprietor of the Lancaster (Pa.) *Journal*. In 1845–51 he edited and published the Philadelphia *Pennsylvanian*, for which he gained a national reputation. In 1851 he came to Washington to serve four years as clerk of the House of Representatives. Strongly opposed to slavery, in 1857 he returned to Philadelphia and founded the *Press*, through which he waged an unrelenting attack on the proslavery Democrats. Returning to Washington, he was again elected clerk of the House in 1859, then secretary of the Senate in 1861, a position he still held. Also in 1861 he founded the Republican *Sunday Chronicle*, which became a daily newspaper the following year. His extensive acquaintance with leading statesmen, and his comprehensive knowledge of public affairs, gave his newspaper wide influence.

[2]On 10 January, in noticing the lecture, both the Washington *National Republican* and the Washington *National Intelligencer* announced that Clemens would repeat it on Saturday, 11 January ("Amusements," Washington *National Republican*, 10 Jan 68, PH in CU-MARK; "Mark Twain's Lecture on the Frozen Truth," Washington *National Intelligencer*, 10 Jan 68, 3). Clemens sent a presumably identical copy of this letter to the *National Intelligencer* (and perhaps to other newspapers as well), which, like the *Morning Chronicle*, published it on 11 January. (For an account of the slight variants between the *Chronicle* text and the text published in the *Intelligencer*, see the textual commentary for this letter.)

To Jane Lampton Clemens and Family
14 January 1868 • Washington, D.C.

(MS and transcript: NPV and
Washington *Evening Star*, 13 Jan 68)

2 AM, 13th

Dear ~~Fold~~ Folks—I thought you might like to read my speech, which Speaker Colfax said was the best dinner-table speech he ever heard at a banquet.[1]

Yrs afly
Sam

[*enclosure:*]

> The twelfth—"Woman: The Pride of the Professions, and the jewel of ours"—was responded to by Mr. Clemens, better known as "Mark Twain."
>
> Mr. Twain remarked as follows:
>
> *Mr. President*:[2]—"I do not know why I should have been singled out to receive the greatest distinction of the evening—for so the office of replying to the toast to woman has been regarded in every age. [Applause.] I do not know why I have received this distinction, unless it be that I am a trifle less homely than the other members of the Club. But be this as it may, Mr. President, I am proud of the position, and you could not have chosen any one who would have accepted it more gladly, or labored with a heartier good-will to do the subject justice, than I. Because, sir, I love the sex. [Laughter.] I love *all* the women, sir, irrespective of age or color. [Laughter.]
>
> Human intelligence cannot estimate what we owe to woman, sir. She sews on our buttons, [laughter,] she mends our clothes, [laughter,] she ropes us in at the church fairs—she confides in us; she tells us whatever she can find out about the little private affairs of the neighbors—she gives us good advice—and plenty of it—she gives us a piece of her mind, sometimes—and sometimes all of it—she soothes our aching brows—she bears our children—ours as a general thing. In all the relations of life, sir,

it is but just and a graceful tribute to woman to say of her that she is a brick. [Great laughter.]

Wheresoever you place woman, sir—in whatsoever position or estate—she is an ornament to that place she occupies, and a treasure to the world. [Here Mr. Twain paused, looked inquiringly at his hearers and remarked that the applause should come in at this point. It came in. Mr. Twain resumed his eulogy.] Look at the noble names of history! Look at Cleopatra!—look at Desdemona!—look at Florence Nightingale!—look at Joan of Arc!—look at Lucretia Borgia! [Disapprobation expressed. "Well," said Mr. Twain, scratching his head doubtfully, "suppose we let Lucretia slide."] Look at Joyce Heth![3]—look at Mother Eve! [Cries of "Oh!" "Oh!"] You need not look at her unless you want to, but, (said Mr. Twain reflectively, after a pause,) Eve was ornamental, sir—particularly before the fashions changed! I repeat, sir, look at the illustrious names of history! Look at the Widow Machree![4]—look at Lucy Stone!—look at Elizabeth Cady Stanton!—look at George Francis Train![5] [Great laughter.] And, sir, I say it with bowed head and deepest veneration, look at the Mother of Washington! she raised a boy that could not lie—*could not lie*—[Applause.] But he *never had any chance.* [Oh! Oh!] It might have been different with him if he had belonged to a newspaper correspondent's club. [Laughter, groans, hisses, cries of "put him out." Mark looked around placidly upon his excited audience and resumed.]

I repeat, sir, that in whatsoever position you place a woman she is an ornament to society and a treasure to the world. As a sweetheart she has few equals and no superiors—[laughter;]—as a cousin she is convenient; as a wealthy grandmother, with an incurable distemper, she is precious—as a wet nurse she has no equal among men! [Laughter.]

What, sir, would the peoples of the earth be, without woman? . . . . They would be scarce, sir—almighty scarce! Then let us cherish her—let us protect her—let us give her our support, our encouragement, our sympathy—ourselves, if we get a chance. [Laughter.]

But, jesting aside, Mr. President, woman is lovable, gracious, kind of heart, beautiful—worthy of all respect, all of esteem, of all deference. Not any here will refuse to drink her

> health right cordially in this bumper of wine, for each and every one of us has personally known, and loved, and honored, the very best one of them all—his own mother! [Applause.]

[1]The second annual banquet of the Washington Newspaper Correspondents' Club began at 7:00 P.M. in Welcker's Restaurant on Saturday, 11 January. Clemens wrote in his *Alta* letter of the next day that he regarded it as "altogether the most brilliant affair of the kind" in his experience. Thirty-seven journalists and nine guests attended, and the celebration went on well past midnight, too late for any report of it to appear in either of the city's two Sunday newspapers, the Washington *Sunday Morning Chronicle* or the *Sunday Herald* (the Sunday form of the *National Intelligencer*, which ran a brief report of the event on Monday morning). But the Washington *Evening Star* for Monday, 13 January, printed a lengthy report of the proceedings, which included a transcript of Clemens's speech, evidently recorded by a stenographer. Although no enclosure now accompanies the letter manuscript, Clemens undoubtedly enclosed at least his speech as it appeared in the *Star*, which (in the absence of newsprint) is reproduced here in type facsimile. His letter must therefore have been written at 2:00 A.M. on 14 (not 13) January. Out of fifteen regular toasts, Clemens responded to the twelfth, "Woman: The Pride of the Professions, and the jewel of ours." Speaker of the House Schuyler Colfax, who would be elected vice-president under Grant in November 1868, was present as one of the guests. He responded to the first regular toast by proposing "The health of the members of the Washington Correspondents' Club: May they always wield the power of the club honestly, conscientiously, and wisely" (SLC 1868dd; "The Press Banquet," Washington *National Intelligencer*, 13 Jan 68, 2; "Annual Banquet of the Corres[pon]dents' Club," Washington *Evening Star*, 13 Jan 68, 2).

[2]The president of the Correspondents' Club was George W. Adams (1838–86), part owner of the Washington *Evening Star* and Washington correspondent of the New York *World* ("The Press Banquet," Washington *National Intelligencer*, 13 Jan 68, 2).

[3]Joice Heth was a slave who attracted public attention in the summer of 1835 when her owners claimed she was over 160 years old and had been George Washington's nurse. P. T. Barnum got his start as a showman when he purchased and exhibited her, until her death in early 1836. Barnum asserted in his autobiography that he was deceived by the claims about her age; her actual age is unknown (Barnum, 73–76).

[4]In the popular song "Widow Machree" the title character is coaxed to leave off her mourning and accept a new husband. Irish author, composer, and artist Samuel Lover (1797–1868) first published the lyrics in an 1842 novel, *Handy Andy: A Tale of Irish Life;* the sheet music was issued soon thereafter (Lover, 45, 284–85; Moffat, 318–19).

[5]Lucy Stone (1818–93) and Elizabeth Cady Stanton (1815–1902), formerly ardent abolitionists, were now prominent leaders in the fight for women's rights. George Francis Train (1829–1904), an eccentric entrepreneur, writer, and lecturer, was an outspoken champion of suffrage for women. Train had recently paid for, and taken part in, a lecture tour of prominent suffragists through major midwestern and eastern cities. The tour ended with a meeting in New York City

on 14 December, at which Train reportedly "nominated himself for the Presidency" ("The Rights of Woman," New York *Tribune*, 16 Dec 67, 8; Lutz, 154–55). Clemens made fun of Train's grandiose schemes in an undated piece published in the New York *Tribune* on 22 January, called him an "insufferable fool" in a letter to the *Enterprise* dated 30 January, and referred to him as "the great Fenian Female Suffrage Ass" in a letter to the Chicago *Republican* dated 21 February (SLC 1868*l*, 1868gg, 1868ii).

To Charles Henry Webb
15 January 1868 • Washington, D.C.

(MS: ViU)

356 C bet. 4½ & 6th
Washington Jan. 15.[1]

Dear Webb—

The books came—am much obliged.[2]

I tackled the Stag—nothing there. He was scared a good deal, but swore hard that all charges were false. If there *was* anything there, I was not able to start it. But it was fun, anyway. I wished all the time, that you were present.[3]

Yrs
Mark

[1]Clemens had recently moved from his quarters at 224 F Street North, which he had shared since November with Senator Stewart. See 9 Feb 68 to Fairbanks, n. 1, and 21 Feb 68 to JLC and family, n. 1, for further details about his several Washington addresses.

[2]The "books" were three copies of *The Celebrated Jumping Frog of Calaveras County* which Clemens had requested (10 Jan 68 to Webb). Clemens sent one of the copies to Charles Langdon, who inscribed it "C. J. Langdon, Elmira, New York, Feby. 5th, 1868." Another was probably sent to Mrs. Fairbanks, and others had already been promised to Henry Ward Beecher and to Emma Beach's mother, both of whom Clemens saw in Brooklyn before the month was out (Parke-Bernet Galleries 1941, lot 90; 20 Feb 68 to Fairbanks; 8 Jan 68 to Beach).

[3]Clemens and Webb had probably known Cornelius Stagg (b. 1827 or 1828) in San Francisco through their mutual friend Frank Soulé, collector for the Department of Internal Revenue, whom Stagg served for a year as deputy until relieved of his post in December 1866. He soon left San Francisco for New York,

where, on 2 February 1867, Clemens reported seeing him (SLC 1867n). On 31 May Stagg received a 150-day appointment (that is, until the end of October 1867) as a special revenue agent—the kind of position that Clemens wanted to secure for Harvey Beckwith (9 Jan 68 to Field), except that special agents were free to exercise their police powers anywhere in the United States, not just in one city. A citizen of Chicago characterized this group of special agents as

> spies and informers who, under color of some kind of an authority from the department at Washington, and under the name of Revenue Agents, prowl around the country with the nominal object of detecting frauds upon the revenue, but with the real design of making all the money they can out of seizures and confiscations. . . .
>
> These men walk into your office, demand your books and papers and open private letters, look at your safe, and then close your store. . . . They then go rum[m]aging around for evidences of fraud. No charge is made—no specific allegation; . . . and wo[e] betide the man, however innocent or honest, in whose books an error is found, . . . unless, indeed, he "comes down" (as it is termed) and pays this harpy what he thinks is a fair compensation for his trouble. (Shufeldt, 2)

Webb and Clemens had evidently heard rumors that Stagg was suspected of extorting bribes from whiskey dealers under cover of enforcing the two-dollar-per-gallon whiskey tax. In late November and early December, after Stagg's appointment had ended, at least one (unidentified) Chicago journalist insinuated repeatedly in print that Stagg was being investigated for such extortion. On 28 November he wrote that the "United States grand jury . . . is now on a grand Stagg hunt. It is exhilarating sport; but the chances are that the Stagg won't be caught" (Chicago *Times*, 4). On 1 December he came close to direct accusation:

> The late Stagg hunt in Chicago was a very exciting affair. . . . The chief huntsmen were Parker, Lawrence, Gen. Norton [local revenue agents], the United States grand jury, and any number of whippers-in, in the shape of detectives and other similar rabble of lesser note[.]
>
> This Stagg, thus hunted, is the one which we alluded to some days since. It started from the revenue recesses of New York, and ran through pretty nearly the entire country. Some small dogs got after it in Peoria, and it was barked at by the various curs of Pekin, Cincinnati, and St. Louis. A regular hunting party was not organized till the animal reached Chicago. . . . but the Stagg is not yet caught.
>
> It is a Stagg of more than average size, strength, and speed. Its antlers are immense. It is a Stagg of ten—that is, ten thousand dollars. . . . But it is to be feared that the antlers of this Stagg will never be nailed as a trophy to the walls of the revenue lodge of this city. ("Stagg-Hunting," Chicago *Times*, 1 Dec 67, 4)

As late as 15 December, the unidentified journalist published similar, though briefer, innuendos: "A meeting of whisky men at the national capital may be accepted as evidence that somebody has just made a raid—*a la* Stagg—among the distilleries." And, "Stagg was once a Christian. There was a time when he listened to the whisper of a '*still* small voice'" ("The Whisky Men in Washington," Chicago *Times*, 4). Formal charges were evidently never brought against Stagg. By late November he was back in Washington, probably to seek reappointment, although apparently without success: he is listed without occupation in the 1868 San Francisco directory (San Francisco City and County 1867, s.v. "Stagg, Cornelius"; Langley 1865, 592; "Cornelius Stagg . . . ," Virginia City *Territorial Enterprise*, 5 Dec 66, 2; McCulloch, 8; "Personal," Washington *Evening Star*, 27 Nov 67, 1; SLC 1868c, 1868o; Langley 1868, 518).

To Jane Lampton Clemens and Pamela A. Moffett
24 January 1868 • Hartford, Conn.

(MS: NPV)

‸☞ Read this *only* to the family, & then burn it—I do *hate* to have anybody know anything about my business. Don't mention the *terms*, herein, on your life. It is business secret.‸

Hartford, Conn., Jan. 24.

Dear Mother & Sister—

This is a good week for me. I stopped in the *Herald* office as I came through New York, to see the boys on the staff, & young James Gordon Bennett asked me to write impersonally twice a week for the *Herald*, & said if I would, I might have full swing, & abuse anybody & everybody I wanted to. I said I must have the very fullest possible swing, & he said, All right. I said "It's a contract"—& that settled *that* matter. I'll make it a point to write *one* letter a week, anyhow.[1]

But the *best* thing that has happened was here. This great American Publishing Company kept on trying to bargain with me for a book till I thought I would cut the matter short by coming up for a *talk*. I met Rev. Henry Ward Beecher in Brooklyn, & with his usual whole-souled way of dropping his own work to give other people a lift when he gets a chance, he said, "Now here—you are ‸one‸ of the talented men of the age,—nobody is going to deny that—but in matters of business, I don't suppose you know more than enough to come in when it rains,; I'll tell you what to do, & how to do it." And he *did*.[2] And I listened well, & then came up here & have made a splendid contract for a Quaker City book of 5 or 600 large ~~paper~~ pages, with illustrations, the manuscript to be placed in the publishers' hands by the middle of July. My per centage is to be a fifth more than they paid Richardson.[3] They pay me more than they have ever paid any author except Horace Greeley.[4] Beecher will be surprised, I guess, when he hears this. But I had my mind made up to *one* thing—I wasn't going to touch a book unless there was *money* in it, & a good deal of it. I told them so. I had the misfortune to "bust out" one author of standing. They had his manuscript, with the understanding that they would publish his book if they could not get a book from me (they only publish two books at a time, & so my book & Richardson's Life of Grant will fill the bill for next fall & winter,)—so that manuscript was sent back to its author to-day. These publishers get off the most tremendous editions of their books you can imagine.[5] [*in margin:* I have to make a speech at the annual Herald dinner on the 6th of May.][6]

I shall write to the Enterprise & Alta every week, as usual, I guess, & to the Herald twice a week—occasionally to the Tribune & the magazines (I have a stupid article in the Galaxy, just issued,)[7] but I am not going [to] write to this, that & the other paper any more. The Chicago Tribune wants letters, but I hope & pray I have charged them so much that they will not close the contract.[8] I am gradually getting out of debt, but these trips to New York do cost like ~~sin.~~ Sin.[9]

I hope you have cut out & forwarded my printed letters to Washington—please continue to do so as they arrive.[10]

I have had a tip-top time, here, for a few days (guest of Mr. Jno. Hooker's family—Beecher's relatives—& ~~of~~ ‸in a general way of‸ ~~the hea~~ Mr. Bliss, ‸also, who is‸ head of the publishing firm.) Puritans are mighty straight-laced, & they won't let me smoke in the parlor, but the Almighty don't make any better people.[11]

Now *don't* go & read this letter to *anybody* outside the family circle—I am sensitive on this point. If you have to talk, *talk*—but don't *read* my letters.

I expect I have made the Alta people mad, but I don't care. They did not telegraph me soon enough.[12]

That cursed, infernal Patent Office ~~business~~ Commissionership has changed round again & gone into Cox's hands. I expect that thing is going to ~~both~~ take me months to accomplish it. The way I'll waltz into some of those people in the Herald the first thing they know, will make them think the Devil himself has got loose for another thousand years. If I ever *do* start in,‸ ~~to~~ in good earnest, to fiddle for them I'll bet they'll dance. I want just one private talk with Andrew Johnson when I get back to Washington, & then I'll know what course to pursue. If they don't want any clerks in the Departments immediately, I will "show up" their damnable rottenness for *not* wanting clerks.[13] Love to all—good-bye. I shall be in New York 3 days—then go on to the capital.

Yrs aff'ly especially Ma,
Yr Sam.

[1]Clemens arrived in New York sometime between 17 and 19 January, remaining there and in Brooklyn until at least the evening of 21 January. He then went to Hartford for several days, returning to New York on 25 January (SLC 1868cc, 1868kk). Members of the *Herald* editorial staff whom Clemens might have known are identified in 20 Nov 67 to JLC and family (2nd of 2), n. 2. At least three letters Clemens may have written from Washington (dated 1, 8, and 15 February) appeared, without signature, in the *Herald* for 3, 10, and 18 February: the first under the heading "Gossip at the National Capital," the others under "Washington Gossip," and all three identified as "Special Correspondence of the Herald" (Budd, 5–9; see SLC 1868r, 1868v, 1868bb).

[2]Beecher's expertise in such matters was demonstrated earlier in January when he executed a contract with J. B. Ford and Company, a recently founded New York subscription publisher, from which he received a "bonus" (probably an advance) of $10,000 for his still-to-be-written *Life of Jesus, the Christ*, the first volume of which was published three years later, in 1871 ("A New Work by Henry Ward Beecher," New York *Times*, 13 Jan 68, 2; Howard, 215; Wilson 1868, 368, 522).

[3]According to Paine, Elisha Bliss had been too ill to respond to Clemens's 2 December letter "in detail" until 24 December; his reply survives only in a now-incomplete typescript, of unknown origin (CtHMTH):

OFFICE OF AMERICAN PUBLISHING CO.

Hartford, Conn. Dec. 24, 1867

Samuel L. Clemens Esq.
Tribune Rooms, Washington D.C.
Dear Sir:

I have a few moments leisure and I shall spend them in writing you as I promised. Have you seen Mr. Richardson at your office? I suppose you have. I spoke to him about your work as talked of by us and asked him to give you some particulars or information regarding our operation, manner of doing business etc. I hope he has done so. I see it announced in one of our morning papers that you are engaged in writing a book or preparing one and that we are to publish it. How it got there is beyond my comprehension. Now about the book, We would like to have you get us up one. We can handle it we think to the advantage of both of us. We shall probably bring out Richardson's new work and we can swing yours also easily and successfully. We think we see clearly that the book would sell; a *humorous* work, that is to say, a work *humorously inclined* we believe it, and Richardson's work we think owe a good deal of their popularity to their *spicy* nature. The first thing then is, will you *make* a book? For material we should suggest your collected letters, *revamped and worked* over and all the other matter you can command, connected [*single extant page ends here*]

Bliss had evidently seen the following announcement, whose source has not been discovered:

> Mark Twain, one of the funniest writers of the day, who was one of the Quaker City excursionists, is preparing a volume descriptive of their voyage. It will be published by the American Publishing company of this city, and those who have laughed over Mark's story of the Jumping Frog of Calaveras, Jim Wolfe and the Cats, or his inimitable letters from Italy and Palestine, will be apt to buy it. ("City and Vicinity," Hartford *Courant*, 24 Dec 67, 8)

Paine, who had access to a complete version of Bliss's letter, paraphrased the rest of its contents: Bliss "recited the profits made by Richardson and others through subscription publication, and named the royalties paid. Richardson had received four per cent. of the sale price" for each copy of his *Beyond the Mississippi;* Bliss "added that they had two arrangements for paying authors: outright purchase, and royalty" (*MTB*, 1:351). Clemens held out for a 5 percent royalty on each copy of *The Innocents Abroad*, rejecting a guaranteed fee of $10,000 "cash in hand" for outright purchase, which Bliss offered as an alternative (*MTL*, 1:146–47; see 27 Jan 68 to Bliss for further details of the contract). Clemens's choice ultimately proved financially wise: *The Innocents Abroad* earned him about $14,000 in its first year of publication; in 1903 he claimed that his royalties from the first American edition had totaled $35,000 (Hirst 1975, 317–18).

[4] Since Bliss's company did not publish Greeley (1811–72)—politician, lecturer, author, founder and editor of the New York *Tribune*—Clemens may have misunderstood what Bliss, or Beecher, had said to him. Greeley did publish by subscription, however, beginning with *The American Conflict* in two volumes (1864, 1866), which issued through O. D. Case and Company of Hartford, and he was about to publish *Recollections of a Busy Life* (1868) through J. B. Ford and Company, Beecher's new publisher (see note 2). His royalty percentage on these books remains unknown, but by 1 January 1867, the first volume of *The American Conflict* had sold nearly 125,000 copies, and the second, nearly 50,000 (Van Deusen, 355).

[5] Richardson's biography aimed "to tell the life-story of Grant the Man, rather than of Grant the General and the Statesman." *A Personal History of Ulysses S. Grant* was issued by the American Publishing Company in late July 1868, but *The Innocents Abroad* did not appear until the following July. The "author of standing" temporarily displaced by Clemens may have been Junius Henri Browne, another *Tribune* writer, whose *Great Metropolis; A Mirror of New York* was issued by the American Publishing Company in January 1869 ("Biography of General Grant," New York *Tribune*, 24 Dec 67, 4; Bliss to SLC, 29 July 68, CU-MARK; SLC to Bliss, 22 July 69, transcript at WU, in *MTLP*, 22–24).

[6] Clemens did not, in fact, speak at this dinner because in May he was living in San Francisco.

[7] "General Washington's Negro Body-Servant" in the February 1868 *Galaxy*, which had appeared by the time Clemens wrote this letter (SLC 1868p; "The Deadliest Inhabitant Extant," Washington *Evening Star*, 24 Jan 68, 1).

[8] Since Clemens does not mention that within a week (on 31 January) he would write the first of six signed letters to the Chicago *Republican*, he may well have confused that newspaper with the Chicago *Tribune*. Nothing in the *Tribune* for 1868 has so far been identified as his. Clemens probably knew at least one newspaper editor who might have approached him on behalf of either the *Tribune* or the *Republican:* for most of 1867, V. B. Denslow was the managing editor of the Chicago *Republican*, having earlier been an editor on the Chicago *Tribune*. In September 1867 Denslow accepted a position on the editorial staff of the New York *Tribune* (SLC 1868t; "Personal," New York *World*, 7 Sept 67, 4; Cummings 1868b, 107).

[9] The creditor, cause, and extent of Clemens's indebtedness remain unknown.

[10] That is, his letters to the *Alta* from the *Quaker City* excursion.

[11] Clemens stayed from 22 to 25 January at the home of John and Isabella Hooker, thus accepting the invitation he reported to his family on 8 January. In an *Alta* letter describing Hartford he explained,

I hear no swearing here, I see no one chewing tobacco, I have found nobody drunk. What a singular country it is. At the hospitable mansion where I am a guest, I have to smoke surreptitiously when all are in bed, to save my reputation, and then draw suspicion upon the cat when the family detect the unfamiliar odor. I never was so absurdly proper in the broad light of day in my life as I have been for the last day or two. So far, I am safe; but I am sorry to say that the cat has lost caste. (SLC 1868kk)

[12] One of the three principal *Alta* editors at this time, Noah Brooks, recalled in 1898 that

while Clemens was in the Eastern States, there came to us a statement, through the medium of the Associated Press, that he was preparing for publication his letters which had been printed in the "Alta California." The proprietors of that newspaper were wroth. They regarded the letters as their private property. Had they not bought and paid for them? Could they have been written if they had not furnished the money to pay the expenses of the writer? (Brooks 1898, 99)

The "statement" was probably an announcement like the one in the *Courant*, or a similar, briefer one that had appeared in the New York *World* on 23 December and was reprinted in the *Alta* on 14 January: "A book is imminent, on the voyage of the *Quaker City*, from the pen of 'Mark Twain'" ("Personal," New York *World*, 23 Dec 67, 4; "Personal," San Francisco *Alta California*, 14 Jan 68, 1). The proprietors evidently telegraphed Clemens protesting his decision to republish his letters without asking their permission. Clemens's comment here suggests that he may have sent a somewhat intemperate reply to this telegram, which probably reached him before he left Washington on 17–19 January en route to Hartford. See 1 Feb 68 to Young, n. 1, for further details.

[13] The clerkship Clemens hoped to secure, either in the Patent Office or in some other government department, was for Orion Clemens. Although the president had not yet sent the Senate any nominations for commissioner of patents, the Washington *Evening Star* reported the names of likely nominees as early as mid-December, a month before Commissioner Theaker's resignation took effect on 15 January. Colonel John Cooke Cox (d. 1872), first mentioned in this connection on 14 December, was mentioned again on 17 January as one of the top three candidates. A former Union army officer from Pennsylvania and now chief clerk in the Department of the Interior, Cox was Secretary Browning's choice as the new commissioner of patents. Clemens's casual reference to Cox may imply that his candidacy was common knowledge, or that Clemens had mentioned him earlier, in a letter no longer extant. The appointment went ultimately to Elisha Foote (1809–83), a lawyer, inventor, and examiner for the Patent Office, who was confirmed on 25 July (Washington *Evening Star:* "The Vacant Commissionership," 14 Dec 67, 1; "Commissioner of Patents," 2 Jan 68, 1; "Hon. T. C. Theaker," 17 Jan 68, 1; "Commissioner of Patents," 17 Jan 68, 1; Senate 1887, 16:325, 368; Interior Department, 143, 150; Boatner, 206).

To Mary Mason Fairbanks
24 January 1868 • Hartford, Conn.

(MS: CSmH)

Hartford, Conn., Jan. 24.

Dear Mother—

Don't abuse me on ~~t~~ account of that dinner-speech in reply to the toast to Woman, if you should see it floating around in the papers.[1] It had slang in it, but they had no business to report it so *verbatimly*. They ought to have left out the slang—*you* know that. It was all their fault. I am not going to make any more slang speeches in public. You will forgive me, now, won't you?

I saw Dan as I came through New York, & I staid part of two days at Mr. Be~~e~~ach's, in Brooklyn. That is a hospitable family, if there ever was one. Mr. Beach has been so liberal & so generous toward some of the cabin crew of the Quaker City, & has treated me so well, also, that I am ashamed to think I ever thought uncharitably of him.[2] Mrs. Beach is a very fine woman, & certainly one seldom finds as good a girl as Emma, anywhere.

I am to do up the Excursion in a vast 5 or 600-page book, for the American ~~p~~Publishing Company of Hartford. It is to be sold only by subscription. They pay most liberally~~,~~—but then my newspaper & magazine contracts were worth six or eight hundred dollars a month, & as I would have to throw away half of them if I prepared the book I was not inclined to do it unless I saw more profit in the said book. I have a very easy contract. I have from now till the middle of July in which to get the manuscript ready. I shall use nearly all my old letters (revamped,) but still many a chapter will be entirely new. What would you call the book?—the "Modern Pilgrim's Progress"—"Cruise of the Quaker City"—or what?

I am tired of writing wishy-washy squibs for the Tribune, & have joined the Herald staff—2 impersonal letters a week. Mr. Bennett says I may have full swing, & say as many mean things as I please.[3] Now don't say a word Madam, because I just mean to abuse people right & left~~,~~, in case the humor takes me to do it. There are lots of folks in Washington who need villifying. I expect I ‸shall‸ ~~will~~ shock you sometimes, anger you occasionally, provoke your motherly uneasiness often—but ~~woul~~ wound your feelings, never!

I have not sworn an oath since I wrote you last—& yet I have not a button on my clothes hardly. The fortitude I have shown under these exasperating circumstances fills me with admiration. I have a splendid opinion of myself, now—& I owe it all to you. Long may you ~~lif~~ live—& long may I live also, to sing your praises.

I am the guest of Mr. Hoo~~p~~‸k‸er's (Henry Ward Beecher's brother=in-law) family here for a few days, & I tell you I have to walk mighty straight. I desire to have the respect of this sterling old Puritan community, for their respect is well worth having—& so I don't dare to smoke after I go to bed, & in fact I don't dare to do *anything* that's comfortable & natural. It comes a little hard to lead such a sinless life, but then you know it won't be for long—I can let myself out when I get to Washington. I have promised to be Mrs. Hooker's special Washington correspondent, & so I shall have to be particular again. I am in a pretty close place—I can't put my slang into your letters—I can't put it into hers—I guess I shall have to deluge Charley Langdon with it.

But I guess I have written bosh enough for the present. Good-bye. I am ever so grateful to you for sending me those copies of the *Herald*. I see a good many ideas in your letters that I can steal.[4] Remember me most kindly to Mrs. Severance & that good old husband of hers.

Sincerly yr friend

Sam Clemens

[1] See 14 Jan 68 to JLC and family.

[2] Beach had undertaken to help the unpaid crew of the *Quaker City:* see 12 Dec 67 to Fairbanks, n. 4. His defense of the *Quaker City* ladies in reply to Clemens's critical remarks in the *Tribune* would have prompted uncharitable thoughts, but what further provocation occurred (if any) remains unknown (see 24 Oct 67 to Goodman, n. 2).

[3] In December and January 1867–68 Clemens published three signed sketches in the *Tribune:* "Information Wanted" on 18 December, "The Facts Concerning the Recent Resignation" on 27 December, and "Information Wanted" on 22 January (SLC 1867bbbb, 1867ffff, 1868*l*). He may have considered these "wishy-washy" because they were politically neutral. On 9 February he wrote "The Facts Concerning the Recent Important Resignation" (SLC 1868x), which was more politically satirical, although still nonpartisan, ridiculing both Republican and Democratic congressmen. For Clemens's "impersonal" letters to the *Herald*, see the previous letter, n. 1.

[4] Mrs. Fairbanks's twenty-seven *Quaker City* letters to her husband's newspaper, the Cleveland *Herald*, which she signed "Myra." Clemens wanted the let-

ters to refresh his memory of the trip for his own account in what became *The Innocents Abroad*. The writing and publication dates of these letters are listed in the headnote to Appendix D.

To William Bowen
25 January 1868 • New York, N.Y.

(MS: TxU)

‸☞ Tell these contents to *nobody* but Mollie.‸[1]

New York, Jan. ~~24~~ 25.

Dear Will—

I have just come down from Hartford, Conn., where I have made a tip-top contract for a 600-page book, & I feel perfectly jolly. It is with the heaviest publishing house in America, & I get the best terms they have ever offered any man save one.[2] The manuscript is to be ready the middle of July. It would take a good deal of money to buy out the ~~s~~ undersigned now, old boy.

I put that postscript at the top of the letter because the above paragraph contains business matters, & *they* ought always to be kept reasonably dark.

Mr. Bennett of the New York Herald tells me that if I will correspond twice a week from Washington, I may abuse & ridicule anybody & *every* body I please. Well, I said, "We will just take one drink on that—all I have been wanting, for a year, is to find a paper that will give me room according to my strength—& pay me double price." He said the Herald would do both. I have two weekly Pacific coast correspondences—I'll raise on them, also, & write very seldom for the Tribune—& then I'll sail in & write that book. If it were not for that book, I would just show these newspaper men how easy it is to make a stack of greenbacks every week—but the book is going to crowd me some—I shall have to cut off *all* outside work, & it is growing pretty lucrative. I *could* make eight hundred a month so easily if I didn't have the book to write.

Will, I was ever so sorry to hear of your bereavement[3]—but at the same time I could not help reflecting that you are still *very*, *very* fortunately situated, for you have a most excellent wife—a good, kind, affectionate comrade in all the vicissitudes of life & one who will always prefer rather to overlook your shortcomings than criticise them—a treasure you have long ago learned the value of. I wish I had been as fortunate. To labor to secure the world's ~~pl~~ praise or its blame either, seems stale, flat & unprofitable,[4] compared with the happiness of achieving the praise or the abuse of ~~a~~ so dear a friend as a wife.

God bless old Bart, I *do* hope he will come out strong & hearty again.[5]

I have been thinking of school-days at Dawson's, & trying to recall the old faces of that ancient time—but I cannot place them very well—they have ~~g~~ faded out from my treacherous memory, for the most part, & passed away. But I still remember the louse you bought of poor Arch Fuqua. I told about that at a Congressional dinner in Washington the other day, & Lord, how those thieves laughed! It *was* a gorgeous old reminiscence. I just expect I shall publish it yet, some day.[6]

But I have a dozen more letters to write, & time presses.

Goodbye, old shipmate.

Forever—
Sam Clemens

1 Mary Bowen, Will's wife.

2 Clemens mistakenly thought this was Horace Greeley (see 24 Jan 68 to JLC and PAM, n. 4).

3 Probably the death of the Bowens' eldest child, Mattie, in September 1867, two months before her eighth birthday (des Cognets, 66).

4 *Hamlet*, act 1, scene 2.

5 Will's older brother Bart had been injured by scalding steam in a steamboat wreck of unknown date. He failed to recover his health and died on 31 May (Anderson, 91; "Death of a Steamboat Captain," San Francisco *Times*, 23 June 68, 1).

6 Clemens and Bowen both attended the Hannibal school run by John D. Dawson (b. 1812?) from its opening in 1847 until Dawson went to California in 1849. Archibald Fuqua (b. 1833?), another classmate, was the son of a Hannibal tobacco merchant. Clemens and Bowen became so absorbed in teasing the insect bought from Fuqua that they were unaware until too late that schoolmaster Dawson was watching them watch the louse. Clemens first published the incident in chapter 7 of *Tom Sawyer*, but his earliest known literary use of it occurs in "Boy's Manuscript," which he wrote in October or November 1868 but left unpublished (*Inds*, 317, 319). No report of the "Congressional dinner in Washington" has been found.

To Elisha Bliss, Jr.
27 January 1868 • New York, N.Y.
(MS: CU-MARK)

SLOTE & WOODMAN, BLANK BOOK MANUFACTURERS,[1]
NOS. 119 & 121 WILLIAM STREET,

NEW-YORK, January 27, 186 8.

M r. E. Bliss, Jr.
Sec'y American Publishing Co.
Hartford, Conn.

DEAR SIR:

Your favor of Jan. 25th is received,[2] & in reply, I will say that I accede to your several propositions, viz: That I furnish ~~you~~ to the American Publishing Company, through you, with MSS sufficient for a volume of 500 to ~~1~~ 600 pages, the subject to be the trip of the Quaker City, the voyage, description of places, &c., & also embodying the substance of the letters written by me during that trip, said MSS to be ready about the first of August, ‸next,‸ I to give all the usual & necessary attention in preparing said MSS for the press, & in preparation of illustrations, in correction of proofs—no use to be made by me of the material for this work in any way which will conflict with its interest—the book to be sold by the American Publishing Company by subscription—& for said MSS & labor on my part, said ~~c~~‸Company to pay me a copyright of 5 per cent. upon the subscription price of the book for all copies sold.[3]

As further proposed by you, this understanding, herein set forth, shall be considered a binding contract upon all parties concerned, all minor details to be arranged between us hereafter.[4]

Very Truly Yours,
Sam. L. Clemens.

[*ten lines blank; new page begins:*]

(Private & general.)

I was to have gone to Washington to-night, but have held over, a day, to attend a dinner given by a lot of newspaper ~~men~~ Editors & literary scalliwags, at the Westminster Hotel. Shall go down tomorrow, if I survive the ~~d~~ banquet.[5]

Yrs Truly

Sam. Clemens

✉

[*letter docketed:*] ✓ Author [*and*] Samuel J Clements | Jan 27/68

1 Clemens used Dan Slote's business stationery, in part because he was again staying with Slote while in New York.

2 Bliss's letter, recapitulated here, has not been found.

3 The price of subscription books varied with the kind of binding the buyer selected. *The Innocents Abroad* could cost as little as $3.50 (in cloth covers) or as much as $8.00 (in "Full Turkey Morocco"), earning Clemens from $.175 to $.40 per copy (Bliss to SLC, 13 Feb 71, CU-MARK).

4 A more formal contract executed on 16 October 1868 contained further stipulations about proofreading and correcting, electrotyping, and promotion of sales. It is fully transcribed in Appendix F.

5 No report of the dinner mentioned here has been found.

To Mary Mason Fairbanks
30 January 1868 • Washington, D.C.

(MS: CSmH)

. . . .

Jan. 30.

P. S.—I confess, humbly, that I deserve all you have said, & promise that I will rigidly eschew slang & vulgarity in future, even in foolish dinner speeches, when on my guard.[1]

And now, won't you cut out ~~s~~ & send to me all your printed letters,[2] for I need notes very badly to write from. My book is to make about 600 pages, & I find that my published letters, even copiously illustrated, will only make 250 pages.[3] I am afraid that to write 5 or 6 newspapers letters a week & a book beside, is going to be more than I can do.

Always your grateful

Debtor & your friend

Sam. L. Clemens,

[1]As Clemens predicted on 24 January, Mrs. Fairbanks had since seen and criticized his "*verbatimly*" reported response to the toast to "Woman" delivered at the Newspaper Correspondents' Club dinner on 11 January. Neither her letter, which awaited him on his return to Washington, nor the body of his, to which this postscript presumably belonged, has been found.

[2]Mrs. Fairbanks's *Quaker City* letters to the Cleveland *Herald;* see 24 Jan 68 to Fairbanks, n. 4.

[3]By 26 January, the *Alta* had published thirty-six *Quaker City* letters, and Clemens had received clippings of fewer than that.

To Emeline B. Beach
31 January 1868 • Washington, D.C.

(MS, *damage emended:* Feldman)

224 F street,
Washington, Jan. 31.

Shipmate, Ahoy!

It is all very well to counterfe~~e~~‸it cheerfulness & say Shipmate, Ahoy! in that fraudulently brusque way, but it is only a swindle, at best~~,~~. One cannot go up & skirmish about New York for a week without paying for it in sorrow & tribulation when he returns. I have not been out of the house since I ~~returned,~~ ‸came home,‸ & have not left the writing table, except to ~~to~~ sleep, & take my meals~~,~~. I have written seven long newspaper letters & a short magazine article in less than two days.[1] It is the most extravagant instance of industry that ever came under your notice, I have no sort of doubt. In two more days I shall have made up for all my lost time. Then I shall feel ~~j~~ less tired, & much jollier than I do now.

You ought to see the letter from Mrs. Fairbanks I found awaiting me here. It was a scorcher—if I may use so unseemly a term to convey what no other will express. It seems I have been using slang again. I am so unfortunate. I know I never, never, never shall ~~become~~ get reformed up to the regulation standard. Every time I reform in one direction I go overboard in another. Now, once & for all, I will *not* use any more slang. But I suppose I shall make some other blunder that is just as bad, & get into trouble again.

I should have thought you might have dropped me a line by this time, Miss Emma. I don't see that you have anything to do wherein to employ your ~~time.~~ ‸leisure.‸ It is immense fun to write, when one hasn't anything to do. Try it. It will eventually perfect your style. Write your compositions to me, instead of to your prejudiced teacher. I will send your teacher Congressional speeches in place of them~~,~~—& Patent Office Reports, & beautiful romantic dissertations on yams, from the Agricultural Department.

I wasted a good deal of strategy trying to make Mrs. Beach invite me to call again, but I didn't succeed. She had concluded she wouldn't—~~s~~ and as she had concluded she wouldn't, why she just *wouldn't*, that was all~~,~~; I was ~~handsomely~~ conquered that time, but she needn't think I am going to stay conquered. No—I shall come without any invitation. I shall come & stay a month! She shall mourn over that victory of hers in ~~allegorical~~ ‸metaphorical‸ sackcloth & ashes. I know I shall be doing wrong—but then I do wrong every day, anyhow.

Now if you will be so kind as to drop me about a hundred & fifty lines, or more, or less, & tell me the names of the Consuls at Gibraltar & Marseilles, Miss Emma, you will confer a favor for which I shall be very greatly obliged to you. Mr. Beach or Capt. Duncan doubtless remember the~~ir~~ names. And please tell me the names of the Murillo pictures that delighted you most—& say all you can about them, too. Remember, I am in a great straight, now, & it is hard to have to write about pictures when I don't know anything about them. Hang the whole gang of old masters, *I* say! The idea that I have to go to driveling about those dilapidated, antediluvian humbugs at this late day, is exasperating. Why I don't ~~ever~~ even remember their names—except Titian, & Tintoretto, & some ‸of‸ those other infamous Italian Vandals. If you will help me, now, I will go to church every Sunday for a month—& ~~behave~~ steadily continue reforming.[2]

Yrs Truly
Sam Clemens

Miss Emma Beach | 66 Columbia street | Brooklyn, N. Y.

[1]Only two of Clemens's known newspaper letters were completed—that is, datelined—on 30–31 January: one to the Chicago *Republican* and one to the *Enterprise* (SLC 1868t, 1868gg). Three others include portions that may have been written on those two days: another to the *Enterprise*, one to the *Alta*, and one to the New York *Herald* (SLC 1868jj, 1868kk, 1868r). An untitled manuscript sketch, left unpublished by Clemens (and now known as "Colloquy between a

Slum Child and a Moral Mentor"), was also written at about this time, as was "My Late Senatorial Secretaryship," published in the May 1868 *Galaxy* (SLC 1868j, 1868ww).

[2]Horatio J. Sprague of Massachusetts had served as United States consul at Gibraltar since 1848; Emma's father mentioned his "kindness" and his "pleasant home and family" in a letter dated 9 July 1867 to the New York *Sun*. Martin F. Conway of Virginia was appointed United States consul at Marseilles in 1866. Neither consul was ultimately mentioned in *The Innocents Abroad*. Traveling with her father and four other passengers in July 1867, Emma had seen in the museums of Seville and Cádiz several paintings of Bartolomé Esteban Murillo (1617?–82), which Clemens could also have seen, albeit with less leisure, in October (Beach 1867b; Interior Department, 3, 4; State Department, 16; Senate 1887, 14 [2]: 857, 883; 24 Oct 67 to JLC and family, n. 1; Newell 1867c).

To John Russell Young
1 February 1868 • Washington, D.C.

(MS: DLC)

~~Tribune~~ 224 F street
Washington / Feb. 1.

Jno. Russell Young Esq

Dear Sir= I smouched those 3 Holy Land letters from the Alta & added 3 ~~in~~ at the end of the list to make up the deficiency, but ~~the~~ as you will see by the inclosed telegram, they don't seem to understand it.[1] So I wish you would tell Mr Hazard to forward them to me, & I will ship them out.[2]

Yrs Truly Sam L. Clemens

P.S. I told Jim Young all you said. You said you didn't write that Washington letter & I had to believe it, ~~thought~~ but by George, Horace himself says you wrote it! And besides, they papers here call it the Occasional Editorial.[3] Mrs. Wright told me what Mr Greeley said. His family has been stopping with the Wrights. I don't say that these things look suspicious—I only insinuate that ~~Horace~~ when Horace comes down here to look over his spectacles & beam on Congress, he has no business to circulate canards, you know![4]

There is nothing here of an exciting nature, except that the Intelligencer woke up in the most astonishing way this morning & told the world that there had been an eruption at Vesuvius. It is a wonderful paper.[5]

S L C.

[*letter docketed:*] ~~File. JRY~~ | *M*r. *Hassard* | *File.*

[1] The enclosure has not been found, but it was doubtless a recent telegram to Clemens from the editors or proprietors of the *Alta California*, pointing out that among his still unpublished Holy Land letters, numbers 40, 41, and 42 were missing (see 24 Nov 67 to Young, n. 1). The *Alta* people had, in fact, grown suddenly touchy, probably—as Clemens himself predicted on 24 January—because of his plan to reuse the letters without permission (see 24 Jan 68 to SLC and PAM, n. 12). On 19 January, for instance, when the *Alta* published letter number 35 (which describes famous places in the Holy Land and briefly recounts several Bible stories), they added an uncharacteristically testy remark:

> [Note by the Editors.—We have received a private letter from our correspondent, in which we expected some explanation of his strange conduct in presenting the above information to the public with such a confident air of furnishing news, but he offers none. He does not refer to the subject of the letter at all, except in the postscript, and then only to mention casually that he has inserted noth[ing] in it but what can be substantiated.] (SLC 1868i)

And on 21 January they published an emphatic claim to ownership of the Holy Land letters which went much beyond the simple copyright notice published at the top of each letter. The most immediate cause of their assertion was the Sacramento *Union*'s recent reprinting of a Mark Twain letter without a credit to the *Alta:*

> As this series of letters were paid for in advance of the departure of "Mark Twain" on the expedition and are the exclusive property of the Alta, as well by purchase as copyright, neither the *Union* nor any other paper has the legal or moral right to publish them. To say the least, if the Sacramento *Union* needed the humorous letter of our correspondent to brighten up its heavy, dull columns, they could have partially atoned for the act of piracy by stating that they had copied the letter in question from the Alta California. If the *Union* is altogether destitute of that courtesy which generally obtains among journalists, and cannot afford to credit its contemporaries with matter which their own enterprise has procured for them, it might, at least, have a wholesome respect for the law of copyright, which protects us in this particular instance. ("The Sacramento *Union* . . . ," San Francisco *Alta California*, 21 Jan 68, 2)

The *Union* replied by claiming that the omission of credit was unintentional ("credit was marked in the copy, but omitted by mistake in the setting up") ("A Small Matter," Sacramento *Union*, 23 Jan 68, 2). But the *Alta* editors rejoined even more aggressively, saying in part:

> This is a small matter, to be sure, and the *Union* is welcome to continue its depredations, but it must not feel hurt if we speak out when its thefts are specially flagrant. It is the only paper in the State that has failed to recognize the legal protection of the law of copyright. It has no right to copy Mark Twain's letters to the Alta, with or without credit. ("The Sacramento *Union* . . . ," San Francisco *Alta California*, 24 Jan 68, 2)

[2]John Rose Greene Hassard (1836–88) joined the *Tribune* staff in 1866. By December 1867 he had "taken charge of the musical column," while also serving as managing editor when Young was absent ("Personal," New York *World*, 2 Dec 67, 4). According to his fellow *Tribune* employee Amos J. Cummings, Hassard was

> a tall, straight gentleman, with a light complexion, blue eyes, regular features, sandy mustache and side whiskers, and legs like those of President Lincoln. . . . Mr. Hassard writes English as smooth as the music of a rippling brook, and frequently dashes off an editorial article steeped in an original solution of humor and sarcasm. (Cummings 1868b, 107)

[3]"The Political Situation. From an Occasional Correspondent," dated "Washington, Jan. 4, 1868," appeared on page one of the 6 January New York *Tribune*. The author of this bold article was an advocate of military enforcement of all Radical Reconstruction measures, and in favor of impeaching President Johnson. He attacked his fellow Republicans for their "halting, cowardly, and time-serving policy" and accused them of "eating turkey and plum pudding" while Johnson and his Southern supporters ignored all the Reconstruction laws. The author also seriously questioned the apparent choice of Grant as the 1868 Republican presidential candidate. He thought it was a sign of weakness to run a victorious general with no political experience, and further believed that Grant was controlled by a wealthy class of Northern investors who were selfishly demanding repayment of war bonds in gold from a financially vulnerable federal government. John H. Riley, Clemens's friend and fellow *Alta* correspondent, was among those who attributed the piece to John Russell Young, who was responsible for many of the *Tribune*'s editorials at this time (Riley 1868b). Its author, however, remains unidentified: the *Tribune* had not yet come out in favor of impeaching President Johnson. Young himself had been forced by Greeley in September 1867 to quash a pro-impeachment editorial; not until late February did he dare to defy his editor-in-chief and put the paper "firmly into the impeachment camp" (Broderick, 124–25).

[4]Greeley had married Mary Youngs Cheney (1814–72) of Cornwall, Connecticut, in 1836. Mrs. Greeley was known as an ill-tempered eccentric who adhered to rigid dietary practices and dabbled in spiritualism. Only two of the seven children born to the Greeleys were still alive: Ida (b. 1848) and Gabrielle (b. 1857). George Washington Wright (1816–85) was a merchant, banker, and former congressman from California (1850–51), who had declined the post of secretary of the interior under President Johnson. The Wrights' daughter, Eunice, was a special friend of Ida Greeley's. Mrs. Wright has not been further identified (Henry Luther Stoddard, 37–38, 106–7, 154, 319; Van Deusen, 148–53; Ida L. Greeley to Mrs. Wright, 3 Sept 67 and 5 Dec 67, George Washington Wright Papers, DLC).

[5]In late November, after a prolonged period of inactivity, Mount Vesuvius began to erupt, remaining active for several months. On 29 January the New York *Tribune* mentioned the continuing flow of lava, and on 30 January it reported that a landslide from the volcano had buried several houses and killed an unknown number of people. The Washington *National Intelligencer* failed to report this "unusual and very fatal catastrophe" until 31 January. On that date Clemens wrote the Chicago *Republican* that the *Intelligencer* "regularly comes out in the most sensational and aggressive manner, every morning, with news it

ought to have printed the day before." That same afternoon, however, the Washington *Evening Star* declared the landslide story a hoax, and on 1 February both the *Tribune* and the *Intelligencer* retracted their reports (SLC 1868t; New York *Tribune:* "Eruption of Vesuvius," 9 Dec 67, 1; "The Eruption of Mount Vesuvius," 29 Jan 68, 1; "The Eruption of Vesuvius," 30 Jan 68, 1; "A Hoax—No Caving in of Vesuvius," 1 Feb 68, 1; Washington *Evening Star:* "The Eruption of Mount Vesuvius," 30 Jan 68, 1; "The Vesuvius Story a Hoax," 31 Jan 68, 1; Washington *National Intelligencer:* "Eruption of Mount Vesuvius," 31 Jan 68, 3; "The Eruption of Mount Vesuvius," 1 Feb 68, 3).

To Elisha Bliss, Jr.
4 and 6 February 1868 • Washington, D.C.

(MS: CU-MARK)

‸N. Y. Tribune Bureau,‸
~~224 F street~~
Washington, Feb. 4,/68.

E. Bliss, Jr. Esq.

Dear Sir: If you ever do such a thing as give an author an advance, I wish you would advance me a thousand dollars. I have cut my newspaper correspondence down a good deal, but I believe that in order to ~~th~~ give to the book the amount of attention it really requires I shall have to cut loose from everything but one, & sometimes two, newspaper letters a week. One of our Senators suggested that I apply for the San Francisco postmastership, because, in case I got it I could perform its duties by Deputy, & then, in receipt of a large salary & perquisites, I could give myself up exclusively to scribbling.[1] So I went to work & ~~I believe I~~ have eternally ruined the chances of the most prominent of the swarm of candidates. But upon looking further into the matter I believe I have *created* work for myself instead of lightening prospective duties. It is a mistaken idea that the postmaster of San Francisco, ~~the~~ an office which wields a vast political power throughout the ~~whole~~ Pacific coast, can be an idle man. I have made a stupid blunder. ~~One~~ A Justice of the Supreme Court[2] has pledged himself to secure my nomination without difficulty; the Pacific Senatorial delegations[3] pledge themselves to secure its confirmation beyond a peradventure.

FEB. 6.—I have thrown away that office, when I had it in my grasp, because it was plain enough that I could not be postmaster & write the book, too. I can get another office when I want it, maybe. But it was worth from ten to twelve thousand a year.[4] In consideration whereof, if you can stand an advance, I wish you *would*, & relieve me of this newspaper corresponding until July. I think the book will be largely the gainer by it. I am satisfied of it, for the correspondence has a constant tendency to snatch me out of the ¢Excursion just as I am getting well interested in it.

If I can stand the *loss*, on the correspondence, of $300 a month for three months, don't you think you can stand the *loan* of it, you being capitalists & I being considerably otherwise? I am not making a demand—I am only making a request.[5]

If you have any curiosity as ‸to‸ that notable postoffice sacrifice, a note from you to Mr. Justice Field, of the Supreme Bench, & another to Senator Conness of California, will satisfy you. I perceive that I have a good deal of work before me. As nearly as I can figure it, my printed letters will fall considerably short of making *one-half* the book.

Yrs Very Truly
Sam L. Clemens

[*letter docketed:*] ✓ auth [*and*] Samuel J Clements | Feb 4/68

[1] This suggestion came from John Conness, senator from California. Conness (1821–1909), originally from Ireland, immigrated to the United States in 1833; after moving to California in 1849 he engaged in mining and mercantile pursuits. He twice served in the state legislature (1853–54, 1860–61), but was an unsuccessful candidate for governor in 1861. From 1863 to 1869 he served as a United States senator, first as a Democrat but later as a Union Republican. He was currently a member of the Committee on Post Offices and Post Roads, which reported to the Senate on presidential nominees for postmasterships. Since Lincoln's term of office, it "was generally conceded that the recommendation of a Republican congressman was the only qualification needed for appointment as postmaster," and that "Republican senators should control the appointment of postmasters in their own home towns" (Poore, 42; Cullinan, 79).

[2] Stephen J. Field.

[3] Senators John Conness and Cornelius Cole (California); William M. Stewart and James W. Nye (Nevada); and George H. Williams and Henry W. Corbett (Oregon).

[4] The official salary of the San Francisco postmaster was only $4,000, but since postal fees collected in that city amounted to nearly $117,000 in 1867, an unscrupulous postmaster could undoubtedly contrive to supplement his official income (Interior Department, 348). In January 1869, Clemens told Olivia Langdon that

the previous year he had "pledged our delegations to support me for Postmaster of San Francisco, but gave up *that* scheme as soon as I found that the place, honorably conducted, was only worth $4,000 a year & was too confining to allow me much time to write for newspapers" (SLC to OLL, 24 Jan 69, CU-MARK, in *LLMT*, 60). For a somewhat different explanation of Clemens's decision, see the next letter.

[5] Bliss's reply to this letter has not been found, but in 1912 Paine reported that Clemens obtained some kind of advance immediately before he sailed for California on 11 March. Newspaper rumors sometimes indicated that Clemens had received $10,000 in advance, but so large a sum seems improbable, and is not corroborated by what is known of Clemens's royalty payments, from which any advance would have been deducted (*MTB*, 1:362; "Books and Authors," Elmira *Advertiser*, 13 Aug 68, 3).

To Jane Lampton Clemens and Pamela A. Moffett
6 February 1868 • Washington, D.C.

(MS: NPV)

224 F street
Washington Feb. 6.

My Dear Mother & Sister—

For two months there have been some fifty applications before the government for the postmastership of San Francisco, which is the heaviest concentration of political power on the coast & consequently ~~m~~ is a post which is much coveted. When I found that a personal friend of mine, the Chief editor of the Alta was an applicant I said I didn't want it—I would not take $10,000 a year out of a friend's pocket.[1] The two months have passed. I heard day before yesterday that a new & almost unknown candidate had suddenly turned up on the inside track, & was to be appointed at once. I didn't like that—& when I heard that he had been recommended to make a friend of me & he said he didn't stand in need of me, I went after his case in a fine passion. I hunted up all our Senators & representatives & found that his name ~~wo~~ was ~~al~~ actually to come from the President at noon yesterday. I got a dozen Senators pledged against him, & had Judge Field of the Supreme Bench get out of his sick bed & visit the President early in the morning. It was jolly. In just no time at all I knocked that complacent idiot's kite so high that it never *will* come down.[2] Then Judge Field said if I wanted the place he could Pledge me the President's appointment—& Senator Conness said he would *guarantee* me the Senate's confirmation. It was a great temptation, but it would render it impossible to fill my book contract, & I had to drop the idea. I have to spend August & September in Hartford—which isn't San Francisco.[3] Mr. Conness offers me my choice out of five influential California offices—now some day or other I shall *want* an office & then, just my luck, I can't get it, I suppose. They want to send me abroad, as a Consul or a Minister.[4] I said I didn't want any of the pie. God knows I am mean enough & lazy enough, now, without being a foreign consul.

Some time in the course of the present century I think they will create a Commissioner of Patents,[5] & then I hope to get a berth for Orion.

I published 6 or 7 letters in the Tribune while I was gone[6]—now I cannot get them. I suppose I must have them copied.

Love to all.

Yrs

Sam,

[1] Clemens described this editor as "one of my best old friends" (10 Feb 68 to Beach). He was Matthias (or Matthew) Gilbert Upton (1829?–97), principal editor of the San Francisco *Alta California* since 1861 and now presumably first among equals with editors Noah Brooks and John S. Hittell. Born in Ireland and educated at Dublin University, Upton began his journalism career on the New York *Herald*, where he became city editor. He moved to California in about 1852 and worked on the San Francisco *Herald* before joining the *Alta* staff. In 1866 and early 1867 he was on recreational leave "after a long and unremitting attention to duty," but he was still writing "editorial correspondence" from the East for the *Alta* until the newspaper sent him to Paris in mid-April. By 1 September, however, he had returned to his post in San Francisco (SLC 1868tt; Rowell, 11; Langley 1868, 111, 282, 550; Upton 1867a–c; San Francisco *Alta California:* "Arrival of the 'Golden City,'" 2 Sept 67, 1; "Editorial Notes," 26 June 72, 2; "His Trenchant Pen at Rest Forever," San Francisco *Call*, 6 Feb 97, 14; San Francisco City and County 1867, s.v. "Upton, Matthias Gilbert").

[2] The "new & almost unknown candidate" was Charles A. Kennedy, a San Francisco merchant known to be a "party Democrat." Senator Cole and California Congressman Samuel B. Axtell supported Kennedy, while Congressman James A. Johnson (also from California) opposed him, as did Senator Conness, who favored Upton (Langley 1868, 318; Rincon 1868b; Jorkins 1868a and 1868b). On 2 March Clemens wrote to the *Enterprise*, "It seems the President not only promised the gentleman [i.e., Field] I requested to go to him that he would cancel the horseman's [i.e., Kennedy's] appointment, but with aggravated generosity said he believed he would not appoint anybody at all for the present" (SLC 1868tt). "Kite" is an archaic spelling of "kyte," which means "belly." Clemens's metaphor ("knocked that . . . kite so high") echoes one he

used in a July 1867 *Alta* letter, where he said that the Italian navy had been completely obliterated, "knocked higher than Gilderoy's kite." The expression alludes to a "celebrated robber" hanged in Edinburgh in 1636 "on an unusually high gallows" (SLC 1867zz; *Lex*, 94).

[3]Clemens expected to deliver the manuscript of his book to the American Publishing Company at the beginning of August, and to stay in Hartford long enough to undertake any necessary manuscript revisions and attend to other aspects of book production (27 Jan 68 to Bliss).

[4]In January 1869 Clemens recalled this period for Olivia Langdon, explaining his decision in rather more purposeful terms:

> Why, a year ago, in Washington, when Mr. Conness, one of our Senators, counseled me to take the post of United States Minister to China, when Mr. Burlingame resigned (the place was chiefly in Mr. C.'s gift,) I said that even if I could feel thoroughly fitted for the place, I had at last become able to make a living at home & wished to settle down—& that if I roamed more, it must be in pursuit of my regular calling & to further my advancement in my legitimate profession. (SLC to OLL, 24 Jan 69, CU-MARK, in *LLMT*, 60)

Anson Burlingame had resigned as minister to China in November 1867 when he accepted an appointment from the Chinese government (see 19 Feb 68 to Burlingame [1st of 2], n. 2). The minister's position went ultimately to Clemens's friend and fellow writer J. Ross Browne, who had been nominated minister to China in late January 1868 and was confirmed in March (Senate 1887, 16:156, 194; see 17 June 67 to Fairbanks, n. 7).

[5]See 24 Jan 68 to JLC and PAM, n. 13.

[6]Clemens published six letters in the *Tribune:* see 20 Nov 67 to JLC and family (2nd of 2), n. 1.

To Mary Mason Fairbanks
9 February 1868 • Washington, D.C.

(MS: CSmH)

‸76‸ ‸76‸
‸76‸ ~~79~~ Indiana Avenue } ‸76‸
‸76‸ Washington, Feb. 9. } ‸76‸[1]

My Dear Mother—

Glory, I have found it! I have found your long-lost letter—the best one you ever wrote me. It was in my pocket all the time—placed, for greater security, along with my sister's photograph, in an envelop about four years old. They have written to me several times to know how I like her picture, & I have been dodging that question with masterpieces of ingenuity that filled me with admiration but kept me in a state of constant worry. Sometimes I was almost driven to come right out with the truth & say I had lost it. And I just expected to "catch it" from you, too. "Catch it" is slang, but it is of the mild sort—I am tapering off with the fullest satisfaction to myself.

I am sick in bed, & *have* been, for four or five days; but I am so glad I found that letter that I am very well able to sit up & write. I am glad, & grateful, to be placed upon your list of friends, for I honor & esteem you more than I can tell. I am *bound* to wander out of the straight path & do outrageous things, occasionally, & I believe I have ~~got~~ a genuinely bad heart ‸anyhow‸—but in the course of time I will get some of the badness out of it or break it.

. . . .

[1]Clemens had presumably just moved to this address, possibly from 356 C Street North, which he had given as the return address of his 15 January letter to Webb. It is also possible that he left the C Street address when he went to New York and Hartford in January, and then stayed again briefly with Senator Stewart at 224 F Street North upon his return to Washington. On 21 February he would tell his family that he had moved five times since leaving Stewart's rooms, but only the C Street address and 76 Indiana Avenue—his current address—are known. Because he was moving frequently throughout this period, Clemens sometimes used 224 F Street for his return address, on the assumption that he could always collect his mail from Stewart, who still lived there.

To Emeline B. Beach
10 February 1868 • Washington, D.C.

(MS: Feldman)

‸☞ P S.—Don't skip any of this letter, now—because it is just *full* of wisdom.

———————————————————————————‸

76 Indiana Avenue
Washington, Feb. 10.

~~Well,~~ Shipmate, ‸Avast! (whatever *that* may mean—but it is a good sea-going word, anyhow)‸—I am sick in bed. I have had a long siege of it, now, & am getting very, very much opposed to it. I did a vast quantity of work during the first few days & nights after I arrived here; then I heard that a blundering adventurer whom nobody knows had quietly ingratiated himself with the officials here & was about to get the San Francisco Postmastership, a place that one of my best old friends has long been a candidate for. I started out at 7 in the evening, ~~in a~~ & by ~~min~~ midnight I had seen every Senator of the Pacific delegation, & had had *such* a time bullying & badgering & persuading them—but I gained my point—they pledged themselves to kill the nomination if it ever got into the Senate. But I did not want it to get even that far. I arranged to go with a friend to see the President early in the morning & see if he would not take some more time before appointing this man—& then I came home & went to bed & have been there ever since. But the nomination ~~is n~~ has not gone to the Senate & *is* not going. My good friend argued the case well with his Royal Highness, & I might have spoiled it. That was a most excellent night's work—& the excitement of it was fine. I think those people never knew before that I had any energy in me. They were really complimentary. They said ~~the~~ *I* should have the nomination & the confirmation too, beyond any question, if I would say the word.[1] Ah, but wouldn't I throw dignity into that position?—and wouldn't I wield its vast political power with a royal spirit?—& moreover wouldn't I send all my friends' letters through the mails free of postage?—aye, & their baggage too, for that matter~~?~~,—& finally wouldn't I tyrannize over all the newspapers, from Utah & Montana, to Japan & China; & from Alaska to the Isthmus, if they didn't speak respectfully of me? I would soon let the public know what it is to have a cruel despot over them. I shall certainly have to be Postmaster under the new dispensation that comes into power a year hence. But I shall always guard against another burst of energy; it ~~m~~h has made me sick once—it might destroy me next time.

I think you were ever so kind to write me a long letter when you were so busy. Very few young ladies would take so much trouble to do me a kindness, I can tell you. And so I am cheerfully willing to bear them the bitterest malice on account of it. Dinner, gymnasium, French, German, music, letter-writing, practicing—it makes my head ache to think of it. It is well that by nature you move quickly—~~as if you ‸were‸ hung on watch-springs, as it were.~~ ‸for otherwise I am afraid that some of those duties would have to go by default.‸

Ah—Harrison, is it?—Miss Harrison. Now you must pardon me, but really I ~~haven't a bit of~~ ‸won't acknowledge full‸ confidence in Miss Harrison's critical judgment. "And now he **feels** the **nicest** *distinctions* of beauty, etc." To get the right word in the right place is a rare achievement. To condense the diffused light of a page of thought into the luminous flash of a single sentence, is worthy to rank as a prize composition just by itself. Now, I don't ~~honestly~~ think H. can do that.[2] Why, I could take sentences from your letters that would rather ~~sir~~ surprise that young woman. You know very well that I am particularly fond of a happy expression, & that I never tired of reading that Howajji in Syria, simply because it could furnish that charm in such profusion.[3] *Any*body can have ideas—the difficulty is to **express** them, without squandering a quire of paper on an idea that ought to be reduced to one glittering paragraph. I charge you to believe that I am not trying to flatter you, for I am not. I am only defending what I have said in a former letter—for when ‸that‸ dreadful teacher "glances" at a composition & throws it aside, it looks, to a casual spectator, somewhat as if my point is not well taken—as they say in the House. Yes—you are right—I *would* rather receive a letter written to me, even though it were short, than a composition, albeit if you did send the latter *I* wouldn't be so criminal as to throw it aside with a "glance"—no sir-*ee!* That was just like Mr. Beecher, for the world. I might have known where ~~that~~ ‸it‸ came from. I sent to a San Francisco paper, the other day, a first-rate anecdote about Mr. Beecher which was told me by old Richelieu Robinson, your jolly member of Congress from Brooklyn. *It* was just like Mr. B., too.[4]

And now while I think of it, Ancient Mariner, I wish you would just hint to Mr. Beecher in a sort of general way, some time or other, that you doubt if I ever returned him the change ~~owing~~ ‸due‸ from that $10 he entrusted to me that night at your house—do you remember?—when he wanted some funeral notices published. Now don't **ask** him—that won't do at all—but say you think I would be likely to steal it—you might mention that I used to steal things in the ship—say anything, you know, that will be likely to make him say whether he ever received that change or not. The amount is a matter of no consequence, but the idea of resting under even the remotest suspicion of having deliberately swindled a minister out of three dollars, is almost disagreeable to me. Now I wouldn't speak so boastingly to everybody, but I will say to *you*, that in the whole course of my life I hardly remember ‸ever having‸ ~~one instance of having~~ stolen money from a minister. Why, I have been so strictly reared that sometimes I look upon a thing like that almost in the light of a crime. Ah, very few people ~~h~~ are fettered with the moral sensibilities that warp *my* judgment. But don't you pay any attention to all this nonsense. You have enough to do without my sitting up nights to invent new schemes for bothering you. I just drifted into this subject because it occurs to me a little unpleasantly sometimes that that mail *might* have miscarried. But you know that it cannot have distressed me unbearably else I would have written Mr. Beecher on the momentous subject long ago.

"Do I suppose that you are going to tell me about those pictures & go into ecstasies over them, only that I may make fun of them?" Now *what* can you mean by such conduct as those? Don't you accuse me of such things. Put you to all that trouble, ‸—a task‸ which you have done so well, & with such an honest good will and with such self-evident earnestness, & then make fun ~~—eith~~ of the subject of it? Upon my word & honor I would not do anything of the kind. I have joked about the old masters a good deal in my letters, but nearly all of that will have to come out. I cannot afford to expose my want of cultivation too much. Neither can I afford to remain so uncultivated—& shall not, if I am capable of rising above it. In this I am freely acknowledging what you have said in this connection. With your letter to ~~go~~ ‸be guided‸ by, I can talk learnedly about Murillo, & appreciatively, withal—& I mean to do it, too.[5] That will rather surprise ~~Mr.~~ Mrs. Fairbanks, who looks upon me as a heretic in art. You say the legend of St Catherine is enchanting when given in full—cannot you try & give it me in full yourself? I wish you would.[6] If you can't recollect accurately, *invent—invent*—let the sin be upon my head. I think that book of mine will be full of inventions anyhow. Give me some more art essays—do. It just suits your pen, because you take so much interest in the subject—& I think some wiseacre has said people write with most facility upon matters they feel an interest in. Tell me about any of those old geniuses. I shan't make fun. Why did you go & lose that note-book?—hadn't you better hunt it up?

I had no difficulty at all in reading your "scrawl," as you call it—but I claim no credit on that account—it was distinct & legible. ~~If you~~ I did not have to "throw it in the fire." If you *want* to "write better next time," I am entirely willing that you should humor yourself to that extent, but I assure you that I am well able to decipher what you put upon the paper even without your taking that pains. Try me, ~~, & see.~~ ‸& verily you shall see.‸ There is no proof like circumstantial evidence.

I came near neglecting to thank you for furnishing me those consul~~'~~s' names—but I do it now, & right heartily.[7] You see I "survived."

You came near being sarcastic that time, my honored correspondent. *That* will never do. ‸You just barely escaped a lecture.‸

I expect you to read all this, ø even if you miss a lesson or two—no, don't miss the lessons—let your dinner go over till next day—this thing of eating dinner *every* day grows monotonous after a while, anyhow.

I have ~~worked~~ ‸written‸ myself up into a comfortable state of convalescence, I believe—& forthwith I will make use of it and write a newspaper letter. ‸Please drop me a line or two—say several hundred.‸

Yrs Truly
Sam L. Clemens

[1] See 6 Feb 68 to JLC and PAM.

[2] Miss Harrison, Emma Beach's teacher, has not been further identified.

[3] *The Howadji in Syria* by George W. Curtis (New York: Harper and Brothers, 1852). In 1907 Emma (Beach) Thayer recalled for Paine that on board the *Quaker City* Clemens

> used to stay up late at night. The way he put it was "I've got to stay up till two o'clock—keep me company—it is beautiful under the stars." He got up late—about ten in the morning. . . . He would call my attention to the beauty of Curtis' language in The Howaji in Syria, reading passages aloud. (Thayer to A. B. Paine, 22 June 1907, Davis 1967a, 2)

[4] Clemens's anecdote about Henry Ward Beecher has not been recovered. "Richelieu Robinson" was William Erigena Robinson (1814–92). Born in Ireland, he immigrated to the United States in 1836 and was graduated from Yale College in 1841. Joining the staff of the New York *Tribune* as an assistant editor in 1843, he then served until 1848 as one of its Washington correspondents, signing himself "Richelieu." He was now a Democratic congressman from Brooklyn (1867–69). Robinson was among the several "honorary members" who had attended the annual dinner of the Washington Newspaper Correspondents' Club on 11 January (see 14 Jan 68 to JLC and family, n. 1) (Marbut, 71; "The Press Banquet," Washington *National Intelligencer*, 13 Jan 68, 2).

[5] See 31 Jan 68 to Beach.

[6] Beach evidently complied with this further request, for some months later, Clemens included an account of the legend in a chapter devoted to his trip through Spain and intended for, but ultimately omitted from, *The Innocents Abroad:*

> The legend of St Catherine (everybody believes it in Spain,) is curious. She was a rich queen, who devoted herself to philosophy. Her subjects did not like the reclusive life she led, & determined she should marry. So the best, the purest, the most learned, & in every way the most perfect man, was sought—for he indeed must be good that should be worthy of her. She ~~desired~~ declared that she would have none that was not her equal, for she desired not to marry. Finally, a monk sent her a picture of Christ, & one also of the Virgin—who, he said, had declared her Son should be husband to Catherine. She slept with the picture in her room, & dreampt that a throng of angels conducted her into the presence of Christ, but that he refused her, saying she was not worthy. Her grief awoke her, & she went to the monk. He told her she must become a Christian. She was consequently baptised.

The next night she dreampt she was again conducted into the presence of Jesus, who then accepted her, & as a pledge of their union, put a ring on her finger. When she awoke in the morning she found the ring was still on ~~fin~~ her finger & knew that the ~~vis~~ seeming vision was a reality. The cruel Maximin tried to make ~~Mrs. C.~~ her renounce her faith, but so far from doing it she ~~con~~ ~~went~~ converted the forty doctors ‸he‸ sent to convince her! This system was not profitable. ~~It was~~ Another was substituted. She was ordered to be placed between two sharp-pointed wheels (hence the "Catherine-wheel" so popular in ~~fir~~ modern fire-works,) revolving with great velocity in different directions. But the moment she was put there the wheels flew asunder & killed her executioners & three thousand people, thus creating ~~great~~ ‸considerable‸ diversion, & angels descended & carried her body over the Red Sea to Mount Sinai, where they buried it. One sees often in America the beautiful engraving of the angels bearing the body of St. Catherine away through the clouds. I shall always look upon it with interest hereafter, & think of the scatterment ~~that~~ ‸the‸ wheel made when it ~~collapsed its flue.~~ ‸burst.‸ (SLC 1868hhh, 1324–28†)

[7] See 31 Jan 68 to Beach.

To Anson Burlingame
19 February 1868 • (1st of 2) • Washington, D.C.
(Cyril Clemens, 18–19)

224 F street,
Washington, Feb. 18.[1]

Your Excellency—

Don't neglect or refuse to keep a gorgeous secretaryship or a high interpretership for me in your great embassy—for pilgrim as I am, I have not entirely exhausted Europe yet, & may want to get converse with some of those Kings again, by & bye.[2]

I am writing a prodigious 600-page *book*, now—a seductive book with pictures on every page—for the great subscription Publishing Co., of Hartford, who publish for Greeley & I exclusively[3]—but I shall have this book done before autumn, & then I think I shall want to be an interpreter. I always *did* want to be an interpreter. It is the only ambition I have.

Please remember me most kindly & respectfully to Mrs. Burlingame, & tell that boy of yours to drop me a line, for I doubt not you are too busy to write to people yourself.[4]

Yours Very Truly,
Samuel L. Clemens.

[1] The manuscript of the next letter, a "duplicate" of this one, shows that the date was probably 19 February. It is not known whether this letter ever reached Burlingame; its provenance and current location are likewise unknown.

[2] In June 1866 in Honolulu, Burlingame (1820–70), who had been "envoy extraordinary and minister plenipotentiary from the United States to China" since 1861, met and befriended Clemens, inviting him to come and stay with him in Peking. Burlingame resigned as minister in November 1867, and thereupon accepted a post offered him by the emperor of China as "envoy on behalf of the Chinese government to all the treaty powers," charged with visiting these nations in order to express China's "sincere desire to be friendly and progressive" and to discuss its position on renewal or revision of treaties in effect since 1858 (SLC to JLC and PAM, 27 June 66, *L1*, 347–48; Burlingame to William H. Seward, 21 Nov 67 and 14 Dec 67, Congress, 1:493–94; S. Wells Williams to Seward, 23 Dec 67, Congress, 1:495–96). At the time of this letter, which Clemens probably directed to San Francisco, Burlingame was about to leave Hong Kong on his way to Washington (via San Francisco), the first stop on his tour of the capitals of western nations, which was to include (among others) London, Paris, Berlin, and St. Petersburg ("Arrival of the 'China' from China and Japan," San Francisco *Alta California*, 1 Apr 68, 1). Clemens did not accompany or later join Burlingame; he did, however, publish an article in the New York *Tribune* about the Chinese mission (SLC 1868nn). Burlingame died of pneumonia in Russia in 1870, on the verge of completing his diplomatic assignment.

[3] See 24 Jan 68 to JLC and PAM, n. 4.

[4] Burlingame married Jane Cornelia Livermore in June 1847. Their son, Edward Livermore Burlingame (1848–1922), left Harvard College in his first year and accompanied his father as a secretary upon the latter's return to China in the summer of 1866, when Clemens met both of them in Honolulu. Clemens later recalled Edward as "a handsome boy of nineteen, and overflowing with animation, activity, energy, and the pure joy of being alive" (AD, 20 Feb 1906, CU-MARK, in *MTA*, 2:125).

To Anson Burlingame
19 February 1868 • (2nd of 2) • Washington, D.C.

(MS: DLC)

224 F street,
Washington, Feb. ~~18~~ 19.

Your Excellency

This is to duplicate a letter I wrote you today by the unreliable Overland Mail[1],—wherein was set forth that I shall have completed my book in the course of a couple of months or so, & then I would like to go with your Embassy as a dignitary of some kind or other, & privately on my own hook as Herald & Tribune correspondent. I want to be a mild sort of dignitary, though, particularly. Pray save me a place. Correspondents will hover about the Expedition anyhow, & so it will be best for the interests of China & the world, that one of them, at least, should be *reliable*.

With kindest regards to ~~you~~ my ~~s~~ Sandwich Islands acquaintances among your now exceedingly large family,[2] I remain,

Yours Very Truly
Mark Twain

[*letter docketed:*] M. Twain, *etc.*

[1] See the previous letter. Presumably this duplicate was sent by the slower but more reliable Pacific Mail Steamship line; it did, in fact, reach Burlingame, in whose papers it has survived.

[2] Clemens makes a playful reference to the large size of Burlingame's household staff, some of whom he apparently met in Honolulu. Burlingame's current entourage numbered nearly thirty officials, servants, and translators ("Arrival of the Chinese Embassy," San Francisco *Alta California*, 1 Apr 68, 1).

To Mary Mason Fairbanks
20 February 1868 • Washington, D.C.

(MS: CSmH)

76 Indiana avenue,
Wash= Feb. 20.

My Dear Mother=

Your most welcome letter is by me, & I must hurry & write while your barometer is at "fair," ~~but~~ ‸for‸ it isn't within the range of possibility that I can refrain long from doing something that will fetch it down to "stormy~~,~~," again.

I ac‸k‸nowledge—I acknowledge—that I *can* be most laceratingly "funny without being vulgar." In proof whereof, I responded again to the regular toast to Woman at a grand banquet night before last, & was frigidly proper in language & sentiment. Read the enclosed notice & see if they accuse me once.[1] *Now* haven't I nobly vindicated myself & shed honor upon my teacher & done credit to ~~my lessons~~ her teachings? With head uncovered, & in attitude ~~unostentatious~~ ‸suppliant‸ but yet expressive of conscious merit, I stand before you in spirit & await my earned "Well done," & augmented emolument of bread & butter—to the end that I may go & slide on the cellar door & be happy.

You just smother me with compliments about that book![2] There is nothing that makes me prouder than to be regarded by intelligent people as "authentic." A name I have coveted so long—& secured at last! *I* don't care anything about being humorous, or poetical, or eloquent, or anything of that kind—the end & aim of my ambition is to be authentic—is to be considered authentic. But don't italicise it—don't do that—~~such a~~ there isn't any need of it—*such* a compliment as that, wouldn't have escaped my notice, even without the underscore.

So far, I believe I haven't indulged in any "flings" that people will mind much. Only one occurs to me just now that I revel in with peculiar ecstasy. It is in the first chapter & just touches Dr. Gibson on a raw place. If he were a man of any appreciation, it would be a royal pleasure to see him waltz around when he reads that. But bless you it will all be lost. That complacent imbecile will take it for a compliment. I do not mention his name, but I *think* all the passengers will know who is meant. Now I know that you will begin to worry about this, & so I will just put in a part of it here so that you may see that it really amounts to nothing. You will not find any fault with it:

‸[I am supposed to be reading the passenger list at 117 Wall st.]‸

"I was proud to observe that among our excursionists were three ministers of the gospel, eight doctors, sixteen or eighteen ladies, several military & naval ~~chef~~ chieftains with sounding titles, an ample crop of Prof~~f~~essors of various kinds, & a gentleman who had "COMMISSIONER OF THE UNITED STATES OF AMERICA TO EUROPE, ASIA & AFRICA" thundering after his name in one awful blast! I had carefully prepared myself to take rather a back seat in that ship, because of the uncommonly select material that would only be permitted to pass through the camel's eye[3] of that committee on credentials; I had schooled myself to expect an imposing array of military & naval heroes, & to have to set that back seat still further back in consequence of it, maybe; but I state frankly that I was all unprepared for *this* crusher! ~~¶~~ I fell under that titular avalanche a torn & blighted thing. I said that if that potentate *must* go over in our ship, why, I supposed he must—but that to my thinking, when the United States considered it necessary to send a dignitary of that tonnage across the ocean, it would be in better taste, & safer, to cart him over in several ships.

"Ah, if I had only known, then, that he was only a common mortal, & that his mission had nothing more overpowering about it than the collecting of seeds, and uncommon yams, & extraordinary cabbages for that poor useless, innocent, harmless old fossil, the Smithsonian Institute, I would have felt *so* much relieved."[4]

Now there is *all* of it, instead of part—& it is *so* mean, & depreciative, & rascally, that I just turn it over as a sweet morsel under my tongue! [Barometer swinging surely around to "Stormy."] Goodness, how I *would* like to see that fellow skip! But he won't—he won't—I shall lose all that. He will think it is a compliment, & go around spelling it over to his asinine neighbors. Now *you* think I bear that man ~~male~~ malice—but upon my sacred word I don't. I would ask him to dinner with me in a minute if I were to meet him—& what he did there or said there, I never would mention disrespectfully, of course—but what he did in the ship is fair ~~pray~~ prey, & *don't you plead for him*~~,~~—you nor Mrs. Severance either—I have your pictures, & I'll distort them & put them in the book. And I'll represent old Mr. Severance as propelling donkeys in the Azores with a ~~g~~ stick with a nail in the end of it at forty cents a day.[5]

No, I don't need a guardian *now*, because I am reformed, now—I have finished up since I wrote last. As soon as I got well enough I began a regular system of working all day long & taking the whole night for recreation—*and* sleep. I don't write *any*thing at night, now. I can write about ten pages of the book a day, pretty comfortably—fifteen, if necessary. Unless I get too much pushed for time I think I will write ~~the~~ almost the entire book new—I don't like *any* of those letters that have reached me from California so far.[6] I may think better of those you weeded of slang, though. There will not be any slang in this book except it should occur in a mild form in dialogues.

You are right. One should not bring sympathy to a sick man. It is always kindly meant, & of course it has to be taken—but it isn't much of an improvement on castor oil. One who has a sick man's true interest at heart will forbear spoken sympathy, & bring him~~,~~ surreptitious~~ly~~ soup, & fried oysters & other trifles that the doctor has tabooed. That is much better than saying, "O, I am *so* sorry you are so ill; you look meaner & meaner all the time, poor man; your eyes are turning yellow & your nose looks like a wen; O, if you were to be taken away from us in your present state, how sad it would be; I will make you some weak gruel & send you up some tracts." Gruel & tracts for a spirit that is famishing for salt-horse & duff![7]

YES, I want your *Herald* letters, of course. I have Dr Jackson's, & Foster is trying to collect his for me. I only want to steal the *ideas*—I am not going to steal the language. Now please hurry them up—there's a good mother.[8]

What has Beach done? Why he has been a regular Good Samaritan in hunting up employment & giving material aid to the bankrupt cabin crew of the Quaker City—& I am sure they deserved little kindness at *his* hands.[9]

You wasn't one of the "frisky old veterans"—don't insinuate such a thing.[10] Remember me to Mr & Mrs S.[11] & *all your* family—whereof I shall be proud to be "Head Cub."

Al~~l~~ways yr friend
Sam L. Clemens.

[*enclosure:*]

Fourth. Woman :
"**All honor**, to woman, the sweetheart, the **wife;**
The delight of the fireside by night and by **day,**
Who never does anything wrong in her life,
Except when permitted to have her own **way.**"

To this toast the renowned humorist and writist, Mark Twain, responded, and it is superfluous to say that while he stood upon the floor declaiming for the fair divinities all that banqueting crew laid down with laughter. His sliding scene; his trials and tribulations; those he had paid for—and not; his valentine; his sublime inspirations and humorous deductions set the very table in a roar. He's a phunny fellow and no mistake, and blessed, indeed, were the G. F.'s with the honor of his company.

[1]The "grand banquet" at which Clemens spoke took place on 14 February, not on the "night before last," as he indicated. In an *Enterprise* letter dated merely "February" (but presumably written on the fifteenth) Clemens enclosed another copy of the flattering "notice," explaining that he

was at a banquet given to the honorable "Society of Good Fellows," last night, and it was a particularly cheerful affair. I mention this subject more particularly, because I wish to introduce in this connection what I consider to be a genuine, uncompromising and unmitigated "first-rate notice." Let the Washington *Express* be your model in matters of this kind hereafter. (SLC 1868*ll*)

The notice appeared on the fourth page of the Washington *Evening Express*, edited by J. D. and A. P. Hoover, where it was part of a much longer report, "Ye Banquet," published on 15 February. The quatrain to which Clemens was asked to respond was "the last poetical production" of Fitz-Greene Halleck (1790–1867), inscribed "in a lady's album," presumably shortly before his death in November 1867; it had apparently been widely quoted in print since then (Rowell, 15; "A Bachelor-Poet's Idea of Woman," New York *Ledger* 23 [1 Feb 68]: 4). Although the clipping enclosed here was pinned, then pasted, to the first leaf of the manuscript, it is unlikely that Clemens attached it in either way, and it therefore appears as a simple enclosure after his signature.

[2] *The Celebrated Jumping Frog of Calaveras County.*

[3] Matthew 19:24: "It is easier for a camel to go through the eye of a needle, than for a rich man to enter into the kingdom of God."

[4] Months before the *Quaker City* departed in June, William Gibson, M.D. (1813–87), of Jamestown, Pennsylvania, had written to the Department of Agriculture and the Smithsonian Institution, offering to collect specimens and information while traveling with the excursion party. On 5 April Commissioner Isaac Newton accepted on behalf of the agriculture department, sending Gibson a letter of introduction addressed "To the United States Ministers & Consuls in Europe, Asia & Africa." The letter stated that Gibson was "hereby commissioned, and accredited by this Department, during his tour through Europe and Asia, to make investigations, observe and collect facts in all matters that may in his opinion be of interest to the Agriculture of the United States." In a letter of further instructions on 24 April Newton directed Gibson to collect data on such things as "the appearances of crops, prices of food and labor," as well as "specimens of cereals and sea shells, etc." On 2 May Joseph Henry of the Smithsonian Institution declined to receive articles such as these, of which it already had "an abundant supply," but added that "we shall be most happy to obtain by your aid any additions of rare or choice mineral specimens, to be deposited in the National Museum under our charge" (Pommer, 386–87). Somewhat later in May, when Gibson appeared in the passenger list posted at Duncan's office, he had not quite become a "Commissioner of the United States of America," but he was identified as "Wm. Gibson, Esq., of the State Department, special agent of the government." And when in September he and the other passengers received a copy of the Arabic New Testament (see 1–2 Oct 67 to Moffett), the printed inscription in his copy read, in part: "Wm. Gibson M.D., Jamestown, Pa. Special Commissioner, commissioned by the State Department Washington, D.C. U.S.A. To Palestine, Arabia, and Egypt" ("The Mediterranean Excursion," New York *World*, 10 May 67, 2; Leamington Book Shop, lot 131). Gibson proved to be a zealous collector of mementoes and specimens. Although there is no evidence that he ever contributed anything to the Smithsonian or to the Department of Agriculture, in late 1868 or early 1869 he donated his *Quaker City* collection to the "Historic Relic and Geological Committee of the Young Men's Christian Association" in Erie, Pennsylvania, not far from Jamestown. In reporting this gift early in 1869, the Erie *Dispatch* characterized his appointment as "a commission of the late administration" and explained that as "an official he

Autographed *carte de visite* of Dr. Gibson, preserved by Colonel William R. Denny. Collection of Mrs. Theodore Whitfield. See p. 192 n. 4.

possessed many facilities for collecting geological specimens, curiosities and relics not possessed by the ordinary tourist, and which were well improved." A list of the "most interesting" items consisted of some forty specimens of water, rock, pebbles, mosaics, broken sculpture, petrifactions, and other samples—including "specimens from the highest point of the Pyramid Cheops, Egypt," "specimen from the Rock of Gibraltar," and "specimen from a broken column in front of the Amphitheatre, where stood the temple of the goddess Diana at Ephesus" ("Historical Relics," Erie [Pa.] *Dispatch*, undated clipping, probably Jan–June 69, CU-MARK; Pommer, 389). The paragraphs that Clemens quoted here from his manuscript of *The Innocents Abroad* (now lost) appeared in chapter 2 virtually without change.

[5] Like most of the passengers, Clemens exchanged photographic *cartes de visite* with several of his friends, and he undoubtedly had such photographs of Mrs.

Fairbanks and the Severances. He also collected commercially produced photographs of historical figures, buildings, and sites, as well as at least some of the stereographic photographs made by the ship's photographer, William E. James, of the actual sights witnessed by the travelers. Clemens evidently turned this collection over to Bliss in October 1868 to be engraved as illustrations for *The Innocents Abroad*. Pictures of several passengers appeared in the book, clearly engraved from their photographs, but neither Mrs. Fairbanks nor the Severances were among them. (See Hirst and Rowles, 15–33, and Hirst 1975, 198–222, 390–412, which reproduces photographic *cartes de visite* of some forty-five *Quaker City* passengers and crew from the collection of William R. Denny.)

[6] In 1883 an unidentified journalist who knew Clemens in Washington at this time provided a description of him at work on his book in his "room in Indiana Avenue":

> And there was Mark Twain in a little back room, with a sheet-iron stove, a dirty, musty carpet of the cheapest description, a bed, and two or three common chairs. The little drum stove was full of ashes, running over on the zinc sheet; the bed seemed to be unmade for a week, the slops had not been carried out for a fortnight, the room was foul with tobacco smoke, the floor, dirty enough to begin with, was littered with newspapers, from which Twain had cut his letters. Then there were hundreds of pieces of torn manuscripts which had been written and then rejected by the author. A dozen pipes were about the apartment—on the wash-stand, on the mantel, on the writing table, on the chairs—everywhere that room could be found. And there was tobacco, and tobacco everywhere. One thing, there were no flies. The smoke killed them, and I am now surprised the smoke did not kill me too. Twain would not let a servant come into his room. He would strip down his suspenders (his coat and vest, of course, being off) and walk back and forward in slippers in his little room and swear and smoke the whole day long. Of course, at times he would work, and when he did work it was like a steam engine at full head. I do believe that if Clemens had not been under contract to write for the Hartford firm his "Innocents Abroad," he never would have done it.
>
> Of course, at that time, we never thought that Twain's book would amount to anything, and probably he did not think it would either, but he was writing for the money his naked MS. would bring from his Hartford publishers. He needed that money, and so he wrote. ("How 'Innocents Abroad' Was Written," New York *Evening Post*, 20 Jan 83, 3)

[7] Salt horse was the "standard army ration of pickled beef preserved in brine so strong that it was inedible unless soaked thoroughly in water before cooking. Often the pickling process was not successful" (Boatner, 719). "Duff" was a slang term for "any sweet food, such as candy, cake, or cookies" (Wentworth and Flexner, 166).

[8] See 24 Jan 68 to Fairbanks, n. 4. Clemens had secured copies of Dr. Jackson's letters to the Monroe County (Pa.) *Democrat*, and was hoping to obtain the letters that Colonel J. Heron Foster, owner and chief editor of the Pittsburgh *Dispatch*, sent to his own newspaper. Clemens probably did find some remarks to jog his memory in both Jackson's and Mrs. Fairbanks's letters. The burlesque of the address to the tsar performed by the *Quaker City*'s crew was a detail mentioned only by her which found its way into chapter 38. Jackson's descriptions of the glove-buying incident in Gibraltar (chapter 7), and the hiring of a guide in Paris (chapter 13), may also have supplied useful hints for Clemens (Hirst 1975, 132–33, 153–54; Mary Mason Fairbanks 1867b; Abraham Reeves Jackson 1867b, 1867d). But it is not known whether Clemens ever saw Foster's letters: the *Dispatch* files are lost, and Foster himself was fatally ill, succumbing to tuberculosis on 26 April at the age of forty-six. When Clemens read a report of his death in

the 20 May San Francisco *Morning Call*, he drafted a long footnote for chapter 20 of *Innocents* (later reduced to two brief sentences) in which he described Foster as a "firm friend & a genial comrade," praising his "sparkling wit, his cheerful spirit & his soldierly will" (SLC 1868bbb, 1–2†; "Death of an Old Californian," San Francisco *Morning Call*, 20 May 68, 1).

[9] See 12 Dec 67 to Fairbanks, n. 4.

[10] Mrs. Fairbanks, aged thirty-nine, had evidently identified herself with the passengers as Clemens described them in his summary letter to the New York *Herald* (see 20 Nov 67 to JLC and family [2nd of 2], n. 4). There he had said:

> Three-fourths of the Quaker City's passengers were between forty and seventy years of age! . . . Let us average the ages of the Quaker City's pilgrims and set the figure down at fifty years. Is any man insane enough to imagine that this picnic of patriarchs sang, made love, danced, laughed, told anecdotes, dealt in ungodly levity? In my experience they sinned little in these matters. No doubt it was presumed here at home that these frolicsome veterans laughed and sang and romped all day. . . . If these things were presumed, the presumption was at fault. The venerable excursionists were not gay and frisky. (SLC 1867sss)

[11] Solon and Emily Severance.

To Jane Lampton Clemens and Family
21 February 1868 • Washington, D.C.

(MS: NPV)

~~76~~ 224 F street
(Keep your eye on the address)
Wash^{n} Feb. 21.

Dear Folks—

I was at 224 first—~~s~~ Stewart is there yet—I have moved five times since—shall move again, shortly. Shabby furniture & shabby food—*that* is Wash^{n}—I mean to keep moving.[1]

I have received all the printed letters you mention—Ma's last, containing one, to-day—& one from Mollie containing 3—the file is complete, *as published* & numbered. But I see no letters from various places in France, Italy, Spain, Egypt, & so on—though it runs in my head that I wrote them. However, it is of no consequence—the Alta contract is completed.[2]

I was at the Illinois State reception last night[3]—a stranger—but after I got on good friendly terms with everybody, a Michigan lady gravely complimented Annie, through me, on her excellent letter in the Jumping Frog![4] I said the letter was genuine, & I would convey the compliment to the proper source. You may give it to my niece, with her uncle's best love.

I couldn't accept the Postoffice—the book contract was in the way—I could not go behind that—& besides, I did not *want* the office. I might want such a thing under the next administration, & if it shall so happen, it will be in my favor that I did not serve under this one. It would not do to take the office, & then have the book company sue me & take away the first year's salary for breach of contract. Love to Sammy & Annie & all—I have many letters to write.

Yrs aff
Sam.

[1] In an 1870 sketch in the *Galaxy*, Clemens recalled that he and Riley frequently "lodged together in many places in Washington during the winter of '67–'8, moving comfortably from place to place, and attracting attention by paying our board—a course which cannot fail to make a person conspicuous in Washington" (SLC 1870, 726). And in an 1889 interview, he mentioned rooming "in a house which also sheltered George Alfred Townsend, [Hiram J.] Ramsdell, George [W.] Adams, and Riley, of the San Francisco *Alta*. . . . A little later that winter William Swinton and I housed together" ("Mark Twain. An Interview with the Famous Humorist," New York *Herald*, 19 May 89, 19).

[2] On 12 February Orion, who was living with his sister and mother in St. Louis, wrote to his wife, still staying with her family in Keokuk:

> Sure enough those papers were sent to you by mistake. Not knowing what had become of the account of Russian bathing [SLC 1867nnn], and the others, Pamela sent 50 cents to the Alta for them; but they have not come. I believe I cut them out for you. Put them in an envelop and send them here or to Sam L. Clemens (Mark Twain) 224 F street, Washington City, D.C. as soon as you can. (OC to MEC, 12 Feb 68, CU-MARK)

The file "*as published* & numbered" could not have included anything later than letter number 39, published the previous Sunday, 16 February, and since Clemens was receiving clippings relayed to him through his family in St. Louis, the file he had almost certainly included less. The first gap in the numbering occurred following letter 39, which was written from Nazareth. Any letters Clemens may have written the *Alta* about Spain or Egypt would not yet have been published—and in fact no such letters ever appeared in the newspaper. For a discussion of letters Clemens may have written in France and Italy but that the *Alta* never published, see 1–2 Sept 67 to JLC and family, nn. 2–4.

[3] Clemens described this occasion in his 21 February dispatch to the Chicago *Republican:*

> This Illinoisan reunion was lively, void of restraint, and eminently pleasant. This is the most agreeable way in which Senators and Representatives can meet their flitting constituents, and the idea is well worthy of adoption by the representatives of other States here. Americans are not by nature, inclination, or home teaching, courtly enough to enjoy the formal humbuggery of an orthodox "reception." (SLC 1868ii)

[4] Young Annie Moffett's "model letter" appeared in "An Open Letter to the American People" (SLC 1866b), first published in the New York *Weekly Review*

on 17 February 1866 and reprinted as "A Complaint about Correspondents" in *The Celebrated Jumping Frog of Calaveras County*.

To Orion Clemens
21 February 1868 • Washington, D.C.

(*MTL*, 1:150–51)

224 F street,
Wash., Feb. 21.

My dear Bro.,

I am glad you do not want the clerkship, for that Patent Office is in such a muddle that there would be no security for the permanency of a place in it. The same remark will apply to all offices here, now, & no doubt will, till the close of the present administration.

Any man who holds a place here, now, stands prepared at all times to vacate it. You are doing, now, exactly what I wanted you to do a year ago.[1]

We chase phantoms half the days of our lives.

It is well if we learn wisdom even then, & save the other half.

I am in for it. I must go on chasing them—until I marry—*then* I am done with literature & all other bosh,—that is, literature wherewith to please the general public.

I shall write to please myself, then. I hope you *will* set type till you complete that invention, for surely government pap must be nauseating food for a *man*—a man whom God has enabled to saw wood & be independent.[2] It really seemed to me a falling from grace, the idea of going back to San Francisco nothing better than a mere postmaster, albeit the public would have thought I came with gilded honors, & in great glory.

I only retain correspondence enough, now, to make a living for myself, & have discarded all else, so that I may have time to spare for the book. Drat the thing, I wish it were done, or that I had no other writing to do.

This is the place to get a poor opinion of everybody in. There isn't one man in Washington, in civil office, who has the brains of Anson Burlingame—& I suppose if China had not seized & saved his great talents to the world, this government would have discarded him when his time was up.

There are more pitiful intellects in this Congress! Oh, geeminy! There are few of them that I find pleasant enough company to visit.

I am most infernally tired of Wash. & its "attractions." To be *busy* is a man's only happiness—& I *am*—otherwise I should die.

Yrs. aff

Sam.

[1]Orion was setting type for the St. Louis *Missouri Democrat*, working as a "sub" and hoping for a "regular situation." On 17 February he wrote Mollie:

> I worked Saturday in the Democrat newspaper office, from 10 A.M. till 5 P.M., and Sunday from 2 P M till 3.45 A.M. All this work together only amounts to $3.68½. . . . The foreman of the newspaper at the Democrat office [William McKee], who is an old friend, had put my name on the sub list before I got back from Keokuk, and says it will result in a regular situation. (OC to MEC, 17 Feb 68, CU-MARK)

In a later letter he explained why, in part, his situation was so precarious:

> The art of printing is so far, with me, a lost art, that I cannot hold a situation in a job or book office, and I cannot set type fast enough for an evening paper. I have not capital to go into practice of law. So there is nothing left, as I know no other business, but to work on a morning paper. (OC to MEC, 8 Apr 68, CU-MARK)

[2]Orion had been working on some invention since at least the previous November. The device in question may have been the "modest little drilling machine" that was reputed to be "favorably thought of by Munn & Co." in June of 1870 (OC to MEC, 26 Nov 67, CU-MARK; SLC to PAM, 12 June 70, NPV†). Or it may have been a "wood-sawing machine" that Clemens recalled his brother had invented:

> He . . . patched it together himself, and he really sawed wood with it. It was ingenious; it was capable; and it would have made a comfortable little fortune for him; but just at the wrong time Providence interfered again. Orion applied for a patent and found that the same machine had already been patented and had gone into business and was thriving. (AD, 6 Apr 1906, CU-MARK, in *MTA*, 2:329)

The phrase "saw wood and be independent" echoes a proverbial steamboat expression, "as independent as a wood-sawyer's clerk," which refers to the importance of wood suppliers to the river economy (see *L1*, 18 n. 6).

To Mary E. (Mollie) Clemens
22? February 1868 • Washington, D.C.

(*MTB*, 1:359–60; Paine, 938;
MS, envelope only, ViU)

. . . .

I have made a superb contract for a book, & have prepared the first ten chapters of the sixty or eighty—but I will bet it never sees the light.

Don't you let the folks at home hear that. That thieving *Alta* copyrighted the letters, & now shows no disposition to let me use them. I have done all I can by telegraph, & now await the final result by mail.[1] I only charged them for 50 letters what (even in) greenbacks would amount to less than two thousand dollars, intending to write a good deal for high= priced Eastern papers, & now they want to publish my letters in book form themselves, to get back that pitiful sum.[2]

. . . .

I rather expect to go with Anson Burlingame on the Chinese embassy.[3]

. . . .

Mrs. Orion Clemens | Keokuk | Iowa [*postmarked:*] WASHINGTON D.C. FEB 22 '68 FREE [*franked by Clemens:*] W^m M Stewart | USS

[1] In both of the printed sources for this letter, the manuscript of which is lost, Paine said it was addressed to Orion—not Mollie—Clemens. But the letter's injunction not to "let the folks at home hear" of the *Alta* problem makes sense only if Clemens was writing to someone *away* from home. Orion would have been puzzled by such an instruction, since he was living "at home" in St. Louis, but Mollie was living with her parents in Keokuk, Iowa. And since Clemens had already told the St. Louis family (Jane, Pamela, and Orion) about his "superb contract" (24 Jan 68 to JLC and family), it seems unlikely that he would repeat himself to them a month later. Having recently received from Mollie three clippings of his *Alta* dispatches (mentioned as received in 21 Feb 68 to JLC and family), Clemens did have reason to write her a letter, and soon he demonstrably did so, as the envelope he addressed to her, postmarked 22 February, establishes. In another letter written at this time but now lost, Clemens must have also informed Pamela of his problem, swearing her to strict confidence even with members of the family (just as he later did in respect to his pending engagement to Olivia Langdon). Pamela evidently confided the information to Orion, but not to Mollie, and probably not to Jane—for in April, Orion was obliged to explain to Mollie why he had known about the problem but had not told her: "Pamela thought Sam had enjoined strict privacy on her, and I said nothing [to you] because she thought Sam would be displeased if privacy to that extent was not kept" (OC to MEC, 10 Apr 68, CU-MARK). Paine reported that when Clemens first heard about the *Alta*'s plans (ostensibly from Joseph Goodman), he "got confirmation of the report by telegraph" (*MTB*, 1:359). Clemens must have learned the bad news and "done all [he could] by telegraph" within a day of writing the previous letter to Orion (on 21 February), which does not mention the problem. It is therefore extremely likely that the envelope transcribed here, and the letter fragment that Paine said was addressed to Orion, belong in fact to each other, and that the letter itself was written no earlier than 21 and no later than 22 February, the date of the postmark.

[2] Noah Brooks recalled the *Alta* editors' response to the news—which they had certainly heard by 14 January—that Clemens planned to reuse his *Quaker City* letters:

Although up to that moment there had been no thought of making in San Francisco a book of Mark Twain's letters from abroad, the proprietors of the "Alta California" began at once their preparations to get out a cheap paper-covered edition of those contributions. An advance notice in the press despatches sent from California was regarded as a sort of answer to the alleged challenge of Mark Twain and his publishers. This sent the perplexed author hurrying back to San Francisco in quest of an ascertainment of his real rights in his own letters. (Brooks 1898, 99)

No copy of this "advance notice" has been found, but whether Clemens saw it or was otherwise apprised of the *Alta*'s plans, he was evidently persuaded on or about 22 February to telegraph for permission to reuse the letters, something he had declined to do earlier (24 Jan 68 to JLC and PAM). The "final result by mail" which he then awaited came about two weeks later, on or about 8 March. A California newspaper, reprinting an item from a still-unidentified "Eastern exchange" (published sometime in mid-March), summarized the situation with some authority:

Mark Twain has got a scrape on his hands. He had written several hundred MS. pages for a book for one of the Hartford publishing houses, expecting to make his letters to the *Alta California* useful for the bulk of his book. These letters were fifty, for which $2,500 in gold coin had been paid. Mark telegraphed to California for permission to use the letters. His telegram was, of course, an admission that the *Alta* had the right to the letters. He got a letter last week, refusing the requested permission. This broke up the Hartford contract, and sent him spinning to the Pacific coast, to break somebody's head. ("Mark Twain in Trouble," Marysville [Calif.] *Appeal*, 9 May 68, 3)

Clemens had, in fact, received his $1,250 fare in currency, or "greenbacks," plus $500 in gold (equivalent to $700 in currency), for a total of about $1,950, or "less than two thousand dollars" (see 15 Apr 67 to JLC and family, n. 1).

[3] In *Mark Twain: A Biography* (1912), Paine implied that this closing comment about Burlingame and the previous paragraph both belonged to the 21 February letter to Orion. But Paine's redaction of this same passage, published in the May 1912 issue of *Harper's Monthly Magazine* (Paine, 938), included the comment about Burlingame and the previous paragraph, but omitted any part of the 21 February letter to Orion. Likewise, when he published the letter to Orion in *Mark Twain's Letters* (1917), he omitted both the Burlingame comment and the previous paragraph. It is therefore much more likely that the Burlingame comment is part of this letter to Mollie than part of the earlier letter to Orion.

To William C. Church
22 February 1868 • Washington, D.C.

(Mott 1957, 364)

. . . .

Friend Church—Confound it, when a man sends you an article & you don't want it, why in the mischief don't you return it at once & give him a chance to use it elsewhere? . . . This isn't right, you know.[1]

. . . .

[1]The article may have been the "short magazine article," not further identified, which Clemens said he wrote at the end of January (31 Jan 68 to Beach). William Conant Church (1836–1917) was one of the editors of the *Galaxy* magazine, which had just published Mark Twain's "General Washington's Negro Body-Servant" in its February issue (SLC 1868p). Church had begun his editorial career assisting his father on the New York *Chronicle*. Later he published the New York *Sun* for a short time, and served as Washington correspondent for the New York *Times* during the war. He and his brother, Francis Pharcellus Church (1839–1906), founded the *Galaxy* in May 1866 and served as co-editors until its demise in 1878, according to Frank Luther Mott. Mott is the only source for the letter text, the original of which he saw in the "Willard Church Collection," whose location is now unknown. Mott is therefore the chief authority for which of the two brothers Clemens here addressed. Some doubt may arise because Mott, in quoting several other letters written by Clemens to the *Galaxy* in 1870, identified their addressee as William, even though all the *Galaxy*'s known replies were written and signed by Francis (Mott 1957, 361–67; Francis P. Church to SLC, various dates, 1870–71, CU-MARK). But Mott might well have seen envelopes or dockets for one or more of Clemens's letters; and even without such evidence, the possibility remains that Francis routinely replied on his brother's behalf.

To Jane Lampton Clemens and Family
8–10 March 1868 • Washington, D.C., or New York, N.Y.

(*Paraphrase:* Paine, 938, and *MTB*, 1:361–62)

A reply came from the *Alta*, but it was not promising. It spoke rather vaguely of prior arrangements and future possibilities. Clemens gathered that under certain conditions he might share in the profits of the venture. There was but one thing to do; he knew those people, some of them—Colonel McComb and a Mr. McCrellish—intimately. He must confer with them in person.

He was weary of Washington, anyway. The whole pitiful machinery of politics disgusted him.

Furthermore, he was down on the climate of Washington. He decided to go to San Francisco and see "those *Alta* thieves face to face." Then, if a book resulted, he could prepare it there among friends. Also, he could lecture.

He had been anxious to visit his people before sailing, but matters were too urgent to permit delay.[1]

[1]Although Clemens apparently confided the seriousness of his difficulty with the *Alta* to Pamela, Orion, and Mollie, he seems to have enjoined such "strict privacy" on them that the bad news did not at the same time reach their mother (see 22? Feb 68 to MEC, n. 1). He presumably informed her, however, shortly before all further secrecy became impossible—that is, when he was obliged to depart for California on 11 March in the steamer *Henry Chauncey*, without first visiting St. Louis. The letter in which he apprised her of his plans survives only in Paine's paraphrase of and brief quotation from it, and Paine himself did not explicitly acknowledge the letter's existence. The span of dates during which Clemens might have written it is limited by his date of departure (11 March) and the date he claimed (in a 1 May dispatch to the Chicago *Republican*) he had received the *Alta*'s letter, confirming its earlier telegram and refusing him permission to reuse his Holy Land letters:

> Three months of wintry weather in New York and Washington had begun to make me restive, and I almost wished for a good excuse to try a change of scene. It came about the eighth of March—a business call to California, and I left Washington instantly, and sailed from New York, in the steamer of the eleventh. (SLC 1868aaa)

To Mary Mason Fairbanks
10 March 1868 • New York, N.Y.
(MS: CSmH)

New York, March 10.

Dear Mother—

A day or two ago I found out that the *Alta* people meant to publish my letters in book form in San Francisco—also that they refuse to let me use them in my book. Neither suits me. My publishers want me to write the book all over new, & not mind ~~the~~ what the Alta does—but *that* won't do. Consequently I have packed my trunk this afternoon, & sail for California to-morrow, to return in June. Good-bye, & good luck. I am in a great hurry.

Saw Mrs. Duncan last night. She said the Captain had gone to Cleveland.[1]

I am *so* glad of an excuse to go to sea again, even for three weeks.

My mother will be grieved—but I *must* go. If the ~~a~~ *Alta's* book were to come out with those wretched, slangy letters unrevised, I should be utterly ruined.

I shall write you from California. And although I am just now "out of luck," I know that I shall be all the more kindly remembered by the forgiving mother of an erratic "cub."

Always Respectfully &
Affectionately
Sam L. Clemens
Occidental Hotel,
San Francisco.[2]

[1] Hannah Tibbets Duncan (1821–69), Captain Duncan's wife of twenty-seven years, had accompanied her husband (and two young sons) on the *Quaker City* voyage. Captain Duncan delivered his lecture about the excursion, which was sponsored by the Christian Associations, on 10 March in Cleveland's Case Hall before a "fair audience" (John E. Duncan, viii, 156; Cleveland *Leader:* "Lecture This Evening," 10 Mar 68, 4; "The Lecture Last Evening," 11 Mar 68, 4).

[2] Clemens was planning to stay at the lavishly furnished Occidental Hotel, at Bush and Montgomery streets. Opened in January 1863 under the management of his friends Lewis and Jerome Leland, it was Clemens's favorite stopping place in San Francisco (*ET&S1*, 474). In January 1868 the hotel had been sold to Edwin Chapin and Gardner Wetherbee ("Occidental Hotel," San Francisco *Evening Bulletin*, 2 Jan 68, 3).

To Jane Lampton Clemens and Family
15 March 1868 • SS *Henry Chauncey* en route from New York, N.Y., to Aspinwall, Panama

(MS: NPV)

‸P. S. Got Pamela's letter—will be no scoffing at sacred things in my book or lectures.‸[1]

At Sea, Sunday,
March 15, Lat. ~~26~~ 25.

Dear Folks—

I have nothing to write, except that I am well—that the weather is fearfully hot—that the Henry Chauncey is a magnificent ship[2]—that we have twelve hundred passengers on board—that I have two staterooms, & so am not crowded—that I have many pleasant friends here & the ~~d~~ people are not so stupid ~~& old~~ ~~&~~ as on the Quaker City—that we had Divine Service in the main saloon at 10.30 this morning—that we expect to meet the upward bound vessel in latitude 23, & this is why I am writing now.[3]

We shall reach Aspinwall Thursday morning at 6 oclock, & San Francisco less than two weeks later. I worry a great deal about being obliged to go without seeing you all, but it could not be helped.

Dan Slote, my splendid room mate in the Quaker City & the noblest man on earth, will call to see you within a month. Make him dine with you & spend the evening. His house is my home always in New York.[4]

Yrs aff'ly

Sam.

[1] As Clemens's later letters to the *Alta* came into print (one every Sunday for most of the spring), it became more obvious that he was willing to "scoff at"—express irreverence toward—the Holy Land. It is not known which *Alta* dispatch prompted Pamela's cautioning remark, which Clemens presumably received shortly before his departure on 11 March, but it is unlikely that she had seen anything published later than 1 March, letter number 44 (SLC 1868hh).

[2] At 25° latitude, the *Henry Chauncey* was just below the tip of Florida. A wooden-hulled sidewheeler of 2,656 tons built in New York in 1865, it was owned and operated by the Pacific Mail Steamship Company (Lytle, 83; "For California via Panama," New York *Tribune*, 7 Mar 68, 3).

[3] The Pacific Mail Steamship Company's "upward bound" steamer left Aspinwall (now Colón) on 15 March, "met and communicated with" the *Henry Chauncey* on 16 March, and arrived in New York on 22 March. Clemens described his fellow passengers and their pastimes on the *Henry Chauncey* in a letter to the Chicago *Republican* dated 1 May ("Marine Intelligence," New York *Times*, 23 Mar 68, 8; "Miscellaneous," San Francisco *Alta California*, 24 Mar 68, 1; SLC 1868aaa).

[4] Slote's visit to St. Louis has not been documented.

To Mary Mason Fairbanks
18 March 1868 • SS *Henry Chauncey* en route from New York, N.Y., to Aspinwall, Panama

(MS: CSmH)

SS. Henry Chauncey,
At Sea, 18th, P.M.

Dear Mother—

We shall reach the Isthmus tomorrow morning.[1] It is getting very hot. Cuba was such a vision!—a perfect garden!

We have twelve hundred passengers on board—half of them in the cabin. But we are not unpleasantly crowded at all. It would crowd the little Quaker City, though, wouldn't it? This is a magnificent ship—my stateroom is twice as large as No. 10[2] (but the other staterooms ain't,.) I haven't anything to write, but nonsense,—which I am furnishing you to let you know we haven't gone down.

Good bye & good luck
The Reformed
Prodigal
Sam L. Clemens

[1]Clemens and his fellow passengers left the *Henry Chauncey* at Aspinwall on the morning of 19 March and traveled across the Isthmus in one day, mainly by train (see John P. Vollmer to A. B. Paine, 26 Dec 1911, Davis 1967b, 3, for an account of this trip). The travelers boarded the *Sacramento* at Panama City on the evening of 19 March and arrived in San Francisco on 2 April ("Arrivals" and "Arrival of the Sacramento," San Francisco *Alta California*, 3 Apr 68, 1).

[2]The number of the stateroom that Clemens and Slote had shared on the *Quaker City*.

ONLY ONE LETTER has been found for the period between 18 March and 14 April, during which Clemens arrived in San Francisco. His negotiations with the owners of the *Alta California* may have begun promptly upon his arrival, late on the afternoon of 2 April, but no public reference to their disagreement, or its resolution, has been found. For the next two weeks, however, his attention was also to a great extent directed toward arranging and publicizing a lecture engagement in the city, which would provide some much-needed income.

Clemens's publicity efforts were very public indeed. On 3 April the *Alta*—apparently without rancor—reported that "the genial and jolly humorist" had arrived the previous day and that he proposed "to lecture in a few days." On 4 April the *Critic* identified his lecture topic as "the results of his pilgrimage to the Holy Land." By 10 April the *Examiner* (among others) reported a definite time and place: 14 April at Platt's Hall, where Clemens had had his largest audience in 1866. And by 12 April the *California Weekly Mercury* reported that when "the Pilgrim has finished his story here, he will tell it to the people of the interior," which suggests that Clemens was now planning to tour California and Nevada towns, despite his intention of the previous November to limit himself to "3 nights in San Francisco, 1 in Sacramento & *maybe* 1 in Virginia" ("Arrival of the Sacramento" and "Arrivals," San Francisco *Alta California*, 3 Apr 68, 1; "Mark Twain's Lecture," San Francisco *Critic*, 4 Apr 68, 3; "Mark Twain's Re-Appearance," San Francisco *Examiner*, 10 Apr 68, 3; "Miscellaneous Items," *California Weekly Mercury* 12 [12 Apr 68]: 5; 24 Nov 67 to Fuller).

The principal San Francisco newspapers frequently reprinted extracts from Clemens's correspondence with the *Alta*, *Enterprise*, New York *Tribune*, Chicago *Republican*, and other journals. And many San Francisco editors treated him as a celebrity, reporting his activities no matter how slight. The *Alta*, for instance, reported that on 6 April he spoke informally at the monthly meeting of a "Literary Society" recently formed by the "younger members of Rev. Dr. [Charles] Wadsworth's [Calvary Presbyterian] Church" in order to "indulge in readings, declamations, vocal and instrumental music, etc." Clemens was "in the audience, and in reponse to an invitation by the management, took the platform in place of an absent singer, and made a speech, which was received with the liveliest applause" ("New Literary Society," San Francisco *Alta California*, 7 Apr 68, 1; reprinted by the Virginia City *Territorial Enterprise*, 10 Apr 68, 2; see also *ET&S2*, 536–37).

Similarly, on 7 and 9 April the *Times* announced a "musical and literary entertainment . . . for the benefit of the Methodist Episcopal Church" in Oakland, which would be served by a special ferry to Alameda, "leaving the wharf on this side at 6 o'clock, and returning at 11." In the second notice the editor added, "In addition to the entertainment already announced, it is understood that Mark Twain will have a few words to say on this occasion" ("Amusements," San Francisco *Times*, 7 and 9 Apr 68, 1). Clemens did speak in Oakland on 9 April, but his difficulties in getting across the bay were more fully reported than the speech itself. It was probably his friend James F. Bowman, now the local editor for the Oakland *News* as well as for the San Francisco *Dramatic Chronicle*, who published the following account:

Yesterday afternoon, about four o'clock, Mark Twain might have been seen rushing madly about in the neighborhood of the Oakland and Alameda ferry landings, on the San Francisco side, inquiring in a bewildered manner of all whom he met, "which boat he ought to take in order to get to the place where the dinner is to come off?" "What dinner?" inquired a benevolent looking citizen, who seemed to think that something was the matter with the pilgrim from the Holy Land. "Well," responded Mark, with a bewildered look, "that's the question. I agreed yesterday, or the day before, or the day before that, or some time or other, to go somewhere to a dinner that was to come off to-day, or maybe to-morrow, or perhaps to-morrow night, at some d—m place across the Bay. I don't know exactly *where* it is, or *when* it is, or who I agreed with. All I know is, I'm *advertised* in the newspapers to be some where, some time or other this week, to dine, or lecture, or something or other—and I want to find out *where* the d—l it is, and how to get there." ("Mark Twain Lost," Oakland *News*, 10 Apr 68, 3; reprinted by the Virginia City *Territorial Enterprise*, 14 Apr 68, 2)

Personal items aside, the San Francisco newspapers frequently reminded readers of the forthcoming lecture, no doubt in part because Clemens purchased advertising space from most of them. His advertisements for "Pilgrim Life, Being a Sketch of His Notorious Voyage to Europe, Palestine, Etc., on Board the Steamship Quaker City" ran routinely from 11 through 14 April. On 10 April, however, the San Francisco *Evening Bulletin* volunteered the following as an item of news:

Mark Twain will give a rollicking sketch of the *Quaker City Pilgrimage* at Platt's Hall on Tuesday of next week. We are sure that the bare announcement of the fact will be sufficient to insure a crowded house. Our citizens have a pleasant recollection of his lecture on the Haw[a]iian Islands last year, and the desire to hear him rehearse his experiences of travel in Europe, Egypt and the Holy Land, will be very general. ("Lecture by Mark Twain," 10 Apr 68, 3)

The next morning, 11 April, the *Alta* followed suit:

"Mark Twain's" reputation as a humorist is so well established that it is only necessary to make the announcement of the evening set apart for his lecture to ensure a crowded Hall; his letters have caused a sensation greater than anything ever before published in California, and all the readers will wish to see the man who has given them so much amusement, while those who enjoy his acquaintance will deem it a duty to be numbered in the audience, for most of them believe that he will give some amusing details that he would not trust to print. ("'Mark Twain's' Sermon on Pilgrim Life," 11 Apr 68, 1)

Such hints about unpublishable "amusing details" of the voyage doubtless originated with Clemens himself, but the trick was picked up and elaborated for him by journals such as the *Golden Era*, which remarked that he "announces his intention to enter minutely into the scandal of the *Quaker City*, . . . and how his innate morality was unsuccessfully assailed during his brief but perilous career." And the *Alta* soon returned to this theme as well: "If he tells on the platform one-half the personal incidents he relates in conversation the audience will have a rare treat: his repartee on Captain Duncan, of the *Quaker City*, is very comical" ("PLATT'S HALL is engaged Tuesday . . . ," *Golden Era* 16 [12 Apr 68]: 4; "'Mark Twain's' Lecture, To-night," San Francisco *Alta California*, 14 Apr 68, 1).

On 14 April, Clemens gave his first performance—before a full house at Platt's Hall, sixteen hundred strong. The lecture itself was evidently a reworking of material already developed for "The Frozen Truth" lecture, delivered in early January in Washington (see 8 Jan 68 to JLC and PAM, n. 7). For reasons explained in the second of the next two letters, however, no text or summary of it has survived.

To Mary Mason Fairbanks
2–14 April 1868 • San Francisco, Calif.

(MS: CSmH)

. . . .

The Prodigal in a far country chawing of husks,[1]

Sam. L. Clemens

P. S.—& with nobody to molest or keep him straight.

(!)mild exultation.

[1] The allusion is to Luke 15:13–16:

> And not many days after the younger son gathered all together, and took his journey into a far country, and there wasted his substance with riotous living.
>
> And when he had spent all, there arose a mighty famine in that land; and he began to be in want.
>
> And he went and joined himself to a citizen of that country; and he sent him into his fields to feed swine.
>
> And he would fain have filled his belly with the husks that the swine did eat: and no man gave unto him.

Clemens could have written this letter, the body of which has not been found, anytime between his arrival in San Francisco on 2 April and his lecture there on 14 April, the income from which must have obviated any need for "chawing of husks" (see 1 and 5 May 68 to Fairbanks). The likelihood is strong, in fact, that it was written toward the beginning of this span of dates, perhaps to announce his safe arrival in San Francisco.

To Samuel Williams
14 April 1868 • San Francisco, Calif.
(MS: CtHMTH)

San Francisco,
April 14.

Friend Williams—

Please see that no reports or synopses (even the most meagre one) are made of my lecture.[1] I must repeat, here & elsewhere, & every point that appears in print must be left out—which is *ruinous* to me. I ask this as a particular, personal favor,~~. A synop~~ & beg that you will guard me against the injury of a synopsis.[2]

Your friend
Mark Twain

[1] Williams (1824?–81) was the San Francisco *Evening Bulletin* editor responsible for "dramatic criticism, and book reviews," according to his fellow editor William C. Bartlett. He had probably helped to puff the lecture, and was very likely the one who reviewed it for the *Bulletin*. Born in Utica, New York, Williams served as a printer's apprentice on the Utica *Herald* before working his way through Williams College, after which he rejoined the *Herald* as an associate editor until about 1854 or 1855, when he traveled for two years in Germany, France, Egypt, and the Holy Land. Returning home, he was invited to join the Albany *Evening Journal* as associate editor. He remained with the *Journal* until 1865, when he accepted an offer from the *Bulletin* and moved permanently to California. By then he had had some experience as a lecturer "who both amused and instructed," according to Bartlett, who also praised his "sound literary judgment and catholic spirit," as well as his "vigorous, condensed, and nervous style" (Bartlett 1881, 324–27; San Francisco *Evening Bulletin:* "Deaths," 1 July 81, 3; "Samuel Williams," 2 July 81, 1, reprinting the Oakland *Tribune*). Clemens not only wrote this request to Williams, and possibly to other journalists as well, he evidently passed out cards with his message at the lecture itself: the reporter for the San Francisco *Dramatic Chronicle* explained that

> just before leaving the hall, we received a card, on the back of which was written in Egyptian hieroglyphics, (under which of course was a translation) the following words: "As I intend to repeat my troubles to-morrow night, don't give any of my good sayings in the morning papers. Yours, Mark Twain." ("Platt's Hall," 15 Apr 68, 3)

Clemens's efforts were apparently successful: no synopsis of his lecture appeared in any of the extant San Francisco newspapers.

[2] The lecture was a financial success for Clemens, earning him about sixteen hundred dollars (at one dollar per ticket). He had made all seats "reserved," and the demand for tickets was so great that he agreed to repeat the lecture on 15

April, "in order to accommodate the thousands of besiegers who were repulsed at the door" (advertisement, San Francisco *Times*, 15 Apr 68, 2). But the lecture itself drew mixed reviews. The *Bulletin* critic (presumably Williams) published what the Virginia City *Territorial Enterprise* later called, in reprinting it, "the most appreciative notice of any of its cotemporaries" ("Of Mark Twain's lecture . . . ," 18 Apr 68, 2). Yet even the *Bulletin* expressed disappointment with the lecture:

> Mark Twain . . . asked his friends of the press to refrain from publishing any synopsis of his discourse, and, having arranged that matter satisfactorily, he proceeded with his lecture. There were many telling points in it—flashes of humor which convulsed his hearers with laughter, and gleams of sentiment which almost induced the wish that he might not resume the humorist's vein. Several passages—descriptive of the solemn grandeur of Rome's gray ruins, and the dreary desolation of the cities of Palestine—were really eloquent. But, on the whole, the lecture was not as completely prepared or warmly received as his first one on the Hawaiian Islands, and after he dismissed the audience there was a general expression of regret that he had not said more about Palestine, etc., and less about the bald-headed, spectacled and sedate old pilgrims on the *Quaker City*. ("Mark Twain's Lecture," 15 Apr 68, 3)

The *Alta* agreed, noting that the "lecture was not so well prepared as the first one delivered on the Sandwich Islands, though two bursts of eloquence called out hearty applause—on the ruins of Palestine, and on what the Pilgrims will not forget" ("'Mark Twain's' Lecture," 15 Apr 68, 1). Similar, though usually briefer, notices appeared in the *Critic*, the *Examiner*, the *Times*, the *Golden Era*, and doubtless other newspapers as well ("Mark Twain's Lecture," San Francisco *Critic*, 15 Apr 68, 3; "Amusements," San Francisco *Examiner*, 15 Apr 68, 3; "Amusements," San Francisco *Times*, 15 Apr 68, 1; "Mark Twain's Lecture," *Golden Era* 16 [18 Apr 68]: 4). After the second performance, the *Alta* editor did his best to smooth over Clemens's earlier lapse:

> The repetition of the lecture on the Holy Land Excursion last night, was vastly gratifying to the audience and the lecturer; he had "got the hang of the sermon" and delivered it with more nonchalance, assuming that confidential conversational tone that breaks down all barriers between the man on the stage and the people occupying the seats. The description of Palestine as it is, the compressed substance of a dozen volumes of travels, is the gem in the lecture, though for poetic eloquence, the summary of things that cannot be forgotten, bears off the palm. ("Mark Twain's Lecture Repeated," 16 Apr 68, 1)

Two weekly journals, on the other hand, were much more critical. The San Rafael *Marin County Journal* was disgusted that "this miserable scribbler, whose letters in the *Alta*, sickened everyone who read them, and of which the proprietors of that paper were heartily ashamed has the audacity and impudence to attempt to lecture to an intelligent people" ("Sickening," 18 Apr 68, 2). And the *California Weekly Mercury* called the lecture "a most palpable failure . . . foul with sacrilegious allusions, impotent humor, and malignant distortions of history and truth" ("Mark Twain," 12 [19 Apr 68]: 5). Before he could learn of these remarks, however, Clemens took the California Steam Navigation Company's daily steamer to Sacramento on 16 April, where he lectured the following night. After also lecturing in nearby Marysville (18 April), Nevada City (20 April), and Grass Valley (21 April), he returned to Sacramento, and on 23 April took the 6:30 A.M. Central Pacific train for Nevada (Langley 1867, "Advertising Department," vii; "Railroads and Stages," San Francisco *Alta California*, 23 Apr 68, 4).

To Joseph T. Goodman
per Telegraph Operator
23 April 1868 • Coburn Station, Calif.

(*Paraphrase:* Virginia City
Territorial Enterprise, 24 Apr 68)

We received the following telegram from him last night dated at Coburn's: "I am doing well. Have crossed one divide without getting robbed anyway. Mark Twain."[1]

[1]Coburn Station (now Truckee, California) "came into existence when the Central Pacific surveyed the route across the pass in 1863–64"; it was named for the owner of a local saloon (Gudde, 328). Clemens had just crossed the Sierra Nevada by way of Donner Pass, which ostensibly reminded him of the bogus holdup perpetrated on him by Denis McCarthy and Steve Gillis (disguised as highwaymen) while he was crossing a lesser "divide" on his way from Gold Hill to Virginia City in November 1866, toward the end of his first lecture tour (*Roughing It*, chapter 79; *L1*, 366–67 n. 4). Clemens was not amused by this practical joke and had departed Virginia City without forgiving his tormentors. Goodman printed this telegram on 24 April, and the next day also published the following item: "Mark Twain arrived here at 5 o'clock yesterday morning in good health and without meeting a single footpad on the way. He will lecture at the Opera House on next Monday and Tuesday nights—sure" ("Arrived," Virginia City *Territorial Enterprise*, 25 Apr 68, 3).

To Mary Mason Fairbanks
1 and 5 May 1868 • Virginia City, Nev., and San Francisco, Calif.

(MS: CSmH)

Virginia, Nevada, May 1.

My Dear Mother =

I cannot go a-Maying today, because it is snowing so hard—& so I have been writing some newspaper letters &[1]

San Francisco, May 5.

I didn't finish—& now I have just arrived home again a few minutes ago. I find your kind letter of April 2 & Charley's of April 1 awaiting me.[2] I have had the *hardest* trip over the Sierras. Steamboat to Sacramento (balmy summer weather & the peaches & roses all in bloom)—railway to the summit (snow thirty feet deep on level ground & 100 in the drifts)—6-horse sleighs to Donner Lake—mail coaches to Coburn's—railway to Hunter's—stage-coaches to Virginia—*all* in the space of 24 hours.[3] Distance 150 miles. Coming back last night in a snowstorm, the two & a half hours' sleighing (part of the time clear weather & superb moonlight,) was something ~~maj~~ magnificent—we made ten miles an hour straight along. We had no such thrilling fun in Palestine.[4]

I lectured here—a little over sixteen hundred dollars in the house—gold & silver. The seats were all taken & paid for long before night, & then I stopped the sale of tickets, which made a large number of people mad—people who came at 7 P. M. & had to go away again. But *I* couldn't help that. I didn't want them standing up & bothering me. It was a miserably poor lecture. I shall write a better one the next time I come to San Francisco.

I wish I could have been there during Charley's visit. I~~t~~ was having a tolerably cheerful time of it at sea at that time, however, & I had rather be afloat than anywhere else—*except* at your house *ma mère*.

The *Alta* has given me permission to use the printed letters. It is all right, now.[5]

I could not go with Mr. Burlingame, though I wanted to do it badly. I told him I would join him in Europe before his mission was finished.[6]

I must try & send my photograph with this. It is better looking than I am, & so I ordered two hundred. I mean to order a thousand more. I will send you five hundred to put in your album.[7]

I find letters here from Mrs. Hooker (Did you~~r~~ meet her?—Mr. Beecher's sister)—& Julius Moulton~~,~~—& a dozen letters from other people.

But I see that I can't keep my eyes open. It is near midnight. I am utterly & completely worn out. I intended to sleep on the boat—they gave me the bridal chamber as usual—(a ghastly sarcasm on my lonely state, but intended as a compliment) but I knew so many people on board that I staid up to talk—& now I cannot write—I can hardly see, for that matter.[8] I was determined to write *at* you tonight, though, ~~bef~~ because I shall have so little spare time for two or three weeks to come that I was afraid I might neglect it.

Under these circumstances I know you will overlook the stupidity of this effort, & write me just the same as if I had done ever so well. *Won't* you?

Remember me most kindly to the family, & when you write Charley tell him I am going to answer very shortly.

Your always friend
& ~~dis~~ far away cub
Sam L. Clemens

P.S. You *must* remember me to Mr & Mrs Severance. I got S's post-script.[9] Thanks.

[1] Probably part or all of two dispatches to the Chicago *Republican* dated 1 and 2 May, both from Virginia City. In the second, Clemens mentioned the trip up from San Francisco which he described in the 5 May portion of this letter (SLC 1868aaa, 1868ccc).

[2] Charles Langdon's 1 April letter was probably written during or shortly after his recent visit to the Fairbankses in Cleveland. On 29 March, Langdon's mother wrote Mrs. Fairbanks, "Charlie may be today with you. . . . Won't he enjoy a visit with you & a rehearsal of the past, & also be delighted to see Mr & Mrs Severance?" (CtHMTH).

[3] The delayed spring of 1868 allowed the train from Sacramento to run only as far as Cisco—fourteen miles from, and eleven hundred feet below, the summit at Donner Pass. The short stretch of existing track beyond Cisco was still covered with deep snowdrifts, requiring passengers to continue from there by sleigh to Donner Lake. At Donner Lake, a railroad construction crew of several thousand laborers—mostly Chinese—was at work blasting and cutting Tunnel No. 9 through solid granite, to close a seven-mile gap that had remained in the track since the onset of the previous winter. Stagecoaches could travel the road from Donner Lake to Coburn Station, where the railroad track resumed, running northeast toward Reno as far as John M. Hunter's station on the Truckee River, about nine miles inside the Nevada state line. The gap at the summit was not closed until 18 June, when it became possible to ride the train continuously from Sacramento to Reno in under ten hours (Lewis, 76–85; Carlson, 140; Angel, 643; "Across the Sierra Nevadas," San Francisco *Alta California*, 20 June 68, 1).

[4] After lecturing at Piper's Opera House in Virginia City on 27 and 28 April, Clemens appeared twice in Carson City, on 29 and 30 April. (The second performance was a school benefit, for which he revived his old Sandwich Islands lecture.) He then returned briefly to Virginia City, where he undoubtedly enjoyed having a few more days "to shake hands and swap yarns with his old friends," as Goodman had predicted upon his arrival ("Mark Twain," Virginia City *Territorial Enterprise*, 24 Apr 68, 2; see Lorch 1968, 79–81, for a fuller account of the Nevada tour). In a newspaper dispatch written on 2 May (see note 1), Clemens remarked that he was not looking forward to his pending return trip from Virginia City to San Francisco on 3 May:

> I rather dread the trip over the Sierra Nevada to-morrow. . . . It is more irksome than it was before—more tiresome on account of your being obliged to shift from cars to stages and back again every now and then in the mountains. We used to rattle across all the way

Two *carte de visite* photographs of Clemens taken at the studio of Bradley and Rulofson, San Francisco. Mark Twain Papers, The Bancroft Library (CU-MARK). See p. 215 n. 7.

> by stage, and never mind it at all, save that we had to ride thirty hours without stopping. (SLC 1868ccc)

[5] Many years later the author recalled his discussion with Frederick MacCrellish of the *Alta:*

> I said that if they had acted fairly and honorably, and had allowed the country press to use the letters or portions of them, my lecture-skirmish on the coast would have paid me ten thousand dollars, whereas the *Alta* had lost me that amount. Then he offered a compromise: he would publish the book and allow me ten per cent. royalty on it. The compromise did not appeal to me, and I said so. I was now quite unknown outside of San Francisco, the book's sale would be confined to that city, and my royalty would not pay me enough to board me three months; whereas my Eastern contract, if carried out, could be profitable for me, for I had a sort of reputation on the Atlantic seaboard acquired through the publication of six excursion-letters in the New York *Tribune* and one or two in the *Herald*.
>
> In the end Mr. Mac agreed to suppress his book, on certain conditions: in my preface I must thank the *Alta* for waiving its "rights" and granting me permission. I objected to the thanks. I could not with any large degree of sincerity thank the *Alta* for bankrupting my lecture-raid. After considerable debate my point was conceded and the thanks left out. (SLC 1904, 76–77)

This summary seems to imply that the discussion with the *Alta* owners occurred after Clemens had returned from his failed "lecture-raid." But the discussion probably preceded the start of that tour, for on 1 May, in a dispatch to the Chicago *Republican*, Clemens wrote: "When I had finished the business that brought me home, I lectured for the mutual benefit of the public and myself"

(SLC 1868aaa). MacCrellish's deliberations may nevertheless have continued until Clemens's return to San Francisco on 5 May.

[6]Burlingame and his retinue arrived in San Francisco on 31 March, two days before Clemens, and "took rooms at the Occidental Hotel," where Clemens also stayed. Burlingame sailed for the East Coast on 30 April, before Clemens returned from his inland tour (San Francisco *Alta California:* "Arrival of the Chinese Embassy," 1 Apr 68, 1; "Eastward Bound," 30 Apr 68, 1).

[7]Sometime between 2 and 16 April, Clemens had his photograph taken at the "Photographic Art Gallery" of Bradley and Rulofson, at the corner of Montgomery and Sacramento streets in San Francisco. William Herman Rulofson (1826–78) was born in Canada; he went to California in 1849 and worked in Sonora (Tuolumne County) before moving his business to San Francisco in 1863, where he became partners with Henry W. Bradley (b. 1812 or 1813), a photographer and wealthy dealer in photographic supplies. Rulofson directed the gallery and soon became one of the most famous portrait photographers of his day, receiving in the 1870s numerous national and international awards for his work. His 1878 catalog claimed that his files contained "negatives of every person of note who . . . visited this coast since 1849." After Rulofson's death, his collection of plates was purchased by the poet Joaquin Miller, who had them scraped clean to build a greenhouse on his property in Oakland (Langley 1867, 99, and "Advertising Department," 33; Haas, Part 1:289, 292–95, Part 2:48–49; Lloyd, 420–21). Two of Rulofson's 1868 portraits of Clemens (different views taken at the same sitting) are extant in three *carte de visite* prints and one postcard-sized enlargement; it is not known which one he sent to Mrs. Fairbanks.

[8]Clemens apparently spent the night of 4 May in Sacramento and at 2:00 P.M. the next day departed for San Francisco on the California Steam Navigation Company's *Capital*, captained by his friend Edward A. Poole (1823–81) ("River Travel," Sacramento *Union*, 5 May 68, 4; *ET&S2*, 514; "Death of a Pioneer," San Francisco *Chronicle*, 9 Nov 81, 2).

[9]Solon Severance's postscript, presumably.

To Elisha Bliss, Jr.
5 May 1868 • San Francisco, Calif.

(Transcript: WU)

San Francisco
May 5./68

E. Bliss Jr Esq

D[r] Sir:

The Alta people, after some hesitation, have given me permission to use my printed letters, & have ceased to think of publishing them themselves in book form. I am steadily at work, & shall start east with the completed manuscript about the middle of June.[1]

I lectured here on the trip the other night—over sixteen hundred dollars in gold in the house—every seat taken & paid for before night.

Yrs Truly
Mark Twain

[1]Clemens's intention was probably to depart on the Pacific Mail Steamship Company's *Golden City*, scheduled for Saturday, 13 June. The company routinely dispatched its steamers for the Isthmus of Panama (and hence for New York) on the sixth, fourteenth, twenty-second, and thirtieth of each month, except when the date fell on a Sunday, which occasioned departure one day earlier or later ("Ocean Steamers," San Francisco *Alta California*, 4 June 68, 4).

To Mary Mason Fairbanks
12 May 1868 • San Francisco, Calif.

(*MTMF*, 27 n. 1)

San F. May 12.

Dear Mother—

I beg pardon for forgetting the picture when I wrote, the other day.[1] I send it now.

Kind regards to all.
Yours

[1]See 1 and 5 May 68 to Fairbanks.

To Frank Fuller
12 May 1868 • San Francisco, Calif.

(Transcripts: CU-MARK and Parke-Bernet Galleries 1956, lot 90)

San Francisco, May 12.

. . . .

I want to preach in the States all winter. I mean to get up a lecture on California, another on "Paris & Pompeii," & revamp my Sandwich Islands talk & put in this superb eruption 3 weeks ago.[1] I go east the 1st of July.[2] My book, (subscription, only—$4.50 per copy, 600 pages octavo, illustrated,) will be issued from the press early in December & the canvassers will be all over the country two or three months before that. Had $1605 in the house first night here. In haste,

Yr friend,
Mark Twain alias Sam
L. Clemens

[1] No trace of a lecture on "Paris & Pompeii" has been found. Clemens had planned to write a lecture about California as early as January 1867 (see 15 Jan 67 to Hingston), but is not known to have done so until May 1869, when he wrote to his agent, James Redpath of the Boston Lyceum Bureau, about a lecture to be called "Curiosities of California," saying that he had not "written it yet, but it is mapped out, & suits me very well. . . . Nearly all the societies wanted a Cal. lecture last year" (SLC to Redpath, 10 May 69, CtY-BR†; Lorch 1952; SLC 1869b). "Curiosities of California," which included a description of Clemens's 1868 experiences in crossing the Sierra, was only partly drafted and never performed. Instead, Clemens substituted a reworked version of his original Sandwich Islands lecture, calling it "Our Fellow Savages of the Sandwich Islands" (*MTSpk*, 14). This lecture, however, apparently did not include details of the March–April 1868 volcanic and seismic activity on the island of Hawaii, vividly described in the *Alta* on 7 May. A crater near the summit of Mauna Loa erupted on 7 March, spewing forth fountains of lava; this spectacular but brief eruption was followed by ten days of severe earthquakes, mud flows, and tidal waves, which in combination destroyed several villages and killed over a hundred people. On 7 April the volcano again erupted, and rivers of lava flowed for five days from the lower slopes of the mountain into the ocean ("From Hawaii. Grand and Terrible Convulsions of Nature," San Francisco *Alta California*, 7 May 68, 1; Coan, 556–59). Clemens had visited Kilauea, an active crater on the eastern slope of Mauna Loa, in June 1866, and routinely included a description of it in his Sandwich Islands lecture (see 21 June 66 to JLC and PAM, *L1*, 343–46).

[2] See 5 May 68 to Bliss, n. 1.

To Elisha Bliss, Jr.
28 May 1868 • San Francisco, Calif.

(MS: ViU)

San Francisco, May 28.

E. Bliss Esq

D[r] Sir—H H. Bancroft & Co, Publishers, here, are anxious to have the agency for my book for this coast & Japan & China. Their subscription department is entirely separate from their other departments, & is superintended by a man who has no other duty to perform. They say they have sold 2,500 copies of Richardson's Mississippi, & will sell about as many more. But the winter has been severe, & they would not let the agents go out & spoil the field for spring labor. They say they have an energetic corps of canvassers, & one which has been sifted of inefficient material; & that their subscription business ~~in~~ is ciphered down to a careful system.[1]

I said I would write you, because I have a large number of personal friends in Japan & China, & ∅ Mr. Burlingame told me not to overlook that trade.[2] Bancroft has agencies there, & is establishing more. The paper I correspond for here (the *Alta*,) is taken by all the mercantile houses in that part of the Orient.

I shall have the MSS finished in twenty days & shall start east in the steamer of the 1st July. If delayed beyond that time I shall go overland. I have the R.R.$ Co's invitation to do so.[3]

Very Truly, &c
Sam. L. Clemens

[*letter docketed:*] *Author* [*and*] Samuel J Clements | May 28/68 | Author letter

[1] Hubert Howe Bancroft (1832–1918) opened a San Francisco book and stationery store in 1856. It soon grew into a publishing firm that issued (among other things) law books, school texts, maps, and music, and also employed a large staff of subscription-book salesmen. The Bancroft subscription department was the West Coast agency for A. D. Richardson's *Beyond the Mississippi*, published by Bliss's company in June 1867. A total of 33,000 copies of this book were sold by the end of 1867, when a second edition was published, of which an additional 23,000 copies had already been sold by the date of this letter. Richardson's current book, *A Personal History of Ulysses S. Grant* (which Bliss was to issue in late July), would be handled in San Francisco by R. J. Trumbull and Company, publishers and general agents. Even so, Bancroft did become the West Coast general agent for *The Innocents Abroad* (American Publishing Company, entries for *Beyond the Mississippi*, May 67–May 68; "A Valuable Book," Marysville [Calif.] *Appeal*, 14 Mar 68, 3; "Richardson's Life of Grant," San Francisco *Alta California*, 31 May 68, 2).

[2] Presumably between 2 and 16 April, the only time Burlingame and Clemens were both in San Francisco.

[3] The Pacific Mail Steamship Company's *Sacramento* was scheduled to sail on 30 June. By late July 1868, passengers could make the overland trip from San

Francisco to New York in only thirteen days, despite having to travel some of the distance by stagecoach, while the steamship voyage took about three weeks. At that time the Central Pacific Railroad tracks had reached only as far as Wadsworth, Nevada, about thirty-five miles east of Reno, while the Union Pacific Railroad, building west from Omaha, Nebraska, had reached a point about halfway across Wyoming. One year from the time of this letter, in May 1869, the two lines were joined at Promontory Point, Utah ("Across the Continent via Pacific Railroads and Wells, Fargo & Co.'s Stages," San Francisco *Alta California*, 23 July 68, 2; Sabin, 171, 183, 225).

To Jane Lampton Clemens and Family
7 June 1868 • San Francisco, Calif.

(MS: CU-MARK)

San F. June 7.

Dear Folks—

A son of Parson Brownlow of Tennessee, introduced himself to me today (he is a Captain in the Regular army)[1] & in the course of conversation mentioned Fentress County, & said he had been there & was connected ~~to~~ with the Emigration Society of which Gen. Thomas is head—& he said *don't* sell the land, because if Grant is elected the land will be very valuable as soon as the R.R.s are finished.[2]

I only write this to cheer you somewhat in case you have failed to sell—though I hope you *have* sold, even though it be for a mere song.

Capt. B. says, let Orion write letters to the Knox~~v~~ville *Whig* (of which his brother John is editor,)[3] mentioning my name, & inquiring about Tennessee~~e~~ land, & so get up an interest in it—which is all very well, but is bosh. Bother the land.

I shall ~~be~~ start east July 1st

Yrs aff.

Sam

[1] Clemens had just met James P. Brownlow (1841?–79), second son of William Gannaway Brownlow (1805–77), the current governor of Tennessee (1865–69). The father began his career as an itinerant Methodist preacher and gained prominence as the editor of the Knoxville *Whig*, earning himself the nickname "fighting parson" for his fiery editorials and courageous political views. During the

war he was an outspoken pro-Union leader. His son James fled from Knoxville through the Confederate lines in the winter of 1861–62 to join the Union Army. As a captain in the infantry, then in the cavalry, he fought in some seventy battles, distinguishing himself by his bravery and winning the affection of his regiment. President Johnson promoted him to the rank of brevet brigadier general of the United States Volunteers in June 1865. In 1866 he joined the Eighth Cavalry, based in San Francisco, but resigned his commission in March 1868 (*Knoxville Census*, 107; Boatner, 93; "Gen. James P. Brownlow," New York *Times*, 29 Apr 79, 4; Heitman, 1:255).

[2]Clemens refers to the seventy-five thousand acres of land in Fentress County, Tennessee, purchased by his father, John Marshall Clemens, for $400 in about 1830. In 1866 Clemens had washed his hands of all attempts to sell this property, but for much of the last eighteen months, Orion had been making a concerted effort to sell it—traveling to Tennessee in order to pay overdue taxes, survey boundaries, and acquire necessary documents. As recently as November 1867, however, he lamented that it would "take many months yet, it may take years, to straighten up all these titles." By early 1868 he had found an interested buyer, but no sale was ever concluded (*L1*, 79 n. 11; SLC to MEC, 22 May 66, *L1*, 341–42; OC to JLC and PAM, 21, 26, and 28 Nov 67, NPV; OC to MEC, 12 Feb 68 and 5 Mar 68, CU-MARK). Tennessee, like other Southern states, began after the war to try to attract new immigrants from Europe as well as emigrants from the Northern states. The "intolerant and proscriptive spirit" of the Confederates, according to Governor Brownlow, had discouraged "men of capital and enterprise" from settling in Tennessee, in spite of its "mild and healthy climate, fertile soil, magnificent scenery, and pure and abundant water." Upon Brownlow's recommendation, a state board of immigration was established, which was authorized to "do all and everything which may and will advance and encourage immigration" (Hesseltine 1932, 108). Partly through it, numerous local "immigration societies" were formed throughout the state, with the aim of populating their respective regions (Bokum, 60–79, 161–62). Neither General Thomas nor the Fentress County society of which he was presumably head has been identified. Captain Brownlow, like his father, believed that the election of Grant to the presidency would mean "peace; it means that carpetbaggers are not to be molested . . . that capital, coming to us from abroad . . . is not to be spurned," thus ensuring economic growth and increased land values (Hesseltine 1957, 132). Grant and Colfax had just been nominated at the Republican National Convention on 20 and 21 May; the Democratic candidates, Horatio Seymour and Francis P. Blair, Jr., were nominated in July.

[3]John Bell Brownlow (1839–1922), eldest son of Governor Brownlow, was a soldier, journalist, and historian. Shortly before the war he joined his father in editing the Knoxville *Whig*, then became its editor when his father was elected governor in 1865. During the early months of the war, the *Whig* was the only pro-Union newspaper published within Confederate territory. It was suppressed by Confederate authorities from October 1861 to October 1863. John Brownlow's editorial style so resembled his father's that "many things the son wrote were as much the father's as if he had written them" (Coulter, 263–64, 402–3).

To Mary Mason Fairbanks
17 June 1868 • San Francisco, Calif.

(MS and transcript: CSmH and
San Francisco *Morning Call*, 17 June 68)

Occidental Hotel,
San F, June 17.

My Dear Mother=

I am back to the old place again. ~~I was sail~~ At our table at the Lick House they had a fashion of fining delinquents champagne for the party when they absented themselves from dinner without leave. I never could remember to ask leave, & yet often went out to dinner. The fines cost me more than my board. It was too much luxury. I came home again. Now I can go out to dinner as much as I please,‸ ~~; I~~ in case any one chooses to invite me, & therefore rejoice thou, for I am happy.[1]

This letter of May 26th is the best you have written me—& it convinces me that you are steadily improving, because I always ~~think~~ ‸recognize‸ your last ‸to be‸ the best. I was ever so glad to receive it, & have begun at once to answer it, instead of going on moralizing over the Sphynx. The Sphynx has "kept" for several thousand years, & will doubtless continue to keep until I write to my faithful mother.

No, I am not going to Europe yet. I talked the matter over with Mr Burlingame, for two [or] three hours, & saw that it was both impracticable & inexpedient.

What did I ever write about the Holy Land that was so peculiarly lacerating? The most straight-laced of the preachers here cannot well get through a sermon without turning aside to give me a blast~~?~~. The last remark reported to me from the pulpit is ~~to~~ "this son of the Devil, Mark Twain!" It is a fine flight of fancy, anyway, isn't it? If I only get time to write the article I have in my head, I will make that parson climb a tree. Don't you distress yourself. It is only the small-fry ministers who assail me. All those of high rank & real influence I visit, dine & swap lies with, just the same as ever. They have complained of nothing save the rudeness & coarseness of those Holy Land letters which you did not revise.[2]

Yes'm, I am going to settle down, now, right away. And when I get settled down I will weight myself down so that I shall stay. I will put a brick in my hat the very first thing. And others on top of it from time to time.[3] But ~~josh~~ joking aside, I *am* going to settle down some day, even if I have to do it in a cemetery. I say these things to encourage you, more than ~~t~~ anything else. I do not wish to see you despondent. And you shall NOT be, as long as I know how to spell, & put up comforting sentences.

O, Geeminy! [That stands for a sigh.] I shall get the Sphynx & the rest of Egypt off my mind to-day, & to-morrow set sail from Alexandria, *homeward bound!* You cannot imagine what a broader world of pleasant significance is in those words to me, now, voyaging drearily over accumulating reams of paper, than ~~ever~~ they bore to my mind when the Quaker City turned *her* bows westward. *Then*, it was the most regretful day to me, of the whole ~~w~~ voyage—*now*, it is the happiest. Cuss the cussed book, anyhow. I wish I were a profane young man—how I would let fly the adjectives sometimes. ‸But I am staunch & true.‸

I am writing page No. ~~1,843.~~ ‸2,343.‸ I wish you could revise this mountain of MSS. for me. There will be a great deal more than enough for the book when it is finished, & I am glad. I can cut out a vast deal that *ought* to perish. I mean to only *glance* at Spain & the islands of the return voyage. If I talked much about the week in Spain I should be sure to ~~char-~~ caricature Miss Newell. It would surely creep in somewhere.[4]

According to the contract, I have to put in that N. Y. *Herald* valedictory squib which worried you so much—but that is all right. I read it over yesterday, & found that it gave a perfectly accurate idea of the excursion. I have marked ~~som~~ out some sentences. That article is so mild, so gentle, that I can hardly understand how I ever wrote such literary gruel. But I shall not make it more savage. I must have been full of charity & generous feeling when I wrote that—let it stand as a testimony that I *am* moved by gentle impulses sometimes. You know what they said about me at Gibraltar when I was absent—& O, I could have said *such* savage things about *them*, ~~in~~ ~~&~~ ‸—‸ ~~w~~ & would have done~~,~~ it, too, if they had had full swing in the metropolitan newspapers to reply. Trust me for that, Madam.[5]

I would so much like to write ~~a letter~~ some letters for the Cleveland

Herald, but I have gotten myself buried, at last, under such a hill of unliquidated literary obligations that I dare not think of it. I have neglected the Chicago Republican almost entirely, & the New York Tribune & the Magazines completely. I am very thankful to Mr. Fairbanks for the offer, though, & appreciate his kindness thoroughly. I hope to be less pushed for time, when the book is off my hands.[6]

I have more letters from splendid friends in China & Japan, offering me princely hospitalities for months. Can't go, now. Did you ever know a China-bred Merchant prince? No? Then you have yet to look upon ~~man in his most~~ the fairest type of man. Ross Browne will be here in a few days with a nice sinecure in his Embassy for me—I gave my word that I would take it—& now my stateroom is engaged for the States. I sail ‸in the "Sacramento"‸ June 30,—arrive in New York in the "Henry Chauncey" July 22^{d}.[7]

~~Sp~~ It was splendid for Mollie![8] I have a second appreciative relative in the family, at any rate. To tell the truth I have a sort of sneaking fondness for "people that it is hard for them to be good," myself. We shall get along well when the "re-union" transpires. Did Mr. Beach & Emma arrive? Did you go east? Have you seen the other cub?[9] How is the dog? If he neglects to wipe his feet on the mat before he comes in, & is in all places & at all times blundering & heedless, he will do no discredit to his name. But don't *chain* him. It makes me restive to think of it.[10]

"When will I come?" Just as soon as engagements in New York & Hartford will permit. Write me, care of Dan Slote, 121 William street, & say when any of the other pilgrims will be likely to be there. As I am "touching them on the raw" ~~of~~ occasionally in the book—albeit very gently—I would like to shake hands with them—Church especially, who is a bully pilgrim. [There it goes again.][11]

My kindest regards & fervent good wishes unto yourself & all your household.

And now I will tackle the Sphynx again.

Your Returning Prodigal
Sam L. Clemens.

[*in margin:*] This good-natured, well-meaning ass, "Pipes," is Stephen Massett—just from Calcutta & Hong-Kong, where he has been giving readings of mine & Artemas Ward's articles.[12]

[*enclosures:*]

Important to Whom it May Concern.

MESSRS. EDITORS: I was expecting to sail for New York in the Pacific Mail Steamship Company's steamer of the 18th June, but unforeseen circumstances compel a delay of a few days. I cannot sail till the 30th of the month. It is therefore proper that I should give this notice to those friends who have entrusted articles to my care for delivery to their relatives in the Atlantic States, so that they can send by parties who sail on the 18th such of them as demand expedition. I will give a list of the things I am speaking of, and those which will admit of delay until the 30th, can remain in my possession: 1 violin; 1 double-barreled gun; 1 package books; 1 ditto sheet music—negro ballads; 1 set casters—vinegar cruet missing; 2 scratch wigs for repair; 1 woman; 7 boxes and 1 barrel ore specimens; 1 amalgamating pan, for repair; 1 parrot; 1 pup; 1 cage canaries—two dead; another woman; 18 mining company prospectuses, marked "Please circulate;" 1 valise—appears to be nothing in it; 6 photographs, consigned to different parties; 1 volume Tennyson; 1 white woman; 1 box salve; 2 accordeons; 1 overcoat; 1 set chessmen; 1 cow; 1 sandalwood fan; 1 rosewood dressing case; 4 meerschaum pipes; 2 specimen pins; some grass widows; 1 hoe steam-press, for repairs; 1 Unabridged Dictionary; 9 bandboxes; 1 lunatic for asylum; 1 idiot for Paris; 1 gridiron; 1 baby; 68 letters; 1 package gold coin; 1 ditto greenbacks; 23 trunks; another woman.

Beside these articles I have to carry along a valise for myself, and a jug, and I may be discommoded unless some of the things go by the steamer of the 18th. The baby is not well, and appears to get worse all the time. I think maybe it has got the mumps, or the consumption, or something of that kind. Those are things I do not know anything about. It must be one of those, because I have doctored it for fits and measles, and all those things, but still she grows worse. She had better go by the steamer of the 18th. I do not think she will keep for the 30th. To tell the plain truth, I am sorry I agreed to take this baby along. A baby is too troublesome—altogether too troublesome. I have had a baby at sea, and I know. Once I had twins on a ship, and I never suffered so much in my life. Please come and get this one, and ship it per steamer of the 18th.

Most of the other articles had better go at the same time, especially the cow and the idiot. If I were relieved of those I could take some more women, and maybe another trunk or two. MARK TWAIN.

"PIPES" TO "MARK TWAIN," ESQ

MY DEAR SIR:—Understanding you are about leaving for the East in the course of the next year or two, by the way of Egypt, will you do me the favor to take a barrel of pipe-stems and some lager beer to my friend, the Pasha, whom I met at the Egyptian Hall, Piccadilly, in London, last year, in poor "Artemus Ward's" company. I know you have a good many "things" to carry for different persons, such as cigars, and clothes, and nuggets and bricks, but I thought from the intimacy that has never existed between us in the mountains, that I might ask of you this favor. I heard that the Emperor Norton was going as your private secretary. If you accede to my request, write me through the columns of the London *Times* or the *Round Table*. Yours, JEEMS PIPES,
Room 1848, Bedlam Block,
Hammersmith, London.

San Francisco, June 14, 1868.

[1]Clemens had returned to the Occidental after a stay of unknown length, in May and June, at the even more opulent Lick House, on the opposite side of

Dining room of the Lick House, San Francisco, 1871. The Bancroft Library (CU-BANC).

Montgomery at Sutter Street. A burlesque menu (almost certainly composed by Clemens) for a 16 May 1868 "Lick House State Banquet given by Messrs. Clemens and Pierson . . . At the expense of the Proprietors of the Hotel" suggests the conviviality he found there (see the illustration below).

2 The cleric responsible for this "fine flight of fancy" has not been identified, but Clemens certainly did encounter such criticism while in San Francisco, and he made several efforts to write a reply to it. One month earlier, on 20 May, George E. Barnes's *Morning Call* described (in all likelihood with Clemens himself as a contributing source) two rather different encounters on Sunday, 17 May, both of which tend to support what Clemens said here to Fairbanks:

> Mark Twain has been to church. He attended twice last Sunday. Since he returned from the Holy Land he has carefully avoided ministers, the promptings of a guilty conscience

LICK HOUSE

STATE BANQUET

GIVEN BY

Messrs. Clemens and Pierson,

(At the expense of the Proprietors of the Hotel.)

TO THEIR

Customary Dinner Companions.

The seats will remain in their usual order or arrangement, thus:

Mr. Coghill.	Mrs. Coghill.	Mr. Ensign.	Mrs. Sherwood.	Capt. Osgood.
	Mr. Latham.	Mr. Clemens.	Mr. Pierson.	

Dinner begins at 6 P. M.

San Francisco, Saturday, May 16th, 1868.

Clemens's announcement for a 16 May 1868 Lick House banquet, page 2 of a four-page folder (whose verso is probably blank).

BANQUET.

Soup.

Ku-Klux-Klan. Soupçon de soupe.

Fish.

Whale, Esquimaux style. Tadpoles.
Angle Worms.

Cold.

Ham, *also*, Shem and Japhet.
Devilled Crabs. Devilish Lobsters,
Corned Beef. Corned Boarders,
Coffee.

Boiled.

Job (*obscure, but Scriptural*), Owl.

Entrees.

Grand Entrée from the Circus.
Terrapin, Seraphim, Cherubim and sich.
Grass Widows a la Sherwood.
Veal Pie (made out of horse, there being no veal in market.)
Broiled Missionary, with mushrooms, a la Fi-ji islands
Beefsteak, Goodyear's patent.
Veuve Fell, "twin" sauce.
Double Eagles on toast.

Roast.

Invited Guest, stuffed.
Shoulder of Mountain, mint sauce.
Buzzard.
Saddle of Mutton, with bridle and other harness.

Relishes.

Horse Radish. (If a radish horse is not agreeable, a greenish one will be provided.)
Pain Killer. Castor Oil.
Mexican Mustang Liniment, S. T. 1860 X.
Spaulding's Prepared Glue. Benzine.

Vegetables.

Green corns, bunions, etc. Brickbats. Mucilage.
Poison Oak. Sherry Blossoms.

Pastry.

Humble Pie. Pie Ute.
Duff. Doughnuts.
Grasshoppers, Digger style. Oil Cake.
Nut-crackers, Screw-drivers, Anvils.

Dessert.

Forty Mile. Great Sahara.
Nicholson Pavement Oases.
Ice Cream and Onions. Strawberries and Garlic.

Clemens's burlesque menu for the banquet, page 3 of the folder. From a photograph in the Mark Twain Papers, The Bancroft Library (CU-MARK). See p. 224 n. 1.

having admonished him to beware of them, lest they should "give him a blast," to use the language of the ungodly. He would dodge around the corner at the sight of a clergyman, as a dog runs from the pound-keeper. But, last Sunday morning he was prevailed upon to attend church, and his mind was greatly relieved upon his being cordially received after service by the officiating clergyman, who, in warm terms, complimented his letters from the Holy Land. He left the church an altered man, and on his way home deviated from the shortest route, in order to pass boldly by numerous churches. He was suddenly seized with a church-going mania, and in the evening hurried to another house of worship. He entered boldly, walked up the aisle with head erect, and took a seat almost immediately "under the droppings of the divine sanctuary." The clergyman was a new comer, of the Baptist persuasion, and his sermon was eloquent and impressive. He told of the visit of Onesimus to Rome, and the impression made upon the mind of the simple rustic at the sight of such splendor and magnificence, and when he inquired for Paul, how the crowd in that great city jeered and ridiculed him. "And what is ridicule?" asked the clergyman. "It is the argument of small minds on subjects far above their comprehension; it is the weapon of cowards." In short, he was particularly severe on the subject of ridicule; "and," said he, "there are the letters of this person, Mark Twain, who visits the Holy Land and ridicules sacred scenes and things. The letters are sought after and eagerly read, because of his puerile attempts at wit, and miserable puns upon subjects which are dear to every Christian heart. It is not right that he should take away the faith of a people without giving them something in return." In fact, he handled the funny traveller without gloves, and caused many eyes to be turned toward Mr. Twain, who manifested considerable signs of uneasiness. After the service had concluded, Mark advanced to the preacher, and, holding out his hand, said: "Sir, I never receive a good dressing-down which I deserve unless I thank the party for it. I am Mark Twain. I feel that I deserve everything which you have said about me, and I wish to heartily thank you." The minister was surprised and embarrassed. He had not intended to speak unkindly or unjustly. "Oh, of course not. I could easily see that, by your manner and tone," replied Mark. "I think you are wrong in the positions you have frequently taken in regard to the Holy Land," said the clergyman. "I know I am," replied Mark, "but not altogether." "Well, no: perhaps not, altogether," replied the clergyman. After a few more remarks of a kindly nature, Mark retired gracefully, running the gauntlet of the eyes of the whole congregation, who had gathered on the church steps to witness his exit. The scene was witnessed, and the conversation overheard, by a number of the audience. Mark has been heard to say since, that he is aware that he went to great lengths in his Holy Land letters; but then, "Those Pilgrims, you know," they so worried and annoyed the "missionary," that, in the heat of momentary passion, he has written many words which his cooler judgment did not approve, and which will not appear in his forthcoming book, which is being prepared in the quiet of his study, away from "Pilgrim" influences. ("Mark Twain at Church," San Francisco *Morning Call*, 20 May 68, 1)

Although this report has been dismissed as a fabrication (see Lauber, 228), Clemens himself identified and replied to his critic in a signed manuscript written sometime later that week, addressed to—but never published in—Frederick Marriott's San Francisco *News Letter and California Advertiser* (Rowell, 12):

If the Rev. D^{r}. Thomas, who gave me such a terrific setting-up in his sermon last Sunday night—& in very good grammar, too, for a minister of the gospel—had only traveled with me in the Holy Land, I could have shown him how much real harm is done to religion by the wholesale veneration lavished upon things that ‸are‸ mere excrescences upon it; which mar it; & which should be torn from it by reasoning or carved from it by ridicule. They provoke the sinner to scoff, when he ought to be considering the things about him that are really holy. It is all very well to respect the devotee's feelings, but let us ~~respect~~ ‸have a thought for‸ the sinner's ~~failings, ‸at the same time‸ —~~ ‸failings, in the meantime—‸ he has a soul to be saved, as well as the devotee. . . . The devotee being safe, had better in charity suffer a little, than ~~he~~ ‸that the sinner‸ be damned. (SLC 1868zz, 10–11)

The Reverend Jesse Burgess Thomas, D.D. (1832–1915), was the new pastor of the First Baptist Church. A graduate of Kenyon College and Rochester Theological Seminary, Thomas left his position at the Pierrepont Street Church, Brooklyn, to take this appointment in San Francisco, preaching there for the first time on 1 March. On 17 May he preached at 1:00 and 7:45 P.M. (San Francisco *Examiner:* "Religious Intelligence," 27 Jan 68, 3; "The New Pastor," 2 Mar 68, 3; "Religious Notices for To-morrow," San Francisco *Evening Bulletin*, 16 May 68, 5). Clemens also defended himself in general against the "abuse" he received for what he had written or said about the Holy Land:

> I acknowledge that I have written irreverently, but I did ‸it‸ heedlessly, or when out of temper—never in cold blood. I *did* fail somewhat in reverence for Jacob, whose character all the bookmake[r]s pra‸ise so highly, but that was honest. I revered the *really* holy ‸~~persons & things &~~‸ places, & ‸deliberately & intentionally‸ derided only the ~~sham~~ manifest shams. The bookmakers all deride them in private conversation, ‸themselves,‸ but weep over them in their books. (SLC 1868zz, 7–9)

In May and June Clemens attempted to write at least three other replies to his clerical critics: one early in May, which was left unpublished; another condensed from the first, probably in the first two weeks of June, intended as part of chapter 46 of *The Innocents Abroad* but ultimately not included; and a third, probably in mid- to late June, which likewise remained unpublished (SLC 1868xx, 1868ddd, 1868fff). In the last attempt Clemens said in part:

> The Savior & ~~him crucified~~ his doctrines we can all accept, & all revere. "Love one another;" "Do unto others as ye would that they should do unto you." This religion is good & pure—and rational, & capable of being understood. The Savior *lived* his doctrine. His example, ‸just‸ as well as ~~his words~~ the mere words of his teachings, are full of usefulness to the world.
>
> ~~Very well.~~ But I do claim the right to protest against the ancient children of Israel & the patriarchs being set up for veneration; against their very bad characters being studiously left uncriticised, & their exceedingly slim virtues ~~being~~ as studiously brought forward & glorified until~~, the world is deceived into the idea that they~~ the world is ~~defrauded~~ ‸persuaded‸ into the idea that ~~they~~ ‸these men‸ were nothing whatever but miraculous concentrations of virtue ‸& wisdom‸ unalloyed by any demerit; against the~~ir wandering,~~ nomadic, unprogressive, pure savagery of their manner of life‸~~; being~~ ‸~~and~~‸ ~~&~~ their insubordination, to rulers & to God, & their cruelty, ferocity, ‸& love of ‸raiding,‸ rapine, & pitiless slaughter of women & children; ‸I do protest against such deeds & customs‸ being offered for praise & emulation. . . .
>
> I wish to say one very suggestive thing in this connection. I cannot find a man—be he preacher, church member or writer—who will speak well of Jacob or the Children of Israel, in private conversation; & I cannot find one who will speak *otherwise than well* of them in the pulpit or in print. Perhaps some one will explain *this* mystery to me? If a man think a thing, why not say it? (SLC 1868fff, 1–2, 22–23†)

Clemens could have socialized with any of several San Francisco clergymen he knew, including, among others: the Reverend Horatio Stebbins (1821–1902), pastor of the First Unitarian Church; the Reverend Charles Wadsworth, pastor of Calvary Presbyterian Church (1814–82); Henry Martyn Scudder (1822–95), pastor of Howard Presbyterian Church; and Andrew Leete Stone (1815–92), pastor of the First Congregational Church. Stebbins and Wadsworth were two of the more prominent clergymen in San Francisco; both men delivered morning sermons on 17 May (unlike Scudder and Stone, who preached only in the evening), and therefore either might have been the clergyman who, according to the *Call* reporter, "complimented his letters from the Holy Land" (*L1*, 369 n. 2;

SLC 1868c; "Religious Notices for To-morrow," San Francisco *Evening Bulletin*, 16 May 68, 5; Langley 1868, 596, 737, 741–42, 744). They were also the clergymen to whom Clemens turned, later in 1868, when he needed character references from San Francisco (see 29 Dec 68 to Langdon, n. 2).

[3] To put a brick in one's hat is to become intoxicated. Clemens used the phrase as early as 1852 (Mathews, 1:187; *ET&S1*, 70).

[4] Clemens's apostrophe to the Sphinx was ultimately part of chapter 58 in *The Innocents Abroad:* a three-page draft of the passage survives, numbered 1256 through 1258 (SLC 1868ggg). A manuscript chapter about his week in Spain, intended for but never published in chapter 59 (very near the end of the book), also survives: it was numbered 1289 through 1331. The page numbers that Clemens wrote here have not been explained. He portrayed Julia Newell in the rejected chapter on Spain with some restraint, merely referring to "our lady with her short traveling dress" (SLC 1868hhh, 1315, quoted in 24 Oct 67 to JLC and family, n. 1). But despite the promise he made Emma Beach not to "make fun," he did indulge in a highly irreverent treatment of Murillo's paintings (10 Feb 68 to Beach).

[5] The contract for *The Innocents Abroad*, dated 16 October 1868 (Appendix F), contains no such stipulation about the 19 November letter to the New York *Herald*, which Fairbanks and several other passengers had complained of at the time (SLC 1867sss; 20 Nov 67 to JLC and family [2nd of 2]). Bliss, however, may well have asked Clemens to include it, and it was reprinted as chapter 61, ostensibly for that reason: "partly because my contract with my publishers makes it compulsory" (SLC 1869a, 643). Clemens toned down the language, substituting "refreshments" for "cigars or drinks," for instance, and he omitted satirical passages on the frequency of prayer meetings and the attempted sale of the ship. The allusion to "what they said about me at Gibraltar when I was absent" is explained in 24 Oct 67 to Goodman, n. 2.

[6] Clemens wrote nothing expressly for Abel Fairbanks's Cleveland *Herald* until November, when he published "A Mystery" there (SLC 1868ppp). Since coming to San Francisco, he had sent nothing to the *Tribune*, and only two dispatches to the Chicago *Republican* (SLC 1868aaa and 1868ccc).

[7] Clemens had been personally acquainted with humorist, author, and traveler John Ross Browne (1821–75) since at least December 1866, when he was a guest at Browne's home in Oakland (SLC to JLC and family, 4 Dec 66, *L1*, 368, 370 n. 6). They had recently renewed their acquaintance in Washington, and on 1 February Clemens informed his *Alta* readers of Browne's nomination to replace Burlingame as minister to China:

> J. Ross Browne's nomination to the Chinese Mission has been sent to the Senate by the President, and there is very little doubt that it will be confirmed. I cordially hope so, partly because he is a good man and a talented one; a literary man and consequently entitled to high honors; and also because he has kindly invited me to take a lucrative position on his staff in case he goes to China, and I have accepted, with that promptness which so distinguishes me when I see a chance to serve my country without damaging my health by working too hard. . . . I am the only man that can fill the bill. I am able to write a hand that will pass for Chinese in Peking or anywhere else in the world. (SLC 1868kk)

Clemens persisted in saying publicly that he intended to visit China when his book was finished, but he never did so (SLC 1868iii; "Mark Twain," San Francisco *Alta California*, 6 July 68, 1). Browne, accompanied by his family, arrived in San Francisco from New York on 4 July and left for China on 3 August. He soon decided, however, that he could no longer support the terms of the Burlingame treaty, and in July 1869 resigned his post when the Grant administration hinted its intention to replace him (San Francisco *Alta California:* "Arrival of the 'Japan,'" 4 July 68, 1; "The Chinese Mission," 3 Aug 68, 2; Williams, 199–205). Had Clemens traveled on 30 June, he would have taken the *Sacramento* from San Francisco and connected with the *Arizona* (not the *Henry Chauncey*) for New York ("Ocean Steamers," San Francisco *Alta California*, 17 June 68, 4). In fact, he postponed his trip until the following week (see 5 July to Bliss).

[8] Mary Paine Fairbanks.

[9] Between 10 and 16 June Mrs. Fairbanks and three of her children (Alice, Charles, and Mary) stayed with the Langdons in Elmira, where she almost certainly did see Charles Langdon, the "other cub" ("Langdon Guest Book,"4).

[10] The Fairbankses had named their recently acquired pet after Clemens; no independent evidence has been found to support Dixon Wecter's assertion that they had "christened him Mark Twain" (*MTMF*, 32 n. 1).

[11] In Colonel Denny's journal, William F. Church is described as "a tall man rather slender in form with open good countenance and a lip that shows determination of purpose, head whitening with the frosts of about fifty two years, a christian of the Congregational church" (Denny 1867, entry for 11 Sept). According to Paine, when Dan Slote became ill on the trip through the Holy Land, several of the party decided to travel on without him, but Clemens refused, saying: "Gentlemen, I understand that you are going to leave Dan Slote here alone. I'll be d—d if I do!" (*MTB*, 1:337). Paine reported the effect of this statement on Church, "a deacon with orthodox views" who "did not approve" of Clemens, indeed finding him "sinful, irreverent, profane": "'He was the worst man I ever knew,' Church said; then he added, 'And the *best*'" (*MTB*, 1:336). Paine had this story from Clemens's Hartford neighbor George H. Warner, who presumably had it from Church himself, but it has not been independently documented (*MTN*, 89–90). Moreover, this anecdote is strikingly similar to Clemens's account of his own illness in Damascus (see 10 Dec 67 to JLC and family, n. 6).

[12] Although the newspaper clippings Clemens enclosed have not survived, it is reasonably clear what they were, and their texts are therefore reproduced here as enclosures. On 13 June Clemens had published "Important to Whom It May Concern" in the San Francisco *News Letter and California Advertiser* (SLC 1868eee), reproduced here in photofacsimile. An imitative and—from Clemens's perspective—exploitative response to it had appeared on the front page of the 17 June San Francisco *Morning Call*, reproduced here in type facsimile (newsprint of the *Call* is unavailable). Clemens's postscript alluded to the second item ("This . . . Massett") but not to the first; yet his purpose for enclosing the second would not have been intelligible to Mrs. Fairbanks without the first. Stephen C. Massett (1820–98), who called himself "Jeems Pipes of Pipesville," was a popular California-based entertainer with experience both there and abroad. His usual performance incorporated recitations, anecdotes, impersonations, and songs of his own composition. Shortly after his return from an Asian tour, on 17 May, and probably just before Clemens wrote this letter to Mrs. Fairbanks, the two men were introduced by editor and proprietor George E. Barnes in the offices of the *Call* (Hart, 264; "Arrival of the 'New York' from China and Japan," San Francisco *Alta California*, 19 May 68, 1; Massett to SLC, 29 Jan 81, CU-MARK).

To Elisha Bliss, Jr.
23 June 1868 • San Francisco, Calif.
(MS: PPiU)

San Francisco, June 23.

E. Bliss, Jr., Esq.

The book is finished, & I think it will do. It will make more than 600 pages, but I shall reduce it at sea.[1] I sail a week hence, & shall arrive in New York in the steamer Henry Chauncey, about July 22. I may tarry there a day or two at my former quarters (Westminster Hotel,) & then report at Hartford.[2]

Yrs Truly,
Sam L. Clemens

[*letter docketed:*] Mark Twain | June 23/68 | *Author*

[1] In 1904, when Clemens recalled that he wrote *The Innocents Abroad* in "sixty days" by working "every night from eleven or twelve until broad day in the morning" and averaging "more than three thousand words a day," he was thinking principally of the two months between 5 May, when he returned to San Francisco from Virginia City, and 6 July, when he finally departed San Francisco (SLC 1904, 78). As early as 7 June the *Call* reported that he had "been industrious of late, strange as it may seem. By dint of almost superhuman application, he has nearly prepared for press the narrative of his travels in the East" ("Nearly Completed," San Francisco *Morning Call*, 7 June 68, 1). More than half the manuscript, however, consisted of printed dispatches from the *Alta*, *Tribune*, and *Herald*, pasted to separate leaves and revised in the margins. And when Clemens began his intensive stint in May, he already had in hand "the first ten chapters" completed earlier in Washington (22? Feb 68 to MEC). In fact, Clemens seems to have completed his manuscript draft in less than "sixty days," for he began to "reduce" it sometime in mid- to late June, when he asked Bret Harte, who was then struggling to complete the first issue of the *Overland Monthly* for publication by 1 July, to read "all the MS of the 'Innocents.'" Harte did so, and told him "what passages, paragraphs & *chapters* to leave out," and Clemens "followed orders strictly. It was a kind thing for Harte to do, & I think I appreciated it" (SLC to Charles Henry Webb, 26 Nov 70, ViU†). At Harte's suggestion, Clemens may have omitted as many as sixty-five pages of manuscript, most of which survive—some with Harte's penciled suggestions on them. Clemens also recalled that he told Harte "to take such matter out of it as he pleased for the Overland free of charge" (SLC to Milicent Washburn Shinn, 27 Oct 82, CU-MARK†). The *Overland* was announced as "now ready" on the evening of 30

June, and it included, among other things, the first of four extracts from the *Innocents* manuscript which Harte had selected and edited for the new magazine (advertisement, San Francisco *Evening Bulletin*, 30 June 68, 2; SLC 1868jjj). Harte's reading and suggested revisions of the manuscript must therefore have been completed shortly after this letter to Bliss. For a full discussion of Harte's editorial advice, see Hirst 1978.

[2]Clemens had agreed to deliver his manuscript to the American Publishing Company "about the first of August" (27 Jan 68 to Bliss).

To Elisha Bliss, Jr.
5 July 1868 • San Francisco, Calif.

(MS facsimile: Daley)

San F. July 5./68.

E. Bliss, Esq.

I waited over, one steamer, in order to lecture & so ~~rob~~ ‸persecute‸ the public for their lasting benefit & my profit[1]—but I shall surely sail to-morrow, & shall hope to arrive in New York per steamer "Henry Chauncey" about July 28.[2]

Yours Very Truly
Sam L. Clemens

N. Y. address, Westminster Hotel.

[*letter docketed:*] ✓ [*and*] Samuel J Clements | July 5/68

[1]Clemens made this change in his travel plans probably no sooner than the evening of 28 June. His advertisement in the 29 June *Alta California* (page 2) announced a single lecture on the evening of 2 July, a "farewell benefit of the future widows and orphans of Mark Twain," which was entitled "The Oldest of the Republics, VENICE, Past and Present." Clemens also wrote and published an elaborate handbill, dated 30 June, in the form of a burlesque "call," ostensibly signed by prominent San Francisco institutions and individuals who, having learned "with the deepest concern that you propose to read a chapter or two of that book in public before you go," expressed their "cordial desire that you *will not*." Clemens's ostensible reply was:

> No, gentlemen, ask of me anything else and I will do it cheerfully; but do not ask me not to afflict the people. I wish to tell them all I know about VENICE. . . . I wish to furnish a deal of pleasant information, somewhat highly spiced, but still palatable, digestible, and eminently fitted for the intellectual stomach. My last lecture was not as fine as I thought it

was, but I have submitted this discourse to several able critics, and they have pronounced it good. (SLC 1868iii)

The lecture must, in fact, have been taken more or less wholesale from the manuscript that later became chapters 22 and 23 of *The Innocents Abroad*, if only because Clemens had no time to prepare anything else.

2 Clemens sailed on the *Montana* on 6 July, boarded the *Henry Chauncey* at Aspinwall (Panama) on 20 July, and arrived in New York on Wednesday, 29 July ("Mark Twain," San Francisco *Alta California*, 6 July 68, 1; "Passengers Arrived" and "Arrived," New York *Times*, 30 July 68, 8). He described both legs of this journey in a dispatch to the *Alta* dated "August, Recently, 1868" (SLC 1868mmm).

To Mary Mason Fairbanks
5 July 1868 • San Francisco, Calif.

(MS: CSmH)

San F, July 5.

Dear Mother—

I lectured on Venice night before last—large audience & fashionable—& gave so much satisfaction that I feel some inches taller, now. Mind, I do not forget that I am right among personal friends, here, & that a lecture which they would pronounce very fine, would be entirely likely to prove a shameful failure before an unbiased audience such as I would find in an eastern city or on board the Quaker City. I only claim that these citizens *here* call this a good lecture—I do *not* claim, *myself*, that it is. I am satisfied it would be pretty roughly criticised in an eastern town.

But one thing I know—there is no slang, & no inelegancies in it—& I never swore once/,, never once was guilty of profanity.[1]

My steamer ticket is bought (at least I insisted on buying it, but they would not take the money,) & I sail tomorrow, *sure*—& hope to reach New York about July 28 in the "Henry Chauncey." I always stop at the N̸ Westminster Hotel. Can't you drop me a line there, or to Dan's care—121 W^m.^ st.?

Saw our engineer, Harris, last night. He is just in, from around the Horn—is 1st assistant in the Japan—new steamer, & Oh, such a perfect palace of a ship. I do want to sail in her so badly. I̸ She leaves for China shortly.[2] Harris's berth is a good one. I am going to introduce him to all the nabobs of the Pacific Mail Steamship Company & make them promise to keep him in service & promote him to a chiefship as soon as they can.[3] Kind regards to all.

Yrs, ‸(on the isthmus,
when you get this,)‸ Sam L. Clemens.

[1]Clemens's lecture (on 2, not 3, July) was well received by the critics. The *Dramatic Chronicle* noted its "wit without vulgarity" and called it "a decided success." The *Californian* reported, "The first part of the lecture was devoted to a graphic and concise history of the past Venice, which was summed up in a very able manner. . . . and during the latter part of his lecture—that describing modern Venice—he sprang all kinds of concealed jokes, drolleries, flashes of humor and sarcasm . . . till the hall echoed with their cachinations." Even the *California Weekly Mercury*, which had lambasted his April lecture for its "sacrilegious allusions" and "malignant distortions," pronounced this performance "a fine affair, superior in many respects to his last—one or two words and one anecdote being all that could possibly be questioned" ("Mark Twain," San Francisco *Dramatic Chronicle*, 3 July 68, 2; "Mark Twain's Lecture," *Californian* 8 [4 July 68]: 3; "Mark Twain," San Francisco *California Weekly Mercury* 12 [5 July 68]: 4).

[2]In mid-April the Pacific Mail Steamship Company launched its new luxury steamer, the *Japan*, from New York. It arrived in San Francisco on 3 July after an eighty-two-day voyage around Cape Horn. A sidewheel steamer of 4,350 tons, with accommodations for over a thousand passengers, it was lavishly fitted out with black-walnut woodwork and furniture and decorated "in the most exquisite style of fresco; peach blossom, lavender, purple, pea green, constitute the principal colors, with gold ornamental work." The *Japan* departed San Francisco for the Far East on 3 August with (among others) J. Ross Browne, American minister to China, and his family aboard (San Francisco *Alta California:* "The New Steamer 'Japan,'" 24 Apr 68, 1; "Arrival of the 'Japan,'" 4 July 68, 1; "Departure of the 'Japan'—An Incident," San Francisco *Evening Bulletin*, 3 Aug 68, 3).

[3]See the next letter.

To Mathew B. Cox
11 July 1868 • SS *Montana* en route from San Francisco, Calif., to Panama City, Panama

(MS facsimile: CaNBFUA)

At Sea, lat. 24.15 N. July 11.

How are you Old Salt?[1]

Well & hearty I hope. I am, & am in splendid condition. It is a jolly good ship & ~~ever~~ a good commander,[2] & everything goes along comfortably & just right. Only I miss *you*. There isn't any one to talk to after I get to bed. I thought I would drop you a line to say the weather is superb, now, but will be as hot as sin to-morrow; & I also wished to report that up to this time I have behaved myself & have not been tight once. Please report the same to Capt. Eldridge,[3] with my kindest regards. And Captain, look out for Harris, 1st assistant engineer of the Japan—splendid fellow & good old friend of mine. He is a stranger in a strange land[4]—therefore treat him well. We are expecting to meet the Golden City every minute—that is why I am writing here at sea. I thought I might be able to send back a note or two if we met her before night.[5] Blackguard Charley Dickinson for not coming down to see us off.[6] Cultivate Col. McComb of the *Alta*—one of the "whitest men in America" as the steerage passenger said about us when we gave him the gin that morning.

I will now take a stiff cocktail to your everlasting good health—& wishing right heartily you were here. Your brandy makes *good* cocktails.

Always your friend
Sam L. Clemens

[1] Mathew Bold Cox (1818?–80) was born in England, but grew up in New York. He served as superintendent of the Pacific Mail Steamship Company's docks from 1849, when he arrived in San Francisco, until he resigned in 1872. During Clemens's voyage from New York to San Francisco in March and April, Cox was a fellow passenger on the *Henry Chauncey* and his cabinmate on the *Sacramento*. On 1 May Clemens wrote the Chicago *Republican*, "My royal roommate, Capt. Cox, of the San Francisco department of the Pacific Mail, was the life and soul of this voyage." He recalled "that splendid old chief, slaving night and day to make everybody else comfortable and happy, and never once thinking of himself," remembered him "turning out of his bunk at unreasonable hours of the morning, swallowing my smoke, and coughing and barking, and yet swearing all the time that tobacco smoke never inconvenienced him," and concluded that "in all the varied phases and circumstances of a long sea voyage" he could not recall one moment when Cox "was not a generous, and a willing helper of all in time of need, and a gentleman in the best sense of the term" (SLC 1868aaa). In "Ye Equinoctial Storm," one of the poems Clemens wrote on board the *Sacramento*, he mentioned Cox and "virtuous Marcus Twain" among those who rebuked a "disgraceful mob" of revelers for setting "their lungs afloat in floods of tangle-foot whiskee" (SLC 1884). Long after Cox's death another acquaintance recalled him as "a noble hearted Englishman and a charming companion when sober," but suggested that "whiskey got away with him at last" (Hopkins, 182–83; "The Ranks Thinning," San Francisco *Alta California*, 19 Apr 80, 1).

[2] The *Montana* was commanded by John M. Cavarly (1832–95), a former clipper-ship captain from New London, Connecticut, who had worked for the Pacific Mail Steamship Company since 1864. Clemens may have known him at

the Lick House, his San Francisco residence ("Ocean Steamers," San Francisco *Alta California*, 6 July 68, 4; San Francisco *Morning Call:* "Items from Sea and Shore," 8 Feb 91, 3; "Died," 31 Oct 95, 15; San Francisco City and County 1869, 19).

[3]Oliver O. Eldridge (1818–1902), originally from Yarmouth, Massachusetts, was the West Coast manager and booking agent for the Pacific Mail Steamship Company. He was one of the San Francisco citizens whom Mark Twain's lecture handbill had represented as signing the "call" for him to leave rather than lecture ("Deaths," San Francisco *Chronicle*, 18 Dec 1902, 12; San Francisco City and County 1867, s.v. "Eldridge, Oliver"; "Grand Dinner to the Chinese Embassy," San Francisco *Alta California*, 29 Apr 68, 1; SLC 1868iii).

[4]Exodus 2:22.

[5]According to the *Montana*'s memoranda, the ship could not have been at latitude 24°15′ on 11 July, as Clemens's dateline indicates: at 12:09 A.M. on that day the ship arrived at Cabo San Lucas, at roughly latitude 23°, and was at about 21° by nightfall. His comment here, however, that the *Montana* was "expecting to meet the Golden City every minute," implies that the date is correct but not the latitude reading: the two ships seem to have passed—without sighting each other—early in the morning of 12 July. Furthermore, their schedules would normally bring them into proximity late on the *Montana*'s fifth day out of San Francisco, at about latitude 20°, as occurred on their next trip (San Francisco *Evening Bulletin:* "Arrival of the 'Golden City,'" 18 July 68, 5; "Arrival of the 'Montana,'" 11 Aug 68, 3; "Arrival of the 'Montana,'" 16 Sept 68, 3).

[6]Charles Dickinson had also been a fellow passenger on the *Henry Chauncey* and the *Sacramento*, presumably the "young Dickinson" who assisted at the drunken festivities of the "brawling gang" (SLC 1884; "Passengers for California," San Francisco *Alta California*, 16 Mar 68, 1).

To Mary Mason Fairbanks
3 August 1868 • New York, N.Y.

(MS, *damage emended:* CSmH)

WESTMINSTER HOTEL, COR. OF IRVING PLACE AND 16TH ST.
NEW YORK ROBERTS, PALMER & FERRIN PROPRS

Aug. 3d.

Dear Mother—

I wrote you Wednesday last, when I arrived—I have the letter in my pocket yet—forgot to mail it. I wrote my other mother at the same time. I have both letters in my pocket. I am always particular to write to my friends. Don't scold. I have met many friends, & have been very,

very busy. I have not seen Capt. Duncan, or the Beaches, but have Dan & Jack Van Nostrand.

I have worked hard on an article for the Tribune, concerning the Chinese Treaty, & I promised to send it down to-day. It isn't finished. If I don't finish it to-day I shall not finish it at all.[1] I did not come east to work, except on the book. I expect to go to Hartford tomorrow, & begin.[2]

I wish I *could* go immediately West, & comply with your kind invitation, but I suppose it will be impossible to do it before 1st October. Written contracts are pretty binding, you know.

Dan says you were in Elmira a short time ago. I wish I could have arrived soon enough to see you. Cannot you come East now? *You* haven't got anything to do.

I knew that dog would die. I knew perfectly well you had invoked a fatal disaster for him when you gave him my name. He received all my sins along with the name, perhaps, & no dog could survive that.

Remember me most kindly, to all the family, & herewith know that I hold you to an extension of your invitation, to take effect two months hence. Whereupon, you will please stand ready to trot out your fatted calf.[3]

[*closing and signature cut away*]

[1] The next day, a six-thousand-word article, "The Treaty with China," signed "Mark Twain," appeared on the front page of the New York *Tribune*, explicating the treaty just ratified by the Senate on 24 July. By Clemens's own admission, the article was "concocted" by him with the Burlingame family and J. McLeavy Brown, first secretary of Burlingame's Chinese mission (SLC 1868kkk; Senate 1887, 16:355–56; 7 Oct 68 to Burlingame; Anson Burlingame to William H. Seward, 14 Dec 67, Congress, 1:494). Alert to Clemens's close personal relationship with Burlingame, the *Tribune* evidently commissioned the article on 30 July, the day after his arrival at the Westminster Hotel, where Burlingame and the Chinese delegation also arrived on 29 July, "at a late hour" ("The Chinese Embassy," New York *Evening Post*, 30 July 68, 2). John Russell Young, still the *Tribune*'s managing editor, noted in his diary for 30 July: "Came down late, and called on Anson Burlingame and Mark Twain. Chatted for an hour and had a pleasant chat." It may have been Young who explained that the article was "furnished . . . by a gentleman who thoroughly understands whereof he writes" (John Russell Young, entry for 30 July; "A full explanation . . . ," New York *Tribune*, 4 Aug 68, 4). The chief makers of the Burlingame treaty, as it came to be known, were Secretary of State William Seward, who drafted the eight articles, and Burlingame, who, as Chinese envoy to the West, was empowered to negotiate on behalf of the Chinese government. The main provisions of the treaty

recognized China's right to unmolested dominion over her own territories, with China conceding her control over inland trade and navigation; granted China the right to appoint consuls to American ports; insured freedom from persecution for followers of foreign religions in either country; allowed unrestricted voluntary migration between China and the United States; and admitted reciprocal rights of travel and residence. (Tsai, 28)

In his impassioned analysis, Clemens expressed a strong belief that the treaty would help to prevent persecution of Chinese immigrants, since a Chinese consul could "call to a strict account all who wrong them":

It affords me infinite satisfaction to call particular attention to this Consul clause, and think of the howl that will go up from the cooks, the railroad graders, and the cobble-stone artists of California, when they read it. They can never beat and bang and set the dogs on the Chinamen any more. These pastimes are lost to them forever. In San Francisco, a large part of the most interesting local news in the daily papers consists of gorgeous compliments to the "able and efficient" Officer This and That for arresting Ah Foo, or Ching Wang, or Song Hi for stealing a chicken; but when some white brute breaks an unoffending Chinaman's head with a brick, the paper does not compliment any officer for arresting the assaulter, for the simple reason that the officer does not make the arrest; the shedding of Chinese blood only makes him laugh; he considers it fun of the most entertaining description. . . . I have seen Chinamen abused and maltreated in all the mean, cowardly ways possible to the invention of a degraded nature, but I never saw a policeman interfere in the matter and I never saw a Chinaman righted in a court of justice for wrongs thus done him. (SLC 1868kkk)

Clemens also understood the purpose of making emigration easier:

Chinamen work hard, and with tireless perseverance; other foreigners get out of work, and labor exchanges must look out for them. Chinamen look out for themselves, and are never idle a week at a time; they make excellent cooks, washers, ironers, and house servants. . . . The Chinamen, able to work for half wages, will take their rough manual labor off the hands of . . . white men. (SLC 1868kkk)

[2]On the day of his arrival, 29 July, Clemens telegraphed Elisha Bliss, apparently indicating that he was on his way to Hartford. But Bliss was about to release Richardson's new book, *A Personal History of Ulysses S. Grant*, and therefore suggested postponing Clemens's Hartford visit:

Your favors have been received & your telegraph, today. How are you? Glad to hear of your safe arrival Expected to see you tonight, but not neccessary to discomode yourself. I replied "I shall be in N.Y. on Monday" to your dispatch— Now what I wish to say is we are just bringing out Richardson's "*Grant*" Book will make its appearance *tomorrow*— Therefore we do not need to press this business unless you wish it. I thought perhaps you would prefer to send your manuscript up by Express to me, let me look it over—& see you on Monday in N.Y. & arrange things there. I should then be able to express an opinion as to the thing, & whether any alterations would suggest themselves to my mind. I mean of course *minor ones* such as arrangements of chapters, styles &c.— I could talk with you more knowingly as to our future steps &c— Having seen you there, you would probably find it neccessary to come to Hartford soon after & stay perhaps a few days with us. (Bliss to SLC, 29 July 68, CU-MARK)

Clemens probably did not send his manuscript, and he did postpone the trip. Bliss and Clemens could have met in New York anytime between 3 and 7 August, when Clemens evidently traveled to Hartford (SLC 1868*lll*).

[3]Luke 15:23.

To Frank Fuller
15 August 1868 • Hartford, Conn.
(MS: CLjC)

☞ Don't make a d—d mistake, now, & send *both* these letters to Dubuque.

148 Asylum st.[1]
Hartf[d] 000 000

Dear Fuller,

You old fool. Why don't you publish your private letters in book form? They would take like everything. Write me a humorous lecture on California, as soon as you can. Or if you will furnish the humor, I will get up the statistics.

Bully for you and Clapp.[2]

Those societies out there can't afford to pay much, & I have been thinking it would be well to get in with them by means of low prices now, & then charge them heavy next season. But you know more about business than I do. If you think well of what I have said in the enclosed letter, mail it—if not, don't.[3] I expect to arrive in New York (at the Everett House, Union Square,)[4] two days hence (viz. Monday, 17.[th.]) Then I'll talk to you. A Pittsburgh society offers me $100 to preach in November—open their course for them.[5]

Speaking of "courses,"[6] I have mine, now. Please forward one dozen Odorless Rubber Cundrums—I don't mind them being odorless—I can supply the odor myself. I would like to have your picture on them.[7]

Yrs
Mark.

[1] The address of the American Publishing Company. The meaning of the zeros following "Hartf[d]" remains unknown: see the textual commentary for this letter.

[2] Possibly Henry Clapp, Jr., whose New York *Saturday Press* had published "Jim Smiley and His Jumping Frog" in November 1865, and who was now on the staff of De Witt Van Buren's New York *Leader*, a weekly (Wilkins, 310; Rowell, 73). The reason for Clemens's congratulations has not been discovered.

[3] The enclosed letter has not been found, but it was almost certainly addressed to G. L. Torbert of Dubuque, secretary of the Associated Western Literary Societies. Torbert's organization had evidently repeated its offer of November 1867 to sponsor a lecture tour for Clemens (see 24 Nov 67 to Fuller; Clemens's 1868 lecture-tour schedule may be found in Appendix E).

[4] A small but fashionable residential hotel on the north side of Union Square at Seventeenth Street (Morris, 110; Browne, 397).

[5] Clemens lectured in Pittsburgh, for a $100 fee, on 19 November (see 20 Nov 68 to JLC and family).

[6] Menstruation.

[7] Fuller was now co-owner, with George H. Munroe, of a New York rubber-goods business, which evidently produced condoms, among other items. The rubber was "odorless" because it contained very little sulfur (Wilson 1868, 384, 789; note by Fuller on the verso of 24 Sept 68 to Fuller). Clemens told his readers in an *Alta* letter dated 22 October: "Frank Fuller, ex-Acting Governor of Utah, is located at 19 Park place, New York, and is making money hand over fist in the manufacture and sale of a patent odorless India rubber cloth, which is coming greatly into fashion for buggy-tops and such things" (SLC 1868ooo).

To Mary Mason Fairbanks
17 August 1868 • Hartford, Conn.

(MS: CSmH)

Hartford, Aug. 17.

My Dear Mother =

You didn't answer my letter from New York. Suppose you are mad about something. You'll get over it—that is all right.

It is very late—been writing a letter to Chicago Republican.[1] Shall leave for New York tomorrow.[2] Shall be there 3 to 5 days. Then shall spend a few days with the other cub[3] in Elmira—& then both of us will go to Cleveland to see the old bear.[4] Good-bye.

~~M~~ Yrs
Sam Clemens

Mrs. Mary M. Fairbanks | Care Daily *Herald* | Cleveland | Ohio [*return address:*] FROM | AMERICAN PUBLISHING CO., | HARTFORD, CONN. | IF NOT CALLED FOR WITHIN | TEN DAYS, PLEASE RETURN. [*postmarked:*] HARTFORD CONN. AUG 17

[1] Clemens's dispatch of 17 August to the Chicago *Republican* discussed the recent increase in emigration to California, described the busy railroad linking Panama City with Aspinwall, and gave an account of what turned out to be his final meeting with Captain Edgar (Ned) Wakeman, the garrulous seaman who inspired his literary interest for many years (SLC 1868*lll*; *L1*, 370 n. 8; for Wakeman, see *N&J1*, 241–43). Clemens ended the letter with a flattering description of Hartford and a request to direct his mail to the "Everett House, Union Square" during his upcoming visit to the Midwest.

[2] Since on the morning of 18 August Clemens was reported at the Everett House, he presumably took a late train on 17 (not 18) August ("The City," New York *Tribune*, 18 Aug 68, 8).

[3] Charles J. Langdon.

[4] Mary Mason Fairbanks.

To Charles J. Langdon *per* Telegraph Operator 21 August 1868 • En route from New York to Elmira, N.Y.

(Jervis Langdon, 5)

Train stops every fifteen minutes and stays three quarters of an hour, figure out when it will arrive and meet me.[1]

[1] On Friday, 21 August, Clemens took the train to Elmira, New York, to visit for a "few days" with the Langdon family (17 Aug 68 to Fairbanks). Charles Langdon's son, Jervis, recalled that "without further consulting the time table Mr. Clemens characteristically chose that train with the biggest sounding name (the Cannon Ball, I believe it was), and towards the middle of the day my father received this telegram." According to Paine, Clemens "meant to go by a fast train, but, with his natural gift for misunderstanding time-tables, of course took a slow one, telegraphing his approach from different stations along the road. Young Langdon concluded to go down the line as far as Waverly to meet him" (Jervis Langdon, 5; *MTB*, 1:367). If Clemens had taken the "Day Express," which departed New York at 7:30 A.M., he would have reached Elmira at about 6:00 that evening, but he seems instead to have taken the 10:00 A.M. "Express Mail," which did not reach Elmira until almost midnight (advertisement, Elmira *Advertiser*, 20 Aug 68, 2; advertisement, New York *Evening Post*, 20 Aug 68, 1). Jervis Langdon added:

> Accompanied by an old friend, my father went down the road to meet the new friend, whose entertaining humor and irresistible magnetism he hoped would balance up with the family for all the uncouth manners and looks, and make a short visit endurable. They

found him in the smoker, in a yellow duster and a very dirty, old straw hat. His wardrobe was compressed into such small compass that it didn't really appear he had brought any. (Jervis Langdon, 5)

Langdon intercepted the train at Waverly, some fifteen miles from Elmira; Paine described the moment:

Langdon greeted him warmly but with doubt. Finally he summoned courage to say, hesitatingly:

"You've got some other clothes, haven't you?"

The arriving guest was not in the least disturbed.

"Oh yes," he said with enthusiasm, "I've got a fine brand-new outfit in this bag, all but a hat. It will be late when we get in, and I won't see any one to-night. You won't know me in the morning. We'll go out early and get a hat."

This was a large relief to the younger man, and the rest of the journey was happy enough. True to promise, the guest appeared at daylight correctly, even elegantly clad, and an early trip to the shops secured the hat. (*MTB*, 1:367)

The Elmira *Advertiser* reported Clemens's arrival:

MARK TWAIN arrived in the City last evening, to be the guest of CHARLES LANGDON, for a few days. It is hoped—indeed, it is the *on dit*, that he will be induced to give a lecture at the Opera House during his stay. He has already attained a great notoriety in California, as a writer and editor, and his Quaker City experiences gave him a wide reputation throughout the country. It will be remembered, that he was one of the excursionists on the Quaker City to the Holy Land, last year, and at the time, established a close fellowship with CHARLES LANGDON, of this City. ("Personal," Elmira *Advertiser*, 22 Aug 68, 4)

Clemens did lecture in Elmira, but not until 23 November.

To Jane Lampton Clemens and Family
24 and 25 August 1868 • Elmira, N.Y.

(MS: NPV)

Elmira, N. Y. Aug. 24.

Dear Folks—

You see I am progressing—though slowly.[1] I shall be here a week yet—maybe two—for Charley Langdon cannot get away until his father's chief business man[2] returns from a journey—& a visit to Mrs Fairbanks, at Cleveland, would lose half its pleasure if Charley were not along. Moulton, of St. Louis ought to be there, too. We three were Mrs. F.'s' "cubs," in the Quaker City. She took good care that we were at church regularly on Sundays; at the 8-bells prayer meeting every night; & she kept our buttons sewed on & our clothing in order—&, in a word, was as busy, & considerate & as watchful over her family of uncouth & unruly cubs, & as patient & as long-suffering, withal, as a natural mother. So we expect

Aug 25th—

Didn't finish yesterday. Something called me away. I am most comfortably situated here. This is the pleasantest family I ever knew.[3] I only have one trouble, & that is that they give too much thought & too much time & invention to the object of making my visit pass delightfully. It needs

. . . .

1 Clemens intended to visit his family in St. Louis after his stay in Elmira and his trip to Cleveland with Charles Langdon.

2 Unidentified, but see note 3.

3 Jervis and Olivia Lewis Langdon were both natives of New York State. They were married in 1832, and settled in Elmira in 1845. Langdon soon became prosperous in the lumber business and then quite wealthy in the coal trade, which he entered in 1855. His extensive operations included mines in Pennsylvania and Nova Scotia, and a huge rail and shipping network that enabled him to become a pioneer supplier of anthracite coal to western New York State, Chicago, and the Far West. In 1865 he dissolved his old partnerships, and from 1866 operated independently as "J. Langdon, Miner & Dealer in Anthracite & Bituminous Coal." His principal business associates were Theodore W. Crane, the husband of Susan Langdon Crane, his adopted daughter; Charles, his only son; and John D. F. Slee. These four men formally became partners in J. Langdon and Company in May 1870. Langdon was known to be a man of great integrity with a strong social conscience. An ardent abolitionist, he had served as a "conductor" on the Underground Railroad, and counted Frederick Douglass, whom he had helped escape from slavery, among his friends (Towner, 610–17; "In Memoriam," Elmira *Saturday Evening Review*, 13 Aug 70, 5; 3 Sept 68 to Crane; Siebert, 414; Douglass to Olivia Lewis Langdon, 9 Nov 70, CtHMTH). The Langdons had been founding members of Elmira's antislavery Park Congregational Church, whose pastor, Thomas K. Beecher, testified in his eulogy of Jervis Langdon:

> At a time when opposition to slavery was costly . . . Mr. Langdon was a pronounced and determined anti-slavery man.
>
> Very few fugitives from slavery have passed through this region without receiving a benefit from him. . . . And when at last, by the costly compulsions of civil war, the system of slavery was abolished, Mr. Langdon's redoubled exertions in behalf of the now freed men were sufficient testimony that his previous zeal had not been a cheap destructiveness, . . . but a true and tender-hearted philanthropy. (Thomas K. Beecher, 27–28)

See also the Langdon family genealogy in Appendix A.

To Elisha Bliss, Jr.
3 September 1868 • Elmira, N.Y.

(Transcript: WU)

Elmira Sept 3—'68

Mr Bliss

Dear Sir:

Inclosed you will find that "Eulogy." I found it today in the "Excelsior Magazine." Please hand it to your neighbor next door who asked for it.[1]

If any letters come for me between now & the 17th please send them to Cleveland, "*care of the Daily Herald.*"[2]

Regards to all the family.[3] How do you come on with the engravings—& in what manner have you decided to illustrate?[4]

Yrs Truly

Sam L. Clemens

[1] The actual clipping enclosed was presumably given to Bliss's unidentified neighbor and is therefore lost. But it was doubtless a single leaf (pages 99–100) torn from the August issue of *The Excelsior Monthly Magazine, and Public Spirit*, which reprinted Clemens's response to the toast to "Woman" delivered at the Washington Correspondents' Club dinner on 11 January; it is reproduced in photofacsimile in Appendix E. The *Excelsior* was a New York periodical "devoted to the elevation of the race," which had published only two previous issues, for June and July. The magazine's ultimate source for Clemens's speech, so far as this can be determined, was the text that appeared in the New York *Evening Post* on 15 January ("A Eulogy of Woman by 'Mark Twain,'" 1). Either the *Excelsior* editors, Miles N. Olmsted and Thomas A. Welwood, or some unidentified intervening copy, omitted one sentence that was in the *Post:* "She bears our children—ours as a general thing" (Wilson 1869, 335, 830, 1143, and "City Register," 25).

[2] The newspaper owned in part by Abel Fairbanks.

[3] Bliss's family consisted of his wife, Amelia Crosby Bliss—whom he had married in 1856—and their three children: Walter (1858–1917), Emma (b. 1860), and Almira (b. 1865). Bliss also had one surviving child by his first wife, who had died in 1855: Francis (Frank) Edgar Bliss (1843–1915) (biographical information on Bliss, CtHSD; Donald T. Bliss to Hamlin Hill, 11 Nov 1964, CU-MARK; New York *Times:* "Obituary Notes," 17 Mar 1917, 13; "Francis Edward Bliss," 10 Nov 1915, 13).

[4] Bliss evidently replied that he wanted to have "pictures sandwiched in with

the text" as well as full-page illustrations (5 Oct 68 to Mary Mason Fairbanks). *The Innocents Abroad* ultimately contained more than 230 engravings, some of which were made from photographs Clemens himself had acquired during his trip, while others were based on pictures collected and made available by fellow passenger Moses S. Beach (Hirst and Rowles, 31). The engravers may not have even begun yet to prepare the illustrations: by early February 1869 only 150 had been completed (Bliss to SLC, 10 Feb 69, CU-MARK).

To Henry M. Crane
3 September 1868 • Elmira, N.Y.

(MS: WU)

J. LANGDON, MINER & DEALER IN ANTHRACITE & BITUMINOUS COAL OFFICE NO. 6 BALDWIN STREET

ELMIRA, N.Y. Sept 3, 186 8

H. M. Crane, Esq

D[r] Sir—

Your favor of Aug. 28 is just to hand. In reply, I ~~must~~ can say that I am willing to lecture, but I cannot tell just yet what the subject would be—either "Venice" or "California," I think. You may set me down for some day in January, if you will—& let me know the date. As to terms, I only want your usual price—what is it? ‸My usual price is $100.‸[1] My address, for the next 3 weeks, will be "*1312 Chesnut street, St Louis, Mo.*"

Yrs Truly
Sam. L. Clemens
(Mark Twain.)

C. M. Crane, Esq[2] | Care Lincoln Literary Society | Rondout | New York. [*postmarked:*] ELMIRA N.Y. SEP 5 [*postage stamp removed*] [*return address:*] RETURN TO J. LANGDON, | ELMIRA, N. Y., | IF NOT DELIVERED WITHIN 10 DAYS. [*docketed:*] Sept 1868 | Twain | Ans[d] 8th was marked for Jan 6[3] [*and*] 850
125
75
1050

[1]In November 1868 the New York *Evening Post* reported that the highest-paid speaker currently represented by the American Literary Bureau in New York was author and women's-rights advocate Olive Logan, who earned up to $250 per lecture. Several other celebrities could command from $150 to $200 at this time, such as Henry Ward Beecher, Anna Dickinson, John Bartholomew Garth, and Horace Greeley. Clemens averaged $100 even during the 1869–70 season, and in 1871 still considered $150 a high fee ("The Price of Lectures," New York *Evening Post*, 28 Nov 68, 2; Higginson, 54; Eubank, 134, 137; SLC to George L. Fall, 20 July 71, *MTL*, 1:189–90).

[2]Clemens's difficulty in reading Crane's handwriting continued (see 20 May 67 to Crane), causing him to mistake Crane's first initial, at least in addressing the envelope.

[3]Crane apparently first booked Clemens to lecture in Rondout on 6 January 1869. Clemens must have rescheduled his lecture in a later letter (now lost), since he actually performed in Rondout on 2 December 1868; in early January he was touring the Midwest.

To Olivia L. Langdon
7 and 8 September 1868 • Elmira, N.Y.

(MS: CU-MARK)

Monday, Midnight.[1]

My Honored "Sister"—

The impulse is strong upon me to say to you how grateful I am to you and to all of you~~,~~ for the patience, the consideration & the unfailing kindness which has been shown me ever since I came within the shadow of this roof, and which has made the past fortnight the sole period of my life unmarred by a regret. Unmarred by a regret. I say it deliberately. For I do not regret that I ~~love you~~ have loved you, still love & shall always love you. I accept the situation, uncomplainingly, hard as it is. Of old I am acquainted with grief,[2] disaster & disappointment, & have borne these troubles as became a man. So, also, I shall bear this last & bitterest, even though it break my heart. I would not dishonor this worthiest love that has yet been born within me by any puerile thought, or word, or deed. It is better to have loved & lost you than that my life should have remained forever the blank it was before. For once, ‸at least,‸ in the idle years that have drifted over me, I have seen the world all beautiful, & known what ~~is~~ it was to hope. For once I have known what it was to feel my sluggish pulses stir with a living ambition. The world that was so beautiful, is dark again; the hope that shone as the sun, is gone; the brave ambition is dead. Yet I say again, it is better for me that I have loved & do love you; that with more than Eastern devotion I worship you; that I lay down all of my life that is worth the living, upon this hopeless altar where no fires of love shall descend to consume it. If you *could* but—

But no more of this. I have said it only from that impulse which *drives* men to speak of great calamities which have befallen them, & so seek relief. I could not say it to give you pain. The words are spoken, & they have fallen upon forgiving ears. For your dear sake my tongue & my pen are now forbidden to repeat them ever again.

And so, henceforward, I claim only that you will let me freight my speeches to you with ~~only~~ ‸simply‸ the sacred love a brother bears to a sister. I ask that you will write to me sometimes, as to a friend ‸whom‸ you feel will do all that a man may to be worthy of your friendship—or as to a brother whom you know will hold his sister's honor as dearly as his own, her wishes as his law, her pure judgements above his blinded worldly wisdom. Being adrift, now, & rudderless, my voyage promises ill; but while the friendly beacon of your sisterly love beams ‸though‸ never so faintly through the fogs & the mists, I cannot be hopelessly wrecked. I shall not shame your confidence by speaking ‸to you in ~~the~~ future letters‸ of this dead love whose requiem I have been chanting. No, I will not offend. I will not misunderstand you.

My honored sister, you are *so* good & so beautiful—& I am so proud of you! Give me a little room in that great heart of yours—only the little you have promised me—& if I fail to deserve it may I remain forever the homeless vagabond I am! If you & mother Fairbanks will only scold me & upbraid me now & then, I shall fight my way through the world, never fear. Write me *something* from time to time—texts from the New Testament, if nothing else occurs to you—or dissertations on ~~the sin of~~ smoking—or extracts from your Book of Sermons[3]—*anything*, whatever—the reflection that my matchless sister wrote it will be sufficient. If it be a suggestion, I will entertain it; if it be an injunction, I will honor it; if it be a command I will obey it or~~, break my royal neck~~ ‸exhaust my energies‸ trying.

And now, good-bye, my precious sister—& may all the sorrows which fate has ~~adorne~~ ordained for you fall upon this foolish head of mine, which would be so glad & so proud to suffer them in your stead. I leave you to the ministering angels—for, daughter of earth as you are, they throng the air about you—they are with you, & such as you, always.

~~B~~ Sincerely & affectionately,

Sam L. Clemens.[4]

Miss Olivia Langdon, | Present. [*docketed by OLL:* Sept. 1868— | 1st][5]

[1]Clemens completed this letter in the early morning hours of Tuesday, 8 September. Later that morning, he and Charles Langdon left for Cleveland to visit the Fairbankses.

[2]Isaiah 53:3.

[3]Unidentified.

[4]Harriet Lewis (later Paff), Olivia's cousin, stayed with the Langdons throughout Clemens's initial visit, from 21 August to 8 September (she is more fully identified in 19 and 20 Dec 68 to OLL, n. 9). Nearly thirty years later she gave the following account:

> I really felt that I had one advantage over my cousin, but only one. She was rich, beautiful and intellectual, but she could not see through a joke, or see anything to laugh at in the wittiest sayings unless explained in detail—I could. The day came for his arrival—Whatever opinion we had formed of his appearance, at least we were not overawed by his presence, or greeting. He said—"How do you do," just as any one would, except with that lazy drawl which has added much flavor to his wit and humor. . . . Our acquaintance progressed to our mutual enjoyment. We rode, walked, talked & sang together, for Mr. C. had a very sweet tenor voice. But alas—I soon discovered that my quickness at seeing the point of a joke and the witty sayings that I had considered almost irresistible were simply nothing in comparison to my cousin's gifts. Mr. C evidently greatly preferred her sense to my nonsense. I told him later that I should never understand why he did. I think I discovered the fact almost as soon as he did, himself, and I thought it would be a most suitable match for both, and anything I could do to help them along should be done. I had been intending to go to N.Y. for a visit, but had postponed it on account of Mr. C's coming. I now decided to go, thinking the courtship might progress better if I were out of the way. Olivia was very unsuspicious, therefore, before leaving I gave her a hint of what I thought Mr. C. had in his mind & heart and said that on my return I should ask a question, in regard to a question I was quite sure would be asked her, and I wanted a favorable answer to both.
>
> My visit was prolonged until a month had passed, when a preemtory message came for my immediate return, which was obeyed. What was my disappointment to learn that the question had been asked, and a refusal given. (Paff, 2–4)

[5]"Present" was the customary term to write on a letter to be personally delivered rather than sent through the mail (Smiley, 410–11). Olivia numbered each of Clemens's courtship letters, beginning with this one, until their marriage in February 1870. It is not known whether she numbered each upon receipt, or after several had arrived, but the numbers appear to be largely contemporaneous with the correspondence itself (see also the textual commentary for this letter). Only one of her replies is known to survive (OLL to SLC, 13 Nov 69, CU-MARK).

To Olivia L. Langdon
21 September 1868 • St. Louis, Mo.
(MS: CU-MARK)

St Louis, Sept. 21, 1868.

My Honored Sister:

I cannot frame language so that it will express to you how grateful I am for that large charity & thoughtful consideration which prompted you to speak so gently when you could have wounded so deeply. I had wished ever so much to receive a reply from you, & yet dreaded it—for I could not believe it possible, under the circumstances, that you could write a letter that would not give me pain, no matter how hard you might try to avoid it. But you did.—It was almost a miracle. Therefore, is it strange that I am grateful?

And I thank you for the happy surprise the picture brought—I thank you more than I can tell—though I never blamed you in the least for withholding it ~~before.~~ ‸formerly.‸ I never dreampt of such a thing—for I believed then, & still believe, that whatever you do is ~~always~~ right. And ‸so,‸ now that you have set aside that just & proper rule of conduct to give me this gratification, I know that you have done it with a free will, & that the gift is sent without reluctance or distrust. You know too well the high honor & respect I hold you in, my sister, to fear that you can ever have cause to repent your transgressed law.

You say to me: “I shall pray for you daily.” Not any words that ever were spoken to me have touched me like these. They have recurred to my mind often & again—& so I have been thinking, thinking, thinking—& what I have arrived at, is the conviction that I would be less than a man if I went on in my old careless way while you were praying for me—if I showed lack of respect, worthiness, reverence, while the needs of one like me were being voiced in the august presence of God. ~~I had not thought of this before, ◊◊◊~~ I beg that you will continue to pray for me—for I have a vague, far-away sort of idea that it may not be wholly in vain. In one respect, at least, it *shall* not be in vain—for I will so mend my conduct that I shall grow *worthier* of your prayers, & your good will & sisterly solicitude, as the days go by. Furthermore, (—it has taken me long ~~time~~ to make up my mind to say these grave words, which, once said, cannot be recalled,) I *will* "pray with you," as you ask: and with such faith & such encouragement withal, as are in me, though feeble & of little worth I feel they must be. It seems strange enough to me—this, reverence, this solemnity, this supplication—& yet, you must surely have some faith that it will not necessarily be useless, else you would not have suggested it. *You* do not speak carelessly. ~~[And you~~ ‸[You‸ perceive that I do *not* think you have written "too earnestly."]

I was so sorry Charlie could not come further West with me, for he is a good traveling comrade, & if he has any unworthy traits in his nature the partiality born of old companionship has blinded me to them. Mrs. Fairbanks was very proud of him that night of the reception ~~in~~ at her house. But I am glad, now, that he did not come to St. Louis. He would have had no rest here—I have none—& it is a muddy, smoky, mean city to run about in. I am called East.—Must finish my ~~f~~ visit here in January. I leave Thursday—24th.[1] I shall rest in Chicago & in Cleveland, & I desire also to tarry a day & a night in Elmira ‸(Monday 28th)‸ if your doors are still open to me & you have not reconsidered your kind invitation.

I fear you did not expect to hear from me so soon—but still you will forgive this letter, will you not? Consider, my indulgent sister, that after all it is only I that so offend. Good-night. The peace that belongeth unto the good, the just & the beautiful, abide with you alway!

—Which is the prayer of him who is proud to write himself—

Your affectionate Brother

Saml. L. Clemens.

Miss Olivia L. Langdon | Elmira | New York. [*postmarked:*] ST LOUIS MO. SEP 22 [*docketed by OLL:*] 2nd

[1]Clemens did not, in fact, complete his visit in January, nor did he leave St. Louis on 24 September.

To Mary Mason Fairbanks
24 September 1868 • St. Louis, Mo.

(Transcript: CU-MARK)

St. Louis, Sept. 24

My Dear Mother—

Yours of the 20th came to hand this morning, & I am glad enough to hear that my visit did not lessen me in your regard. I dimly feared the contrary. Don't be afraid to write sermons—I am perfectly willing not only to receive them but to try to profit by them. Your advice about the building of the lecture I shall strictly follow. I shall try very hard to make it a creditable one. If diligent effort will do this I shall accomplish it. What I want, a hundred times more than "study," is a cheerful day—an untroubled spirit. I hope for such a day.

I shall start day after to-morrow (Saturday) at 8 A.M., which will bring me to Cleveland Sunday morning. Then I will leave Cleveland Monday morning. I have some idea of spending Tuesday in Elmira—will talk with you.[1]

I have received a very jolly letter from Mr. Langdon & one from Charlie. Mr. L. was very low spirited when we saw him last.[2]

I have thought over & over again of writing that squib for the Herald, but I have not once been in a happy humor, & could not do it. There is something in my deep hatred of St. Louis that will hardly let me appear cheery even at my mother's own fireside. Nobody knows what a ghastly infliction it is on me to visit St. Louis. I am afraid I do not always disguise it, either.

I missed Mr. Fairbanks' friend Cleland,[3] in Chicago—couldn't happen to catch him in. I was mighty busy in that town, too.

I wish Mr. Fairbanks would see that photographer & get my imperial-size pictures & hold them for me, till I come.[4]

I shall probably telegraph my approach from some point along the line of the railroad on Saturday night.

. . . .

[1] Clemens evidently did leave St. Louis on the morning of 26 September, and stayed that same night with the Fairbankses. He proceeded to Elmira on 27 Sep-

Clemens and Charles J. Langdon in Cleveland, September 1868. Mark Twain Papers, The Bancroft Library (CU-MARK). See p. 254 n. 4.

tember, staying with the Langdons until the evening of 29 September, when he departed for New York (5 Oct 68 to Mary Mason Fairbanks; OLL to Alice B. Hooker, 29 Sept 68, CtHSD; "Mark Twain . . . ," Elmira *Advertiser*, 30 Sept 68, 4).

[2] Jervis Langdon was suffering from stomach cancer, which would prove fatal in a little less than two years; at this time the gravity of his condition was still unknown.

[3] Cleland has not been identified. Clemens passed through Chicago while traveling from Cleveland to St. Louis.

[4] Clemens and Charles Langdon were photographed together by James F. Ryder during their visit to the Fairbankses; this picture is reproduced above. A second photograph of Clemens, dressed identically, was probably also taken at this time, although the extant print—reproduced as the frontispiece for this volume—was evidently ordered some years later when Ryder was at a different address. Both prints (now in CU-MARK) are "imperial-size"—roughly 4″×6″—rather than the smaller *carte de visite* size.

To Frank Fuller
24 September 1868 • St. Louis, Mo.

(MS: CLjC)

St Louis, Sept 24.

Noble Chief:

~~I~~ Your six-line letter is just to hand, but no cundrum. However, never mind the cundrums. I can get along without them, I suppose. My aunt never uses them. Some people can do things as well as others.[1]

Mr. Torbert appears to be getting along well enough ~~in~~ ‸with‸ the lecture tour. I have made several other appointments to preach.[2]

I hope you are well, Judge, & I hope your Company is well, also. I like Odorless Rubber Companies. I like them because they don't stink.[3]

Yrs always,

Mark.

[1] "Some things can be done as well as others" was one of the mottoes rendered proverbial by Sam Patch (1807?–29), a daredevil who became a folk hero in 1827 when he jumped from a seventy-foot cliff at Passaic Falls. Two years later he was killed in a jump from the top of Genesee Falls, near Rochester (Dorson, 133–38).

[2] See 15 Aug 68 to Fuller, n. 3. Clemens's winter tour began in Cleveland on 17 November 1868 and ended in mid-March 1869. Torbert was responsible for midwestern engagements only: according to Clemens, by late November he had

booked twenty-one dates between 23 December (later moved up to 22 December) and 18 January. Clemens himself arranged ten appearances in November and December, mainly in eastern towns, in part through the agency of the American Literary Bureau in New York, which as early as 3 October was listing "Saml. L. Clemens (Mark Twain)" as an available lecturer on "Americans in the Old World." Later in the tour, Torbert continued to add new engagements until Clemens told him to stop (29? Nov 68 to PAM; "The Price of Lectures," New York *Evening Post*, 28 Nov 68, 2; "The Lecture Season," *Round Table* 8 [3 Oct 68]: 234; SLC to OLL, 29 Jan 69, CU-MARK; Clemens's lecture schedule for November 1868–January 1869 is given in Appendix G).

3 See 15 Aug 68 to Fuller, n. 7.

To Olivia L. Langdon
4–5 October 1868 • Hartford, Conn.

(MS: CU-MARK)

. . . .

P.S.[1]—I suspect that I have unsettled Mrs. Fairbanks' mind, somewhat, concerning her Elmira visit, by telling her how much more prostrated in health I found Mr. Langdon than I had expected, & how inopportune I feared my late visit was, for that reason—for I could not be blind to the truth that he needed quiet & repose more than anything else, & I don't carry much quiet among my baggage. And so you must mend this matter if you have ~~n~~ it in your power. You must write her that Mr. Langdon is a great deal better—that is, if you can do it & still approximate to the truth.[2] Of course you needn't go & tell the *whole* truth, as I have done, my dear contrary, obstinate, wilful, but always just & generous sister—I can't *help* telling the whole truth, (being similar to young George Washington,) but you *must*. Otherwise I ~~m~~ will muss your hair again. I am afraid to write any more, because you were just a little severe the other day, you know. Good-bye, & God give you His peace.

Yr affectionate Brother.

Mark L Clemens.

1 Clemens's third letter to Olivia, to which this postscript must have belonged, has been lost. But on 5 October Clemens alluded to having written her "a little while ago," and one week later he suggested the letter's import by saying "I'll

bet I have written a letter that will *finish* me. I wish I had it back again—I would tone it down some" (5 Oct 68 and 12 Oct 68 to Mary Mason Fairbanks). Presumably, then, he had broken his promise to express only fraternal affection toward Olivia, which may explain why only this playful postscript survives. In his next (18 October) letter to her (which she numbered "4th"), he apologized for having written "in hot-blooded heedlessness."

2 By the time Clemens left Elmira on 29 September, Langdon was feeling well enough to travel, for on that day Olivia wrote to a friend, "Father and Mother go this afternoon to Baltimore where they will be for a few days" (OLL to Alice B. Hooker, 29 Sept 68, CtHSD). According to a letter seen by Dixon Wecter but now lost, the Fairbankses did in fact postpone a fall visit to Elmira because of Langdon's condition (Olivia Lewis Langdon to Mary Mason Fairbanks, 17 Nov 68, paraphrased in *MTMF*, 48 n. 1).

To Mary Mason Fairbanks
5 October 1868 • Hartford, Conn.

(MS: CSmH)

148 Asylum street,
Hartford, Oct. 5.

Dear Mother:

I have been here two or three days—& staid a day in New York.[1] They sent a letter from here to St Louis for me the day before I arrived—could it have been from you?—& with the heads for my lecture in it? If so, do please hurry & write it again—for I want to go to work. The cold I caught the night I came into Cleveland, is still with me & I can do no work now. I thought it was well, else I would not have left Elmira. They warned me against it, & Miss Livy[2] ~~promised~~ prophesied a relapse if I went. The prophecy was fulfilled within ten hours. It has been a terrible cold. It may take its course though—it can't last always. After I had been a night & a day at Mr. Langdon's, ~~c~~Charley & I got into the wagon at 8 PM, ~~& just~~ to leave for New York, & just as we sat down on the aftermost seat the horse suddenly started, the seat broke loose, & we went over backwards, Charley falling in all sorts of ways & I lighting ~~on~~ exactly on my head in the gutter & breaking my neck in eleven different places. I lay there about four or five minutes, completely insensible—& then the water ~~they~~ the young ladies were pouring on my head brought me to.

The seat followed Charley out & split his head wide open, so that you could look~~in~~ through it just as if you were looking through a gorge in a mountain. There wasn't anything to intercept the view—which was curious, because his brains hadn't been knocked out. They took us in the library & laid us out—& then came the inquest—& so we were all ready for the funeral in the morning. They buried us both in one grave, but it was too crowded to suit *me*, because I am not used to sleeping double, anyhow, dead or alive, & so I left, & am here. I despise to be buried along with another man—it is too sociable. I like to be planted by myself—under a monument. But seriously, it came very near being a fatal mishap to both of us. I had rather not take the chances on it again.[3]

I had an exceedingly pleasant time of it at Mr. Langdon's. I can't *write* about that matter that is in your mind & mine, but suffice it that it bears just a *little* pleasanter aspect than it did when I saw you last & I am *just about* that much more cheerful over it, you know. The letter I wrote a little while ago was not to *you*.[4] We must not be too fast with our interpretations—yet still ~~it *will* seem a *little* bit~~—nothing—nothing. The ‸(friendly)‸ correspondence was argued against & objected to before, but not this time. Is—*is* the sign worth anything? I wish it were—but then all signs fail in a dry time.

We have had a long talk about the book, & concluded that it cannot be illustrated profusely enough & get it out in December, & therefore we shall make a spring book of it & issue it the first of March. The publishers are ready to snatch it out ~~now~~ at once, with the usual full-page engravings, but they prefer to have pictures sandwiched in with the text, & [I] do too. So I shall have an idle month, now, on my lecture, if I ever get at it.

Give my love to all the family, please. Good-bye—

Yours Affectionately
Sam. L. Clemens.

Mrs. A. W. Fairbanks, | Care "Herald." | Cleveland | Ohio. [*return address:*] FROM | AMERICAN PUBLISHING CO., | HARTFORD, CONN. | IF NOT CALLED FOR WITHIN | TEN DAYS, PLEASE RETURN. [*postmarked:*] HARTFORD CONN. OCT 5

[1]Clemens had returned to Hartford, where he again stayed with the Blisses, to continue preparation of the printer's copy, particularly the illustrations, for

The Innocents Abroad. The exact date of his return and the date of his one-day stay in New York have not been determined.

[2]Olivia L. Langdon.

[3]Olivia gave the following account of this mishap in a letter to Alice Hooker, written just after Clemens's departure:

Mr Clemens spent two days here on his way back to Hartford from St. Louis, he intended only to remain one day, but as he and Charlie started for the Depot, they were thrown out of the back end of the waggon (it was a democrat-waggon and the seat was not fastened) both striking on their heads, Charlie's head was quite badly cut Mr Clemens was stunned— It did not prove to be serious in either case— We all enjoyed Mr. Clemens stay with us very much indeed— (OLL to Alice B. Hooker, 29 Sept 68, CtHSD)

Paine reported that at the end of the first day, Clemens confided his love for Olivia to Charles, who did not consider him a suitable match for his sheltered sister and recommended that he leave immediately (*MTB*, 1:368). Clemens later said that he had exaggerated the seriousness of his injury to gain time with Olivia (AD, 14 Feb 1906, CU-MARK, in *MTA*, 2:106–9).

[4]That is, 4–5 Oct 68 to OLL.

To Abel W. Fairbanks
5 October 1868 • Hartford, Conn.

(MS: CSmH)

148 A~~y~~sylum st.
Hartford, Oct. 5.

Dear Mr. Fairbanks[1]—

When I was in St Louis the other day, I received a tired & travel-worn letter, originally from Columbus, Ohio, proposing that I should lecture there during the coming winter. The ~~s~~Society that sent it may have forgotten the circumstance by this time, for that letter had been browsing around a good while, & had more postmarks on it than there was room for, & so some were sticking over the edge. It had been to San Francisco; & back to New York; then to Washington; to Hartford, ~~Cleveland,~~ Elmira, & finally to St Louis. I suppose it would have gone to the ~~devil,~~ ‸dickens,‸ eventually, if it had kept on following me. It was the most faithful letter I ever saw. I conceived a fellow feeling for it, which ripened at once in‸to‸ a ~~strong~~ warm personal friendship—& I sat down ‸immediately‸ to answer it—which was considerable promptness for *me*. But something called me away, & when I came back the letter was gone. It had got used to going, I suppose, & couldn't wait. I thought of holding on ~~t~~ till it gets back from San Francisco again, or wherever it has gone, but it loafs around too much, & wanders out of the straight track too often to be depended on, & so I fear me the winter may be over before it turns up again. Therefore, my object in ~~wr~~ dropping you this formal business note is to ask that you will ~~send~~ request some friend of yours in Columbus ~~to~~ (I am a stranger there,) to find out what Society that was, ~~&~~ (my memory is as faithful as ever about forgetting things,) & present to them my compliments & regrets, & request them to write Mr. G. L. Torbert, Secretary of the Associated Western Library[2] Associations, Dubuque, Iowa, on the subject of that lecture. I am sorry I have to take such an excessively roundabout & unbusinesslike way of communicating with the Columbus Society, but I know of no better one under the circumstances.

~~M~~ Yrs always
Mark.

P. S. ~~I~~ My love to the family. I wrote Mrs. F. to-night. I suppose if you sent this letter ‸of mine‸ straight to some friend of yours in Columbus it would ~~save~~ state the case itself & save you trouble.[3]

[1] Abel Whitmore Fairbanks (1817–94) was born in Cornish, New Hampshire, and learned the printing trade as a very young man. In 1836 he was in charge of the job office of the Detroit *Advertiser*, and several years later purchased the defunct Toledo *Blade* and successfully revived it. He moved to Cleveland in 1849 and early the next year bought a half-interest in the *Herald* (Lorenzo Sayles Fairbanks, 551–52; Rose, 232).

[2] Clemens meant "Literary."

[3] Fairbanks did exactly what Clemens suggested, forwarding the letter with the following note inscribed on the verso:

John T. Short,
The Enclosed letter is from Sam'l L Clemens, or "Mark Twain." Please read its contents, and comply with the requests, if you can. He will give a good lecture without doubt— After you have got throgh, please return the letter to me—
Yours truly
A.W. Fairbanks
Cleveland, Oct. 7, 1868.

On 5 February 1869 Clemens wrote to Mrs. Fairbanks, "Got the invitation from Columbus, but know of no date I can give them" (CSmH, in *MTMF*, 69). Clemens did not perform in Columbus during his four-month tour.

To Frank Fuller
5–30 October 1868 • Hartford, Conn.
(MS: CLjC)

. . . .

If a man were to signify however which he was not & could not if he had the power, which being denied him he will endeavor anyhow, merely *because* he don't, would *you?* I should think not.

Good-bye,
Yrs always,
Mark.[1]

[1] This manuscript fragment survives among Fuller's personal papers and was presumably addressed to him. The top half of the single sheet (written on one side only), which contained between thirty and sixty words, has been cut away. Fuller wrote an undated note on the verso of the backed manuscript: "This puzzling paragraph was evidently cut from something which Mark decided not to send me. F.F." The letter was written sometime before the last two months of 1868, for the text of the first surviving sentence (lacking only "& could not") appeared in a 28 November San Francisco newspaper item, which read in its entirety:

> MARK TWAIN ON MORAL SCIENCE.—Some one sent the following "question in moral science" to Mark Twain for solution, and, after working on it for three weeks, Mark submits it to Judge Charles F. Cady, of Illinois:
>
> "If a man were to signify, however, which he was not if he had the power, which being denied him he will endeavor anyhow, merely *because* he don't, would *you?*" (San Francisco *Examiner*, 28 Nov 68, 1).

The stationery, ink, and handwriting of the manuscript are virtually identical to those of the previous two letters, both written from Hartford—an indication it too might have been written on 5 October. It was probably written no later than 30 October, the last day Clemens spent in Hartford before returning to New York, where he had no need to write to Fuller. It is likely, but not certain, that the San Francisco *Examiner* reprinted the item from a still-unidentified eastern newspaper. Fuller was a likely source for such an item: it was he who earlier gave the New York *Evening Telegram* information gleaned from one of Clemens's 1867 letters (see 24 Nov 67 to Fuller, n. 6).

To Edward L. Burlingame
7 October 1868 • Hartford, Conn.

(Cyril Clemens, 18)

148 Asylum St.,
Hartford, Conn., Oct. 7.

Dear Ned—

I am here, getting out a book. I saw your father & mother & Gerty often in New York—& also Mr. Brown of the Legation. We all concocted a Treaty article together, for the *New York Tribune*.[1]

Do you remember your Honolulu joke?—"If a man compel thee to go with him a mile, go with him Twain." I have closed many & many a lecture, in many a city, with that. It always "fetches" them.[2] Send me your Picture—I enclose mine.[3]

Your friend,
Mark Twain.

[1] See 3 Aug 68 to Fairbanks, n. 1. "Gerty" was Edward's sister, Gertrude.

[2] Clemens himself had been recently "fetched" by Burlingame's joke. After Clemens's second lecture in Virginia City, the *Territorial Enterprise* reported that he

> was yesterday made the recipient at the hands of Mr. Conrad Wiegand, the well known assayer, of a very beautiful and highly-polished silver brick, worth some $40. The brick bears the following inscription: "Mark Twain—Matthew, V: 41—Pilgrim." All our readers will recollect at once that the verse referred to reads as follows: "And whosoever shall compel thee to go a mile, go with him twain." Twain would never object to going even farther, if sure of getting a fellow to the bar presented him by Mr. Wiegand, and provided he was furnished a seat in a good, easy-going and softly-cushioned carriage. ("A Neat and Appropriate Present," 29 Apr 68, 3)

Eventually, however, Clemens grew tired of the joke, saying in 1906:

> When it was new, it seemed exceedingly happy and bright, but it has been emptied upon me upwards of several million times since—never by a witty and engaging lad like Burlingame, but always by chuckle-heads of base degree, who did it with offensive eagerness and with the conviction that they were the first in the field. (AD, 20 Feb 1906, CU-MARK, in *MTA*, 2:125)

[3] The enclosure has not been found, but it was probably a small, *carte de visite* print of the Bradley and Rulofson photograph recently made in San Francisco, rather than an "imperial-size" print of the one taken in Cleveland (see 1 and 5 May 68, n. 7, and 24 Sept 68, n. 3, both to Fairbanks).

To Henry M. Crane
7 October 1868 • Hartford, Conn.

(MS: ODaU)

148 Asylum st
Hartford, Oct. 7.

C. M. Crane, Esq

Dear Sir: If I have heretofore told you the title of my proposed lecture I beg to alter it. I had not then written the lecture. I have just finished writing it now, & it has taken a little different shape from what I had expected—so I now call it: "*The American Vandal Abroad.*"[1] I am one of those myself.

Yrs Truly.
Mark Twain

[1] Clemens composed his ninety-minute lecture by extracting short passages from the manuscript of *The Innocents Abroad*, assembling them to produce an abridged account of the *Quaker City* voyage (Hirst 1975, 174–75; see also the following letter). The surviving draft of the lecture, although incomplete, shows that Clemens was conscious that he would speak in Cleveland under Mrs. Fairbanks's watchful eye, as well as in Elmira before the Langdon family: he therefore avoided castigating his fellow *Quaker City* passengers and made no mention of the Holy Land (SLC 1868nnn). The lecture was first announced in advertisements of the American Literary Bureau as "Americans in the Old World," but on 24 October the title became "American Vandals in the Old World" (*Round Table* 8 [3 Oct 68 and 24 Oct 68]: 234, 282).

To Mary Mason Fairbanks
12 October 1868 • Hartford, Conn.

(MS: CSmH)

148 Asylum st,
Hartford, Monday.

Dear Mother:

Yes, "how well we timed it—what a beautiful tableau," &c. Plague take it, there wasn't enough of it. If I had broken a leg, I would have been infinitely better satisfied. As you say, "No place *could* have been better chosen."

Why didn't I get your letter sooner, & so used your cool head instead of my hot one? I'll bet~~ter~~ I have written a letter that will *finish* me. I wish I had it back again—I would tone it down some.[1]

And thunder, I wrote the *lecture* the day before your letter came, too. That is to say, I "smouched" a lecture out of my ~~bood~~ book—a good part of it, at least/, came from the book. I had planned the lecture *just about* as you did, & wrote & wrote & kept writing till I saw that I was never going to weave a web that would suit me. So then I altered the tittle to "The American Vandal Abroad," & began again. ~~Ther~~ I treat him gently & good-naturedly, except that I give him *one* savage blast for aping foreign ways (illustrating with your friend late from Paris who gave a *French* pronunciation to his Cleveland friend's name).[2] To tell the truth there isn't a great deal of Vandal in the lecture. I glance at him in the Boulevards & at the *Opera Comique*—make him moralize poetically over the tomb of Napoleon—& I mention his execrable French. Then I describe the Park at Versailles—brief. Trot the gentleman to Genoa & Milan & let him see that hideous statue of a *skinned man* in the Cathedral ('twill make you shudder)[3]—then shoot him by Como to Venice, where I become elaborate on the gondola in its queer aspect as a private carriage. And then I observe that:

"*Our* Vandals hurried away from Venice, & scattered abroad everywhere. You could find them breaking specimens from the dilapidated tomb of Romeo & Juliet, at Padua—& infesting the picture-galleries of Florence—& gravely seeking information concerning sausages, at Bologna—& risking their necks on the Leaning Tower at Pisa—& snuffing sulphur fumes from the crater of Vesuvius—& burrowing among the exhumed wonders of Herculaneum & Pompeii. And you could behold ~~him~~ ‸them‸, with specu~~ul~~‸t‸a‸cles on & blue cotton umbrellas under their arms, benignantly contemplating Rome from the venerable arches of the Coliseum."[4]

Now that isn't ill-natured, *is* it? Then some more description: the Acropolis, the Parthenon & then, Athens by moonlight. Then a glance at the Emperor of Russia—then the *moral* of the lecture, which is Let the Vandal continue to travel—it liberalizes him & makes a better man of him (though the moral is an entirely gratuitous contribution & will be a clear gain to the societies employing me, for it isn't deduced from anything there is in the lecture)—& *then*, we close with a starchy & a high-toned glimpse at each of the most imposing pictures we saw—Gibraltar, St Peters, Venice, the Pyramids, Damascus, &c—fireworks, you know—then, finis.[5]

Of course, scattered all through, are the most preposterous yarns, & all that sort of thing. But I *think* it will *entertain* an audience, this lecture. I *must not* preach to a select few in my audience, lest I have only a select few to listen, next time, & so be required to preach no more. What the societies *ask* of me is to *relieve* the heaviness of their didactic courses—& in accepting the contract I am just the same as *giving my word* that I will do as they ask.

Blame the fine arts & the Old masters, mother mine—that is forbidden ground for me—*couldn't* say a word without abusing the whole tribe & their works like pickpockets. Only a wholesome dread of *you* kept me from doing it anyhow.[6]

Col. Herrick writes & asks if I can lecture in Cleveland in Nov. at all.[7] I've a notion to say I *will*, any time between the 1st & 15th. I would like *you* to write the first critique on this lecture—& then it wouldn't be *slurred over* carelessly, anyhow.

Give my love to all the family.

Your dutiful brick,
Sam*l* L. Clemens

[1] See 5 Oct 68 to Mary Mason Fairbanks. The "letter that will *finish* me" was the one Clemens wrote on 4–5 October to Olivia. The present letter was therefore written on 12 October, the only "Monday" between 5 October and Clemens's next, penitent letter to Olivia, dated 18 October.

[2] In his manuscript draft of the lecture Clemens wrote, "A lady passenger of ours used to tell of a fellow citizen of hers—in Pittsburgh—who spent 8 weeks in Paris & then went back home & addressed his dearest old bosom friend Herbert as 'Mr. *Erbair!*'"; he went on to identify this Frenchified tourist as "Mr. Gordon" (SLC 1868nnn, 7–8†). Almost a year later he told Olivia that his description of Gordon in chapter 23 of *Innocents* (partly repeated in the lecture draft) was intended as a "portrait" of George Ensign, a San Francisco dandy: "When I uttered [it] in a lecture on Venice in San Francisco there was a perceptible flutter all over the house, because they recognized the portrait—& poor George was present, though I didn't know he was there—only thought it likely he *would* be" (SLC to OLL, 3 Sept 69, CU-MARK, in *LLMT*, 107).

[3] Baedeker's *Italy. Handbook for Travellers* described this statue of Saint Bartholomew by the late-sixteenth-century sculptor Marcus Agrate as "anatomically remarkable" because "the saint is represented flayed, with his skin on his shoulder" (Baedeker 1879, 120). Clemens commented in his lecture draft that it

looked natural, because it looked somehow *as if it were in pain.* A skinned *man w^{d} be likely to look that* way—unless his attention were occupied by some other matter. It was a hideous thing, & yet there was a fascination about it somewhere. I am very sorry I saw it, because I shall *always* see it now. I shall dream of it, sometimes. I shall dream that it is resting its corded arms on the bed's head & looking down on me with its dead eyes; I shall dream that it is stretched between the sheets with me & touching me with its exposed muscles & its stringy cold legs. (SLC 1868nnn, 22–23†)

[4] In his lecture draft Clemens wrote:

> *Our* Vandals hurried away from Ven. & scattered abroad everywhere. You could find them breaking specimens from the ‸dilapidated‸ tomb of Romeo & Juliet at Padua—& infesting the picture-galleries of Florence—& risking their necks on the Leaning Tower ~~at~~ ‸of‸ Pisa—& snuffing sulphur fumes on the summit of Vesuvius—& burrowing among the exhumed wonders of Hercul & Pom—& you might see them with spectacles on & ‸blue cotton‸ umbrellas under their arms ~~benevolently~~ ‸benignantly‸ contemplating Rome from the venerable arches of the Coliseum. (SLC 1868nnn, 42†)

[5] The "starchy" closing Clemens describes here does not survive in the lecture draft, but the "moral" does:

> If there is a moral to this lecture it is an injunction to all Vans to *travel.* I am glad the Am. Van *goes* abroad. It goes him good. It makes a better man of him. It rubs out ‸a multitude‸ [of] his old unworthy biases & prejudices. ‸It aids his religion for it‸ It enlarges his charity & his benevolence ~~& makes~~ ‸—it‸ broadens his views of men & things; it deepens his ~~charity~~ ‸generosity‸ & his compassion for the failings & shortcomings of his fellow-creatures. Contact with men of various nations & many creeds, teaches him that there are *other* people in the world besides his own little clique, & other opinions as worthy of attention & respect as his own. He finds that he & *his* are not the most momentous matters in the universe. Cast into trouble & misfortune in strange lands & being mercifully cared for by those he never saw before, he begins to learn that best lesson of all, ‸—that one w^{h} culminat[e]s in the conviction that‸ that God puts *something* good & something lovable in every man his hands create~~.—that the men are not~~—that the world is *not* a cold, harsh, cruel ~~& degraded~~ prison-house, stocked with all manner of selfishness & hate & wickedness. It *liberalizes* the Van to travel—you never saw a bigoted, opinionated, stubborn, narrow-minded, self-conceited, *almighty mean man* in your life but he had stuck in one place ~~all~~ ever since he was born & thought God made the world & dyspepsia & bile for *his* especial comfort & satisfaction. So I say, *by all means,* let the Am. Van. *go on* traveling/‸—& let no man discour him.‸ (SLC 1868nnn, 55–57†)

[6] Clemens nevertheless did include a paragraph about the Vandal's opinion of *The Last Supper:* "The Vandal goes to see this picture, which all the world praises—looks at it with a critical eye & says it's a perfect old nightmare of a picture & he wouldn't give $40 for a million like it—(& I endorse his opinion,) & then he is done with Milan" (SLC 1868nnn, 27†).

[7] Lieutenant Colonel John French Herrick (1836–1909) was elected corresponding secretary of the Cleveland Library Association in May 1868. He also served on its lecture committee, which eventually arranged for Clemens to appear in Cleveland on 17 November. Having won distinction in the Civil War as commander of the Twelfth Ohio Volunteer Cavalry, Herrick was now practicing law in partnership with his brother and acting as a United States court commissioner for northern Ohio (Cleveland *Leader:* "Cleveland Library Association," 6 May 68, 1; advertisement, 17 Nov 68, 4; Van Tassel and Grabowski, 500; *Cleveland Directory* 1868, 186, 349).

To Olivia L. Langdon
18 October 1868 • Hartford, Conn.
(MS: CU-MARK)

148 Asylum st. ‸Sunday,‸
Hartford, Oct. 18.

My Honored Sister:

You have rebuked me. I sinned, ~~against~~ but it was in hot-blooded heedlessness—not deliberate intent to do wrong. ~~I~~ You have treated my letter[1] as it deserved, since it offended you ~~wi~~‸with silent - - - - - - - (*not* contempt—I cannot think of the proper word)—as it deserved, I say, for it is not a brother's ~~p~~ right to offend a sister who has never harmed him. I accept the rebuke, severe as it was, & surely I ought to thank you for the lesson it brings. For it has brought me back to my senses. I walk upon the ground again—not in the clouds. It is hard to speak of one's own humiliation—to see one's pride brought low, & *tell* of it to another. I do not know that I could write these words to any one but you—& not to you but that I feel you will not ridicule them. It has taken me two days to master this false pride & make the reparation that is your due—shall I *never* be a man? But it is over—& now I come to you with all trust, all confidence—simply as a reproved, repentant brother seeking a sister's pardon—& ask that you will forget & forgive my fault. I have no fears, no doubts. I have confessed. I am sorry. I will not offend again. It is the easier to come to you so, because that I have not been criminal—only heedless. You will restore to me your respect & your esteem, which I have forfeited.

And so the clouds are gone, & I am cheerful again. I make no apology for writing this letter—for in word & spirit it shall be inoffensive—& more than that, who shall take away from ~~the bro~~ a brother his privilege of writing to his sister when the spirit moveth him?—yea, & even though she chooses to take her own time about answering? You *are* my sister, for you did not take me for a brother to cast me off the first time I went astray, but to bear with me when I am wrong, & forgive me when I right myself again. And to assist me ~~som~~ sometimes with the power that is in your good influence—you know too well how much I need it.

But whatever may befall, you will always seem to me a sister, & Mrs. Fairbanks a mother, for between you you have made me turn some of my thoughts into worthier channels than they were wont to pursue, & benefits like that, the worst of us cannot forget.

I̸ Set a white stone—for I have made a friend.[2] It is the Rev. J. H. Twichell. I have only known him a week, & yet I believe I think almost as much of him as I do of Charlie. I could hardly find words strong enough to tell how much I *do* think of that man. ‸(And his wife, too.)‸[3] I met him at a church sociable,̸, (where I made a dozen pleasant acquaintances, old & young & of both sexes.)[4] He made me promise to spend Wednesday evening at his house[5]—it was not hard to do. On Tuesday his pretty, young wife walked three blocks by my side (I didn't know who in the mischief she was, & she was not certain that I was myself,)—I would drop back, ‸now & then,‸ thinking it must annoy her to be elbow to elbow with a stranger so long—& behold, *she* would drop back alongside! I would march ahead—& she would just range up alongside again! It was the most absurd performance you ever saw. At last, y̸ just as I was going to ~~shout "Police!"~~ ‸call the police,‸ she changed her course & left me. But she came into the publication office pretty soon & had them introduce me, & then the mystery was solved. She had simply wanted to tell me to come to *tea*, & *then* spend the evening—but not being sure that I was the right man she walked all that long distance with me without being able to ~~make~~ muster courage enough to introduce herself. I had a splendid time at their house. I had my "manners" with me, & got up to go at 9.30 PM, & never sat down again—but he said he was bound to have his talk out—& ~~bless you~~ *I* was willing—& so I only left at 11. And then he made me carry off the choicest books in his library. Splendid fellow! I went last night at 7 to carry them home—& I was in a hurry, for I was writing to Charlie & wanted to mail the letter before 9—but the clock struck 10 before I got away. He had his sermon to write, but he said never mind the sermon, it would be all the better for a little talk beforehand—(~~it~~ &‸ it *was* good, too—I heard it this morning.) This man ~~keeps apologedizing~~ ‸apologized‸ to me for talking so much about religion. He would not have done me that wrong if he had known how much I respected him for it & how beautiful his strong love for his subject made his words seem. When religion, coming from your lips & his, shall be distasteful to me, I shall be a lost man indeed. This morning he ran out

& overtook me in Farmington Avenue, & walked a quarter of a mile. His eyes were flashing with pleasure—& he said: ~~"Clem~~ "I have just been visiting an invalid parish[i]oner, who will never rise from her bed any more—& she says she prays for me every day! Clemens, you don't know what limitless *power* there is in a woman's prayers!—the prayers of a hundred men cannot lift me up like one prayer ~~for~~ ‸from‸ a woman!—I pity you from the bottom of my heart, for you do not know what it is to have a pure, sinless, noble Christian woman pray daily for you." It is what he said—*word for word*. I said "I *do* know it—my sister." "Ah, yes, but it is not so strong—your sister *has* to pray for you—it is not the generous tribute that comes uncompelled from the lips of another woman, for this has no dross of earth, no selfishness about it." You seem so much my sister that I could say naught against his argument, & so said nothing. But I was glad to hear him speak so. He & his wife are to drive me about the country tomorrow afternoon, & I am to sup with them & spend the evening, which is to last till midnight. He is about my age—likes my favorite authors, too, just as you do (except Mrs. Browning, whom I *would* like, if I could ever get that "string of lamp-posts" straightened out in my head.)[6] After church, at noon to-day, I went with him to the alms house & helped him preach & sing to the inmates/, (I helped in the singing, anyhow.) Heaven & earth, what a sight it was! Cripples, ~~id~~ jibbering idiots, raving madmen; ‸thieves, rowdies, paupers;‸ little children, stone blind; blind men & women; old, old, men & women, with that sad ~~inward~~ absent look ‸in their faces‸ that tells of thoughts that are busy with "the days that ~~come~~ ‸are‸ no more."[7] I have not had anything ~~move my pity~~ ‸touch me‸ so since I saw the leper hospitals of Honolulu & Damascus. As we came along the road—

However, enough of a thing is too much, I take it. Never mind my writing so much—I am *always* diffusive—& please don't say that I *persecute* you with letters. You must consider the circumstances that called this one forth. When you can find an idle moment pray write—& if you haven't but a page to write, why let it *be* a page—I hope I have not grown selfish & exacting in my old age. Do not say anything that is unkind, please. Give me back your trust again—for I *know* that in a larger measure than before, I am worthy.

Good-bye. ~~(My sense of shame is back again—& yet it does seem that I am punished enough. Shall I *never* learn anything?)~~ Happy dreams visit you, & peace abide with you always.[6] I will not scratch *that* out, *anyhow*.

Your affectionate Brother,
Sam[l]. L. Clemens.

Miss Olivia L. Langdon | Elmira | New York. [*postmarked:*] [HARTFOR]D CONN. OCT 18 [*docketed by OLL:*] 1868 | 4th

[1] Clemens's 4–5 October letter to Olivia.

[2] Setting a white stone has been understood "from classical times as an expression for commemorating any piece of good fortune or any lucky day" (Hazlitt, 2:568).

[3] Joseph Hopkins Twichell (1838–1918) was pastor of the Asylum Hill Congregational Church at 814 Asylum Street in Hartford. Born in the nearby town of Southington, Twichell—the oldest son of a prosperous factory owner—was graduated from Yale College in 1859 and entered the Union Seminary in New York, which he left in 1861 to serve for three years as chaplain in the Seventy-first New York Volunteers. In 1865 he completed his divinity studies at Andover Seminary in Massachusetts and was offered the Asylum Hill pastorate upon the recommendation of Horace Bushnell (1802–76), a prominent Congregational minister and theologian, whom he had met while on furlough in Hartford. The cornerstone of the Asylum Hill Church was laid in May of 1865, and its new minister was installed in December of that year. Julia Harmony Cushman Twichell (1843–1910) was born in Exeter, New York, but was living in Orange, New Jersey, when she and Twichell were married on 1 November 1865. They had been introduced by her cousin Diodate Cushman Hannahs, a classmate of Twichell's at Yale. In August 1868 Harmony gave birth to a son, Edward Carrington, the first of nine children (Strong, 11, 45–47, 52; Mansfield, 10–11).

[4] Paine reported that Elisha Bliss's wife introduced Twichell to Clemens, who

> was at an evening reception in the home of one of its [the Asylum Hill Church's] members when he noticed a photograph of the unfinished building framed and hanging on the wall.
>
> "Why, yes," he commented, in his slow fashion, "this is the 'Church of the Holy Speculators.' "
>
> "Sh," cautioned Mrs. Bliss. "Its pastor is just behind you. He knows your work and wants to meet you." Turning, she said: "Mr. Twichell, this is Mr. Clemens. Most people know him as Mark Twain."
>
> And so, in this casual fashion, he met the man who was presently to become his closest personal friend and counselor, and would remain so for more than forty years. (*MTB*, 1:370–71)

[5] The Twichells lived in the parsonage at 125 Woodland Street, a few blocks from Asylum Street (Strong, 52; Geer, 24, map facing 25).

[6] Evidently an allusion to Elizabeth Barrett Browning's *Aurora Leigh* (1857), one of Olivia's favorite poems (OLL to Alice B. Hooker, 7 June 67, CtHSD):

> . . . . His breath against my face
> Confused his words, yet made them more intense,—
> As when the sudden finger of the wind

Will wipe a row of single city-lamps
To a pure white line of flame, more luminous
Because of obliteration. . . .
(Browning, 395)

On 12 January 1869 Clemens again mentioned this poem to Olivia: "You will translate Aurora Leigh & be gentle & patient with me & do all you can to help me understand what the mischief it is all about" (CU-MARK†).

[7] The Hartford Almshouse—on Huntington, near Asylum Street—was built in 1851, within the walls of its predecessor, which had been gutted by fire: some form of the institution had existed on this eight-acre site since 1822. The present building served as a workhouse for paupers as well as a hospital for the old and infirm (Geer, map facing 25, 27; Trumbull, 1:362–64). Clemens quoted from part 4 of Tennyson's *Princess* (1847):

Tears, idle tears, I know not what they mean,
Tears from the depth of some divine despair
Rise in the heart, and gather to the eyes,
In looking on the happy Autumn-fields,
And thinking of the days that are no more.
(Tennyson 1847, 66)

To Jane Lampton Clemens and Family
24?–27 October 1868 • Hartford, Conn.

(*Paraphrase:* OC to MEC, 30 Oct 68, CU-MARK)

We had an excellent letter from Sam,[1] inquiring kindly after you and me and my machine,[2] and conveying the idea that he is likely to become a Christian

He has a friend, a Presbyterian minister,[3] about his own age, with whom and his wife he spends much time; and Mrs. Fairbanks, (dear good woman) and others, write him sermons. His book is ~~to~~ not to be issued till March. He is going to commence his lecturing soon—beginning at Cleveland.

[1] This paraphrase of Clemens's letter survives in a letter written on 30 October by Orion Clemens, living with his mother and sister in St. Louis, to Mollie, visiting her family in Keokuk (she had apparently joined Orion in St. Louis the previous spring). Since three days of transit time must be allowed for a letter to reach St. Louis from Hartford, the latest date Clemens's now-lost letter could have been sent was 27 October (Alexander W. Randall, 82). But Orion's 30 October letter responded to Mollie's "note of day before yesterday just received"—that is, 28 October. It seems most likely that Mollie's note of 28 October was an immediate response to a letter from Orion written on 26 October (although it

remains possible that she was answering a letter received from him some days earlier). If as of 26 October Orion had not yet received his brother's letter, then, still allowing for three days' transit time, it could have been sent no earlier than 24 October.

[2] See 21 Feb 68 to OC, n. 2.

[3] Joseph H. Twichell, actually a Congregational minister (see the previous letter). The Clemenses were Presbyterians, even though Annie Moffett had for a time attended a Congregational Sunday school (*MTBus*, 24; Angel, 215).

To Olivia L. Langdon
30 October 1868 • Hartford, Conn.

(MS: CU-MARK)

Hartford, Oct. 30.

My Honored Sister:

Your welcome letter made me entirely *satisfied*. And so I have dispatched all lagging work contentedly since, & am unmanacled, now, & free to go whither I list.[1] I owe you many thanks for this assistance. And I thank you for the assurance that I still have your respect & esteem—& particularly that "they have not been changed"—for I would not willingly have them diminished in any degree.

"It may sometimes seem to you that Christ is far from you, that his indwelling spirit is not with you." You have said truly. I pray as one who prays with words, against a firm-set mountain of sin. I pray *too* hopefully, sometimes, & sometimes hopelessly. But I still pray—& shall continue to pray. Mr. Twichell has confidence that I shall succeed, & says that I will be a most useful man in the world then—& you know it is pleasant to think that at any time you have been useful or are going to be. The idea of that party of ministers at his house the other night thanking me fervently for having written & published certain trash which they said had lit up some gloomy days with a wholesome laugh was a surprise to me. I had not flattered myself before that a part of my mission on earth was to be a benefactor to the clergy. I believe I have only one good hope to keep me in heart in this search after a better life, & that is, that indolent as I seem, I know I possess a deal of persistence, & that I shall keep on coming to the surface again after each discouragement & beginning the contest afresh until ——. Time must decide what the result shall be. I believe, appreciate, & have treasured up what you say about religion & what was in the little printed slip, & I trust that this kindness & consideration of yours will not be lost upon me.

Mrs. & Mrs. Twichell & myself, & two young ladies, sisters of Mrs. T., drove 10 miles out in the country & back the other day,[2] & in the course of the conversation Mr. T. uttered several things that struck me forcibly. I was speaking at length about the present wonderful method of communicating with the deaf & dumb almost wholly by word-signs instead of letters,[3] & said it was so particularly curious because some of these people were *born* deaf & dumb & consequently knew no *words* at all—then how is it that we, who *think in words*, can convey *such* thoughts to these people? He said we *didn't* always think in words—that our highest, grandest, most brilliant thoughts were far beyond our capacity to frame into words, & that we *had* no words that would express them—that often a radiant thought-vision lit up our plodding brains with its wierd beauty, & vanished instantly to the heaven it surely came from, while we stood amazed, delighted, yet utterly incapable of determining *what* it was like, but only ejaculating helplessly, "Heavens! *what* was that!" And he said something like this—I have the substance I think, but I have forgotten his language: But some day this tramelling flesh will be stripped away, this prison-house thrown open & the soul set free—free to expand to its just magnitude—& *then* what thoughts we shall have! what visions! The celestial visitants that haunt us now, exquisite but without form & void,[4] will be stately temples of thought, ornate, symmetrical, full of grace, & gorgeous with dissolving lights that stream from that far-off world we dream of!—*not* the shapeless magnificent chaos they seem to us here in the dark! I never heard this idea suggested before, but I think it is very beautiful.

Twichell is splendid. And he has one rare faculty—he is thoughtful & considerate. He lends me his overcoat when I go there without one, lends me his umbrella, lends me his slippers. I asked for a pair of slippers only once—I never have to ask for them now. These are small things, but they show the man, you know—he thinks of others people's comfort before his own—& thus reminds me of you—& to my own disadvantage. For I know of many instances of your inconveniencing yourself to satisfy some persistent petition of mine, when it would have looked better if I had been thinking more of your pleasure & less of my own. I know very well what you would say to this, but that couldn't alter the *facts* any. The facts simply are, that I ought to be ashamed of myself—and I ain't. I still reflect with pleasure upon every time I persuaded you to do anything. It was wrong to persuade you to go to see the Misses Spaulding that day when you wanted to write.[5] But I would do it again. I do not mind doing *any*thing that is wrong when I know I am right. No, I am unrepentant. I regret to this day that the horse was not there.

"Each soul must fight its own battle, & human friendship is impotent to help." I even think I am glad to find an imperfection in you, for it makes you more like other people—glad to find a most ungenerous sentiment reposing in a bosom where it has no company. The little child, trusting its mother, trusts her God—having faith in its mother, has faith in whom *she* worships—loving its mother, loves the Savior toward whose gracious presence she turns with such a yearning tenderness—& so led, so guided, *it* is saved, while the doctors, learned & wise, grope among premises & arguments, testimonies, doubts & logic, & are lost. The preacher helps his flock—the missionary exiles himself from all of earth his love holds dear, to help the friendless & forsaken in every hapless land—even Jesus saith, "If two of you shall agree on earth as touching anything that they shall ask, it shall be done for them of my Father which is in Heaven."[6] And so you, only you, are left to say "human friendship is impotent to help." You have read Matt. XXV, 44–45? & XVII, 18–20? However, you make the strongest point against your own doctrine, once in every four & twenty hours—when you pray for me—& so what need is there that *I* should say a word by way of argument?

But I still stick to what I said at first—I am glad you hold this extravagant doctrine—I am glad you have it—I would not that it should be otherwise, my sister—& with that perversity that belongs to human nature, I simply love you all the better for it.

But after all, I must unsay those arguments of mine—for I cannot pit a few flippant fancies against the years of patient study that have revealed to you the *truth*. And when I come to search my understanding & my heart, neither will consent that you are capable of thinking a wrong thing any more than you are of doing one. I do not *want* to think you are—I do not want to harbor such an idea at all—~~for then I think I should not have faith in my species any more.~~ [Now I *didn't* want to scratch that out, but then ~~you would have wrapped my knuckles, maybe,~~ ~~&~~ I thought ‸maybe‸ I had better do it. Curiosity is a virtue of your sex—I don't mind your exercising it, sister mine.]

Yes, I will be sure to write Mrs. F. to send you that book. No, I'll get a new one & mark it again. That one is soiled by railway travel. I have been reading such an exquisite book![7] I'll tell you all I— No indeed, you are *not* given to saying unkind things, & I am very, very thankful for it—but I knew you *could*, if you believed it necessary, & that is why I pleaded. Get your Browning ready—for lo, I come like a lamb to the slaughter![8] You know very well that I enjoyed my lessons before, ~~noth~~ notwithstanding I couldn't get the gas-lamps right.[9]

I shall spend the first week of Nov. in New York, & shall surely call on Mrs. Brooks ("not Brown"—yes, I remember.)[10] Then I shall be in Cleveland till the 17th Nov. Won't you please write me at the Everett House, Union Square, N.Y? Remember it is already "unfrequently" since you wrote. Try—& if you can't, why then be sure to write "Care Herald, Cleveland~~,~~"—long before the 17th. Now remember that I am not where I can "persist" until I persuade you—& so be generous.

You see that I am *trying* not to abuse my privilege of writing as much as I please—& not succeeding worth a cent. Somehow 9 pages don't seem to hold anything.[11] ~~But I've got to ‸must‸ have relief. I'll inflict the rest on Mrs. Fairbanks, who's *got* to put up with it.~~

What was the name of that hymn we fancied so much in church one day? "Fading, Still Fading" is beautiful~~,~~—old, but beautiful.[12]

P. S.—~~You~~ Good-bye & pleasant dreams.—Your affectionate Brother, Saml. L. Clemens.

[*on back of letter as folded:*]

P. S. I have got mother Fairbanks in a stew again. I named that lecture just for her benefit. And I sent her ~~ab~~ an absurd ~~pretended~~ synopsis of it that I knew would provoke her wrath—& intimated that I was idling somewhat.[13] I like to tease her because I ~~love~~ like her so. ~~I would tease you, only you take everything in such dreadful earnest it hurts my conscience. I never could venture farther than to convince you that there was 16 in a cribbage hand that hadn't *any*thing in it.~~

~~Good-bye—.~~

P. S.—Have just received an imperative invitation from the Webb sisters to attend a party in New York to-night—to which is added an urgent note from several eminent newspaper men & "Many New Yorkers & Californians"—& now, my sister, *my* curiosity is fearfully excited! I do *wonder* what it is? I shall take the cars at noon.[14]

~~*Good* bye.~~

P. P. S—I am going to a Yale College re-union with Mr. Twichell, & then go on to N. Y.[15]

I will sieze the opportunity offered by all this blank space to say ~~Good bye—may peace & prosperity attend you.~~[16]

[I did not scratch it out to excite your curiosity, or to tease you, but because it was surplusage.]

~~Goo~~

✉

Miss Olivia L. Langdon. | Elmira | New York. [*postmarked:*] NEW HAVEN CON. OCT 30 [*docketed by OLL:*] 5th

[1] In an *Alta* dispatch dated 28 October Clemens wrote: "I have not been working very hard, but I have got this book of mine ready for the engravers and electrotypers at last, though it will not be issued from the publishing house till March. Not knowing what else to name it, I have called it 'THE NEW PILGRIM'S PROGRESS.' I am told that Bancroft is to be the agent for it on the Pacific Coast and in China" (SLC 1868qqq).

[2] It is not known which two of Harmony Twichell's six sisters were present on this outing, which Clemens informed Olivia on 18 October would take place "to-morrow." His reference to "young ladies," however, suggests that neither Delia Cushman Hannahs (aged about thirty-nine), Maria Cushman (aged about thirty), nor Dora H. Cushman (aged about twenty-eight) were along, but that Mary D. Cushman (aged about twenty-two), Harriet E. Cushman (aged about eighteen), or Charlotte Cushman (aged about sixteen) might well have been (18 Oct 68 to OLL; "Sudden Death of Mrs. Twichell," Hartford *Courant*, 25 Apr 1910, 2; *Exeter Census*, 11).

[3] Clemens's "speaking at length" about sign language may have been prompted by the proximity of the American Asylum at 690 Asylum Street, the first school for the deaf in the United States. Founded in 1817 by Thomas Hopkins Gallaudet (1787–1851), the school moved to this large tract of land, granted it by Congress, in 1821. Gallaudet studied French techniques for teaching deaf mutes, eventually bringing to the United States a system of signs and gestures developed in the late eighteenth century by Abbé Charles Michel de l'Epée, which, together with the manual alphabet, evolved into modern American Sign Language (Trumbull, 1:425–27; Geer, 27).

[4] Genesis 1:2.

[5] Clara (1849–1935) and her older sister, Alice (d. 1935), were the daughters of Captain Henry Clinton Spaulding, a wealthy Elmira coal and lumber dealer, and his wife, the former Clara Wisner. The incident referred to here has not been further identified (Salsbury, 433; Towner, 128; Boyd and Boyd, 197; Herbert A. Wisbey, Jr., to Dahlia Armon, 12 Jan 1987, CU-MARK). In 1906 Clemens described Clara as "my wife's playmate and schoolmate from the earliest times," who was "about my wife's age, or two or three years younger—mentally, morally, spiritually, and in all ways, a superior and lovable personality" (AD, 26 Feb 1906, CU-MARK, in *MTA*, 2:140).

6 Matthew 18:19.

7 Neither book has been identified. Clemens's references to the "exquisite" book in two later letters to Olivia (5 and 7 Dec 68, and 31 Dec 68) imply that it was one, or all, of the four parts of *The Angel in the House*, a popular verse narrative by Coventry Kersey Dighton Patmore (1832–96): *The Betrothal* (1854), *The Espousals* (1856), *Faithful for Ever* (1860), and *The Victories of Love* (1862), published together in one volume in 1866 (London: Macmillan). The first two parts trace the growing love, courtship, and marriage of Honoria Churchill and Felix Vaughan. The last two concern the courtship and marriage of Honoria's cousin, Frederick Graham, and Jane, a chaplain's daughter. Clemens quoted from or discussed these books elsewhere in his letters to Olivia (4 Dec 68, 23 and 24 Dec 68, and 31 Dec 68).

8 Isaiah 53:7.

9 See 18 Oct 68 to OLL, n. 6.

10 Fidele A. Brooks (b. 1837) was the wife of Henry J. Brooks, a New York leather merchant. The Brookses were close friends of the Langdons', and were particularly fond of Olivia; they had signed the Langdons' guestbook on 19 August, just two days before Clemens arrived for his first visit, but it is not known just when, or even whether, Clemens had met them. His mistake of "Brown" for "Brooks" has not been found, perhaps because it occurred in the now largely lost letter of 4–5 October ("Langdon Guest Book," 5; Wilson 1868, 134; Fidele A. Brooks to SLC, 2 Jan 1910, CU-MARK; SLC to PAM, 23 June 69, CU-MARK).

11 At this point in his letter Clemens was only one line from the bottom of the ninth page, which he had begun with the paragraph "But after all" (273.29). Eight words into that paragraph's second sentence ("understanding," 273.31), he had started writing in a noticeably smaller hand, making two lines of script fit into each ruled line of stationery. He went on to squeeze the rest of his letter into the margins and onto the back of this same page.

12 "Fading, Still Fading," an anonymous vesper hymn sung to a Portuguese melody, had been popular in America since its first publication in the *Sacred Minstrel* (1830). The words were included in Henry Ward Beecher's *Plymouth Collection of Hymns*, which was probably the hymnal of the Langdons' church (Park Congregational) and had been "frequently used" on board the *Quaker City* (Julian, 362; McCaskey, 3:62; SLC 1867sss):

> Fading, still fading, the last beam is shining,
> Father in heaven! the day is declining,
> Safety and innocence fly with the light,
> Temptation and danger walk forth with the night;
> From the fall of the shade till the morning bells chime,
> Shield me from danger, save me from crime.
> (Henry Ward Beecher 1855, 822)

13 See 12 Oct 68 to Fairbanks.

14 Neither the "party" alluded to, nor the signers of the "urgent note," have been identified. The Webb sisters, Emma and Ada, were moderately well-known professional actresses and singers. They debuted in 1860 as the "Fairy Star Sisters" at New York's recently opened New Bowery Theater. Clemens had met them in April when they were on tour in Virginia City, billed in the *Trespass* as the "beautiful and accomplished Artistes," appearing in "a choice selection from their Repertoire of Dramas, Burlesques, [and] Musical Farces." They canceled their last two performances in order to make Piper's Opera House available

to Clemens (Odell, 8:244; Odell, 7:230; "Amusements," Virginia City *Trespass*, 25 Apr 68, 2; Virginia City *Territorial Enterprise:* "Piper's Opera House," 16 Apr 68, 3; "Mark Twain," 24 Apr 68, 3; "Piper's Opera House," 26 Apr 68, 3).

[15] Nothing further is known about this 30 October "re-union"; but see 18 Nov 68 to the president of the Yale College Scroll and Key Society.

[16] Clemens was writing on the back of his ninth and final page, after folding the letter for mailing, in a "blank space" of about one-sixth of a page.

To Mary Mason Fairbanks
31 October 1868 • New York, N.Y.

(MS: CSmH)

Everett House,
New York, Oct. 31.

Dear Mother—

Don't worry—*I*'m all right. I'll be in Cleveland Nov. 8—lecture there Nov. 17—so you can get ready to scratch. I'll expunge every word you want scratched out, cheerfully.[1] Love to all. (In a great hurry,)

Your Cub
Mark.

P. S.—~~I~~ Some few castles in Spain going up. I wrote an awful letter—but followed with another that set it all right. The answer was satisfactory to the subscriber.[2]

Mark.

[1] See 12 Oct 68 to Fairbanks.

[2] See 4–5 Oct 68 to OLL, n. 1.

To Jane Lampton Clemens
4 November 1868 • New York, N.Y.

(MS: NPV)

Everett House N.Y.
Election Day.

Dear Mother—

I have just received your letter with the murder in it—haven't read the latter—it is midnight & I shall go to bed in a minute & read it there. I like murders—especially when I can read them in bed & smoke.[1]

I made two calls, yesterday, in 49th & 53d street, & at the last place I heard of Clara Wiley—through a little Miss Po~~h~~lhemus—got the address & went there—in 45th street, I think it was—& took dinner & staid till 9:30 & then had to walk all the way home, clear down here to 17th street, because the omnibuses were all full & the weather cold as the mischief. Clara is very pretty & the boys very handsome. Mrs Wiley & Geo. are not a day older than they were when I saw them last, 12 or 15 years ago. Geo. was only at home a moment—business called him away—but I have to call on some more friends in that neighborhood day after to-morrow & shall call on him again in the evening.[2] I called on Mrs. Garth & the girls to-day in Brooklyn, but could only stay a moment as I ~~w~~ had gone over to dine with some friends. Jno. & Helen have gone to Baltimore to live.[3]

. . . .

1 Election day was 3 November, but since it was midnight, Clemens actually wrote his letter on 4 November. His mother had either described—or, more likely, enclosed a clipping about—a recent "horrible and strange" murder in St. Louis. On 23 October, Henry D. Christian, a government detective who "paid special attention to the hunting up of tobacco frauds," was found in an alley, unconscious with a serious head wound. He remained in a coma until his death the next day. His murderers were not identified, but were thought to be men he had informed against, since in the course of his duties he was known to have "brought down maledictions upon himself as well as threats of vengeance" ("Murder. Assassins at Work. Terrible Struggle for Life," St. Louis *Missouri Democrat*, 26 Oct 68, 4).

2 The object of Clemens's second call (on "53d street") was Olivia's friend Fidele Brooks, who lived at 675 Fifth Avenue, on the corner of Fifty-third; Clemens had recently promised to visit her (30 Oct 68 to OLL). Mrs. Brooks's younger sister, Josephine Griffiths Polhemus, was also staying there, in order to attend what her daughter Anne later described as a "fashionable girls school of that time," which was "Miss Meeker's English and French Boarding and Day School for Young Ladies." The recipient of Clemens's first call, ostensibly in Forty-ninth Street, remains unidentified, but since the Wileys lived at 54 East Forty-ninth Street, near Madison Avenue—not, as Clemens wrote here, "in 45th street"—he may have inadvertently reversed the Wileys' address with that of his first call. Clara Wiley (b. 1851) was the daughter of George Washington Wiley and the former Elmira Gregg. The "boys" were Clara's brothers: James (b. 1847 or 1848), George Lourie (1848?–1924), Will (1853?–82), and Snowden (b. 1856 or 1857). (George later married Josephine Polhemus, in 1873.) The Wileys were friends of the Brookses' and, coincidentally, old friends and neighbors of Clemens's family, who had known them since the late 1840s, both in Hannibal and in

St. Louis. George Washington Wiley had lived in Hannibal until the gold rush of 1849 lured him to California, but by the early 1850s he was back in Missouri, where he became a partner in a St. Louis wholesale grocery firm. Sometime after mid-1860 he moved his family to New York (Anne Wiley Leek to Dixon Wecter, 3 Jan 1948, CU-MARK; "Instruction," New York *Evening Post*, 22 Aug 68, 3; Wilson 1868, 1161; "George L. Wiley," New York *Times*, 17 Apr 1924, 19; *St. Louis Census* 1860, 209; *MTBus*, 34, 101; Josephine Polhemus Wiley to OLC, 24 Jan 74, CU-MARK; Hagood and Hagood, 85, 87; Knox, 8, 206). Clemens did call on the Wileys again, sometime before leaving for Cleveland on 7 or 8 November. In 1944 Clara's younger sister, Margaret (b. 1858 or 1859), wrote to Clemens's nephew, Samuel C. Webster, about this second visit:

After dinner, he & my father sitting smoking and *I at desk, but listening* doing lessons—your uncle with hands deep down in his pockets—usual attitude—he suddenly said "George—I want your advise I am DESPERTATLY IN LOVE with the most exquisite girl—*so beautiful, unfortunately* very rich. She is quite an invalid—I have proposed & been *refused* a dozen times—*what* do YOU think?" Father said Sam are you *crazy to think* of *such* a thing— "Thats what I was afraid you would say. I know I'm too rough—knocking around the world." And the tears came. He took out his handkerchief and wiped them away. Father said: "Sam, are you fooling? Is this one of your blank jokes?" He saw he was terribly serious and hurt. So father jumped up, ran over, took him by the shoulders, gave him a shake and said: "Sam you old Galoote, you. You're not rough; you're the most perfect gentleman—the cleanest, most decent man I know today. There is no girl in the world too good for you. Go for her, and get her, and God bless you, Sam." Mr. Clemens said, "Well, I will go see her again tomorrow, and I'll harass that girl and harass her till she'll *have* to say yes! For George, you know I never had wish or time to bother with women, and I can give that girl the purest, best love any man can ever give her. I can make her well and happy." So he got her, and made her happy. (Margaret Wiley to Samuel C. Webster, 16 Nov 1944, item C73, NPV, and *MTBus*, 101–2)

[3]Clemens had known the Garth family, Hannibal tobacconists, since they arrived from Virginia in 1842. Susan E. Garth (b. 1814 or 1815) was the wife of the older son, David J. Garth (1822–1912); their two "girls" were Elvira (b. 1844 or 1845) and Mary (b. 1846 or 1847). "Jno. & Helen" were David's younger brother, John H. Garth (1837–99), and his wife, the former Helen V. Kercheval (1838–1923), also of Hannibal; Clemens later described her as "one of the prettiest of the schoolgirls" (AD, 9 Mar 1906, CU-MARK, in *MTA*, 2:184). By 1862 the Garth brothers had moved to New York City. David, who had been the young Clemens's Sunday school teacher (and tobacconist), lived on Henry Street in Brooklyn. In 1868 he was a partner in the Manhattan banking firm of Garth, Fisher, and Hardy. John, one of Clemens's closest Hannibal friends, operated a tobacco-processing factory in Brooklyn until 1866 or 1867, when he evidently moved to Baltimore (*Portrait*, 776–77; Wilson 1866, 369; Wilson 1867, 376; Wilson 1868, 394; *Inds*, 320, 328).

To Jane Lampton Clemens and Family
18 November 1868 • Cleveland, Ohio
(MS: NPV)

Cleveland, Nov. 18.

Dear Folks—

Have received letters from Ma, Pamela & Orion, but haven't a *bit* of time to write. Made a *splendid* hit last night & am the "lion" to-day. Awful rainy, sloppy night, but there were 1,200 people present, any-how—house *full*. I *captured* them, if I *do* say it myself.[1] I go hence to Pittsburgh—thence to Elmira, N. Y.

Yrs

Sam.

[1] Clemens delivered "The American Vandal Abroad" for the first time on the evening of 17 November at Case Hall, Cleveland's new cultural center. He was well received: the Cleveland *Leader* called the performance "a most auspicious beginning" for the lecture course arranged by the local library association, while the *Plain Dealer* claimed that Clemens was the "most popular of American humorists since the demise of poor Artemas [i.e., Artemus Ward]," who had been its most celebrated editor ("Mark Twain," Cleveland *Leader*, 18 Nov 68, 1; "Mark Twain," Cleveland *Plain Dealer*, 18 Nov 68, 3). The *Herald* review, written by Mrs. Fairbanks (as Clemens himself had requested on 12 October), was predictably exuberant, calling the evening "brilliant entertainment" during which Clemens firmly held the attention of the audience with the "magnetism of his varied talent."

> We expected to be amused, but we were taken by surprise when he carried us on the wings of his redundant fancy, away to the ruins, the cathedrals, and the monuments of the old world. There are some passages of gorgeous word painting which haunt us like a remembered picture.
>
> We congratulate Mr. Twain upon having taken the tide of public favor "at the flood" in the lecture field, and having conclusively proved that a man may be a humorist without being a clown. He has elevated the profession by his graceful delivery and by recognizing in his audience something higher than merely a desire to laugh. (Mary Mason Fairbanks 1868)

Many years later Clemens claimed that his Cleveland performance was rescued from disaster by a friend in the audience:

> I came here once with a new lecture about the Innocents Abroad that I had prepared. I thought that I had mastered it; but alas, I found out otherwise. I had launched out and was sailing along beautifully when a gentleman and lady who perhaps had to take an early train got up to go out. The little occurrence threw me off the track. Suddenly I forgot where I was. I couldn't for the life of me tell where I left off. I paused and tried to think, and the pause became very embarrassing—finally seemed to become amusing to the audience. I

assure you it was not so to me. As the laughter increased I grew frantic and frankly admitted that I had lost my place, and said that I would be everlastingly obliged if some one in the audience would tell me where I left off. The effect of this was to make the audience laugh harder than before. They thought it was a joke, although I still insisted that it was not. Finally, when the suspense had become overpowering, an angel—with a bald head—arose and asked me if I was really in earnest in desiring to know which lie I was telling. I said I was, and the gentleman kindly told me. I shall never forget that good man. It was Mr. Solon Severance. ("When Mark Twain read . . . ," New York *Evening Post*, 22 Dec 84, clipping in CtY-BR)

To the President of the Scroll and Key Society, Yale College 18 November 1868 • Cleveland, Ohio

(MS facsimile: CtY)

Cleveland, Nov. 18.

Mr. President
of the S. & K.[1]

Allow me the privilege (in haste,) of remembering myself most kindly to my esteemed & honored brethren of the S & K,—whom God preserve!

Fraternally
Mark Twain

[*enclosure:*][2]

Yrs Truly
Sam*l* L. Clemens
Mark Twain

[1]On 5 November Clemens became an honorary member of the Scroll and Key, a secret society for Yale College seniors and alumni, founded in 1842 for the pursuit of fellowship, moral and literary self-improvement, and charity. Clemens's membership was sponsored by Joseph Twichell, who had been active in the society since 1859, his senior year. Twichell requested permission for Clemens to join under a provision that allowed for the election of public figures who had attained eminence in literature or art (Maynard Mack, 46, 214–15 n. 14).

[2]Clemens enclosed his card, together with some "paragraphs"—possibly reviews of his Cleveland lecture—which do not survive (see the next letter).

To Joseph H. and Harmony C. Twichell
18 November 1868 • Cleveland, Ohio
(MS: CtY-BR)

Cleveland, Nov. 18.

Dear ~~J~~ T.‸'s.‸—

Congratulate me, my often remembered friends—for lo, the child is born! It was most flatteringly received—1200 applausive & appreciative people present. I have dropped a note to the S. & K., Yale College, inclosing the paragraphs. I speak in Pittsburgh tomorrow & Elmira 23$^{d.}$ Love to you both. Good-bye. Yrs

~~Alf~~ Always—
Mark.

To Jane Lampton Clemens and Family
20 November 1868 • Cleveland, Ohio
(MS: NPV)

Cleveland, Nov. 20.

Dear Folks—

I played against the eastern favorite, Fanny Kemble, in Pittsburgh, last night. She had 200 in her house, & I had upwards of 1,500.[1] *All* the seats were sold, ~~wi~~ (in a driving rain storm, 3 days ago,) as reserved seats at 25 cents extra, even those in the second & third tiers—& when the last seat was gone the box office had not been open more than 2 hours. When I reached the theatre they were turning people away & the house was crammed. 150 or 200 stood up, all the evening.[2] I go to Elmira to-night. I am simply lecturing for societies, at $100 a pop.

Yrs
Sam.

[1] Frances (Fanny) Anne Kemble (1809–93), of the renowned English theatrical family, was an acclaimed actress, author, and lecturer who had gained great popularity for her public readings of Shakespeare. She began a series of readings in Pittsburgh's Lafayette Hall on 19 November, the same evening Clemens lec-

tured at its Academy of Music. The Pittsburgh *Gazette* commented that Kemble's "audience, though of a first-class order as regards intelligence and appreciation, was not such a one as the entertainment should receive, which, however, was no doubt influenced by the lecture attraction in another part of the city" (Pittsburgh *Gazette:* "Amusements," 19 Nov 68, 8; "Mrs. Fanny Kemble," 20 Nov 68, 8).

[2]The Pittsburgh *Gazette* reported that Clemens had spoken "before one of the largest and most intelligent audiences ever assembled in our city," adding that he

> is a pleasing talker and puts just enough jest into his composition to make it pleasing and palatable. He does not fall into the error of those who have taken the lecture field to amuse rather than instruct an audience, of extravagant joking or straining of words to make sentences appear funny. There is no extravagance about Mark Twain's style, and yet he is entitled above all living men to the name of American humorist. ("Mark Twain at the Academy," 20 Nov 68, 8)

The Pittsburgh success occasioned comment even on the West Coast. On 17 December the San Francisco *Alta California* reported:

> By the Pittsburg[h] papers we see that "Mark Twain," our travelling correspondent, has struck a harvest with his lecture "The American Vandal Abroad." He was requested to repeat his lecture in Pittsburg[h], with a promise of a full house at "reserved seats" price (every seat was taken the first night), but as he had made engagements for twenty-one lectures in twenty-five nights at different places, he was obliged to decline. The banks will soon be bidding for the privilege of keeping his account. ("Success of the 'American Vandal,'" 1)

But the Pittsburgh lecture was not unanimously applauded, for in his 29 December letter to Jervis Langdon, Clemens reported that an "unjust & angry criticism" of it appeared in the Pittsburgh *Dispatch*, presumably in the issue of 20 November. Although no copy of the newspaper or its review has been found, the Pittsburgh *Post* recalled a year later that the *Dispatch* had "styled him a great fraud, said there was nothing in him, and as a lecturer he was a failure. Yes, and even ventured to tell the Young Men's Library Association that if they wished to make their lectures a success, they would not engage Twain" (Vandal, 1).

To Mary Mason Fairbanks
26 and 27 November 1868 • Elmira, N.Y.

(MS: NN-B and CSmH)

PRIVATE.

~~Paradise, Nov~~
Elmira, Nov. 26.
Thanksgiving Day.

My Dear Mother—

It is MY thanksgiving ~~D~~ day, above all other days that ever shone on earth. Because, after twenty-four hours of persecution from me, Mr. & Mrs. L. have yielded a *conditional* consent—Livy has said, over & over again, the word which is so hard for a maiden to say, & if there were a church near here with a steeple high enough to make it an object I should go & jump over it. What do you think? She felt the first faint symptom ~~Monday night~~ *Sunday*, & the lecture *Monday* night brought the disease to the surface.[1] She isn't my sister any more—but some time in the future she is going to be my wife, & I think we shall live in Cleveland.

I think that, because I think you will persuade Mr. Fairbanks to sell me ~~an in~~ a living interest in the *Herald* on such a credit as will enable me to pay for it by lecturing & other work—for I have no relatives to borrow money of, & wouldn't do it if I had. And then we shall live in the house next to yours. I am in earnest, now, & you must not cease your eloquence until you have made Mr. Fairbanks yield.[2]

I do *wish* you were here. You see it is a grave matter I have so suddenly sprung upon them, & they are bewildered. And yet they are (sensibly) more concerned about what I am likely to be in the future than what I *have* been in the past. They think you could build up their confidence—I *know* that is why they so wish you were here.[3]

Mr. L. has plenty of fun to-day, breaking in on our private drawing=room confidences under pretense of measuring the room to see if it is large enough for *three*.

Congratulate me, my darling Mother—(that brings the tears to your eyes & a smile ~~of~~ to your lips~~)~~—because you know you *do* congratulate me, away down in the depths of your loving heart.) And you *know* I am so happy that I am almost beside myself.

I touch no more spirituous liquors after this day (though I have made no promises)—I shall do no act which you or Livy might be pained to hear of—I shall seek~~s~~ the society of the good—I shall be a *Christian*. I shall climb—climb—climb—toward this bright sun that is shining in the heaven of my happiness until all that is gross & unworthy is hidden in the mists & the darkness of that lower earth whence *you* first lifted my ~~ascend ascen~~ aspiring feet. Have no fears, my mother. I shall be *worthy*—yet. Livy beli[e]ves in me. You believe in me, too, whether you say it or not. I believe in *myself*. I believe in God—& through the breaking clouds I see the star of Hope rising in the placid blue beyond.

I bow my reverent head. Thy blessing, mother!

For Livy's sake (not mine,) keep this secret from Allie, & my precious little Mollie,[4] & from *all*. Give my cordial love to Mr. F. & all your blessed household.

Yrs in ecstasy
Mark.

P. S. Write *instantly*, for I leave on the 1st. for Rondout[5] & then Dan Slote's.

P. S.—*Friday*—Dear Mother, you are to understand that we are not absolutely *engaged*, because of course ~~Livy~~ Livy would not fall in love Sunday & engage herself Thursday—she must have time to *prove* her heart & make *sure* that her love is permanent. And I must have time to *settle*, & create a new & better character, & prove myself in it—& *I* desire these things, too. That she loves me I would be a fool to doubt. That she shall *continue* to love me is the thing that I must hope for & labor to secure.

But I must not stay here, & so I leave for New York to-night—for idle tongues will be busy with her name soon enough. ~~I~~ On the score of her health it is better that I should go, too—so her parents ~~think~~ thought, this morning, for they knew she had hardly eaten or slept for 48 hours. But she slept last night, & is not so like a lovely, peerless, radiant ghost to-day. [Laughter & applause.] She is serene & happy, to-day, & ate a roast turkey for luncheon.[6] [Cheers.] And for all the old gentleman is so concerned he knows he has not been so jolly himself for months, or had such noble opportunities for poking fun at helpless people. [Hear, hear.] He makes her face [*in margin:* (over) over] crimson, & enjoys it. But he don't embarrass *me* any to speak of. [Vociferous applause.] Mother, I verily & absolutely *worship* her. [Thunders of applause.] And she knows it & likes it. [Hip—hip—hurrah!]

Write me at once—address 121 William st., New York.[7]

Charley says: "All well, & father better."

Yrs lovingly

Mark

[*on back of previous page:*]

~~Elmira~~[8]

[*centered on page:*]

P. S. *Please* come & see the Langdons right away—they are *so* anxious you should. They want so much to question you about me. *Won't* you?

[1] According to Paine, Clemens arrived at the Langdons' on the morning of 21 November, while the family was still at the table, and said, "The calf has returned; may the prodigal have some breakfast?" On Monday evening, 23 November, Clemens delivered "The American Vandal Abroad" at the Elmira Opera House for the benefit of a local volunteer fire company of which Charles Langdon was an active member. With Olivia and her family in the audience, Clemens was nervous enough not to give his best performance; in fact, he was so distressed that he "closed with a fervent apology for my failure" (see the next

letter, and SLC to OLL, 13 and 14 Jan 69, CU-MARK, in *LLMT*, 49). The Elmira *Advertiser* commented that he "was not in good voice," but described the lecture as "pleasing and satisfying" and "well received throughout." On 25 November it reported that the fire company would "clear a very handsome sum from the MARK TWAIN Lecture of Monday evening" (*MTB*, 1:375; Jerome and Wisbey, 69; Elmira *Advertiser:* "Mark Twain and the American Vandal," 24 Nov 68, 4; "City and Neighborhood," 25 Nov 68, 4).

[2] For Clemens's own account of his negotiations with Abel Fairbanks to become a partner in the Cleveland *Herald*, see 29 Dec 68 to Langdon.

[3] Although the Langdons had been very grateful for Charles's friendship with Mrs. Fairbanks since at least November 1867, they evidently first met her during her week-long visit to Elmira in June 1868 (17 June 68 to Fairbanks, n. 9). Within a few days of the present letter, Mrs. Langdon wrote the following remarkable letter to Mrs. Fairbanks (ViU):

Elmira Dec 1st 1868

My dear Mrs Fairbanks

I feel drawn to write you today. I WOULD that I could see you for an hour!——— In one of your 'Holy Land' letters which I cannot conveniently refer to now, you speak of holding your pen, (amid the multitude of things that were eager to be spoken, and perhaps the much greater number, that your own mind, desired should remain unspoken); in indecision about what to write, or where & how to begin. I do not quote your words of course.

But I by no means occupy your situation, as I have but one subject of which to speak.— —— —

By this time you have begun to anticipate of whom I am about to write; and I the more readily ask you to become *our* confidante, our counselor, as Mr Clemens has told Livia, that you were already his.— — — —

I earnestly desire, (and here my perplexity in writing begins, & the feeling that I could so much better talk with you,) that every word of this communication should be such that the subject of it, could now, or at any future day, read it not only without pain, but with the consciousness that it was prompted by feelings of the highest generosity & kindness toward him.

I cannot, & need not, detail to you the utter surprise & almost astonishment with which Mr Langdon & myself listened to Mr Clemens declaration to us, of his love for our precious child, and how at first our parental hearts said no.—to the bare thought of such a stranger, mining in our hearts for the possession of one of the few jewels we have. All this I must pass by, for today I have to deal with that, with which the judgment only has to do.—

You, my dear friend have known Mr Clemens, more or less intimately since your and his embarkation on the 'Quaker City'—you knew him first, as a somewhat celebrated personage next you knew him as a fellow-traveller, and as your acquaintance with him increased into the time of weeks & months, you began to look upon him from your higher standpoint of maturer experience & closer estimate & appreciation of men, (out of your Christian heart, that was so earnestly desirous to do good to all around you, God bless & reward you for it) without criticism, but with those counsels, and it may be rebukes that hasten to do men good. And now you have known him in your family, at the fireside day by day, almost as if he were your own son.— — —

Now what I am about to write, must be plainly & frankly spoken. I do not ask as to his standing among men, nor do I need to be assured that he is a man of genius that he possesses a high order of intellectual endowments, nor do I scarcely crave your opinion of his affectional nature, but what I desire is your opinion of him as a *man;* what the kind of man he *has been*, and what the man he now is, or is to become.

I have learned from Charlie & I think the same idea has pervaded your conversation, or writing or both,—that a great change had taken place in Mr Clemens, that he seemed to have entered upon a new manner of life, with higher & better purposes actuating his conduct.——

The question, the answer to which, would settle a most weaning anxiety, is,—from what standard of conduct,—from what habitual life, did this change, or improvement, or reformation; commence?
Does this change, so desirably commenced make of an immoral man a moral one, as the *world* looks at men?—or—does this change make of one, who has been entirely a man of the world, different in this regard, that he resolutely aims to enter upon a new, because a Christian life?———

— — — — — — — —

I think my dear friend that to you my meaning will not be obscure, & that your maternal heart will make every allowance for me I never feel so much the change that has taken place in my physical strength, as when I try to use my brain for any purpose whatever, so soon does my head become weary, & my thoughts indistinct & confused.

Mr Langdon is slowly gathering up his strength but much more slowly than we hoped & expected, but I am confidently hoping that he will now in a short time be comfortably well. Mr & Mrs Crane leave for Florida tomorrow evening, we feel much more encouraged to hope that Sue will be benefitted by the travel & the sojourn in the South than we did a month ago.——
Livia & Charlie (as well as my neice whom we have come to love very much) are well Charlie has now installed himself quite thoroughly in his 'Hardware business' & seems quite happy.—I cannot express to you how much I prise your letters to him, nor what a wealth I feel that they are to him.——
We do feel very anxious to see you & Mr Fairbanks here & to have a good long visit from you both, then will it not be delightful to rehearse everything that interests us all. Will you remember us very kindly to Mr & Mrs Severance & please tell them that at the next reunion appointed we confidently expect they will be present.

Our warmest love to all your dear family

Very faithfully yours
Olivia Langdon

An early answer to this letter will increase our already great obligations to you.
O.L.

4 Alice and Mary Fairbanks.

5 See 3 Sept 68 to Crane, n. 3.

6 Although Olivia is not known to have suffered at this time from a specific ailment, she had become "an invalid at sixteen, through a partial paralysis caused by falling on the ice, and she was never strong again while her life lasted," as Clemens recalled in 1906:

After that fall she was not able to leave her bed during two years, nor was she able to lie in any position except upon her back. All the great physicians were brought to Elmira, one after another, during that time, but there was no helpful result. In those days both worlds were well acquainted with the name of Dr. Newton, a man who was regarded in both worlds as a quack. . . .

One day Andrew Langdon, a relative of the Langdon family[,] came to the house and said: "You have tried everybody else, now try Dr. Newton, the quack. . . ."

Newton came. He found the young girl upon her back. Over her was suspended a tackle from the ceiling. It had been there a long time, but unused. It was put there in the hope that by its steady motion she might be lifted to a sitting posture, at intervals, for rest. But it proved a failure. Any attempt to raise her brought nausea and exhaustion, and had to be relinquished. Newton made some passes about her head with his hands; then he put an arm behind her shoulders and said "Now we will sit up, my child."

The family were alarmed, and tried to stop him, but he was not disturbed, and raised her up. She sat several minutes, without nausea or discomfort. Then Newton said that that would do for the present, he would come again next morning; which he did. He made some passes with his hands and said, "Now we will walk a few steps, my child." He took her out of bed and supported her while she walked several steps; then he said "I have reached the limit of my art. She is not cured. It is not likely that she will *ever* be cured. She will never be able to walk far, but after a little daily practice she will be able to walk one or two hundred yards, and she can depend on being able to do *that* for the rest of her life." (AD, 13 Feb 1906, in *MTA*, 2:103–5)

[7] Slote's business address.

[8] Clemens wrote the following postscript on the back of the first page of the previous two-page postscript, centering it as a block in the middle of an otherwise blank page. He abandoned, but did not literally strike out, this word—presumably the beginning of his normal dateline for a letter he must have completed elsewhere, if at all.

To Olivia L. Langdon
28 November 1868 • New York, N.Y.

(MS: CU-MARK)

☞ Please address "Everett House, Union Square, New York."

~~121 William street~~
New York, Nov. 28.

My Dear, Dear Livy:

When I found myself comfortably on board the cars last night (I see Dan has just come in from breakfast, & he will be back here, within five minutes & interrupt me,)—when I found myself comfortably on board the cars, I said to myself: "Now whatever others may think, it is **my** opinion that I am blessed above all other men that live; I have known supreme happiness for two whole days, & now I ought to be ready & willing to pay a little attention to necessary duties, & do it cheerfully." Therefore I resolved to go deliberately through that lecture, without notes, & so impress it upon my memory & my understanding as to secure myself against any such lame delivery of it in future as *I* thought characterized it in Elmira. But I had little calculated the cost of such a resolution. Never was a lecture so full of parentheses before. It was Livy, Livy, Livy, Livy, all the way through! It was one sentence of Vandal to ten sentences about *you*. The insignificant lecture was hidden, lost, overwhelmed & buried under a boundless universe of Livy! I was sorry I had ever made so reckless a resolve, for its accomplishment seemed entirely hopeless. Still, having *made* it, I *would* stick to it till it was finished, & I *did*—but it was rather late at night. Then, having a clear conscience, I prayed, & with good heart—but it was only when I prayed for you that my tongue was touched with inspiration. You will smile at the idea of *my* praying for *you*—I, who so need the prayers of all good friends, praying for you who surely need the prayers of none. But never mind, Livy, the prayer was honest & sincere—it was *that*, at least—& I know it was heard.

I slept *well*—& when I woke my first thought was of you, of course, & I was so sorry I was not going to see you at breakfast. I hope & ~~belive~~ believe you slept well, also, for you were restful & at peace, darling, when I saw you last. You needed rest, & you still need it, for you have been so harassed, & so persecuted with conflicting thoughts of late—*I* could see it, dear, though I tried so hard to think my anxiety might be misleading my eyes. *Do* put all perplexing reflections, all doubts & fears, far from you for a little while, Livy, for I dread, dread, *dread* to hear you are sick. No mere ordinary tax upon your powers is likely to make you ill, but you must remember that even the most robust nature could hardly hold out against the siege of foodless, sleepless days & nights which you have just sustained. I am ~~t~~ not talking to you as if you were a feeble little child, for on the contrary you are a brave, strong-willed *woman*, with no nonsense & no childishness about you—but what I am providing against is your liability to indulge in troubled thoughts & forebodings. Such thoughts *must* come, for they are *natural* to people who have brains & feelings & a just appreciation of the responsibilities which God places before them, & so *you* must have them,—but as I said before, my dearest Livy, temper them, *temper* them, & be *you* the mistress & not *they*. Be cheerful—always cheerful—you can *think* more coolly, & calmly, & justly for it. I leave my fate, my weal, my woe, my *life*, in your hands & at your mercy, with a trust, & a confidence & an abiding sense of security which nothing can shake. I have no fears—none. I believe in you, even as I believe in the Savior in whose hands our destinies are. I have faith in you—a faith which is as simple & unquestioning as the faith of a devotee in the idol he worships. For I know that in their own good time your doubts & troubles ~~with~~ will pass away, & ‸then‸ you will give to me your *whole* heart & I shall have nothing more to wish for on earth.

This day I prize above every earthly gift so much of your precious love as I *do* possess, & so am satisfied & happy. I feel no exacting spirit—I am grateful, grateful, unspeakably grateful for the love you have already given me. I am crowned—I am throned—I am sceptred. I sit with the s/ Kings.

I do love, love, *love* you, Livy! ~~And I do~~ My whole being is permeated, is renewed, is leavened with this love, & with every breath I draw its noble influence makes of me a better man. And I shall yet be *worthy* of your priceless love, Livy. It is the ~~ta~~ glad task of my life—it is the purest ambition & the most exalted, that ever I have known, & I shall never, never swerve from the path it has marked out for me/, while the goal & *you* are before me. Livy, I could not tell your honored father & mother how deeply I felt for them, & how heartless it seemed in ~~my~~ me to come, under cover of ~~ther~~ their trusting, generous hospitality, & try to steal away the sun out of their ‸domestic‸ firmament & rob their fireside heaven of its angel. I could not tell them in what large degree (& yet how feebly in comparison with the reality,) I appreciated & do still appreciate the tremendous boon I was asking at their hands. I could not tell them how grateful I was, & how I loved them for pausing to listen to my appeals when they could have upbraided me for my treachery & turned me out of doors in deserved disgrace. I call these things by their right names, Livy, because I *know* I ought to have spoken to them long before I spoke to you—& yet there was nothing criminal in my *intent*, Livy—nothing wilfully & deliberately underhanded & dishonorable—I could say it in the high court of Heaven. *You* know I would scorn to do a shameful act, my darling—you know it & will maintain it/—for never yet had any friend a stauncher, braver defender than YOU—you—you Perfection! Ah, how "deluded" I am, & how I do love to be so "deluded!" I could not tell them those things, Livy, but if it shall seem necessary, I know that *you* can. And moreover you can always say, with every confidence, that I have been through the world's "mill"—I have traversed its ramifications from end to end—I have searched it, & ~~prov~~ probed it, & put it under the microscope, & I *know* it, through & through, & ‸from‸ back to back;/,‸—‸its follies, it[s] frauds & its vanities—all by personal **experience** & not through dainty *theories* culled from nice moral books in luxurious parlors where temptation never comes & it is easy to be good & keep the heart warm & one's ~~generous~~ ‸best‸ impulses fresh & strong & uncontaminated—& now I know *how* to be a better man, & the *value* of so being, & when I say that I *shall* be, it is just the same as if I *swore* it! *Now!*[1]

Good-bye, Livy. You are so pure, so great, so good, so beautiful. *How* can I help loving you? Say, rather, how can I keep from *worshipping* you, you dear little paragon? IF I could only see you! I do *wish* I could. Write me im-*mediately*. Don't wait a minute. You are never out of my waking thoughts for a single fraction of a second, & I do so want to hear from you. Ah, well, I suppose I shall lecture to those Rondout pirates about *you*, & yet, poor confiding creatures, they think I am going to talk about the Vandal. But such is life. And mind you just keep on, writing until you ~~bef~~ begin to feel tired,—but not a moment afterward, my peerless Livy, for I love you too dearly to wish to ~~see you~~ have you ~~tire yoursel~~ do irksome things, even to gratify **me.**

Tell me the name of that book you were going to lend me, Livy, so that I can get it. I shall send *those* books by Ed, if I can find him.[2]

I saw an old friend of mine at breakfast a while ago, (ex-Gov. Fuller,) & he gave me a lot of notices of my New York lecture delivered 18 months ago. I inflict them on you,—for why *shouldn't* I? The house was ~~full o~~ crowded, on that occasion, but it was not my popularity that crowded it. The exertions of my friends did *that*. They got up the whole thing—suggested it, engineered it, & carried it through successfully. If any man has ~~p~~ a right to be proud of his friends, it is I, thy servant. The *Tribune* notice is by Ned House, who ranks as the most eminent dramatic critic in the Union.[3]

Good-bye, Livy. All this time I have felt just as if you were here with me, almost—& part of the~~m~~ ~~t~~ time as if I could *see* you standing by me. But you are vanished! I miss a gracious presence—~~I l~~ a glory is gone from about me. I listen for a dear voice, I look for a darling face, I caress the empty air! God bless you, my idol. Good-bye—& I send a thousand kisses—pray send *me* some.

Most lovingly, Yours
Forever—~~Mark~~ Samuel.

P. S.—I do LOVE you, Livy!

P. P. S.—I enclose a ~~melain~~ ferrotype—don't you see how soft, rich, expressive, ~~*human, the featur*~~ ‸the‸ lights & shades are, & how *human* the whole picture is? If you can't get me the porcelain ~~or~~ picture, Livy, do please ~~s~~ have a ferrotype taken for me. This pretty little sixteen-year-old school-girl is Gov. Fuller's daughter—Fuller gave it to me this morning. I never saw the young lady but once—at a party in Brooklyn a short time ago—& then I petrified her by proposing with frozen gravity, (just after introduction,) to kiss her *because I was acquainted with her father*[.] *He* enjoyed the joke immensely (because he has known me so long & intimately,) but *she* didn't.[4]

P. P. P. S.—I do *love*, LOVE, LOVE you, Livy, darling. Write immediately—*do*.

[*in margin:*]

If any of the family inquire of me, ~~give th~~ remember me kindly to them—& please convey to Mr. & Mrs. Langdon my love & respectful duty. They know *that* is sincere enough, no matter what may befal you & I. I *love* you, Livy!

[*on back of letter as folded:*]

Livy, shan't you come to New York this winter?

I love, love, *love* you, Livy!

PPPPP.S—I *do* love you, Livy!

Miss Olivia L. Langdon | Present.[5] [*docketed by OLL:*] 6th [*and in pencil*] Nov. 29th 1868

[1]Clemens's remarks about Mr. and Mrs. Langdon filled three manuscript pages: "Livy" (290.12) is the third word on the eighth page, and "*Now!*" is the last word on the tenth page. Olivia could therefore have easily shown them to her parents without revealing anything else in the letter.

[2]The book Olivia intended to lend Clemens has not been identified. The books he planned to send her may have been Coventry Patmore's four-part verse narrative, *The Angel in the House* (see 30 Oct 68 to OLL, n. 7). By early December Clemens had evidently not carried out his plan, since the book he elsewhere called "exquisite"—possibly part of the Patmore tetralogy—was still in his possession (see 5 and 7 Dec 68 to OLL). "Ed" was almost certainly Olivia's cousin Captain Edward L. Marsh (1842–1906), who stayed with the Langdons from late November until 16 December. Marsh, whom Clemens later described as "a handsome young bachelor," was the son of Mrs. Langdon's twin sister, Mrs. Sheppard Marsh; the Marshes had lived in Iowa since leaving Elmira in 1857. Marsh served as captain of the Second Iowa Regiment during the war and later went into the real-estate business (OLL to Alice B. Hooker, 16 Dec 68, CtHSD; AD, 26 Mar 1906, CU-MARK, in *MTA*, 2:250–51).

[3]The enclosed clippings, notices of Clemens's 6 May 1867 Sandwich Islands lecture, do not survive. In addition to House's New York *Tribune* review, they may have included, among others, favorable brief reviews in the New York *Herald*, *Times*, *Evening Post*, and *Evening Express* (7 May); the Brooklyn *Union* and *Eagle* (9 May); the New York *Dispatch* (12 May); the New York *World* (13 May);

Street and Smith's *New York Weekly* (30 May). House's review appeared on 11 May 1867; it is reprinted in full in Appendix E.

[4]The enclosure has not been found. "Melainotype" (or "melanotype") was an early name for a ferrotype, later known as a tintype: a positive photograph produced by the wet collodion process on sheet-iron plates (Jones, 240). Fuller and his wife, Mary F. Fuller (1829?–1906), had two daughters: Ida F. (b. 1849 or 1850), now aged eighteen or nineteen, and Anna Cora (b. 1853 or 1854), now aged fourteen or fifteen (*Portsmouth Census*, 740). The "party in Brooklyn" has not been further identified.

[5]Beginning with this letter, the first after their informal engagement, Clemens sent his letters to Olivia sealed within a second envelope addressed and mailed to her brother, Charles. Only the "inside" envelopes directed to Olivia survive; on many of them Clemens wrote "Present" or "Politeness of" Charles—conventional ways to inscribe letters entrusted to another for delivery. According to Olivia's cousin Harriet Lewis, this procedure was adopted because of Clemens's "prominence and also because there was no engagement," and Olivia "did not wish their names coupled together in the newspapers" (Paff, 5).

To Joseph H. Twichell
28 November 1868 • New York, N.Y.

(MS: ViU)

DANIEL SLOTE.
WEBSTER WOODMAN.
WM. A. MAUTERSTOCK.
FRANK BOWMAN.
P. O. BOX 21.

SLOTE, WOODMAN & CO., BLANK BOOK MANUFACTURERS,
NOS. 119 & 121 WILLIAM STREET,

NEW YORK, Nov. 28 1868.

Private.

My Dear J. H.

Sound the loud timbrel![1]—& let yourself out to your most prodigious capacity,—for I have fought the good fight[2] & lo! I have won! Refused three times—warned to *quit*, once—accepted at last!—& beloved!—Great Caesar's ghost, if there were a church in town with a steeple high enough to make it an object, I would go out & jump over it! And I persecuted her parents for 48 hours & at last they couldn't stand the siege any longer & so they made a *conditional* surrender:—which is to say, if *she* ~~don't~~ makes up her mind thoroughly & eternally, & I prove that I have done nothing criminal or particularly shameful in the past, & establish a good character in the future & *settle down*, I may take the sun out of their ¢ domestic firmament, the angel out of their fireside heaven. [Thunders of applause.] She felt the first symptoms last Sunday—my lecture, Monday night, brought the disease to the surface—Tuesday & Tuesday night she avoided me & ~~c~~would not do more than be simply polite to me because her parents said NO absolutely (almost,)—Wednesday they capitulated & marched out with their side-arms—Wednesday night—she said over & over & over again that she loved me but was sorry she did & hoped it would yet passes away—Thursday I was telling her what ~~a~~ *splendid, magnificent* fellows you & your wife were, & when my enthusiasm got the best of me & the tears sprang to my eyes, she just jumped up & said she was *glad* & *proud* she loved me!—& Friday night I left, (to save her sacred name frome the tongues of the gossips[)]—& the last thing she said was: "Write *immediately* & just as often as you can!" Hurrah! [Hurricanes of applause.] There's the history of it.

Oh, no—there isn't any persistence about *me*—certainly not. But I am so happy I want to scalp somebody.

My fervent love to you both. Write me, now—address 121 William street.

I walk in the clouds again. I bow my reverent head—thy blessing!

Mark.

[1] Thomas Moore's "Sound the Loud Timbrel. Miriam's Song," in *Sacred Songs* (1816): "Sound the loud Timbrel o'er Egypt's dark sea! / Jehovah has triumph'd—his people are free" (Moore, 244).

[2] 1 Timothy 6:12: "Fight the good fight of faith, lay hold on eternal life."

To Pamela A. Moffett
29? November 1868 • New York, N.Y.

(MS facsimile, *damage emended:* Davis)

DANIEL SLOTE. SLOTE, WOODMAN & CO., BLANK BOOK MANUFACTURERS,
WEBSTER WOODMAN. NOS. 119 & 121 WILLIAM STREET,
WM. A. MAUTERSTOCK.
FRANK BOWMAN.
P. O. BOX 21. NEW YORK, Nov. 29[1] 1868.

[*eleven or twelve lines (about 70 words) missing*]

Rondout & Newark & one or two other places, I go West to deliver 21 lectures at $100 a piece—beginning at Detroit, Michigan Dec. 23, &

ending at some Wisconsin town Jan. 18[2]—after which I have promised to preach in New York city for the Fireman's Fund.[3] I would send Ma some money, but Dan has gone home (he is my banker,)[4]

[*twelve or thirteen lines (about 80 words) missing*]

Now—*Private*—Keep it to yourself, my sister—do not even *hint* it, to *any* one—I make no exceptions. I can trust you. I love—I *worship*—Olivia L. Langdon, of Elmira—& she loves me. When I am permanently *settled*—& when I am a Christian—& when I have *demonstrated* that I have a good, steady, reliable character, her parents will withdraw their objections, & she *may* marry me—*I* say she *will*—I intend she *shall*—the earth will cease to turn round & the sun to traverse his accustomed courses when I give it up. Cool, deliberate, critical Mrs. Fairbanks says her peer does not exist upon earth—& cool, deliberate, critical Mrs. Brooks of New York, says the same, & I endorse it with all my heart. Both have informed me frankly that neither I nor any other man is worthy of her & that I can never get her. What will they say *now*, I wonder? Her parents have refused to permit the attentions of *anybody*, before, but I was mean enough to steal a march on them. They are not *very* much concerned about my *past*, but they simply demand that I shall prove my *future* before I take the sunshine out of their house. I have made that household spend several sleepless nights lately. But they all like me, & they can't help it. *Now* you know why I was so savage & crazy in St Louis. I had just been *refused* by my idol a few days before—was refused again afterward—was warned to *quit* after that—& have won the fight at last & am the happiest man alive. If I were in St Louis *now* you would see me in my *natural* character, & love me. I drink no spirituous liquors any more—I do nothing that is not thoroughly *right*—I am *rising*. I think Mrs. Fairbanks (who loves me like a son,) will go beside herself for joy when she hears of my good fortune. For in her eyes & mine, Livy Langdon is *per***fection** itself. Mind—*no word of this to anybody*. ‸The above is my address for ten days.‸[5]

Affectionatly
Sam.

[1] The missing portion of this letter (the top two-thirds of its first leaf) was cut away from its surviving, "*Private*," portion. The letterhead and date have therefore been supplied from other evidence. Clemens's statement below (see note 5) that Slote's New York address was to be his for the "next ten days" indicates,

depending on how precise he was being, that he wrote the letter on 29 or 30 November. Twenty-nine November has been supplied here chiefly because the "private" portion of this letter resembles so closely the previous 28 November letter to Twichell (also marked "private"). Both letters are similar in content and tone, both are inscribed on Slote and Woodman stationery (in the case of this letter, the letterhead stationery survives only from the second leaf), and both were returned to Clemens at some point, since their provenance is the Samossoud Collection (see pp. 515–16). These similarities have led to the conjecture that the two letters were probably written within a day of each other, and have provided part of the rationale for restoring the missing letterhead to page one (see the textual commentary for this letter).

2 Clemens would lecture in Rondout, New York, on 2 December; Newark, New Jersey, on 9 December; Norwich, New York, on 11 December; Scranton, Pennsylvania, on 16 December; and at Fort Plain, New York, on 19 December. Appendix G lists his known lecturing appearances in the "West" from late December through 18 January. Several changes were made while the tour was in progress; the engagements scheduled at this time were, so far as is known, in the following seventeen cities. Michigan: Detroit, 23 December; Charlotte, 25 December; and Tecumseh, 26 December. Ohio: Akron, 30 December, and Dayton, 31 December (see 21 and 23 Dec 68 to OLL). Indiana: Fort Wayne, 29 December, and Indianapolis, 4 January. Illinois: Rockford, 6 January; Chicago, 7 January; Monmouth, 8 January; Galesburg, 10 January; Peoria, 11 January; Bloomington, 12 January (see SLC to OLL, 2 Jan 69, CU-MARK); and Ottawa, 13 January. Iowa: Davenport, 14 January, and Iowa City, 15 January. The "Wisconsin town" was probably Sparta, where he was scheduled to appear on 17 or 18 January (see SLC to OLL, 17 Jan 69 [misdated 16 Jan] and 19 Jan 69, CU-MARK, in *LLMT*, 54, 55).

3 Clemens had been asked to give a benefit lecture for the old New York Volunteer Fire Department (now apparently operating solely as a charity), probably by Dan Slote (a member) or Alonzo Slote (its treasurer). The Slotes, now living at the same address, were almost certainly brothers ("Daniel Slote," New York *Herald*, 14 Feb 82, 5; "Amusements," New York *Times*, 14 Dec 68, 7; Wilson 1868, 1005).

4 According to Jane Clemens's own record, in 1868 she received $50 from Clemens on 13 March, $50 on 5 May, $100 on 7 August, $50 on 19 September, $20 (twice) on 8 December, and $20 again on 11, 14, 17, and 28 December (JLC, no page).

5 Although Clemens left New York briefly several times in early December, he departed for a more extended period on 10 December, spending that night at the Delavan House in Albany, presumably en route to his lecture the next day at Norwich and then to Elmira (12 Dec 68 to OLL). The "above" address to which Clemens refers is the address of Slote, Woodman & Co., given in the letterhead, which in the surviving manuscript appears only at the top of the fourth and last page (beginning at "the sunshine out of their house," 295.20).

To Jervis Langdon
2 December 1868 • New York, N.Y.
(MS: CtHMTH)

‸A. M.‸
Everett House
N. York, N Dec. 2.

Dear Mr Langdon—

I wish I hadn't come away, now. I might just as well ~~as~~ have spent two or three days persuading Mrs. Langdon to let me stay longer. I don't know what I could have been thinking about, that I hadn't sagacity enough to think of that. However, during the last day or two I suppose my head was so full of lecturing, & writing for newspapers, & other matters of a ~~strictly~~ business nature, that I couldn't think of *anything* I *ought* to have thought of. You may have noticed that I was a good deal absorbed—in business. You may n have noticed that I hadn't much time to be around with family.— Well, it was because I had to get off in the drawing-room by myself, so I could think about those lectures & things. I can always think better when I get off in a drawing-room by myself. So you see that was how it was. I thought I ought to make this explanation, because, latterly, you know, I was not as sociable as I might have been. I *meant* to be sociable. I meant to be ~~uncommonly~~ ‸very‸ sociable with all the family. And I *did* make as fair a start for it as I could—but I never got very far—~~there wasn't enough to go around, maybe. I suppose.~~ ‸I never finished the list.‸

But notwithstanding all this pretended cheerfulness, I am *not* boisterously cheerful. I know from what Miss Langdon said the night I left, that she would have answered my letter yesterday if she had been well. There is nothing tranquilizing about that reflection. I— — however, I will not try to wet-blanket *your* spirits. You will need all your hopefulness & all your cheer when Mrs. Crane goes from you—when every heart in your household shall yield up a sunbeam & take to itself a shadow. Even the dumb brutes will know that a friend is gone from among them. And the flowers will, I am sure—& if they exhale a sweeter incense that day, you may know it for a ~~payer~~ prayer they are sending up for their lost mistress. Everything & everybody will miss her, from Mrs. Ford down to the captive birds in the cages—& missing her will grieve that she is gone. Without knowing ~~Mr~~ Mrs. Crane very well—certainly not as well as I wish to—I know how you all regard her & how keenly her going forth from your midst is going to be felt.[1]

But I am not cheering you up as much as I meant to when I sat down. Dan & I had conspired to get Jack over to my Newark lecture, ~~ten~~ ‸7‸ days hence, & I was to tell the "Moses Who?" story in most elaborate detail & enlarge on Jack's peculiarities unstintedly—but I fear the scheme must fail, because Dan cannot get any tickets. They have used the plan of reserving seats at an extra price, & that has persuaded the people that I am a prodigy of some kind—a gorilla, maybe—& so the seats are all sold. {The truth is, it is not my popularity that has caused this, I think, but the fact that I am to lecture for an energetic, well⸗organized Association.}[2] Dan says he wishes he was out of the blank⸗book business, because he believes it is more respectable to be a fraud & go around deluding the ignorant, like me! But Dan's an old fool—I mentioned it to him. I am invited back to Pittsburgh to repeat—& by people of standing, too—& by the same lecture committee, ~~all~~ also—& that shows that when I delude people they don't KNOW it—& consequently it is no sin.

John Russell Young (the Managing Editor,) tells me that the price of *Tribune* shares is $7,000 each, & none in market just now. There are 100 shares, altogether, & a share yields $1,000 a year—sometimes as high as $2,000. He wants me to buy—told him I would take as many shares as I could mortgage my book for, & as many more as I could pay for with labor of hand & brain. I shan't make up my mind~~, yet~~ ‸in indecent haste‸ (because I haven't heard from Cleveland & am waiting,)[3] ~~but if I *do* make it up in that direction I will own in that high-toned stuck-up institution yet. But in the midst of these grave delibera-~~ ‸but if I *do* buy, I shall retain Horace Greeley on the paper.‸

Chase of the Herald says Frank Leslie wishes to see me—thinks he wants me to edit a new paper he designs issuing, but don't know. ~~*I*~~ *I* can't make pictures. However, I will go & see him.[4]

If you hear that I didn't get away in the 11.30 train this morning, & didn't lecture in Rondout to-night, you will know that the reason was because I was writing to you, & so you will be responsible for the damage done to my pocket—but you can come back on the Rondouters, you know, for the damage you have saved *them*.[5]

If you please, I wish you would say to Mrs. Langdon that I wish to go ‸back‸ to Elmira—for a little while—*only* a little while—only just long enough to say to Miss Langdon a few things which I hadn't quite finished telling her—it will only take a couple of weeks, or a couple of months, or such a matter? Will she let me? But really, I suppose I *could* get along with just one evening—or just one *hour*—if I couldn't do any better. Now be *good*—you are the splendidest man in the *world!*—be generous, now—be merciful—*do* ask~~e~~ her, please? I'll call you all the nice names I can think of if you will enter into this little conspir—

Time's up—good-bye—love to all—

Yrs ever

Saml. L. Clemens

Please don't let Miss L. hear the first part of this letter—she won't like to be w[6]

[1] Eunice Ford (1782–1873) was Jervis Langdon's mother. Born Eunice King, she was married three times: first to Jervis's father, Andrew Langdon (1774–1811); then to Jonathan Williams; and finally to Jonathan Ford, who died in 1843. She now lived with the Langdons (Towner, 609–10; Jerome and Wisbey, 236–37). Susan Langdon Crane, Jervis's thirty-two-year-old adopted daughter, was about to leave on an extended southern vacation with her husband, Theodore. On 16 December, Olivia wrote to Alice Hooker: "Sue and Theodore left us for the South two weeks ago tomorrow night— They staid in Washington about a week, then were in Richmond a few days. I suppose that they are now in Charleston, they will go on to Florida— We hope a great deal from the change for Sue's throat" (CtHSD).

[2] Clemens first published his anecdote about Jack Van Nostrand in chapter 6 of *Roughing It*, as it was ostensibly "set down in my Holy Land note-book" (SLC 1872, 57). But he evidently told the story on various occasions after September 1867, when Colonel Denny's "impressive speeches" about Moses first elicited Van Nostrand's innocently irreverent remark, "Moses who?" (*MTB*, 3:1290). In May 1868, while writing *The Innocents Abroad* in California, Clemens expressed mock indignation that "here, all of a sudden, this anecdote, all garbled & mutilated, turns up in San Francisco,, ~~I~~ and *I* am accused of making that remark. I did *not* make it, & never thought of ~~do~~ making it. I get enough abuse, without having to suffer for the acts of others" (SLC 1868zz, 7). The manuscript for "The American Vandal Abroad" contains some evidence that Clemens considered using the anecdote in that lecture, and he is known to have done so at least three times: in Newark (New Jersey) on 9 December 1868, in Tecumseh (Michigan) on 26 December 1868, and in Peoria (Illinois) on 11 January 1869. It was not included in *The Innocents Abroad* (SLC 1868nnn, 42; Lorgnette, no page; SLC to OLL, 14 Jan 69, CU-MARK; "Mark Twain's Lecture," Peoria *Transcript*, 12 Jan 69, PH in CU-MARK). Clemens's Newark lecture was sponsored by the Clayonian Society, which remained a favorite: even three years later

he said he preferred "to talk for my same old society—the Clayonians—good boys" (SLC to James Redpath and George L. Fall, 10 June 71, NHi†).

[3] For Clemens's account of his negotiations with the Cleveland *Herald*, see 29 Dec 68 to Langdon.

[4] It is not known when or whether Clemens consulted with Frank Leslie about "a new paper." Leslie, whose real name was Henry Carter (1821–80), was the son of an English glove manufacturer. He began his career as an artist and engraver, became (while still very young) superintendent of the art department of the London *Illustrated News*, and in 1855 in New York began to issue *Frank Leslie's Illustrated Newspaper*, which by 1868 had achieved a circulation of 70,000, largely because of its numerous and timely engravings. During the postwar period, Leslie created and managed a virtual journalistic empire, which included as many as ten illustrated papers: among them were *Frank Leslie's Illustrirte Zeitung* (a German-language edition of his newspaper, circulation 25,000); *Frank Leslie's Boys' and Girls' Weekly* (circulation 27,000); and two monthly publications, *Frank Leslie's Ladies' Magazine* (circulation 50,000) and *Frank Leslie's Budget of Fun* (circulation 25,000). In 1871, William H. Chase, whom Clemens knew as an editor on the *Herald*, went to work for Leslie (Rowell, 72, 76; "Death of William H. Chase," New York *Times*, 24 June 81, 4).

[5] Clemens presumably caught the Hudson River Railroad's 11:30 A.M. express to Albany and Troy, leaving the train en route to cross the Hudson River to Rondout. The next such train left at 3:30 P.M.—evidently too late for comfort ("Railroads," New York *Evening Post*, 2 Dec 68, 4).

[6] Clemens broke off in the middle of a line, probably to catch his train.

To Olivia L. Langdon
4 December 1868 • (1st of 2) • New York, N.Y.

(MS: CU-MARK)

Metropolitan Hotel }
New York, Dec. 4. }

My Dear, Dear Livy:

A blessed peace has folded its wings over my spirit, & I am at rest. For your letter is come! It seemed to me that my feet could not carry me fast enough—to my room, to read it. Now that I *have* read it, & re-read it, I am perfectly satisfied & happy—for you are well. And you are not only well, but you are coming to love me better & better. I know it, albeit you may not know it yourself. You are building up this love as I would have it built—upon a basis of **reason,** not **passion.** You are raising this edifice gradually, course by course, & proving each as it is laid. And when, in the fulness of time, it is finished, its walls shall be eternal! *Pas-*

sion ~~is born without~~ springs *full-grown* from the heart (& ~~hea~~ the heart alone)—& when lagging Reason follows & strips off its finery & exposes the skeleton beneath, Passion dies. The love that lasts, & ~~it~~ is genuine, is that love which is born of both *heart & brain.* It has an ~~i~~‸I‸nfancy—a Youth—a Maturity. The ~~heat~~ heart siezes upon each stage, & accepts it, & takes it to itself—but not until the grave, calm, ~~i~~‸I‸nspector-General, *Reason*, has passed upon it & endorsed it with his approval. Livy, was *ever* the love of an ill-matched couple born of both ~~heat~~ heart & brain? Do superiors ever *love, revere & honor* inferiors with the **brain's** consent? Hardly, I think. Mrs. Brooks & Mrs. Fairbanks, brilliant women both, have married away down below them—& it would be hard to convince me that they did not love first & *think* afterward.

Yes, my own dear Livy, paradoxical as it may sound, your first page *did* pain me—& sharply, too—& yet I *wanted* to hear you say it. ~~It~~ I knew it would hurt, & yet I *coveted* the words—because they would so surely prove that eternal **love** was growing up in your heart of hearts, right under the ~~exe~~ exacting eye of *Reason—love*, that shall stand calmly above ~~b~~ vanquished doubts & bodings, at last, ~~as~~ even as ‸at times‸ Gibraltar stands above the slumbering sea that so lately wasted its wrath against his everlasting walls. I can bide my time, my Livy, being full of faith in you & without fear—for your love is growing, growing, growing (you proved it before you reached your final page,) & it will reach its maturity all in good time. And then, pray Heaven enlarge my capacity!—for lo! such degree of your love as I already possess does so fill all my being with happiness that it is a mystery to me how I am to accommodate an increase! This is not idle talk, Livy—I *am* so happy I hardly know what to do with myself—& I bless you, & give honest gratitude to God that it is so. How *easy* it was to pray, when your letter came—for the heart ~~looks~~ **naturally** looks *upward for something to* THANK when a great generous wave of *gratitude* sweeps over its parched & thirsty deserts. This thought struck me, then: How vapid & inefficient the loves of the gods of mythology—the loves of Jove~~s~~ & Juno—for when the music of love ~~wov~~ woke its grand symphonies in their hearts, *there was none above them to thank*. I prayed that at last you might come to love me freely & fully, & that He would prepare me to be worthy of it—which could only be, in ~~its~~ utter completeness, through my investment with His spirit. Some of my other prayers have seemed only faint-hearted words, words, words, compared to this, which ~~surged up~~ came surging up out of my *heart*—a great tide of *feeling*, which scorned set phrase & tricks of speech, & prayed *itself!*

Your letter was due here Wednesday, & yet only reached me to-day (Friday.) What a world of distress it would have saved me if it had come when it ought to have come! But never mind—it is over now. The fault was in the New York postoffice—for the Elmira postmark was Dec. 1. This morning when the postman came without the longed-for letter, I could bear it no longer, & so I wrote & mailed a little note beseeching you to write.[1] I must close, now, & mail this much of my letter right away, to keep you from being uneasy about *your* letter.

I kiss you, darling—& thank you from my heart for the wished-for kiss you sent to me.

Lovingly & devotedly,
Sam*l*. L. C.

[*in margin:*]
I forgot Mother Fairbank's letter—I will write again tomorrow, & inclose it. You *knew* I would tell *her*—& *I* knew it would make her so proud & happy.

Miss Olivia L. Langdon | Present. [*docketed by OLL:*] 8th

[1] Clemens's "little note," his seventh letter to Olivia, does not survive. That she received it, however, is established by the docket number "8th" on the envelope of the present letter.

To Olivia L. Langdon
4 December 1868 • (2nd of 2) • New York, N.Y.

(MS, *damage emended:* CU-MARK)

Dec. 4.

☞ The last page of the last letter (to-day) was 5.[1]

———

Now! I got down stairs with my letter just *after* the mail had gone to the postoffice, but I bribed a bell-boy to break his neck getting there with it before the mail should close—& so I suppose it is all right.[2]

You have done right, Livy. Put before me *all* your doubts & fears—all your troubles. As you say, & as you *know*, you may feel sure of my "patience toward, & brave words to," you. And you saw how your confessions soothed you & revived your love. We *will* "help to bear one another's burdens," Livy, & both shall be t better, & stronger, & happier for it. I am grieved to see you harassed with misgivings—& yet am I cruelly content that it is so, for only I o through such can come a love that shall be noble, lasting, & without alloy or blemish. ~~Your~~ Gold must pass through the batteries, the concentrators, the amalgamators, ~~the assay office,~~ the smelting furnace, the assay office, the refiner's exquisitely fervent & cleansing fires—all before it can become minted coin & bear the stamp that shall testify its perfected worth to men. It was gold *at first*, Livy—it was only hidden from sight among base metals in homely quartz. Let your doubts & your fears pass one by one to death & oblivion, in ~~ther~~ their due & proper season, Livy, even as the galena, the antimony & the pyrites drift from the batteries & are lost.

"Do not believe in any mortal as you believe in your Savior." Forgive me, Livy, if I uttered such a thing *irreverently*—for it could not fail to wound you. I am thinking, thinking, thinking—but nothing comes back to me now but something I said about an "eastern ~~ded~~ devotee & his idol."[3] The thought of unquestioning devotion *always* brings m before me some pictures I saw in a Sunday School book when I was a boy, of Hindoo devotees swinging on hooks thrust into their backs—holding out an arm till it withered—making incredible journeys on their knees & s bruising their heads against the ground at every third step—casting themselves under the Car of Juggernaut,[4] etc,—all to find favor with ~~hideous~~ majestic idols that smiled not nor gave any sign. But you will forgive me, Livy. I did not mean to hurt you. I *could* not do that, with deliberate intent.

And you are *not* "Perfection"—no? And I shan't *say* you are? ~~There you go, again, you dear little concentration of lLiteralness!~~ Why, ~~bless your good old heart,~~ nobody said *you* considered yourself perfection—*no!* It is *I*—& Mrs. Brooks—& Mrs. Fairbanks—& all else that know you—that considers you perfection—& I warn you that we shall *go on* saying it (to ourselves,) notwithstanding your tyrannical, illegal & outrageous edict stops us henceforth from saying it to *you!* If I were to bring the Constitution of the United States to bear upon this question, ~~I co~~ (where it speaks of free speech & freedom of the press,) I could easily show you that I have a perfect right to say it to *you*, too—~~I~~ & I *would*, too, if I dared to disobey you, you awful tyrant! Oh, ~~w~~ don't you mind what I shall "discover some day"—I shall just discover what I have *already* discovered—that I love, love, love, love, love, LOVE~~l~~ you!—multiplied by a hundred & fifty! And so loving you I note your faults, & knight them with my love, & call them the *perfection of faults* (for I have searched them out & I know what they are.) They are—1, The using of slang (but you didn't know it was slang, my little angel by brevet, else you wouldn't have used it); 2. The leaving off of blue ribbons at times (which is unconstitutional & unsustain[e]d by law); 3. The appearing five minutes late at breakfast, every morning, when I have been watching the door for ages & ages to see you enter, radiant & beautiful, & fill all the dull air with sunshine;) 4. But your most heinous fault is in loving *me*—& I pray that it may grow, & grow, & grow, till it shall usurp all your being & leave you nothing but one stately, magnificent, concentrated, sublimated, overwhelming *Fault*, for all Time! Livy, you are a true Woman—for when did ever a woman condescend to show *why* one of her imperious assertions should be received as incontrovertible *fact?* I couldn't help smiling at the truly feminine confidence with which you simply *asserted* that you were not perfection, & then calmly changed the subject without ever~~y~~ offering ~~a~~ word or hint of argument or testimony to support it! {But I take it all back, my darling, my idol—for you are sensitive to irony, & must feel it, even though you *do know* that ‸when‸ it goes from *me* to *you*, it can never be aught else ~~that~~ ‸than‸ *loving badinage* & ~~is~~ forbidden to bear with it a sting. And beside, your simple *word*, which never yet was doubted, stands superior to all argument & evidence—when you speak, it is the King that speaks—the monarch's word is Truth, & unimpeachable—& when you say & I doubt, I shall no longer stand worthy to be called leal & true subject of thine, O loved & honored liege!}

Livy, I am doing according to the valued privilege you have accorded me—I am telling you all I feel & think & do—~~I~~ & I am grateful that you give to me *your* confidence. The very least little thing you do, is full of interest to me & I pray you tell it me. If another tells me he ~~w~~ rode or walked, sat, sang or went to church, it is nothing—but when you tell me *you* did it, I devour it as though I were absorbing priceless learning. When you said you were quietly located in your room, ready to have a little visit with me, I *saw* you, just as plainly as if I had been there beside you, with my eager arms about you & looking into your dear eyes. If I could only take you to my arms *now*, & imprint upon your forehead the kiss of reverent Honor, & upon your lips the kiss of Love, imperishable & undefiled!

Livy, I wrote your father Wednesday (whose honor & respect, & ~~yo~~ likewise your mother's I hope always to deserve & hold,) & I tried to seem lively, but somehow I couldn't get over the dread that you were ill—& so I begged him to let me come up, if only for an hour or two—but I am reassured & comfortable now. If he dares to ridicule me I shan't inflict another letter on him for three or ‸four‸ weeks! But do you know, if I hadn't got your letter to-day I would have arrived in Elmira tomorrow night? Indeed I would. You were saved as by fire.[5] I wouldn't have passed another such a day as yesterday for *any*thing. [*torn in order to cancel:*] I [◇◇◇pose] I ru[i◇◇◇ ◇◇◇ ◇an's]

[*twenty lines (about 120 words) torn away*]

[keep ◇◇th◇◇◇ ◇◇◇◇ y◇]u, el[◇◇] I wouldn't have been betrayed into this confession[6]—& so I rely on you not to take advantage of my confidence to go & make yourself sorry.

And now, being in a confessing mood, I bow my expectant head for your forgiveness, & proceed to reveal to you that I told *Dan*—& have told the *Twichell's*—& my *sister*—& Mrs. *Fairbanks*. What a load is off my conscience now! But observe, Livy, I know *who* to tell. These several parties are very, very dear to me—& each is a sealed book. Our secret is safe in their hands—as safe as though it were shut within the fabled copper vessel of Arabian story & sealed with the seal of Solomon, lord of the genii.[7] I do *wish* you could read Twichell's letter—magnificent fellow! Let me give you an extract or two:

"Receive my benediction, Mark—my very choicest! I breathe it toward you—that particular doxologic & hallelujah formula thereof which I use on occasions which but for the sake of propriety I should celebrate by a smiting of my thigh, a grand *pas seul* & three cheers with a tiger!—a style of Te Deum which somehow I never *could* manage to execute successfully in the pulpit. Bless you, my son!—yea, Bless you, my children both!!"

And here is another:

"I do congratulate you, dear friend, with all the power of congratulation that is in me, (I speak for my wife, of course, when I say "I," as I always do when writing to any of our common loves) & I congratulate *her*. If I could do anything to help you in the matter, I would, joyfully.

Command me if you have any use for me. I don't know anything about your past; but it does seem to me that a fellow, whom I have found so thoroughly lovable for a whole fortnight of quite free intercourse can't have become incapable of a character worthy any man's or woman's respect. I don't care very much about your past, but I do care very much about your future. I hope & expect, that it will be a nobly lived, happy, pure & useful future, ending with the dear life eternal which our Savior gives for repentance & faith. Now is the best time you will ever see for giving your heart to God. Your heart, with this new, sacred love in it is a more precious thing to offer God than it was without it. You never have been able to bring so worthy a gift to ~~h~~ Him as now. And while you are in the mood of gratitude, as I know you are, & all full of tender feelings, begin with genuine diligence to pray for & seek that peace in believing in Jesus Christ & knowing Him that is so sweet as to sweeten even the most joyful earthly joys. Be assured, my friend, I have not forgotten you in my secret hours with God, & I shall not."

It is just like him—the gorgeous, whole-souled fellow! What splendid nights we had together!—& how gently & how tenderly he taught the religion that is all in all to him. And shall be to me, likewise, I hope & pray. You can see that he knew all about it before! He & his ~~wi~~ dear little wife used to try to comfort me, but they made slim progress at it! But when they would grow discouraged & down-hearted, it made me sorry & forthwith I lifted them up—I told them that even though you remained adamant for five years, a love like mine must melt you at last—for I *could* not & *would* not give you up! Bold ~~worl~~ words, my precious Livy, but not the words of base egotism—only words of strong love, & courage, faith & deathless hope—none else. I do not inclose Twichell's entire letter, simply because I am sending you enough MS. of my own to tire you out—I *want* you to read it *all*, ‸(his letter, I mean,)‸ whenever I can learn to write a shorter letter myself.

Livy, while I think of it, if you want a perfectly fascinating study, & one that will exercise your noble analytical faculty, try phonographic short-hand. It is worth~~y~~ a dozen languages, for pure usefulness.[8]

~~I freely send Mrs. Fairbanks' letter to you,~~

I don't cut Mrs. F.'s letter in two to tease you, Livy—I only do it because I want to show it to you *myself* & talk with you about it some day. There are no secrets in it, & nothing to be concealed from you. I shall not lose my half of it, for I will put it with your letter received to=day—& you know I shall not lose it *then*, unless I lose my coat. But *wouldn't* you like to know ~~what~~ the rest of that sentence about the Sphynx? Well, ~~I can't refuse you anything—& so you may~~ add this:

"- - - sesame to her ~~pole~~ poetical nature. I know it will be that richness of a pure imagination, the *royal* part of yourself, that will hold her in your spell."

See how trustingly I furnish you with armor to shield you from my love & shut me out of your heart. She says, likewise:

"Your sweet secret is safe—but I have no secrets from my husband," &c, &c, &c., & tells how that good old fellow ~~she~~ let his eyes fill with tears over my letter. They tell me in Cleveland that very few people have bored through the shell & got into his heart, as *I* have done. It pleased Mrs. Fairbanks, you may depend. Livy, I don't claim to *fascinate* ANY creature—but I *do* claim that ~~I~~ sooner or later, when I love a friend, I *prove* to him that I am worthy of *every* confidence, *every* trust—& I say to you, now, Livy, on ~~the honor of a man~~ my word of honor as a man, that I never yet made ~~‸an individu‸~~ ~~a man~~ ‸an individual‸ a friend, *called* him my friend, & lost him. Gracious, how you do make me say unseemly things! I would hardly dare to say that to any but you, lest I should be set down for a loud-mouthed boaster.

Further, Mrs. F. says she fully understands my caution to remember that my fate was still in your hands & undecided—that our projected & expected engagement was not yet consummated, because you wanted to make *sure* that you loved me, first, & your father & mother wanted to see whether I was going to prove that I have a private (& improving) character as well as a public one. And then she says:

"True, ~~a~~—~~a~~ but all those conditions rest with *your~~self~~*—& could a man play such treason with himself as to let go what you have so nearly won?"

Bless her good old soul, she knows perfectly well that though conditions & obstructions were piled as high as Chimborazo[9] I would climb over them all! I *would*, Livy. For my *life* is in it. ~~Possibly *more*—who but He, shall say?~~

[*in margin:* I relent, Livy, & enclose such of that nonsense as has not been destroyed.]

[*six lines (about 35 words) torn away*]

[*torn in order to cancel:*] e[a◊◊◊]y.

And she says: "Of course you must live in Cleveland." That is what *I* want to do. Don't *you?* Now say you *do*, Livy, there's a dear good girl.

Mrs. Fairbanks, & Mrs. Severance, & little Mrs. Foote, & sweet Mother Crocker, would so love you & minister unto you that you would hardly know you were not at home.[10] But bless me, I am doing an inconsiderate thing to scare you in this way. I am too premature—& so I seem to be always trying to *hurry* you—but I don't mean to, Livy—kiss me & be friends again.

The rest of her letter is all splendid good advice—nearly all—& I shall keep it. I always do try to follow that venerable woman's advice—& yours too—you whom I love, love, LOVE, Livy.

I am in *such* a fidget to get the picture! Please send it right away, Livy—never mind how you look. Why you are not more ~~wan~~ ‸worn‸ now than you were when I was there, for you have slept & rested since—& I do *know* that no human being was ever so beautiful as you were when you came in, that last afternoon, regally robed in blue.

[*twenty-nine lines (about 180 words) torn away*]

Monday & write me, *won't* you? Please do, Livy, & direct it to the Metropolitan Hotel, & I shall get it Tuesday. And if I don't, I shall walk clear up to the Everett House, thinking that possibly you have misdirected it—& there'll be snow on the ground, & such a walk as that will be ~~tr~~ terrible, Livy. And I must lecture in Newark the very next night (Wednesday,) & shall need a kiss & a kind word from you to help me do my duty by those people—& you know who they are, Livy—they are first-class, intelligent people, who do business in New York & reside in Newark. Next comes my lecture here, Dec. 14 (unless I manage to get out of it—which prospect begins to look dark, now)—[11] Next is Scranton, Pa., Dec. 16—next is Fort Plain, (New York)—next comes my long Western tour, beginning with Detroit, Dec. 23. Now *can't* I stop and see you—*only* for two or three hours—on Dec. 20? Can't I ~~li~~ Livy? I ~~do~~ shan't mind walking there from Fort Plain. Please ask Mrs. Langdon. Tell her I will cheerfully scalp all the gossips that venture to comment on it. [*in margin:* ☨ Tell "grandma"[12] I *will* help her out of trouble if she will give me a chance when she gets into it.]

I have read VI Corinthians,[13] Livy, & shall read more in the Bible before I go to bed—& *be sure* I shall do *all* I can to profit by what you have written concerning religion. And I shall pray (& for you as well,)—not only at stated hours, but often. I have increased courage, now. [*in margin:* Livy, I see you are troubled because you have small faith ~~in~~ ‸that‸

my efforts to become a Christian will succeed,—or because you believe I still lean on you. Be comforted, dear. I have given up the latter, long ago. *I* hope—& with high courage—in the former—why cannot you?]

I was at Old Trinity[14] last Sunday (now I am commencing again!—*do* bear with me, Livy,) & in the afternoon I called on Mrs. Brooks & staid till 10 at night.

[*marginal note (about 15 to 20 words) torn away*]

Upon my word it was *not* my fault, Livy. *She* kept talking—*I* knew I was a fool for not going—knew it all the time—but she kept talking about you, & I *couldn't* go. She never gave me a chance to go, anyhow. But I am honestly ashamed, & I shan't go there again, soon, except to ask her pardon. *I* didn't talk about you—I didn't *dare* to—at the third sentence she'd have guessed our secret, & then—why, you couldn't have told her yourself, you know. Two hours of this time I spent at church with Josie Polhemus—& on the way, she asked after Mr. Langdon's health & I said he had been *very* sick for many days, but was getting well, now. She said: "Why, Miss Livy didn't write *that*—she only said he was unwell—why *didn't* she say it?"

[*marginal note (about 15 to 20 words) torn away*]

I said it was because you forgot it. Then this young woman clapped her hands for very joy!—joy that you had a fault,! ~~in your charac~~—joy that the model so persistently held up for her emulation, had betrayed a blemish!—for behold, you could *forget* such a thing! Ah, Livy, how noble it is to do good! How much worthier it was in me to confer this precious happiness upon this innocent young creature than it would have been to have spent the time in frivolous conversation! Bless me, ◇◇◇ Livy—for have I not been doing good in an humble way?

Good-bye—& rest & peace be thine. ◇◇◇ I *love* you, Livy!

Forever yours,

Saml. L. C.

P. S.—*Late at night.* Now that I have read your letter over again, slowly & carefully, I seem convinced that I am *not* making a progress toward a better life worthy any one's faith, or hope, or regard. And so, —forth I drift again into the moonless night of despondency. Since I saw you, I have not said one word, or done one deed, that I take blame to myself for—no, nor even thought one such thought, maybe—I remember none now. And yet what is there in my heart at this moment but bitterness—& hatred of myself for my clinging wickedness—& contempt for myself for putting such easy faith in these aspirations after better things, that breathe the word of promise to our ear & break it to our hope? *What* is there in my heart but sinking confidence—what in the earth I stand upon but graves—what in the air about me but phantoms—what in the firmament above my head but clouds & thick darkness, closing the gates of heaven against me?

I thought to burn this letter—but it is the reflex of—no matter.

Pray for me—if you can. For *I* cannot‸, ~~pray.~~ And yet I *will*, if the words choke me.

And so I mail this—so happily begun, so sadly ~~finished.~~ ended.

~~[From that Book.]:~~
~~"My Mother, would I might~~
~~But be your little child to-night,~~
~~And feel your arms about me fold,~~
~~Against this loneliness & cold!"~~[15]

‸I do *love* you, Livy, & so I scratched it out—for it might have made you unhappy. I kiss you.‸

Will the sun come again in the morning? I hate myself for being so unmanned—so fallen—so debased. Where is your ~~love~~ love *now*, Livy?

[*on back of letter as folded:*] I have torn up several sheets *trying* to reduce this to a decent length. But I can't.

[*on back of envelope:*]

I took out some of
this letter—& tore
up some of it—
but still I can't
get it short
enough—
however, I shall succeed
better next time.

[*docketed by OLL:*] 9th

[1] The present letter, which begins with a page numbered "6," is a continuation of the previous letter of five pages. As first written, before Clemens tried to "re-

duce" it, it consisted of twenty-seven pages (twenty-five numbered consecutively from 6 through 30, plus a two-page postscript). Clemens tore off parts of pages 14, 15, 24, and 25, and removed page 26.

[2] "West Mail (via Erie R.R.) closes at 5 A.M. and 4 P.M., and arrives at 7.30 A.M., 1, 4 and 10.30 P.M." ("Postoffice, New York," New York *Evening Post*, 28 Nov 68, 4).

[3] In his letter of 28 November to Olivia, Clemens said his faith in her was "as simple & unquestioning as the faith of a devotee in the idol he worships."

[4] In Puri, India, the followers of the Hindu cult of Juggernaut (or Jagannath), an incarnation of Vishnu, perform an annual ceremony in which they remove images of the god and his sister from their temple and pull them on immense carts to a summer home one mile away. These carts represent the moving world over which Juggernaut—whose name means lord of the world—presides. Although many devotees have committed suicide by throwing themselves under the wheels of the carts, this is not a part of the ritual.

[5] 1 Corinthians 3:15: "If any man's work shall be burned, he shall suffer loss: but he himself shall be saved; yet so as by fire."

[6] Clemens explained his suppression here in the next letter to Olivia (5 and 7 Dec 68). The first and last lines of the suppressed passage may be conjectured: "I suppose I ruined one man's" and "keep *nothing* from you, else. . . ."

[7] Since boyhood Clemens had been familiar with the tale of Aladdin and the magic lamp in *The Arabian Nights' Entertainments*, a collection of Oriental tales first published in English in 1792. The genii of Arabian mythology were ruled by a race of kings named Suleyman. See *HF*, 380–81.

[8] Clemens's interest in—and respect for—shorthand was stimulated by his friendship with stenographic reporter Andrew Marsh, who in 1868 published *Marsh's Manual of Reformed Phonetic Short-Hand: Being a Complete Guide to the Best System of Phonography and Verbatim Reporting* (see also 29 Dec 68 to Langdon, n. 6). Marsh's system was essentially the phonetic one introduced by Isaac Pitman in 1837, which soon gained wide popularity in the United States. Olivia was studying French "with the nuns" at this time (OLL to Alice B. Hooker, 29 Sept 68, CtHSD).

[9] A dormant, snow-capped volcano, the highest mountain in Ecuador (20,577 feet), not scaled until 1880.

[10] Mary E. Foote (b. 1816 or 1817) was the wife of John A. Foote, a prominent Cleveland attorney whose friendship with the Severance family may have begun as early as 1837, when he and Solomon L. Severance, Solon's father, served as officers of the newly founded Cuyahoga County Anti-Slavery Society. The Footes lived near the Severances on Kinsman Street. Eliza P. Crocker (b. 1831 or 1832) was the wife of Timothy D. Crocker (b. 1822 or 1823), a former lawyer and banker who was currently president of the Cleveland Petroleum and Refining Company. The Crockers, both *Quaker City* passengers, lived near the Fairbankses on St. Clair Street (Rose, 157; *Cleveland Census* 1860, roll 952:89, roll 953:738; Severance, 1; *Cleveland Directory* 1868, 138, 155, 161, 282). None of Mrs. Fairbanks's letter to Clemens is known to survive.

[11] Clemens had apparently agreed to lecture for the New York Volunteer Fire Department on 14 December, instead of sometime after 18 January as he originally planned (see 29? Nov 68 to PAM, n. 3). No record has been found, however, that the lecture ever took place.

[12] Mrs. Eunice Ford.

[13] Probably 2 Corinthians: "We . . . beseech you also that ye receive not the grace of God in vain" (6:1). Less likely is 1 Corinthians: "Know ye not that he which is joined to a harlot is one body? for two, saith he, shall be one flesh" and "Flee fornication. . . . he that committeth fornication sinneth against his own body" (6:16, 18).

[14] Trinity Protestant Episcopal church occupies a "stately Gothic edifice" on Broadway at the head of Wall Street, designed by Richard Upjohn and built in 1841–46. At this time it was the second-oldest and wealthiest religious institution in New York City (King, 341–42).

[15] These lines, canceled so heavily that Olivia could not have read them without great difficulty, are quoted from Book 1, letter 4, of *Faithful for Ever*, the third part of Patmore's verse narrative. The speaker is a rejected lover who, having lost all hope of winning his beloved's hand, addresses a lament to his mother.

To Olivia L. Langdon
5 and 7 December 1868 • New York, N.Y.

(MS: CU-MARK)

~~F~~ Saturday Night.
Dec. 5, 1868.

My Dearest Livy:

I feel better, now—ever so much better—after last night's mental storm. But *why* I should, I do not know. Yes, I *do* know, too—at least I *think* I know. But I cannot write it, though I could *tell* it you, easily. I can even write it, ‸too,‸ after a fashion: I think it is because I have been praying that I might seek the Savior for his *own* sake, & from no selfish motive—*not* to secure your loving approbation—not to sweep away Mrs. Fairbanks uneasiness concerning my eternal future & make her heart glad—*not* to crown my mother's & my sister's long generation of prayers for me with tidings that they are answered & all is well—*not* that I may thus achieve what all true men desire, the good opinion of good men—*not* for the sake of these things, but for the sake of Christ alone. Now ‸you‸ will say: "Then the storm passed, the thunders ceased & a great calm was upon the ~~face of the~~ troubled waters—& you were at peace."[1] No, it was not so, Livy. I simply ~~feet~~ felt less despondent—nothing more. I will not exaggerate it. And I prayed that no word, & no act of mine, might deceive you, even in the faintest degree—that I might *do* nothing, *say* nothing, which could in any way mislead you—that you might not fancy me already a Christian, in some sense, by what I write, when the Father knows I am only *trying* to be—only groping in the dark—only ~~h~~ still hoping, still endeavoring, when peradventure it may be that there shall be no fruition for the hope, no victory for the endeavor. It is hard to have to speak such truths as these, but then I so love you, Livy, that I cannot bear the idea of your thinking better of me than I am—for then, unwittingly, I should be in a manner playing a false part toward you. And Livy, neither last night nor tonight, have I found anything in the Bible but *conviction & condemnation*—save & except one little verse. It is Romans, 8th chapter & 24th verse.[2] It seemed to me that a sunbeam rested there.

Livy, it was a mangled letter I sent you yesterday—but then I was in a mangled mood when I wrote the postscript & mailed the letter. I found I had abused my privilege of writing you, & had written at least two letters in one. Common decency demanded that I should reduce it—& in doing it I was not much guided by rhyme or reason. The "confession" I destroyed was that I had refused to ~~deliver~~ lecture a week hereabouts ~~for $600, because—Oh,~~ I *can't* tell it again—you would say I was a‸n‸ ~~love-sick~~ idiot. ~~[And between ourselves, I *am!*] I could not be so reckless as to write the above if you had any curiosity in your composition. [Oh!]~~[3]

You want me to *succeed*. Bless you for saying it, Livy—& I pray you, say it again—for I love to hear it. And with the favor ‸& the ~~be~~ blessing,‸ of Him who rules our destinies, I *shall* succeed, Livy—do not fear. Why *you* love me, Livy—you love me *well*—better than you think for—much better than you could be brought to thoroughly comprehend at this time except it were revealed to you by seeing me shrouded & coffined,~~,~~ ‸& dead.‸ *Then* you would know. ‸Death startles many a torpid love into life.‸

~~Liv~~ I have found in the "exquisite" book to-night a passage which is the ~~very~~ soul & spirit of what I have been trying to tell you with tongue & pen.[4] It is *confirmation*. It is prophecy. Read it, Livy, & you will see yourself in it—& you will see that you need have no doubts & no misgivings when you wish that I shall succeed. You will see—~~I~~ as I *have done all along*, ever since Thanksgiving day of blessed memory—that your ~~anxietie~~ natural anxieties & perplexities will fade away & you will end by giving me all your heart & all your priceless love. For this is the process of the loftiest phase of Love—a love ~~in~~ ‸upon‸ which heart & intellect, ~~judgment~~ & calm reason sit in judgment—& *their* verdict gives birth to the highest type of Love—to the only "*True*" Love—a love that is deathless—a love that *grows*, & never diminishes. You said once, in the drawing-room, that you were *glad* you loved me—& you will *infallibly* find that you can say it again, & before very long, Livy. *Do* say it, *just* as soon as you can.~~, Livy.~~ Try to say it now—please say it in your very next letter—for I do so long to hear it, Livy. It is high honor I am asking—an honor to which all earthly honors else seem tame & of little worth—but yet I dare to crave it, Livy. But if you cannot say it now, my faith will remain the same—it cannot falter—for your prayers to ~~g~~ God will be answered & He will yet enable you to say it. *Still* pray that we may be all in all to each other for life, Livy. Still pray—pray unceasingly. I shall so pray—sinner that I am, & all unworthy to approach the Throne. And fearful, too, & courageless, save when I bear your blameless name upon my lips. It is easy to pray for *you*, but it seems dreadful *presumption* to ask favors for myself. You have earned them—but I do not deserve them. Why Livy, think of it for a moment—think of a son dishonoring a generous earthly father all his life & then going at the last hour & asking for food & shelter under his roof. Cannot you know how that son would approach the door—then retire to the shadows—approach again & again—hesitate—knock feebly—& when the door was opened find his tongue sealed to the roof of his mouth & feel humbler than the very dogs that snuffed the air suspiciously about him? But if he came partly to ask a kindness for his sister—faithful always, & well-beloved of the household—how then? You ~~know me &~~ can ~~c~~ understand me.

Livy, I don't like the "exquisite" book, now, as I did before. I don't want you to read it now.~~, do~~ I will keep it for you, & you shall read it another time. That will do, will it not? *I* forgive *you*, you know, for forbidding me to read the "Home Life"—& so I shall read "A Life for a Life" instead—& shall like it, no doubt, because you do—otherwise I should take it up with a prejudice against the author of ~~"J.~~ "Halifax."[5]

I think I will run up to Hartford, Monday morning, to see the Twichell's & look after my book—& return Tuesday night. You didn't seriously mind my telling Dan & the Twichells, did you? They will never mention it—& what's the use of loyal & true friends, Livy, if you can't ~~divi~~ share joys as well as griefs with them? *They*~~,~~ & my sister & Mrs. F. are *all* I shall tell.

Do hurry the picture, Livy, please.

I believe I will enclose part of yesterday's long letter in this, instead of burning it. ‸No ~~I won't~~—it would make *this* too long.‸

Livy, you ought to get this ~~Tuesday~~ ‸Monday,‸ or at furthest ~~Wednesday.~~ ‸Tuesday.‸ Now, can't you write a line Tuesday & dispatch it at once, so that I can get it Wednesday? I̸ If you can do this, address it to *Everett House, Union Square*—for I have concluded not to quit the Everett finally & forever for the Metropolitan until I get back from my next little trip. But if you *can't* write Tuesday,—~~but~~ then please write Wednesday & direct it to Norwich, NEW YORK (spell *that* strong ‸or they'll send it to Connecticut;‸) care of *Geo. M. Tillson*—for I lecture there Friday the 11th. You needn't be afraid, for if it don't reach me there I will instruct Tillson to forward it to me at ~~FORT *Plain, N. Y., care* of George Elliott.~~ *Scranton, Pa., care of A. Crandall*[6]—I lecture there Wednesday the 16th. Why you can write me a *second* letter, to Scranton yourself, Livy—& another to *Fort Plain, N.Y., care of Geo. Elliott*—where I lecture the 19th. *Do*, please—& let me stop & see you the 20th,̸—I wish I dared to stop on the 12th. I kiss you & bless you. Good-bye.

Devotedly & sincerely
& with imperishable affection
S L. C.

[*in margin:* Livy there are ~~som~~ s̸—*so many* things—& important ones—that I wish to tell you—& I can only *tell* them—I couldn't *write* them, in a month.]

P. S.—Monday Morning—I got your kind little letter (written Friday night,) & thank you very much for it, Livy. You must forgive my ~~wile~~ wild, distempered language when speaking of you. It only looks wild on paper, for then there is no voice to modulate it. It is simply the overflowings of a strong love—& is *not* deliberate flattery,̸ ‸or self=deception,‸ as you mistake it to be, Livy. But I will curb it, for your sake. Livy, please do not wrong my intelligence so much as to fear seriously for that "awakening." Your way of taking everything *literally* has made you so accept from me such words as Perfection & Paragon—& thus I find you gravely worrying your/ gentle spirit with the conviction that I regard you as absolutely *perfect*, & so must necessarily wake up to a ghastly consciousness of my mistake on some sad morning of wedded life. No, no, no, Livy,—I am grateful to God that you are *not* perfect—~~I am~~ & when we *are* husband & wife, ~~as~~ ‸(&‸ I hope & pray & do believe that He in His goodness will permit me to see that welcome day,) I shall see you, Livy, as I see you now: a *Woman*—nothing more & nothing less—a Woman, with the faults, the failings, the weaknesses of her sex & of her race; but with a more generous share of the merits & virtues of our nature than falls to the lot of many; a *Woman*, Livy, mortal, & so of necessity imperfect—a *Woman* only—God forbid that you should be an angel. I am not fit to mate with an angel—I could not *make* myself fit. But I can reach to your altitude, in time, & I *will*. I mean as near to it as God ~~has~~ will permit. Livy, *how* can you talk as if I might wake up to something dreadful, when you *know* that the contrary is in evidence before my eyes—when you know that the love & reverence ~~of~~ all your household ‸bear you‸ stand~~s~~ before me the splendid evidence of what you have been from infancy?—proof beyond & above suspicion or refutation, that you are a *true Woman* & *cannot* be else than a true & noble Wife. Livy, if you had ~~only~~ studied the human face for a lifetime—not as an elegant pastime, but *eagerly, anxiously*, in strange lands & friendless, to see if it were a good face or an ill, a kind face or a cruel, a generous face or a selfish, a face to be trusted or shunned—so conning faces *knowing* that if you read ~~it~~ ‸them‸ wrongly you ~~may~~ ‸would‸ suffer—if you had done this, Livy, you could look in your glass & find there proofs stronger than the sworn evidence of men—proofs that you~~r~~ are ~~& long have~~ as good & pure & noble a woman as any that walks the earth to-day. Do not fear for the "awakening," Livy. I see the faults you have, as plainly as you see them (two really grave ones whose existence you do not suspect, yourself,)—I know you *well*—I have not been educated to require weeks & months to learn a person in—& I respect you, & honor you, & love you, above all things else in the wide earth. Livy, you think it "so strange" that I love you. No, ‸(you must pardon me,)‸ you really think it so strange that you love *me*, in any degree—but I hope the strangeness of it will pass away. It is *not* strange that I love you—or that any one who knows you loves you. I have written all the foregoing calmly & dispassionately, & have said no word that I could not take an oath to before ~~maj~~ magistrate or minister, ~~we~~—& so, gravely seriously & earnestly I beg you to receive it as *truth—truth*, Livy. Let your mind be at rest—I know you never can be "perfect"—& am thankful that it is so. I am glad Mrs. Crane is ready to love me—I am sure I am ready to love *her*. The little poem[7] *could not* have come in better time, I think—I do thank you for it. I am so bitterly disappointed at the news from Mr. Langdon. Oh, he was looking so *well*, when I left, & *promising* so well. Try to tell me better news next time.

P. P. S.—*Monday, 4 P. M.*—Livy, I received Twichell's welcoming dispatch too late, for the train, & so it is a question whether I shall go to Hartford at all. I *may* go to-night, though, for I suppose I ought to see the publishers.

I have just received a letter from my Western friend,[8] appointing me to begin at Detroit *one day earlier*—that is, on Dec. 22^{d}—& so I could hardly dare to stop on the 20th to see you, even if I had permission. Now this is to ask Mrs. Langdon, through you, if I may stop *just a night*, Dec. 12~~,~~—not a moment longer, if it be her will. Please urge this for me Livy—will you? I would not ask it, but it does look as if I shall have *no other* opportunity of seeing you for four months. It is too long. And I have things to *say* which *should* be said, ~~w~~ & which I could not *write* in a month. I am sure I might be permitted to come, considering all the circumstances. Still, if her judgment says No, I submit. Livy, if I do not get a decided *No*, by letter or telegraph, at "Norwich, New York," (see address,) on Dec. 11, I SHALL arrive at your house some time on the evening of the 12th if I can possibly get there. Because I shall have no opportunity of waiting for an answer. No—that course would be wrong, & so I must not do it. But please get me the permission, Livy—do. Bless me, I am so tied hand & foot with these lecture appointments that I don't know whether I am standing on my head or my heels.

✉

Miss Olivia L. Langdon | Present. [*on back of envelope:*] + [*docketed by OLL:*] 10th [*OLL, in pencil:*] A son dishonoring a loving earthly Father &c

[1] Mark 4:39: "And he arose, and rebuked the wind, and said unto the sea, Peace, be still. And the wind ceased, and there was a great calm."

[2] "For we are saved by hope."

[3] Clemens removed his "confession" from the previous letter by tearing it out of the pages. Nothing further has been learned about the offer for six lectures which he refused. He wrote and crossed out the last two sentences of the cancellation solely to tease Olivia about her curiosity in such matters. He made the bracketed final word slightly more difficult to read than the rest, because it is the punch line—representing Olivia's reaction upon discovering that the sentence she has just deciphered expresses too much confidence in her lack of curiosity.

[4] As suggested earlier (30 Oct 68 to OLL, n. 7), the "exquisite" book may have

been all, or one, of the four parts of Patmore's *Angel in the House*, although no specific passage matching Clemens's description has been identified.

5 *The Home Life: In the Light of Its Divine Idea* (1867) by James Baldwin Brown (1820–84) was a study of the Christian ideal of marriage and child rearing which emphasized the role of the wife as the guardian of "truth, purity, dignity, goodness, and charity" (Brown, 21). Olivia's objections to it are not known. *A Life for a Life* (1859) was by English author Dinah Maria Mulock Craik (1826–87), who had earlier published *John Halifax, Gentleman* (1857), which in an 1863 letter to the San Francisco *Morning Call* Clemens had described as a "high-flown batch of contradictions and inconsistencies" (*ET&S1*, 283). Craik's more recent novel concerned the courtship of a sheltered young woman by a man some years her senior. Lacking her family's blessing, the courtship was conducted largely through letters that extolled the sanctity of womanhood and marriage, and urged equal purity and high purpose for both man and woman. Clemens read and "marked" a copy of *A Life for a Life* some weeks later, assuring Olivia that he liked it "right well" (SLC to OLL, 17 Feb 69, CU-MARK†).

6 Tillson and Crandall were representatives of Clemens's sponsors in Norwich and Scranton, respectively, and have not been further identified. For Elliott, see 19 and 20 Dec 68 to OLL, n. 11.

7 Unidentified.

8 G. L. Torbert.

To Olivia L. Langdon with a note to Charles J. Langdon 9 and 10 December 1868 • New York, N.Y.

(MS: CU-MARK)

New York, Dec. 9.

My Dearest Livy:

At 1 o'clock this morning, Twichell & I were ~~playing~~ ‸praying‸ for you. You were asleep & knew nothing of it, but I hope that your slumbers were none the less peaceful, or your dreams less pleasant for it. We had been sitting alone in his parlor since 10 P. M., & I was to leave in the 1:20 A.M. train. We had talked a great deal about you, of course; & we had also held a long & earnest conversation upon the subject of religion. I told him, Livy, what was the truth—that although I had been praying ‸more or less‸ since ~~th~~ about the middle of September, & here latterly day by day & earnestly, I feared I had ‸not‸ made as much progress as I ought to have done—& that *now* I began clearly to comprehend that one *must* seek Jesus for himself alone, & uninfluenced by selfish motives.

And so my perplexities had increased; for wheresoever I turned to seek the ~~sav~~ Savior I was confronted by the phantom of a selfish impulse: first, my measureless love for you & the impossibility of my remaining content to give you daily pain by my separation from the Christian fold if you were my wife ‸(which, may God grant you shall be,)‸—second, my natural desire to cheer my aged mother's closing days with those tidings that would make her old heart young again & her failing pulses leap for joy—third the great calm that would descend like a benediction upon my sister's spirit to know that the gates of God were open to me—& finally the great wave of happiness that would sweep athwart the breast of that faithful pilgrim mother of mine[1] & erase in a single instant the mighty debt of gratitude scored there against me. I said I was warring against these human impulses, now, but ~~wa~~ the tide of battle was against me. I *would* succeed at last, but when? And Livy, that most excellent friend told me *clearly* & *concisely* HOW to seek the better life—& showed me how to *utilize* these fettering impulses & make of them aids, in some sense, when they could not be driven away, instead of fatal obstacles. Then I was glad I went to Hartford. And at last, in the midst of the solemn night, he prayed fervently for my conversion, & that your love & mine might grow until it was made *perfect* love by the approving spirit of God—& that hand in hand & ‸with‸ hearts throbbing in unison we might compass that only worthy journey of life whose latest steps ushered the wayfarer into ‸the‸ home of eternal peace. But when he ~~do~~ dropped his voice to a gentler tone, & prayed so touchingly & so tenderly for *you*, Livy, & that you might be shielded from all harm & spared all suffering & sorrow, I felt as if ~~I were almost~~ the light from the Better Land shot its rays above the dark horizon of my mind & gilded its barren wastes with its glory. I am a hundred times thankful that I made this little journey to Hartford. The Twichell's send the‸ir‸ warm love & friendship & esteem to you, Livy, for I told them it would be acceptable. I took two sets of their pictures, on purpose that I might send one set to you.[2] They do not do them justice, of course. [*in margin:* P P P S.—Don't you kiss Twichell's picture—I can't permit it, by any manner of means.]

I was sorry the ferrotype had not come, so that I might show them a picture more like you than my little bosom friend the photograph. When *will* it come, Livy?

Of course I did not sleep a wink, coming down in the cars—being excited—& I must not go to bed till after the Newark lecture. And now

I am going down to the Metropolitan to get your letter.‸ ~~& your picture, & shall be disappointed.~~ ‸I *may* be disappointed.‸ But I shall love & bless you just the same, since I cannot help it. I *shall* get ~~a~~ them at Scranton, Pa., the 16th—please make up your mind that I shall, Livy. [You see I have already lost hope that I am to be permitted to look upon your face on the 12th.] I *wish* I had begged for one more day in Elmira.

I fully appreciated your grief at parting with Mrs. Crane & was as sorry for you as if the grief had been my own. But I did & do think *so* much of you for hiding it from the rest of the household, hard as the task was, for I know they can bear anything else better than to see you in distress.‸ ~~, Livy.~~

If I~~'~~ had the time, now, I would write & ask Mrs. Langdon to forgive my impatient demands upon her leniency, & would also drop a line to Mr. Langdon—but I suppose I must not attempt it. Tender to them my loving honor, Livy, if I may offer it. Livy, whom I do love more tenderly than ever, ~~so~~ be good & generous, now, & send me a kiss & *all* the love you can spare. Good-bye. I kiss you.

In honor & unfailing love,
Yrs, always
S. L. C.

Wednesday Night.

I just can't estimate how many thanks I owe you, Livy, for your good, long, delightful letter. It *saved* me—saved me from another Elmira failure before a great audience in Newark. I felt so heavy & stupid from want of rest & sleep, & from wearing excitement at Twichell's, ~~th~~ that when I went down town at noon it was with many misgivings about to-night's work. So much so that I began to think of leaving some of the *serious* paragraphs out of the lecture rather than read them badly. I knew I had asked you to write a cheery letter for to-day, & I knew you had done it, because you are always faithful to every legitimate & ~~useful~~ reasonable trust, & ~~are~~ so are always to be depended upon—but I feared that the letter had not yet arrived. I was *so* glad to find it *had* come, I do assure you. It brightened me up so much that I *knew* perfectly well I was entirely safe for every line of the lecture. I said to myself, "I can make that audience *laugh* whenever I please—so I will talk the humorous to *them;* but when I come to the serious passages, I will enthrone my matchless little princess (the same being *you*,) in the chief seat in the house, & talk *that* to *her*.” And ~~“~~Livy, I would have given *anything* if you had really been there. *Then* you would have heard a lecture delivered as it *should* be delivered; you would have seen a lecturer perfectly at his ease; you would have seen a brilliant audience pretty completely at the mercy of the speaker, too, & swung “from grave to gay, from lively to serene,”[3] without the least perceptible effort in the world. It was splendid. I *enjoyed* every sentence of the discourse, & was sorry to quit ~~was~~ ‸when‸ it was finished. I wished it had been before a metropolitan audience of 5,000; I could have persuaded them with just as much ease—I could have carried them with me with just the same facility.[4] Tonight you would not have recognized this as the same dull harangue I dragged ~~my self~~ myself through so painfully in Elmira. Of course the people came trooping to the stage to be introduced & offer congratulations (they always do after a startling *success*, but they promptly *don't* under other circumstances,) & so I missed the New York train & was delayed an hour—but they did n't succeed in champaigning me, Livy—I took one glass of ale & refused to be fèted further. It isn't a bit of trouble to refuse. I elaborated my closing “moral” somewhat, & one gentleman said that that gave the lecture a sort of Sabbath-school cast. I said if he meant that it gave it a *religious* cast, it was precisely what I intended—whereupon he hastened to say that he had meant no offense & was finding no fault. The Society tried to bind me to open their course next season, but I said I could not make promises so far in advance—*would* comply, however, in case I entered the lecture field ~~no~~ any more. But what a string of boastful confidences I am making! I wouldn't ~~dare~~ *think* of so unbosoming myself on paper to anybody but you—but then there isn't anything I *wouldn't* dare to unbosom to you, you fascinating rascal! [No, you are *not* a rascal—you are the very dearest girl in all the wide world, & anybody who says the contrary is taking his life into his own hands.] Livy, I do thank you *ever* so much for that happy letter, & I want you to write many, many more like it. You were just your dear little *self* in it, & you talked just as you would talk if I were by your side & Mrs. Hayloft & Bement were far away. [It tickles me every time I think of your adventure with Bement that day, poor fellow!][5] I can pray with great good heart this night, Livy, no fear of that~~,~~—for I am grateful to God. I shall not forget *you* in my petitions.

Livy it makes me proud & glad to hear you give voice to such invincible faith in my sure conversion—glad to know that your faith in me rests upon a foundation that is firm & *certain*, & proud to know that I possess ~~the~~ nine-tenths of the heart of the best & purest girl I ever have known. Nine-tenths, Livy—if you deny it I shan't believe you; & so you needn't waste time denying it at all. Your denial would only be premature, ‸anyhow,‸ because I *will* have the nine-tenths—& the other tenth too—I *will*, I WILL—& so *restez tranquille*, as we Frenchmen say. [*in margin:* PPPPPS—I can't correct this, Livy—guess out the mistakes.] And I am glad, ever so glad, to perceive that you really know me better than *any one* else does. Mrs. Fairbanks often says you are a surprisingly shrewd reader of character, & I believed her from the first.

"If there is any change," you "love me *more* instead of less." Scratch out all the first part, & simply say you *do* love me more—& more—& more—do, Livy, there's a dear, good, *honest* girl. Be honest, Livy, just for once! {Now *don't* you apply your damaging ~~litt~~ *literal* test to that—I *know* you are *always* good & honest.}

Livy, I am *glad* you wrote me that little lesson about the proper manner of applying the gift of humor—& you knew perfectly well I would be, for all you pretended you didn't—you wise bundle of Innocence! It gratifies me to have you make such suggestions, & I want you to make them as much as you will. There won't be anything to ‸"‸forgive,‸"‸ at all. I honor & appreciate the sentiments you expressed, & shall follow out your suggestion—for it is sound & right. And I won't tear up any more pages, Livy, to make my letters shorter—your ban upon such conduct delighted me, for I do love to scribble long letters to you. I seem *with* you, & having *my* little visit when I am writing you.

[*in margin:* P. P.-S.—I *will* obey the order, Livy, & send the removed pages of that letter—but next time, please, ~~m~~ dear—let me hurry to bed, now.][6]

I was so glad to ~~her~~ hear of your long walk, Livy—& yet it makes me a little uneasy, too, for fear you *may* injure yourself in this way. [*in margin:* P. S.—And now I pray for you, my own heart's love.] But tell me *all* such exploits, Livy—tell me everything you can think of about yourself—you will always ~~had~~ have a glad & loving listener. And write your religious thoughts freely—I like to read those, too.

I shall be sure to call on ~~m~~ Miss Emma Nye.[7]

I glory in your womanly "impulse[")]—down with ~~"ja~~ "judgment" when it interferes! Livy, please do write me just as often as you can—never mind "judgment." And don't you know, I asked you for a kiss, &

you didn't send it—give it to me now, Livy, please. Your dear letter isn't *half* answered, but I am so worn out (it is 2 A M—must be up at 8) &—having had *no* sleep for two days & more than one night—& I am *so* sleepy. [*in margin:* Doubt your love? *No*—I never *seriously* thought of such a thing for a moment, Livy. Never once.] Good-bye. I *do* love you so tenderly, Livy. *Please* write me to Scranton, Pa., right away.

Always yrs, $ in love & faith.

Sam L. C.

[*on back of page 1, used as a wrapper:*] Do—do—*do* send the picture, Livy—$ to Scranton, care of A. Crandall.

[*on back of wrapper as folded:*]

Livy, I *am* giving my whole
heart to God.

[*on envelope:*]

‸Charley it would look better if you would write occasionally yourself, instead of occupying your time teaching your betters how to make S's. How do you like *that?*‸

Miss Olivia L. Langdon
Present.

Politeness of Charley
(who isn't polite enough to write to a fellow.)

[*across envelope end:*] P. S. It was happy news about Charlie & Miss Ida—I am glad. Tell the lazy cub to write me all about it.[8] [*docketed by OLL:*] 11th

[1] Mary Mason Fairbanks.

[2] The photographs Clemens enclosed have not been found. A photograph of Joseph Twichell is reproduced on p. 438.

[3] Clemens's variation on a line from Pope's "Essay on Man" (1734): "From grave to gay, from lively to severe" (Pope, 59).

[4] Sponsored by the Clayonian Society, Clemens's "American Vandal Abroad" lecture was enthusiastically received on the evening of 9 December at the Newark Opera House, which was filled to capacity. Clemens himself made, or was sent, clippings of at least two newspaper notices: the Newark *Press* (a weekly) and the Newark *Courier*, whose reviewer, "Lorgnette," wrote:

> It was beyond all question the most enjoyable lecture of the season, and never went away an audience better satisfied with an hour's entertainment. . . .
>
> His descriptive passages, wherein he painted Venice, Rome, and Athens, in all the varied hues and phases of their marvelous beauty, showed the ideality of the real poet under

the kindly satire of the genuine humorist. A most delicious talker, drawing his purposely homely words up out of a heart overflowing with generous sentiments of true manliness. (Lorgnette, no page)

[5] "Mrs. Hayloft" (or "Haycroft," as Clemens called her in a later letter) has not been further identified. Edward P. Bement was an Elmira friend of the Langdons'. Clemens came to regard him as one of Olivia's disappointed suitors, a circumstance which may be alluded to here (31 Dec 68 to OLL; Boyd and Boyd, 67; SLC to OLL, 27 Feb 69, CU-MARK, in *LLMT*, 70).

[6] If Clemens ever did send these suppressed pages and parts of pages from his 4 December letter, they have not been found.

[7] Emma M. Nye (1846?–70) was the daughter of Catherine and George M. Nye, an Elmira water-pipe manufacturer (*Elmira Census*, 534). Emma had been a schoolmate of Olivia's. She was visiting friends in Detroit, where Clemens was scheduled to lecture on 22 December.

[8] Since at least the spring of 1868, Charles Langdon had been quietly courting Ida B. Clark (1849–1934), daughter of Elmira businessman Jefferson Burr Clark and his wife, Julia (Susan L. Crane to Ida B. Clark, 19 Mar 69, owned by Jervis Langdon, Jr., PH in CU-MARK; Salsbury, 430). In a letter to Alice Hooker probably written sometime in the last ten days of November, he indicated that he had not yet told his parents of his intentions toward Ida:

> Please be a little careful about what you say in regard to Ida in the presence of either Father or Mother, because they are a little exercised on the subject, as they are watching Libbie & hate to have me fall into the same error. Therefore if you will please say nothing in their presence I will thank you very much. I have had a delightful talk with you tonight & have already set you down among my best & most respected friends. . . . If Libbie wants or asks to hear this you can read it to her. CJ (CtHSD)

He must, nevertheless, have informed them shortly thereafter, for in a 25 November 1869 letter to Mrs. Fairbanks, Mrs. Langdon said in part:

> And what a family! such a change has come over it in one short year that sometimes I can hardly recognize it as my own. It is just a twelve-month tomorrow since Mr Clemens first talked with me of his love for Livia. . . . One short year ago Charlie was with us, & he also had just told us of his love for Ida. (CtHMTH)

To Jane Lampton Clemens and Family
10 December 1868 • New York, N.Y.

(MS: NPV)

Everett House,[1]
N. Y. Dec. 10.

Dear Folks—

I didn't move to the Metropolitan—shall when next I come to town. I ought to write you fully, now, but can't—am just ready to leave the city for Norwich, N. Y., Fort Plain, N. Y. & Scranton, Pa—all these are before 20th Dec. Then I begin at Detroit, Mich, Dec. 22 & talk nearly every night for some time, through the West. Shan't get a chance to go to St Louis—lecture engagements interfere.

I could not write you last night—was tired out. Had not slept for 36 hours. Went over in the evening & lectured in Newark (most superb success I ever achieved)—then returned here at midnight & had to stand around the ferry house twenty minutes before I could get a carriage, & so got chilled through. Couldn't write—can't now. Good-bye. Love to all. When you write, address letter simply to "Mark Twain, Care Lecture Committee"—no use for both names—my *own* is little known. I could have cleared ten thousand dollars this lecture season if I had entered the field before the various lecture courses were filled. As it is, I shall not clear *more* than $2,000, if so much.[2]

Always Yrs
Sam.

The little town is Stamford—2 hours from New York. I will think of the Western New York towns.[3]

---

[1] This letter was written on the three blank sides of a folder announcing a bankruptcy sale at John A. Reed's "Diamond Parlor," a jewelry store at 791 Broadway, six blocks south of the Everett House. The sale began on 7 December and continued for several days (Wilson 1867, 849; "A Large Sale of Diamonds and Other Gems," New York *Evening Post*, 11 Dec 68, 2).

[2] Clemens would have had to lecture well over a hundred times during the four-month lecture season, at $100 per lecture, in order to "clear" $10,000. He actually made about forty appearances between November and March. In June 1869 he claimed to have made $8,000 or $9,000 from lecturing during the previous fourteen months, of which only $3,600 was still in the bank, because his "expenses were something frightful during the winter" (SLC to JLC and family, 4 June 69, NPV, in *MTL*, 1:158).

[3] Clemens's mother and sister had expressed an interest in moving from St. Louis to some smaller, eastern town. Clemens had evidently praised (but not identified) Stamford, Connecticut, through which he had passed several times on the train between New York and Hartford. In April 1870 the Moffett household (including Clemens's mother) moved to Fredonia, New York, a small town near Lake Erie, chosen because "Uncle Sam lectured there [in January 1870] and was struck by the intelligence of the audience" (SLC to OC, 21 Apr 70, CU-MARK; *MTBus*, 103; "From Dunkirk," Buffalo *Express*, 24 Jan 70, 4).

To Mary Mason Fairbanks
12 December 1868 • Norwich, N.Y.
(MS: CSmH)

‸[Priveight.]‸

Norwich, Dec. 12.

Dear Mother:—

It is noon, & snowing. I am here, the guest of Judge Mason—& happy. Mrs. Mason is ~~g~~ *so* good, & so kind, so thoughtful, so untiring in her genuine hospitality, & lets me be just as troublesome as I want to, that I just love her, & it seems as if she were *you*—or your double. She lets me smoke in the house, & bring in snow on my boots, & sleep late, & eat at unseasonable hours, & leaves my valise wide open ~~& un~~ on the floor & my soiled linen scattered about it just exactly as I leave it & as it *ought* to be to make life truly happy. I tell you I *like* that. It is being at *home*, you know. They are going to let me stay till Monday. And I shall enjoy every moment of the time. Don't you wish *you* were here? But we have two pleasant young ladies, & so we don't need you & haven't got any use for you, mother mine.[1]

And I have pestered Mrs. Langdon through Livy, till she has surrendered & says I may call on the 17th & stay one day & night. Hip—hip—hurrah! Livy is growing stronger & better. ~~I~~ She will soon be a perfect Hercules in a small way. Last Monday she walked up to the Spauldings & back, in a driving snow-storm. What do you think of that? If she embarks in any more desperate enterprises like that, there is going to be war in our family.[2] I don't want to lose her *now*. Don't you be worried about *us* (though your awful croak about looking from Pisgah upon the Promised Land yet failing at last to enter it[3] was~~,~~ perfectly reasonable & made me feel properly uncomfortable.) She isn't demonstrative, a bit, (who ever supposed she would be?) but she sticks like a good girl, & answers every letter just as soon as she has read it—& lectures me like smoke, too. But I like it. And I never do or think or say anything now that isn't right, (except being slow about answering the letters of good indulgent mothers,) & so if I am not to be a Christian at last, it will take many & many a month of discouragement to *prove* it to me.

I am to lecture in Fort Plain, N. Y., on the 19th, & in Detroit the 22d. I *wonder* if I dare to stop in Cleveland an hour or two. Have to go down town. Good-bye.

Lovingly,
Mark.

[*in margin:*] Lectured last night—full house—gave satisfaction.

✉

Mrs. A. W. Fairbanks, | Care "Herald" | Cleveland | Ohio. [*postmarked:*] NORWICH N.Y[.] DEC 14

[1] Judge William N. Mason (1820–93)—Mrs. Fairbanks's cousin—and his wife, Sarah Cary Mason (1821–1912), were Clemens's hosts. Judge Mason began practicing law in Norwich in 1841, and was elected a justice in 1850, holding that position for some twenty years. The Masons had two unmarried sons, aged sixteen and twenty-three. The "young ladies" have not been identified (Smith, 330; "James Mason Family," 1–2; "William Mason Family," 1–2).

[2] The Spauldings lived only a few doors from the Langdons on Main Street (Boyd and Boyd, 142, 197).

[3] Deuteronomy 34:1–4.

To Olivia L. Langdon with a note to Charles J. Langdon 12 December 1868 • Norwich, N.Y.

(MS: CU-MARK)

Norwich, Dec. 12.

My Dearest Livy—

It is splendid! gorgeous! unspeakably magnificent! I am to see you, *you*, YOU on the 17th! "Move eastward, happy earth," as Tennyson according to Twichell, says.[1] Familiarity with disappointment has taught me to school myself to *expect* nothing, & then I am fortified when No is the answer to any petition I offer—& when Yes is the answer the joy is all the wilder & happier for the delicious *surprise* of it. [¶] But for the human egotism that is in me, I would not have put that forward as a system of philosophy original with myself, but would have said "Familiarity with disappointment teaches *us*"—for it does teach that lesson to *all* but absolute fools, sooner or later—& now having lectured myself my conscience is easy again.] So I *shall* be there the 17th, if God permits, & shall try to arrive very early in the morning, in order to make the most of my visit—& in order that I may go into the closet in my room & bang on the door till you get up in time for breakfast *once*—& then I will go down *with* you to make sure of you, my little angel by brevet. [It did tickle Twichell excessively to hear me speak of you as an angel by brevet, for he was a chaplain in the army & so he recognized the felicity of the expression & enjoyed it as only a military man could. I told him anybody could see that you ~~*were*~~ ‸*are*‸ an angel by brevet, & that you are in the ‸"line of promotion"—but that I was glad & happy to know that you couldn't attain your *full rank* on this earth—otherwise I should be a miserable wretch who must drag through this weary life unmated.]

Why *Livy!* (‸"Oh, *Char*lie!") *Don't* scare a body that way again. I *always* look at the end of a letter *first*, to see how it is signed (because the *mood* of the writer crops out there & you know what to expect,)—& behold, ‸there was‸ your *entire* name displayed in frozen & awful solemnity! I expected what I so love to see (& if *must* confess such lack of decorum, *kiss*,) viz., "Lovingly, Livy"—& found (as I thought,) **only** "LIVY *L.* LANGDON." I imagined all kinds of horrors at once. I am the guest of Judge Mason & family for 2 or 3 days, & had just been introduced to two young ladies at the moment your letter was handed me in the parlor. And I had begun a most brilliant conversation, ~~tw~~ too, (as *I* thought,) but I said, "Excuse me, please, till I open this & see who it is from & whether the business is pressing or not"—as if I didn't *know* perfectly well who it was from. But that name took the life all out of me, & I couldn't keep my attention on the conversation after that—I did *wonder* what was in a letter signed so portentously! But I was only tortured with a very mildly painful curiosity, *not* distress—& merely said to myself: "In my infamous heedlessness I ~~w~~ have written something which has hurt her feelings—possibly angered her—but never mind, it is all right—long before this her calm judgment has told her that it was not deliberate & intentional & *could not* be—& so, even if her letter be grieved or angry *she* is neither, *now*." And so, with what I supposed was your written punishment for high crime & misdemeanor[2] in my pocket, Livy, I had the hardihood to march down to the ~~church~~ crowded church & deliver as cheerful a lecture as ever you listened to in all your life! I knew you couldn't *keep* angry feelings, any more than I could. Somehow they *will* slide off, you know, do what one will to remain dignifiedly malignant! Anger won't stick unless you know that the offender *meant* to offend—& the idea of my *meaning* to offend *you*, was just simply preposterous.

Well, I can't *tell* how thankful I am to Mr & Mrs. Langdon for their generous permission, because there are no words in the dictionary long enough or strong enough; & so I will be content to *feel* thankful—all over!

I went to bed at the Delavan House, in Albany,[3] night before last, with my cigar & my library at my elbow—which library consisted of the Bible, your last letter & a Harper's Monthly. And I read the 27th Psalm, & pondered long over the probable meaning of the last verse.[4]

"*Wait* on the Lord"—~~Unil~~ Until: Selfish motives are gone from you; until your heart is purified of evil passions, your hands grown unaccustomed to evil deeds, your brain become unused to framing evil thoughts, your lips no longer prone to utter tainted speeches; until the pride of your own might is humbled; until its impotency is demonstrated; until that strength which comes from God's puissance is recognized as the *only* strength that can avail; until struggling hath exhausted you; until your finite wisdom is proven folly; until hope is dead within you; until patient study & patient groping in the dark has brought you at last to the eminence whence you can see the light, & *comprehension of the Word* dawns upon you; until you learn you are *nothing* of yourself alone; until finally you dimly perceive what a tremendous, what a colossal thing it is you ~~are~~ have been so complacently asking, as if it were a cheap & common favor—ETERNAL LIFE!—a life whose drifting years are as the sands of the sea drawn out into infinite procession, & each a lingering century of light, & love, & unimaginable bliss! "*Wait*" till you are thus prepared to vaguely *appreciate* the magnitude of this prodigious favor you are seeking, & *then* "HE WILL STRENGTHEN YOUR HEART"—He will revive it with *H*is Spirit—He will lift it up out of its humiliation, & all will be well. And so, conning my lesson with "good courage" & with firm faith, I "WAIT." I "wait"—in His own good time my hope will be crowned with its fruition. And *then!* my life will have an object! What an amazing value the thought gives to this life of mine, which was so perfectly valueless before! Perhaps you may appreciate that last remark when I tell you that for many years, & up to much less than a year ago I absolutely loved to look upon dead men & envy them! I *couldn't* keep from envying them—& in *all* moods—joy & sorrow the same. I was well nigh a savage, Livy.

Last night I went to bed & took my library along, again,—your new letter, a book,[5] & a Bible which I found in my room. I looked immediately for the passages referred to in your letter, but alas! the Bible was German! I couldn't read a word. However, to-night the matter shall be different. I do not carry my own Bible with me because it is a little too large for convenience, & besides I can always get one in the hotels. I am rather sorry I left mine, though, for it isn't always merely in one's room that he wishes to read. It is well to *keep at* a thing if one hopes to accomplish an end. I appreciate *that*, by old experience.

Livy, you are the best little encourager in the world. ~~W~~ One *couldn't* lose hope, with your earnest trust & confidence to inspire him. I can only be grateful, Livy, & I *am*—such services are beyond the possibility of adequate repayment. Bless your brave, true heart, you are *so* dear to me, Livy, & I am so unworthy. And I am so proud of you, my peerless!

"Which have been sounding in my ears *much of the time* since." Livy, *don't* say that. It makes me feel as if I have grieved you, wounded you, by speaking of your faults. I cannot *bear* that. I had rather hurt myself, five hundred times over. Oh, I would have you always, *always* happy—for you so well *earn* such a state—you so well *deserve* it, Livy. For you do *right*—as nearly as *any* human being *can*. Forgive me, Livy—I am sorry. "Help" you? Whensoever *I* can help you, & do not, I shall have changed my nature. My strong love shall help you in whatsoever love **can** help. *Our* love shall ~~be~~ make us strong to guide, sustain & help each other in all circumstances, at all times & in all seasons. With religion to order life, & love to fulfill its ~~deg~~ decrees, what life could be a failure, what life unworthy?

I know you are proud, Livy (God pity all men & women who are not, for they shall need it!) & I am glad you feel that it does not shame ~~it~~ ‸that pride‸ to open your heart to me—for nothing shows such exalted confidence in one as to fearlessly lay bare one's pride before him. I can tell you *anything*, without any fear, or any misgivings—& that you have this ~~tr~~ sort of trust in me in such a large degree, is very, very gratifying.

But they hurry me to go visiting. And so I bid you a loving good-bye, & go—to *talk* to other people, but *thinking* of you all the time, & loving & honoring you above all created things,—for I shall bear you with me. I waft a phantom kiss upon this messenger breeze that is journeying toward you. To think that I shall *see* you so soon! Oh! happiness!

Yrs forever & always,

Samuel Langhorne Clemens!

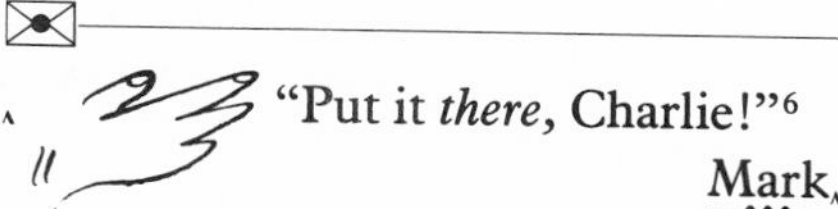

"Put it *there*, Charlie!"[6]

Mark

Miss Olivia L. Langdon

Present.

[*docketed by OLL:*] 12th [*OLL, in pencil:*] Wait on the Lord

[1] "Move Eastward, Happy Earth" appeared in *Poems* (1842). It expresses a lover's yearning for the dawn, his "marriage-morn" (Tennyson 1862, 371–72).

[2] From article 2, section 4, of the Constitution of the United States, which defines the grounds for removal of federal officers: "impeachment for, and conviction of, treason, bribery, or other high crimes and misdemeanors." President Johnson's impeachment trial in the Senate had ended with his acquittal on 26 May 1868.

[3] Charles E. Leland (1843–1906) became sole proprietor of the Delavan House in late 1867, remaining in that position for twenty years. He belonged to the second generation of Lelands in the hotel business, and may have been the brother of Clemens's friend Lewis Leland ("Topics Uppermost," Elmira *Advertiser*, 2 Dec 67, 1; New York *Times:* "Charles E. Leland," 1 Mar 1906, 9; "Mrs. Agnes Leland," 1 Jan 1909, 11).

[4] "Wait on the LORD: be of good courage, and he shall strengthen thine heart: wait, I say, on the LORD" (Psalms 27:14).

[5] Possibly Dickens's *Old Curiosity Shop* (1841), since, one week later, Clemens arrived in Fort Plain with a copy in his pocket (19 and 20 Dec 68 to OLL, n. 11).

[6] Clemens presumably offered his congratulations for Charles's successful negotiation of his engagement to Ida Clark. The hand is reproduced in facsimile from the manuscript (cf. *L1*, xxx).

To Joseph H. Twichell
12 December 1868 • Norwich, N.Y.

(MS facsimile: Davis)

Norwich, N.Y., Dec. 12.

Dear Twichell—

Hip—hip—Hurrah! She just goes on "accepting the situation" in the most ~~natural~~ innocent, easy-going way in the world. She writes as if the whole thing were perfectly understood, & would no doubt be unpleasantly astonished ~~to find~~ if she only knew I had been regarding it differently & had been ass enough to worry about a cousin whom she merely gives the passing mention accorded to the humblest guests.[1] *She* don't know anything about beating the devil around the bush[2]—she has never been used to it. She simply calls things by their right names & goes straight at the appalling subject of matrimony with the most amazing effrontery. I am in honor bound to regard her grave, philosophical dissertations as *love letters*, because they probe the very marrow of that passion, but there isn't a bit of romance in them, no poetical repining, no endearments, no adjectives, no flowers of speech, no nonsense, no bosh. Nothing but solid chunks of wisdom, my boy—love letters gotten up ~~in~~ on the square, flat-footed, cast-iron, inexorable plan of the most approved commercial correspondence, & signed with stately & exasperating decorum. "Lovingly, LIVY L. LANGDON"—*in full*, by the Ghost of Caesar! They are more precious to me than whole reams of affectionate superlatives would be, coming from any other woman, but they *are* the darlingest funniest *love* letters that ever were written, I do suppose. She gets her stateliness of ~~English~~ epistolary composition from her native dignity, & she gets that from her mother, who was born for a countess.

Hip—hip—Hurrah! I have badgered them & persecuted them until they have yielded, & I am to stop there for one day & night, on Dec. 17!

I am full of gratitude to God this day, & my prayers will be sincere. Now write me a letter which I can read to her, & let it reach Elmira a day or so before I get there—enclose it in an envelop directed to "*Chas. J. Langdon, Elmira, N.Y.*"[3] Good-bye. My love to you *all*.

Yrs always—

Mark.

[*in margin:*] P.S. She knows you & Mrs. T. know all about it~~,~~—she likes that.

[1] Edward L. Marsh (see 28 Nov 68 to OLL, n. 2).

[2] Evidently a conflation of "beat about the bush" and "whip the devil round the stump," meaning "to get round or dodge a difficulty or dilemma by means of a fabricated excuse or explanation" (Whitney and Smith, 2:1580).

[3] The same cautious procedure that Clemens himself used in writing to Olivia, here presumably to avoid alerting mail handlers that he was again visiting the Langdons.

To Olivia L. Langdon
19 and 20 December 1868 • Fort Plain, N.Y.
(MS: CU-MARK)

Fort Plain, Dec. 19.

My Dearest Livy—

Here at dead of night I seem to hear the murmur of the far Pacific—& mingled with the music of the surf the melody of an old familiar hymn is sounding in my ear. It comes like a remembered voice—like the phantom of a form that is gone, a face that is no more. You know the hymn—it is "Oh refresh us."[1] It haunts me now because I am thinking of a steadfast friend whose death I have just learned through the papers—a friend whose face must always appear before me when I think of that hymn—the Rev. Franklin S. Rising. I hear he was lost in the late disaster on the Ohio river.[2] He was rector of the Episcopal church in Virginia City, Nevada—a noble young fellow—& for 3 years, there, he & I were fast friends. ~~A~~ I used to try to teach him how he ought to preach in order to get at the better natures of the rough population about him, & he used to try hard to learn—for I *knew* them & he did not, for he was refined & sensitive & not intended for such a people as that. ~~And~~ [I mentioned him once in an absurd sketch entitled "Information for the Million" in that "Jumping Frog" book.~~*~~][3] Afterward I stumbled on him in the Sandwich Islands, where he was traveling for his health, & we so arranged it as to return to San Francisco in the same ship. We were at sea five Sundays. He felt it his duty to preach, but of the 15 passengers, none even pretended to sing, & he was so diffident that he hardly knew how he was to get along without a choir. I said, "Go ahead~~—don't be afraid~~—I'll ~~bac~~ stand by you—*I*'ll be your choir." And he *did* go ahead—& I was his choir. We could find only *one* hymn that I knew. It was "Oh, Refresh us." Only one—& so for five Sundays in succession he stood in the midst of the assembled people on the quarter-deck & gave out that same hymn twice a day, & I stood up solitary & alone & sang it! And then he went right along, happy & contented, & preached his sermon. We were together *all* the time—pacing the deck night & day—there was no other congenial company. He tried earnestly to bring me to a knowledge of the true God. In return, I read his manuscripts & made suggestions for their emendation. We got along well together (I never acquired a good man's friendship & lost it again, in all my ~~live~~ life, Livy.) A month ago, after so long a separation, he saw by the *Tribune* that I was at the Everett House, & came at once & left his card—I was out & did not see him.[4] It was the last opportunity I was ever to have on earth. For his wanderings are done, now; his restless feet are still; he is at peace. *Now* the glories of heaven are about him, & in his ears its mysterious music is sounding—but to me comes no vision but a lonely ship in a great solitude of sky & water; & unto *my* ears comes no sound~~s~~ but the complaining of the waves & the softened cadences of that simple old hymn—but Oh, Livy, it comes freighted with *infinite* pathos!

Tunes are good remembrancers. Almost every one I ~~know~~ am familiar with, summons instantly a face when I hear it. It is so with the Marseillaise, with ~~the~~ Bonny Doon & a score of others; when I hear "We 3 Kings of Orient" I think of Mrs Severance, *sure*—& whenever I hear the "Prodigal" I shall as surely think of you, my loved & honored Livy.[5]

At Utica, this morning, I saw Miss Anna Dickinson pass along & enter the drawing-room car, & I *wanted* to follow & talk with her a while, but I was unshaven & very shabby in dress in consequence of early rising, & so I just sat still & we traveled many miles together & yet *not* together. Scold me, Livy, dear. I suppose I deserve it. And yet see the sacrifice I made—& all for *you:* I *wouldn't* go there & tell her that such a looking object as *I* was, was regarded with respect & esteem by *you* & your family.[6] ‸Shucks, I am *always* making sacrifices.‸

Sunday Night, 10 o'clock. I got that far, late last night, & then felt tired out. So I desisted, & shortly went to bed. And the first thing I noticed when I opened the little Testament, was, that you hadn't written your name in it anywhere. I was sorry, then, that we tore out that fly-leaf. I ~~wa~~ had been afraid, at the time, that some profane eye might see it there & some common tongue make a flippant remark about it & so cause me to insult its owner. But who would ever see it Livy? Nobody ~~m~~ but me. And so *why* did we tear it out? Find it, ~~Livy,~~ & send it to me, please. And hurry up the ferrotype, Livy. I am half sorry, now, that I parted with the other, though unquestionably it *was* a most inferior picture of you. Already I yearn to see you again; already I begin to miss you more & more. Last night I dreamed of you—but you were only with me a single moment & then instantly the vision faded & passed away.

I wish we had persuaded Mr. & Mrs. Langdon to visit longer with us in the drawing-room in the afternoon, for we never had a right *good* visit with them afterward. I thought at the time, that maybe we might not have so pleasant an opportunity again—& yet the temptation to have you all to myself was very, very strong, Livy. I have written Mr. Leland of the Metropolitan[7] to forward Mr. Langdon's letter to me at Lansing, ~~W~~ Mich. I guess there's a mild scolding in it—but it couldn't be *very* severe, coming from *him*.

Please tell Miss Lewis that I am pining for her, & thinking about her all the time. I was as much distressed as she was, with the fear that our conduct toward each other would attract attention, especially as we were in the room together when the Misses Spaulding came—but never mind, they will think I only came to see Charley. She was out of the way when the Swiss Bell-Hangers[8] were there, & so they only saw you & I together. Tell her I dream about her sometimes, & whenever I do I snore. She is a good girl, Livy.[9] Now that I think of it, I didn't even call on Mrs. Ford—but then I had such a short visit, ~~Livy~~ that I couldn't really afford to see anybody, but you. I should have grudged the time a little, & that would have taken the grace all out of the visit.

I have been the guest, all day, of my poet-friend, Mr. Elliott, & his wife. He is editor of the paper here. They are very handsomely housed, & I have enjoyed their free & hearty hospitality exceedingly. [*in margin:* Writing facilities are not good here, & so I use a pencil.][10] Mrs. Elliott is a good, genuine little woman, & although I had never seen her before (she is the original of the "Bonnie Eloise" of the old song so popular ten years ago,) she immediately took a ~~kind~~ motherly interest in me & urged & beseeched me most feelingly to marry—but I said No, no use—I didn't know but one young woman whom I would like to have for a wife, & she wouldn't give her consent.[11] Then she pitied me, with all her kind heart—& I suppose I have left her in the sad conviction that because that young woman won't give her consent *now*, I am going to let her alone. Which is a mistake, my darling Livy, as you will surely find. I have had a venerable ex-Member of Congress praising me so lavishly about the serious passages in the lecture all the evening at Elliott's that I am half ashamed of being a professional Humorist any more! Such strength hath a compliment. His wife & daughters sent to invite me to come to breakfast & be their guest tomorrow, but unfortunately I leave in the westward train two hours after midnight.[12]

If I can ~~rel~~ recollect it, I will send my sister's letter with this, though somehow it seems to me that I read it to you. You would like her, ever so much. She is a Christian after your own heart.[13]

I *love* you, Livy. And I am happy in the possession of half your heart. I would rather hold half of your heart than all of anybody's else—& so I am tranquil & satisfied. I was wrong to urge you so to give it all to me at this time, but I didn't mean any harm, Livy, none at all. It was an honest impulse, & honest impulses are always forgivable. I shall have it some day, my dear, dear little tormentor. [*in margin:* I do not & *shall* not neglect my prayers, Livy, but somehow they do not seem as full of *life* as when you or Twichell are by.]

And now I have to bid you good night & good-bye—& so I leave you with fitter comrades—the viewless spirits of the air,[14] the ministering angels of God. I kiss your forehead in reverent blessing, & on your dear lips I place the kiss of loving trust & affection. Peace be with you & with all your household, my darling.

With loving devotion,

Saml L. C.

P. S.—I shall get letters from you in all those places in my list of appointments shan't I? Do try to have it so, Livy! At any time that you are tired or sleepy & can't write much, write & send a few lines *anyhow*, Livy—for I could not help feeling a little uneasy about you, otherwise, & it is such a royal pleasure to hear from you. I shall be sure to call on Miss Emma Nye. Do you know you never told me what Mr. & Mrs. Langdon said about my proposed clandestine visit? I didn't *forget* to speak to them about it myself, but every time it came to my tongue's end they were in such a good humor that I hadn't the heart to spoil it. It was very, very shabby in me, because now you will have to defend me *yourself*—no, but you mustn't—you ‸must‸ let them scold me just as much as I deserve. Why, it looks as if I had done a thing I was afraid or ashamed to acknowledge—& I don't & *wouldn't* do anything of that kind, Livy. I was openly doing wrong, but I didn't mean to shirk any of the blame of it. When you said they would "welcome me with their hearts," I didn't *begin* to take *that* as forbidding me the house, you little dear—but you seemed to think you had very broadly conveyed that impression to me! You wasn't quite literal *enough*, that time if you meant *that*, you darling little woman.

Miss Olivia L. Langdon | Present. [*docketed in ink by OLL:*] 13th

[1] This hymn, more commonly known by its first line, "Lord, dismiss us with thy blessing," was written in 1773 by the Reverend John Fawcett (1739–1817), an English Baptist (Sims, 48–49).

[2]Rising was only about thirty-five years old when he perished, along with some eighty-five other passengers and crew, in the 4 December collision of the Ohio River steamboats *America* and *United States*. He had been on a tour of official duty as financial secretary of the American Church Missionary Society. Although news of the disaster appeared early and often in the New York newspapers, including telegraphic reports the next day, Rising was not identified as among the fatalities until 10 December, when the *Tribune* described him as "a clergym[a]n of marked devotion to his work, and one who, during the last few years, has become very widely known by his successful efforts to awaken interest in the field of domestic missions. He was about 30 years of age, and unmarried, of exceedingly pleasing manners, and one whose place cannot easily be supplied." Clemens may not have learned of Rising's death until a memorial service in Brooklyn was reported on 18 December ("Dreadful Disaster on the Ohio River," New York *Evening Post*, 5 Dec 68, 3; New York *Tribune:* "The Ohio River Steamboat Disaster," 10 Dec 68, 5; "The Ohio River Disaster," 17 Dec 68, 2; "The Ohio Steamboat Disaster—Memorial Meeting," 18 Dec 68, 5; *Annual Cyclopaedia 1868*, 583–84; *L1*, 354 n. 3).

[3]First published as "Washoe.—'Information Wanted'" in the Virginia City *Territorial Enterprise* sometime in early May 1864 (*ET&S1*, 365–71, 742–46). Mark Twain referred to Rising, by name, as "our Episcopalian minister," who had "done as much as any man among us to redeem this community from its pristine state of semi-barbarism" (*ET&S1*, 369).

[4]Rising could have seen either of two *Tribune* announcements, on 2 and 5 November, that Clemens was staying at the Everett House ("The City," New York *Tribune*, 2 Nov 68, 8, and 5 Nov 68, 5).

[5]The words and music of "La Marseillaise," the French national anthem, were written in 1792 by Rouget de Lisle. Robert Burns's "Ye Banks and Braes o' Bonie Doon," a paean to the River Doon, was possibly the most popular of his songs; it was first published in 1792, set to a tune composed by James Miller in the style of a traditional Scots air (Lindsay, 73). The Christmas carol "Kings of Orient" was written and composed in 1857 by John Henry Hopkins, rector of Christ's Church in Williamsport, Pennsylvania; its connection with Emily Severance is not known (Dearmer, Williams, and Shaw, 451–54). The last song mentioned was probably "Prodigal," written by Ananias Davisson and published in his 1820 *Supplement to the Kentucky Harmony* (Harrisonburg, Va.):

> Afflictions, tho' they seem severe,
> Are oft in mercy sent;
> They stopt the prodigal's career
> And caused him to repent,
> Altho' he no relenting felt
> Till he had spent his store;
> His stubborn heart began to melt
> When famine pinch'd him sore.
> (George Pullen Jackson, 80–81)

[6]Anna E. Dickinson (1842–1932), a lecturer and author, was a good friend of the Langdons', with whom she sometimes stayed while lecturing or visiting in Elmira. Born in Philadelphia to a family of poor Quaker abolitionists, by the age of seventeen she was speaking publicly in defense of both abolition and women's rights. At twenty-three she formally entered the lyceum circuit, where she immediately became the most successful woman in the field, earning $200 a night by 1868. Clemens was correct in his fear that she would not approve of him: she

later termed him a "vulgar boor" (Chester, 10, 12, 15–18, 292; Higginson, 54; James Harvey Young, 40–41).

[7]Probably Lewis Leland (1834–97), whom Clemens said on 29 December either was, or was soon to become, "proprietor" of New York's Metropolitan Hotel, long owned and managed by the Leland family business, Simeon Leland and Company (29 Dec 68 to Langdon; H. Wilson 1868, 634; advertisement, New York *Evening Post*, 8 Dec 68, 3). Leland had entered the hotel business in 1847 at the Clinton House in New York City (*ET&S2*, 49, 367; New York *Times:* "Lewis Leland Retires," 9 May 89, 2; "Died," 21 Dec 97, 7; San Francisco City and County 1867, s.v. "Leland, Lewis").

[8]Unidentified. Clemens may have meant to write "Bell-Ringers."

[9]Harriet Lewis (later Paff) was the daughter of Mrs. Langdon's brother, who had moved from New York to Illinois in the 1840s; she was about the same age as Olivia. In the spring of 1868 she came from her home in Ottawa, Illinois, for a year-long visit with the Langdons, during which time she became Olivia's—and later Clemens's—confidante (Paff, 1; SLC to OLL, 12 Jan 69, CU-MARK; SLC to Mary Mason Fairbanks, 10 May 69, CSmH, in *MTMF*, 94–98). In an 1897 reminiscence, she explained that Olivia

> had felt sensitive all the time about the public knowing that she was the object of Mr. C's attentions and would be until she could come to a decision, therefore when guests came or when we were out together Mr. C. and I appeared to be devoted to each other, and unlikely as it may seem, we did succeed in deceiving people, much to the amusement of us all. (Paff, 5)

[10]The entire letter was written in pencil.

[11]Clemens's hosts in Fort Plain, New York, were George W. Elliott (1830–98) and his wife, the former Mary Bowen. Clemens had known Elliott since sometime in late 1867, when he may have been invited to lecture in Fort Plain (9 Jan 68 to JLC and PAM, n. 1). Elliott, who began his career in journalism on the Rochester (N.Y.) *American*, was now an associate editor of the *Mohawk Valley Register* (Diabolis, no page). In addition, he had a reputation as a poet:

> His best known production is "Bonny Eloise, the Belle of the Mohawk Vale," which has become the song of the Valley. It is said he composed the words to this popular melody while on a railroad journey from New York to Fort Plain, addressing his song to his sweetheart, Mary Bowen (with a change of name). The work bears [a] copyright date of 1858 and J. R. Thomas was the composer of the plaintively sweet melody to which Mr. Elliott's words are sung. "Bonny Eloise" was a favorite air played by the military bands of both the North and South during the Civil war. (Greene, 2:1739)

One week after Clemens's visit Elliott wrote this account of his arrival:

> As the eastward bound express train halted at this station, in that glorious flood of sunlight of last Saturday afternoon, there stepped from the drawing-room car a little merry-eyed, curly-headed, intelligent-looking gentleman, whose age is hardly thirty-five. From one of his overcoat pockets peeped out a copy of DICKENS' "Old Curiosity Shop;" and from the other, as he walked along chatting with a friend, he drew and leisurely shelled and ate a handful of peanuts. This was Mr. SAMUEL L. CLEMENS, familiarly known to the reading public as "*Mark Twain*," and acknowledged, wherever the English language is spoken, as *par excellence* the "Humorist of America." With his calm self-possession and winning geniality of manner, added to a slight "Down East" accent, he is the impersonation of the shrewd, fun-loving, genuine "live Yankee." . . .
>
> We have an unwavering faith in "*Mark Twain.*" We count upon his success as confidently as upon the coming of an expected comet. (Elliott, 3)

Of Clemens's lecture Elliott observed: "Mr. CLEMENS . . . drew upon the passive minds of his listeners pictures as strongly lined and as indelible as the memory of a delicious dream" (Elliott, 3).

[12]Clemens had probably met Peter Joseph Wagner (1795–1884), a representative from New York in the Twenty-sixth Congress (1839–41). Born in Montgomery County, Wagner moved to Fort Plain at the age of ten, graduated from Union College in Schenectady in 1819, and, except for his term in Congress, practiced law continuously in Fort Plain until his retirement in 1873. He and his wife, Margaret, had two daughters: Gozina, aged about twenty-three, and Caroline, aged about twenty-two (*Minden Census*, 287).

[13]Pamela's letter has not been found.

[14]An amalgam of "the sightless couriers of the air" (*Macbeth*, act 1, scene 7, line 23), "the viewless wings of poesy" (John Keats, "Ode to a Nightingale," line 33), and "the viewless spirit of the tempest" (Sir Walter Scott, *The Pirate*, chapter 6). Clemens had used the phrase at least once before, in 1863 (see *ET&S1*, 290).

To Olivia L. Langdon with a note to Charles J. Langdon 21 and 23 December 1868 • Detroit, Mich.

(MS: CU-MARK)

Detroit, Dec. 21.

My Dearest Livy—

I am *almost* tired out. It has been 22 hours since I wrote you, & ever since that time I have been drifting along over the *slowest* railways. I have just arrived here, & it is almost midnight. I can't get any supper—too late—but I don't mind that—

I am so inexpressibly tired & drowsy!—not tired, either, but worn, you know, & dreary. I wish I never had to travel any more. And I *won't*, after we come to anchor, my dear—I won't for any light cause. How I long to have a home & never leave it! You don't thoroughly appreciate the luxury of having a home, Livy—but you could before long, if you had to go, go, go, all the time, from one of these hated hotels to another, as I do. Now this room is large & well furnished, & the open fire looks cheerful—but it is stupid & lonesome,—& there is that indescribable something or other about the disposal of the curtains & the bureau ornaments which tells that the place ~~does not~~ ‸seldom‸ knows the gentle presence of a woman. I wish you—but you *can't* be here, of course—& so there isn't any use in wishing it. I——but I am falling asleep. I *do* LOVE you, Livy. Good-night. Our Father have you in ~~his~~ His holy keeping.~~, my blameless one.~~

22ᴰ—MIDNIGHT.—I have just this moment parted with my newspaper friends—I don't get a moment's time to myself. ~~I~~ The whole day long I have been driving or visiting, with first one & then another—& I found an old friend or two here, as usual—I find them everywhere—how they do wander! It was move, move, move—all the day long—& so I got no time to ~~write~~ finish my letter—I barely got time to shave before time for the lecture (1,000 or 1,100 people there—they seemed to like it.) I called on Miss Nye and Mrs. Sill[1] at 4 P.M., & staid to tea at 6, because the place looked homelike & I wanted to get away from the dreariness of the hotel. I am not going to tell you what Miss Nye said about you, Livy, because you would simply say she was blinded by love, & you would *believe* it, too. Why *won't* you let us praise you all we want to?—it is ever so pleasant to us, & it don't do you any harm, you dear little woman. But *one* thing she said which I will tell you, anyhow—it supports what Mrs. Fairbanks says, & what I say: She said your English composition was wonderful for the charm there was about it—& *I* say its simplicity, its naturalness & its unconsciousness are just *matchless*. Now ruffle your feathers!—but it isn't of any use, Livy—I am not on the sofa & you can't stop my mouth. {If I *were* I would stop yours with a kiss precious soon, I can tell you.} I was very stupid, at Mr. Sill's, but I think it was mostly because I was ashamed of being there unshaven~~,~~—though of course I was drowsy from driving two hours & a half in the cold & snow. Mr. Sill was not at home, & the ladies could not attend the lecture, but Miss Nye sent a note inviting me ~~to fo~~ (for Mrs. Sill) to come there Christmas Day to attend some sort of Santa Claus fandango—but you know I can't be here then. Please won't you write Miss Nye so, in your next letter?—there's a dear good girl. You see the note does not require an answer, & even if it did, *when* shall I get a chance to answer it?

No letter from you, Livy—but I know it will come in the morning, ~~be~~ unless circumstances have interfered to prevent your writing it—for I know you *meant* to do it.

Don't write to *Dayton*, AT ALL—the date has been changed—but please write ~~so that~~ one letter to *Cleveland* (care Herald) to hit that date (Dec. 31.) I shall be there.

Livy, I ought to be ashamed to send you such a shabby, incoherent, yea, ~~trifling &~~ trivial ~~a~~ letter as this—but dear, it has been written in fatigue & drowsiness at such odd moments as I could catch late & night—& you will forgive. It is 1 o'clock A.M. now, & I must get up this morning (23^d) & go & lecture at Lansing to-night. I am very sleepy. My fire has gone out & I am catching cold. Give my loving duty to Mr. & Mrs. Langdon, please.

Good night. I shall remember you in my prayers, five minutes hence, my life, my hope, my darling!

Always your
Loving subject
& Obedient—
Saml. L. C.

‸The picture, the picture, Livy!‸

[*in margin of page 1:*] Now, Livy *please don't* answer this with a short letter just because this is short, but consider the circumstances, dear, & write a good long one.

‸Charley, please give a world of my respect & esteem to Miss Ida,[2] & a homeopathic dose of my love.

Do, you new-fashioned nail-grab,[3]

& Oblige
Sam.‸

‸Charlie, if you will send me a keg of nails for a Christmas present, I will send you one of my old second-hand lectures.‸

[*on the back:*] Please give letters 4 days in which to reach any point in the list, Livy—the mails are so unreliable that this seems necessary.

[*docketed in ink by OLL:*] 14th

[1]Emma Nye's hosts in Detroit, Mr. and Mrs. Sill, have not been further identified.

[2]Ida B. Clark.

[3]Charles Langdon had recently entered the hardware business in Elmira. In his mother's 1 December letter to Mrs. Fairbanks, she noted that "Charlie has now installed himself quite thoroughly in his 'Hardware business' & seems quite happy" (26 and 27 Nov 68 to Fairbanks, n. 3). According to the Elmira *Adver-*

tiser, Charles had formed a partnership with Miles Ayrault, Stephen Rose, and Irving D. Booth (Boyd and Boyd, 61, 70, 185):

The new year brings to the Hardware House of AYRAULT, ROSE & CO., on Lake street, a new partner in the person of Mr. CHARLES J. LANGDON, who enters upon the practical business of a merchant with the same characteristic energy which he has heretofore exhibited in the pursuit of knowledge or pleasure. ("Our Business Men," Elmira *Advertiser*, 4 Jan 69, 4)

To Olivia L. Langdon with a note to Charles J. Langdon 23 and 24 December 1868 • Lansing, Mich.

(MS, *damage emended:* CU-MARK)

Lansing, Mich., Dec. 23.

My Dearest Livy—

Twenty minutes after I had mailed my Detroit letter to you this morning, (in Detroit,) your letter reached me. I was sorry it had not come a little sooner, so that I could have told you, because you will fear I did not get it at all. I was not at all satisfied with my performance in Detroit, for notwithstanding I had the largest audience they had seen there for a long time, I was awkward & constrained—ill at ease—& did not satisfy them, I think.[1] But if I had only had your letter in my pocket, then, how different it would have been—! Livy, dear, you don't know what inspiration flows from your pen. I can please *any* audience when I have a new letters of yours by me. It is because I always feel a tranquil gladness, a glow of happiness, then, & it is easy to impart it to the multitude about me. Now tonight we had the largest audience that has ever attended any lecture ‸here‸ but Gough's,[2] & I honestly believe I pleased every individual in the house. The applause of the serious passages was cordial & unstinted. The gentlemen of the Society pledged me to come again (in case I lecture another season—I always make that reservation, because I don't want to run about any more unless I *must*.)[3]

As usual, I found an old friend[4] here, & we have had a glorious talk over old times. I am to dine with him & other friends tomorrow. I shall spend my Christmas Eve in this delightful little city.

"Are you interested in these profound matters of the evening?" Bless your dear old heart, Livy, I am interested in *everything* you do & say—nothing that concerns you is unimportant to me. And those little personal details are the very things that please me most—because they bring *you* before me—& to me you are the *world*—you are the universe! I so love you, Livy, & am so proud of you, that I *cannot* hear too much about you. Your letter brings you back to me, & I see you in your dainty room, among your books & pictures—I see the south window & the hanging basket of flowers—& more than all, I see your precious little figure bending over that fanciful portfolio—the one vision in all the world that my eyes most love to look upon.

Why yes—you *must* have "banished all suspicion" from ~~Mis~~ Mr. Coleman's[5] mind by calling him by my name twice in the same evening! You dear little concentration of gravity, *that* looks very much to me like a modest ebullition of humor! Look out—you are on dangerous ground—be careful, or you will blossom into a humorist when you least expect it, & so distress yourself beyond measure! But your humor is kindly & gentle, Livy, & will not make anybody unhappy.

No indeed, Livy, you cannot tell me too much about yourself. When you tell me what you ~~have~~ are doing, I *know* it—but at other times I can only guess. And so I am always guessing. At 8 in the morning—(or *ten minutes after*)—I say to myself, "Now she is at breakfast"—just after noon, "Now she is at luncheon"—at six in the evening, "Now she is at dinner"—but after that, & during the odd hours of the day, I can only form random conjectures of what you are about. But ø there is one thing that I am always conscious of, & that is, that whatever you are doing or saying, I would like ever so much to know all about it.

Ladies don't usually like those books, Livy, I don't know why—because those same books praise them so much, maybe.[6] ~~Hor~~ Honoria is a great-souled, self-sacrificing, noble woman like you (I can see you in everything she does) & she is so happy in the weal of others & so compassionate of their woes‸. And she is so thoughtful, & so tender, & so exquisitely womanly. One learns to love poor Jane, ‸by & bye,‸ & feel a longing to caress her secret sorrows away & do something to make glad the grieving little heart that so yearned to be loved. And how death hallows her!—how it shames away all ungenerous criticism of her little faults, ennobles her virtues & makes sweet womanly graces of what seemed blemishes before! Even the reader feels that *he himself* has somehow lost something when poor Jane is gone.

Did I scare you, Livy? And did I make you sad, talking of the home in Cleveland? I know it—I know I did. Oh, child! you~~r~~ write so tenderly, so beautifully of it! "To think of having them grow used to my being absent, so that at last they would cease to miss me, made me feel as if I wanted father to put his arms about me & keep me near him always." English literature cannot show a finer passage than that, Livy. "Honesty is the best policy," in literature, *always*. One who writes from his *heart*, can never write badly—~~&~~ ‸but‸ the daintiest paragraph that was ever written cannot deceive if it is a lie—if it is a pretense of what is not *felt*. No one ever wrote well, who wrote ~~wa~~ what was not in his heart. I said you wrote well—*more* than well, Livy—& I *knew* I could bide my time ~~in~~ with confidence—I knew I could *prove* it, whenever I chose. Write whatever an honest impulse dictates, Livy, without ever stopping to think whether it will be better to say it or not, or to consider much how it ought to *be* said—it will find its own proper language. What would Mrs. Fairbanks say to that passage? She would say it was worthy of Sterne. I don't know what reminded me of Sterne—but do you remember Uncle Toby & the ~~woul~~ wounded soldier? (I hope not, because the book is coarse, & I would not have you soil ~~your~~ ‸your pure‸ mind with it.) But the incident I speak of is ~~match~~ beyond praise in its treatment—it is such a noble burst of generous feeling. The ~~poor~~ wounded soldier (wounded unto death,) pleads so touchingly that the doctors will make him a little better, so that he can go & see his home & its idols again—& good old Uncle Toby's ~~honest~~ whole honest heart is in the matter. Then in the midst of his ~~generous~~ ‸kindly‸ enthusiasm some one comes & tells Toby that it cannot be—it cannot be—the soldier must die—he will never march again. And *then* old Toby's ire bursts out in a great avalanche of generous wrath,—& forgetting his gout, he rises up & tries to take the grand step of a soldier (for his heart is full & his body *must* act his thought,) & he thunders:

"He shall *not* die! He shall march!—by God he *shall* march again!"

[*six lines (about 30 words) torn away*]

[*insertion on a page left partly blank:*]

‸[*in top margin:* ‸~~(M~~‸]

"*And the ministering spirit that flew up to Heaven's chancery with the oath blushed as he gave it in; & the recording angel, as he wrote it down, dropped a tear upon the word & blotted it out forever.*"[7]

[Made a mistake of memory before.]

[*fourteen blank lines*]‸

Livy, that is the finest thought in the English language—& no thought could be more exquisitely expressed. It is one of the most famous passages in our literature, too—& when~~ever~~ everything else that Lawrence Sterne ~~ever~~ wrote shall have been forgotten, that one little paragraph will still secure to him an enduring fame—a fame that shall last while English is written & noble impulses still stir in the human heart. You touch one as nearly as Lawrence Sterne, if I *do* say it myself—but I have a *right* to say it, because if you are not *my* Livy you are not anybody else's Livy that I know of—not with my consent, you ain't, anyhow~~?~~.

I just don't wonder that it makes you sad to think of leaving such a home, Livy, & such household Gods—for there is no other home in all the world like it—no household gods so lovable as yours, anywhere. And I shall feel like a heartless highway robber when I take you away from there—(but I *must* do it, Livy, I *must*—but I shall love you so dearly, & try so hard all the days of my life to make you happy, & shall so strive to walk as you do in the light & the love of God, that some of the bitterness of your exile shall be spared you.) But Oh, they *never* would cease to miss you, darling—they—

I'll *not* read that passage again for an hour!—for it makes the tears come into my eyes every time, in spite of me. You shall visit them, Livy—& so often that they *cannot* ~~much~~ well realize ~~than~~ that you are an absentee. You shall never know the chill that comes upon me ~~when~~ sometimes when I feel that long absence has made me a stranger in my own home—(not that *I* ever seem a stranger to my mother & sister & my brother, for their love knows no change, no modification[)]—but then I see them taking delight in things that are new to me, & which I do not comprehend or take an interest in; I see them heart-&-heart with people I do not know, & who are nothing to me; & so I can only *look in* upon their world without entering~~,~~; & I turn me away with a dull, aching consciousness that long exile has lost to me that haven of rest, that pillow of weariness, that refuge from care, & trouble & pain, that type & symbol of heaven, HOME—& then, away down in my heart of hearts I yearn for the days that are gone & the phantoms of the olden time!—for the faces that are vanished; for the forms I loved to see; for the voices that were music to my ear; for the restless feet that have gone out into the darkness, to return no more forever!

But *you* shall not know this great blank, this awful vacancy, this *something missed, something lost*, which is felt but cannot be described, this solemn, mysterious desolation. No, ~~you~~ ~~I~~ with my experience, I should dread to think of your old home growing strange to you. Don't be sad, Livy—any more than you can help—we'll have all the folks out in our home *often*—& we will make them sorry to go away again, too. Cheer up, Livy, you dear good girl, & go & *invite* them. We'll have no sorrow, darling, that shall abide with us!—we'll model our home after the old home, & make the spirit of Love lord over all the realm—& Sorrow shall be banished the royalty! Smile again, Livy, & be of good heart. Turn toward the Cross & be comforted—I turn with you— What would you more? The peace of God shall rest upon us, & all will be well.

Good-bye, Livy, dear—& good night. It was~~n't~~ not midnight when I began, but I have written so leisurely (for this room is very, *very* pleasant—reminds me of my room in your house) that it is half-past 2 in the morning, now, & so it is Christmas Eve. I guess I shall sleep rather late. Good bye, & God bless you for the coveted words that close your letter: "With a kiss & *increasing love*." So may it increase till it can go no farther—till it ~~is~~ ‸be‸ *perfect*, darling, & our two hearts pulse in unison, our hands be joined one with the other, & our feet & our eyes be turned, together, toward ~~& th~~ the far shores of eternity.

Good-bye. Write me *all the letters you can*, Livy, to reach Cleveland on the 28th, 29th, 30th, 31st, of Dec., & 1st of Jan.—now you *will*, won't you, you dear little woman? I talk in Akron, but I shall return to Cleveland the same day. And send the picture, dear, so I can show it to my good, noble old Mother Fairbanks, & make her heart glad. *Please*, Livy.

In spirit I kiss you—would it were ~~real.~~ ‸in *reality*.‸

In loving devotion, always

Sam*l*. C

[*in top margin:*] You know I don't talk in Dayton, Livy.

Miss ~~L. L~~ Livy L. Langdon

Present.

Christmas gift, Charley!—send me a keg of nails.[8]

[*docketed by OLL:*] 15th [*OLL, in pencil:*] Home, & the quotation from Sterne

[1] At least one reviewer confirmed Clemens's opinion of his 22 December performance in Detroit: "The lecture itself was decidedly good, but its delivery was

not what might have been expected, an assumed drawl, though very taking and appropriate at times, spoiling the effect of many of the finest sentences" ("Mark Twain," Detroit *Free Press*, 23 Dec 68, 1).

[2] John Bartholomew Gough (1817–86) had been giving well-attended temperance lectures since he signed the pledge in 1842.

[3] The Young Men's Society of Lansing sponsored Clemens's 23 December lecture, which was well reviewed:

> He talked easily, walking up and down the stage at a pace that slowly marked the time of his words. His delightful description of Venice by moonlight, the Sphinx, the Acropolis at Athens, were as fine specimens of word painting as can be drawn by any other lecturer. ("The Lecture of Mark Twain," Lansing *State Republican*, 31 Dec 68, 3)

[4] Unidentified.

[5] Unidentified.

[6] "Those books" were the four parts of Patmore's *Angel in the House* (see 30 Oct 68 to OLL, n. 7); Clemens may have given them to Olivia during his recent visit to Elmira, on 17–18 December.

[7] *The Life and Opinions of Tristram Shandy, Gentleman* (1762), volume 6, chapter 8. The first paragraph Clemens recalls here, containing Uncle Toby's oath, is not an exact quotation, but the second paragraph accords verbatim with the first-edition text, except for the substitution of "ministering" for "accusing." It is not known what edition of the book Clemens had read nor, therefore, whether the alteration was his.

[8] See the previous letter, n. 3.

To Pamela A. Moffett
24 December 1868 • Lansing, Mich.

(MS: NPV)

‸*N°. 6.*‸

Lansing, Mich, Dec. 24.

My Dear Sister:

I have nothing new to report concerning that matter, save that it moves along entirely to my satisfaction. I thank you ever so kindly for your letter—which I exhibited.[1] I am not afraid of your betraying the secret.

I have nothing to write except to wish you all a merry Christmas & a happy new year. I have lectured in Newark, Rondout, Norwich, Scranton, Fort Plain[,] Detroit & Lansing, & am fairly under way, now. The above places are in New York, New Jersey, Pennsylvania & Michigan. I go into Ohio again, in a day or two, & shall spend New Year's in Cleveland, it being very close to my other appointments. I shall be the guest of the "Herald" folks,[2] of course. I hardly get time to turn around, much less write.

Give my love to all the family. I enclose some money—$20 for Ma, & $10 for the children, to buy holiday nonsense with, or to give to the missionaries, or to expend in any other ~~specious~~ species of dissipation that may engage their fancy.[3]

I think you will like Norwich, New York, very much. If you will send Orion in the spring to rent a house (you only have to pay $150 to $200,) I will pay his way.[4] Good-bye.

Yrs affectionately

Sam.

[1] Presumably the same letter Clemens mentioned in his 19 and 20 December letter to Olivia.

[2] Abel and Mary Mason Fairbanks.

[3] Jane Clemens recorded the receipt of $20 from her son on 28 December as the sixth installment of that amount received from him that month, which explains Clemens's own notation ("*No. 6.*") at the top of his letter (29? Nov 68 to PAM, n. 4).

[4] As he had earlier promised, Clemens here suggested one of the towns in western New York to which his mother and sister might want to move (10 Dec 68 to JLC and family, n. 3).

To Mary Mason Fairbanks
24 and 25 December 1868 • Lansing, Mich.

(Transcripts and MS facsimile: copy by Dixon Wecter, CU-MARK; Cleveland *Herald*, 16 Jan 69; Sotheby, lot 5; and Sotheby Parke Bernet 1976, lot 42)

Lansing, Mich., Dec. 24

Dear Mother—

I shall arrive at your house Dec. 28—& shall leave again Jan. 2,—except that I shall lecture in Akron Dec. 30. I skip Dayton for the present.

Don't you know, I just kept on begging & worrying Mrs. Langdon by letter, till she had to say come, to get rid of me. And so I broke a lecture engagement & stopped there from 7 p.m. 17th to 7 p.m. 18th. It was splendid. I had a hard time getting permission to come, but after I *was* there, none of them were anxious to have me go again—so that was a point gained, wasn't it? I think so. Mr. Langdon is well again, & was perfectly jolly—bothered us & interrupted us all he could—& appeared to enjoy it.

I begin to think that Livy's letters are going to miscarry wofully on this trip—but I shall fix it as I go along. I have written her to write Cleveland & never mind the other places for the present—& so you take care of them if any chance to arrive before I do. You say she writes well. I should *think* so. This paragraph from her letter received yesterday, so touches me with its simple pathos & so stirs my pity for the poor child, withal, that I feel like a monstrous sort of highwayman when I think of tearing her from the home which has so long been her little world, her shelter, her refuge:

"I think that you must have scared me a little, yesterday, talking about the home in Cleveland, because to-day I have been feeling sad at the thought of ever leaving this home of mine, ever going out from among those who have always made a part of my life. *To think of having them grow used to my being absent from them, so that at last they would cease to miss me,* MADE ME FEEL AS IF I WANTED FATHER TO PUT HIS ARMS ABOUT ME & KEEP ME NEAR HIM ALWAYS—ALWAYS."

It is one's *heart* that writes, Madam—mere art could never teach any one to put words together like that. Further along, she says: "He said last night that if he could live as long as I did, he would never let any man take me away from him; & he said that when I left home he was going to sell out—he is good at making threats."

That girl is one in a million. She is fearfully & wonderfully made. Do *you* know her superior anywhere?

My dear good mother, she read me your letter to Mrs. Langdon & re-read & dwelt with particular delight upon the passage wherein you speak of placing *full* confidence in me—told her mother that that was just what *she* ought to do.[1] And I believe she does—& it is all owing to your cordial, whole-hearted endorsement of me, my loved & honored mother—& for that, & for your whole saving letter, I shall be always, *always* grateful to you. And when I prove unworthy of the service you have done me in this matter, & the generous trust you have placed in me, even in the slightest degree, I shall be *glad* to know that that day is the last appointed me to live. There is *no* way in which I shall not prove your judgment perfect. Across the wastes of frozen snow that lie between us, mother, I waft a filial kiss so warm that such idle citizens as be abroad this night shall think the Spirit of the South Wind went by. Amen. And *that* is honest.

Write to Livy, please. I guess she don't owe you a letter. And maybe she does, too. Sometime ago I shamed her so about not answering your letter to her about our contemplated visit, that she verily thought she had committed something akin to high treason. She was going to hurry off & write at once—but I saw that what I had said had distressed her so, that I stopped her & told her it was only *talk*—& that her mother's letter was sufficient. I didn't exactly *think* so, but then the girl was in so much trouble, *how* could I do otherwise? And so maybe she didn't write.[2] Writing is a great labor to her, & the close application it requires taxes her strength—but I will tell her to skip me, for once, & write you.

About this time (past midnight, & so, Christmas is here,) eighteen hundred & sixty nine years ago, the stars were shedding a purer lustre above the barren hills of Bethlehem—& possibly flowers were being charmed to life in the dismal plain where the Shepherds watched their flocks—& hovering angels were singing Peace on earth, goodwill to men. For the Savior was come. Don't you naturally turn, in fancy, now, to that crumbling wall & its venerable olives, & to the mouldy domes & turrets of Bethlehem? And don't you picture it all out in your mind as we saw it many months ago? And don't the picture mellow in the distance & take to itself again the soft, unreal semblance that Poetry & Tradition give to the things they hallow? And now that the greasy monks, & the noisy mob, & the leprous beggars are gone, & all the harsh, cold hardness of *real* stone & unsentimental glare of sunlight are banished from the vision, don't you realize again, as in other years, that Jesus *was* born there, & that the angels *did* sing in the still air above, & that the wondering Shepherds *did* hold their breath & listen as the mysterious music floated by? *I* do. It is more real than ever. And I am glad, a hundred times glad, that I saw Bethlehem, though at the time it seemed that that sight had swept away forever, every pleasant fancy & every cherished memory that ever the City of the Nativity had stored away in my mind & heart.

Please give my love to Mollie,[3] & to Old Mr. Fairbanks, & to *all* the family. I am coming. When you write our most excellent & well-beloved Mrs. Mason, please say to her that I warned you to ORGANIZE! against my coming. I guess she'll understand. I have just written her to-day.

Good-bye. Peace unto your household—& a very happy Christmas.

Your promising scrub,

Mark.

1 Mrs. Fairbanks's reply to Mrs. Langdon's 1 December letter (see 26 and 27 Nov 68 to Fairbanks, n. 3) has not been found.

2 Olivia had written, albeit belatedly. Her visit to Cleveland, in the company of her brother, had originally been scheduled for May 1868, but was then postponed—at her request—until "the Fall." When Mrs. Fairbanks wrote to confirm a fall visit, Mrs. Langdon replied on Olivia's behalf, saying that "for several reasons (which I could easily explain to you could I see you,) we do not either of us feel that it is just the time for her to go now" (OLL to Mary Mason Fairbanks, 30 Apr 68, CtHMTH; Olivia Lewis Langdon to Mary Mason Fairbanks, 4 Sept 68, CtHMTH). Mrs. Langdon's reluctance to let Olivia accompany Clemens and her brother on their September visit to the Fairbankses suggests that she already suspected Clemens's special interest in her daughter. Olivia did not herself reply to Mrs. Fairbanks until 26 October, presumably after Clemens chided her about the matter:

> In looking at your letter I find it dated Aug. 20th— Who would have thought that so long a time would elapse after the rec'pt of it, before I should send you one word (directly) of thanks for your heartily expressed wish that I should visit you? If shame would set me free from blame worthiness, I should be free, for I am ashamed that in appearence you should have been so long neglected— (CtHMTH)

3 Mary Paine Fairbanks.

To Olivia L. Langdon
25 December 1868 • Lansing, Mich.

(MS: CU-MARK)

TO LIVY.

Long after supper Christmas Eve, & long before Breakfast Christmas morning—1868.

~~It~~ I have been writing letters to ~~all my~~ a number of my friends, my darling Livy, but it is not near daylight yet, & so I can't resist the temptation to write a line to you before I go to bed. I do it only for the pleasure of talking to you, for I haven't really anything to write—nothing at all except that I love you, Livy—I love you more than I can tell. And now is the *time* to love—for on this day the Savior was born, whose measureless love unbarred the gates of Heaven to perishing men. All this long night my thoughts have somehow wandered to that subject—all the night long my memory has been drifting back to Bethlehem, & more & more vividly the *reality* of what occurred there so many ages ago has seemed to dawn upon me—until now, even *I* can half comprehend the grandeur of the old *first* Christmas night.

I wish you a *glad* Christmas—a painless Christmas—a Christmas of rest, & peace, & thanksgiving, Livy, ~~dear.~~ O, crowned & sceptred queen of my true heart! [I *must* get a little magniloquent in speech every time I think of you, Livy—I can't help it. For—I—*love* you.] Never mind the foolishness of it, I *love* you—& I wish I were near enough to touch your dear forehead with the benediction of a kiss, this Christmas morning.

I have n't received any letter from you, to-day, but *maybe* I may to= morrow. I am full of *hope* that you have written, though I know that many things can & do occur to delay & prevent your writing. I shall hear from you at Charlotte, *sure*. And maybe at Tecumseh—& *certainly* at Cleveland,—send *several* letters to Cleveland, Livy, be sure & do that. And send the picture—I am just in a fidget to see it. ~~You dear~~ You little humbug, you went out for Miss Hooker's basket, & I really suppose you never went near the daguerrean rooms. O, Livy, why *will* you be guilty of such conduct as those? But you may consider that I don't call you a little humbug at all, if you will only send the picture. PLEASE, Livy.

This isn't a *letter*, Livy—I have already written up everything I knew, tonight, long ago—& so I am simply scribbling this merely to be communing with you & putting my arm about you, as it were, & looking into your eyes. Forgive.

I must to bed. I ride 20 miles in a cutter to-day, & lecture tonight at Charlotte. Good-bye, & happy dreams, my peerless Livy. I am obeying all your orders strictly, except ~~not~~ in the matter of sitting up late—that one I *do* overstep just a mere trifle, but nothing to signify.

Devotedly,

Saml. L. C.

I wrote a letter to your father & mother an hour ago—or so.

Miss Olivia L. Langdon

Present.

[*docketed by OLL:*] 16th

To Olivia L. Langdon
27 December 1868 • Tecumseh, Mich.
(MS: CU-MARK)

Tecumseh, Dec. 27.

I got your letter at Charlotte, my dear, dear Livy, & I rather hoped to get one here, but it did not come. However, if one *should* come, it will be mailed to me at Cleveland. I find I shall be there at noon to-morrow, which is much sooner than I expected. [*in margin:* It is too bad, Livy, that I have to write so much in pencil.][1]

Yes, Livy, I *do* like to have you give me synopses of Mr Beecher's sermons—& you need not suppose that I read them over once & then lay them aside for good, for I do not. I read ~~&~~ them over & over again & try to profit by them.[2] I got the printed sermon also, & have read that several times.~~, also.~~ Everything convicts me—so does this sermon. "A Christian is a fruit-bearer~~,~~—a moral man is a vine that does not bear fruit." That is me, exactly. *I* do not swear, I do not steal, I do not murder, I do not drink. My "whole life is *not*." *I* am "*not* all over."[3] "Piety is the right performance of a common duty, *as well as the experience of a special moral emotion*."[4] I now perform all my duties as well as I can, but see what I lack!—I lack the *chief* ingredient of piety—for I lack (almost always) the "special moral emotion"—that inner sense which tells me that what I do I am doing *for love* of the Savior. I *can* be a Chirstian—I *shall* be a Christian—but when I feel as I feel to-day, it seems a far journey away. I would be discouraged, but for the reflection that one learns a foreign language only by patient study, not by a single lesson; we cannot cross the Continent at a stride, we cannot bridge the sea with a shingle. Therefore, why should I spurn the Savior for a lifetime & then hope to gain pardon save through long toil & striving & supplication? I will *not* be discouraged. I am glad you marked the sermon, Livy—why didn't ~~p~~ you put in the margin what you & your father & mother *said* about the prominent passages? Yes, my little dear, I *shall* be glad to receive the Plymouth Pulpit as often as you will send it—& I *shan't* care to have an opinion of my own in the matter, notwithstanding your quiet sarcasm upon yourself, but shall certainly like what you like—in jest or earnest you are right about *that*. Mark them, Livy.

As to the social drinking, give yourself no more uneasiness about it, O, my loved, my honored, my darling little Mentor!—for it had bothered my conscience so much ever since it seemed to me that day in the drawing-room that you gave your consent to it *with a little reluctance*, that I have hardly taken a glass of ale or wine since but it seemed to me your kind eyes were upon me with a sort of gentle reproach in them—& so—well, I don't drink *anything*, now, dear, & so your darling noble old heart has been troubling itself all ~~to no~~ for nothing! But please don't let my *motive* distress you, Livy. You know the child must crawl before it walks—& I must do right for love of you while I am in the infancy of Christianity; & then I can do right for love of the Savior when I shall have gotten my growth. And especially don't give *this* instance any ~~p~~ importance, for it is *no sacrifice*, because I have not now, & *never had*, any love for any kind of liquors, & not even a ~~passing~~ passable *liking* for ~~an~~ any but champagne & ale, & only for these *at intervals*. I ought to be ever so grateful to you, Livy, for your brave confidence in me, & for the consideration you show for me in simply *suggesting* reforms when you could be such an absolute little tyrant if you chose. I do not know of anything I could refuse to do if you wanted it done. I am reasonably afraid that you'll stop me from smoking, some day, but if ever you do, you will do it with such a happy grace that I shall be swindled into the notion that I didn't *want* to smoke any more, anyhow!

I shall try to recollect to enclose the little Manual in this. I studied it carefully, & *it* convicts me, in some two or three of its clauses.[5] I will talk with you about them when I see you, for it would be hard to explain the whole matter by letter.

Livy, I do wish you were here, for it is very lonely in this solemn room on this solemn cloudy Sabbath. If I could only take you to my heart, now, & talk to you & hear your voice, I could want no other company, no other music. *This* letter of yours isn't cold, Livy—it couldn't be, when you say that the better you know me the better you love me. That is pleasant to hear from your lips. I do hope you may not cease to be able to speak those words until you shall have given me *all* your love & so shall have no more to give. I do LOVE you, Livy! And don't you worry because you do not love me as well as I love you, Livy. It isn't strange at all, that you can't do it—because I am not as lovable as you are—I lack a great deal of being as lovable as you, Livy. It makes me glad to hear of Mr Langdon saying he loves me better the better he knows me—for it seems to me that I could not love him, or Mrs. Langdon or

Mrs. Fairbanks more than I do, or reverence them more deeply. It ~~was~~ ‸is‸ such a pity we did not persuade your father & mother to stay longer with us in the drawing-room that day, Livy—it touches me yet when I remember that Mrs. Langdon looked, as she went out at the door, as if she thought she had been intruding. We shall not let either of them ever think such a thing again, Livy.

Of course I now think of many things that ought to have been said when I was with you, dear, but couldn't think of them then. I think I shall have to make out a *list*, against my next visit. Some of them I *did* think of—they were confessions—but they seemed of such trifling import that it appeared not worth while to waste priceless time upon them—& I think so yet. Still, I shall always be ready & willing to confess *anything* & *everything* to you, Livy, that you could possibly wish to know.

The supper bell has rung. Tomorrow I shall see mother Fairbanks! Hip—hip—hurrah! I am getting all in a fidget, now, as the time approaches. We'll have a royal jollification to-morrow night‸.‸ ¶ I'll kiss little Mollie as a substitute for you, Livy, because she said privately to her mother, in her innocent way, "I do *love* Mr. Clemens!" And do you appreciate what it is to have a child like that, love you? Do you know her? Just listen. She used to have a green silk dress which she was very proud of, & was always glad when Sunday came, so she could wear it to church. But on one occasion she was to go to church with a little guest of hers, & to the amazement of everybody she steadily refused to wear anything but her every-day dress—& she would give no explanation. But at night, in privacy, she told her mother it was because the other little girl had no fine dress, & she didn't want to make her feel badly!

She ~~bo~~ didn't *boast* of this thing; she simply *explained* her conduct to her mother. Livy, it was the noblest thing I ever knew a child to do. Who shall say the angels did not visit her bedside that night? ¶ How many men & women are there who have in them so grand a spirit of magnanimity as this little Mollie Fairbanks showed?

Good bye, darling—over these leagues of weary distance I cast a loving kiss. Sam*l*. L C.

[*letter docketed in ink by OLL:*] 17th

[1] The entire letter was written in pencil.

[2] Olivia might have synopsized Henry Ward Beecher's sermons from any of several sources, such as the two-volume selection published in early November

by Harper and Brothers (advertisement, New York *Evening Post*, 7 Nov 68, 2; Henry Ward Beecher 1868).

[3]Although the actual "printed sermon" that Olivia sent has been lost, Clemens's quotations show that it was the first number of the new weekly *Plymouth Pulpit*, which on 26 September had begun to print each of Beecher's sermons "in neat pamphlet form," six days after its delivery, as "reported by Mr. T. J. Ellinwood, who has been the authorized reporter at Plymouth Church for the last ten years" ("Literary," New York *Evening Post*, 24 Sept 68, 2; "New Publications," New York *Times*, 26 Sept 68, 5). The first issue contained Beecher's sermon of 20 September—"The Duty of Using One's Life for Others"—in which he said:

> Contrast with this idea, also, the life of moral men who think they are good, and good enough, because they simply avoid evil. A moral man, as distinguished from a Christian man, is one who is negative. A Christian is one who is positive. A Christian is a fruit-bearer. A moral man is a vine that does not bear fruit. . . . A Christian man is one that develops graces into positivity. He acts out of himself and upon others. . . . A moral man, I repeat, is negative. He does *not* swear, and he does *not* steal, and he does *not* murder, and he does *not* get drunk, and his whole life is *not*. His law is, "Thou shalt *not*," and, "Thou shalt *not*," and, "Thou shalt *not*." He is *not* all over, and nothing more! (Henry Ward Beecher 1869, 10)

[4]Clemens quoted from an earlier passage in the same sermon:

> Now, he who devotes the active hours of his life to those spheres to which Providence calls men, is really giving himself for others. It is not necessary that a man should go apart from life in order to do the work of piety. Piety is the right performance of a common duty, as well as the experience of a special moral emotion. Too often men think that religion, like music, is something that belongs to a department which is exceptional and quite outside of the ordinary routines of life. We leave religion to go to our work and duty. We forsake work and duty, at appropriate periods and pauses, to go back to religion. But a better conception of religion is, that it is the conduct of a man's disposition *in* work *by* work. (Henry Ward Beecher 1869, 5)

[5]Possibly the *Manual of the Plymouth Church, Brooklyn, N.Y.* (New York: Baker and Godwin, 1867). Its eighty-one pages included the "Articles of Faith" and "Covenant with the Church" which prospective church members were expected to embrace. On the other hand, Clemens may have been referring to *The Confession of Faith, Covenant, Ecclesiastical Principles, Forms of Admission, Etc.*, a briefer booklet that Plymouth Church issued periodically—or even to a similar publication from Thomas K. Beecher's Park Congregational Church in Elmira.

To Jervis Langdon
29 December 1868 • Cleveland, Ohio

(MS facsimile: Davis)

Cleveland, Dec. 29.

Dear Mr. Langdon

I wrote to the Metropolitan Hotel for your letter (of Dec. 8,) & it overtook me two or three days ago at Charlotte, Mich.[1] I will not deny that the first paragraph hurt me a little—hurt me a good deal—for when you speak of what I said of the drawing-room, I see that you mistook the harmless overflow of a happy frame of mind for criminal frivolity. This is a little unjust—for although what I said may have been unbecoming, it surely was no worse. The subject of the drawing-room cannot be more serious to you than it is to me. But I accept the rebuke, freely & without offer of defence, & am as sorry I offended as if I had *intended* offense.

All the rest of your letter is just as it should be. The language is as plain as ever language was in the world, but I like it all the better for that. I don't like to mince matters myself or have them minced for me. I think I am safely past that tender age when one cannot take his food save that it be masticated for him beforehand~~,~~—& I would much ~~pefer~~ ‸prefer‸ to suffer from the clean incision of an honest lancet than from a sweetened poison. Therefore it is even as you say: I have ‸“too much good sense” to blame you for that part of ~~your~~ ‸the‸ letter. Plain speaking ~~only increases one's esteem & respect for the speaker.~~ ‸does not hurt one.‸

I am not hurrying my love—it is my love that is hurrying *me*—& surely no one is better able to comprehend that than you. I fancy that Mrs. Langdon was the counter part of her daughter at the age of twenty=three—& so I refer you to the past, for explanation & for pardon of my conduct. At your time of life, & being, like you, the object of an assured regard, I shall be able to ~~talk~~ urge moderation upon younger people, & shall do it relentlessly—but now I feel a larger charity for such. Your heart is big enough to feel all the force of that remark~~,~~—& so believing, you will not be surprised to find me thus boldly knocking at it. It does not seem to me that I am otherwise than moderate—it cannot seem so from my point of view—& so while I continue as moderate as I am now & have been, I think it is fair to hope that you will not turn away from me your countenance, or deny me your friendly toleration, even though it be under a mild protest.

It is my desire as truly as yours, that sufficient time shall elapse to show you, beyond all possible question, what I *have been, what I am*, & what I am *likely to be*. Otherwise you could not be satisfied with me, nor I with myself. I think that much of my conduct on the Pacific Coast was not of a character to recommend me to the respectful regard of a high eastern civilization, but it was not considered blameworthy there, perhaps. We go according to our lights. I was just what Charlie would have been, similarly circumstanced, & deprived of home influences. I think all my references can say I never did anything mean, false or criminal.

They can say that the same doors that were open to me seven years ago are open to me yet; that *all* the friends I made in seven years, are still my friends; that wherever I have been I can go again—& enter in the light of day & hold my head up; that I never deceived or defrauded anybody, & don't owe a cent. And they can say that I attended to my business with due diligence, & made my own living, & never asked anybody to help me do it, either. All the rest they can say about me will be *bad*. I can tell the whole story myself, without mincing it, & will if they refuse.[2]

I wish to add to the references I gave Mrs. Langdon, the following: Hon. J. Neely Johnson, Carson City, Nevada. He was ~~one~~ Governor of California some ten years ago, & is now Chief Justice of the Supreme Court of Nevada, if my memory serves me. He has known me about seven years—he & his wife—we were next door neighbors—& his house~~h~~ is always my home, now-a-days when I am in Carson, & has been for a year or two past.[3] Then there is the present Governor of Nevada, H. G. Blaisdel—he has known me four or five years—don't know whether he has known any good of me or not. He is a thoroughly pure & upright man, & a most excellent.[4] And I give you, also, Joseph T. Goodman (reared in Elmira, I believe,) proprietor & chief editor of the "Daily Enterprise," Virginia City, Nevada & C. A. V. Putnam, his ~~N~~ news= editor—the first of whom has known me six years (I was his ~~c~~‸City editor 3 years without losing a day,) ‸& the latter five years, &‸ neither of whom would say a damaging word against me for love or money or hesitate to throttle anybody else who ventured to do it—& so you will perceive at once that they are not the ~~best people~~ most promising sources to refer you to for information. Those ~~t~~ two fellows are just the salt of the earth, in my estimation.[5] Now, however, being appealed to seriously, in so grave a matter as this, it is very possible—even likely—that they would override their ancient friendship for me, & speak the whole truth. I shall not write to them—or to any of these references, of course—& so their testimony will be unbiased. Then there is A. J. Marsh, ‸who is a‸ Phonographic Reporter, in San Francisco, my close friend for five or six years,—he & his wife & family are utterly without reproach, & would be in *any* community.[6] And Frank Gross & wife (of the San Francisco "Bulletin"[)]—& Sam Williams & Rev. Mr. Bartlett of the same editorial staff,‸—the two latter don't know me so *intimately* as the other.‸[7] There is Lewis Leland[8] (I think he is proprietor of the Metropolitan Hotel in New York—& if he is not now he soon is to be, if I understand the matter rightly.) He has known me intimately for 3 or 4 years—I boarded at his Occidental Hotel 2 or 3 years—& he will surely know my general character & standing in San Francisco. And R. B. Swain & family, San Francisco. Mr. Swain is Superintendent of the U.S. Mint, & is also one of the "merchant princes"‸ there. He is ~~a man~~ the Schuyler Colfax of the Pacific Coast—being regarded by high & low, rich & poor, Tom, Dick & Harry, as a man against whose pure ~~na~~ reputation *nothing* can be said. He don't know much about me, ‸*himself*‸ maybe, though ~~I~~ we were pretty intimate latterly, but he ought to know a good deal through his Secretary Frank B. Harte, (editor of the Overland Monthly & ~~one of~~ the finest writer~~s~~ out there) for *we* have been very intimate for several years. This morning I received from Mr. Swain a letter which has been following me some time. I think a great deal of him, else I wouldn't write to him. You have no antipathy to thoroughly good men, & so I beg that you will give his picture a place on the mantelpiece.[9]

As to what I am *going to be*, henceforth, it is a thing which must be *proven* & established. I am upon the right path—I shall succeed, I hope. Men as lost as I, have found a Savior, & why not I? I have hope—an earnest hope—a long-lived hope.

I wrote you & Mrs. Langdon a letter from Lansing, which will offend again, I fear—& yet no harm was meant, no undue levity, no disrespect, no lack of reverence. The intent was blameless—& it is the *intent*, & not the *act* that should be judged, after all. Even men who take life are judged by this rule only.

They say the desire is so general, here, to have this public distressed again by a repetition of my lecture, that Mr. Fairbanks offers me $150 to repeat it ~~in~~ the third week in January, & Mrs. Fairbanks offers to let me repeat it for the benefit of the Orphan's Home ~~at~~ ~~(of which~~ at a dollar a head & pay me nothing for it. I have accepted the latter proposition.[10] I have received a second invitation from the Association I lectured for in Pittsburgh to come there & talk again. They have gotten up some little feeling there because of an unjust & angry criticism upon the lecture ~~which~~ ‸(it‸ appeared in the "Dispatch,")‸ & ‸I think maybe‸ that is the cause of these calls. I shall try to go, though really I am not disposed to quarrel with the Dispatch's opinion or make myself ~~sorrowful~~ ~~ful~~ ‸sad‸ about it, either. I always liked to express my opinions ~~rather~~ freely in print, & I suppose the Dispatch people have a taste that runs in a similar direction.[11]

The folks here are all well, & we are having a very pleasant time of it. I shall lecture in Akron to-morrow night, & then return here & spend New Year's.

I like the Herald ~~better~~ ~~bet~~ as an anchorage for me, better than any paper in the Union—its location, politics, present business & prospects, all are suitable. Fairbanks says the concern (with its lot & building,) inventories $212,000; its earnings were ~~$22,000~~ ‸$42,000‸ for the past year, which is a good percentage for such safe & lasting property as a newspaper. He owns half & the Benedicts the other half. He wants me in very much—wants me to buy an eighth from the Benedicts, so that the control would rests with him when I gave my vote so—~~& said~~ price about $25,000. He says if I can get it he will be my security until I can pay it all by the labor of my tongue & hands, & that I shall not be hurried. That suits me, just exactly. It couldn't be better. ~~I don't like~~ He says the salaries of himself & the elder Benedict are $3,000—& mine would be $3,000. Yet he would *hire* me & pay me more. I don't understand these things. It is a slim salary—& so I should *have* to make the paper make money, to save myself. However, I shall see Mr. Benedict & try to make the arrangement.[12]

I believe I have nothing further to say, except to ask pardon for past offenses against yourself, they ~~being~~ having been heedless, & not deliberate; & that you will

{Mrs. Fairbanks has just come in & she says: "For shame! cut that letter short—do you want to wear out what endurance the poor man has left after his siege of illness?" This is a woman, Sir, whose commands are not to be trifled with,—& so I desist.}

With reverent love & respect
I am
Sincerely
Sam[l]. L. Clemens

[*on back of letter as folded:*] J. Langdon Esq | Present.

[1]Clemens arrived and lectured in Charlotte on Christmas, leaving for Tecumseh, Michigan, the next day. Langdon's 8 December letter, which evidently replied to his of 2 December, has not been found.

[2]In 1906 Clemens recalled a "private talk" with Langdon, which must have occurred during his Elmira visit ending on 27 November:

Mr. Langdon called my attention to something I had already noticed—which was that I was an almost entirely unknown person; that no one around about knew me except Charley, and he was too young to be a reliable judge of men; that I was from the other side of the continent, and that only those people out there would be able to furnish me a character, in case I had one—so he asked me for references. I furnished them, and he said we would now suspend our industries and I could go away and wait until he could write to those people and get answers. (AD, 14 Feb 1906, CU-MARK, in *MTA*, 2:109–10)

Clemens further recalled that he had referred Langdon to "six prominent men, among them two clergymen (these were all San Franciscans), and he himself had written to a bank cashier who had in earlier years been a Sunday school superintendent in Elmira and well known to Mr. Langdon" (in *MTA*, 2:110). Langdon wrote to James S. Hutchinson, then a cashier for the San Francisco banking firm of Sather and Company, who "had formerly been in Langdon's employ in Elmira," according to a relative, asking him to interview Clemens's six references (Hutchinson, 36; Langley 1868, 295, 487). Only two of these references have been identified: the Reverend Horatio Stebbins and the Reverend Charles Wadsworth, with both of whom Clemens felt he was on good terms. Hutchinson did in fact call on Stebbins, and he spoke to one of Wadsworth's deacons; he may also have tried to contact Wadsworth himself (SLC to Charles Warren Stoddard, 25 Aug 69, Freeman and Co., lot 68).

[3] John Neely Johnson (1825–72), originally from Indiana, was admitted to the Iowa bar at the age of twenty-one; he went to California in 1849, where within a year he was elected city attorney of Sacramento. In 1855 he was nominated for governor by the American (Know-Nothing) Party, elected, and served a two-year term (1856–58). In 1860 he moved to Carson City, where he practiced law. There, in 1861, he met Orion and Samuel Clemens, who in late 1862 became his neighbors (and tenants) on Curry Street. In 1851 Johnson married Mary Zabriskie (b. 1833 or 1834), with whom he had a son, William, and then a daughter, now about twelve years old. He served as a delegate from Ormsby County to the 1863 and 1864 Nevada constitutional conventions, and was elected president of the latter. In May 1867 Governor Henry G. Blasdel (see note 4) appointed Johnson to serve as an associate justice of the Nevada Supreme Court, in place of Cornelius M. Brosnan, deceased. On 3 November Johnson was elected for the remaining two years of Brosnan's original six-year term, during which Brosnan had been scheduled, according to the Nevada State Constitution (article 6, section 3), to serve as chief justice. Johnson may have assumed that he would fill that position as well, but it went instead to former Chief Justice James F. Lewis. Johnson remained on the bench until the end of his term in January 1871, but did not run for re-election and was never chief justice. Like Clemens, he was a Mason. Clemens apparently stayed with the Johnsons while lecturing in Carson City in November 1866 and late April 1868 (SLC to OC, 17 May 67, *L1*, 213; OC 1862–63, item 19; Angel, 81, 86, 87n, 90, 336, 679; Melendy and Gilbert, 66–79; *Carson City Census*, 262; "Utah," Virginia City *Territorial Enterprise*, 1 Sept 72, 3; "Obituary," Salt Lake City *Tribune*, 2 Sept 72, 1; "Funeral of Governor Johnson," Salt Lake City *Herald*, 3 Sept 72, 3; Carson City *Appeal:* "The Vacancy on the Supreme Bench," 24 Apr 67, 2; "The Vacant Judg[e]ship Fitly Filled," 12 May 67, 2; "National Union Republican Nominations," 17 Sept 68, 2; "Hon. H. O. Beatty" and "Appointed to the Supreme Bench," 10 Nov 68, 2 and 3).

[4] Henry Goode Blasdel (1825–1900), also from Indiana, went to California in 1852 and to Virginia City in 1860, "where he engaged successfully in mining and in the reduction of gold and silver ores, and was the superintendent of the celebrated Potosi, Hale and Norcross mines." He became the state of Nevada's first governor in 1864, holding that office through 1870. Blasdel was also a Mason and

"a strong advocate of total abstinence" (*NCAB*, 2:200; *L1*, 317 n. 1). Both Blasdel and Johnson were among the prominent citizens of Carson who invited Clemens to lecture there in 1866, saying in part that the "people of Carson City . . . have none other than the most kindly remembrances of you" (SLC to Abraham V. Z. Curry and others, 1 Nov 66, and SLC to Henry G. Blasdel and others, 1 Nov 66, *L1*, 363–64).

5 Goodman was born in Masonville, New York, about one hundred miles east of Elmira. Clemens claimed in 1906 that he had not given Goodman's name until well after Langdon had heard from his other references, reasoning that his old and close friend would not have offered "unprejudiced testimony" (Emrich, 263; AD, 14 Feb 1906, CU-MARK, in *MTA*, 2:111). This letter shows, however, that even before Langdon could receive replies from the "six prominent men" named in November, Clemens sought to mitigate the result with evidence from ten friendly references. Charles A. V. Putnam (b. 1823 or 1824), a printer originally from Maine, moved to the West in 1852. He had been Joseph Goodman's "telegraph, paragraph and scissoring editor" on the Virginia City *Territorial Enterprise* since May 1863. The recent discovery of rich mineral deposits in the White Pine district of Lander County would soon prompt him to leave Virginia City temporarily in order to establish a newspaper in the region (*Virginia City Census*, 119; Rasmussen, 4:51; Doten, 3:2227–28; *ET&S1*, 457; Angel, 330, 649). Clemens's 1866 characterization of Putnam in "Ministerial Change" was, if anything, even more emphatic about his loyalty to his friends (see SLC 1866a).

6 Andrew Jackson Marsh (1826–83) was born in Binghamton, New York. He served in the Mexican War and worked for the New York *Herald* before moving to California in 1860. In 1861–62 he wrote correspondence from Carson City for the Sacramento *Union* (see Marsh 1972). Marsh and Clemens had been acquainted since at least 1862, and had collaborated in reporting the 1863 Nevada Constitutional Convention. Marsh was now the shorthand reporter for the Fifteenth District Court in San Francisco; nothing is known about his family (Marsh, Clemens, and Bowman, 462 n. 2 and passim; SLC to OC, 23 July 62, *L1*, 229; Langley 1868, 365, 735).

7 Frank Wells Gross (1839–86) was born in Illinois and reared in Massachusetts, moving to San Francisco with his father in 1856. He joined the staff of the San Francisco *Evening Bulletin* in 1860, eventually serving as its local editor; he had recently left that position and was now a reporter for the *Morning Call*. Gross and his wife (who is not further identified) had one daughter. Like Johnson and Blasdel, he was a Mason ("Death of Frank W. Gross," San Francisco *Morning Call*, 6 Dec 86, 3; "Biographies of Some of the Candidates," San Francisco *Alta California*, 20 June 79, 1; San Francisco City and County 1867, s.v. "Gross, Frank Wells"; Langley 1868, 251). Samuel Williams, the *Bulletin*'s drama and music critic, has been previously identified (14 Apr 68 to Williams, n. 1). William Chauncey Bartlett (1818–1907) was born in Connecticut but as a young man went to Ohio, where in the early 1850s he practiced law. In 1860 he moved to California and entered the ministry, serving as pastor of the First Congregational Church in Santa Cruz in 1860–64. He became a correspondent for the *Bulletin* in about 1867 and soon thereafter accepted an editorial position; like Williams, he was also a contributor to Harte's *Overland Monthly* ("Veteran Journalist Answers Final Call," San Francisco *Call*, 9 Dec 1907, 4; "Dr. William C. Bartlett,

Famous Pioneer, Expires," Oakland *Tribune*, 9 Dec 1907, 3; Langley 1868, 83; Robinson et al., 44–45).

[8] Leland is identified in 19 and 20 Dec 68 to OLL, n. 7.

[9] Robert Bunker Swain (1822–72) was born in Massachusetts and went to California in 1855. From 1863 to 1869 he was superintendent of the United States branch mint in San Francisco, as well as head of R. B. Swain and Company, commission merchants and insurance agents. He and his wife, the former Clara Ann Fillmore, had one son. Swain had named Bret Harte his secretary, a sinecure that by 1868 paid $270 per month. Their offices were in the *Call* building on Commercial Street. Clemens had known and worked with Harte on the *Californian* long before he became editor of the *Overland Monthly*. His opinion of Harte's literary talents was much the same in 1866: see SLC to JLC and PAM, 20 Jan 66, *L1*, 328 (Langley 1868, 531; *CofC*, 12, 227–28; O'Connor, 68–69, 90; Bartlett 1898, 41; Brooks 1898, 99).

[10] Clemens's lecture at Case Hall in Cleveland on 22 January 1869 netted $564 for the Cleveland Orphan Asylum ("Cleveland Orphan Asylum," Cleveland *Herald*, 17 Feb 69, 3).

[11] See 20 Nov 68 to JLC and family, n. 2.

[12] The Cleveland *Herald*, a small Republican daily housed in a four-story building on Bank Street, was run by Fairbanks, Benedict, and Company. Abel Fairbanks had, since 1850, owned the paper jointly with various partners, currently father and son George A. and George S. Benedict (1812–76, 1841–71). In 1868 the *Herald* claimed a daily circulation of 7,500 (Rowell, 86; Rose, 231–32, 242; "George H. Benedict," New York *Times*, 15 May 76, 5; "A Railway Horror," New York *Tribune*, 8 Feb 71, 1; "The Railroad Horror," Buffalo *Express*, 10 Feb 71, 2).

To Olivia L. Langdon
30 December 1868 • Cleveland, Ohio
(MS: CU-MARK)

[*postscript on back of page 1, in pencil:*]

‸Dec. 30—Just got your letter & sketch —thank you, dear.‸

Cleveland, Dec. 30. AM.

My dearest Livy, I feel like drawing near you & having your counsel & encouragement, this morning, for I need it. I have passed through another of those seasons when religion seems‸~~e~~ far away & well-nigh unattainable, & when one feels grimly like jesting with holy things & giving up in despair. Why *is* it that godliness flies me? Why is it that prayer seems so unavailing & all my searching & seeking a mockery? I study the ~~t~~Testament every night, I read anything touching upon religion that comes in my way, I keep myself wholly from wrong-doing—but sometimes a chilly apathy comes upon me at last. Last night, with a great effort, I compelled myself to do a disagreeable thing & make a sacrifice of my comfort to the comfort of others because I desired to do right. I thought it was a triumph over selfishness, & felt the better for it for a while, but it is all gone now that I perceive that I did not do right for the *love* of it, & so the *spirit* of the whole thing was wrong at last. I wish you were here to help me, for you are as strong in these things as I am weak & bewildered.

I wrote your father yesterday in answer to his letter about making haste slowly—but I wish I hadn't written him that Christmas letter from Lansing, for I fear he does not know me as well as you do, Livy, & I am apt to pain him with my heedless way of writing, though you know I don't mean any harm. I love him too well & reverence him too much to pain him wantonly.

No letter to-day, dear, none yesterday, none the day before. It seems an age, Livy. I fully expect one tomorrow—*with the picture*—& have written Dayton to see if perchance you have sent a letter there. How my heart goes out to you this day! It seems to me that I could walk fifty miles to see you. Seems!—I *know* I could. You are a little bit of a piece of humanity—there isn't anything of you, hardly—~~h~~ scarcely an armful—but what there is is unspeakably precious, Livy!

Mrs. Fairbanks has been telling me something I like. She says one rational way of seeking Christ is to learn to put yourself out of sight when you are meditating an act, & consider how to do it for the comfort & benefit of others, & so take to itself a Christ-like spirit—& that bye & bye when one has made this a habit & it has become a *pleasure* to consider the weal of others first, that religion will not then be far away. ‸It is like Henry Ward's sermon—send some more, Livy, dear.‸[1] It does not seem that that should be impossible—not at all *impossible*—& so I will make the trial. There are many that are good & true adding their prayers to mine—mine are not neglected on *any* day—& why should not I succeed, in time? Pray for me, Livy—but I know that you will & that you do. I shall be grateful—I *am* grateful.

Livy, one thing has been in my mind ever since I saw Miss Nye in Detroit. It is to ~~ur~~ beg you not to get up so soon in the morning. This is serious, Livy, & sensible. She says you are always sleepy when they call you for breakfast—& do not you know, dear, that the *morning* sleep is by far the most strengthening of all? It is, indeed. Sleep till you have no more *desire* to sleep, & you will be strong. You are wakeful at two in the morning, & you need to sleep late to make up for it. Livy, you who most need rest & renewing sleep of all the household, sleep less than any of the others. You make a sacrifice of yourself—you get up not because you want to, but because you know that ‸to the others‸ the breakfast would lose half its charm, its cheer, its sunshine ~~if your~~ if your dear face were absent—but Livy, *it isn't right*. They don't know that you rise sleepy, or they wouldn't let you do it. Please think of this, won't you, & comply with my petition? *Do*, Livy.

The prettiest & in many ways the most attractive young lady that graced the reception given by Mrs Fairbanks for Charlie & I was dreadfully, perhaps fatally, burned, lately, by ~~the~~ a gas explosion in her father's house. I remember her particularly, because I took her out to supper, & was more drawn to her ~~during~~ than to the others, during the evening, by the gentleness of her manners. Her hands are burned off, almost entirely, & her face is disfigured to ghastliness, it is said. It is terrible.[2]

You may have heard, by this time, that little Mollie Fairbanks broke her wrist while skating, some days ago. An awkward man ran against her, & as she fell she tried to save herself by throwing out her arm. Hence the disaster. She bears it bravely, & is getting on well.

Livy, it is jolly to be here. I was starving to hear somebody speak your name. And now I can talk to Mrs. Fairbanks as much as I please about you. She read ‸to me‸ Mrs. Langdon's letter[3]—it could have been a severe one, easily enough, but it wasn't. It was the reverse. We have talked a deal about Charlie, & Mrs. F., you may be sure, is glad to hear of his satisfaction in his new business, & of his ~~re~~ improved health & his safe passage over the awful chasm that lay between his love for Ida & his father's knowledge of it.[4] She spoke, with ~~the~~ a proud humidity in her eyes, of how Charlie used to leave repentant little notes in her stateroom when he had been rebellious. She ~~say,~~ says he is the best of all boys to repent, because he does it with such a ~~conquering~~ winning grace & with such hearty earnestness withal. I guess we have canvassed & complimented the family pretty thoroughly. I arrived just in time to keep this good woman from publishing my Christmas letter to her. However, since she only wants to print an extract or two because their reverent spirit is more to my credit than my customary productions, we'll let her have her way.[5]

Livy, I guess that after all I shall become interested in this "Herald," & then you shall be MANAGING EDITOR—that is to say, you'll manage the editor. I think we'll live in Clevland, Livy—& then we'll persuade Mr. Langdon to come & live in Euclid Avenue, so that we can have a ~~goo~~ place to go to & get a *good* dinner occasionally when we have got so hungry we can't stand it any longer. But I don't think *we'll* live in the Avenue yet a while, Livy—we'll take a back seat with Mrs. Fairbanks, in St. Clair street.[6] But, then, what of it?—it will be a *pleasant* back seat, *won't* it? It couldn't well be otherwise, with you there.

Solon Severance is coming early with a buggy, ~~n~~ New Year's, & we are going to make calls all day long. He knows everybody—& we are going as a Temperance Phalanx, to shed a beneficent influence far & wide ~~of~~ ‸over‸ this town! Mrs. F. says that if Solon is in a good flow of spirits that day, he & I will make a rare team & not be very unwelcome anywhere. She thinks we'll relieve the dull stupidity of New Year formalities to some extent, & that ~~we'll be~~ our progress through the city will not pass unnoticed. That is kind. I do *wish* Charlie were here to go with us. We mean to have *fun*—& he would *enjoy* it, too. But don't I wish *you* were here, you Koh-i-Noor! you Golconda! you rival of the sun!—you beautiful, ~~lovable~~ lovable, darling Livy! I kiss your forehead, in deep gratitude to the Giver of all Good, for your priceless love. God bless you, always, Livy.

With loving devotion—

Yours,

Saml. L. C.

Of *course* Mrs. F. sends‸ you her love~~,~~—if she didn't I would cut her acquaintance. P. S. I do LOVE you, Livy!

Miss Olivia L. Langdon | Present. [*docketed by OLL:*] 18th 1868

[1] See 27 Dec 68 to OLL.

[2] Clemens had met and dined with Ella F. Hubby, aged about nineteen, during his and Charles Langdon's September visit to the Fairbankses. She was the younger daughter of Leander M. Hubby, president of the Cleveland, Columbus, and Cincinnati Railroad, whose house in East Cleveland was destroyed by a gas explosion on 5 December. Hubby himself was also badly burned, as were his son

and daughter-in-law ("Terrible Gas Explosion," Cincinnati *Enquirer*, 7 Dec 68, 4; "A Strange Accident," New York *Evening Post*, 10 Dec 68, 4; *Cleveland Census* 1860, 243; *Cleveland Directory* 1868, 31, 193).

[3] Transcribed in 26 and 27 Nov 68 to Fairbanks, n. 3.

[4] See 9 and 10 Dec 68 to OLL, n. 8, and 21 and 23 Dec 68 to OLL, n. 3.

[5] In his 7 (dated 6) January 1869 letter to Mrs. Fairbanks, Clemens asked her to return his letter of 24 and 25 December so that he could "fix the extract for publication & return it to you" (CSmH, in *MTMF*, 63). Shortly thereafter the Cleveland *Herald* published a version of the ninth paragraph (350.13–32), titling it "Mark Twain" and prefacing it with these words: "The following charming extracts which we are permitted to make from the private correspondence of that gentleman, will present him favorably to the public, in another role than that of humorist" ("Mark Twain," Cleveland *Herald*, 16 Jan 69, 4).

[6] Euclid Street (not officially an avenue until 1870) was, by the late 1860s, the wealthiest residential area in Cleveland (Rose, 364, 303). Clemens described it to his *Alta* readers on 22 October:

> It is devoted to dwelling-houses entirely, and it costs you $100,000 to "come in." Therefore none of your poor white trash can live in that street. You have to be redolent of that odor of sanctity which comes with cash. The dwellings are very large, are often pretty pretentious in the matter of architecture, and the grassy and flowery "yards" they stand in are something marvellous. (SLC 1868ooo)

The Fairbanks family had lived on attractive (but less expensive) St. Clair Street since 1857, briefly at number 139 and then at 221 (Boyd, 68; *Cleveland Directory* 1868, 155).

To Olivia L. Langdon
31 December 1868 • Cleveland, Ohio

(MS: CU-MARK)

Cleveland, Dec. 31.

My Dearest Livy—

Your Christmas letter arrived an hour before I went on the stage at ~~k~~ Akron, last night, & of course I captured *that* audience. It was much the largest gathering a lecture had called out since Gough talked there 2 years ago. It couldn't have been larger, for all standing room was filled. Then I went to a ~~pr~~ large private dancing party & ~~danced til~~ stayed till 12:30, though I only danced, 3 times. I made it up talking & making friends. There were a large number of comely & companionable young ladies there, & the young gentlemen were cordial, intelligent & agreeable. Fairbanks went down with me, & we were the guests of a pleasant family who have made us promise to come again in ~~January,~~ February (from Ravenna,)[1] & then the young folks are to give a ~~dancing party~~ party in our honor. I escaped a serenade by a brass band by going to the party, & so escaped making a speech. I liked the friendly idea of the serenade, but wouldn't have enjoyed being so pointedly lionized.

Somehow I missed an appointment at Fort Wayne, Ind., for night before last—I wonder what the assembled multitude said about me? I am requested by telegraph to talk there Jan 2, & shall do it. Did *you* know I was to lecture there? No, you didn't—I forgot to put it in the list. And I missed an appointment at Buffalo, for Dec. 15. Never got the notice until to-day.

I am invited to lecture in Norwalk, Ohio, & shall try to do so—say about the 3^{d} or 4th week in January. If I do, I shall inform you. Mrs. Fairbanks is anxious that I should, for she says it is a~~n~~ most intelligent & in every way excellent community.[2]

Your Christmas letter gave me *so much* pleasure, Livy—& some pain—because *you* had suffered. It breaks my heart to see you suffer, whether it be at the thought of leaving your good home, or for *any* cause. And yet I want you to keep no sorrow of yours from me—I would share your griefs & your heart-aches as well as your joys—I would bear *all* your heart-aches myself, & place myself between you & sorrow, taking all your troubles upon myself & shielding you from all the ills of life, if I only could. But since it is impossible, let me at least suffer *with* you, Livy. Do not grieve, Livy, but look at the pleasant side of the picture, as Mrs. Fairbanks does. She builds airy plans of what she would have come to pass some day—your household living here in "the Avenue"—*her* household—Allie~~s~~ & Charlie Stillwell's household[3]—~~you—~~ & you & I, all in pleasant visiting distance of the Avenue mansion—& poor Charlie & Ida[4] out in the cold!—out in the cold in Elmira till they could be persuaded to come here, also, & shed ~~their li~~ the light of their love & hardware wisdom upon the iron interests of Cleveland. Isn't that pleasanter than being down-hearted & looking upon the dark side, my little darling? *Isn't* it, Livy? Cheer up—cheer up you precious, peerless, matchless girl—~~s~~ & say again you love me half as well as I love you. Such words *will* come reluctantly from that pen of yours, do what I can to coax them—but say them *anyhow*, Livy, for I love to read them as much as you hate to write them! And then I will like the cows in the picture, notwithstanding cows in pictures are my aversion. I will march up to that picture, with my proud arm about you, & give in my leal & true allegiance without a whimper. Oh, I do it *now*, in fancy.

I am so glad you like the "exquisite" book, Livy—& if I only had it now I could mark it as it *should* be marked, I think.[5] I was afraid, before, because I feared you might dislike the book ~~at I~~ after all. It seems to me that every line in it is an inspiration, & so is worthy of a mark. I shall always like that book, now, because it makes you think of *me*. I lost my interest in the marking long before I got through, because I had concluded, you know, that it would not do ~~its~~ to send it to you, & so there was no use in marking it further.

I said to Mrs. Fairbanks, in a long, chatty, private talk, a day or two ago, that you were a wonderful girl, & that it was a frequent puzzle to me why I never had happened to meet another like you—& wondered if you were the *only* one in the world like yourself—faultless—faultless at least as compared to other people (for Livy, I have fallen back to my old heresy, & I *will not* be driven or persuaded again into the hopeless task of seeking faults in you, so there!—don't you say a word—I won't let you!) And she said it was a puzzle to her, too—she had never seen the woman worthy to be called your peer—& that if you had ~~a perf~~ an imperfection it was beyond her ability to find it. And then she said she did not say that because it would give me so much pleasure or because she was blinded by her partiality for you, but because her coolest & most critical judgment justified it. I ~~could~~ wanted to just kiss her all to pieces! But I shan't say another word—~~for I shall~~ ‸lest I‸ convince you that you are a great deal too good for me, & then you won't love me,/, O, most excellent among women, O, loved & honored Livy! Honoria was the dainty phantom of a poet's fancy—but you, her superior, live in the flesh. Don't you say a word, Livy.

That *was* the ~~funiest~~ funniest predicament! Poor Bement!! I could see you both, just as if you had been before me—& how I did enjoy it,/! I only wish I could have been behind the door then. So Mrs. Haycroft suspects, & Ed Bement *knows*. What a muddle in—poor Livy! And my curiosity is interested in the Christmas Dinner at Dr Sayles's. Tell me all about it, now. Did Miss Emma throw out any insinuations? What did *you* say? What did you do? Was Greeves happy?—(it is a grievous name for a happy man.) Tell me all about it, please.[6]

Don't read a word in that Jumping Frog book, Livy—*don't*. I hate to hear that infamous volume mentioned. I would be glad to know that every copy of it was burned, & gone forever. I'll never write another like it.

Tell Mr. Langdon he mustn't come in & interrupt you when you are writing to me. It is highly improper,, is "such conduct as those." I am both grieved & surprised at it. And he keeps doing it, too—this is the third time. Why this will never do!

Tomorrow will be the New Year, Livy—& the gladdest that ever dawned upon me. The Old Year is passing. Hour by hour, minute by minute, its life ebbs away, & faintly & more faintly its waning pulses beat. I see it drift‸ing‸ out to join itself to the dead centuries without regret, & yet with many a friendly adieu, with ~~may~~ many a grateful parting word for what it has done for me, for what it ~~still~~ is doing, for what it is still to do. For it found me a waif, floating at random upon the sea of life, & it leaves me freighted with a good purpose, ‸& blessed with‸ a fair wind, a chart to follow, a port to reach. It found me listless, useless, aimless—it leaves me knighted with ~~nobe~~ noble ambition. It found me well-nigh a skeptic—it leaves me a believer. It found me dead—it leaves me alive. It found me ready to welcome any wind that would blow my vagrant bark abroad, no matter where—it leaves me seeking home & an anchorage, & longing for them. It found me careless of the here & the hereafter—it leaves me with faith in the one & hope for the other. It found ~~me.~~ my heart scorched, bitter, barren, loveless—& leaves it filled with softening, humanizing, elevating love for the dearest girl on earth, Livy—& I, the homeless then, have on this last day of the ~~die~~ dying year, a home that is ~~pre~~ priceless, a refuge from all the cares & ills of life, in that warm heart of yours, & am supremely happy! And so with grateful benediction I give Godspeed to this good Old Year that is passing away. If I forget all else it has done for me I shall still remember that it gave me your love, Livy, & turned my wandering feet toward the straight gate & the narrow way.[7] Welcome the New Year, with its high resolves!, its lofty aspirations! its love, & life, & death! its joy & sorrow! its hidden fates, its awful, curtained mysteries!

Your letter ~~of yesterday (~~received day before yesterday, I have not even touched upon yet, ~~&~~ but still must stop now & go out with the family for the evening. You are a malicious little piece of furniture, Livy, to send me that sketch from the Independent, when you ‸knew‸ perfectly well it would make me cry. *I*'ll fix you for it, Miss. But I liked it, you dear good girl, & am glad you sent it.[8] You might have sent me a kiss, too, I should think, these generous Christmas times/, you selfish thing.

Now, I *must* stop. Severance was in, a moment ago, & ~~call~~ says he will be after me with a buggy promptly at 11 o'clock next year to take me calling—which means *to-morrow*.

Good-bye, Livy, dear—can't take time to read this over & correct it—it wouldn't get in the mail.

Lovingly & *most* lovingly
Saml L. C.

[*letter docketed by OLL:*] *19*th 1868

1 Clemens lectured in Ravenna, Ohio, on 13 February (SLC to Mary Mason Fairbanks, 13 Feb 69, CSmH, in *MTMF*, 72).

2 Clemens lectured in Fort Wayne on 2 January and in Norwalk on 21 January (SLC to OLL, 2 Jan 69, 14 Jan 69, 21 and 22 Jan 69, all in CU-MARK).

3 Alice Fairbanks's engagement to Charles B. Stilwell, a bookkeeper, did not end in marriage, as Clemens told Olivia in a letter of 7 and 8 January 1870 (CU-MARK; *Cleveland Directory* 1867, 261).

4 Ida B. Clark.

5 See 30 Oct 68 to OLL, n. 7.

6 Physician Henry Sayles and his family were neighbors of the Langdons'. His daughter, Emma, a good friend of Olivia's, was engaged (or about to become engaged) to marry Mr. Greeves, whose first name Clemens recorded both as "John" and as "Sanford" (Boyd and Boyd, 142, 188; OLL to Alice B. Hooker, 24 May 69, CtHSD; SLC to OLL, 13 May 69, CU-MARK†; SLC to Olivia Lewis Langdon, 23 June 69, NPV†).

7 Matthew 7:14.

8 Possibly Augusta Larned's "Parson Fielder's Christmas Visit," clipped from the 24 December issue of the New York *Independent*, a Congregationalist weekly. It told the story of a country parson with a large family, too poor to give his "hearty support" to holiday celebrations, awaiting two of his deacons, whom he expects to dismiss him. Instead they bring money and gifts, restoring his faith in the joys of Christmas (Larned, 2). Founded in 1848, the *Independent* advocated abolition and, after the war, temperance and women's suffrage. Henry Ward Beecher had edited it in 1861–63, but it was now edited and published by two prominent members of his congregation, Theodore Tilton and Henry C. Bowen (Mott 1938, 367–74).

Appendixes

Appendix A

Genealogies of the Clemens and Langdon Families

THE CLEMENS family genealogy is documented in *Mark Twain's Letters, Volume 1: 1853–1866* (379–81), where it was first published. The Langdon family genealogy, first published here, draws on the following sources.

Documents: Birthday book presented to Eleanor Sayles Langdon by Susan Langdon Crane in 1919, now at the Center for Mark Twain Studies at Quarry Farm, Elmira (confirmation of Jervis Langdon's birthdate); Jervis Langdon, Jr., to Dahlia Armon, 27 Mar 1986, CU-MARK (source of the marriage date of his father and Eleanor Sayles).

Published Sources: Biographical dictionaries (*NCAB, Who Was Who*); a genealogy of the Crane family (Crane, 141); a study of Mark Twain's connection with Elmira, New York (Jerome and Wisbey, 236–37); a history of Chemung County, New York (Towner, 609–17); Thomas K. Beecher's obituary address for Jervis Langdon; and obituaries for: Jervis Langdon (Elmira *Saturday Evening Review*, 13 Aug 70); Ida Clark Langdon (New York *Times*, 17 Dec 1934, 23); Jervis Langdon (Elmira *Star-Gazette*, 17 Dec 1952); Ida Langdon (New York *Times*, 9 Oct 1964, 29); and Eleanor Sayles Langdon (New York *Times*, 16 June 1971, 48).

Clemens Family

John Marshall Clemens
b. 11 Aug 1798
d. 24 Mar 1847

m. 6 May 1823

Jane Lampton
b. 18 June 1803
d. 27 Oct 1890

Orion Clemens
b. 17 July 1825
d. 11 Dec 1897

m. 19 Dec 1854

Mary Eleanor (Mollie) Stotts
b. 4 Apr 1834
d. 15 Jan 1904

Pamela Ann Clemens
b. 13 Sept 1827
d. 31 Aug 1904

m. 20 Sept 1851

William Anderson Moffett
b. 13 July 1816
d. 4 Aug 1865

Pleasant Hannibal Clemens
b. 1828 or 1829
d. aged 3 months

Margaret L. Clemens
b. 31 May 1830
d. 17 Aug 1839

Benjamin L. Clemens
b. 8 June 1832
d. 12 May 1842

SAMUEL LANGHORNE CLEMENS
b. 30 Nov 1835
d. 21 Apr 1910

m. 2 Feb 1870

Olivia Louise (Livy) Langdon
b. 27 Nov 1845
d. 5 June 1904

Henry Clemens
b. 13 July 1838
d. 21 June 1858

Jennie Clemens
b. 14 Sept 1855
d. 1 Feb 1864

Annie E. Moffett
b. 1 July 1852
d. 24 Mar 1950

m. 28 Sept 1875

Charles Luther Webster
b. 24 Sept 1851
d. 26 Apr 1891

- Alice Jane (Jean) Webster
  b. 24 July 1876
  d. 11 June 1916

  m. 7 Sept 1915 — [1 child]

  Glenn Ford McKinney
  b. 15 Feb 1869
  d. 15 Feb 1934

- William Luther Webster
  b. 15 Oct 1878
  d. ? Mar 1945

- Samuel Charles Webster
  b. 8 July 1884
  d. 24 Mar 1962

  m. 1920?

  Doris Webb
  b. ?
  d. 9 July 1967

Samuel Erasmus Moffett
b. 5 Nov 1860
d. 1 Aug 1908

m. 13 Apr 1887

Mary Emily Mantz
b. 19 Aug 1863
d. 2 Oct 1940

- Anita Moffett
  b. 4 Feb 1891
  d. 26 Mar 1952

- Francis Clemens Moffett
  b. 1 Oct 1895
  d. 4 Mar 1927

Langdon Clemens
b. 7 Nov 1870
d. 2 June 1872

Olivia Susan (Susy) Clemens
b. 19 Mar 1872
d. 18 Aug 1896

Clara Langdon Clemens
b. 8 June 1874
d. 19 Nov 1962

m. 6 Oct 1909

1) Ossip Gabrilowitsch
b. 7 Feb 1878
d. 14 Sept 1936

- Nina Gabrilowitsch
  b. 18 Aug 1910
  d. 16 Jan 1966

m. 11 May 1944

2) Jacques Alexander Samossoud
b. 8 Sept 1894
d. 13 June 1966

Jane Lampton (Jean) Clemens
b. 26 July 1880
d. 24 Dec 1909

Langdon Family

Jervis Langdon
b. 11 Jan 1809
d. 6 Aug 1870

m. 23 July 1832

Olivia Lewis
b. 19 Aug 1810
d. 28 Nov 1890

Susan Langdon (adopted)
b. 18 Feb 1836
d. 29 Aug 1924

m. 7 Dec 1858

Theodore W. Crane
b. 26 Sept 1831
d. 3 July 1889

Olivia Louise (Livy) Langdon
b. 27 Nov 1845
d. 5 June 1904

m. 2 Feb 1870

SAMUEL LANGHORNE CLEMENS
b. 30 Nov 1835
d. 21 Apr 1910

Charles Jervis Langdon
b. 13 Aug 1849
d. 19 Nov 1916

m. 12 Oct 1870

Ida B. Clark
b. 7 Mar 1849
d. 17 Dec 1934

[see Clemens genealogy]

Julia Olivia (Julie) Langdon
b. 21 Nov 1871
d. 15 July 1948

m. 29 Nov 1902 — [2 children]

Edward Eugene Loomis
b. 2 Apr 1864
d. 11 July 1937

Jervis Langdon
b. 26 Jan 1875
d. 16 Dec 1952

m. 2 Oct 1902 — [2 children]

Eleanor Sayles
b. 10 Feb 1878
d. 15 June 1971

Ida Langdon
b. 15 Oct 1880
d. 9 Oct 1964

Appendix B

Prospectus of the Quaker City *Excursion*

TWO EDITIONS of this document are known to be extant. The first appeared on or about 25 January 1867, when a Brooklyn newspaper reprinted its text in full ("Up the Mediterranean," Brooklyn *Union*, 25 Jan 67, 4). The second appeared sometime between 5 April, when the selection of the steamship *Quaker City* was first announced in the press, and 3 June, when Sherman's withdrawal became generally known and the excursion managers ceased to mention him in their newspaper advertisements. The second edition is reproduced here from a copy originally owned by Bloodgood H. Cutter, now in the Mark Twain Memorial (CtHMTH). This particular copy was printed before Sherman withdrew, but distributed afterward, for in the postscript (added in the second edition) one crucial phrase has been carefully deleted by hand: "with Gen. Sherman on board" ("The Mediterranean Excursion," Brooklyn *Eagle*, 5 Apr 67, 2; New York *Evening Post:* "General Sherman Declines a Reception in This City," 31 May 67, 2; advertisements, 1 and 3 June 67, 1, 3).

The second edition was a visibly cruder typesetting than the first, but apart from the added postscript, substantive changes were minor. Mark Twain saw both editions. In his *Alta* letter written on 2 March (SLC 1867r) he clearly referred to the first, which noted that "passages must be taken and paid for on or before April 15th," changed in the second to "passages must be paid for when taken." When, however, he published the text of the prospectus in *The Innocents Abroad* (chapter 1), he reproduced an edited version of the second edition.

EXCURSION

TO THE

Holy Land, Egypt, the Crimea, Greece,

AND

INTERMEDIATE POINTS OF INTEREST.

BROOKLYN, February 1st, 1867.

THE undersigned will make an excursion as above during the coming season, and begs to submit to you the following programme:

A first-class steamer, to be under his own command, and capable of accommodating at least one hundred and fifty cabin passengers, will be selected, in which will be taken a select company, numbering not more than three-fourths of the ship's capacity. There is good reason to believe that this company can be easily made up in this immediate vicinity, of mutual friends and acquaintances.

The steamer will be provided with every necessary comfort, including Library and musical instruments.

An experienced physician will be on board.

Leaving New York about June 1st, a middle and pleasant route will be taken across the Atlantic, and passing through the group of Azores, St. Michael will be reached in about ten days. A day or two will be spent here, enjoying the fruit and wild scenery of these islands, and the voyage continued, and Gibraltar reached in three or four days.

A day will be spent here in looking over the wonderful subterraneous fortifications, permission to visit these galleries being readily obtained.

From Gibraltar, running along the coasts of Spain and France, Marseilles will be reached in three days. Here the steamer will remain eight days, giving ample time not only to look over the city, which was founded 600 years before the Christian era, and its artificial port, the finest of the kind in the Mediterranean, but to visit Paris during the great Exhibition; and the beautiful city of Lyons, lying intermediate, from the heights of which, on a clear day, Mont Blanc and the Alps can be distinctly seen. Passengers who may wish to extend the time at Paris can do so, and, passing down through Switzerland, rejoin the steamer at Genoa.

From Marseilles to Genoa is a run of one night. Ten days will be given here in which the excursionists will have an opportunity to look over this, the " magnificent City of palaces," visit the birthplace of Columbus, twelve miles off, over a beautiful road built by Napoleon I. From this point excursions may be made to Milan, Lakes Como and Maggiore, or to Milan, Verona, famous for its extraordinary fortifications, Padua, and Venice. Or if passengers desire to visit Parma, famous for Correggio's frescoes, and Bologna, they can by rail go on to Florence, and rejoin the steamer at Leghorn, thus spending about three weeks amid the cities most famous for Art in Italy.

From Genoa the run to Leghorn will be made along the coast in one night, and six days appropriated to this point in which to visit Florence; its palaces and galleries; Pisa, its Cathedral and "Leaning Tower," and Lucca and its baths, and Roman Amphitheatre; Florence, the most remote, being distant by rail about sixty miles.

From Leghorn to Naples, (calling at Civiti Vecchia to land any who may prefer to go to Rome from that point,) the distance will be made in about 36 hours; the route will lay along the coast of Italy, close by Caprera, Elba, and Corsica. Arrangements have been made to take on board at Leghorn a pilot for Caprera, and, if practicable, a call will be made there to visit the home of Garibaldi.

Eight days will be spent in Naples, in which Rome, [by rail] Herculaneum, Pompeii, Vesuvius, Virgil's Tomb, and possibly the ruins of Paestum, can be visited, as well as the beautiful surroundings of Naples and its charming bay.

The next point of interest will be Palermo, the most beautiful city of Sicily, which will be reached in one night from Naples. A day will be spent here, and leaving in the evening, the course will be taken towards Athens.

Quaker City excursion prospectus, page 1 of a four-page folder. Mark Twain Memorial, Hartford, Connecticut (CtHMTH).

Skirting along the north coast of Sicily, passing through the group of Æolian Isles, in sight of Stromboli and Vulcania, both active volcanoes, through the Straits of Messina, with "Scylla" on the one hand and "Charybdis" on the other, along the east coast of Sicily, and in sight of Mount Etna, along the south coast of Italy, the west and south coast of Greece, in sight of ancient Crete, up Athens Gulf, and into the Piræus, Athens will be reached in two and a half or three days. Remaining here one day, the Bay of Salamis will be crossed, and a day given to Corinth, whence the voyage will be continued to Constantinople, passing on the way through the Grecian Archipelago, the Dardanelles, the Sea of Marmora, and the mouth of the Golden Horn, and arriving in about 48 hours from Athens.

One day will be devoted to Constantinople, which can be extended to two if desirable, and thence the way taken out through the beautiful Bosphorus, across the Black Sea to Sebastopol and Balaklava, a run of about 24 hours. Here it is proposed to remain two days, visiting the harbors, fortifications, and battle-fields of the Crimea; thence back through the Bosphorus, touching at Constantinople to take in any who may have preferred to remain there; down through the sea of Marmora and Dardanelles, along the coasts of ancient Troy and Lydia in Asia, to Smyrna, which will be reached in two or two and a half days from Constantinople. A stay of two days will be made here, to give opportunity of visiting Ephesus, 50 miles distant by rail.

From Smyrna towards the Holy Land the course will lay through the Grecian Archipelago, close by the Isle of Patmos, along the coast of Asia, ancient Pamphylia, and the Isle of Cyprus, Beirout will be reached in three days. At Beirout time will be given to visit Damascus; after which the steamer will proceed to Joppa, and remain there ten or twelve days.

From Joppa, Jerusalem, the River Jordan, the Sea of Tiberius, Nazareth, Bethany, Bethlehem, and other points of interest in the Holy Land can be visited, and here those who may have preferred to make the journey from Bierout *through* the country passing through Damascus, Galilee, Capernaum, Samaria, and by the River Jordan and Sea of Tiberius, can rejoin the steamer.

Leaving Joppa, the next point of interest to visit will be Alexandria, which will be reached in 24 hours, and a stay made here of four or five days. The ruins of Cæsar's Palace, Pompey's Pillar, Cleopatra's Needle, the Catacombs, and ruins of ancient Alexandria, will be found worth the visit. The journey to Cairo, 130 miles by rail, can be made in a few hours, and from which can be visited the site of ancient Memphis, Joseph's Granaries, and the Pyramids.

From Alexandria the route will be taken homeward, calling at Malta, Cagliari (in Sardinia), and Palma (in Majorca), all magnificent harbors, with charming scenery, and abounding in fruits.

A day will be spent at each place, and leaving Palma in the evening, Valencia in Spain will be reached the next morning. A day or two will be spent in this, the finest city of Spain.

From Valencia, the homeward course will be continued, skirting along the coast of Spain, Alicant, Carthagena, Palos, and Malaga, will be passed but a mile or two distant, and Gibraltar reached in about twenty-four hours.

A stay of one day will be made here, and the voyage continued to Maderia, which will be reached in about three days. Captain Marryatt writes: "I do not know a spot on the globe which so much astonishes and delights upon first arrival as Madeira." A stay of one or two days will be made here, which, if time permits, may be extended, and passing on through the islands, and probably in sight of the Peak of Tenneriffe, a southern track will be taken, and the Atlantic crossed within the latitudes of the Northeast trade winds, where fair winds, mild and pleasant weather, and a smooth sea can always be expected.

A call will be made at Bermuda, which lies directly in this route homeward, and will be reached in about ten days from Maderia, and after spending a day with our friends the Bermudians, the final departure will be made for home, which will be reached in about three days.

It will be seen by the foregoing, in which all reasonable allowance is made, that the excursionists will be in Marseilles about the 20th of June; Naples, 20th July; Constantinople, 6th August; Sebastopol, 10th; Joppa, 20th; Alexandria, September 5th; Gibralter, 25th, and New York, about October 20th to 25th, after an absence of about four and a half to five months. And it is believed that in no other way can so much of interest be seen and enjoyed with so little fatigue and annoyance, and at so small a cost.

Already, applications have been received from parties in Europe wishing to join the Excursion there. The ship will at all times be a home, where the excursionists, if sick, will be surrounded by kind friends, and have all possible comfort and sympathy.

Quaker City excursion prospectus, page 2.

Should contagious sickness exist in any of the ports named in the programme, such ports will be passed, and others of interest substituted.

The price of passage is fixed at $1.250, currency, for each adult passenger. Choice of rooms and of seats at the tables apportioned in the order in which passages are engaged, and no passage considered engaged until ten per cent. of the passage money is deposited with the treasurer.

Passengers can remain on board the steamer, at all ports, if they desire, without additional expense, and all boating at the expense of the ship.

All passages must be paid for when taken, in order that the most perfect arrangements be made for starting at the appointed time.

Applications for passage must be approved by the committee before tickets are issued, and can be made to the undersigned.

Articles of interest or curiosity, procured by the passengers during the voyage, may be brought home in the steamer free of charge.

Five dollars per day, in gold, it is believed, will be a fair calculation to make for *all* travelling expenses on shore, and at the various points where passengers may wish to leave the steamer for days at a time.

The trip can be extended, and route changed, by *unanimous* vote of the passengers.

CHAS. C. DUNCAN,
117 WALL STREET, NEW YORK.

RUFUS R. GRAVES, TREASURER.

COMMITTEE ON APPLICATIONS.

J. T. HOWARD, ESQ., R. R. GRAVES, ESQ., C. C. DUNCAN.

COMMITTEE ON SELECTING STEAMER.

~~CAPT. W. W. STORY, *Surveyor for Board of Underwriters,*~~

C. W. COPELAND, *Consulting Engineer for U. S. and Canada.*

J. T. HOWARD, ESQ.,

C. C. DUNCAN.

P. S.—The very beautiful and substantial Side Wheel Steamship "*Quaker City*" has been chartered for the occasion, and will leave New York June 8th, ~~with Gen. Sherman on board~~. Letters have been issued by the government commending the party to courtesies abroad.

1867
1492
375

Quaker City excursion prospectus, page 3. The calculation of years on the lower left, and the faint notes on the lower right, were inscribed by an unidentified writer or writers. The verso, page 4, is blank.

Appendix C

Passengers and Crew of the Quaker City

THE BASIC source for the following names is "List of PASSENGERS—'Quaker City,'" printed at St. George, Bermuda, the ship's last port of call before reaching New York. One copy of this document, originally owned and annotated by Bloodgood H. Cutter, is at the Mark Twain Memorial (CtHMTH). A photocopy of the second, owned and annotated by William R. Denny, is at the University of Virginia (ViU). Denny wrote across the top of his copy, "A correct list of the passengers of the 'Quaker City' steam ship, in their excursion to the East." Following the list of names, the roster concluded: "—Total 74, or, with the addition of Miss Langdon who joins them here, a total of 75. A few of these, however, left the ship at Alexandria or elsewhere." Miss Langdon was Julia L. Langdon, no relation to Charles (Julia L. Langdon Barber to Clemens, 18 Jan 1907, CU-MARK). She, Stephen and Louisa Griswold, Louis McDonald, and M. A. Serfaty were among those who joined the ship after its first arrival at Gibraltar. The number of passengers departing New York on 8 June was therefore no greater than seventy.

The text of the printed roster has been amended to give full names whenever possible—information derived from various documentary sources cited elsewhere in this volume, as well as from signatures and notations on the passengers' *cartes de visite* collected by Denny (Hirst 1975, 390–412). The names of the crew have been supplied chiefly from "Excursion to the Holy Land," New York *Tribune*, 8 June 67, 8, with spelling corrections from other primary documents.

Passengers

Allen, Anthony Bezenet, New York City
Andrews, Dr. Edward, Albany, N.Y.
Barry, Major James G., St. Louis

Beach, Moses Sperry, Brooklyn
  Beach, Miss Emeline B., Brooklyn
Beckwith, Thomas S., Cleveland
Bell, Mr. and Mrs. R. A. H., Portsmouth, Ohio
Birch, Dr. George Bright, Hannibal, Mo.
Bond, Mr. and Mrs. John W., St. Paul, Minn.
  Bond, Miss Ada, St. Paul, Minn.
Bond, Miss Mary E., Plaquemine, La.
Brown, Dr. Marcus, Circleville, Ohio
  Brown, Miss Kate L., Circleville, Ohio
Bullard, the Reverend Henry, Wayland, Mass.
Chadeyne, Miss Carrie D., Jersey City
Church, William F., Cincinnati
Clemens, Samuel Langhorne, San Francisco
Crane, Dr. Albert, New Orleans
  Crane, Albert, Jr., New Orleans
Crocker, Mr. and Mrs. Timothy D. (Eliza P.), Cleveland
Cutter, Bloodgood Haviland, Little Neck, Long Island
Davis, Joshua William, New York City
Denny, Colonel William Ritenour, Winchester, Va.
Dimon, Mr. and Mrs. Frederick, Norwalk, Conn.
Duncan, Mrs. Charles C. (Hannah T.), Brooklyn
  Duncan, George F., Brooklyn
  Duncan, Henry E., Brooklyn
Fairbanks, Mrs. Abel W. (Mary Mason), Cleveland
Foster, Colonel James Heron, Pittsburgh, Pa.
Gibson, Dr. and Mrs. William (Susan), Jamestown, Pa.
Green, Mrs. J. O., Washington, D.C.
Greenwood, John, Jr., New York City
Greer, Frederick H., Boston
Griswold, Mr. and Mrs. Stephen M. (Louisa M.), Brooklyn
Haldeman, Honorable Jacob Samils, Harrisburg, Pa.
Heiss, Goddard, Philadelphia
Hoel, Captain William R., Waynesville, Ohio
Hutchinson, the Reverend Eleazer Carter, St. Louis
Hyde, Honorable James K., Hydeville, Vt.
Isham, John G., Cincinnati
Jackson, Dr. Abraham Reeves, Stroudsburg, Pa.

James, William E., Brooklyn
Jenkins, Frederick P., Boston
Kinney, Colonel Peter, Portsmouth, Ohio
Krauss, George W., Harrisburg, Pa.
Langdon, Charles Jervis, Elmira, N.Y.
Langdon, Miss Julia L.
Larrowe, Mrs. Nina D., San Francisco
Leary, Daniel D., New York City
Lee, Mrs. S. G., Brooklyn
Lockwood, Mr. and Mrs. E. K., Norwalk, Conn.
McDonald, Louis, Bristol, England
Moody, Captain Lucius, Canton, N.Y.
Moulton, Julius, St. Louis
Nelson, Arba, Alton, Ill.
Nesbit, Dr. Benjamin B., Louisville, Ky.
Nesbit, Thomas B., Fulton, Mo.
Newell, Miss Julia, Janesville, Wis.
Parsons, Samuel B., New York City
Payne, Dr. and Mrs. James H., Boston
Quereau, the Reverend George W., Aurora, Ill.
Sanford, Solomon N., Cleveland
Serfaty, M. A., Gibraltar
Severance, Mr. and Mrs. Solon Long (Emily A.), Cleveland
Sexton, Nicholas, New York City
Slote, Daniel, New York City
Van Nostrand, John A., Greenville, N.J., and New York City

Crew

Duncan, Charles C., captain
Bursley, Ira, sailing master and executive officer
Jones, William, second officer
Burdick, Benjamin F., steward
Harris, John, chief engineer
Vail, Robert, purser
Pratt, William A., quartermaster

Appendix D

Itinerary of the Quaker City *Excursion*

THE FOLLOWING sources furnished the documentary basis for this itinerary: Clemens's letters to the San Francisco *Alta California* (beginning with SLC 1867oo); *N&J1*, 329–452; *The Innocents Abroad* (SLC 1869a); journals kept by William R. Denny, Charles C. Duncan (the most reliable source for the ship's arrival and departure times), Charles J. Langdon, Benjamin B. Nesbit, and Emily A. Severance (the above documents, already cited in the notes, are fully described in References); and newspaper letters written by Moses S. Beach, William R. Denny, Charles C. Duncan and Emily A. Severance, Mary Mason Fairbanks, Abraham R. Jackson, William E. James, Julius Moulton, and Julia Newell. We are grateful to Leon T. Dickinson, who in 1969 provided the Mark Twain Papers with copies of these newspaper letters, most of which he discovered. A full record is given below of all the known letters from each newspaper correspondent; explicit case-by-case citation of all supporting (or conflicting) evidence has been deemed impractical.

The hours of departure and arrival given in the itinerary are approximate. When the time of day was recorded differently in two or more sources, either the most probable time or a reasonable average was adopted. Similarly, when the date was recorded differently, the most likely was chosen. Whenever possible, place names are given in English ("Leghorn" rather than "Livorno," for example). Spelling authorities were, in descending order, the *National Geographic Atlas*, *Webster's New Geographical Dictionary*, and Murray.

Sources

Moses S. Beach to the New York *Sun*

NO.	WRITTEN	PUBLISHED	NO.	WRITTEN	PUBLISHED
1	8 June	10 June	3	15 June	18 July
2	9 June	10 June	4	17 June	19 July

NO.	WRITTEN	PUBLISHED	NO.	WRITTEN	PUBLISHED
5	1 July	25 July	22	30 Sept	9 Nov
6	1 July	26 July	23	30 Sept	11 Nov
7	21 June	29 July	24	21 Sept	24 Nov
8	24 June	31 July	25	25 Sept	15 Nov
9	25 June	2 Aug	26	30 Sept	16 Nov
10	4 July	8 Aug	27	3 Oct	18 Nov
11	9 July	12 Aug	28	5 Oct	19 Nov
12	9 July	13 Aug	29	19 Oct	20 Nov
13	12 July	14 Aug	30	9 Nov	20 Nov
14	20 July	16 Aug	31	11 Nov	24 Nov
15	20 July	20 Aug	32	21 Nov	22 Nov
16	15 Aug	16 Sept	33	26 Oct	23 Nov
17	17 Aug	18 Sept	34	3 Nov	25 Nov
18	18 Aug	19 Sept	35	21 Oct	26 Nov
19	26 Aug	23 Sept	36	21 Oct	27 Nov
20	14 Sept	5 Nov	37	22 Oct	28 Nov
21	16 Sept	8 Nov			

William R. Denny to the Winchester (Va.) *Times*

[No extant file of the *Times* has been found; Denny's letters are preserved as clippings in a scrapbook owned by Mrs. Theodore Whitfield, PH in CU-MARK.]

NO.	WRITTEN	PUBLISHED	NO.	WRITTEN	PUBLISHED
none	29 June	unknown	none	10 Aug	unknown
"	30 June	"	"	[August]	"
"	2 July	"	"	28 Aug	"
"	10 July	"	"	[September]	"
"	13 July	"	"	[September]	"
"	19 July	"	"	[September]	"
"	21 July	"	"	[September]	"
"	22 July	"	"	11 Sept	"
"	24 July	"	"	16 Sept	"
"	28 July	"	"	[October]	"
"	30 July	"			

Charles C. Duncan and Emily A. Severance to the New York *Independent*

NO.	WRITTEN	PUBLISHED
none	19 June, 4 July	15 Aug
"	21 and 27 July, 3 Aug	29 Aug

Mary Mason Fairbanks to the Cleveland *Herald*

NO.	WRITTEN	PUBLISHED	NO.	WRITTEN	PUBLISHED
1	8 June	12 June	15	15 Aug	30 Sept
2	9 June	13 June	16	23 Aug	4 Oct
3	16 June	22 July	17	28 Aug	8 Oct
4	22 June	23 July	18	30 Aug	9 Oct
5	29 June	24 July	19	6 Sept	19 Nov
6	2 July	25 July	20	12 Sept	20 Nov
7	10 July	3 Aug	21	17 Sept	22 Nov
8	11 July	14 Aug	22	21 Sept	29 Nov
9	15 July	15 Aug	23	26 Sept	5 Dec
10	18 July	20 Aug	24	30 Sept	7 Dec
11	22 July	23 Aug	25	5 Oct	11 Dec
12	25 July	9 Sept	27 [26]	24 Oct	25 Nov
13	27 July	11 Sept	27	14 Nov	14 Dec
14	3 Aug	26 Sept			

Abraham R. Jackson to the Monroe County (Pa.) *Democrat*

[No extant file of the *Democrat* has been found; Jackson's letters are preserved as clippings in a scrapbook owned by Horace Levy, PH in CU-MARK.]

NO.	WRITTEN	PUBLISHED	NO.	WRITTEN	PUBLISHED
1	22 June	unknown	10	22 July	unknown
2	30 June	"	11	26 July	"
3	2 July	"	12	31 July	"
4	5 July	"	13	11 Aug	"
5	8 July	"	14	19 Aug	"
6	11 July	"	15	2 Sept	"
7	16 July	"	16	10 Sept	"
8	18 July	"	17	14 Sept	"
9	19 July	"	18	[October]	"

William E. James to the Brooklyn *Eagle*

NO.	WRITTEN	PUBLISHED
none	26 July	14 Aug
"	10 Aug	19 Sept
"	30 Aug	20 Sept

Julius Moulton to the St. Louis *Missouri Republican*

NO.	WRITTEN	PUBLISHED
none	23 July	19 Aug[1]
"	30 Aug	14 Oct
"	1 Sept	22 Oct
"	2 Oct	19 Nov
"	3 Oct	24 Nov[2]

Julia Newell to the Janesville (Wis.) *Gazette*

NO.	WRITTEN	PUBLISHED	NO.	WRITTEN	PUBLISHED
none	22 June	23 July	none	10 Aug	17 Oct
"	14 July	1 Aug	"	3 Sept	21 Oct
"	14 July	16 Aug	"	15 Sept	6 Nov
"	20 July	24 Aug	"	October	23 Nov
"	20 July	7 Sept	"	October	30 Nov
"	29 July	12 Sept	"	[October]	7 Dec
"	[August]	3 Oct	"	October	14 Dec

Itinerary

8 June *QC* left the Manhattan wharf, 2:00 P.M., but soon anchored in Gravesend Bay, off Brooklyn.

10 June *QC* departed Gravesend Bay, 12:30 P.M.

21 June *QC* arrived at Horta, island of Fayal, Azores, in the morning.

23 June *QC* departed Horta, 11:00 A.M.

29 June *QC* arrived at Gibraltar, 10:00 A.M.

30 June SLC and companions[3] took a steamer to Tangier.

[1] Contains a reference to his "last," or previous, letter, which has not been found.

[2] Ends "I will write you again," but no subsequent letters have been found.

[3] Barry, Denny, Foster, Greer, Jackson, Slote, and an English merchant named Redman.

1 July	SLC and companions returned from Tangier to Gibraltar in time for the *QC*'s 6:00 P.M. departure.
4 July	*QC* arrived at Marseilles, 7:00 P.M.
5 July	SLC and companions[4] departed Marseilles for Paris by an evening train.
6 July	SLC and companions arrived in Paris in the evening.
11 July	SLC and companions departed Paris for Marseilles by a morning train.
12 July	SLC and companions arrived in Marseilles in the morning.
13 July	*QC* departed Marseilles at noon.
14 July	*QC* arrived at Genoa, 6:00 A.M.
16 July	SLC and companions[5] departed Genoa by train, arriving in Milan that evening.
18 July	SLC and companions traveled by train from Milan to Como, then by steamer to Bellagio on Lake Como.
20 July	SLC and companions traveled by steamer from Bellagio to Lecco, departing Lecco by carriage, 1:00 P.M., for Bergamo, where they caught the train, passing through Brescia, Verona, Vicenza, and Padua, and arriving in Venice, 8:00 P.M.
22 July	SLC and companions departed Venice by train, passing through Bologna and Pistoia overnight.
23 July	SLC and companions arrived in Florence; *QC* departed Genoa, 7:00 P.M.
24 July	*QC* arrived at Leghorn, 7:00 A.M.
?25 July	SLC and companions departed Florence on the noon train for Pisa, where they spent two hours; they arrived at Leghorn in the evening and boarded the ship.
?26 July	SLC and companions, to avoid being quarantined on the *QC* at Naples, took a French steamer to Civitavecchia, then a train to Rome, arriving the following evening.
31 July	*QC* departed Leghorn, 9:00 A.M.

[4] Jackson and Slote.
[5] Jackson and Slote.

1 Aug	SLC and companions probably departed Rome for Naples by train; *QC* arrived at Naples, where it was quarantined for a week.
7 Aug	SLC and companions[6] departed Naples in the morning for two days on the island of Ischia.
9 Aug	SLC and companions returned from Ischia to Naples in the morning; at midnight SLC and companions[7] departed for Mt. Vesuvius.
10 Aug	SLC and companions[8] visited Capri by chartered steamer.
11 Aug	*QC* departed Naples, 8:00 A.M.
14 Aug	*QC* arrived at Piraeus at noon, but the passengers did not disembark; SLC and companions[9] defied the quarantine and visited Athens that night.
15 Aug	*QC* departed Piraeus at noon.
17 Aug	*QC* arrived at Constantinople at daybreak.
19 Aug	*QC* departed Constantinople, 1:00 P.M.
21 Aug	*QC* arrived at Sevastopol, 5:00 A.M., and departed again at 9:00 P.M.
22 Aug	*QC* arrived at Odessa, 4:00 P.M.
24 Aug	*QC* departed Odessa, 11:00 A.M.
25 Aug	*QC* arrived at Yalta at noon.
26 Aug	*QC* party, including SLC, visited Tsar Aleksandr II and family.
28 Aug	*QC* departed Yalta, 8:00 P.M.
30 Aug	*QC* arrived at Constantinople at daybreak.
3 Sept	*QC* party, probably including SLC,[10] visited Scutari during the day; *QC* departed Constantinople, 10:00 P.M.
5 Sept	*QC* arrived at Smyrna, 10:00 A.M.

[6] Clemens identified his party only as "two or three of us" (SLC 1867bbb).

[7] Jackson, Benjamin Nesbit, Newell, and four others—a man and three women, not otherwise identified (see 9 Aug 67 to JLC and family, n. 1).

[8] Unidentified, except for Denny, Newell, and Slote.

[9] Birch, Denny, and Jackson.

[10] See 1–2 Sept 67 to JLC and family, nn. 1, 6.

6 Sept Large *QC* party, including SLC, visited Ephesus during the day; *QC* departed Smyrna, 11:00 P.M.

10 Sept *QC* arrived at Beirut before daylight.

11 Sept SLC and companions[11] departed Beirut on horseback, 3:00 P.M., camping that night ten or twelve miles east of the city.

12 Sept SLC and companions broke camp, 6:30 A.M., and stayed that night in the Lebanon valley at Temnin el Foka, near Zahlah, about two-thirds of the way between Beirut and Baalbek.

13 Sept SLC and companions broke camp, 6:30 A.M., visited Baalbek, returned south, and camped that night at Sirghāyā.

14 Sept SLC and companions arrived in Damascus at sunset.

15 Sept *QC* departed Beirut at midnight.

16 Sept SLC and companions departed Damascus at noon, camping that night at Kefr Hauwar; *QC* arrived at Mt. Carmel, 10:00 A.M., and departed again at noon, arriving at Jaffa (now part of Tel Aviv), 8:00 P.M.

17 Sept SLC and companions departed Kefr Hauwar in the morning and camped that night at Baniyas, formerly the ancient city of Caesarea Philippi.

18 Sept SLC and companions departed Baniyas, 7:15 A.M., and camped that night at Ain Mellahah, near Lake Huleh (now called Bahret el Hule).

19 Sept SLC and companions departed Ain Mellahah, 7:00 A.M., and camped that night at Tiberias, on the Sea of Galilee.

20 Sept SLC and companions departed Tiberias in the morning and camped that night at Nazareth.

21 Sept SLC and companions departed Nazareth, 7:30 A.M., and camped that night at Janīn.

22 Sept SLC and companions departed Janīn, 2:00 A.M., and camped that night at Lubban.

23 Sept SLC and companions departed Lubban, 2:30 A.M., and reached Jerusalem at noon.

[11] Birch, Church, Davis, Denny, Moulton, Slote, and Van Nostrand.

25 Sept SLC and companions departed Jerusalem, 8:00 A.M., for a two-day side trip, camping that night near Jericho.

26 Sept SLC and companions departed Jericho, 2:00 A.M., visited the Jordan River and the Dead Sea, camping that night at Mar Saba.

27 Sept SLC and companions departed Mar Saba, 3:00 A.M., visited Bethlehem and returned to Jerusalem at noon.

29 Sept SLC and companions departed Jerusalem, 3:00 P.M., reaching Ramla in the evening.

30 Sept SLC and companions departed Ramla in the morning and, after three hours, arrived at Jaffa and boarded the ship.

1 Oct *QC* departed Jaffa, 7:30 A.M.

2 Oct *QC* arrived at Alexandria at sunset.

4 Oct SLC and companions[12] departed Alexandria by train, 4:00 P.M., arriving in Cairo late that evening.

5 Oct SLC and companions departed Cairo on donkeys, early in the morning, to visit the Sphinx and the pyramids at Giza, returning to Cairo that night.

7 Oct SLC and companions departed Cairo for Alexandria and boarded the ship; *QC* departed Alexandria, 5:00 P.M.

13 Oct *QC* arrived at Cagliari, island of Sardinia, 9:00 P.M.; departed at midnight without disembarking passengers.

15 Oct *QC* arrived at Algiers, 3:30 P.M.; departed, 5:30 P.M., without disembarking passengers.

17 Oct *QC* arrived at Málaga, 1:00 P.M.; departed, 4:00 P.M., without disembarking passengers, and arrived at Gibraltar, 11:00 P.M.

18 Oct SLC and companions[13] departed Gibraltar at noon, traveling overnight by horseback and carriage to Algeciras, Vejer, and San Fernando.

19 Oct SLC and companions boarded the 4:00 P.M. train for Seville, arriving at midnight.

[12] Unidentified, except for Slote and Van Nostrand (*The Innocents Abroad*, chapter 58).

[13] Jackson, Moulton, Newell, and a guide (Michael Beñunes).

22 Oct	SLC and companions traveled by train to Córdoba.
23 Oct	SLC and companions returned by 9:00 A.M. train to Seville; departed Seville for Cádiz, stopping briefly in Jerez.
24 Oct	SLC and companions arrived in Cádiz; *QC* departed Gibraltar, 6:00 P.M.
25 Oct	*QC* arrived at Cádiz, 7:30 A.M.; SLC and companions boarded at 10:30, and *QC* departed Cádiz, 11:00 A.M.
28 Oct	*QC* arrived at Funchal, island of Madeira, at noon; departed, 8:00 P.M., without disembarking passengers.
11 Nov	*QC* arrived at St. George, Bermuda, at daybreak.
15 Nov	*QC* departed St. George, 8:00 A.M.
19 Nov	*QC* arrived at New York City, 10:00 A.M.

Appendix E

Enclosures with the Letters

ENCLOSURES ARE transcribed here when they are too long to be presented conveniently with the letters themselves. Textual commentaries for these enclosures appear following the commentaries for the letters.

Enclosure with 20 November 1867 To Jane Lampton Clemens and Family (1st of 2) • New York, N.Y.

(New York *Herald*, 20 Nov 67)

THE QUAKER CITY PILGRIMAGE.

Return of the Holy Land Excursionists—The Story of the Cruise—A Serio-Comic Picture of Life on Board—The Expedition Not All Couleur de Rose.[1]

The steamship Quaker City, Captain Duncan, with her excursionists, returned yesterday morning to this port from her cruise to the Holy Land and the Mediterranean. The steamer arrived at Bermuda from Madeira on the 11th instant, which island she left for New York on the 15th, with passengers and crew in good health, who yesterday were safely landed at the foot of Wall street, where the Quaker City is now. The steamer is in good condition, and will probably in about two weeks be placed again on the Charleston line. The expedition has terminated successfully and to the satisfaction of the majority of those participating in the same. The Quaker City, with the excursionists on board, it will be recollected, left New York on the 8th of June, with sixty-seven passengers, sixteen of whom were ladies, who, with the exception of seven pas-

[1] These subtitles, as well as the following introductory paragraph and list of passengers, were provided by the *Herald*.

sengers who left the steamer at Alexandria, in Egypt, returned on board of the vessel; those who left her at Alexandria having returned to the United States by a direct route. At Constantinople a fireman was lost, who, one night when going on board, fell overboard and was drowned. No other mishaps occurred during the whole of the cruise.

The Quaker City brings back the following passengers:—

Captain W. R. Hoel, Colonel James K. Hyde, John G. Isham, Dr. A. R. Jackson, Wm. E. James, Colonel P. Kinney, George W. Krauss, Charles J. Langdore,[2] Mrs. Mina Larrowe, Daniel D. Leary, E. K. Lockwood, Mrs. Lockwood, Louis McDonald, Captain Lucius Moody, Julius Moulton, Arba Nelson, Dr. B. B. Nelson, Thomas B. Nesbitt, Miss Julia Newell, Dr. J. H. Payne and wife, Rev. G. W. Quereau, D. D.; S. N. Sanford, M. A. Serfaty, S. L. Severance and wife, Nicholas Sexton, John A. Van Nostrand, Miss Langdon, Dr. E. Andrews, Major J. G. Barry, Moses S. Beach, Miss E. B. Beach, R. Bell and wife, Dr. G. B. Birch, J. W. Bond, wife and infant; Miss M. E. Bond, Dr. M. Brown, Miss Kate Brown, Rev. Henry Bullard, Miss Carrie Chadeayne, Samuel L. Clemens ("Mark Twain"), Bloodgood H. Cutter, Albert Crane, M. D.; Albert Crane, Jr.; J. D. Crocker and wife, J. W. Davis, Colonel J. W. Denny, Fred. Dunore and wife, Mrs. C. C. Duncan, George F. Duncan, H. E. Duncan, Mrs. A. W. Fairbanks, Colonel J. Heron Foster, Dr. William Gibson and wife, Hon. J. S. Haldeman, Goddard Heiss.

The Cruise of the Quaker City.

TO THE EDITOR OF THE HERALD:—

The steamer Quaker City has accomplished at last her extraordinary voyage and returned to her old pier at the foot of Wall street, after an absence of five months and a half. The expedition was a success in some respects, in some it was not. Originally it was advertised as a "pleasure excursion." Well, perhaps it was a pleasure excursion, but certainly it did not look like one; certainly it did not act like one. Anybody's and everybody's notion of a pleasure excursion is that the parties to it will of a necessity be young and giddy and somewhat boisterous. They will

[2] That is, Charles J. Langdon. Several other passengers' names are misspelled in this list, which has been transcribed here exactly as printed in the *Herald*. The correct names may be found in Appendix C.

dance a good deal, sing a good deal, make love, and pray very little. Anybody's and everybody's notion of a well conducted funeral is that there must be a hearse and a corpse, and chief mourners and mourners by courtesy, many old people, much solemnity, no levity, and a prayer and a sermon withal. Three-fourths of the Quaker City's passengers were between forty and seventy years of age! There was a picnic crowd for you! It may be supposed that the other fourth was composed of young girls. But it was not. It was chiefly composed of rusty old bachelors and a child of six years. Let us average the ages of the Quaker City's pilgrims and set the figure down at fifty years. Is any man insane enough to imagine that this picnic of patriarchs sang, made love, danced, laughed, told anecdotes, dealt in ungodly levity? In my experience they sinned little in these matters. No doubt it was presumed here at home that these frolicsome veterans laughed and sang and romped all day, and day after day, and kept up a noisy excitement from one end of the ship to the other; and that they played blind-man's buff or danced quadrilles and waltzes on moonlight evenings on the quarterdeck; and that at odd moments of unoccupied time they jotted a laconic item or two in the journals they opened on such an elaborate plan when they left home, and then skurried off to their whist and euchre labors under the cabin lamps. If these things were presumed, the presumption was at fault. The venerable excursionists were not gay and frisky. They played no blind man's bluff; they dealt not in whist; they shirked not the irksome journal, for alas! most of them were even writing books. They never romped, they talked but little, they never sang, save in the nightly prayer meeting. The pleasure ship was a synagogue, and the pleasure trip was a funeral excursion without a corpse. [There is nothing exhilarating about a funeral excursion without a corpse.] A free, hearty laugh was a sound that was not heard oftener than once in seven days about those decks or in those cabins; and when it was heard it met with precious little sympathy. The excursionists danced, on three separate evenings, long, long ago (it seems an age), quadrilles, of a single set, made up of three ladies and five gentlemen (the latter with handkerchiefs around their arms to signify their sex), who timed their feet to the solemn wheezing of a melodeon; but even this melancholy orgie was voted to be sinful and dancing was discontinued.

The pilgrims played dominoes when too much Josephus or Robinson's Holy Land Researches, or book writing, made recreation necessary—for dominoes is about as mild and sinless a game as any in the world perhaps, excepting always the ineffably insipid diversion they call playing at croquet, which is a game where you don't pocket any balls and dont't carom on anything of any consequence, and when you are done nobody has to pay, and there are no cigars or drinks to saw off, and, consequently, there isn't any satisfaction whatever about it—they played dominoes till they were rested, and then they blackguarded each other privately till prayer time. When they were not seasick they were uncommonly prompt when the dinner gong sounded. Such was our daily life on board the ship—solemnity, decorum, dinner, dominoes, prayers, slander. It was not lively enough for a pleasure trip; but if we had only had a corpse it would have made a gorgeous funeral excursion. It is all over now; but when I look back, the idea of these venerable fossils skipping forth on a six months' picnic, seems exquisitely ludicrous. The advertised title of the expedition—"The Grand Holy Land Pleasure Excursion"—was a ghastly misnomer. "The Grand Holy Land Funeral Procession" would have been better—much better.

As advertised, the "Plymouth Collection of Hymns" was used on board. It was frequently used. We had a prayer meeting every night. On this part of the subject I wish to touch very lightly. I could not quarrel, no one could quarrel, with the prayer meetings. We are all taught to respect these things. I merely mention them as being a unique feature in pleasure excursions, and worthy of imitation in future picnics. There were those in the ship's company who attributed the fact that we had a steady siege of storms and head winds for five mortal months solely to the prayer meetings. But I was not of that faction. There were those who were abandoned enough to believe that some time or other a particularly aggravating and long-drawn prayer meeting would bring down a storm that would sink the ship. I was not of that party either. I said all along that we hadn't prayer meetings enough; we ought to have them before breakfast, and between meals, and every now and then, and pretty much all the time. Those were my sentiments. I do not brag, but those were certainly my sentiments. The argument that they prayed the same old prayers over again every night was nothing to me. I knew that if they only performed oftener and held out long enough, they were bound to start something fresh after a while. There is nothing that gives startling variety to a picnic like prayer meetings. Especially when the "Plymouth Collection" is used, because as a general thing the tunes are a shade too complicated for the excursionists, and so, when they are properly tangled, they are exceedingly lively.

Wherever we went, in Europe, Asia or Africa, we made a sensation, and I suppose I may add, created a famine. None of us had ever been anywhere before; we all hailed from the interior; travel was a wild novelty to us, and we conducted ourselves in accordance with the natural instincts that were in us, and trammelled ourselves with no ceremonies, no conventionalities. We always took care to make it understood that we were Americans—Americans! When we found that a good many foreigners had hardly even heard of America, and that a good many more knew it only as a barbarous province away off somewhere, that had lately been at war with somebody, we pitied the ignorance of the Old World, but abated no jot of our importance. Many and many a simple community in the Eastern hemisphere will remember for years the incursion of the strange horde in the year of our Lord 1867, that called themselves Americans, and seemed to imagine in some unaccountable way that they had a right to be proud of it. We generally created a famine, partly because the coffee on the Quaker City was unendurable and sometimes the more substantial fare was not strictly first class; and partly because one naturally tires of sitting long at the same board and eating from the same dishes.

The people of those foreign countries are very, very ignorant. They looked curiously at the costumes we had brought from the wilds of America. They observed that we talked loudly at table sometimes. They noticed that we looked out for expenses and got what we conveniently could out of a franc, and wondered where in the mischief we came from. In Paris they just simply opened their eyes and stared when we spoke to them in French! We never did succeed in making those idiots understand their own language. One of our passengers said to a shopkeeper, in reference to a proposed return to buy a pair of gloves, "*Allong—restay trankeel*—maybe ve coom Moonday;" and would you believe it, that shopkeeper, a born Frenchman, had to ask what it was that had been said. Sometimes it seems to me, somehow, that there must be a difference between Parisian French and Quaker City French.

The people stared at us everywhere and we stared at them. We generally made them feel rather small, too, before we got done with them, because we bore down on them with America's greatness until we crushed them. And yet we took kindly to the manners and customs, and especially the fashions of the various peoples we visited. When we left the Azores, we wore awful capotes and used fine tooth combs—successfully. When we came back from Tangier, in Africa, we were topped with fezzes of the bloodiest hue, and hung with tassels like an Indian's scalp lock. In France and Spain we attracted some attention in these costumes. In Italy they naturally took us for distempered Garibaldians, and set a gunboat to look for anything significant in our changes of uniform. We made Rome howl. We could have made any place howl when we had all our clothes on. We got no fresh raiment in Greece—they had but little there of any kind. But at Constantinople, how we turned out! Turbans, scimetars, fezzes, horse pistols, tunics, sashes, baggy trowsers, yellow slippers—Oh, we were gorgeous! The illustrious dogs of Constantinople barked their under jaws off, and even then failed to do us justice. They are all dead by this time. They could not go through such a run of business as we gave them and survive.

And then we went to see the Emperor of Russia. We just called on him as comfortably as if we had known him a century or so, and when we had finished our visit we variegated ourselves with selections from Russian costumes and sailed away again more picturesque than ever. In Smyrna we picked up camels' hair shawls and other dressy things from Persia; but in Palestine—ah, in Palestine—our splendid career ended. They didn't wear any clothes there to speak of. We were satisfied, and stopped. We made no experiments. We did not try their costume. But we astonished the natives of that country. We astonished them with such eccentricities of dress as we could muster. We prowled through the Holy Land, from Cesarea Phillippi to Jerusalem and the Dead Sea, a weird procession of pilgrims, gotten up regardless of expense, solemn, gorgeous, green spectacled, drowsing under blue umbrellas, and astride of a sorrier lot of horses, camels and asses than those that came out of Noah's ark, after eleven months of sea-sickness and short rations. If ever those children of Israel in Palestine forget when Gideon's band went through there from America they ought to be cursed once more and finished. It was the rarest spectacle that ever astounded mortal eyes, perhaps.

Well, we were at home in Palestine. It was easy to see that that was the grand feature of the expedition. We had cared nothing much about Europe. We galloped through the Louvre, the Pitti, the Ufizzi, the Vatican—all the galleries—and through the pictured and frescoed churches of Venice, Pisa and the cathedrals of Spain; some of us said that certain of the great works of the old masters were glorious creations of genius, (we found it out in the guidebook, though we got hold of the wrong picture sometimes), and the others said they were disgraceful old daubs. We examined modern and ancient statuary with a critical eye in Florence, Rome or anywhere we found it, and praised it if we saw fit, and if we didn't we said we preferred the wooden Indians in front of the cigar stores of America. But the Holy Land brought out all our enthusiasm. We fell into raptures by the barren shores of Galilee; we pondered at Tabor and at Nazareth; we exploded into poetry over the questionable loveliness of Esdraelon; we meditated at Jezreel and Samaria over the zeal of Jehu, who slew seventy sons of one gentleman, massacred all the worshippers of Baal in his district, and performed other meritorious missionary services; we rioted, fairly rioted, among the holy places of Jerusalem; we bathed in Jordan and the Dead Sea, reckless whether our accidental insurance policies were extra hazardous or not, and brought away so many jugs of precious water from both places that all the country from Jericho to the mountains of Moab will suffer from drought this year, I think. Yes, the pilgrimage part of the excursion was its pet feature—there is no question about that. After dismal, desolate, smileless Palestine, beautiful Egypt had few charms for us. We merely glanced at it, and were ready for home.

They wouldn't let us land at Malta—quarantine; they wouldn't let us land in Sardinia; nor at Algiers, Africa; nor at Malaga, Spain; nor at Cadiz; nor at the Madeira Islands. So we got offended at all foreigners and turned our backs upon them and came home. I suppose we only stopped at the Bermudas because they were in the programme. We did not care anything about any place at all. We wanted to go home. Homesickness was abroad in the ship—it was epidemic. If the authorities of New York had known how badly we had it, they would have quarantined us here.

We failed to sell the ship. I mention this because to sell the ship seemed to be as much of an object of the excursion as anything else, and so of course to know that we failed to sell her must necessarily be of interest to the public. We were to sell the ship and then walk home, I suppose. That would have given variety to the pleasure excursion at any rate.

The grand pilgrimage is over. Goodby to it, and a pleasant memory to it, I am able to say in all kindness. I bear no malice, no ill will towards any individual that was connected with it, either as passenger or officer. Such persons as I did not like at all yesterday I like very well to-day, now that I am at home, and always hereafter I shall be able to poke fun at the whole gang if the spirit so moves me to do, without ever saying a malicious word. The expedition accomplished all that its programme promised that it should accomplish, and we ought all to be satisfied with the management of the matter, certainly. But that such pleasure excursions as this are calculated to be suffocated with pleasure, I deny; and that a party more ill-fitted, by age and awful solemnity, for skurrying around the world on a giddy picnic, ever went to sea in a ship since the world began, I deny also, most fervently.[3]

Enclosure with 25 November 1867
To Charles Henry Webb • Washington, D.C.

(MS: InU-Li)

Act. I—Scene I.

Capt. Dusenberry's Office in Wall street.

[Enter six old maids, in obsolete costumes, & a dozen veterans of both sexes in all stages of sickness, mutilation & dilapidation.] ‸with cats, parrots, poodles, &c.‸

1st Maid—(D With youthful diffidence)—Good morning sir—is this the office of the Grand Pleasure Excursion all over the hH‸abitable Globe & the Holy Land in Five Months?

Capt.—It is Madam—or Miss, no doubt, judging by appearances, —pray be seated. James (to the clerk)—bring chairs—be seated, ladies & gentlemen.

1st Maid—We have seen by the published programme, that none but persons of the highest respectability & the most stainless morality—

[3]Clemens probably supplied his signature ("Mark Twain") on the actual clipping he enclosed.

Capt—You will be safe ladies, I assure you that *you* need not have any fears if you go with us, of the snares of designing men. *Aside*—Your faces are security for *that*, anyway.

1st M—We are very, *very* glad to ~~you~~ hear you say that. It lifts a *load* of apprehension from our hearts. And we see, also, that Mr. Beecher is going with you—is that true?

~~E~~ Capt—Entirely so.

M—‸Oh, Joy!—‸ And Gen. Sherman?

Capt—Yes—

M—And the Drummer Boy & Maggie Mitchell?[1]

Capt—Both.

M—Rapture!—what a delightful variety!—And it is ~~printed~~ published in the programme that the $1250 fare must be paid in advance & the recommendations of all applicants for passage submitted to the Committee on Credentials. We have brought our money (they pass it in), & some letters endorsing our characters (they hand over a voluminous mass of Manuscripts) & now Captain, if we should be so fortunate ~~&~~ as to meet with favor in the eyes of the Committee,—

Capt (pretending to glance over the recommendations)—No danger in the world, my dear Miss—encomiums like these could never be slighted by any committee.

M—You see, we are poor unprotected young things—

All Maids—Silly unsophisticated creatures—

M—Just of an age to fall into the pitfalls that line the path of thoughtless youth—

All—Gay, & foolish & giddy—

‸1st‸ M—Just in that budding spring of life when ~~b~~ innocence &

[1] Robert Henry Hendershott, known since the Civil War as the "Drummer Boy of the Rappahannock," had apparently intended to join the excursion with his fiancée, the daughter of a wealthy Poughkeepsie merchant. When her parents withheld their consent to the marriage, the couple canceled their plans for the trip and eloped on 31 May (New York *Herald*, 4 June 67, 8). The actress Margaret Julia Mitchell (1837–1918) had been famous since her 1862 appearance in New York City as the elfin child in *Fanchon the Cricket*, an adaptation of George Sand's *La Petite Fadette*. Announced as one of the *Quaker City* passengers until 5 June, she withdrew so late that at least two newspapers included her on their lists of departed excursionists ("The Duncan Excursion," Brooklyn *Eagle*, 5 June 67, 3; "The Mediterranean Excursion," Brooklyn *Union*, 8 June 67, 4; "The Pleasure Excursion to Europe and Palestine—Sailing of the Quaker City," New York *Times*, 9 June 67, 8).

beauty are too apt to prove ~~false beacons~~ the sources of bitterest sorrow to their possessors—

All—Sad, sad ~~lop~~ lot—(snuffling)

1st M—And—and—Will you—will you be our dear guardian & friend & shield us from harm with your manly breast? Speak!

All.—Oh, be our guardian angel!

Capt.—This hand shall defend you from all peril—this breast shall shield you—this heart shall be your refuge! All the ship's company shall know my fatherly care, but ~~you~~ unto you I will be father, mother, brother, uncle, sister-in-law [Excuse these tears]

All—Heaven bless you, sire! [Exit.]

Capt D—[*Aside*]—~~Got~~ Well, a few more old cats like that would make a unique excursion of it, *I* should say.] [To the others.]—Ah, ladies & gentlemen—

1st Cripple—Wher do you stop at first, Capt?

Capt—At the Azores.

1 Cr—Is that a tribe, or is it a mountain~~?~~ or something?

Cap—Oh—neither. It is a group of islands.

1 Cr—Jes so—jes so. Where next?

Cap—At Gibraltar.

Cr—Tribe? Or maybe—maybe, mountain?

Cap (Cursed old fool)—No, Oh, no—kind of a mountain—great rock on a peninsula of Southern Spain.

Cr—That's good. That's powerful good. Wher next?

Cap—Marseilles.

1 Cr.—I-yi—where they make the white vests & sing March on march on ye brave, the ~~e~~ 'venging sword unsheath & so on. That's very good. Marseilles—that's very good—only place in Ireland that's *worth* a d—n.

Cap—I should be glad to converse with you at some length, Mr—Mr.—~~but time~~ for I perceive that you are of an observing turn of mind & endowed with a fund of ~~entertaining~~ interesting information which cannot fail to make your conversation entertaining to ~~such~~ any man in the world who—who—would be likely~~—~~to be entertained by it—[No—no—no thanks]—but time presses, &—did you wish to say anything in particular.

1 Cr—Nothing, only here is my money

The Others—And mine—

1 Cr—And my recommendations—

The Others—And mine, also—

1 Cr—And I guess we're all in the same boat together—~~at~~ leastways; we want to be.

[They pass the compliments,
& exit.]

Capt—(Throwing the stacks of recommendations in the fire)—Committee on Credentials! Humph! Twelve Hundred & Fifty Dollars ~~is the Committee on Credentials~~—*paid!*—(ironically)—well, I guess you'll all pass the Committee without running aground. And here's another stack of recommendations come by mail from Arkansas, & Jersey & other out of the way places. Let's see what *they* say. [Reads.]

Whangwang, Minn.
Jan 67.

~~Dr Capt &c~~

"This is to certify that ~~I~~ we have known the inclosed Deacon Pendergrass for 62 year, & always found him a stunner at awakenins, & hark from the tomb! when it comes to giving in "experience." A square man & ~~fre~~ not knowing of his own gifts.

Jno Smith—Jno W. Smith
Jno. H. Smith—Jno Peter
Smith &c &

$1250 Enclosed.

Cap—Pendergrass will do.
Reads—

Alligator Terrace,
Indiana &c

This is to signify that the within named Jno Butterfield has retired from business and does not keep ‸corner‸ grocery any more. ~~The~~ He has the soap. He comes from the first families of this place & his uncle has been post master once & his grandfather was a Home Guard in the Revolutionary war. He knowed the nigger that was body-servant servant to

Genl. Washington. Notwithstanding that that nigger in a bogus form keeps turning up every year & ~~c~~ dying in the newspapers ~~&~~ at the most cussedest unearthly ages that ~~a~~ ever even Methusalem heard of, but not genuine & not to be relied on. He is 57 years old—Butterfield, not the nigger—& is poorly ‸as to health,‸ but ~~a fair eater.~~ handy with a knife & fork.

Jno Jones, J. B.
Jones, W^{m} H.
Jones, Geore Wash-
ington Jones &c.

$1250 enclosed.]

Cap~~-~~D—Well, I suppose this dazzling acquisition must be added to the ships list, too. The last recommendation is a good one.

Rondout, N.Y. Jan &c

The young gentleman whose‸ ‸~~b sends a note w~~ father sends a note with this requesting that his name may be placed before your Com. ~~of~~ on Credentials, is of stainless reputation & ~~unimpea~~ exalted principles. He is a graduate of Yale College, & although he will necessarily have to remain in ~~the~~ the modest & retiring position proper to him in the midst of such a constellation of intellect & learning as will illuminate your ship, he will still feel only too grateful if allowed to mingle, though ever so little, with these great lights, & borrow ~~a look from~~ ‸of‸ the radiance that falls, ~~unønno~~ unnoted of themselves upon all who come within their orbits. Mr. Livingston~~e~~'s father commanded a brigade in the late war, ~~&~~ his, uncle was a class mate of Gen. Grant at West Point, & another uncle has served in the Senate of the United States for 16 years. Another member of the family ~~has~~ was for many years our Minister at the court of France, &c &c &c—

Cap~~-~~D—No use to read it all—a man could get passage in an Emperor's state barge with half such a recommendation as that. I don't propose to take the young man to *Heaven*. ~~Th~~ His money is received—that is of more consequence to me than it is to know what his respectable old grandfather did. I'll take the money out of the balance of these letters & burn them. I guess I can risk the Com. on Credentials. Oh, that Com. on Cre. was a rare dodge! [Laughs exhaustingly or otherwise.]

[Exit.]

Act. II

Scene I—Quarter Deck of a Steamer

Enter 2 Newspaper Correspondents

They look dejected. A pause.

Mark Twain—Ah, me!

Stiggers—The remark I ~~re~~ was about to make.

M. T.—Well, how does it strike *you?*

S.—Don't mention it.

M. T. ‸(Quoting from the programme)‸—Splendid ship~~—so the programme hath it.~~

S.—Eight miles an hour.

M. T.—~~An abundance of~~ ‸Plenty of instrumental‸ music.

S.—Three wheezy melodeons & a clarinet.

M. T.—Vocal ditto.

S.—Plymouth Collection of Hymns![2]

M. T.—Excessively select company.

S.—Selected out of a camp-meeting & a hospital—some of them sick, some of them crippled & the balance reading sermons & backbiting each other all day long.

~~M. T.—No passenger accepted without a spotless reputation~~

M. T.—~~A~~ Passengers will be lively, young & happy.

S.—Rustiest gang of old fossils since Methuselah's time. There ain't 14 out of the 60 but are over 60 years old.

M. T.—No passenger accepted without a spotless reputation.

Both—How did *you* get here?

M. T.—Committee on Credentials.

S.—Bah! Twelve hundred ~~4~~ & Fifty Dollars in greenbacks! Could have brought Sing-Sing[3] along if they had the money.

M. T.—Beecher!

S.—Backed water—they advertised him to death.

[2] Henry Ward Beecher's *Plymouth Collection of Hymns* (1855), a title on the list of books the excursionists were encouraged to bring with them (see note 4).

[3] A state prison in Sing Sing (now Ossining), New York, built in 1825–28.

M. T.—~~Gen~~ Sherman!

S.—They made him sick, too. They made him ~~an~~ a medium for advertising the Grand Holy Land Funeral Excursion for Pleasure till he got so distressed at last ~~till~~ that he ~~thought he~~ fled to the ‸savages of the plains—‸ ~~Plains—~~preferring a merciful swift death by ~~a~~ the tomahawk to the lingering torture of wearing out his life ~~lugging~~ ‸carrying‸ a bulletin board on his back.

M. T.—Maggie Mitchell.

S.—*She* died of advertising, too. Human nature couldn't stand this infernal advertising!

[A Pause.]

M. T—Well, did you bring your share of the programme list of books~~?~~ ‸for the ship's library?‸

S.—What is *that?*

M. T.—Tent Life in the Holy Land, Pilgrim's Progress & Other Travels, Shepherd of Salisbury Plain, Thompson's Whole Duty of Man,[4] Mother Goose's Melodies—

S.—*I* brought four reams of quarto post, thirty gross of steel pens & a barrel of gin!

M. T.—Stiggers, I *love* you. [They embrace.]

S.—Well, we've been out ten days, now, ~~& at l~~ ‸and‸=here comes the whitest man in the ship!

[Enter Dan Sproat.]

‸(Low, fat, & chunky.‸ ~~& jolly~~‸

Dan—Boys, it's awful. Them ~~old pil~~ venerable old ~~pir~~ pilgrims are going to run the prayer meeting *every* night, now that the most of them are not seasick any more, instead of every *other* night. And they're going to have two sermon's every Sunday. Ain't it a gay pleasure trip, I don't

[4]Clemens explained in an *Alta* letter written from Jerusalem, "Before the *Quaker City* left New York, the passengers were instructed to bring along an assortment of books. A list of the volumes they ought to have, in order to be posted concerning England, France, Spain and the many other countries they were to visit, was furnished to each" (SLC 1868ss). This list included, among other titles, William Cowper Prime's *Tent Life in the Holy Land* (1857), John Bunyan's *The Pilgrim's Progress and Other Travels from This World to That Which Is to Come* (1678), Hannah More's *The Shepherd of Salisbury Plain* (1795), and *The Whole Duty of Man, Laid Down in a Plain Familiar Way for the Use of All* (attributed to Richard Allestree and John Fell, 1658). Clemens may have momentarily confused this last book with William McClure Thomson's *The Land and the Book*, one of his sources of information about the Holy Land.

reckon? I wish we had brought along a corpse, & then we could have a bully funeral every now & then—anything to be cheerful. We'll die with the dry rot if this sort of thing goes on. And don't you know, ~~tha~~ they have been just howling about ~~a~~ ‸the‸ little ~~wine~~ claret & stuff ~~that~~ we take in our room occasionally. They are down on No. 10[5] you know. It's on your account, Mark, not mine. And I say, Stiggers—~~I—here!~~ I—by George there goes that old gong!—here, get behind the booby-hatch! —‸or‸ them old pilgrims will rope you in for the prayer meeting. ~~Just~~ ~~l~~‸Look at old Homily, now, with his nose in the air. He hasn't got his sea-legs, yet—*I* would n't laugh if one of them heavy seas was to fetch him. Would n't *care* a d—n, either. [They hide.]

[Enter Patriarchs, male & female, in procession.]

Elder Homily—(With a sigh)—How wonderful is prophecy! Here we are, brethren & sisters, ~~on~~ far on the briny deep. We are not trusting in our own might, yet are we marvellously upheld. Such protection—such love as this, ought to warm are hearts toward all our fellow creatures & fill them with charity for all their shortcomings & sinful, sinful conduct. Ah yes, it ought. Let us be lenient with the failings of those who are in the ways of iniquity, & the paths of e-*ter*-nal destruction! Ah, me, there is that abandoned Sproat, for instance [Pantomime by Sproat & Co.]—& that Twain [More pantomime] & that ridiculous Stiggers [Extravagant by-play.] They drink & drink & drink, in that No. 10 till ~~is~~ it is horrible—perfectly *hor*rible! And they smoke there—which is against the ship's rules—& they have bribed the cabin crew & the porter & they burn safety lanterns there all night ‸(which is against the rule, too)‸ & say they are writing to the newspapers—which is a *lie*, brethren & sisters—they're playing sinful 7-up‸; ~~—~~That's what they're doing. Ain't it so, sister Whistler?

Sis. S. (fine voice)—Yes, bless goodness, it *is*. It ain't no longer ago than last night that the sea give one of them wretched heaves which it ~~makes~~ pretty nigh fetches my very insides out of me every time it does it, & goodness knows glad am I we don't have 'em on the farm or sure I am that never *I* should survive, *I* know—Glory be to God! And when that sea give that heave I stumbled, sorter, & accidentally fell up ~~aga~~ agin the keyhole & lo & behold you I hear Dan Sproat say "I played the tray for low"—& Twain says "Seventeen for game," & that sinful Stiggers he said he guessed ~~tak~~ he'd take a drink. And the~~m~~ way them heathens was

[5] The number of the stateroom that Clemens had shared with Slote.

a carrying on!—I never ~~see~~ ‸hear‸ the ~~s~~ beat of it in *my* life, bless you. Much *they* care whether the ship goes down or not.

Elder H—Much use it is to wrestle with the Lord for quiet weather with such as these on board. But it is our duty to wrestle—Brother Bascom is over his long hypocritical prayer by this time—

Sis. S—Which it never gets no higher than the fore-spanker-gaff=tops'l-jib-boom, *I* don't ~~them~~ think—as them bejiggered sailors calls it, nobody being able to understand them but a born lunatic.

Elder S—And so *we* will wrestle if Providence be willing. {Exit.}

Stiggers—Now the blamd old bag of bogus piety is going down to pray up another nor-wester. The~~se~~ first time these people get a settled stomach in them they get out their Plymouth Collections & start another storm that sets them to heaving again. If they'd only let up once, we could have some fair weather. But didn't they give it to us! Out of whole cloth, too! I'd like to catch old Whistler at that keyhole once. Here comes BASCOM's flock/, now—stand back.

Enclosure with 3 September 1868 To Elisha Bliss, Jr. • Elmira, N.Y.

(*Excelsior Monthly Magazine*, August 1868, RPB-JH)

EULOGY ON WOMAN.

BY "MARK TWAIN."

AT the dinner given by the Correspondents' Club at Washington, recently, "Mark Twain" was called on to respond to the usual toast to "Woman," which he did in the following characteristic style:

MR. PRESIDENT: I do not know why I should have been singled out to receive the greatest distinction of the evening—for so the office of replying to the toast to woman has been regarded in every age. (Applause.) I do not know why I have received this distinction, unless it be that I am a trifle less homely than other members of the club. But be this as it may, Mr. President, I am proud of the position, and you could not have chosen any one who would have accepted it more gladly, or labored with a heartier good-will to do the subject justice, than I. Because, sir, I love the sex. (Laughter.) I love all the women, sir, irrespective of age or color. (Laughter.)

Human intelligence cannot estimate what we owe to woman, sir. She sews on our buttons (laughter); she mends our clothes (laughter); she ropes us in at the church-fairs; she confides in us; she tells us whatever she can find out about the little private affairs of the neighbors; she gives us good advice—and plenty of it; she gives us a piece of her mind sometimes—and sometimes all of it; she soothes our aching brows. In all the relations of life, sir, it is but just, and a graceful tribute to woman, to say of her that she is a brick. (Great laughter.)

Wheresoever you place woman, sir—in whatever position or estate—she is an ornament to that place she occupies, and a treasure to the world. (Here Mr. Twain paused, looked inquiringly at his hearers, and remarked that the applause should come in at this point. It came in. Mr. Twain resumed his eulogy.) Look at the noble names of history! Look at Cleopatra! look at Desdemona! look at Florence Nightingale! look at Joan of Arc! look at Lucretia Borgia! (Disapprobation expressed. "Well," said Mr. Twain, scratching his head doubtfully, "suppose we let Lucretia slide.") Look at Joyce Heth! look at Mother Eve! (Cries of "Oh! oh!") You need not look at her unless you want to, but (said Mr. Twain reflectively, after a pause), Eve was ornamental, sir; particularly before the fashions changed! I repeat, sir, look at the illustrous names of history. Look at the Widow Machree! look at Lucy Stone! look at Elizabeth Cady Stanton! look at George Frances Train! (Great laughter.) And, sir, I say it with bowed head and deepest veneration, look at the mother of Washington! she raised a boy that could not lie—could not lie. (Applause.) But he never had any chance. ("Oh! oh!") It might have been different with him if he had belonged to a newspaper correspondent's club. (Laughter, groans, hisses, cries of "Put him out." Mark looked around placidly upon his excited audience, and resumed:)

I repeat, sir, that in whatsoever position you place a woman, she is an ornament to society and a treasure to the world. As a sweetheart she has few equals and no superiors (laughter); as a cousin she is convenient; as a wealthy grandmother, with an incurable distemper, she is precious; as a wet nurse she has no equal among men! (Laughter.)

What, sir, would the people of the earth be without woman? . . . . . They would be scarce, sir—almighty scarce! Then let us cherish—let us protect her. Let us give her our support, our encouragement, our sympathy—ourselves, if we get a chance. (Laughter.)

But, jesting aside, Mr. President, woman is lovable, gracious, kind of heart, beautiful—worthy of all respect, of all esteem, of all deference. Not any here will refuse to drink her health right cordially in this bumper of wine, for each and every one of us has personally known, and loved, and honored, the very best one of them all—his own mother. (Applause.)

A Recipe for Happiness.—It is simply, when you rise in the morning, to form a resolution to make the day a happy one to a fellow-creature. It is easily done; a left off garment to the man who needs it; a kind word to the sorrowful; an encouraging expression to the striving—trifles in themselves as light as air—will do it, at least for twenty-four hours: and if you are young, depend upon it that it will tell when you are old; and if you are old, rest assured it will send you gently and happily down the stream of time to eternity. Look at the result: You send one person—only one—happily through the day; that is, three hundred and sixty-five in the course of a year; and suppose you live forty years only after you commence this course, you have made fourteen thousand six hundred human beings happy, at all events, for a time. Now, worthy reader, is not this simple? and is it not worth accomplishing? We do not often indulge in a moral dose; but this is so small a pill, that one needs no red currant jelly to disguise its flavor, and requires to be taken but once in a day, that we feel warranted in prescribing it. It is most excellent for digestion, and a promoter of pleasant slumber.—*London Atlas.*

As a ship having a sure anchor may lie safe in any place, so the mind that is ruled by perfect reason is quiet any where.

A SNAKE IN THE GRASS.

BY JOHN G. SAXE.

OME, listen a while to me, my lad,
Come, listen to me for a spell!
Let that terrible drum
For a moment be dumb,
For your uncle is going to tell
What befell
A youth who loved liquor too well.

A clever young man was he, my lad,
And with beauty uncommonly blessed,
Ere with brandy and wine
He began to decline,
And behaved like a person possessed;
I protest
The temperance plan is the best.

One evening he went to a tavern, my lad,
He went to a tavern, one night,
And drinking too much
Rum, brandy, and such,
The chap got exceedingly "tight,"
And was quite
What your aunt would entitle a "fright."

The fellow fell into a snooze, my lad;
'Tis a horrible slumber he takes—
He trembles with fear,
And acts very queer;
My eyes! how he shivers and shakes
When he wakes,
And raves about horrid great snakes!

'Tis a warning to you and to me, my lad;
A particular caution to all—
Though no one can see
The viper but he—
To hear the poor lunatic bawl,
"How they crawl!
All over the floor and the wall."

Next morning he took to his bed, my lad,
Next morning he took to his bed;
And he never got up,
To dine or to sup,
Though properly physicked and bled;
And I read
Next day the poor fellow was dead.

You've heard of the snake in the grass, my lad,
Of the viper concealed in the grass
But now you must know,
Man's deadliest foe
Is a snake of a different class;
Alas!—
'Tis the viper that lurks in the glass!

Enclosure with 28 November 1868
To Olivia L. Langdon • New York, N.Y.

(New York *Tribune*, 11 May 67)

MARK TWAIN AS A LECTURER.

About a year and a half ago, a communication entitled "Joe Smiley and his Jumping Frog," with the hitherto unknown signature of "Mark Twain," appeared in *The Saturday Press* of this city.[1] The name, though new, was not remarkable, but the style of the letter was so singularly fresh, original, and full of character as to attract prompt and universal attention among the readers of light humorous literature. Mark Twain was immediately entered as a candidate for high position among writers of his class, and passages from his first contribution to the metropolitan press became proverbs in the mouths of his admirers. No reputation was ever more rapidly won. The only doubt appeared to be whether he could satisfactorily sustain it. Subsequent productions, however—most of them reproduced from California periodicals—confirmed the good opinion so suddenly vouchsafed him, and abundantly vindicated the applause with which his first essay had been received. In his case, as in that of many other American humorous writers, it was only the first step that cost. Since that time he has walked easily—let us hope not too easily—over his special course.

His writings being comparatively new to the public, and his position having been so recently established, it might perhaps, have been doubted whether his name, would at present be sufficient to attract an audience of any magnitude to witness his debut as a lecturer. But the proof of the general good-will in which he is already held was manifested last Monday evening by his brilliant reception at the Cooper Institute. The hall was crowded beyond all expectation. Not a seat was vacant, and the aisles were filled with attentive listeners. The chance offering of "The Jumping Frog," carelessly cast, 18 months ago, upon the Atlantic waters, returned to him in the most agreeable form which a young as-

[1] This review of Clemens's 6 May 1867 New York City lecture was written by Edward H. House.

pirant for popular fame could desire. The wind that was sowed with probably very little calculation as to its effect upon its future prospects, now enables him to reap quite a respectable tempest of encouragement and cordiality. His greeting was such as to inspire the utmost ease and confidence, and it is pleasant to add that his performance in every way justified the favor bestowed upon him. No other lecturer, of course excepting Artemus Ward, has so thoroughly succceeded in exciting the mirthful curiosity, and compelling the laughter of his hearers.

The subject of his address "The Sandwich Islands," was treated mainly from a comic stand-point, although scraps of practical information and occasional picturesque descriptions of scenery and natural phenomena peculiar to that region were liberally interspersed. The scheme of the lecturer appeared to be to employ the various facts he had gathered as bases upon which to build fanciful illustrations of character, which were furthermore embellished with a multitude of fantastic anecdotes and personal reminiscences. The frequent incongruities of the narration—evidently intentional—made it all the more diverting, and the artifice of its partial incoherence was so cleverly contrived as to intensify the amusement of the audience, while leaving them for the most part in ignorance of the means employed. As to the manner of the speaker, it is difficult to write explicitly. It was certainly peculiar and original. Perhaps no better idea of it could be conveyed than by saying it is in almost every respect the exact opposite to that of the late Artemus Ward. It suited that admirable lecturer's humor to exhibit a nervous quickness and a vivacity which always communicated itself to those who surrounded him, and his best "points" were made by the droll affectation of complete unconsciousness with which he uttered the most telling jests. Mark Twain's delivery, on the other hand, is deliberate and measured to the last degree. He lounges comfortably around his platform, seldom referring to notes, and seeks to establish a sort of button-hole relationship with his audience at the earliest possible moment. He is even willing to exchange confidences of the most literal nature. Having made an accidental error in figures, last Monday evening, at which there was great laughter, he paused and requested to be informed "what he had said," and was indisposed to proceed until his curiosity should be gratified. Instead of manifesting indifference to his own good jokes, he appears to relish them as heartily as anybody—a characteristic, by the bye, which also belongs to the most eminent "reader" now known to the

British public.[2] The only obvious preconcerted "effect" which he employs is a momentary hesitation or break in his narration before touching the climax of an anecdote or a witticism. But his style is his own, and needs to be seen to be understood. A second opportunity for this, we learn, is presently to be afforded, to which, when it approaches, we shall invite particular attention.

[2]Charles Dickens.

Appendix F

Contract for The Innocents Abroad

ELISHA BLISS, on 16 October 1868, wrote out two copies of a contract between Clemens and the American Publishing Company for publication of an unnamed book, eventually called *The Innocents Abroad; or, The New Pilgrims' Progress*. Clemens's copy, signed by both men, is in the Mark Twain Papers (CU-MARK); Bliss's copy, signed only by Clemens, is in the Beinecke Rare Book and Manuscript Library at Yale (CtY-BR). Clemens's copy is transcribed below. The textual commentary for this appendix records the minor variants between the two copies.

This Memorandum made this Sixteenth day of October A.D. 1868. between the American Publishing Co. of City of Hartford & Samuel J Clemens of City of New York Wittnesseth, that the sd Clemens agrees to furnish to the Said Company manuscript properly prepared & written sufficient to make an Octavo volume of at least 500 pages— Table of contents &c &c to be made out fully & any other matters neccessary, to the book to be attended to & prepared. And the said Clemens agrees with the said Company that they shall have the exclusive use of sd Manuscript & right to publish the same & that he will not use the same in any other manner, or any part of it or of its contained matter The subject of the same to be the trip of the "Quaker City to the Holy Land" And the said Compny agree to publish sd manuscript, bringing it out in Book form with illustrations, & they agree to pay to sd Clemens for the copyright of the same, the royalty of Five (5) per cent. upon the retail price of every volume sold by them payable at the expiration of each & every three months after the book is brought out. No royalty however to be paid him upon any Books given to Editors, or furnished to them or others, for notices, advertisements, or for the purpose of advancing the sale of the

Book. The said Clemens is to give all neccessary time & attention to the reading of proofs & correting the same if necessary & to all other matters connected with the bringing out of the Book usual‸l‸y done by Authors & to do all in his power to promote the sale of the work

The sd Company agree that the work shall be Electrotyped during the next 4 months & be ready to place in the hands of ‸their‸ Agents very early next spring & that they will use all reasonable efforts to sell the same, & ‸will‸ adopt all of the usual forms & methods to so do.

Elisha Bliss Secty
Am. Pub Co

Signed Sam. L. Clemens.[1]

The Mss for book contracted for by within contract by S. L Clemens has been delivered to us—& entitled Inno. Abroad

Am. Pub Co.
per E Bliss for firm[2]

[*on back of contract as folded, in Charles L. Webster's*[3] *hand:*] Contract with Am Pub Co. Oct 16 1868 [*and in an unidentified hand:*] 5% on retail price of each volume [*and in a second unidentified hand:*] ~~Innoc Abroad~~ Innocense *Abroad Innocence Abroad*

1 Clemens inscribed "Signed" as well as his signature.

2 Bliss added the preceding paragraph no earlier than April or May 1869, when Clemens decided on the title of his book.

3 Charles L. Webster (1851–91) of Fredonia, New York, married Clemens's niece, Annie Moffett, in 1875. He began to assist Clemens with his business affairs in 1881. In 1884 Clemens established the New York publishing firm of Charles L. Webster and Company, with Webster as manager.

Appendix G

Lecture Schedule, 1868–1869

THIS SCHEDULE lists Mark Twain's known lecture appearances from 17 November 1868, the start of the winter season, to 15 January 1869, the last date that his agent, G. L. Torbert, originally booked for his midwestern tour. (Torbert later added appearances, extending the tour until mid-February; Clemens finished his season with a lecture in Sharon, Pennsylvania, on 20 March.) For lectures confirmed by a newspaper announcement, review, or report, we cite the newspaper as our source. Unless otherwise indicated, newspapers cited for this purpose were published in the same town or city where Clemens lectured. When a lecture is known only through Clemens's statement in a letter, we cite it as our source; all letters cited that are not published in this volume are in CU-MARK.

DATE	PLACE	SOURCE
7 Nov 68	Cleveland, Ohio	*Herald*, *Leader*, and *Plain-Dealer* (18 Nov 68)
19 Nov 68	Pittsburgh, Pa.	*Gazette* (20 Nov 68)
23 Nov 68	Elmira, N.Y.	*Advertiser* (24 Nov 68)
2 Dec 68	Rondout, N.Y.	2 Dec 68 to Langdon
9 Dec 68	Newark, N.J.	*Advertiser* (10 Dec 68)
11 Dec 68	Norwich, N.Y.	5 and 7 Dec 68 to OLL
16 Dec 68[1]	Scranton, Pa.	5 and 7 Dec 68 to OLL
19 Dec 68[2]	Fort Plain, N.Y.	5 and 7 Dec 68 to OLL; *Mohawk Valley Register* (25 Dec 68)

[1]Clemens "missed an appointment at Buffalo, for Dec. 15" (31 Dec 68 to OLL).

[2]Clemens "broke an engagement" in an unidentified town to be in Elmira "from 7 p.m. 17th to 7 p.m. 18th" (24 and 25 Dec 68 to Fairbanks).

DATE	PLACE	SOURCE
22 Dec 68	Detroit, Mich.	*Advertiser and Tribune* and *Free Press* (23 Dec 68)
23 Dec 68	Lansing, Mich.	*State Republican* (31 Dec 68)
25 Dec 68	Charlotte, Mich.	25 Dec 68 to OLL
26 Dec 68	Tecumseh, Mich.	14 Jan 69 to OLL
30 Dec 68	Akron, Ohio	Cleveland *Leader* (1 Jan 69)
2 Jan 69[3]	Fort Wayne, Ind.	31 Dec 68 and 2 Jan 69 to OLL
4 Jan 69	Indianapolis, Ind.	*Journal* (5 Jan 69)
6 Jan 69	Rockford, Ill.	Galena (Ill.) *Gazette* (26 Jan 69), quoting Rockford *Register*
7 Jan 69	Chicago, Ill.	*Tribune* and *Times* (8 Jan 69)
8 Jan 69	Monmouth, Ill.	7 Jan 69 to OLL [2nd of 2]
9 Jan 69	Galesburg, Ill.	Peoria (Ill.) *Transcript* (cited in Wallace, 17)
11 Jan 69	Peoria, Ill.	*Transcript* and *National Democrat* (12 Jan 69)
12 Jan 69[4]	Decatur, Ill.	*Republican* (14 Jan 69)
13 Jan 69	Ottawa, Ill.	*Republican* (21 Jan 69) (cited in Wallace, 132)
14 Jan 69	Davenport, Iowa	*Democrat* (15 Jan 69)
15 Jan 69	Iowa City, Iowa	*Republican* (6 and 20 Jan 69)

[3]Clemens was originally scheduled to appear in Dayton, Ohio, on 31 December (see 21 and 23 Dec 68 to OLL); he told Mrs. Fairbanks in his letter of 24 and 25 December that he would "skip Dayton for the present."

[4]Clemens mentioned in his letter of 2 Jan 69 to Olivia that he was originally scheduled to appear in Bloomington, Illinois, on 12 January.

Appendix H

Photographs and Manuscript Facsimiles

REPRODUCED HERE are thirty-eight contemporary images—photographs (including many original *cartes de visite*), engravings, a porcelaintype, a watercolor miniature, and an oil painting—chiefly of Clemens's friends, associates, and traveling companions during the period of these letters. Many of these images have not been published before.

Immediately following these documents is a representative selection of seven letters in Clemens's holograph, reproduced in photofacsimile. We provide these documents partly for their inherent interest, and partly to afford the reader a chance to see for himself what details of the manuscript the transcription includes, as well as what it omits. Because of the imperfect nature of the facsimiles, close comparison with the transcription may turn up apparent discrepancies between the two.

Jane Lampton Clemens, probably late 1850s. Mark Twain Papers, The Bancroft Library (CU-MARK).

Charles Henry Webb, mid-1870s. Webb inscribed the back on 21 March 1877 to Charles Warren Stoddard. The Bancroft Library (CU-BANC).

Charles Warren Stoddard, 1869. The Bancroft Library (CU-BANC).

Henry Ward Beecher, 1868, engraving (Beecher 1868, frontispiece).

John McComb, 1880.
The Bancroft Library (CU-BANC).

Senator William M. Stewart, 1865.
The Bancroft Library (CU-BANC).

John Russell Young, 1880.
The Bancroft Library (CU-BANC).

The departure of the *Quaker City* from New York on 8 June 1867 (*Frank Leslie's Illustrated Newspaper*, 29 June 67, 233).

Mary Mason Fairbanks, 1867 or 1868. From an original *carte de visite* formerly owned by her granddaughter, Harriet F. Bolles. Mark Twain Papers, The Bancroft Library (CU-MARK).

Solon L. and Emily A. Severance, ?1867. From an original photograph formerly owned by their daughter, Julia Severance Millikin. Mark Twain Papers, The Bancroft Library (CU-MARK).

Dr. Abraham Reeves Jackson.

Julius Moulton.

Daniel Slote (with autograph).

John A. (Jack) Van Nostrand.

These 1867 *cartes de visite* of *Quaker City* excursionists were preserved and, except for Slote's, identified by Colonel Denny. Collection of Mrs. Theodore Whitfield.

Captain Charles C. Duncan.

Major James G. Barry.

Dr. George Bright Birch.

Bloodgood Haviland Cutter (with autograph).

These 1867 *cartes de visite* of *Quaker City* excursionists were preserved and, except for Cutter's, identified by Colonel Denny. Collection of Mrs. Theodore Whitfield.

(Confederate) Colonel William Ritenour Denny.

Colonel James Heron Foster (with autograph).

Stephen M. and Louisa M. Griswold.

Colonel Peter Kinney.

These 1867 *cartes de visite* of *Quaker City* excursionists were preserved and, except for Foster's, identified by Colonel Denny. Collection of Mrs. Theodore Whitfield.

Elisha Bliss, Jr., probably 1870s. Mark Twain Memorial, Hartford, Connecticut (CtHMTH).

Joseph H. Twichell, probably 1860s. Mark Twain Memorial, Hartford, Connecticut (CtHMTH).

Olivia L. Langdon, 1864. Watercolor by Samuel R. Fanshaw (1814–88), actual size. Clemens said in 1906 that he first saw Olivia "in the form of an ivory miniature" on the *Quaker City*. No painting on ivory survives, but this miniature portrait on cardboard was in Clemens's possession at the time of his death. Mark Twain Papers, The Bancroft Library (CU-MARK).

Porcelaintype of Olivia Langdon, 1866 or 1867. Mark Twain Papers, The Bancroft Library (CU-MARK).

Porcelaintype of Olivia Langdon, 1868. Ida Langdon, Charles Langdon's daughter, mistakenly believed this to be the image that Clemens saw on board the *Quaker City;* Paine likewise misidentified it (*MTB*, facing 1:338). Mark Twain Papers, The Bancroft Library (CU-MARK); donated in 1948 by Jervis Langdon, Jr. (Charles's grandson).

Jervis Langdon, ?1869. Mark Twain Papers, The Bancroft Library (CU-MARK).

Olivia Lewis Langdon, ?1869. Mark Twain Papers, The Bancroft Library (CU-MARK).

Charles Jervis Langdon, probably 1867. Mark Twain Memorial, Hartford, Connecticut (CtHMTH).

Susan Langdon Crane, probably late 1850s. Mark Twain Memorial, Hartford, Connecticut (CtHMTH).

Theodore Crane, ?1880. Mark Twain Memorial, Hartford, Connecticut (CtHMTH).

William Chauncey Bartlett, probably late 1860s. The Bancroft Library (CU-BANC).

John Neely Johnson as governor of California (1856–58), oil painting ca. 1875 by Francis M. Pebbles (1839–1928), probably from a photograph. California Department of General Services, Sacramento.

Horatio Stebbins, probably mid-1870s. The Bancroft Library (CU-BANC).

Robert Bunker Swain, ?1869. The Bancroft Library (CU-BANC).

Charles Wadsworth, 1863, engraving (*North Pacific Review* 2 [May 1863]: facing 273). The Bancroft Library (CU-BANC).

Samuel Williams, ?1869. The Bancroft Library (CU-BANC).

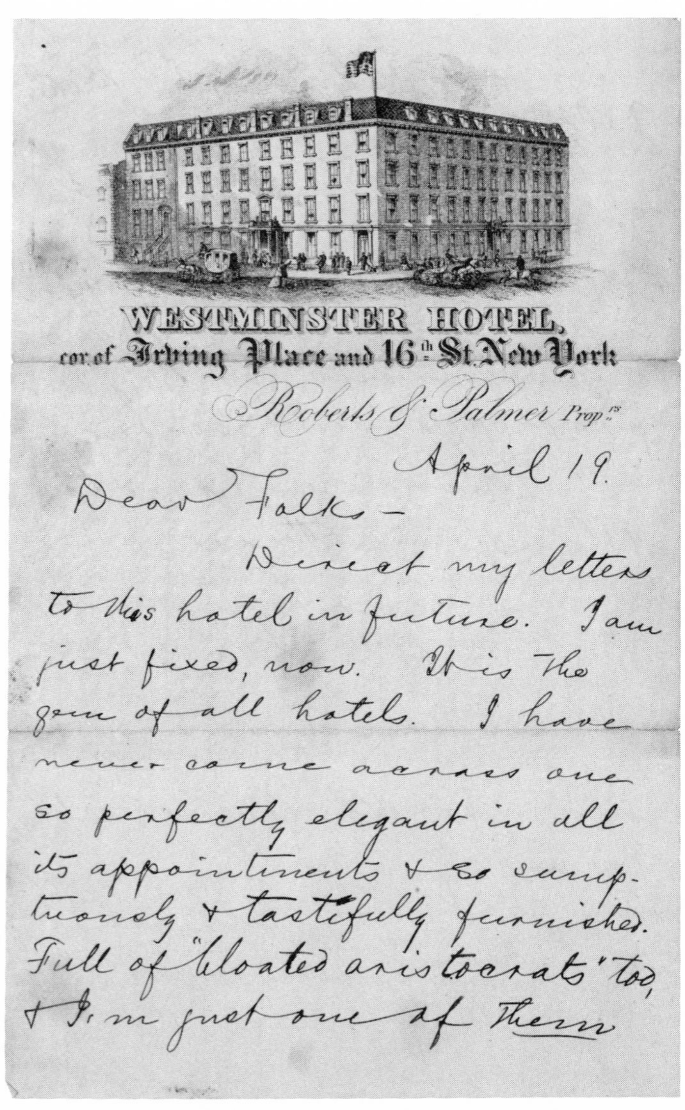

WESTMINSTER HOTEL,
cor. of Irving Place and 16th St. New York
Roberts & Palmer Prop.rs

April 19.

Dear Folks—

Direct my letters to this hotel in future. I am just fixed, now. It is the gem of all hotels. I have never come across one so perfectly elegant in all its appointments & so sumptuously & tastefully furnished. Full of "bloated aristocrats" too, & I'm just one of them

Clemens to Jane Lampton Clemens and family, 19 April 1867, New York, N.Y. Mark Twain Papers, The Bancroft Library (CU-MARK). The letter is written on both sides of a single leaf. Transcribed on p. 27; reproduced at 64 percent of actual size.

kind myself — & so is Beck Jolly.

The book will issue the 25th. James Russell Lowell ("Hosea Biglow,") says the Jumping Frog is the finest piece of humorous writing ever produced in America.

Give my love to all my sweethearts.

Good bye

Sam

Dorsey goes west in a day or two.

Manuscript page 2, to Jane Lampton Clemens and family, 19 April 1867. Verso.

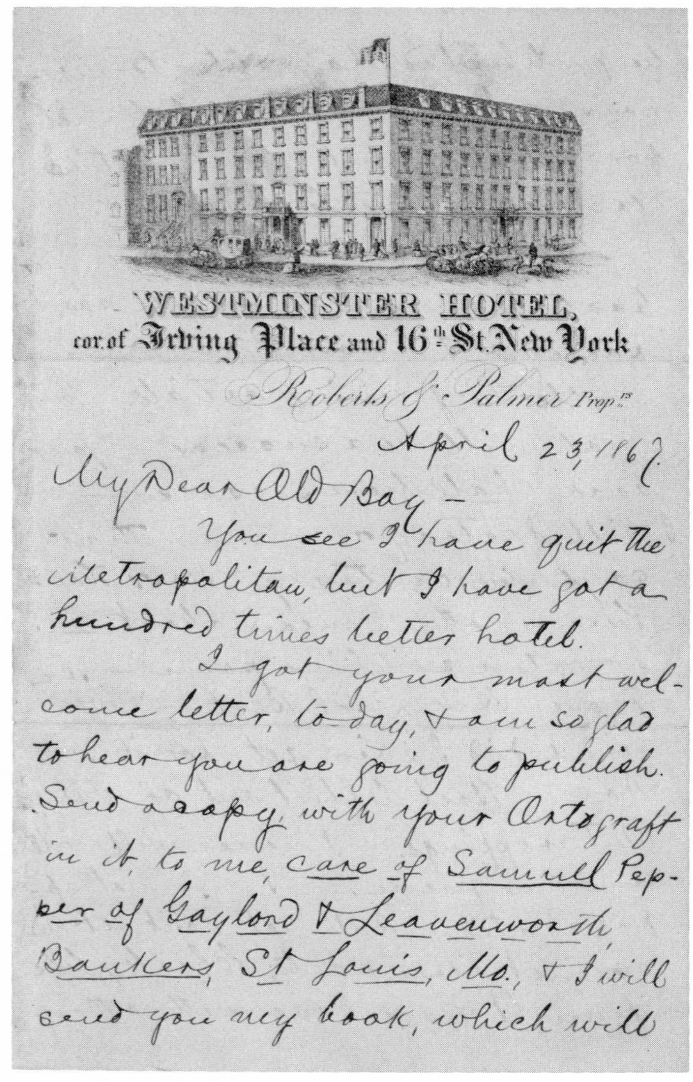
WESTMINSTER HOTEL,
cor. of Irving Place and 16th St. New York
Roberts & Palmer Prop.rs

April 23, 1867.

My Dear Old Boy—

You see I have quit the Metropolitan, but I have got a hundred times better hotel.

I got your most welcome letter, to-day, & am so glad to hear you are going to publish. Send a copy, with your Ortograft in it, to me, care of Samuel Pepper of Gaylord & Leavenworth, Bankers, St Louis, Mo., & I will send you my book, which will

Clemens to Charles Warren Stoddard, 23 April 1867, New York, N.Y. Mark Twain Papers, The Bancroft Library (CU-MARK). The four-page letter is written on both sides of two leaves of a folded sheet. Transcribed on pp. 29–30; reproduced at 64 percent of actual size.

be published day after to-morrow. I suppose I shall sail for Palestine just about the time you receive this—June 8.

I want to endorse your book, because I know all about poetry & I know you can write the genuine article. Your book will be a success—your book *shall* be a success—& I will destroy any man that says the contrary. How's that? There is nothing mean about *me*. I wrote a sublime poem—"He Done His Level Best"—& what credit did I ever get for it?—None. Bret left it out of the Outcroppings. I never will write another poem. I am not appreciated. But that don't set me against other poets, Charley, like it might have done with other

Manuscript page 2, to Charles Warren Stoddard, 23 April 1867. Verso of the first leaf.

men, & so I will back up your book just as strong as I know how. Count on me to-day, to-morrow & *all the time.* And I don't say it in a whisper, but I say it strong.

[Signed & sworn to]—

Mark Twain

I haven't seen Miss Carmichael, but I hope I shall, soon.

I was talking with Willie Winter, the talented reviewer of the Tribune & the Saturday Review, yesterday, & he said a lady had given him some of your poems, in MSS, & he, supposing they had not been published (I think she *told* him they had not,) printed them as original & got scissors for it in the San F. papers. Then he apologised in print, or explained, & the San F. papers scouted his ex-

Manuscript page 3, to Charles Warren Stoddard, 23 April 1867. Recto of the second leaf.

planation as a shabby falsehood. He is one of the finest young men on the press anywhere, & it is a pity to throw away his good will & his really great influence. The Cal. papers ought to let these papers here borrow from us occasionally,—it wouldn't actually help the Cal. paper to receive credit, & it *does* help us to be copied, with signature attached.

How is Bret? He is publishing with a Son of a Bitch who will swindle him, & he may print that opinion if he chooses, with my name signed to it. I don't know how his book is coming on—we of Bohemia keep away from Carleton's.

The papers here say I am going to lecture shortly, & I may. I don't know yet.

Write to me, *sure*, care of Mr Pepper, St Louis (I mean to have my letters forwarded to Europe.)

Good-bye, & God bless you, my boy.

Mark Twain

Manuscript page 4, to Charles Warren Stoddard, 23 April 1867. Verso of the second leaf.

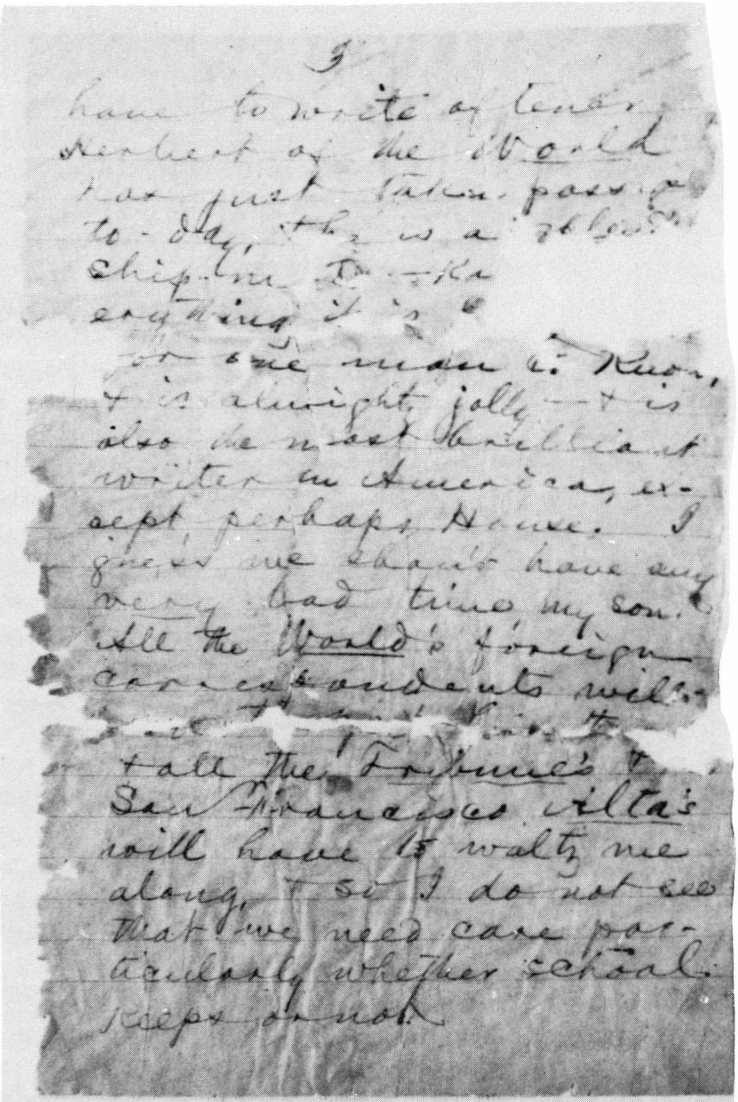

Clemens to William Bowen, 7 June 1867, New York, N.Y. Harry Ransom Humanities Research Center, University of Texas, Austin (TxU). Only two of the four original manuscript pages of this letter survive; they are written on the rectos of two leaves numbered 3 and 4. The letter is transcribed on p. 54, where the text of the missing pages, as well as of the damaged portions of the surviving pages, has been recovered from a complete TS (see the textual commentary); reproduced at 70 percent of actual size.

Manuscript page 4, to William Bowen, 7 June 1867. Recto of the second leaf.

Washington, Dec. 2, 1867.

E. Bliss, Jr. Esq.

Sec'y American Publishing Co.—

Dear Sir:

I only received your favor of Nov. 21st last night, at the rooms of the Tribune Bureau here. It was forwarded from the Tribune office, New York, where it had lain eight or ten days. This will be a sufficient apology for the seeming discourtesy of my silence.

I ~~have written~~ wrote fifty-two letters for the San Francisco "Alta California" during the Quaker City excursion, about half of which number have been printed, thus far. The "Alta" has few exchanges in the east, and I suppose scarcely any of these letters have been copied on this side of the Rocky

Clemens to Elisha Bliss, Jr., 2 December 1867, Washington, D.C. Mark Twain Papers, The Bancroft Library (CU-MARK). The letter is written on the first three pages of a folded sheet cut into two leaves. Transcribed on pp. 119–20; reproduced at 58 percent of actual size.

Mountains. I could weed them of their chief faults of contruction & inelegancies of expression, & make a volume that would be more acceptable in many respects than any I could now write. When those letters were written my impressions were fresh, but now they have lost that freshness; they were warm then—they are cold, now. I could strike out certain letters, & write new ones wherewith to supply their places. If you think such a book would suit your purpose, please drop me a line, specifying the size & general style of the volume; when the matter ought to be ready; whether it should have pictures in it or not; & particularly what your terms with me would be, & what amount of money I might possibly make out of it. The latter clause has a degree of importance for me which is almost beyond my own comprehension. But you understand that, of course.

Manuscript page 2, to Elisha Bliss, Jr., 2 December 1867. Verso of the first leaf.

I have other propositions for a book, but have doubted the propriety of interfering with good newspaper engagements except my way as an author could be demonstrated to be plain before me. But I know Richardson, & learned from him, some months ago, something of an idea of the subscription plan of publishing. If that is your plan invariably, it looks safe.

I am on the N. Y. Tribune staff here as an "occasional," among other things, and a note from you addressed to

Very Truly &c
Sam. L. Clemens

New York Tribune Bureau, Washington, will find me, without fail.

Manuscript page 3, to Elisha Bliss, Jr., 2 December 1867. Recto of the second leaf.

P. S.—Oh, excuse haste, bad grammar & everything. I am in a fidget *all* the time. [I am getting to italicise, like a girl.]

N. Y. Tribune Bureau
Washington D.C. Dec. 2.
1867

My Dear Forgiving Mother—

It all came of making a promise! I might have known it. I never keep a promise. I don't know how. They only taught about the wise virgins & the stupid ones, in our Sunday School—never anything about promises. The truth is, Mr. Bennett sent for me two or three times before I ~~[illegible]~~ approached the Herald. They found me, the last time, within 200 yards of the St Nicholas, whither I was going to dine with you & Charlie. Well, I was bitter on those passengers. You don't know *what* atrocious things women, & men too gray-haired & old to have their noses pulled, said about me. And but for your protecting hand

Clemens to Mary Mason Fairbanks, 2 December 1867, Washington, D.C. Special Collections Department (Clemens 6314-q), Clifton Waller Barrett Library, University of Virginia, Charlottesville (ViU). The letter is written on the first six pages of two folded sheets cut into four leaves (Clemens used the fourth leaf for 2 Dec 67 to Fuller). Only the fifth page is numbered. Transcribed on pp. 121–23; reproduced at 58 percent of actual size.

I would have given them a [illegible] or two that would have penetrated even their muddy intellect & afforded [illegible] them something worth abusing me about. Well, the last time I was sent for, [illegible] it was Mr. Glen, chief of the foreign correspondence department that came, & he just happened to touch the old bitterness [illegible] in the right place. I had had no time to go anywhere or get any money; I wanted fifty dollars; I thought, now, I can make that in two hours, & stir up those Quakers most delightfully [illegible] at the very same time — & yet, say nothing that will sound malicious. I found part of that old article in my pocket, & [illegible] it in. It was well I didn't find it all — & well it was, also, that all real malice passed out of my heart while I wrote. Else I must [illegible] have said bitter things. And yet to this

Manuscript page 2, to Mary Mason Fairbanks, 2 December 1867. Verso of the first leaf.

day I have a strong desire, whenever I think of some of the events of that trip with that ~~sppkkkkgkkkk~~, to print the savagest kind of a history of the excursion. ~~[canceled]~~ I have promised you that I wouldn't, & so I haven't the slightest doubt in the world *but that I will*. I can't keep a promise. When I get married I shall say: "I take this woman to be my lawfully wedded wife, & *propose* to *look out* for her in a sort of a general way, &c &c." It would be dangerous to go beyond that.

But I didn't *promise* you that I wouldn't swear—yet *no* man is freer from the sin of swearing than is thy servant this day; & no man is freer from the *inclination* to swear, than he, whether ^he is^ in a passion or otherwise.

Manuscript page 3, to Mary Mason Fairbanks, 2 December 1867. Recto of the second leaf.

I was the worst swearer, & the most reckless, that sailed out of New York in the Quaker City. I shamed Bursley; I shamed Harris; I shamed the very fo'castle watches, I think. But I am as perfectly & as permanently cured of the habit as I am of chewing tobacco. Your doubts, Madam, cannot shake my faith in this reformation. I have _no_ inclination to swear, albeit I boil over as often as ever; more ~~this~~ than this, I feel the same _uncomfortableness_ in the hearing of oaths that I feel when I listen to things that have always been distasteful to me. Shall these signs pass for nothing? Have not they a deep meaning? Do not they show that it is not merely that the idle tongue has ~~[illegible]~~ been taught a new trick which it may discard when the novelty is gone, but that the lesson has gone down, down, to the spirit that orders the tongue & commands its movements?

Manuscript page 4, to Mary Mason Fairbanks, 2 December 1867. Verso of the second leaf.

5

Verily this is so, O thou of little faith!
And while I remember you, my good, kind
<u>mother</u>, (whom God preserve!) never be-
lieve that tongue or spirit shall forget
this priceless lesson that you have taught
them.

But as for those Quakers, I don't
want their friendship, I don't want
their good opinions, I wouldn't have
their good offices. I don't want any
commerce with people I don't like.
They can hurt me. Let them. I would
rather they should hurt me than help me.
All the friends I wanted in that ship were:
Yourself; Mr & Mrs. Severance; the cub;
Emma Beach; Dan; Moulton; Jack;
I don't remember any others—I don't suppose
there <u>were</u> any others. My opinion of the
rest of the gang is so mean, & so vicious,

Manuscript page 5, to Mary Mason Fairbanks, 2 December 1867. Recto of the third leaf.

& so outrageous in every way, that I could
not collect the terms to express it with-
out of any less than sixteen or seventeen
different languages. Such another
drove of cattle *never* went to sea before.
Select party! Well, *I* pass.

Those vapid, senseless letters I pub-
lished in the Tribune had *one* good effect.
They procured me several propositions
from the book publishers. I like that
of The American Publishing Co. of Hart-
ford, much the best. They publish only
by subscription, & by this means gave A. D.
Richardson's first book 100,000 ~~circle~~ cir-
culation & have already given his last
one 41,000. I have written them to give me
an explicit statement of what they want,
when they want it, &c.

I am Tribune "occasional," *Alta*
"special" & have propositions from the
Herald. I have magazine engagements—but unhap-
pily I have *promised*. I have had, & still receive,
lecturing invitations, but cannot accept, of course.
I am full of work, & as usual am doing nothing. I give
you these foolish details, believing they will interest you.
Give me another sermon! Yr. Improving Prodigal, Saml. Clemens

Manuscript page 6, to Mary Mason Fairbanks, 2 December 1867. Verso of the third leaf.

Clemens to Mary Mason Fairbanks, 3 August 1868, New York, N.Y. Huntington Library, San Marino, Calif. (CSmH). Pages 1 and 2 of this three-page letter are written on the first and fourth sides of a single folded sheet; page 3 is written across sides two and three on the inside. The letter was damaged when the signature on page 3 was cut away. Transcribed on pp. 237–38; reproduced at 50 percent of actual size.

Dan says you were in Elmira a short time ago. I wish I could have arrived soon enough to see you. Cannot you come East now? You haven't got anything to do.

I knew that dog would die. I know perfectly well you had invoked a fatal disaster for him when you gave him my name. He received all my ills along with the name, perhaps, & no dog could survive that.

Remember me most kindly to all the family, & herewith know that I hold you to an extension of your invitation, to take effect two months hence. Whereupon, you will please stand ready to trot out your fatted calf.

Manuscript page 3, whence the signature was removed, to Mary Mason Fairbanks, 3 August 1868.

Hartford, Oct. 30.

My Honored Sister:

Your welcome letter made me entirely *satisfied*. And so I have dispatched all lagging work contentedly since, & am unmanacled, now, & free to go whither I list. I owe you many thanks for this assistance. And I thank you for the assurance that I still have your respect & esteem—& particularly that "they have not been changed"—for I would not willingly have them diminished in any degree.

"It may sometimes seem to you that Christ is far from you, that his indwelling spirit is not with you." You have said truly. I pray as one who prays with words, against a firm-set mountain of

Clemens to Olivia L. Langdon, 30 October 1868, Hartford, Conn. Mark Twain Papers, The Bancroft Library (CU-MARK). The letter is written on nine leaves torn from folded sheets. The first eight leaves have writing on the rectos only. Clemens originally wrote on the recto only of the ninth leaf as well, but added two postscripts on its verso. Transcribed on pp. 271–75; reproduced at 73 percent of actual size.

2

sin. I pray too hopefully, sometimes, & sometimes hopelessly. But I still pray—& shall continue to pray. Mr. Twichell has confidence that I shall succeed, & says that I will be a most useful man in the world then—& you know it is pleasant to think that at any time you have been useful or are going to be. The idea of that party of ministers at his house the other night thanking me fervently for having written & published certain trash which they said had lit up some gloomy days with a wholesome laugh was a surprise to me. I had not flattered myself before that a part of my mission on earth was to be a benefactor to the clergy. I believe I have only one good hope to keep me in heart in this search

Manuscript page 2, to Olivia L. Langdon, 30 October 1868. Recto of the second leaf.

3

after a better life, & that is, that indolent as I seem, I know I possess a deal of persistence, & that I shall keep on coming to the surface again after each discouragement & beginning the contest afresh until—. Time must decide what the result shall be. I believe, appreciate, & have treasured up what you say about religion & what was in the little printed slip, & I trust that this kindness & consideration of yours will not be lost upon me.

Mr. & Mrs. Twichell & myself, & two young ladies, sisters of Mrs. T., drove 10 miles out in the country & back the other day, & in the course of the conversation Mr. T. uttered several things that struck me forcibly. I was speaking at length about the present

Manuscript page 3, to Olivia L. Langdon, 30 October 1868. Recto of the third leaf.

4

wonderful method of com-
municating with the deaf &
dumb almost wholly by word-
signs instead of letters, & said it
was so particularly curious
because some of these people
were <u>born</u> deaf & dumb & con-
sequently knew no <u>words</u> at all
—then how is it that we, who <u>think</u>
<u>in words</u>, can convey <u>such</u> thoughts
to these people? He said we
<u>didn't</u> always think in words—
that our highest, grandest, most
brilliant thoughts were far be-
yond our capacity to frame into
words, & that we <u>had</u> no words
that would express them—that
often a radiant thought-vision
lit up our plodding brains with
its wierd beauty, & vanished
instantly to the heaven it surely
came from, while we stood
amazed, delighted, yet utterly

Manuscript page 4, to Olivia L. Langdon, 30 October 1868. Recto of the fourth leaf.

5

incapable of determining
what it was like, but only
ejaculating helplessly, "Heav-
ens! *what* was that!" And
he said something like this—I have
the substance I think, but I have for-
gotten his language: But some day
this trammelling flesh will be stripped
away, this prison-house thrown open
& the soul set free—free to expand
to its just magnitude—& *then* what
thoughts we shall have! What visions!
The celestial visitants that haunt us
now, exquisite but without form & void,
will be stately temples of thought, ornate,
symmetrical, full of grace, & gor-
geous with dissolving lights that
stream from that far-off world
we dream of!—*not* the shapeless
magnificent chaos they seem to
us here in the dark! I never heard
this idea suggested before, but I
think it is very beautiful.

Manuscript page 5, to Olivia L. Langdon, 30 October 1868. Recto of the fifth leaf.

6

Twichell is splendid. And
he has one rare faculty—he is thought-
ful & considerate. He lends me
his overcoat when I go there without
one, lends me his umbrella, lends
me his slippers. I asked for a pair
of slippers only once—I never have
to ask for them now. These are
small things, but they show the
man, you know—he thinks of
other people's comfort before
his own—& thus reminds me of
you—& to my own disadvantage.
For I know of many instances of
your inconveniencing yourself
to satisfy some persistent petition
of mine, when it would have looked
better if I had been thinking more of
your pleasure & less of my own. I
know very well what you would say to
this, but that couldn't alter the *facts*
any. The facts simply are, that I ought
to be ashamed of myself—and I

Manuscript page 6, to Olivia L. Langdon, 30 October 1868. Recto of the sixth leaf.

7

ain't. I still reflect with pleasure
upon every time I persuaded you
to do anything. It was wrong to per-
suade you to go to see the Misses Spaul-
ding that day when you wanted to
write. But I would do it again.
I do not mind doing <u>any</u>thing that is
wrong when I know I am right. No,
I am unrepentant. I regret to-this
day that the horse was not there.

"Each soul must fight its own
battle, & human friendship is impotent to
help." I even think I am glad to find an
imperfection in you, for it makes you more
like other people—glad to find a most un-
generous sentiment reposing in a bosom
where it has no company. The little child,
trusting its mother, trusts her God—hav-
ing faith in its mother, has faith in Whom
<u>she</u> worships—loving its mother, loves
the Savior toward whose gracious pres-
ence she turns with such a yearning
tenderness—& so led, so guided, <u>it</u> is

Manuscript page 7, to Olivia L. Langdon, 30 October 1868. Recto of the seventh leaf.

8

saved, while the doctors, learned & wise,
grope among premises & arguments, tes-
timonies, doubts & logic, & are lost.
The preacher helps his flock—the mis-
sionary exiles himself from all of earth
his love holds dear, to help the friendless
& ~~f~~ forsaken in every hapless land—even
Jesus saith, "If two of you shall agree
on earth as touching anything that they shall
ask, it shall be done for them of my Father
which is in Heaven." And so you, only you,
are left to say "human friendship is im-
potent to help." You have read Matt. XXV,
44–45? & XVII, 18–20? However, you make
the strongest point against your own doctrine,
once in every four & twenty hours—when you
pray for me—& so what need is there that
I should say a word by way of argument?

But I still stick to what I said at first
—I am glad you hold this extravagant doctrine
—I am glad you have it—I would not that it
should be otherwise, my sister—& with that
perversity that belongs to human nature, I simply
love you all the better for it.

Manuscript page 8, to Olivia L. Langdon, 30 October 1868. Recto of the eighth leaf.

P.S.—Good-bye & pleasant dreams.—Your affectionate Brother, Saml L. Clemens.

But after all, I must unsay those arguments of mine—for I cannot pit a few flippant fancies against the years of patient study that have revealed to you the truth. And when I come to search my understanding & my heart, neither will consent that you are capable of thinking a wrong thing any more than you are of doing one. I do not want to think you are—I do not want to harbor such an idea at all—[illegible] [Now I didn't want to scratch that out, but then maybe [illegible] I thought I had better do it. Curiosity is a virtue of your sex—I don't mind your exercising it, sister mine.]

Yes, I will be sure to write Mrs. F. to send you that book. No, I'll get a new one & mark it again. That one is soiled by railway travel. I have been reading such an exquisite book! I'll tell you all I—No indeed, you are not given to saying unkind things, & I am very, very thankful for it—but I knew you could, if you believed it necessary, & that is why I pleaded. Get your Browning ready—for lo, I come like a lamb to the slaughter! You know very well that I enjoyed my lessons before, notwithstanding I couldn't get the gas-lamps right.

I shall spend the first week of Nov. in New York, & shall surely call on Mrs. Brooks ("not Brown"—yes, I remember.) Then I shall be in Cleveland till the 17th Nov. Won't you please write me at the Everett House, Union Square, N.Y.? Remember it is already "unfrequently" since you wrote. Try—& if you can't, why then be sure to write "Care Herald, Cleveland"—long before the 17th. Now remember that I am not where I can "persist" until I persuade you—& so be generous.

You see that I am trying not to abuse my privilege of writing as much as I please—& not succeeding worth a cent. Somehow 9 pages don't seem to hold anything. [illegible]

What was the name of that hymn we fancied so much, in church one day? "Fading, Still Fading" is beautiful—old, but beautiful.

Manuscript page 9, to Olivia L. Langdon, 30 October 1868. Recto of the ninth leaf.

P.P.S.—I am going to a Yale College re-union with Mr. Twichell & then go on to N.Y.

I will seize the opportunity offered by all this blank space to say

[I did not scratch it out to excite your curiosity, or to tease you, but because it was surplusage.]

P.S. I have got mother Fairbanks in a stew again.—I named that lecture just for her benefit. And I sent her an absurd synopsis of it that I knew would provoke her wrath—& intimated that I was idling somewhat. I like to tease her because I like her so.

P.S.—Have just received an imperative invitation from the Webb sisters to attend a party in New York to-night—to which is added an urgent note from several eminent newspaper men & "Many New Yorkers & Californians"—& now, my sister, my curiosity is fearfully excited. I do wonder what it is? I shall take the cars at noon.

Manuscript page 10, to Olivia L. Langdon, 30 October 1868. Verso of the ninth leaf, inscribed after the letter was folded for mailing.

The envelope, to Olivia L. Langdon, 30 October 1868. Although Clemens wrote this letter in Hartford, the front of the envelope was postmarked in New Haven, where he mailed it later that same day. The back of the envelope bears Olivia's contemporary endorsement ("5th") as well as Clara Clemens's later annotation, "Read."

Editorial Apparatus

Guide to Editorial Practice

THE AIM OF *Mark Twain's Letters* is to publish, in chronological order, the most reliable and the most legible text possible for every personal and business letter written by (or for) Samuel L. Clemens, and to publish the letters he received, selectively, as a part of the annotation. The editorial aim for that annotation is to explain whatever requires explanation, either in notes appended to the letters, or in editorial narrative between them, with cross-references and reidentifications accomplished (as necessary) largely through the index. Three further matters, about which it is useful to be informed only as the need arises, are treated in the textual commentaries at the back of the volume: (a) when and where a letter has been previously published, if at all; (b) where and by whom the original documents have been preserved, or not, as the case may be; and (c) how and on what evidence the text of each letter has been established for this edition.

Fundamentally, the text of any letter is a matter of historical fact, determined for all time by the original act of sending it. Its text therefore includes everything that was originally sent, from the envelope to the enclosures: all nonverbal elements, all words and word fragments, numerals, punctuation, and formal signs—whether canceled or standing, inscribed or adopted, written or stamped by others during the time of original transmission and receipt. There is no necessary or obvious hypothetical limit on which of these elements may be significant. We must begin, in fact, with the assumption that almost any aspect of an original letter might be significant, either to the writer or the recipient, or both—not to mention those for whom the letters are now being published. In principle, therefore, the text of any letter properly excludes only such additions, revisions, and corrections as were made in the documents after the original transmission and receipt—even if such changes were made by the writer or the original recipient, or someone acting on their behalf.

But while there are few limits on what properly constitutes the text of a letter, there are many limits on what constitutes a satisfactory transcription of it. Most of Clemens's letters that survive in the original holograph, for example, lack the original envelope. Some lack one or more of the enclosures, or have been deliberately censored with the scissors, and not a few have been accidentally damaged and partly lost in one way or another, subsequent to their original transmission. All such accidents, however, limit only how much of the letter may be said to survive in its original documents, not how much of it ought to be, or even can be, transcribed. It is commonplace for a letter to survive partly in its original documents, and partly in a copy of originals otherwise missing or lost: any transcription that did not rely on *both* could scarcely be called complete, let alone reliable. The real question is not how transcriptions may be limited because parts of a letter no longer survive, but how much of the text that does survive a transcription may *leave out* and still function as intended.

We assume that the purpose of publishing letters is to make them easier to read than they are in the original documents. On that assumption, a successful transcription must include enough of the text to enable someone to rely on *it*, rather than the original, and it must exclude enough to make the transcribed text easier to read (or at least not more difficult to read) than the original. Thus, when the documents originally sent are intact and available, we transcribe them as fully and precisely as is compatible with a highly inclusive *critical text*—not a literal, or all-inclusive one, but a typographical transcription that is optimally legible and, at the same time, maximally faithful to the text that Clemens himself transmitted.[1] Original documents are therefore emended (changed) *as little as possible*, which means only in order to alter, simplify, or omit what would otherwise threaten to make the transcription unreadable, or less than fully intelligible in its own right. When, however, the original

[1] The transcription is not a *literal text*, even though it is probably as inclusive as most texts for which that claim is made, nor is it a *noncritical text*, as defined by G. Thomas Tanselle, since even though it "aims at reproducing a given earlier text [i.e., the original letter] as exactly as possible," the editor essentially defines what *is* possible by deciding what can be transcribed legibly. The editor is therefore "making decisions about how the new text will differ from the text in the document," with the result that the transcription necessarily "becomes a critical text" ("Textual Scholarship" in *Introduction to Scholarship in Modern Languages and Literatures*, edited by Joseph Gibaldi [New York: Modern Language Association, 1981], 32, 47).

documents are lost, we necessarily rely on the most authoritative *copy* of them. Since copies by their nature contain errors, nonoriginal documents are emended *as much as necessary*, partly for the reasons we emend originals, but chiefly to restore the text of the lost original, insofar as the evidence permits. The only exceptions (each discussed below) are letters which survive (a) only in the author's draft, (b) only in someone else's paraphrase of the original, (c) only in damaged originals or unique nonoriginals, and (d) in originals that, wholly or in part, can be faithfully reproduced only in photographic facsimile. But whether or not a letter survives in its original documents, every departure from the text of the documents used (designated the copy-text) is recorded as an emendation in the textual commentary for that letter, barring only the most trivial kinds of change, which are instead categorized and described here.

Mark Twain's Letters, Volume 1 (1988), first applied this basic rationale for emendation while also deploying a new system of manuscript notation. We called the result "plain text," partly to distinguish it from the alternative methods still used most frequently to publish letters, so-called "clear text" and "genetic text."[2] We require two things of every transcription in plain text: (a) it must be sufficiently faithful to the text of the letter to serve as the most *reliable substitute* now possible for it; and

[2]According to Fredson Bowers, "General methods of transcription divide neatly in two," which is to say (a) *clear texts*, with supplementary apparatus containing all details of revision, and (b) *genetic texts*, without supplementary apparatus because the text itself contains all such details. A clear text transcribes the revised form of a manuscript "diplomatically," meaning that the "transcription exactly follows the forms of the manuscript in spelling, punctuation, word-division, italics (for underlining), and capitalization, but not in matters of spacing or in line-division, nor is a facsimile visual presentation of alterations attempted." A genetic text, on the other hand, includes authorial alterations in the text "by means of a number of arbitrary symbols like pointed brackets to the left or right, arrows, bars, and so on," with the common result that it is often "difficult to read the original text consecutively" and "impossible to read the revised text at all in a coherent sequence" ("Transcription of Manuscripts: The Record of Variants," *Studies in Bibliography* 29 [1976]: 213–14, 248). *Plain text*, however, descends from a kind of transcription not mentioned by Bowers, in which the myriad details of a manuscript (particularly the author's alterations to it) are systematically divided between the text and its apparatus, precisely in order to make the text as complete and informative as possible without destroying its legibility (see *N&J1*, 575–84). The practical result of this division is radically improved by adopting a less obtrusive and more readable system of notation than has been used in the past: plain text manages simultaneously to increase both overall legibility *and* the amount of detail that can be included in the transcription.

(b) it must be *easier to read* than the original letter, so long as its reliability is preserved intact. To the extent that maximum fidelity and maximum legibility come into conflict, this way of linking them ensures that neither goal is maximized at undue expense to the other. The linkage works well for Clemens's letters, in part because they (like many people's letters) were intended to be read in manuscript, and his manuscripts are typically very legible to begin with. But in no small part, the linkage succeeds because the new system of notation is able to make legible in transcription many aspects of manuscript which would otherwise pose the necessity of choosing between maximum fidelity and maximum legibility. The consequence is that a typical letter transcription in plain text, though obviously not a replacement for the original, can still be read, relied on, and quoted from, as if it were the original.

While the notation system is admittedly new, it makes as much use as possible of editorial conventions that are familiar, traditional, and old. We have, for instance, deliberately kept the number of new conventions to a minimum, modifying or adding to them only very gradually, and only as the letters themselves demand it. When editorial conventions are new, they often adapt familiar conventions of both handwriting and typography. New conventions are in general called for by the effort to include, or at least to include more legibly, what has tended to be problematic, or simply ignored, in earlier methods of transcription. Two examples here will suffice. To transcribe printed letterhead in a way that is practical, inclusive, and fully intelligible, plain text uses EXTRA-SMALL SMALL CAPITALS for the printed words and a dotted underscore below whatever the writer put in the printed blanks, such as the date and place. Likewise, to transcribe all cancellations and identify all insertions (even of single characters) where they occur in the text, but without making the result illegible, plain text uses ~~line-through~~ cross-out rules, a̸ slashes, and ‸inferior‸ carets.‸,

Most of these devices can now be produced with the type itself, making them economical both to set and to print. And many can fairly be characterized as type-identical with their handwritten counterparts. A line or a slash through type, crossing it out, needs no interpretation: it simply *means* canceled, just as it would in manuscript. The overall effect therefore contrasts favorably with the effect of arbitrary symbols, such as ⟨pointed⟩ brackets to the left ⟨a⟩ or right, ↑arrows,↓ | bars↑,↓ and so on—editorial conventions that today will seem both new and numerous, that will almost certainly mean something different from one edition to the next, and that in any case must be consciously construed at each occurrence.

A related risk of type-identical signs, on the other hand, is that their editorial function as *signs* will be forgotten—that they will be seen to picture, rather than to transcribe (re-encode), the original manuscript. It thus bears repeating that plain text, despite its greater visual resemblance to the handwritten originals, is emphatically not a type facsimile of them. Like all diplomatic transcription *except* type facsimile, plain text does not reproduce, simulate, or report the original lineation, pagination, or any other formal aspect of the manuscript, save where the writer intended it to bear meaning and that meaning is transcribable—which is exactly why it does reproduce or simulate many formal elements, such as various kinds of indention and purposeful lineation. In fact, it is usually the case that these formal (nonverbal) aspects of manuscript already have more or less exact *equivalents* in nineteenth-century typographical conventions.

Clemens's letters lend themselves to such treatment in part because his training as a printer (1847–53) began a lifelong fascination with all typographical matters, and in part because he lived at a time when the equivalents between handwriting and type were probably more fully developed and more widely accepted than they had ever been before (or are likely ever to be again). The consequence for his handwritten letters was that, while he clearly never intended them to be set in type, he still used the handwritten forms of a great many typographical conventions as consistently and precisely in them, as he did in literary manuscripts that were intended for publication. This habitual practice makes it possible to transcribe his letters very much as if they were intended for type—to use, in other words, the system of equivalents employed by nineteenth-century writers to tell the typesetter how the manuscript should appear in type—but in reverse, to tell those who rely on the typographical transcription just how the letter manuscript appears. In short, Clemens's typographical expertise makes his letters easier to transcribe fully and precisely, as well as easier to read in transcription, than they otherwise would be, assuming that we understand the meaning of his signs and the code for their typographical equivalents exactly as he did—an assumption that cannot always be taken as granted.

1. The Author's Signs

A few of the typographical signs in these letters may seem a bit unfamiliar, if not wholly exotic. Others may seem familiar, even though they in fact no longer have the precise and accepted meaning they had when Clemens used them. Especially because some signs have fallen into disuse and (partly for that reason) been adapted by modern editors for their own purposes, it is the more necessary to emphasize that here they bear only the meaning given them by Clemens and his contemporaries. Purely editorial signs in the transcription are identified on pages xxv–xxvii above, and since they sometimes adapt typographical conventions, they must not be confused with authorial signs. They have, in fact, been designed to avoid such confusion, and especially to avoid usurping the normal, typographical equivalents for authorial signs.

Still, authorial signs present two related but distinct problems for successful transcription: (a) how to explicate those signs whose authorial meaning differed from the modern meaning, but can still be recovered, at least in part; and (b) how to represent authorial signs whose earlier typographical equivalent, if any, remains unknown—at least to the editors. The glossary of SPECIAL SORTS and table of EMPHASIS EQUIVALENTS which follow here are intended to solve these problems—to alert the reader to those changes in meaning which we can identify, and to describe the handwritten forms for which the typographical forms are taken to be equivalent—or, in a few cases, for which they have been *made* equivalent because we lack a better alternative.

The glossary includes signs that do not appear in every volume of *Mark Twain's Letters*, much less in every letter, and it omits some signs that will only be added as they become relevant in subsequent volumes. Like the glossary, the table provides some information that was, and often still is, regarded as common knowledge, which may explain why the contemporary equivalent for some authorial signs has proved so elusive. That no table of comparable detail or completeness has so far been found in any grammar, printer's handbook, dictionary, or encyclopedia, would appear to indicate that the system of emphasis was almost completely taken for granted, hence rarely made fully explicit or published, even by those who relied upon it. The particular meaning for Clemens of all such equivalents between manuscript and type, at any rate, has had to be deduced or inferred from the letters themselves, and from his numerous literary manuscripts, with his instructions for the typist and typesetter (sometimes with the further evidence of how they responded to his instructions), as well as from the consistent but usually partial evidence in a variety of printer's handbooks, encyclopedias, manuals of forms, and other documents bearing on what we take to be the system of equivalents between handwriting and type (*L1*, xlvi n. 3).

Special Sorts

asterisks * * * Always called "stars" by Clemens and by printers generally, asterisks appear in his manuscript as simple "Xs" or crosses (X), or in a somewhat more elaborate variant of the cross (⁕), often when used singly. In letters (and elsewhere) he used the asterisk as a standard reference mark, either to signal his occasional footnotes, or to refer the reader from one part of a text to another part. (The conventional order of the standard reference marks was as follows: *, †, ‡, §, ‖, ¶, and, by the end of the century, ☞.) He also used asterisks for a kind of ellipsis that was then standard and is still recognizable, and for one now virtually obsolete—the "line of stars"—in which evenly spaced asterisks occupy a line by themselves to indicate a major omission of text, or—for Clemens, at any rate—the passage of time not otherwise represented in a narrative. For the standard ellipsis, we duplicate the number of asterisks in the source, thus: * * * * (see also *ellipsis*, below). In transcribing the line of stars, however, the exact number of asterisks in the original becomes irrelevant, since the device is intended to fill the line, which is rarely the same length in manuscript as it is in the transcription. The line of stars in the original is thus always transcribed by seven asterisks, evenly separated and indented from both margins, thus:

* * * * * * *

braces } ⏟ { { Clemens drew the brace as a wavy vertical line that did not much resemble the brace in type, except that it clearly grouped two or three lines of text together. He drew braces intended for three or more lines as straight (nonwavy) lines with squared corners, like a large bracket, usually in the margin. He occasionally used the two- and three-line braces in pairs, vertically and horizontally, to box or partly enclose one or more words, often on a single line. The one-line brace ({ }) was evidently not known to him, and would probably have seemed a contradiction in terms. It appears to be a modern invention, but has sometimes proved useful in the transcription when the original lineation could not be reproduced or readily simulated (see *L1*, 219). Otherwise, the transcription always prints a brace and preserves, or at least simulates, the original lineation.

dashes – — —— ——— = Clemens used the dash in all four of its most common typographical forms (en, em, two-em, and three-em), as well as a parallel dash, shorter than an em dash, which we render by an equals sign. The parallel dash appears to be used interchangeably with the much more frequently used em dash, but almost invariably at the end of a line (often a short line, such as the greeting). Its special meaning, if any, remains unknown. Clemens occasionally used dashes visibly longer than his em dash, presumably to indicate a longer pause: these are transcribed as two-, three-, or (more)-em dashes, by relying on the length of em dashes in the manuscript as the basic unit. That Clemens thought in terms of ems at all is suggested by his occasional sign for a dash that he has interlined as a correction or revision (⊢⊣), which was then the standard proofreader's mark for an em dash. Clemens used the dash as *terminal* punctuation only to indicate abrupt cessation or suspension, almost never combining it with a terminal period. Exceptions do occur (see pp. 250–51), but most departures from this rule are only apparent or inadvertent. For instance, Clemens frequently used period and dash together in the standard typographical method for connecting sideheads with their proper text ('P.S.—They have'), a recognized decorative use of period-dash that does not indicate a pause. The em, two-em and, more rarely, the en and the parallel dash were also used for various kinds of ellipsis: contraction ('d—n'); suspension ('Wash='); and ellipsis of a full word or more ('until——.'). Despite some appearance to the contrary, terminal punctuation here again consists solely in the period. On the other hand, Clemens often did use the period and dash combined when the sentence period fell at the end of a slightly short line in his manuscript ("period.— | New line"), a practice derived from the typographical practice of justifying short lines with an em dash. These dashes likewise do not indicate a pause and, because their function at line ends cannot be reproduced in the transcription, are always emended, never transcribed. Clemens used en dashes in their familiar role with numerals to signify "through" ('Matt. xxv, 44–45'). And he used both the em dash and varying lengths and thicknesses of *plain rule*—in lists, to signify "ditto" or "the same" for the name or word above, and in tables to express a blank. See also *ellipsis* and *rules*, below.

ellipsis ----- ...... **** -------- — — — — Nineteenth-century typography recognized an enviably large variety of ellipses (or leaders, depending on the use to which the device was being put). Clemens himself demonstrably used hyphens, periods, asterisks, en dashes, and em dashes to form ellipses or leaders, in his letters and literary manuscripts. The ellipsis using a dash of an em or more is also called a "blank" and may stand for characters ('Mr. C—'s bones') or a full word left unexpressed. In the second case, the dash is always separated by normal word space from the next word on *both* sides ('by — Reilly'), thereby distinguishing it from the dash used as punctuation ('the ship——, and'), which is closed up with the word on at least one side. When any of these marks are used as leaders, the transcription does not necessarily duplicate the number in the manuscript, using instead only what is needed to connect the two elements linked by the leaders. But for any kind of ellipsis except the "line of stars" (see *asterisks*), the transcription duplicates exactly the number of characters used in the original.

fist ☞ ☜ Clemens used the "fist," as it was called by printers (also "hand," "index," "index-mark," "mutton-fist," and doubtless other names), not as the seventh of the standard reference marks, but for its much commoner purpose of calling special attention to some point in a text. As late as 1871 the *American Encyclopaedia of Printing* characterized the device as used "chiefly in handbills, posters, direction placards, and in newspaper work,"[3] but Clemens used it often—and without apology—in his letters. We transcribe it by a standard typographical device, either right- or left-pointing, as appropriate, except in special circumstances. The following case, for instance, requires facsimile of the original, since Clemens clearly meant to play upon the term "fist" by drawing the device as a distinctly *open hand:*

"Put it *there*, Charlie!" (see p. 331)

[3] *American Encyclopaedia of Printing*, edited by J. Luther Ringwalt (Philadelphia: Menamim and Ringwalt, J. B. Lippincott and Co., 1871), 217.

paragraph ¶ The paragraph sign is both a mark of emphasis and the sixth of the reference marks. It is actually "P" reversed (left for right, and white for black) to distinguish it from that character. Clemens, however, commonly miswrote it as a "P," drawing the hollow stem with large, flat feet, but not the left/right or white/black reversal in the loop. Whenever the sign is used in a letter, we transcribe it by the standard typographical device, with a record of emendation when it has been misdrawn. Clemens used the paragraph sign as a reference mark and as shorthand for the word "paragraph," but most commonly in letters to indicate a change of subject within a passage, one of its earliest meanings. When he inserted the paragraph sign in text intended for a typesetter, he was doubtless specifying paragraph indention. But when he used it in a letter, he was usually invoking the earlier meaning as a substitute for indention. The transcription always prints the sign itself, even when it was inserted (‸¶) or was manifestly an instruction to a typesetter. In the textual commentary, however, the paragraph sign in brackets [¶] is *editorial* shorthand for "paragraph indention."

rules
═══ (a) ═══
═══ (b) ═══
——— (c) ———

Double rules (a), *parallel rules* (b), and *plain rules* (c), or rule dashes, in manuscript are usually, but not invariably, centered on a line by themselves, serving to separate sections of the text. When used within a line of text, they are positioned like an ordinary em dash and may serve as a common form of ellipsis, or to mean "ditto," or simply to fill blank space in a line. This last function may be compared with the original purpose of the eighteenth-century flourish, namely to prevent forged additions in otherwise blank space. But as with the flourish, this function had in Clemens's day long since dissolved into a mainly decorative one. Rules appear in Clemens's manuscript in three distinguishable species, each with two variant forms. We construe wavy lines in manuscript as "thick" rules, and straight lines as "thin" rules, regularizing length as necessary. (a) *Double rules* appear in manuscript as two parallel lines, one wavy and the other straight, in either order. (b) *Parallel rules* appear in manuscript as two parallel lines, either both wavy or both straight (thick or thin). (c) *Plain rules* appear as single lines, either wavy or straight (thick or thin).

EMPHASIS EQUIVALENTS

Clemens used the standard nineteenth-century system of underscoring to indicate emphasis, both within and between words. He indubitably understood the equivalents in type for the various kinds of underscore, but even if he had not, they could probably be relied on for the transcription of his underscored words, simply because the handwritten and the typographical systems were mutually translatable. Although we may not understand this system as well as Clemens apparently did, it is still clear that he used it habitually and consistently, and that anomalies are much more likely to result from our, rather than his, ignorance or error.

Occasionally Clemens used what appear to be two variations of a single underscore—a broken underscore (*not* prompted by descenders from the underscored word) and a wavy underscore (more distinctly wavy than normally occurs with any hand-drawn line). If these are in fact variations of a single underscore, they evidently indicate a more deliberate, or a slightly greater, emphasis than single underscore would imply. They have been transcribed in *l e t t e r s p a c e d i t a l i c* and **boldface** type, respectively, even though we do not know what, if any, typographical equivalent existed for them (both are marked ⋆ in the table). Clemens occasionally used letterspacing, with or without hyphens, as an a-l-t-e-r-n-a-t-i-v-e to italic, but he seems not to have combined it with italic, so that this editorial combination may always signify broken underscore. Wavy underscore in manuscript prepared for a printer did mean boldface, or some other fullface type, at least by 1900, but it is not clear for how long this convention had been in place. And in any case, boldface would now ordinarily be used for a level of emphasis higher than CAPITALS or *ITALIC CAPITALS*, so that the use of boldface type to represent wavy underscore is necessarily an editorial convention.

Clemens also sometimes emphasized capital letters and numerals in ways that appear to exceed the normal limits of the typographical system as we know it. For instance, when in manuscript the pronoun 'I' has been underscored twice, and is not part of an underscored phrase, we do not know what typographical equivalent, if any, existed for it. Since the intention is clearly to give greater emphasis than single underscore, rendering the word in small capitals (I) would probably be a mistake, for that would indicate *less* emphasis than the absence of any underscore at all (I). In such cases (also marked ⋆ in the table), we extend the fundamental logic of the underscoring system and simulate one underscore for each manuscript underscore that exceeds the highest known typographical convention. 'I' in manuscript is therefore transcribed as an italic capital with one underscore (*I*). Otherwise, underscores in the original documents are simulated only (a) when Clemens included in his letter

MANUSCRIPT	TYPE
lowercase	roman lowercase
Capitals and Lowercase	Roman Capitals and Lowercase
lowercase (underscored once)	*italic lowercase*
Capitals and Lowercase (underscored once)	*Italic Capitals and Lowercase*
*Capitals and Lowercase (underscored with a broken line)	**I t a l i c L e t t e r s p a c e d*
*Capitals and Lowercase (underscored with a wavy line)	***Boldface Capitals and Lowercase**
lowercase (underscored twice)	ROMAN SMALL CAPITALS
Capitals and Lowercase (underscored twice)	ROMAN CAPITALS AND SMALL CAPITALS
CAPITALS or lowercase (underscored three times)	ROMAN CAPITALS
CAPITALS (underscored once) or lowercase (underscored four times)	*ITALIC CAPITALS*
*CAPITALS (underscored twice)	**ITALIC CAPITALS* (underlined)
*1, 2, 3, 4, 5 (underscored)	**1, 2, 3, 4, 5* (underlined)

something he intended to have set in type, in which case his instructions to the typesetter must be reproduced, not construed, if they are to be intelligibly transcribed; and (b) when he deleted his underscore, in which case the transcription simulates it by using the standard manuscript convention for deleting an underscore.

Since underscores in manuscript may be revisions (added as an afterthought, even if not demonstrably so), one virtue of the system of equivalents is that it allows the transcription to encode exactly how the manuscript was marked without resorting to simulation. There are, however, some ambiguities in thus reversing the code: for example, a word inscribed initially as 'Knight' or 'knight' and then underscored three times would in either case appear in type as 'KNIGHT'. Clemens also sometimes used block or noncursive capitals or small capitals, simulating rather than signing 'KNIGHT' or 'KNIGHT'. Ambiguities of this kind do not affect the final form in the text, but whenever Clemens used block or noncursive letters, or when other uncertainties about the form in the manuscript arise, they are noted or clarified in the record of emendations.

2. Revisions and Self-Corrections

The transcription always represents authorial *revisions* where they occur in the text, just as it does all but the most ephemeral kinds of *self-correction*. Either kind of change is wholly given in the transcription, except when giving all details of an individual occurrence or all cases of a particular phenomenon would destroy the legibility of the transcription. For *revisions*, the transcription always includes at least the initial and the final reading, with intermediate stages (if any) described in the record of emendations. But in letters, revisions are rarely so complicated as to require this supplemental report.

Self-corrections are sometimes omitted by emendation, and are more frequently simplified by emendation than are revisions, chiefly because if fully transcribed in place they often could not be distinguished from revisions, except by consulting the textual commentary—even though the distinction is perfectly intelligible in the original letter. This limitation comes about in part because causal evidence of errors, such as a line ending ("misspel- | ‸ling") or a physical defect in the pen or paper, cannot be represented in the text without adding a heavy burden of arbitrary editorial signs. Thus a word miswritten, then canceled and reinscribed because of such a defect would, in the transcription, look like a revision, or at least like hesitation in the choice of words. In part, however, the problem with transcribing self-corrections lies in the sheer number that typically occur in manuscript. Self-corrections internal to a word, for example, are so frequent that more than one kind of emendation has had to be invoked to bring their presence in the transcription within manageable, which is to say readable, limits.

Another limitation of the present system is that the transcription does not distinguish between *simple deletions*, which may have been made either before or after writing further, and *deletions by superimposition*, in which the writer deleted one word by writing another on top of it, hence certainly before writing further. Because we have no way to make this distinction legible in the transcription, we represent all deletions as simple deletions. And, in the previous volume, we supplemented the transcription in this respect by recording as emendations "each instance of deletion by superimposition" (*L1*, xxxiv), thereby enabling anyone to ascertain the method of cancellation used, since deletions by superimposition were always described ('x' *over* 'y'), whereas simple deletions were not. The advantage of this procedure was that, while clumsy and expensive, it meant the transcription with its apparatus could always be relied on to provide the method of cancellation, whether or not the editors thought this information was useful in any given case. Its great disadvantage was that it caused the record of emendations to be nearly overwhelmed by reports of superimposition, only a small percentage of which were of any interest.

Pending the invention of an affordable, reliable way to signal this distinction in the transcription, the present volume records deletion by superimposition *only* when it is judged to be useful information—chiefly where the timing of a cancellation can be established as immediate from this evidence in the manuscript, although in the transcription the timing appears indeterminate. For example, where the transcription reads 'Do~~nt~~ you', the manuscript might show either (a) that 'you' followed 'Do~~nt~~' (a simple deletion, hence indeterminate), or (b) that 'you' was superimposed on 'nt' (deletion by superimposition, hence certainly immediate). Since the record of emendation gives *only* those cases where cancellation by superimposition establishes the immediate timing of a change, and only where this fact is deemed relevant, readers are entitled to infer from the *absence* of an entry for two such words ('~~&~~ at,' for example) that simple deletion has occurred. Where it is deemed irrelevant ('~~in order that~~ so that'), the method of deletion is neither transcribed, nor recorded as an emendation.

All transcribed deletions are, with minor exceptions, fully legible to the editors, and were therefore arguably so to the original recipient of the letter. But Clemens clearly did make some deletions easier or more difficult to read than others. His occasional addition of false ascenders and descenders to his normal deletion marks, for instance, has the intended effect of making it quite difficult to read what was canceled, at least so long as the presence of these false clues remains undetected. Such cases show, in fact, that Clemens must have known that his normal methods of cancellation did not prevent most readers from reading what he crossed out. Indeed, we know from letters in this volume that he enjoyed teasing his fiancée about her practice of reading his cancellations—even going so far as to invent a passage which, upon recovery, taunted her gently for having deciphered it (see p. 313).

It is clear that Clemens experimented with a wide variety of cancellations more or less actively *intended* to be read, but even apart from these deliberate and relatively rare cases, his methods of cancellation in letters ranged across a full spectrum of difficulty. The transcription does not, however, attempt routinely to discriminate among these, simply because we lack any conventional means for representing the differences legibly. Cancellations thus actively intended to be read—or not, as the case may be—are identified in the notes when their special character is not otherwise apparent from the transcription. But deletions accomplished by unusual methods *are* simulated whenever possible, for the methods themselves often convey some such intention (see, for example, p. 72). And in letters included in this volume, Clemens used for the first time two methods of cancellation which occupy opposite ends of the spectrum of difficulty, and which the transcription therefore simulates.

Mock, or pretended, cancellations are words crossed out so lightly that they are easily read, visibly distinct from normal deletions, as well as being (for the most part) deletions of words still necessary to the sense. Clemens used various methods for creating mock cancellations, but the transcription renders them uniformly as struck through by a hairline rule, which is visibly thinner and rides higher on the x-height than the half-point rule used for normal deletions. (Compare 'Well, *I* ~~pass.~~' with 'Well, *I* ~~pass.~~'). Clemens also deleted parts of some letters by tearing away portions of the manuscript page, which he then sent, visibly mutilated. By their very nature, such deletions are unlikely to be read by anyone, but occasionally Clemens left enough evidence in the torn page to permit as much as the first or last line of the suppressed passage to be reconstructed. Yet even if the entire excision somehow survived, it would not be included in the transcription, simply because it was not part of the letter he sent. When text canceled in this fashion can be reconstructed, therefore, it is transcribed with wholly missing characters as diamonds and partly missing characters as normal alphabetical characters, bracketed as *interpolations:* 'I [◊◊◊pose] I ru[i◊◊◊ ◊◊◊ ◊an's]'. The result is not, in the ordinary sense, readable—any more than the original manuscript at this point was, except in the sense that one or two characters or words left standing could still be read, out of context. The fully legible reconstructed reading is, therefore, given only in the notes.

It may be added here that some deletions in manuscript, especially of punctuation, were indicated there only by methods not themselves transcribable. For instance, when Clemens added a word or more to a sentence already completed, he rarely struck out the original period. Instead, he signaled his intention simply by leaving only the usual word space between the original last word and the first word of his addition, rather than the larger space always left following a sentence period. Whenever someone reading the manuscript would have *understood* something as canceled, even though it was not literally struck out, the transcription represents it as if it had been deleted in the normal fashion, and the record of emendations reports the fact as an *implied deletion.*

Deletions

■ Single characters and underscores are deleted by slash marks—occasionally even when the deletion is internal to the final form of the word ('privileḏ̸ge'). Single characters include the symbol for illegible character (ø̸) and, more rarely, Clemens's own deleted caret (‸̸), when that alone testifies to his having begun a change.

,̸ ;̸ :̸ !̸ (̸)̸ "̸ "̸ '̸ '̸ !̸ ?̸ -̸ +̸ a̸ b̸ c̸ d̸ j̸ k̸ l̸ t̸ w̸ x̸ y̸ z̸ 1̸ 2̸ 3̸ 4̸ ø̸

A̸ B̸ C̸ D̸ E̸ F̸ G̸ H̸ I̸ J̸ K̸ L̸ M̸ N̸ O̸ P̸ Q̸ R̸ S̸ T̸ U̸ V̸ W̸ X̸ Y̸ Z̸ $̸ &̸

■ Two or more characters are deleted by a horizontal rule ('~~have written~~') —occasionally even when they are internal to the word ('examin~~ed~~ation').

■ Separate, successive deletions of two or more characters are signified by gaps in the horizontal rule ('~~that dwell in~~ ~~all~~ ~~the hearts~~'). These gaps *never* coincide with line ends in the transcription. Thus, horizontal rules that continue from the end of one line to the next ('~~it by any wilful act of her own~~') *always* signify a single, continuous deletion, never separate ones.

■ Deletions *within* deletions are shown by combining the horizontal rule with the slash mark for single characters ('~~thought̸~~'), or two horizontal rules for two or more characters ('~~I was sail~~'). The earlier of the two deletions is always represented by the shorter line: to read the first stage, mentally *peel away* the longer line, which undeletes the second stage.

Insertions

■ Insertions are defined as text that has been placed between two previously inscribed words or characters, or between such a word or character and a previously fixed point (such as the top of the page), thus written *later than* the text on either side of it. Insertions may be interlined (with or without a caret), squeezed in, or superimposed on deleted characters—methods not distinguished in the transcription and not recorded as emendations except when pertinent.

■ Single characters (including punctuation marks) are inserted by a caret immediately beneath them ('& I desire').

■ Two or more characters are shown inserted, either between words or within a word, by a pair of carets ('into').

Insertions with Deletions

■ Insertions may be combined with deletions of one or more words, and in various sequences:

'worth knowing, ~~, the King included, I believe.~~'
'~~Eighteen months~~ A short time ago'
'intended to say, Aunt Betsey, ~~that,~~'

■ Insertions may be combined with deletions within a word:

'Malcolm~~b~~'
'~~m~~May-tree'
'wishes~~ing~~'

In the last two cases here, the carets indicating insertion designate characters that have been superimposed on the characters they delete. Superimposition is, in such cases, a kind of insertion designed to place new characters next to older, standing characters. Clemens might have achieved much the same thing, albeit with greater trouble, by crossing out the old and literally interlining the new characters. The timing of insertions combined with deletions internal to a word must, in any case, be understood as pertaining only to the sequence of change to that word, not as later than any other part of the text.

With the one class of exceptions noted at the end of this paragraph, alterations within a word are transcribed in the text only (a) if the rejected form was a complete word, even though not a possible word in context, or (b) if it was a recognizable start on, or misspelling of, a word possible in context. Thus the reader will find 'litera~~r~~ture' in the text because it contains the beginning of 'literary', which was possible in context, but will not find 'excursi~~i~~on' except in the report of emendations because it contains no other word or part of a word possible in context, nor is it a genuine misspelling. This rule of thumb has been devised partly because the notation for internally altered words is unconventional, and partly because such internal self-corrections occur very frequently in manuscript, so that if always transcribed they would introduce a large number of trivial puzzles throughout the text, threatening if not destroying its legibility. In fact, to reduce the impediment further, the editors may simplify internally altered words, (c) whether or not the original form was a word, or start of a word possible in context, *whenever Clemens reused three or fewer characters* (counting quotation marks, parentheses, dollar signs, and the like). In such cases the transcription gives the canceled and the final form in succession, just as if they had been separately inscribed. Thus we transcribe '~~and~~ any' for what could be accurately, but not as legibly, transcribed as 'anyd̸'—the form that is used to record the occurrence of simplification as an emendation. Altered numerals of more than one place must always be simplified in this way, even if the writer reused more than three characters.

To quote the letters without including the author's alterations, omit carets and crossed-out matter, closing up the space left by their omission. Compound words divided at the end of a line in this edition use the double hyphen (⸗) if and only if the hyphen should be retained.

3. Emendation of the Copy-Text

We emend original documents as little as possible, and nonoriginal documents as much as necessary, but we emend both kinds of copy-text for two fundamental reasons: to avoid including an error, ambiguity, or puzzle that (a) is *not in* the original, or (b) *is* in the original, but cannot be intelligibly transcribed without altering, correcting, resolving, or simplifying it.

Errors made by the writer are not emended if they can be intelligibly transcribed. Some few errors may be corrected by *interpolation*—supplying an omitted character or word within editorial square brackets—but only if the editor is confident that the writer has inadvertently omitted what is thus supplied. Interpolated corrections may be necessary to construe the text at all, let alone to read it easily, and would therefore be supplied by any reader if not supplied by the editor. Permitting interpolated corrections in the text is thus a logical extension of transcribing errors when, and only when, they can be intelligibly transcribed. Interpolated corrections, at any rate, do not conceal the existence of error in the original, and are therefore not *emendations* of it: like editorial description, or superscript numbers for the notes, they are always recognizably editorial, even when they enclose a conjecture for what the writer meant to but did not, for whatever reason, include in the letter sent. Interpolations are therefore not normally recorded in the textual commentaries. Interpolations are not always supplied, even if what is missing seems beyond serious doubt, nor could they be used to correct all authorial errors of omission: mistaken 'is' for 'it', for example, or a missing close parenthesis that must remain missing because it might belong equally well in either of two places.

Most errors in a *nonoriginal* copy-text, such as a contemporary newspaper, are attributable not to the writer, but to the typesetter, and are therefore emended. Yet even here, certain grammatical errors and misspellings may be recognizably authorial, and therefore not emended. On the whole, however, Clemens's precise and meticulous habits were well known in editorial offices before he left the West, and they make it more, rather than less, likely that errors in such a printing are the typesetter's—especially because editors and typesetters were typically committed by their professions not to a literal transcription, but to a "correct" form of any document they published. Typesetting errors are self-evident in such things as transposition ('strated' for 'started'), wrong font ('carriEd'), and some kinds of misspelling ('pouud'). In addition, we know that by 1867 Clemens consistently wrote '&' for 'and' in his letters—except where the word needed to be capitalized, or the occasion was somewhat more formal than usual, as in the document transcribed on pp. 35–37 (where he was just as consistent in spelling out 'and' as he was consistent elsewhere in using '&'). In any nonoriginal copy-text, therefore, 'and' is sure to be a form imposed by the typesetter, who had good professional reasons for excluding '&' as an unacceptable abbreviation. The word is therefore always emended as an error in nonoriginal copy-texts.

But if authorial errors are preserved uncorrected, it may well be asked why it is ever necessary to emend *originals* to avoid including one, not to mention how this can be done without changing the meaning of the original letter, and therefore the reliability of the transcription.[4] The general answer to these questions is that in a transcription which does not re-

[4] G. Thomas Tanselle, "Historicism and Critical Editing," *Studies in Bibliography* 39 (1986): 8 n. 15.

produce the text line for line with the original, some forms in the original must *be* changed if they are not to assume a different meaning in the transcription—in other words, if they are not to become errors in it. Clemens's characteristic period-dash combination at the end of a line is a classic example of something that must be emended because it would become an error if literally transcribed. The period-dash apparently combined as terminal punctuation in Clemens's manuscripts virtually always occurs at a line end, at least until about the mid-1880s, when he seems to have trained himself not to use the dash there, probably because contemporary typesetters so often misinterpreted his manuscript by including it in the type, where it would appear as an intralinear dash between sentences. The typographical origin of this device was probably as an inexpensive way to justify a line of type (especially in narrow measure, as for a newspaper), but Clemens would certainly have agreed with the majority view, which frowned upon the practice.[5] As already suggested (p. 486), when Clemens used a dash following his period, he indicated simply that the slightly short line was nevertheless full, and did not portend a new paragraph. The device may owe something to the eighteenth-century flourish used to prevent forged additions in otherwise blank space, since it sometimes occurs at the end of short lines that are followed by a new paragraph. At any rate, he never intended these dashes to be construed as punctuation. Yet that is precisely what happens if the typesetter or the reader does not recognize the convention and reads it as a pause. Any dash following terminal punctuation at the end of a line is therefore not transcribed, but emended. When "period.— | New line" occurs in a newspaper or other printing of a lost letter, it doubtless reflects the typesetter's own use of this method for right justification, and is necessarily emended. And when "period.—Dash" occurs within a line in such a printing, it is almost certainly the result of the typesetter's misunderstanding the convention in Clemens's manuscript, and is likewise emended.

Ambiguities left by the writer are also not emended if they can be intelligibly transcribed. But both original and nonoriginal copy-texts will inevitably contain ambiguous forms that, because the transcrip-

[5]The dash "is totally inadmissible as something to fill out a line, when that ends with a period and there is hardly enough matter" ([Wesley Washington Pasko], *American Dictionary of Printing and Bookmaking* [New York: Howard Lockwood and Co., 1894; facsimile edition, Detroit: Gale Research Company, 1967], 132).

tion is not line for line, must be resolved, not literally copied. Ambiguously hyphenated compounds ("water-|wheel"), for example, cannot be transcribed literally: they must be transcribed unambiguously ("waterwheel" *or* "water-wheel"), since their division at a line end cannot be duplicated. Using the editorial rule (|) to show line end would introduce a very large number of editorial signs into the text, since consistency would oblige the editor to use the symbol wherever line endings affected the form in the transcription. Even noncompound words divided at the end of a line may sometimes be ambiguous in ways that cannot be legibly preserved in the transcription: "*wit*-|ness" in the copy-text must be either "*witness*" or "*wit*ness." Dittography (of words as well as punctuation) likewise occurs most frequently at line ends—physical evidence that makes it readily intelligible as an error in the source, but that is lost in a transcription which abandons the original lineation. Dittography becomes more difficult to construe readily when it is simply copied, because the result is at least momentarily ambiguous. It is therefore emended, even in intralinear cases, in order not to give a distorted impression of this overall class of error. The general category of manuscript forms affected by their original position at line ends, however, is even larger than can be indicated here.

Puzzles created by the writer are likewise preserved if they can be intelligibly transcribed. On the other hand, we have already described several aspects of the author's alterations in manuscript which would, if transcribed, introduce puzzles in the transcription: the method of cancellation, errors with a physical cause, implied deletions, self-corrections that would masquerade as revisions, and changes internal to a word which the editor may simplify. These alone show that holograph manuscripts invariably contain many small details which we simply have no adequate means to transcribe. But with the system of notation used in plain text, it is technically feasible to include many more of these details in the transcription than we do. For instance, when Clemens wrote the words 'yourself about' in an 1853 letter, he actually made and immediately corrected two small errors: 'yoursef̸lf abot̸ut'. The transcription, following the rules of thumb already described, omits both self-corrections, recording them as emendations: the first because the rejected form ('yoursef') is not a complete word, nor does it begin a possible word in context, nor is it a genuine misspelling; the second because the rejected form ('abot') does not begin any possible word, in or out of context.

The question posed by such details is not simply whether including them would make the text more reliable or more complete (it would), but whether they *can* be intelligibly and consistently included without creating a series of trivial puzzles, destroying legibility, while not adding significantly to information about the writer's choice of words or ability to spell. There are, in fact, a nearly infinite variety of manuscript occurrences which, if transcribed, would simply present the reader with a puzzle that has no existence in the original. For instance, a carelessly placed caret, inserting a phrase to the left instead of the right of the intended word, is readily understood in the original, but can be transcribed literally only at the cost of complete confusion. And when Clemens writes off the right edge of the page and must then reinsert words he has just deleted on the right, but now in the left margin, literal transcription which did not also represent the cause of the changes would create a puzzle where there simply is none in the original.

Exceptional Copy-Texts. When the original documents are lost, and the text is therefore based on a nonoriginal transcription of one kind or another, the normal rules of evidence for copy-text editing apply. When, however, two transcriptions descend independently from a common source (not necessarily the lost original itself, but a single document nearer to the original than any other document in the line of descent from it), each might preserve readings from the original which are not preserved in the other, and these cannot be properly excluded from any text that attempts the fullest possible fidelity to the original. In such cases, no copy-text is designated; all texts judged to have derived independently from the lost original are identified; and the text is established by selecting the most persuasively authorial readings from among all variants, substantive and accidental. Before this alternative method is followed, however, we require that the independence of the variant texts be demonstrated by at least one persuasively authorial variant occurring uniquely in each, thereby excluding the possibility that either text actually derives from the other. If independent descent is suspected, even likely but not demonstrable in this way, the fact is made clear, but whichever text has the preponderance of persuasively authorial readings is designated copy-text, and the others are treated *as if* they simply derived from it, whether or not their variants are published.

Damaged texts (usually, but not necessarily, the original letters) are emended as much as possible to restore the original, though now invisible, parts of the text that was in fact sent. This treatment of an original document may seem to be an exception to the general rule about emending originals as little as possible, but a damaged manuscript is perhaps best thought of in this context as an imperfect copy of the original. And despite some appearance to the contrary, emendation in such cases is still based on documentary evidence: sometimes a copy of the original made before it was damaged, or damaged to its present extent—more commonly, evidence still in the original documents but requiring interpretation, such as fragments of the original characters, the size and shape of the missing pieces, the regularity of inscribed characters (or type) and of margin formation, the grammar and syntax of a partly missing sentence, and, more generally, Clemens's documented habits of spelling, punctuation, and diction. This kind of evidence cannot establish beyond a reasonable doubt how the text originally read. Its strength lies instead in its ability to *rule out* possible readings, often doing this so successfully and completely that any conjecture which survives may warrant some confidence. At any rate, we undertake such emendations even though they are inevitably conjectural, in part because the alternative is to render the text even less complete and more puzzling than it is in the damaged original (since sentence fragments are unintelligible without some conjecture, however tentative), and in part because only a specific, albeit uncertain, conjecture is likely to elicit any effort to improve upon what the editors have been able to perform. For this same reason, a facsimile of any seriously damaged document is always provided, either in an appendix with other manuscript facsimiles or in the textual commentary for that letter.

Letters and, more frequently, parts of letters that survive in the original but cannot be successfully transcribed constitute another exception and will be published in facsimile. For example, two letters that Clemens typed in 1874 (joking the while about his difficulties with the typewriter) clearly exceed the capacity of transcription to capture all their significant details, particularly the typing errors to which he alludes in them. Partly because they were typed, however, the original documents are relatively easy to read and therefore can be published in photographic facsimile, which preserves most of their details without at the same time making them any harder to read than the originals. These are true exceptions in the sense that most of Clemens's typed letters can and will be transcribed. But it is generally the case that facsimile cannot provide an optimally reliable and readable text, even of Clemens's very legible holograph letters, which comprise at least eight thousand of the approximately ten thousand known letters.

Yet by the same principles which justify transcription of most letters into type, facsimile should serve to represent within a transcription most elements of a manuscript which would (a) not be rendered more clearly, or (b) not be rendered as faithfully by being transcribed (newspaper clippings, for instance)—or that simply cannot be faithfully transcribed, redrawn, or simulated (drawings, maps, rebuses, to name just a few of the possibilities). It follows that if an original newspaper clipping enclosed with a letter cannot, for any reason, be reproduced in legible facsimile, it will be transcribed line for line in what approximates a type facsimile of the original typesetting. Long and otherwise unwieldy enclosures may, on the other hand, be reproduced instead in an appendix reserved for that purpose—either in photographic facsimile or in plain text.

Letters which survive only in the author's draft, or in someone else's paraphrase of the original, are also exceptions. In the first case, the source line of the editorial heading always alerts the reader that the text is a draft. In such cases, emendation is confined to those adjustments required for any original manuscript, and is not designed to recover the text of the document actually sent, but to reproduce the draft faithfully as a draft. Likewise, if a letter survives only in a paraphrase, summary, or description, it is included in the volume only if the nonoriginal source is judged to preserve at least some words of the original. And like the author's draft, it is not necessarily emended to approximate the original letter text more closely, since its nonauthorial words usually provide a necessary context for the authorial words it has, in part, preserved. When it is necessary to interlard paraphrase with transcription, the paraphrase appears in italic type and within editorial brackets, labeled as a paraphrase, in order to guarantee that there will be no confusion between text which transcribes the letter and text which does not pretend to.

Silent Emendations. In addition to the method of cancellation, which is usually omitted from the transcription and the record of emendations, several other matters may involve at least an element of unitemized, which is to say silent, change. To save space, we transcribe only routine addresses on envelopes by using the vertical rule (|) to signify line end;

nonroutine text on envelopes is transcribed by the same principles used elsewhere. The text of preprinted letterhead is reproduced in EXTRA-SMALL SMALL CAPITALS, usually in its entirety, but as fully as possible even when unusually verbose, and never to an extent less than what Clemens may be said to adopt or refer to ("I'm down here at the office"). Only substantive omissions from letterhead are reported as emendations, since the decorative variations of job type are literally indescribable. Postmarks are also transcribed in EXTRA-SMALL SMALL CAPITALS, but only unusual postage stamps are transcribed or described. Whenever Clemens used any of the following typographical conventions in his original letter (hence also whenever they occur in nonoriginal copy-texts and are deemed authorial), the transcription reproduces or simulates them, even when it is necessary to narrow the measure of the line temporarily, which is done silently: diagonal indention; hanging indention; half-diamond indention; squared indention; the flush-left paragraph and the half line of extra space, which is its collateral convention; text centered on a line, positioned flush right, or flush left; and quotations set off by quotation marks, indention, reduced space between lines (reduced leading in type), extra space above or below (or both), smaller characters in manuscript (smaller type in nonoriginals), or any combination of these conventions.

In this volume, as in the previous one, normal paragraph indention is standardized at two ems, with variations of one em and three ems often occurring in the same letter. We silently eliminate minor, presumably unintended variation in the size of all indentions, and we place datelines, complimentary closings, and signatures in a default position, unless this position is contradicted by the manuscript, as when extra space below the closing and signature show that Clemens intended them to appear on the same line. But unmistakably large variation in the size of indention is treated as deliberate, or as an error, and reproduced or simulated, not corrected or made uniform. Notes which Clemens specifically did *not* insert within the letter text but wrote instead in its margin are nevertheless transcribed at the most appropriate place within the text, and identified by editorial description: '[*in margin:*] All well', or '[*in bottom margin:* over]'. The editorial brackets in these cases may enclose just the editorial description, or both the description and the text described, depending on which conveys the original most economically. The only alternative to transcribing these notes where they are deemed "appropriate" is to transcribe them in a *completely* arbitrary location, such as the end of the letter. We likewise transcribe postscripts in the order they occur, even if this differs from the order they were intended to be read, so long as the intended order remains clear. Thus a marginal 'P. P. S.' can intelligibly precede a 'P. S.', just as a 'P. S.' inserted at the top of a letter can precede the letter proper, whether or not it was actually intended to be read first. But if, for example, a postscript inserted at the top is written across or at right angles to the main text—a sign it was *not* intended to be read before or with the text it crosses—the intended order must prevail over the physical order, and the postscript is therefore moved to the end of the letter. Only *changes* in writing media are noted where they occur in the text, as in '[*postscript in pencil:*]', from which it may also be reliably inferred that all preceding text was in ink. Line endings, page endings, and page numbers are silently omitted from the transcription, but where they affect the text or its emendation, they are given in the record of emendation.

4. Textual Commentaries

The textual commentaries each contain five (or at most six) sections or parts. ▪ The *headings*, which repeat the editorial headings of the letters themselves, but give the date first, and add the record numbers from the *Union Catalog of Clemens Letters* (*UCCL*) at the end, are designed to serve as a calendar of letters for the volume. ▪ *Copy-text* identifies the document or documents that serve as the basis for the transcription, and from which the editor departs only in the specific ways listed as emendations. ▪ *Previous publication* cites, in chronological order, and may also briefly characterize, known forms of publication before this one. This section does not attempt a complete record of previous publication, but only suggests roughly how and when the letter was first made public and therefore accessible to scholarship. Publications to which frequent reference is made may be described in the first of two prefatory sections, called Description of Texts. ▪ *Provenance* likewise gives what is known about the history of ownership of the original letter. It makes frequent reference to the second of two prefatory sections, called Description of Provenance. ▪ *Emendations and textual notes* records, in a list keyed by page and line number to the edited text, all deliberate departures from the copy-text (barring changes categorized here as *silent emendations*), and may include (a) editorial *refusals* to emend, identified by "*sic*," only when readings are deemed especially at risk of being mistaken for typographical errors in the edited text, and (b) *textual notes*, which are always italicized and within square brackets, to explain the reasoning behind any particular emendation of, or refusal to emend, the copy-text. When no copy-text has been designated because two or more documents descend independently from the lost original, *all variants* are recorded and identified by abbreviations defined under the heading *Copy-text*, and this section is renamed *Emendations, adopted readings, and textual notes*, to signify that no preferred text, or copy-text, exists for that letter. ▪ *Historical collation* appears in the commentaries only rarely and is used to list variants between nonoriginal documents that may have descended independently from a common source, but have not been drawn upon for the text.

All entries in these lists begin with a page and line cue (for example, 120.3, meaning page 120, line 3), followed by the word or passage to be documented, exactly as it stands in the transcription, except where indention [¶], line ending (|), or abbreviation ('Write . . . is') is necessary. As far as possible, entries are confined to the words and punctuation being documented. Line numbers include every line of letter text on a page, even when the page contains text for more than one letter, including all *rules*, and all lines that are wholly editorial, such as '[*about one page (150 words) missing*]', '[*in pencil*]', the editorial ellipsis (. . . .), or the full-measure envelope rule. Line numbers *exclude* all editorial matter in the letter headings and in the notes. Each reading is separated by a centered bullet (•) from the corresponding reading of the copy-text, *transcribed* without change or emendation, insofar as our notation permits, or *described* within brackets and in italic type, as necessary.

Editorial Signs and Terms

[¶]	Paragraph indention.
~	A word identical to that on the left of the bullet (hyphenated compounds are defined as one word).
∧	Punctuation absent in the copy-text but present in the transcription, hence emended.
‖	End of a line at the end of a page; may supplant (|).

above Interlined or written in the space above something else. Compare '*over*' and '*across*'.

across Written over and at an angle to previously inscribed text.

false start Start anticipated, requiring a new beginning, as in a race.

implied Not signaled explicitly, but implicitly.

miswritten Malformed, misshapen—*not* mistaken in any other sense.

over Superimposed on something, thereby deleting it. Compare '*above*' and '*across*'.

partly formed Characters not completed, hence conjectural, are transcribed as if they were complete.

R. H. H.
Revised, August 1989

Textual Commentaries

THE CONTENT and purpose of the textual commentaries, as well as the special symbols and terms used in them, are described in the last part of the Guide to Editorial Practice, pp. 479–506. In what follows here we summarize information about prior publication and provenance which would otherwise have to be frequently repeated in the commentaries for letters in this volume.

1. Description of Texts

Individual commentaries may designate as copy-text one or both of the following publications. When the information given here is pertinent for any reason, the reader is specifically referred to it.

MTB *Mark Twain: A Biography. The Personal and Literary Life of Samuel Langhorne Clemens by Albert Bigelow Paine, with Letters, Comments and Incidental Writings Hitherto Unpublished; Also New Episodes, Anecdotes, etc.* 3 vols. New York and London: Harper and Brothers, 1912. *BAL*, p. 251. *Copy used:* copy #1, CU-MARK. Where *MTB* has served as copy-text, copy #1 (publisher's code H-M on the copyright page of volume 1, signifying the first impression, ordered in August 1912) has been collated against copy #2 (code K-K, signifying an impression ordered in October 1935, which is the latest impression located). In 1935 Paine made a few corrections in the plates, but no variants in the texts of the letters collected in the present volume have been found.

MTB was first issued in three volumes, then in four and later in two, all with the same pagination. Paine said that he had "obtained his data from direct and positive sources: letters, diaries, account-books, or other immediate memoranda" (*MTB*, 1:xv). His industry in this respect was such that several letters he published have not since been found in their original form and are therefore known only from his transcriptions (or occasional facsimiles) in *MTB* and *MTL*. Although the printer's copy for *MTB* has not been found, it is known that Paine's general method of acquiring letter texts was to borrow the original whenever possible, presumably transcribe it himself, probably on a typewriter, and then return the manuscript to its owner. He presumably had full access both to the documents (now in the Mark Twain Papers) that Clemens himself defined and set aside for his official biography, and to those now in the McKinney Family Papers. He also had access to at least some of the letters in the Moffett Collection, but it is not known whether these were ever fully in his hands or transcribed for him. Although he published many of the letters now in the McKinney Family Papers, he published relatively few of those in the Moffett Collection. *MTB* is copy-text for a few letters not republished in *MTL*. But letter texts in *MTB* are generally excerpts and, judging from collation with letters that are still extant in manuscript, they were more freely edited than the corresponding passages published in *MTL*. Excerpts from *MTB* appeared in *Harper's Monthly Magazine* in thirteen installments, running from November 1911 through November 1912, hence, largely before *MTB* appeared in September 1912. Collation shows that when the book and the magazine both include text for a letter, they sometimes contain evidence of having each derived independently from a common source (very likely a typescript and its carbon copy), even though each has been separately copy-edited. Whenever persuasively authorial variants are found uniquely in both texts, the transcription is based on both. When such variants cannot be found, *MTB* is designated copy-text and the magazine, which was generally edited more heavily than the book, is treated as if it simply derived from *MTB* instead of their common source.

MTL *Mark Twain's Letters, Arranged with Comment by Albert Bigelow Paine*. 2 vols. New York and London: Harper and Brothers Publishers, 1917. *BAL* 3525. *Copy used:* copy #1, CU-MARK. As indicated under *MTB*, the letters published in *MTL* are generally more complete as well as more reliable than those extracted or published in full in *MTB*. Because printer's copy for *MTL* has likewise not been found, it is not always clear what relation it bore to the printer's copy for *MTB*. Transcriptions are based on both *MTL* and *MTB* only when persuasively authorial variants occur uniquely in both, thus establishing their independent derivation from the lost manuscripts. Otherwise, if a letter appears both in *MTL* and *MTB*, *MTL* is chosen as copy-text and *MTB* treated as if it simply derived from *MTL* instead of their common source.

Most of the letters published in *MTL* survive as original manuscripts. Collation of these documents with their transcriptions in *MTL* shows, in addition to the expected errors and omissions, that the *MTL* transcription always spelled out ampersands, and always imposed a uniform style on the dateline, greeting, complimentary closing, and signature lines. The uniformity of this house styling is established by a very large body of letter manuscript, and Clemens's consistency in using certain forms is likewise established by an even larger body of evidence. When the copy-text is *MTL*, this evidence is considered sufficient to permit the conjectural restoration of the likely forms in the original letter, at least in these uniformly styled elements. All emendations to remove this nonauthorial styling in *MTL* are, of course, published.

2. Description of Provenance

Brownell Collection The George H. Brownell Collection is housed in the Rare Book Department of the Memorial Library of the University of Wisconsin (WU). George H. Brownell (1875–1950) was a midwestern newspaperman who eventually became a full-time Mark Twain scholar, devoted especially to the task of obtaining photocopies (or originals) of Clemens's uncollected journalism and letters. In 1935 he helped found the Mark Twain Society of Chicago and, in 1941, the Mark Twain Association of America. In January 1939 he became the first editor of the *Twainian*, a position he held until his death. In October 1936, Brownell acquired an unusual collection of Clemens material from a Mark Twain collector, Irving S. Underhill (who died in 1937, in Buffalo). According to Brownell,

> the aged, bed-ridden Irving S. Underhill had begun his preparations for death by shipping the more valuable items in his Twain collection to a New York auction concern. To me, at that time, he shipped two large cartons of miscellaneous Twainiana of no sale value, but having for me an almost inestimable bibliographical value.
>
> Contained in one of those cartons was a box of Mark Twain letters—not the originals, but copies of the originals made by typewriter, pen and pencil. I never

learned from Mr. Underhill how he acquired this strange collection of fully 200 Twain letters. My guess is that the copies were made by some dealer, long ago, at a time when the originals were passing through his hands to the purchaser. Mr. Underhill might then have bought or traded something to the dealer for the copies. (Brownell 1943, 2)

Brownell's conjecture was correct. The copies had been made by Dana S. Ayer of Worcester, Massachusetts, a book and manuscript dealer who had been a salesman (as of the late 1890s) for the American Publishing Company (*BAL* 3521; Second Life Books, lot 764; Samuel R. Morrill to Clifton W. Barrett, 24 Apr 1957, ViU). Brownell compiled a list of Underhill's documents, which included 158 Ayer transcriptions of Clemens letters (Brownell 1941). None of these letters was written earlier than 1867, when Clemens first corresponded with Elisha Bliss of the American Publishing Company. More than half of them were addressed to Bliss or to his son, Francis E. Bliss, who were both officers of the American Publishing Company. Most of the remaining letter transcriptions were addressed to Frank Fuller, Clemens's business agent from the spring of 1867 until sometime in 1868, when Clemens presumably placed Bliss in charge of past as well as his then current business correspondence (Brownell 1941). In the fall of 1942, Brownell loaned the Ayer transcriptions to Bernard DeVoto, who in turn had the majority of them retranscribed, depositing these retranscriptions in the Mark Twain Papers (described below). Brownell ultimately bequeathed the documents to the University of Wisconsin, where they now reside.

The original manuscripts for most of the letter transcriptions in the Brownell Collection have been found and are accessible to the editors, but a few letters are known only by the copy Ayer made of the original. By assessing the overall accuracy of Ayer's transcriptions and identifying the kinds of errors he introduced into them, it is possible to emend the texts of those few letters or parts of letters for which no manuscript survives, in order to restore the likely reading of the lost original.

This volume contains eleven letters from Brownell's list, but only three of them depend wholly or partially on the Ayer transcription: 7 August 1867 to Fuller, now at CtY-BR, and 5 May and 3 September 1868 to Bliss. The manuscripts for three others (2 December 1867, 27 January 1868, and 4 and 6 February 1868, all to Bliss) became part of the Mark Twain Papers with the acquisition in 1957 of the Mendoza Collection (see below). The original manuscripts for two letters (24 November 1867 to Fuller, and 5 July 1868 to Bliss) are privately owned, but both owners have provided a photocopy of the original or permitted direct access to it. The University of Virginia (ViU) owns the manuscript of 7 June 1867 to Fuller, and Lehigh University (PBL) owns the manuscript of 2 December 1867 to Fuller. The manuscript of 5 December 1867 to Fuller is owned by Yale University (CtY-BR).

Bassett Collection (1955). Norman D. Bassett, a Madison alumnus, donated his Mark Twain collection to the University of Wisconsin on 9 July 1955. It contains, among its one hundred seventy-eight items, twenty-three Clemens letters, now housed in the Rare Book Department. In this volume both letters to Henry M. Crane (20 May 1867 and 3 September 1868) belong to the Bassett Collection.

Doheny Collection The Estelle Doheny Collection at the Edward Laurence Doheny Memorial Library, St. John's Seminary, Camarillo, California (CCamarSJ). In 1940 Estelle Doheny (1875–1958), philanthropist and widow of wealthy oil man Edward Doheny, became a major patron of St. John's Seminary, funding the construction of its library facility and donating to that facility "her superb collection of rare books, illuminated manuscripts, paintings, paperweights and works of art" (Mahony, 4). From 1940 until her death, Estelle Doheny donated to the seminary many literary manuscripts and manuscript fragments (about a dozen of which were Clemens's), more than seven thousand rare books (including sixty volumes from Clemens's library), and about fifteen hundred autograph letters (of which approximately fifty were Clemens's). In 1987 St. John's Seminary began liquidating the Doheny Collection at auction, and by February 1989 all the Mark Twain holdings had been sold. In this volume, there are four letters that were in the Doheny Collection, all written to Emeline B. Beach: 5 December 1867, and 1 January, 31 January, and 10 February 1868 (the last two are now in the collection of John L. Feldman). These are all the letters Clemens is known to have written Beach before his marriage, and they were eventually returned to Clemens by the addressee herself. Paine, in preparing *Mark Twain: A Biography* (*MTB*) and *Mark Twain's Letters* (*MTL*), sent out letters of inquiry to Clemens's friends and associates. From Emma Beach Thayer he received a response on 22 June 1907, which read in part: "The following winter [i.e., 1868] Mr. Clemens came several times to our home—went with us I think to hear Mr. Beecher preach, and wrote when he was in Washington. If he wants the letters I have them, I think" (Davis 1967a, 2). Eight months later, Clemens's secretary, Isabel Lyon, made the following entry in her "Daily Reminder" for 1908: "Feb 12—At the King's request I wrote M^{rs}. Thayer to ask if she would send down the letters the King wrote her many years ago just after the Quaker City Expedition, for the King & Paine to see. Copies can be made there or here." The "King" in fact appears to have kept the originals. Paine, however, did not publish them in *MTL* or *MTB*, although in *MTB* he attributed a quotation from one of them to a letter Clemens "wrote home" (1:359). Since the Beach letters were not included in the Mark Twain Papers, they were probably kept with the private papers of Clara Clemens, and eventually sold by her or her husband, Jacques Samossoud. Mrs. Doheny purchased a substantial amount of Mark Twain materials from Maxwell Hunley, a Beverly Hills book and manuscript dealer who bought extensively at a 1951 auction of some of Clara's holdings, and who may have sold additional Mark Twain material for Samossoud (Frederick Anderson to Robert Daley, 2 Sept 1977, CU-MARK). All four Doheny letters in this volume were again sold at auction on 17 and 18 October 1988 (Christie, lot 1186).

Huntington Library Henry E. Huntington (1850–1927), financier, railway executive, and heir to Collis Potter Huntington's railroad fortune, bequeathed his San Marino, California, estate as an endowed public museum and art gallery for his enormous collection of rare books, manuscripts, and paintings. The Clemens material at the Huntington Library includes literary manuscripts and nearly two hundred autograph letters. Over half of these letters are addressed to Mary Mason Fairbanks, and were bought by Henry Huntington from the Fairbanks family in 1918 (Thomas Nast Fairbanks to Dixon Wecter, 4 Dec 1947, and Wecter to Fairbanks, 6 Dec 1947, CU-MARK). There are twenty letters in this volume which belong to the Huntington Library: one to Charles Warren Stoddard, one to Abel W. Fairbanks, and eighteen to Mary Mason Fairbanks.

McKinney Family Papers The Jean Webster McKinney Family Papers, housed in the Francis Fitz Randolph Rare Book Room, Helen D. Lockwood Library, Vassar College, Poughkeepsie, New York (NPV). This collection was given to Vassar in 1977 by Jean and Ralph Connor, of Tymor Farm, LaGrangeville, New York. Jean Connor inherited the papers from her mother, Jean Webster McKinney, who had in turn inherited them from her mother, Annie Moffett Webster, Clemens's niece and the wife of Charles L. Webster, his business partner from 1884 to 1888. The letters and other Clemens materials in the collection represent one of the three principal caches of family letters, which passed from Clemens to his mother, Jane Lampton Clemens (d. 1890), his brother Orion (d. 1897) and sister-in-law Mollie Clemens (d. January 1904), and ultimately to his sister, Pamela A. Moffett (d. August 1904). Some of these documents went eventually to Pamela's son, Samuel E. Moffett (see Moffett Collection, below), and some to her daughter, Annie Moffett Webster. Not surprisingly, therefore, several manuscript letters are now found partly in the McKinney Family Papers and partly in the Moffett Collection.

Mollie Clemens wrote her nephew Samuel Moffett on 31 July 1899, "We never destroyed Sams letters—*excepting* by his request, or a few no one should see" (CU-MARK). At least one partly destroyed (censored) letter survives in this collection (see *L1*, 347–49), but by far the larger toll was probably taken by accidental physical damage or loss, and by the deliberate destruction, following Mollie Clemens's death, of most of Clemens's letters to his mother. As early as 1881, Orion Clemens had assembled a number of his brother's letters written between about 1853 and 1865 as part of a sprawling manuscript for his own never-published autobiography, finding even then that not all the letters had been preserved intact. On 6 October 1899, Pamela Moffett sent an unknown number of original letters to her son, Samuel Moffett, then a journalist in California, saying in part that she "was sorry to see that parts of some of the letters were missing" (CU-MARK). He tried to publish at least a few of these letters in biographical sketches of Clemens, but was eventually told to preserve them for publication after Clemens's death. Some, if not all, of these letters must eventually have become part of the Moffett Collection.

But in 1904, according to a 1935 Associated Press story in an unidentified newspaper clipping, Mollie Clemens's executor, John R. Carpenter, burned "almost four trunks" of Clemens's letters to his mother, "as requested by the famous humorist." Carpenter confided his story, according to this report, to Dr. G. Walter Barr of Keokuk, who gave this account:

> When Mrs. Clemens died [in 1890], . . . her carefully preserved personal and family treasures went into the possession of her son, Orion. When Orion died, his wife had the succession and kept it inviolate until her own death in 1904.
>
> John R. Carpenter was administrator of Orion's wife's estate and the treasured

archives of Mother Clemens were delivered to him. One item was a collection of letters from Mark Twain to his mother, running through many decades, from youth to worldwide fame.

But with those three or four trunks of letters was an admonition. Mark Twain had enjoined his mother that she always burn his letters to her. She had not done so, but had passed on the mandamus to Orion and to the wife of the latter, and Carpenter was familiar with it.

He had a treasure of incalculable value and an imperative order to destroy it.

Carpenter realized fully the value of the material he was about to burn in his library grate. When I exclaimed that to destroy all those letters was a monstrous crime against biography, history and the record of a man who belonged to the whole world, he answered that he agreed with me—but what could be done under the circumstances?

Mark Twain had written those letters to his mother in perfect candor—and about the whole sum of his candid writing was in them—intending and believing that nobody else would ever see them, and had ordered them burned.

And so Carpenter burned every one. It took him several long evenings to complete the job thoroughly. ("Mark Twain Letters to Mother Burned at Direction of Author," unidentified clipping, datelined 14 Dec [1935], PH in CU-MARK; the New York *Times* also published an abbreviated version of this story on 15 Dec 1935, 2)

That this story was not a fiction is suggested by the postscript of Clemens's 14 February 1904 letter to Carpenter, the original draft of which survives in the Mark Twain Papers: "If there are any letters of mine, I beg that you will destroy them."

The McKinney Family Papers consist of Clemens documents typically left by him, at various times, with his sister. They include his eariest surviving notebook (probably written in 1855; see *N&J1*, 11–39); half a dozen literary manuscripts, incomplete and unpublished, written principally between 1859 and 1868 (see *ET&S1–3*); more than six hundred letters and telegrams from Clemens to various members of his family, and to business associates like Webster, as well as family photographs and mementoes, and letters and documents by other family members and close associates (Simpson, 6–14). Twenty-nine letters in this volume, all of them addressed to Jane Clemens and family, to Pamela Moffett, or to Mollie Clemens, belong to the McKinney Family Papers.

Mark Twain Papers The Mark Twain Papers, The Bancroft Library, University of California, Berkeley (CU-MARK). The core of this collection consists of the original documents that Clemens made available to Albert Bigelow Paine for the official biography Paine was to produce, and from which (in part) Paine eventually published his selected editions of letters, notebooks, and the autobiography. Since Clemens's death in 1910, these papers were successively in the care of Paine (1910–37); Bernard DeVoto at Harvard (1938–46); Dixon Wecter at the Huntington Library, San Marino, California, and later at the University of California in Berkeley (1946–50); Henry Nash Smith (1953–63); and Frederick Anderson (1963–79), both of the latter at the University of California in Berkeley, and both successors to Paine, DeVoto, and Wecter as the official literary executor of the Clemens estate. Upon the death of Clara Clemens Samossoud in 1962, the papers were bequeathed to the University of California, and in 1971 they became part of The Bancroft Library, where they now reside.

The original collection segregated by Clemens for Paine included forty-five of the approximately fifty extant notebooks kept between 1855 and 1910; approximately seventeen thousand letters received by Clemens or his family; an estimated six hundred literary manuscripts, most of them unpublished, including the autobiographical dictations; as well as photographs, clippings, contracts, and a variety of other documents originally owned by Clemens. Four letters in this volume are from this original collection: 19 April 1867 and 9 August 1867 to Jane Clemens and family, 14 August 1867 to Charles Duncan, and 24 September 1867 to Mr. Esais. Since Paine's tenure, primary and secondary documents have been added in various ways to the Papers—ranging from gifts of both photocopied and original manuscripts and documents, to large purchases and bequests comprising many hundreds of documents, to the systematic compilation of a secondary archive of photocopies, collected from institutions and private owners of original documents around the world, for the specific purpose of publishing a comprehensive scholarly edition of Mark Twain's Works and Papers.

Samossoud Collection (1952), The Mark Twain Papers. Among the documents in Clemens's possession at the time of his death, but not included in the Mark Twain Papers or made wholly available to Paine, were the letters written to his fiancée and wife, Olivia L. Langdon, and later to their daughters, Susie, Clara, and Jean. Dixon Wecter was permitted to transcribe most of these letters, as well as some others that were still owned and separately housed by Clara. He used these transcriptions as the basis for his selected edition, *The Love Letters of Mark Twain* (*LLMT*), published in 1949, and ultimately deposited all of them in the

Mark Twain Papers. On 21 March 1952, however, the University of California purchased from Clara's husband Jacques Samossoud (d. 1966) approximately five hundred original letters written to Olivia between September 1868 and her death in 1904. Other parts of the large cache of family letters still held by Clara and her husband were sold or given at various times between 1949 and 1962 to other persons and institutions, not all of which have yet been identified. (See, for example, Doheny Collection, above. Clara likewise gave Chester L. Davis and the Mark Twain Research Foundation of Perry, Missouri, a number of Clemens's letters, as well as some of Olivia's.) This volume contains the first eighteen letters in the Samossoud Collection.

Moffett Collection (1954), The Mark Twain Papers. This collection represents the portion of Pamela Moffett's papers which passed to her son, Samuel, instead of her daughter, Annie (see McKinney Family Papers, above). The collection became the property of Samuel Moffett's daughter Anita Moffett (d. 1952), either upon his death in 1908, or upon the death of Anita's younger brother, Francis Clemens Moffett, in 1927. The papers were discovered in 1954 by Jacob Zeitlin in a warehouse sale that included some of Anita Moffett's effects: sixteen hundred letters by Clemens, his family, and associates (including Pamela's letters to her son and daughter); ten scrapbooks of newspaper clippings for the period 1858–98, evidently compiled by Orion and Mollie Clemens, and containing original printings of Clemens's (and Orion's) western journalism, which had been largely unknown to Paine and all subsequent scholars (see *MTEnt*); deeds to 1860s Nevada mining claims owned by Clemens or his brother; family photographs; and a family Bible. The collection was purchased for the University of California in 1954 by a group of anonymous donors. The inventory of Clemens letters made at the time is not always specific enough to enable the editors to be certain whether some letters were part of the Moffett acquisition or were already part of the Mark Twain Papers in 1954. No letters in the present volume are in doubt, however; two belong to the Moffett Collection: 20 May 1867 and 7 June 1868, both to Jane Clemens and family.

Mendoza Collection (1957), The Mark Twain Papers. In January 1957 the University of California purchased a collection of one hundred sixteen Clemens letters written between 1867 and 1905 (all but one of them to Elisha Bliss or Henry H. Rogers), as well as eleven other miscellaneous items. This collection was offered for sale to the University by

Aaron Mendoza of the Isaac Mendoza Book Company, New York City. The Mark Twain Papers now contain about eighty-five letters to Rogers (or members of his family) and forty-nine original letters to Elisha Bliss or Francis E. Bliss. Of the total, all but roughly twenty letters were part of the Mendoza Collection, which contributes three letters to this volume: 2 December 1867, 27 January 1868, and 4 and 6 February 1868, all to Elisha Bliss. See also Brownell Collection, above.

Stanton Collection (1961), The Mark Twain Papers. In 1961 the University of California purchased from Mrs. Alice P. Stanton of Washington, D.C., two letters written to John Stanton (Corry O'Lanus), her husband's grandfather, on 14 May and 20 May 1867. Both letters are published in this volume.

Tufts Collection (1971), The Mark Twain Papers. The James and John M. Tufts Collection was assembled chiefly by James Tufts, an acquaintance of Clemens's and, for more than forty years (1892–1935), a prominent San Francisco journalist who at various times was an editor for the *Call*, the *Chronicle*, and the *Examiner*. The collection was purchased in 1971 from Tufts's son, Dr. John M. Tufts of Kentfield, California. It includes twenty-three original letters by Clemens to various correspondents, literary manuscripts, first printings of his sketches, first editions of his books, and photographs. One letter in this volume belongs to the Tufts Collection: 23 April 1867 to Charles Warren Stoddard.

Appert Collection (1973 and 1977), The Mark Twain Papers. The gift of Mr. and Mrs. Kurt E. Appert of Pebble Beach, California, this collection includes more than fifty letters by Clemens to various correspondents, literary manuscripts, photographs, letters from various hands to Clemens, first editions of his works, and books from his library. No letters in this volume belong to the Appert Collection.

■ 15 January 1867 · To Edward P. Hingston · New York, N.Y. · *UCCL* 00118

■ *Copy-text:* MS, Robert B. Honeyman Collection, Linderman Library, Lehigh University, Bethlehem, Pa. (PBL). ■ *Previous publication:* none known. ■ *Provenance:* The Honeyman Collection, which contains eleven Clemens letters written between 1867 and 1897, was deposited at PBL in March 1957. On the verso of the last leaf of the letter someone has written:

S. L. Clemens | known as | Mark Twain | Samuel Langhorne Clemens | American Humourist | Born Florida Missouri | Nov 30 1835

This is a very interesting letter written evidently in 1866 when Artemuas Ward was in England.

This letter shows the great esteem in which Mr E P Hingston was held by Mark Twain & A. Ward

▪ *Emendations and textual notes:*

8.2 ~~16.~~ 15. • 15.~~6.~~ ['6' *doubtful*]

▪ 2? February 1867 · To Mary E. (Mollie) Clemens · New York, N.Y. · *UCCL* 00119

▪ *Copy-text:* MS, Jean Webster McKinney Family Papers, Vassar College Library (NPV). ▪ *Previous publication: MTBus*, 90–91, dated "*Feb.* [1867]." ▪ *Provenance:* see McKinney Family Papers, pp. 512–14. ▪ *Emendations and textual notes:*

10.16 else, • [*period doubtful*]

10.17 ~~p~~ • [*partly formed*]

10.19 stocked • [*sic*]

▪ 2?–7 February 1867 · To John McComb · New York, N.Y. · *UCCL* 11464

▪ *Copy-text:* Paraphrase, probably written by McComb, "Californian Authors," San Francisco *Alta California*, 15 Mar 67, 1. ▪ *Previous publication:* "Californian Authors," *Californian* 6 (16 Mar 67): 4, which reprints the copy-text. ▪ *Provenance:* The original letter is not known to survive. ▪ *Emendations and textual notes:* none.

▪ 2? March 1867 · To the Proprietors of the San Francisco *Alta California* · New York, N.Y. · *UCCL* 10992

▪ *Copy-text:* "Mark Twain," chapter 51 of *Living Leaders of the World*, edited by Lew Wallace et al. (Chicago: Hubbard Bros., 1889), 333, which quotes the text, probably incompletely. The author of chapter 51 has not been identified. ▪ *Previous publication:* none known except the copy-text. ▪ *Provenance:* unknown. ▪ *Emendations and textual notes:* none.

▪ 19 March 1867 · To Charles Henry Webb · St. Louis, Mo. · *UCCL* 00120

▪ *Copy-text:* MS, Clifton Waller Barrett Library, University of Virginia, Charlottesville (ViU). ▪ *Previous publication: MTLP*, 11, without Clemens's revisions. ▪*Provenance:* deposited at ViU on 17 December 1963. ▪*Emendations and textual notes:* none.

▪ 11 April 1867 · To Howard Tucker · St. Louis, Mo. · *UCCL* 00121

▪*Copy-text:* MS, Keokuk Public Library, Keokuk, Iowa (IaK). ▪*Previous publication:* none known. ▪*Provenance:* The letter has presumably remained in the library since Tucker, treasurer of the Keokuk Library Association in 1867, received it. ▪*Emendations and textual notes:* none.

▪ 11 April 1867 · To Alice J. Hyde · St. Louis, Mo. · *UCCL* 11498

▪*Copy-text:* MS, Department of Special Collections, University Library, University of California, Santa Barbara (CU-SB). ▪*Previous publication:* none known. ▪*Provenance:* unknown. ▪*Emendations and textual notes:*

21.9 Packing • ['P' *possibly mended from partly formed* 'B' *or* 'H']
21.9 to-night • to-|night

▪ 15 April 1867 · To Jane Lampton Clemens and Family · New York, N.Y. · *UCCL* 00122

▪*Copy-text:* MS, Clifton Waller Barrett Library, University of Virginia, Charlottesville (ViU). ▪*Previous publication: MTB*, 1:310–12, paraphrase and brief excerpts. ▪*Provenance:* deposited at ViU on 17 December 1963. ▪*Emendations and textual notes:*

22.10 ~~th~~ • [*partly formed*]

▪ 19 April 1867 · To Jane Lampton Clemens and Family · New York, N.Y. · *UCCL* 00123

▪*Copy-text:* MS of letter, Mark Twain Papers, The Bancroft Library, University of California, Berkeley (CU-MARK); MS of envelope, Clifton Waller Barrett Library, University of Virginia, Charlottesville (ViU). A photographic facsimile of the MS of the letter is on pp. 446–47. The MS consists of one sheet of white wove paper, $5\frac{1}{2}$ by $9\frac{1}{8}$ inches (13.9 by 23.1 cm), inscribed on both sides in black ink, now faded to brown. ▪*Previous publication: MTB*, 1:321, brief quotation. ▪*Provenance:* see Mark Twain Papers, pp. 514–15; the envelope was deposited at ViU on 17 December 1963. ▪*Emendations and textual notes:*

27.5 ~~the~~ this • th~~e~~is
27.7 tastefully • ['e' *mistakenly dotted and the dot canceled*]
27.18 Mo • M[o] [*torn*]
27.19 NEW-YORK • NEW-YO[R]K [*torn*]

■ 22 April 1867 · To Malcolm Townsend · New York, N.Y. · *UCCL* 02444

■ *Copy-text:* MS, Henry W. and Albert A. Berg Collection, The New York Public Library, Astor, Lenox and Tilden Foundations, New York City (NN-B). ■ *Previous publication:* AAA 1924, lot 92, without the salutation and complimentary closing. ■ *Provenance:* On 24 or 25 November 1924, the MS, accompanied by a souvenir menu from the 1900 Lotos Club banquet in Clemens's honor, was sold as part of the collection of "the late William F. Gable of Altoona, Pennsylvania." It is not known when it became part of the Berg Collection, given by Dr. Albert A. Berg to NN in 1940 but continuously enlarged by gift and purchase since then. The MS came to the Berg Collection tipped into a copy of the first American edition of *The Adventures of Tom Sawyer* (1876). ■ *Emendations and textual notes:*

28.7–8 ~~& if you are anythin~~ and a sentiment also: • ['and a sentiment also:' *over wiped-out* '& if you are anythin']

28.12 ~~lit~~ • [*doubtful*]

28.17 school-girls • school-|girls

■ 23 April 1867 · To Charles Warren Stoddard · New York, N.Y. · *UCCL* 00124

■ *Copy-text:* MS, Mark Twain Papers, The Bancroft Library, University of California, Berkeley (CU-MARK). A photographic facsimile of the MS is on pp. 448–51. The MS consists of a folder of off-white wove paper, $5\frac{1}{2}$ by 9 inches (14 by 22.8 cm), inscribed on all four pages in black ink, now faded to brown. ■ *Previous publication:* Pourquoi 1880b, 535. ■ *Provenance:* see Tufts Collection, p. 517. ■ *Emendations and textual notes:*

29.16 *me.* • [*possibly* '*me:*']

30.2 it?—None. • ~?—|~.

■ 27 April 1867 · To Charles Warren Stoddard with a note to the Postmaster · New York, N.Y. · *UCCL* 00125

■ *Copy-text:* MS of letter, Huntington Library, San Marino, Calif. (CSmH, call no. HM 35075); MS of mailing label or wrapping, Charles Warren Stoddard Collection, The Bancroft Library, University of California, Berkeley (CU-BANC). The letter was written in Stoddard's autograph album on pages 204–5, 207, 209, and 211. The mailing label or wrapping has been trimmed to roughly the size of an envelope. ■ *Previous publication:* Pourquoi 1880a, 357, without the epigraph from "Confucius," the salutation, or the mailing label. ■ *Provenance:* Stoddard's autograph album was acquired by CSmH in 1944; the mailing label was acquired by CU-BANC in 1954 as part of the T. W. Norris Collection, which in turn supplied most of the material for the Stoddard Collection. ▪*Emendations and textual notes:*

35.1 **Confucius.** • [*Clemens's simulated Chinese characters are reproduced in facsimile from the MS. Their authenticity or resemblance to real characters has not been established.*]

36.10 A.M. • [*small capitals simulated, not underscored*]

36.12 ¶‸ • [*mistakenly inscribed as a* 'P']

36.22 Eden-land • Eden-|land

36.26 know—I • ~—‖—~

36.37 ¶ • [*mistakenly inscribed as a* 'P']

37.3 NEW-YORK APR 27 • [◊◊◊◊]YORK [◊PR 2]7 [*badly inked*]

▪ 1 May 1867 · To Jane Lampton Clemens and Family · New York, N.Y. · *UCCL* 00126

▪*Copy-text:* MS, Jean Webster McKinney Family Papers, Vassar College Library (NPV). ▪*Previous publication: MTB*, 1:314, with omissions; *MTL*, 1:124. ▪*Provenance:* see McKinney Family Papers, pp. 512–14. ▪*Emendations and textual notes:* none.

▪ 1 May 1867 · To Francis Bret Harte · New York, N.Y. · *UCCL* 00128

▪*Copy-text:* MS, Collection of American Literature, Beinecke Rare Book and Manuscript Library, Yale University (CtY-BR). ▪*Previous publication: MTB*, 1:320, brief excerpt; Phelps 1914, 215; *MTL*, 1:124; Phelps 1939, 492. ▪*Provenance:* bequest of William Lyon Phelps, deposited at CtY-BR in 1944. In *Essays on Books*, Phelps wrote that he was given the letter "in 1908, by Bret Harte's sister, Mrs. Wyman, of Oakland, California" (Phelps 1914, 215 n. 1). ▪*Emendations and textual notes:* none.

▪ 14 May 1867 · To John Stanton (Corry O'Lanus) · New York, N.Y. · *UCCL* 00129

▪*Copy-text:* MS, Mark Twain Papers, The Bancroft Library, University of California, Berkeley (CU-MARK). ▪*Previous publication:* none known. ▪*Provenance:* see Stanton Collection, p. 517. ▪*Emendations and textual notes:* none.

▪ 20 May 1867 · To John Stanton (Corry O'Lanus) · New York, N.Y. · *UCCL* 00131

▪*Copy-text:* MS, Mark Twain Papers, The Bancroft Library, University of California, Berkeley (CU-MARK). ▪*Previous publication:* none known. ▪*Provenance:* see Stanton Collection, p. 517. ▪*Emendations and textual notes:*

46.4 had • ~~ha~~ | had

■ 20 May 1867 · To Henry M. Crane · New York, N.Y. · *UCCL* 02779

■ *Copy-text:* MS, Rare Book Department, Memorial Library, University of Wisconsin, Madison (WU). ■ *Previous publication:* none known. ■ *Provenance:* see Bassett Collection, p. 511. ■ *Emendations and textual notes:*

47.14 ~~th~~ • [*partly formed*]

■ 20 May 1867 · To Jane Lampton Clemens and Family · New York, N.Y. · *UCCL* 00130

■ *Copy-text:* MS, Mark Twain Papers, The Bancroft Library, University of California, Berkeley (CU-MARK). ■ *Previous publication: MTB*, 1:321, excerpts. ■ *Provenance:* see Moffett Collection, p. 516. ■ *Emendations and textual notes:*

48.7 write~~. I~~ for • [*period wiped out and* 'for' *written over partly formed* 'I']

48.12 ~~I~~ It • ~ | ~ [*deletion implied*]

48.17 Affty • [*possibly* '~~I~~ Affty']

■ 1 June 1867 · To Jane Lampton Clemens and Family · New York, N.Y. · *UCCL* 00132

■ *Copy-text:* MS, Jean Webster McKinney Family Papers, Vassar College Library (NPV). ■ *Previous publication: MTB*, 1:321–22, excerpts; *MTL*, 1:125–26. ■ *Provenance:* see McKinney Family Papers, pp. 512–14. ■ *Emendations and textual notes:*

49.9 ~~un~~ • ['n' *partly formed*]

50.14 ~~whole~~ whose • who/se

■ 1 and 8 June 1867 · To Frank Fuller · New York, N.Y. · *UCCL* 00136

■ *Copy-text:* MS, Mark Twain Memorial, Hartford (CtHMTH). ■ *Previous publication: MTLP*, 11–12. ■ *Provenance:* donated to CtHMTH on 8 February 1944 by the Hartford War Bond Committee. ■ *Emendations and textual notes:* none.

■ 7 June 1867 · To William Bowen · New York, N.Y. · *UCCL* 00133

■ *Copy-text:* TS (a transcription), Mark Twain Papers, The Bancroft Library, University of California, Berkeley (CU-MARK), is copy-text for 'Westminster . . . I' (54.1–17); MS, pages 3–4, Harry Ransom Humanities Research Center, University of Texas, Austin (TxU), is copy-text for the remainder (54.17–34); extensive damage has been emended. MS pages numbered '3' and '4', the only ones known to survive, have been silked to prevent further loss, a process that immobilized the several fragments but did not always perfectly align them as they were originally written. A photographic facsimile of the MS is on pp. 452–53. The MS consists of two leaves of off-white wove paper, originally measuring approximately 5¼ by 8⅛ inches (13.2 by 20.8 cm). Inscribed on one side only in black ink (now faded to brown), each leaf has twenty-two horizontal rules. TS is a carbon copy of a modern typescript of the entire letter, including what was presumably on MS pages 1–2, which are lost, but also parts of the text now missing from MS pages 3–4. TS was made in 1940 by Theodore Hornberger while preparing *Mark Twain's Letters to Will Bowen*. He typed it not from the MS, which was even then reduced to something very close to its present condition, but from a document he described to Bernard DeVoto as "some kind of a proof-sheet or off-print" from the weekly humor journal *Texas Siftings*, supplied to him "by Mr. R. B. Bowen" (Hornberger to DeVoto, 13 Jan 1941, CU-MARK). When Hornberger published the letter, however, he described this same source as "a typescript of a letter the original of which is incomplete," and, again, as "a typescript on a letterhead of *Texas Siftings*, now in the possession of Mr. R. B. Bowen." Royden Burwell Bowen (born 18 May 1883) was one of William Bowen's sons; it was he who "presented to the Rare Book Collections [at the University of Texas] the fragments of the third and fourth pages of this letter, which he found among his papers" (*MTLBowen*, 3–4, 7 n. 12, 10, 29). Neither Hornberger nor the present editors were able to find the letter in the extant (but broken) file of *Texas Siftings*, which began publication in 1881 and ceased in 1897, four years after William Bowen's death. The document owned by Royden Bowen is now lost, and its precise nature (whether proofsheet, offprint, or typed transcription on magazine letterhead) cannot now be verified, even though Hornberger's published conclusion is probably correct. Collation of MS pages 3–4 with the corresponding part of TS shows that the missing document must have transcribed the letter not only when all four pages were present, but also in a relatively undamaged state. It is clear, for instance, that the references to Miriam and Mrs. Robbins in the final paragraph, which are not now legible in the damaged MS, could not have been supplied solely by conjecture. Since independent evidence confirms their accuracy (see p. 56 n. 7), the only reasonable inference is that the missing document transcribed by TS contained a more complete text derived directly (or indirectly) from the original. Where TS can still be compared with MS, however, it contains several errors in spelling, punctuation, and emphasis, as well as one substantive error, the omission of 'that' (54.25). It consistently renders '&' as 'and' (ten times) and represents Clemens's normal em dash as four hyphens (two times). These errors were probably introduced both by the earlier, missing document, and by Hornberger's typescript of it (TS), for in the transcription that Hornberger published, he reproduced some twelve of them, despite the contrary evidence even of the damaged MS, while he also corrected others, such as all but one 'and' for '&', by relying on that same damaged MS. (Hornberger's handwritten corrections of TS, in ink, are here ignored because they were all drawn from the extant MS, not the missing document of which TS was a copy.) Where TS is the sole source for the text, therefore, it almost certainly contains similar errors in spelling, punctuation, and emphasis, which cannot now be confidently identified or corrected. For instance, TS has no underscored words—not even where the extant MS shows Clemens consistently underscoring newspaper names like the *World* and the *Tribune*—perhaps because the nineteenth-century typewriter used to copy the letter lacked an underscore key. In other letters written at about this time, however, Clemens omitted the underscore more frequently than he supplied it, and often did both even in a single letter. On the evidence, therefore, unitalicized 'Tribune' (54.16) may be accurate, or in error. Only the most likely departures from the lost original are here corrected: 'and' is emended to '&' (seven times), and a four-hyphen dash is emended to an em dash (once). On the other hand, where MS is copy-text, but so damaged as to be illegible, TS has independent authority because it derives from the relatively undamaged original. The TS reading is therefore adopted as an emendation, insofar as it is consistent with the remaining textual and physical evidence in MS. All variants between the edited text, MS, and TS are therefore recorded here, even when the reading of TS is manifestly mistaken. ▪*Previous publication:* possibly in an unidentified issue of *Texas Siftings* (see *Copy-text*); *MTLBowen*, 15–16. ▪*Provenance:* MS was deposited at TxU by Royden Burwell Bowen in 1940. Theodore Hornberger sent TS to DeVoto in the Mark Twain Papers in 1941, when the archive was at Harvard (Hornberger to DeVoto, 13 Jan 1941, CU-MARK). ▪*Emendations and textual notes:*

[*TS is copy-text for* 'Westminster . . . I' *(54.1–17)*]

54.1–2 Hotel, | New • ~, ~ (TS) [*The place and date are on one line in TS, too long to have fit on a single line in the MS. They are emended here to follow Clemens's practice in manuscripts for 1 May 67 to JLC and family, 1 May 67 to Harte, 14 May 67 to Stanton, and 1 June 67 to JLC and family.*]

54.6 & • and [*also at 54.9, 12, 13, 15, 16, 17*] (TS)

54.7 then— • ~---- (TS)

[*MS is copy-text for* 'have . . . Clemens' *(54.17–34)*]

54.17 Herbert . . . *World* (MS) • ~, . . . World, (TS)

54.18 to-day, & (MS) • today and (TS)

54.18 a splendid ship-mate— • a [s]ple[n]d[i◇] | ship-m[◇]t[◇]— [*torn*] (MS); a splendid shipmate---- (TS)

54.18–19 knows everything (TS) • k[n◇◇◇ ◇◇◇]|erything [*torn*] (MS)

54.19 is possible for (TS) • is [p◇◇◇◇◇◇◇] | for [*torn*] (MS)

54.19 & . . . —& (MS) • and . . . ----and (TS)

54.21 shan't (MS) • shant (TS)

54.21 *very* (MS) • very (TS)

54.21 *World's* (MS) • World's (TS)

54.22 will have (TS) • will | [◇◇]ve [*torn*] (MS)

54.22 to put him through, & • t[◇]p[◇t him] t[h◇◇◇◇◇◇] | & [*torn*] (MS); to put him through, and (TS)

54.22 *Tribune’s* & the San • *Tribune’s* & [◇◇◇] | San [*torn*] (MS); Tribune’s and the San (TS)

54.23 *Alta’s* (MS) • Alta’s (TS)

54.23 & (MS) • and (TS)

54.25 Mrs (MS) • ~. (TS)

54.25 & (MS) • and (TS)

54.25 that (MS) • [*not in*] (TS)

54.26 walking into a furnace, I will do it. I (TS) • wa[◇]king int[◇ ◇] furnace[◇ | I ◇ill do it◇] I [*torn*] (MS)

54.26 want to be (TS) • w[ant | ◇◇] be [*torn*] (MS)

54.26–27 remembered to all your (TS) • reme[◇]bered to | [◇◇]l your (MS)

54.27 mother’s family & its branches • [m]other’s famil[◇] | & its branches [*torn*] (MS); mother’s family and its branches, (TS)

54.28 St Louis 3 days & • St Louis 3 day[s] | & [*torn*] (MS); St. Louis three days and (TS)

54.28–29 me, & • m[◇◇] | & [*torn*] (MS); me, and (TS)

54.29 I could find *him*, is infamous. • I | [c]o[ul]d f[in]d *him*, i[s i◇]-| [◇a]mo[u◇]. [*torn*] (MS); I could find him, is infamous. (TS)

54.29–30 I’ll recollect the scoundrel. (TS) • I’[l]l re[◇◇◇◇◇◇◇] | the scoun[d◇◇◇◇] [*torn*] (MS)

54.31 Miriam? Tell (TS) • Mi[◇◇◇◇◇] | Tell [*torn*] (MS)

54.31 dream of her still. (TS) • dream [◇◇ ◇◇◇] | still. [*torn*] (MS)

54.31–32 dream of Mrs. Robbins • drea[◇ ◇◇ ◇◇◇◇] | Robbins [*torn*] (MS); ~ ~ ~. ~, (TS)

54.32 not so much (TS) • no[◇ ◇◇] | much (MS)

54.32 Good bye, my oldest • Good bye, [m◇ ◇◇◇◇]|est (MS); Good-bye, my oldest (TS)

54.33–34 Yrs Ever, | Sam Clemens • Yrs Eve[◇◇] | Sam Cle[◇◇◇◇] [*torn*] (MS); yours ever, | Sam Clemens (TS)

▪ 7 June 1867 · To Jane Lampton Clemens and Family · New York, N.Y. · *UCCL* 00134

▪*Copy-text:* MS, Jean Webster McKinney Family Papers, Vassar College Library (NPV). ▪*Previous publication: MTB*, 1:320, 322–23, excerpts; *MTL*, 1:127–28, with omissions. ▪*Provenance:* see McKinney Family Papers, pp. 512–14. ▪*Emendations and textual notes:*

57.5 *any*thing • *any*-|thing

57.19 ~~me~~ two • [‘two’ *over* ‘me’]

57.20 ~~L’a~~ Lac • L‸ac‸~~’a~~

57.25 & • [*possibly* ‘ø &’]

57.28 it • [*sic*]

57.30 ~~it in~~ • [‘n’ *partly formed*]

58.2 visit. But • ~.—|~
58.4–5 conduct • co[n]-|duct [*torn*]

■ 7 June 1867 · To Frank Fuller · New York, N.Y. · *UCCL* 00135

■ *Copy-text:* MS, Clifton Waller Barrett Library, University of Virginia, Charlottesville (ViU). ■ *Previous publication:* none known. ■ *Provenance:* deposited at ViU on 17 December 1963. An Ayer transcription of this letter is at WU; see Brownell Collection, pp. 509–11. ■ *Emendations and textual notes:* none.

■ 8 June 1867 · To John McComb · New York, N.Y. · *UCCL* 00137

■ *Copy-text:* MS facsimile. The editors have not seen the MS, which is in the collection of Robert Daley. ■ *Previous publication:* Carnegie Book Shop, lot 461, excerpts; Bryce B. Miller, 1L, with omission; Sotheby Parke Bernet 1974, lot 82, excerpts. ■ *Provenance:* William D. Morley, Inc., of Philadelphia, offered the MS for sale in 1941 (TS in CU-MARK); Charles Neider acquired it (probably from Carnegie Book Shop) in 1963 and provided a typed transcript to CU-MARK; Robert Daley acquired the MS (probably from Sotheby Parke Bernet in 1974) and in August 1976 provided CU-MARK with a photocopy thereof. ■ *Emendations and textual notes:*

60.16 ~~di~~ • [*doubtful*]

■ 21 and 29 June; 1, 3, and 5 July 1867 · To Jane Lampton Clemens and Family · Island of Fayal, Azores; Gibraltar; Tangier, Morocco; SS *Quaker City* en route from Gibraltar to Marseilles; and Marseilles, France · *UCCL* 00139

■ *Copy-text:* MS, Jean Webster McKinney Family Papers, Vassar College Library (NPV). ■ *Previous publication: MTL*, 1:129–31, with omissions. ■ *Provenance:* see McKinney Family Papers, pp. 512–14. ■ *Emendations and textual notes:* The postcard of Cape Spartel, which Clemens probably enclosed in this letter, is reproduced courtesy of the Vassar College Library.

67.4 Sau • [*possibly* 'San']
67.8 ~~p~~ • [*partly formed*]
68.25 sunsets • sun-|sets
68.34 to-morrow • to-|morrow

■ 12 July 1867 · ~~To Eliza (Lillie) Hitchcock~~ (*not sent*) · To Jane Lampton Clemens and Family · Marseilles, France · *UCCL* 00140

■ *Copy-text:* MS, Jean Webster McKinney Family Papers, Vassar College Library (NPV). ■ *Previous publication: MTBus*, 93–94, including a complete photofacsimile following 98. ▪*Provenance:* see McKinney Family Papers, pp. 512–14. ▪*Emendations and textual notes:*

72.11–12 ~~Fre~~ Ferris • Ferris~~re~~ [*doubtful*]
72.14 woould • [*sic*]

▪ 15 July 1867 · To Jane Lampton Clemens and Family · Genoa, Italy · *UCCL* 00141

▪*Copy-text:* MS, Jean Webster McKinney Family Papers, Vassar College Library (NPV). The MS is inscribed in pencil on a single leaf of cream-colored notebook paper, measuring $3\frac{15}{16}$ by $6\frac{1}{2}$ inches, with twenty-four horizontal blue rules. Clemens almost certainly wrote the letter in a notebook (now lost) which he presumably used in the period between 2 July 1867 (the last entry in the surviving Notebook 8) and 11 August (the first entry in the surviving Notebook 9) (CU-MARK; see *N&J1*, 370–71). The dimensions of the MS page match both these notebooks, and it is ruled in exactly the same way as Notebook 9. When Clemens ripped the letter out of the notebook, it damaged several characters, all easily supplied. ▪*Previous publication:* none known. ▪*Provenance:* see McKinney Family Papers, pp. 512–14. ▪*Emendations and textual notes:*

74.8 midnight • mid-|night
74.12 to-day • to-|day
74.15 gas-lit • gas-|lit
74.17 goo[d] • goo[d] [*torn away*]
74.19 [of] • [◇◇] [*torn away*]
74.20 formerly[.] • ~[◇] [*torn away*]

▪ 7 August 1867 · To Frank Fuller · Naples, Italy · *UCCL* 00142

▪*Copy-text:* Photocopy of a transcript (handwritten, in pencil) made by Dana S. Ayer of Clemens's now-lost MS. The editors have not seen the transcript itself, which is in the Collection of American Literature, Beinecke Rare Book and Manuscript Library, Yale University (CtY-BR). Emendation to restore the likely reading of the lost original has been carried out only where Ayer's habitual errors can be confidently identified: Ayer's invariant 'and' for Clemens's invariant '&'; Ayer's flush-left paragraphs for Clemens's normal indented paragraphs; and Ayer's omission of terminal punctuation where Clemens habitually supplied it. ▪*Previous publication:* none known. ▪*Provenance:* see Brownell Collection, pp. 509–11. ▪*Emendations and textual notes:*

75.4 thing, • [*comma possibly a stray mark*]
75.5 [¶] Shall • [*flush* ¶] ~
75.6 [¶] It • [*flush* ¶] ~

75.6 us, • [*possibly no comma*]

75.6 & • and [*also at 75.7, 8, 10, 12, 76.5, 7, 8 (twice), 12 (three times), 14, 19, 20, 21*]

75.12 that, • [*possibly* '~.']

75.13 Washington. • ~^

76.1 [¶] I • [*flush* ¶] ~

76.3 [¶] I • [*flush* ¶] ~

76.4 [*no* ¶] I will • [*possible flush* ¶] ~ ~

76.13 weeks. • ~^

76.14 [¶] Good-bye • [*flush* ¶] ~

76.17 (over) • [*Since the versos of all three pages of Ayer's transcription are blank, there can be no doubt that Ayer copied this instruction from the MS, and that Clemens wrote the postscript on the verso of the last page of the body of the letter.*]

■ 7 August 1867 · To Daniel Slote · Naples, Italy · *UCCL* 00143

■ *Copy-text:* MS, *not sent*, Harry Ransom Humanities Research Center, University of Texas, Austin (TxU). Albert Bigelow Paine had this MS in his possession at the time of his death, presumably having received it from Clemens; this fact suggests that Clemens never gave—and perhaps never even showed—his unfinished note to Slote. Paine wrote on the MS: "1867 | (Quaker City trip) | Mem. for 'Dan'." ■ *Previous publication:* AAA / Anderson Galleries 1937, lot 68. ■ *Provenance:* Paine owned the letter when he died in 1937; it is not known when TxU acquired it. ■ *Emendations and textual notes:* none.

■ 9 August 1867 · To Jane Lampton Clemens and Family · Naples, Italy · *UCCL* 00144

■ *Copy-text:* MS, *damage emended*, Mark Twain Papers, The Bancroft Library (CU-MARK). ■ *Previous publication: MTB*, 1:346 n. 1, brief excerpt. ■ *Provenance:* see Mark Twain Papers, pp. 514–15. On the first MS page, Paine wrote, in pencil now erased, "No. 3," and on the second page, also erased, "This page." ■ *Emendations and textual notes:*

78.4 daylight • day-|light

78.8 midnight • mid-|night

78.17 Orion Clemens, Esq. • [O◇i◇◇] Clem[◇◇◇◇ ◇◇]q. [*torn*]

78.17 1312 Chesnut street • [◇◇]12 Chesn[ut s]treet [*torn*]

78.17 United • [◇◇◇◇e]d [*torn*]

78.18 9 AGO • [9] AGO [*badly inked*]

78.19 UF° SUCCURSALE • U[F]° SU[C]CU[R]SALE [*badly inked*]

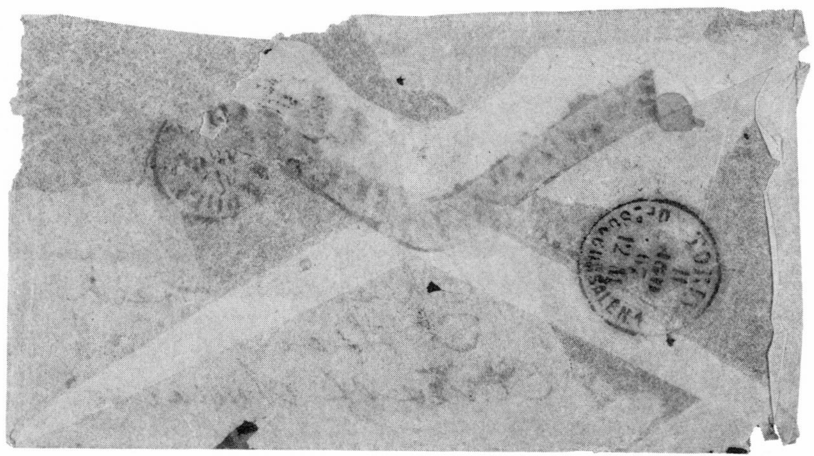

9 August 1867 to JLC and family, front and back of envelope (CU-MARK).

▪ 14 August 1867 · To Charles C. Duncan · Piraeus, Greece · *UCCL* 11496

▪*Copy-text:* MS, *draft*, Notebook 9, Mark Twain Papers, The Bancroft Library, University of California, Berkeley (CU-MARK). This unsigned draft is written in pencil, upside down on the eleventh and twelfth lined pages from the back of Notebook 9. This notebook is one of three that survive from the period of the *Quaker City* voyage. The signatories of this petition, if there were any, have not been identified. It is not known if any version of it was ever delivered to Duncan. ▪*Previous publication: N&J1*, 386–87. ▪*Provenance:* see Mark Twain Papers, pp. 514–15. ▪*Emendations and textual notes:*

79.8 ~~have~~ ‸having‸ • hav~~e~~‸ing‸

79.11 ~~have~~ ‸having‸ • hav~~e~~‸ing‸ ['e' *partly formed*]

80.1 altar • [*sic*]

▪ 26 August 1867 · To Jane Lampton Clemens and Family · Yalta, Russia · *UCCL* 00145

▪*Copy-text:* MS, Jean Webster McKinney Family Papers, Vassar College Library (NPV). Clemens enclosed what is evidently his first draft of the address to Tsar Aleksandr II. The MS of the letter and its enclosure are independently paginated. Mark Twain made a fair copy of this draft in his notebook under the entry dated 25 August (Notebook 9, CU-MARK). ▪*Previous publication: MTL*, 1:131–33, without the enclosure. The notebook copy of the enclosure was published in *MTN*, 78–79, and in *N&J1*, 406–7. ▪*Provenance:* see McKinney Family Papers, pp. 512–14. ▪*Emendations and textual notes:*

81.8 fortnight • fort-|night

81.23 aid-de camp • aid-||de camp [*sic*]

82.3–4 Emperor [thanked us for] the address • [*Any interpolation here is to a degree uncertain, but since some verb is necessary in order to construe the sentence, we have supplied the same words Clemens used in reporting the event on 27 August in his dispatch to the* Alta California *(SLC 1867ooo). Toward the end of that same newspaper dispatch, he also said*, 'Inasmuch as the Emperor approved the document'. *But in chapter 37 of* The Innocents Abroad, *Mark Twain retained the first phrase from his* Alta *dispatch:* 'He thanked us for the address, and said he was very much pleased to see us'. *A Russian newspaper columnist named* 'Ready Pen' *reported in an August 1867 issue of the Odessa* Vestnik *that* 'the Emperor was pleased to hear an address' *and that he* 'immediately reciprocated with kind words of his own' *(Startsev, 119)*.]

82.8 ~~ther~~ their • the~~r~~ir

82.15 dint • [*sic*]

82.17 to-morrow • to-|morrow

82.33	countrymen • country-|men
82.35	far‸ far • [*Possibly dittography; Clemens wrote* 'far' *only once when he copied this draft into his notebook.*]
82.36	~~th~~ • [*partly formed*]
83.6	Russia, • [*deletion implied*]
83.12	~~&~~ or • ['or' *over* '&']
83.16	& to • [*possibly* '& ~~to~~ to'; '~~t~~' *partly formed*]

■ 26 August 1867 · From Samuel L. Clemens and Others to Daniel D. Leary · Yalta, Russia · *UCCL* 09123

■ *Copy-text:* Transcript, Mark Twain Papers, The Bancroft Library, University of California, Berkeley (CU-MARK). The transcript is a carbon copy of a typescript prepared by Lewis Leary from another transcript, now lost, presumably made from the original document by retired Columbia University administrator Philip M. Hayden. (Hayden mistakenly thought that Lewis Leary was related to Daniel D. Leary.) The petition of thanks was almost certainly not composed by Clemens, nor was it in his hand, except for the signature. ■ *Previous publication:* Leary, 202. ■ *Provenance:* deposited at CU-MARK on 18 September 1967. ■ *Emendations and textual notes:* On the assumption that the names were signatures, and therefore difficult to transcribe accurately, we have emended the transcript to restore the likely correct reading of the lost original.

86.9	W. • E.
86.10	Crocker • Crocher
86.12	S. • A.
86.13	Payne • Paine
86.16	J. • I.
86.21	P. • F.

■ 1–2 September 1867 · To Jane Lampton Clemens and Family · Constantinople, Turkey · *UCCL* 00146

■ *Copy-text:* MS, Jean Webster McKinney Family Papers, Vassar College Library (NPV). ■ *Previous publication: MTB*, 1:335, excerpt; *MTL*, 1:134–36, with omission. ■ *Provenance:* see McKinney Family Papers, pp. 512–14. ■ *Emendations and textual notes:*

88.8	Pastachio • [*possibly* 'Pestachio']
88.37	I • I | I
89.17	to-night • to-|night
89.23	~~him~~ his name • hi‸s~~m~~-| name

■ 10 September 1867 · To Jane Lampton Clemens and Family · Beirut, Syria · *UCCL* 00148

■ *Copy-text:* MS, Jean Webster McKinney Family Papers, Vassar College Library (NPV). ■ *Previous publication: MTL*, 1:136. ■ *Provenance:* see McKinney Family Papers, pp. 512–14. ■ *Emendations and textual notes:* none.

■ 24 September 1867 · To Mr. Esais · Jerusalem, Syria · *UCCL* 00149

■ *Copy-text:* MS, Mark Twain Papers, The Bancroft Library, University of California, Berkeley (CU-MARK). ■ *Previous publication:* none known. ■ *Provenance:* see Mark Twain Papers, pp. 514–15. Mr. Esais presumably returned the letter with the Bible, both of which are in CU-MARK. ■ *Emendations and textual notes:*

94.2 ~~21~~ 24 • 24~~1~~ (‸)

■ 1–2 October 1867 · To Samuel E. Moffett · SS *Quaker City* en route from Jaffa, Syria, to Alexandria, Egypt · *UCCL* 00154

■ *Copy-text:* MS, *damage emended*, Jonathan Goodwin Collection, Mark Twain Memorial, Hartford (CtHMTH). Clemens inscribed this now-incomplete letter on the back and front flyleaves of his copy of an 1866 Arabic translation of the New Testament (Beirut, Syria: American Mission Press). Some seventy copies of this book were given to the *Quaker City* passengers by the American Mission. Each copy presumably included a printed presentation sheet, with the passenger's name inscribed in Arabic, pasted to the front flyleaf (see pp. 96–97 nn. 3–4). Clemens wrote a single line—'This rose has a history.' (95.2)—on the back flyleaf; he began his letter proper ('At Sea, October, 1867.') on the page facing this flyleaf (95.4); and he probably continued and signed his letter near the top of the printed presentation sheet, almost all of which has since been cut away and lost, leaving only two holograph insertions partly visible, plus the final line of type (see the illustrations below). On the assumption that the printed presentation sheet in the copy of the book given to Charles Langdon (also at CtHMTH) was identical with the one in Clemens's copy—save only the Arabic names inscribed on each—the missing part of the printed text has been supplied from Langdon's copy. The books themselves measure 4$\frac{13}{16}$ by 7$\frac{3}{4}$ inches (12.2 by 19.7 cm); the presentation sheets measure 4$\frac{1}{4}$ by 5$\frac{5}{16}$ inches (10.7 by 13.5 cm). (A second Arabic inscription below the last printed line in Langdon's copy transliterates "Nizam Mushaqa," a proper name or possibly "rule of Mushaqa," a modification of the printed date. This second Arabic inscription is absent from Clemens's copy, but the difference should not affect the reconstitution of the printed lines above it.) Clemens's name in Arabic (a transliteration of "Samu'il Clemens") has also been recreated—in this case, by relying on the expertise and generosity of Michael Fahy in the Department of Anthropology at the University of Michigan, and professors Mounah A. Khouri and Muhammad Siddiq in the Department of Near Eastern Studies at the University of California, Berkeley, who analyzed the transliterated name in Langdon's copy (which reads "Karlus Landon") and wrote out Clemens's name in a comparable style (that of a Western missionary, not a native speaker) for reproduction in this transcription of Clemens's letter. ▪*Previous publication:* City Book Auction, lot 88; Brownell 1945. ▪*Provenance:* It is not known when the damage to this letter occurred, but the earliest description of it now known was published in 1945 in an auction catalog (City Book Auction, lot 88). The letter was donated to CtHMTH in 1972 by Connecticut collector Jonathan Goodwin as part of a large gift of Mark Twain books and manuscripts. ▪*Emendations and textual notes:*

96.4–10	ARABIC . . . (Sam. L. • [◇◇◇◇◇◇ . . . ◇◇◇◇]. L. [*cut away*]
96.11–12	PASSENGER . . . CITY, • [*cut away*]

▪ 13, 15, and 17 October 1867 · To Jane Lampton Clemens and Family · SS *Quaker City* at Cagliari, Sardinia; Algiers, Algeria; Málaga, Spain; and Gibraltar · *UCCL* 00151

▪*Copy-text:* MS, Jean Webster McKinney Family Papers, Vassar College Library (NPV). ▪*Previous publication: MTL*, 1:137, without the postscript at the top of the letter (97.1). ▪*Provenance:* see McKinney Family Papers, pp. 512–14. ▪*Emendations and textual notes:* none.

▪ 24 October 1867 · To Jane Lampton Clemens and Family · Cádiz, Spain · *UCCL* 00152

▪*Copy-text:* MS, Jean Webster McKinney Family Papers, Vassar College Library (NPV). Although this text fills a single MS leaf, beginning with a dateline at the top of the recto and ending with a signature at the bottom of the verso, the absence of Clemens's normal greeting after his dateline strongly suggests that the leaf was originally a continuation from a previous page of MS, now lost. For some indication of what, in addition to his normal greeting, the now-missing leaf (or leaves) may have contained, see p. 99 n. 1. ▪*Previous publication: MTB*, 1:340–41, with omission; *MTL*, 1:137–38, with a greeting ('DEAR FOLKS,—') clearly not in the transcribed MS. ▪*Provenance:* see McKinney Family Papers, pp. 512–14. ▪*Emendations and textual notes:*

99.4	quarantine,) • [*no open parenthesis*]
99.4	horseback • horse-|back
99.8	tired. Since • ~.—|~
99.15	infatuated • infatu~~ed~~ated

This rose has a history

At Sea, October, 1867.

To Sammy Moffett—

From his Uncle Sam.

Read this book carefully, Sammy, & study its precepts well. In urging this, I am inspired by the hope that you will derive as much satisfaction from its perusal as I have done. No words can express the comfort this little book has been to me. Often, in lonely nights at sea, I have taken her down & tackled her, first at one end & then at the other, & finally sailed in at the middle & waltzed out at both ends, while tears of gratitude suffused my eyes for the blessed missionary brick that

The back flyleaf and facing page of the Arabic volume, MS pages 1–2, reproduced at 53 percent of actual size

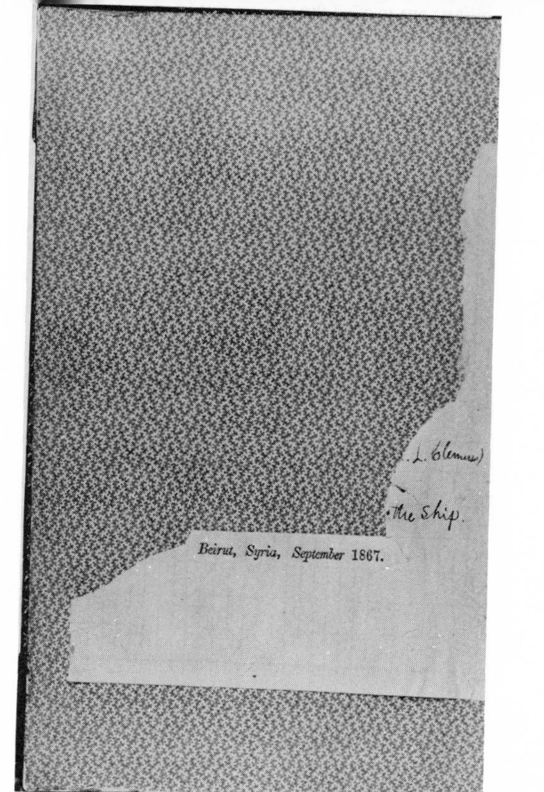

Beirut, Syria, September 1867.

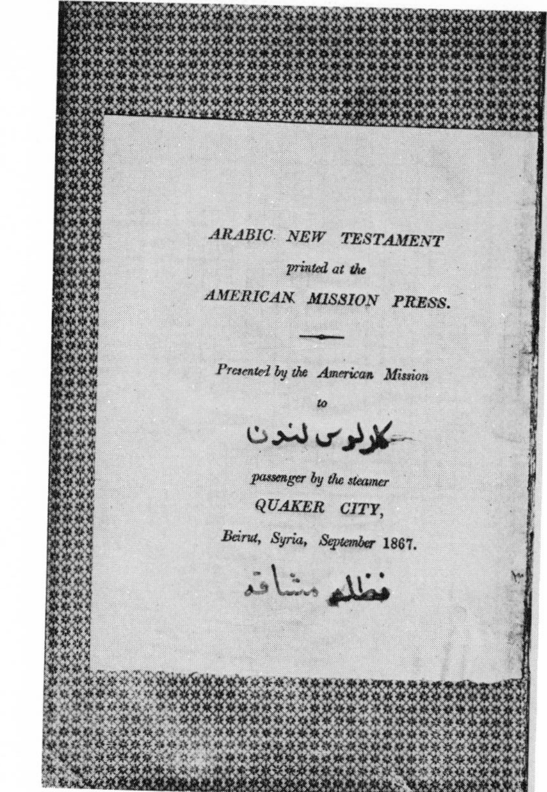

ARABIC NEW TESTAMENT
printed at the
AMERICAN MISSION PRESS.

Presented by the American Mission
to

passenger by the steamer
QUAKER CITY,
Beirut, Syria, September 1867.

Printed presentation sheet pasted to the front flyleaf in Clemens's copy (left) and in Charles Langdon's copy (right), each reproduced at 55 percent of actual size. Mark Twain Memorial, Hartford, Connecticut (CtHMTH).

■ 24 October 1867 · To Joseph T. Goodman · Cádiz, Spain · *UCCL* 00153

■ *Copy-text:* Paraphrase, probably written by Goodman, "Mark Twain," Virginia City *Territorial Enterprise*, 1 Dec 67, 2, microfilm in The Bancroft Library, University of California, Berkeley (CU-BANC). ■ *Previous publication:* "Mark Twain," San Francisco *Examiner*, 13 Dec 67, 1, which reprints the copy-text. ■ *Provenance:* The original letter is not known to survive. ■ *Emendations and textual notes:* none.

■ 20 November 1867 · To Jane Lampton Clemens and Family · (1st of 2) · New York, N.Y. · *UCCL* 00155

■ *Copy-text:* MS, Jean Webster McKinney Family Papers, Vassar College Library (NPV). The MS is written in pencil on both sides of a single leaf subsequently torn from Notebook 10 and sent. Clemens evidently turned to a part of the notebook not yet used for notes, and he wrote with the notebook inverted (CU-MARK; see *N&J1*, 453–95). For further details, see the commentary for the next letter. ■ *Previous publication: MTBus*, 94–95. ■ *Provenance:* see McKinney Family Papers, pp. 512–14. ■ *Emendations and textual notes:*

104.8 midnight, • mid-|night. [*deletion implied*]
104.12 to-morrow • to-|morrow

■ 20 November 1867 · To Jane Lampton Clemens and Family · (2nd of 2) · New York, N.Y. · *UCCL* 00156

■ *Copy-text:* MS, Jean Webster McKinney Family Papers, Vassar College Library (NPV). The MS was written in pencil on two sides of one leaf, but only the first side of a second, both subsequently torn from Clemens's notebook and sent (Notebook 10, CU-MARK; see *N&J1*, 453–95). The second leaf has room for a signature but is unsigned. The likelihood of a third, now-missing leaf, presumably with a signature, has therefore been examined in light of physical evidence from the notebook itself. The two extant leaves of the letter prove to be the conjugate halves of two folders in a gathering, originally consisting of five folders (ten leaves), from which Clemens also tore the single leaf used for the previous letter. The conjugate half of that leaf is the only leaf now missing and unaccounted for from the original gathering: the surviving evidence would permit it to fall in any of four different positions, only one of which might have allowed its use as a third leaf of the letter. But even if the missing leaf fell in that position, it would be unusual for Clemens to use it as such before he used the last (ruled) line and the whole second side of the second leaf, both of which are blank. More likely than a missing third leaf, therefore, is that he intentionally left the second leaf partly blank and unsigned. ■ *Previous publication: MTBus*, 95–96. ■ *Provenance:* see McKinney Family Papers, pp. 512–14. ■ *Emendations and textual notes:*

106.3 room-mate's • room-|mate's

106.7 ~~sociable~~ sociable • ∼ | ∼ [*Since the cancellation marks run off the torn edge of MS page 2 and onto the corresponding page stub left behind in Notebook 10, Clemens clearly wrote his letter before tearing out the notebook leaves.*]

■ 22 November 1867 · To John Russell Young · Washington, D.C. · *UCCL* 00157

■ *Copy-text:* MS, Papers of John Russell Young, Library of Congress (DLC). ■ *Previous publication:* Dickinson, 117–19, with omissions. ■ *Provenance:* donated to DLC in 1924 by Mrs. John Russell Young and Gordon R. Young. ■ *Emendations and textual notes:* After inscribing only the first four lines on the last leaf of the MS ('[¶] If . . . anyhow', 108.33–109.1), Clemens trimmed the right margin, probably to make it more nearly the same size as the two previous leaves, which were a different kind of paper. He inadvertently trimmed off the end of the last word in those four lines, then repaired some of the damage by deleting the damaged words and reinscribing them at the beginning of the line below.

108.13 ~~F~~F • ∼ | ∼

108.19–20 ~~censer~~ censor • ∼ | ∼

108.33 know[n] the • kno[w◇] | the [*trimmed*]

108.33 were • ~~w~~[◇◇◇] | ‸were‸ [*trimmed*]

109.1 have • ~~ha~~[◇◇] | ‸have‸ [*trimmed*]

109.1 anyhow • any‸~~-ho~~[◇] | ‸how‸ [*trimmed*]

■ 24 November 1867 · To Frank Fuller · Washington, D.C. · *UCCL* 00158

■ *Copy-text:* MS, collection of Mrs. Robin Craven. ■ *Previous publication:* AAA / Anderson Galleries 1934, lot 121, excerpt; Davis 1954, excerpt. ■ *Provenance:* Mrs. Craven provided CU-MARK with a photocopy of the MS on 21 April 1969. An Ayer transcription of this letter is at WU; see Brownell Collection, pp. 509–11. ■ *Emendations and textual notes:*

111.6–7 rip. In • ∼.—|∼

111.14 ~~my~~ me • m~~y~~e

111.22 ~~c~~‸Congress~~.~~ • [*deletion of period implied*]

112.6 ~~Ch~~ • ['h' *partly formed*]

112.11 $400~~.~~—$400 • ∼.—|∼ [*deletion implied*]

112.14–15 *& charitable.* • & charitable. [*squeezed in at the bottom of MS page with no room below for an underscore*]

■ 24 November 1867 · To John Russell Young · Washington, D.C. · *UCCL* 00159

■ *Copy-text:* MS, Papers of John Russell Young, Library of Congress (DLC). ■ *Previous publication:* none known. ■ *Provenance:* donated to DLC in 1924 by Mrs. John Russell Young and Gordon R. Young. ■ *Emendations and textual notes:*

113.6 gently • ~~gently~~ gently [*corrected miswriting*]

■ 25 November 1867 · To Charles Henry Webb · Washington, D.C. · *UCCL* 00160

■ *Copy-text:* MS, Josiah K. Lilly, Jr., Collection, Lilly Library, Indiana University (InU-Li). ■ *Previous publication:* SLC 1927, [4–5], in facsimile. ■ *Provenance:* donated to InU-Li in 1955. The MS is bound with its original enclosure, the twenty-eight MS pages of Clemens's unfinished *Quaker City* play, transcribed in Appendix E. ■ *Emendations and textual notes:*

114.2 F̸ • [*partly formed; possibly* 'T̸']

■ 25 November 1867 · To John Russell Young · Washington, D.C. · *UCCL* 00161

■ *Copy-text:* MS, Papers of John Russell Young, Library of Congress (DLC). ■ *Previous publication:* none known. ■ *Provenance:* donated to DLC in 1924 by Mrs. John Russell Young and Gordon R. Young. ■ *Emendations and textual notes:*

116.3 signature/ • [*deletion implied*]

■ 25 November 1867 · To Jane Lampton Clemens and Family · Washington, D.C. · *UCCL* 00162

■ *Copy-text:* MS, Jean Webster McKinney Family Papers, Vassar College Library (NPV). ■ *Previous publication: MTB*, 1:346–47; Davis 1954, excerpt. ■ *Provenance:* see McKinney Family Papers, pp. 512–14. ■ *Emendations and textual notes:* none.

■ 1 December 1867 · To John Russell Young · Washington, D.C. · *UCCL* 00164

■ *Copy-text:* MS, Papers of John Russell Young, Library of Congress (DLC). ■ *Previous publication:* none known. ■ *Provenance:* donated to DLC in 1924 by Mrs. John Russell Young and Gordon R. Young. ■ *Emendations and textual notes:*

117.11 w̸ • [*partly formed*]

■ 2 December 1867 · To Elisha Bliss, Jr. · Washington, D.C. · *UCCL* 00165

■ *Copy-text:* MS, Mark Twain Papers, The Bancroft Library, University of California, Berkeley (CU-MARK). A photographic facsimile of the MS is on pp. 454–56. The MS consists of a cut folder (two leaves) of blue-lined off-white laid paper, $7\frac{5}{8}$ by $9\frac{3}{4}$ inches (19.4 by 24.8 cm), inscribed on the first three pages in black ink, now faded to brown. The first leaf has been silked and the second backed to prevent further damage. ■ *Previous publication: MTB,* 1:350–51; *MTL,* 1:141–42; *MTLP,* 12–13, without Clemens's revisions. ■ *Provenance:* see Mendoza Collection, pp. 516–17. An Ayer transcription and a Brownell typescript of this letter are at WU; see Brownell Collection, pp. 509–11. ■ *Emendations and textual notes:*

119.9 fifty-~~f~~two • ['~~f~~' *partly formed*]
119.23–24 ‸has‸ ~~possess~~ a • ~ ~ | ~
120.2 ~~also.~~ • [*period doubtful*]
120.5 New • Ne~~Y~~w [*false start;* 'Y' *partly formed*]

■ 2 December 1867 · To Mary Mason Fairbanks · Washington, D.C. · *UCCL* 00166

■ *Copy-text:* MS, Clifton Waller Barrett Library, University of Virginia, Charlottesville (ViU). A photographic facsimile of the MS is on pp. 457–62. The MS consists of three sheets (cut from folders) of blue-lined off-white laid paper, $7\frac{5}{8}$ by $9\frac{3}{4}$ inches (19.4 by 24.8 cm), inscribed on all six sides in black ink, now faded to brown. The leaves have been partially repaired with tape to prevent further damage. ■ *Previous publication: MTMF,* 3–6. ■ *Provenance:* deposited at ViU on 17 December 1963. ■ *Emendations and textual notes:*

121.15 ~~old~~ gray-haired • ['gray' *over wiped-out* 'old']
122.31 has • has ~~has~~
123.7 with out of • [*sic*]
123.22 [¶] Give me • ‸Give me‸ ~~Give me~~ ['Give me' *indented as a paragraph but miswritten, then canceled, and rewritten to the left of the original margin.*]

■ 2 December 1867 · To Frank Fuller · Washington, D.C. · *UCCL* 00167

■ *Copy-text:* MS, Robert B. Honeyman Collection, Linderman Library, Lehigh University, Bethlehem, Pa. (PBL). ■ *Previous publication:* none known. ■ *Provenance:* The Honeyman Collection, which contains eleven Clemens letters written between 1867 and 1897, was deposited at PBL in March 1957. See also Brownell Collection, pp. 509–11. ■ *Emendations and textual notes:*

124.1 Washngton • [*sic*]

124.5	delivered • [*first* 'e' *dotted as* 'i', *then dot deleted*]
124.6	other • oth~~r~~er ['r' *mended to* 'e']

■ 4 December 1867 · To John Russell Young · Washington, D.C. · *UCCL* 00168

■ *Copy-text:* MS, Papers of John Russell Young, Library of Congress (DLC). ■ *Previous publication:* none known. ■ *Provenance:* donated to DLC in 1924 by Mrs. John Russell Young and Gordon R. Young. ■ *Emendations and textual notes:*

125.1	~~T~~ • [*partly formed*]
125.5	Land • ~~Lan~~ Land [*corrected miswriting*]
125.7	but • ~~but~~ | but [*corrected miswriting*]

■ 5 December 1867 · To Emeline B. Beach · Washington, D.C. · *UCCL* 00169

■ *Copy-text:* MS, Estelle Doheny Collection, The Edward Laurence Doheny Memorial Library, St. John's Seminary, Camarillo, Calif. (CCamarSJ). ■ *Previous publication:* Booth, 220–21; *MTMF*, 2, brief excerpt; Christie, lot 1186, excerpts. ■ *Provenance:* see Doheny Collection, pp. 511–12. ■ *Emendations and textual notes:*

126.4	~~ha~~ • [*possibly* '~~kn~~']
126.9	Herald • Her[a◇]d [*torn*]
126.19	year • yea[◇] [*torn*]
127.3	~~seeker a~~ • [*possibly* '~~seeker o~~']
127.5	to-day • to-|day
127.9	am • a[m] [*torn*]

■ 5 December 1867 · To Frank Fuller · Washington, D.C. · *UCCL* 00170

■ *Copy-text:* MS, Willard S. Morse Collection, Collection of American Literature, Beinecke Rare Book and Manuscript Library, Yale University (CtY-BR). ■ *Previous publication:* Cyril Clemens, 16–17, with alterations; Kaplan, 59, excerpt. ■ *Provenance:* donated to CtY-BR in 1942 by Walter F. Frear. ■ *Emendations and textual notes:*

128.12	Missippi • [*sic*]

■ 10 December 1867 · To Jane Lampton Clemens and Family · Washington, D.C. · *UCCL* 00171

■*Copy-text:* MS, Jean Webster McKinney Family Papers, Vassar College Library (NPV). ■*Previous publication: MTB*, 1:327, excerpt; *MTBus*, 96–97. ■*Provenance:* see McKinney Family Papers, pp. 512–14. ■*Emendations and textual notes:*

129.9 Bench‸ • [*followed by a small stroke, part of the insertion, possibly intended as a dash, but here treated as a stray mark*]

129.14 ~~You have writt~~ *You* are no common • ['*You* are no common' *written over wiped-out* 'You have writt']

129.15 best • ~~bes~~ best [*corrected miswriting*]

129.16 write • ~~w~~ write [*corrected miswriting*]

130.7–8 days. [¶] I • ~.—| [¶] ~

130.9–10 ~~may,~~ ‸maybe • [*comma mended to a caret*]

130.17 ~~Y~~ • [*partly formed*]

130.26–27 again. She • ~.—|~

■ 12 December 1867 · To Mary Mason Fairbanks · Washington, D.C. · *UCCL* 00172

■*Copy-text:* MS, Huntington Library, San Marino, Calif. (CSmH, call no. HM 14219). ■*Previous publication: MTMF*, 6–9. ■*Provenance:* see Huntington Library, p. 512. ■*Emendations and textual notes:*

133.4 your & son • [*sic*]

133.10 ~~th~~ • [*partly formed*]

133.13 Shakspeare • Shaksp[◇◇]re [*inkblot*]

133.16 you • ~~you~~ you [*corrected miswriting*]

133.18 paid. I • ~.—|~

■ 13 December 1867 · To Frank Fuller · Washington, D.C. · *UCCL* 00173

■*Copy-text:* MS, collection of Mrs. Robin Craven. ■*Previous publication:* AAA / Anderson Galleries 1934, lot 122, excerpt. ■*Provenance:* sold on 6 or 7 November 1924 by Anderson Galleries, New York City, sale no. 1870, lot 84 ("Autographs and Manuscripts of the Late F. Hopkinson Smith"). Mrs. Craven provided CU-MARK with a photocopy of the MS on 21 April 1969. ■*Emendations and textual notes:*

136.10 respond/ • [*period doubtful*]

■ 24 December 1867 · To Emily A Severance · Washington, D.C. · *UCCL* 02780

■ *Copy-text:* MS, Western Reserve Historical Society, Cleveland (OClWHi). ■ *Previous publication:* Severance, 218–19, with omissions; *MTMF*, 9, 11–12. ■ *Provenance:* Julia Severance Millikin (Emily Severance's daughter) owned the MS at least as late as 1938, the year she published it. The MS was deposited at OClWHi ca. 17 May 1986. ■ *Emendations and textual notes:*

137.27 ‸if‸ • ~~‸if‸~~ ‸if‸ [*corrected miswriting*]

■ 30 December 1867 · To the Brooklyn *Eagle* · New York, N.Y. · *UCCL* 11062

■ *Copy-text:* "The Holy Land Excursion. Did the Pilgrims Keep Sober?—A Letter from Mark Twain," Brooklyn *Eagle*, 31 Dec 67, 3. ■ *Previous publication:* none known except the copy-text. ■ *Provenance:* Clemens's MS is not known to survive. ■ *Emendations and textual notes:*

141.34 didn't • did'nt
142.2 ship—— • ~ ——

■ 8 January 1868 · To Jane Lampton Clemens and Pamela A. Moffett · Washington, D.C. · *UCCL* 00175

■ *Copy-text:* MS, Jean Webster McKinney Family Papers, Vassar College Library (NPV). ■ *Previous publication: MTB*, 1:352, 355, excerpts and paraphrase; *MTL*, 1:142–43. ■ *Provenance:* see McKinney Family Papers, pp. 512–14. ■ *Emendations and textual notes:*

144.13 night-hawks • [*possibly preceded by a canceled partly formed* 'h']
145.3 ~~Beech~~ ['h' *partly formed*]
145.9 title • ~~tiltl~~ ‖ title

■ 8 January 1868 · To Emeline B. Beach · Washington, D.C. · *UCCL* 00174

■ *Copy-text:* MS, Estelle Doheny Collection, The Edward Laurence Doheny Memorial Library, St. John's Seminary, Camarillo, Calif. (CCamarSJ). ■ *Previous publication:* Booth, 221–23; Christie, lot 1186, excerpts. ■ *Provenance:* see Doheny Collection, pp. 511–12. ■ *Emendations and textual notes:*

147.7 ~~wat~~ what • wh‸at‸~~at~~
147.10 worded • ~~worded~~ worded [*corrected miswriting*]
148.4 ~~I~~is • ['i' *over partly formed* 'I']

148.7 to-morrow • to-|morrow
148.20 ~~them.~~ • [*deletion of period implied*]
149.21 ~~ref~~ reproofs • re~~f~~proofs

■ 9 January 1868 · To Stephen J. Field · Washington, D.C. · *UCCL* 00177

■ *Copy-text:* MS, Mark Twain Papers, The Bancroft Library, University of California, Berkeley (CU-MARK). ■ *Previous publication:* none known. ■ *Provenance:* donated to the University of California as part of the Stephen Johnson Field Collection by Mrs. George E. Whitney (born Mary Lewis Swearingen), the sister of Field's wife of forty years, the former Sue Virginia Swearingen. Mrs. Field died in 1901, two years after her husband's death in 1899 (Hogan and Schnitzer, 41, 44, 45, 52). In 1970, the Field collection was transferred from the Rare Book Room of Doe Library to The Bancroft Library. This letter was deposited in CU-MARK in 1971. ■ *Emendations and textual notes:*

150.5 distilleries • dist~~er~~illeries ['il' *over* 'er']
150.6 them. Beckwith • ~.—|~

■ 9 January 1868 · To Jane Lampton Clemens and Pamela A. Moffett · Washington, D.C. · *UCCL* 00176

■ *Copy-text:* MS of letter, Jean Webster McKinney Family Papers, Vassar College Library (NPV); MS of envelope, Clifton Waller Barrett Library, University of Virginia, Charlottesville (ViU). The date in the postmark ('10') is badly inked and therefore uncertain: it may be '15' or '13' instead, in which case the envelope would belong to Clemens's 14 January 1868 letter to JLC and family, or to some other letter, now lost, written on 12 or 13 January. ■ *Previous publication: MTB*, 1:356, excerpt; *MTL*, 1:144–45, without postscript and envelope. ■ *Provenance:* see McKinney Family Papers, pp. 512–14. The envelope was deposited at ViU on 17 December 1963. ■ *Emendations and textual notes:*

151.12 door-keeper • door-|keeper
152.5 them. I • ~.—|~
152.12 D.C. • D.C[◊] [*badly inked*]
152.12 COLLECTED • COLL[EC]T[ED] [*badly inked*]
152.12 10 • 1[◊] [*possibly* '13' *or* '15'; *badly inked*]

■ 10 January 1868 · To Charles Henry Webb · Washington, D.C. · *UCCL* 00178

■ *Copy-text:* None. The text is based on two auction-catalog transcriptions that derive independently from the lost MS:

P[1]	AAA 1927, lot 109
P[2]	Parke-Bernet Galleries 1940, lot 188

Although P[2] is more complete than P[1], both lack (at least) a salutation. Like many catalogs, P[1] and P[2] use italic type for text quoted from manuscript, a convention not followed here. ▪*Previous publication:* none known except P[1] and P[2]. ▪*Provenance:* The MS was once owned by Henry Goldsmith, New York (before 1927), and then by John Gribbel, Philadelphia (before 1940). Its present location is unknown. ▪*Emendations, adopted readings, and textual notes:* Adopted readings without sigla are editorial emendations of the source readings.

153.1	Jan. 9 • Jan. 9 [1903] (P[1]); January 9 [1867] (P[2])
153.3	Please . . . 3 (P[2]) • Asks Webb to send him three (P[1])
153.3	the Jumping (P[2]) • dee Jumping (P[1])
153.4	me (P[1]) • [*not in*](P[2])
153.4	for (P[2]) • [*followed in* P[1] *by three ellipsis points, which stand for the dropped words described in the next entry*]
153.4–5	I . . . mail. (P[2]) • [*not in*] (P[1])
153.5	A.M. (P[1]) • AM (P[2])
153.6–7	Yr. . . . Clemens. (P[2]) • [*not in*] (P[1])

▪ 10 January 1868 · To the Washington *Morning Chronicle* · Washington, D.C. · *UCCL* 00127

▪*Copy-text:* "Mark Twain," Washington *Morning Chronicle*, 11 Jan 68, 1. This letter was also published on the same morning by the (tri-weekly) Washington *National Intelligencer* ("Mark Twain's Lecture," 11 Jan 68, 1), and possibly by other Washington morning papers that the editors have not seen, evidently from separate holograph copies which Clemens presumably wrote out and delivered to them. Although Clemens probably introduced some differences from copy to copy (he would have altered, for example, 'EDS. CHRONICLE' to '*Editors National Intelligencer*', or vice versa), most of the variants between the copy-text and the *Intelligencer* are probably errors or unauthorized changes. The *Intelligencer* almost certainly replaced 'last night' with 'Thursday night' (154.2–3) in its copy, whereas the *Chronicle* probably preserves the original reading. In fact, none of the variants in the *Intelligencer* printing, the salutation apart, is a convincingly authorial revision, or even more clearly authorial than the variant in the *Chronicle*. ▪*Previous publication:* see *Copy-text*. The letter also appeared in "Letter from Mark Twain," Washington *Evening Express*, 11 Jan 68, 1, which probably copied the text from the *Intelligencer* printing; in "Mark Twain's First Lecture in Washington—What the Press Say of Him," Virginia City *Territorial Enterprise*, 30 Jan 68, 1 (which reprinted the *Chronicle* version, incorrectly dating it 10 January); and in "'Mark Twain' Lecturing on the Frozen Truth," San Francisco *Alta California*, 1 Feb 68, 1 (which reprinted the *Enterprise*, crediting only the *Chronicle*). ▪*Provenance:* No MS for any of the copies distributed by

Clemens is known to survive. ▪*Emendations and textual notes:* Only the variants between the copy-text and the *Intelligencer* are recorded here; the copy-text has not been emended.

154.1 EDS. CHRONICLE: • *Editors National Intelligencer:*
154.2 I • It
154.2 understood • ~,
154.2–3 last night • Thursday night, [*Clemens wrote his original letter on Friday, 10 January, the day after his lecture. It is likely that the* Intelligencer *staff rather than Clemens made this alteration, because had the need for the change occurred to Clemens himself, he would have changed both copies, which he presumably wrote at the same time.*]
154.3 lecture, • ~;
154.5 (I • ‸~
154.6 him, but • ~; ~,
154.6 honor • ~,
154.7 that.) • ~.‸
154.9 time • ~,

▪ 14 January 1868 · To Jane Lampton Clemens and Family · Washington, D.C. · *UCCL* 00179

▪*Copy-text:* MS, Jean Webster McKinney Family Papers, Vassar College Library (NPV), is copy-text for the letter; for an envelope that may belong to it, see 9 Jan 68 to JLC and PAM; copy-text for the enclosure, which does not survive in the original document sent, is that portion of "Annual Banquet of the Corres[pon]dents' Club" (Washington *Evening Star*, 13 Jan 68, 2) which published a stenographic transcription of Clemens's speech. Although he might have enclosed his manuscript for the speech (if he wrote one), none has been found, and it seems more likely that he would send a more legible and less bulky clipping, if possible: the *Star* is the only known printing that appeared in time to be included. The *Star*'s full report of the dinner ran to more than half a large page of newsprint, and included (in addition to Clemens's speech) full transcriptions of the remarks by the club's president, George W. Adams, as well as letters to the club from Edwin B. Haskell (Boston Press Club president) and John Russell Young. On the assumption that Clemens would not have sent his speech still embedded in these several columns of reportage, only his speech has been reproduced as the enclosure. ▪*Previous publication: MTB*, 1:348–49, brief paraphrase and an inaccurate excerpt from the letter proper. The enclosure, or some variant thereof, was widely reprinted at the time: "A Eulogy of Woman by 'Mark Twain,'" New York *Evening Post*, 15 Jan 68, 1; "Woman. Mark Twain's Eulogy of the Fair Sex," St. Louis *Missouri Republican*, 22 Jan 68, 3 (an original clipping of the *Republican*, annotated by Paine, is in CU-MARK, box 3A, no. 41); "Woman—Mark Twain's Opinion of Her," Virginia City *Territorial Enterprise*,

2 Feb 68, 1; "A Eulogy of Woman by 'Mark Twain,'" San Francisco *Examiner*, 3 Feb 68, 1; "Woman—Mark Twain's Opinion of Her," Oakland (Calif.) *News*, 10 Apr 68, 4; "A Eulogy of Women, by 'Mark Twain,'" unidentified clipping, TxU; "Mark Twain's Eulogy of the Fair Sex," unidentified clipping (misidentified as the Washington *Star*), reproduced in photographic facsimile in Meltzer, 109; "Eulogy on Woman. By 'Mark Twain,'" *Excelsior Monthly Magazine*, August 1868, 99–100 (reproduced in Appendix E); *MTS* 1910, 104–6; *MTB*, 3:1612–13; *MTS* 1923, 31–33. All of the above appear to derive directly or indirectly from the *Evening Star*. Four of them (the St. Louis *Missouri Republican*, the clipping in Meltzer, the *Excelsior*, and *MTB*, 3:1612–13) omit part or all of two phrases that were presumably considered indelicate for some readers: 'she bears our children—ours as a general thing' (155.37–38) and the proposal to drink Woman's health 'right cordially in this bumper of wine' (157.1). In addition, one text has been found which was not based on the *Star*'s report: a separate stenographic record published in 1868 by Clemens's friend Andrew J. Marsh (Marsh 1868, 91–92). Among the variants in this transcription is a probably more authorial (and certainly more risible) version of one remark: 'look at Frances——Frances——George Francis Train!' (see 156.25–26). ▪ *Provenance:* For the letter, see McKinney Family Papers, pp. 512–14; for a possible envelope, see the commentary to 9 Jan 68 to JLC and PAM; the original enclosure is not known to survive. ▪ *Emendations and textual notes:* For the enclosure, because no example of the original newsprint was found that would reproduce legibly in photographic facsimile, the original typesetting in the *Star* has been transcribed line-for-line. In copies of the *Star* which the editors have seen, several characters at line ends failed to print; they have been emended, where possible, on the assumption that not all originals were identically defective. No other emendations have been made.

[*MS is copy-text for* '2 . . . Sam' *(155.1–6)*]

155.2 ~~Fold~~ Folks • Fol~~d~~ks

[Evening Star *is copy-text for* 'The . . . [Applause.]' *(155.8–157.4)*]

155.17 know • know[◇] [*Either an unidentified character failed to print, or a space was mistakenly set at the end of a line.*]

155.25 Laughter.] • ~.[◇]

155.28 we • w[e]

155.29 buttons, • ~[◇]

155.30–31 laughter,] she • ~,[◇] ~

155.31 confides • confide[◇]

155.32 out • ou[◇]

155.33 neigh- • neigh[◇]

156.3 ter.] • [◇]er.]

156.53 all of • [*sic*]

▪ 15 January 1868 · To Charles Henry Webb · Washington, D.C. · *UCCL* 00181

▪*Copy-text:* MS, Clifton Waller Barrett Library, University of Virginia, Charlottesville (ViU). ▪*Previous publication:* none known. ▪*Provenance:* deposited at ViU on 17 December 1963. ▪*Emendations and textual notes:* none.

▪ 24 January 1868 · To Jane Lampton Clemens and Pamela A. Moffett · Hartford, Conn. · *UCCL* 00182

▪*Copy-text:* MS, Jean Webster McKinney Family Papers, Vassar College Library (NPV). ▪*Previous publication:* Paine, 937, and *MTB*, 1:357–58, excerpts; *MTL*, 1:145–46, excerpt; Davis 1954, brief excerpt. ▪*Provenance:* see McKinney Family Papers, pp. 512–14. ▪*Emendations and textual notes:*

160.14	I • I̸ | I
160.23	~~paper~~ pages • pages~~per~~
161.17	who • ~~who~~ who
161.37	Yr • [*possibly* 'Ys']

▪ 24 January 1868 · To Mary Mason Fairbanks · Hartford, Conn. · *UCCL* 00183

▪*Copy-text:* MS, Huntington Library, San Marino, Calif. (CSmH, call no. HM 14221). ▪*Previous publication: MTMF*, 13–16; Davis 1954, brief excerpt. ▪*Provenance:* see Huntington Library, p. 512. ▪*Emendations and textual notes:*

165.3	t̸ • [*partly formed*]
165.4	papers. It • ∼.—|∼
165.18	subscription. They • ∼.—|∼
165.27	wishy-washy • wishy-|washy
166.2–3	~~woul~~ wound • woul̸nd
166.20	Good-bye • Good-|bye
166.24	Sincerly • [*sic*]

▪ 25 January 1868 · To William Bowen · New York, N.Y. · *UCCL* 00184

▪*Copy-text:* MS, Harry Ransom Humanities Research Center, University of Texas, Austin (TxU). On the back of the letter as folded, someone (possibly Bowen himself) has written several sums, in pencil. ▪*Previous publication: MTLBowen*, 16–18; Davis 1954, brief excerpt. ▪*Provenance:* purchased by TxU in 1940 from William Bowen's daughter, Eva Laura Bowen (Mrs. Louis Knox) (*MTLBowen*, 7 n. 12, 10). ▪*Emendations and textual notes:*

167.2	~~24~~ 25 • 25‸~~4~~
167.5	tip-top • tip-|top
168.2	the • the ‖ the
168.2	~~pl~~ praise • p~~l~~raise
168.7	school-days • school-|days
168.9	~~g~~ • [*partly formed*]

▪ 27 January 1868 · To Elisha Bliss, Jr. · New York, N.Y. · *UCCL* 00185

▪*Copy-text:* MS, Mark Twain Papers, The Bancroft Library, University of California, Berkeley (CU-MARK). ▪*Previous publication: MTL*, 1:147–48; *MTLP*, 13–14. ▪*Provenance:* see Mendoza Collection, pp. 516–17. An Ayer transcription of this letter is at WU; see Brownell Collection, pp. 509–11. ▪*Emendations and textual notes:*

169.11	~~1~~ 600 • [‘6’ *over* ‘1’]
169.14	‸next,‸ • ‸~~ne,~~‸ | ‸next,‸

▪ 30 January 1868 · To Mary Mason Fairbanks · Washington, D.C. · *UCCL* 00186

▪*Copy-text:* MS, Huntington Library, San Marino, Calif. (CSmH, call no. HM 14220). Clemens gave this single MS leaf its own dateline and labeled it a postscript, probably to a now-lost letter to Fairbanks. A less likely possibility is that he intended it as a delayed addendum to his 24 January letter to Fairbanks, separately mailed six days later. ▪*Previous publication: MTMF*, 16–17. ▪*Provenance:* see Huntington Library, p. 512. ▪*Emendations and textual notes:*

170.8	30 • [‘0’ *malformed and easily misread as* ‘1’ *or* ‘d’]
170.9	promise • pr~~n~~omise

▪ 31 January 1868 · To Emeline B. Beach · Washington, D.C. · *UCCL* 00187

▪*Copy-text:* MS, *damage emended*, collection of John L. Feldman. ▪*Previous publication: MTB*, 1:359, brief excerpt described as a letter “home”; Booth, 223–25; Christie, lot 1186, excerpts. ▪*Provenance:* see Doheny Collection, pp. 511–12. ▪*Emendations and textual notes:* The damaged text of the envelope has been emended in part by reference to Clemens’s own comments in an earlier letter to Beach (see 149.10–11). Both the postage stamp and the postmark have been completely torn away.

171.9	~~t◇~~ • [‘t’ *partly formed;* ‘◇’ *malformed*]

171.19 another. Now • ~.—|~
172.9 s̸ • [*partly formed*]
172.14 I do • [*possibly* 'I I̸ do'; 'I̸' *partly formed*]
172.16 Gibraltar & • [*possibly* 'Gibraltar &̸ | &'; *deletion implied: doubtful* '&' *written off edge of page*]
172.25 ~~ever~~ even • ever̸n
172.27 ~~behave~~ steadily • ['steadily' *over wiped-out* 'behave']
172.32 Emma Beach • Emma [◇◇◇◇◇] [*torn*]
172.32 Columbia street • Colum[◇◇◇ ◇◇◇◇◇◇] [*torn*]
172.32 Brooklyn, N. Y. • Brook[◇◇◇◇ ◇◇ ◇◇] [*torn*]

Courtesy of John L. Feldman.

■ 1 February 1868 · To John Russell Young · Washington, D.C. · *UCCL* 00188

■ *Copy-text:* MS, Papers of John Russell Young, Library of Congress (DLC). ■ *Previous publication:* none known. ■ *Provenance:* donated to DLC in 1924 by Mrs. John Russell Young and Gordon R. Young. ■ *Emendations and textual notes:*

173.15 only • ~~only~~ only
174.3 S • [*possibly* 'ø S'; '◇' *partly formed uppercase character*]

■ 4 and 6 February 1868 · To Elisha Bliss, Jr. · Washington, D.C. · *UCCL* 00189

■ *Copy-text:* MS, Mark Twain Papers, The Bancroft Library, University of California, Berkeley (CU-MARK). ■ *Previous publication:* *MTLP*, 14–15, without

Clemens's revisions. ▪*Provenance:* see Mendoza Collection, pp. 516–17. An Ayer transcription of this letter is at WU; see Brownell Collection, pp. 509–11. ▪*Emendations and textual notes:*

176.8 ~~th~~ • [*partly formed*]

▪ 6 February 1868 · To Jane Lampton Clemens and Pamela A. Moffett · Washington, D.C. · *UCCL* 00190

▪*Copy-text:* MS, Jean Webster McKinney Family Papers, Vassar College Library (NPV). ▪*Previous publication: MTB*, 1:359, excerpts; *MTL*, 1:148–49. ▪*Provenance:* see McKinney Family Papers, pp. 512–14. ▪*Emendations and textual notes:*

178.6 m̸h • [*partly formed, possibly* 'w']
178.15 ~~wo~~ was ~~al~~ actually • wo̸as al̸ctually

▪ 9 February 1868 · To Mary Mason Fairbanks · Washington, D.C. · *UCCL* 00191

▪*Copy-text:* MS, Huntington Library, San Marino, Calif. (CSmH, call no. HM 14222). The MS, a single leaf inscribed on both sides and unsigned, is almost certainly incomplete. ▪*Previous publication: MTMF*, 17–18. ▪*Provenance:* see Huntington Library, p. 512. ▪*Emendations and textual notes:* none.

▪ 10 February 1868 · To Emeline B. Beach · Washington, D.C. · *UCCL* 00192

▪*Copy-text:* MS, collection of John L. Feldman. ▪*Previous publication:* Booth, 225–29; Christie, lot 1186, photofacsimile of MS page 5 and excerpts. ▪*Provenance:* see Doheny Collection, pp. 511–12. ▪*Emendations and textual notes:*

181.15 76 • [*underscored twice*]
182.3–4 ~~min~~ midnight • min̸d-|night
182.20 matter.̸,— • [*deletion of period implied; possibly* '~.̸,—']
182.26 m̸h • [*partly formed*]
183.4 ~~sir~~ surprise • s~~ir~~urprise [*canceled* 'i' *not dotted*]
183.8 them,̸ • [*deletion implied*]
183.15–16 albeit • ~~alb~~ albeit [*corrected miswriting*]
183.30 not. The • ~.—|~
184.2 bothering • ~~bothering~~ bothering [*corrected miswriting*]
184.19 ~~Mr.~~ Mrs. • Mr.̸s.
184.27 fun. Why • ~.—|~
184.34 pains. Try • ~.—|~

■ 19 February 1868 · To Anson Burlingame · (1st of 2) · Washington, D.C. · *UCCL* 00194

■ *Copy-text:* Cyril Clemens, 18–19. ■ *Previous publication:* none known except the copy-text. ■ *Provenance:* In 1932, when Cyril Clemens published the letter, it belonged to Frederick A. Burlingame. The MS has not since been found. ■ *Emendations and textual notes:*

186.6 & • and [*also at 186.7, 10, 11, 14, 15*]
186.8 *book,* • ~,* [*Cyril Clemens's note explained that* The Innocents Abroad *was the book in question.*]
186.10 I exclusively • I (sic) exclusively
186.18 Samuel L. Clemens • SAMUEL L. CLEMENS

■ 19 February 1868 · To Anson Burlingame · (2nd of 2) · Washington, D.C. · *UCCL* 00195

■ *Copy-text:* MS, Papers of the Burlingame Family, Library of Congress (DLC). ■ *Previous publication:* none known. ■ *Provenance:* donated to DLC in 1955 by Roger Burlingame. ■ *Emendations and textual notes:*

187.2 ~~18~~ 19 • 19~~8~~
187.5 Mail, • [*period doubtful*]
188.7 ~~you~~ my • ['my' *over wiped-out* 'you']

■ 20 February 1868 · To Mary Mason Fairbanks · Washington, D.C. · *UCCL* 00196

■ *Copy-text:* MS, Huntington Library, San Marino, Calif. (CSmH, call no. HM 14223). ■ *Previous publication: MTMF*, 18–23. ■ *Provenance:* see Huntington Library, p. 512. ■ *Emendations and textual notes:*

189.28 ~~chef~~ chieftains • ch~~ef~~ieftains [*canceled* 'f' *partly formed*]
189.29 Proff~~f~~essors • ['f' *deleted after word was completed*]
189.37 ø • [*partly formed*]
190.3 the • ~~the~~ the [*corrected miswriting*]
190.15–16 ~~male~~ malice • mal~~e~~ice
190.26 *any*thing • *any*-|thing
190.28 time • [*possibly* '~~I~~ time'*;* '~~I~~' *partly formed*]
191.17 Al~~f~~ways • [*possibly* 'Al~~f~~ways'*;* 'f' *partly formed*]

■ 21 February 1868 · To Jane Lampton Clemens and Family · Washington, D.C. · *UCCL* 00197

■ *Copy-text:* MS, Jean Webster McKinney Family Papers, Vassar College Library (NPV). ■ *Previous publication: MTB*, 1:359, brief excerpt; *MTBus*, 98–99.

■ *Provenance:* see McKinney Family Papers, pp. 512–14. ■ *Emendations and textual notes:*

195.10 *published* • *pub-*|lished

■ 21 February 1868 · To Orion Clemens · Washington, D.C. · *UCCL* 00198

■ *Copy-text: MTL*, 1:150–51. Excerpts were also published in chapters 65 and 66 of *MTB* (1:360–61): 'We . . . then.' (197.11–16) and 'This . . . Congress!' (197.26–198.3). In addition, *MTB* paraphrased one sentence that does not appear in *MTL:* 'He closes by saying that he rather expects to go with Anson Burlingame on the Chinese embassy.' (1:360). Although *MTL* and *MTB* probably derive independently from a common source, none of the variants found in *MTB* has been deemed superior to *MTL*, and none has been adopted, including the paraphrased sentence, which is judged to belong to the next letter, 22? Feb 68 to MEC (see p. 200 n. 3). ■ *Previous publication:* none known, except for *MTL* and *MTB*. ■ *Provenance:* The location of the MS is not known. ■ *Emendations and textual notes:* The rationale for emending *MTL* to restore ampersands and the like is given on p. 509. Although uniformly rejected, all *MTB* variants are recorded and identified here. An asterisk (*) follows the line number for each emendation of the copy-text.

197.1–2* F street . . . 21. • F. STREET, WASH., *Feb. 21. (1868)*
197.3–4* [*no* ¶] My dear Bro., [¶] I • [¶] MY DEAR BRO.,—I
197.6* & • and [*also at 197.12*, 14*, 18*, 21*, 23*, 28 (twice)*, 198.5*, 6**]
197.12 [¶] It • [*no* ¶] ∼ (*MTB*)
197.12 & • and [*also at 197.14, 28 (twice)*] (*MTB*)
197.13 them— . . . marry— • ∼, . . . ∼, (*MTB*)
197.14 bosh,— • ∼‸— (*MTB*)
197.16 [¶] I • [*no* ¶] ∼ (*MTB*)
197.17* government • gov-|vernment
197.26 the • a (*MTB*)
197.26–198.2 There . . . Washington, . . . office, . . . Burlingame— . . . world, . . . up. • ∼ . . . ∼‸ . . . ∼‸ . . . ∼, . . . ∼‸ . . . ∼. [*follows* 'There . . . Congress!' *(198.3)*] (*MTB*)
198.3 [¶] There . . . more . . . Congress! • [*no* ¶] There . . . some . . . Congress! [*precedes* 'There . . . up.' *(197.26–198.2)*] (*MTB*)
198.6* die. • ∼‸
198.8* Sam • SAM

■ 22? February 1868 · To Mary E. (Mollie) Clemens · Washington, D.C. · *UCCL* 00199 (letter) and 11421 (envelope)

■ *Copy-text:* MS, envelope only, Clifton Waller Barrett Library, University of Virginia, Charlottesville (ViU). There is no copy-text for the letter itself, which is based on two independent transcripts:

P[1]	Paine, 938
P[2]	*MTB*, 1:359–60

P[1] and P[2] derive independently from a common source, a transcript made directly or indirectly from the now-lost letter MS, either by or for Paine (see pp. 508–9). Although the transcript may have been a copy of the complete MS, both P[1] and P[2] are manifestly incomplete. It is also possible that the MS itself was incomplete when Paine or his transcriber copied it, which might explain why Paine thought the letter was to Orion in St. Louis, even though the text indicates that the person being addressed was not 'at home' in St. Louis (see p. 199 n. 1). In both P[1] and P[2], the first four sentences are apparently quoted directly from Paine's transcript, and the final sentence (199.9) is paraphrased. In P[2], however, Paine inserted four lines of commentary and an extract from the previous letter to Orion (21 Feb 68) between the quotation and the paraphrase, thus apparently attributing the paraphrased sentence to the earlier letter. In P[1], however, Paine clearly attributed the sentence to this letter, and he did not include it in the *MTL* text of 21 Feb 68 to Orion (see the previous commentary). ▪*Previous publication:* none known except P[1] and P[2]. ▪*Provenance:* The MS of the letter is not known to survive; the envelope was deposited at ViU on 17 December 1963. ▪*Emendations, adopted readings, and textual notes:*

[*Based on* P[1] *and* P[2] *for* 'I . . . embassy.' *(198.10–199.9)*]

198.10 & (P[1]) • and [*also at 199.2, 3, 6*] (P[2])
198.11 eighty— (P[1]) • ~, (P[2])
199.4 50 (P[2]) • 50 [*sic*] (P[1])
199.7 themselves, (P[1]) • ~$_\wedge$ (P[2])
199.9 I rather expect • He closed by saying that he rather expected (P[1]); He closes by saying that he rather expects (P[2])

[*MS is copy-text for* 'Mrs. . . . USS' *(199.12–13)*]

199.12–13 D.C. . . . FREE • D[◇]C[◇] . . . [◇REE] [*badly inked*]

▪ 22 February 1868 · To William C. Church · Washington, D.C. · *UCCL* 00020

▪*Copy-text:* Mott 1957, 364 and 364 n. 13. The text is quoted on 364 and cited in the footnote as "Letter to W. C. Church, dated February 22, 1868 (Willard Church Collection)." ▪*Previous publication:* none known except the copy-text. ▪*Provenance:* The location of the MS is not known: it is not among the William Conant Church Papers at NN or DLC. At the time Frank Luther Mott saw it, the MS was part of "Mr. Church's file of *Galaxy* correspondence," then in possession of Church's son, Willard Church (d. 1944) of Montclair, New Jersey (Mott 1957, 361 n. 4). ▪*Emendations and textual notes:*

200.2 Friend • "~
200.2 & • and [*also at 200.3*]
200.4 know. • ~."

■ 8–10 March 1868 · To Jane Lampton Clemens and Family · Washington, D.C., or New York, N.Y. · *UCCL* 11489

■ *Copy-text:* None. The text is a paraphrase of the original letter (now lost) based on two versions of the paraphrase published by Paine. Although in neither version did Paine explicitly mention his source, the unattributed quotation, ' "those *Alta* thieves face to face." ' (201.10), is a strong sign that it was a letter (see p. 202 n. 1). Each of the two versions appears to derive independently from a common source—probably the typescript (and carbon copy) of Paine's biography, which he condensed and serialized in *Harper's Magazine* before publishing it as a book (see pp. 508–9):

P^1	Paine, 938
P^2	*MTB*, 1:361–62

Collation shows that P^1 and P^2 are in the following relation to the letter MS:

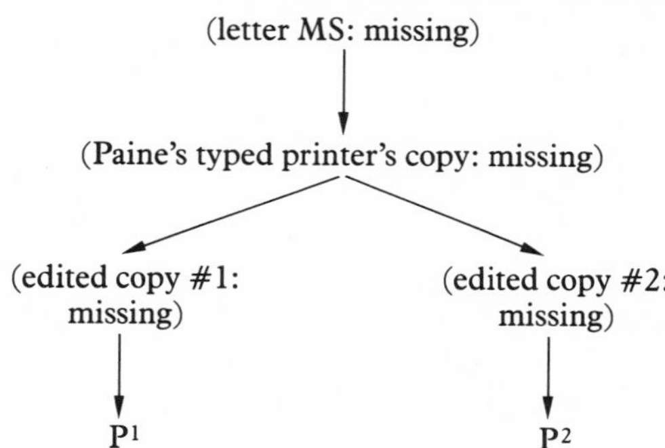

Copies #1 and #2 were initially identical, or nearly so, before Paine edited each for its respective publication. The chief difference between the two versions is that P^1 aimed at an abbreviated form of the work eventually published in *MTB*. But we cannot rule out the possibility that some differences arose because Paine added material for P^2 after the copy for P^1 had been separated from it. The objective here is thus to reconstruct the relevant portion of Paine's printer's copy before it was separately edited for P^1 and P^2, and to depart from that reconstruction only insofar as it does not represent a paraphrase of the missing letter MS. ■ *Previous publication:* none known except P^1 and P^2. ■ *Provenance:* It is not known whether Paine had direct or indirect access to the now-missing MS. ■ *Emendations, adopted readings, and textual notes:*

201.4 do; (P^2) • ~: (P^1)

201.4 people, (P^1) • ~— (P^2)

201.5 McCrellish— (P^1) • $\sim_\wedge$ (P^2)

201.7 pitiful (P^2) • beautiful (P^1)

201.8 him. (P^1) • him. In his notebook he wrote: [¶, *reduced type:*] Whiskey is taken into the committee rooms in demijohns and carried out in demagogues. [*regular type, flush left:*] And in a letter:

[¶, *reduced type:*] This is a place to get a poor opinion of everybody in. There are some pitiful intellects in this Congress! There isn't one man in Washington in civil office who has the brains of Anson Burlingame, and I suppose if China had not seized and saved his great talents to the world this government would have discarded him when his time was up. (P^{2}) [*These two quotations came from Notebook 10 (see* N&J1, *488) and from 21 Feb 68 to OC (see 197.26–198.3), respectively. They are not in* P^{1} *and were probably removed from the copy for* P^{1} *during the process of condensation, but they might have been added to the copy for* P^{2} *after* P^{1} *had been separated from it. In either case, they are not adopted here because they are clearly not part of the letter paraphrase.*]

201.9 [¶] Furthermore . . . Washington. (P^{2}) • [*not in*] (P^{1})

201.10 thieves . . . face." (P^{2}) • ~" . . . ~.∧(P^{1})

201.11 Also (P^{2}) • Furthermore (P^{1})

▪ 10 March 1868 · To Mary Mason Fairbanks · New York, N.Y. · *UCCL* 00200

▪*Copy-text:* MS, Huntington Library, San Marino, Calif. (CSmH, call no. HM 14224). Mrs. Fairbanks wrote the words "And my" as well as a series of practice strokes, in ink, to the left of the closing and signature. ▪*Previous publication: MTMF*, 23–24. ▪*Provenance:* see Huntington Library, p. 512. ▪*Emendations and textual notes:*

202.6 mind • ~~mind~~ | mind [*corrected miswriting*]

▪ 15 March 1868 · To Jane Lampton Clemens and Family · SS *Henry Chauncey* en route from New York, N.Y., to Aspinwall, Panama · *UCCL* 00201

▪*Copy-text:* MS, Jean Webster McKinney Family Papers, Vassar College Library (NPV). ▪*Previous publication: MTL*, 1:152, without the postscript. ▪*Provenance:* see McKinney Family Papers, pp. 512–14. ▪*Emendations and textual notes:*

203.11 ~~26~~ 25 • 25~~6~~

▪ 18 March 1868 · To Mary Mason Fairbanks · SS *Henry Chauncey* en route from New York, N.Y., to Aspinwall, Panama · *UCCL* 00202

▪*Copy-text:* MS, Huntington Library, San Marino, Calif. (CSmH, call no. HM 14225). ▪*Previous publication: MTMF*, 24. ▪*Provenance:* see Huntington Library, p. 512. ▪*Emendations and textual notes:*

205.4 nonsense~~,~~ • [*deletion implied*]

■ 2–14 April 1868 · To Mary Mason Fairbanks · San Francisco, Calif. · *UCCL* 02737

■ *Copy-text:* MS, Huntington Library, San Marino, Calif. (CSmH, call no. HM 14228). The surviving MS consists of the bottom third of a single leaf, inscribed on one side, and cut from a full leaf containing at least one additional line of text, now lost: two descenders from the line above show below the cut edge. There is a residue of dried glue on the otherwise blank back of the fragment (indicating it may have once been mounted), and there are faint, possibly caprine, teeth-marks on the lower left corner. ■ *Previous publication: MTMF*, 33, dated by Dixon Wecter, "in the midst of this California sojourn." ■ *Provenance:* see Huntington Library, p. 512. ■ *Emendations and textual notes:* none.

■ 14 April 1868 · To Samuel Williams · San Francisco, Calif. · *UCCL* 02781

■ *Copy-text:* MS, Cyril Clemens Collection, Mark Twain Memorial, Hartford (CtHMTH). ■ *Previous publication:* Cyril Clemens, 15; Lionberger, 123. ■ *Provenance:* The verso of the MS page is annotated by a previous owner: "From A.J Roll | 1342 Bellamy St | Santa Clara | California | U.S.A. | To whom it may concern: The Mark Twain letter on the other side was put in Mr. Williams's scrapbook by Mr. Williams himself. I procured the page as is from his son. A.J. Roll." Cyril Clemens published the letter in 1932, and Lionberger cited him as its owner when he reprinted it in 1935. The Cyril Clemens Collection was donated to CtHMTH in November 1985. ■ *Emendations and textual notes:*

209.8 synopsis • synop/sis ['s' *over partly formed* 'i']

■ 23 April 1868 · To Joseph T. Goodman *per* Telegraph Operator · Coburn Station, Calif. · *UCCL* 00203

■ *Copy-text:* Paraphrase, probably written by Goodman, "Mark Twain," Virginia City *Territorial Enterprise*, 24 Apr 68, 3, microfilm in The Bancroft Library, University of California, Berkeley (CU-BANC). ■ *Previous publication:* none known except the copy-text. ■ *Provenance:* The original telegram is not known to survive. ■ *Emendations and textual notes:*

211.3 Twain." • $\sim_{\wedge}$"

■ 1 and 5 May 1868 · To Mary Mason Fairbanks · Virginia City, Nev., and San Francisco, Calif. · *UCCL* 00204

■ *Copy-text:* MS, Huntington Library, San Marino, Calif. (CSmH, call no. HM 14226). ■ *Previous publication: MTMF*, 25–27. ■ *Provenance:* see Huntington Library, p. 512. ■ *Emendations and textual notes:*

212.6 snowstorm • snow-|storm

212.8 ~~maj~~ magnificent • ma~~j~~gnificent
212.17 I~~t~~ • ['t' *partly formed*]
212.28 Julius • Juli~~s~~us
212.28 Moulton~~,~~ • [*deletion implied*]
212.35–36 ~~bef~~ because • be~~f~~cause

▪ 5 May 1868 · To Elisha Bliss, Jr. · San Francisco, Calif. · *UCCL* 02731

▪*Copy-text:* Transcript (handwritten, in ink) of the MS (now lost) made by Dana S. Ayer, Rare Book Department, Memorial Library, University of Wisconsin, Madison (WU). *MTB* (1:363) paraphrased and excerpted 'I am . . . night.' (215.7–216.2); *MTL* (1:152–53) published the entire letter. The *MTB* and *MTL* texts may derive independently from the MS through a common transcript, possibly the Ayer transcript itself, or another, now lost. Since none of the variants in *MTB* and *MTL* has been deemed superior to the readings in Ayer, however, Ayer is designated copy-text, and both *MTL* and *MTB* are treated as if they derive from it: all their variants are recorded, though none is adopted. ▪*Previous publication:* see *Copy-text*. ▪*Provenance:* see Brownell Collection, pp. 509–11. ▪*Emendations and textual notes:* none. ▪*Historical collation:*

215.1–7 San . . . form. (*MTL*) • [*not in*] (*MTB*)
215.1–2 San . . . 68 [*brace*] • SAN FRANCISCO, *May 5, '68*. [*no brace*] (*MTL*)
215.3 Bliss Jr Esq • BLISS, Jr. Esq. (*MTL*)
215.4–5 D[r] Sir: [¶] The • DR. SIR,—The (*MTL*)
215.6 & • and (*MTL*)
215.7–8 [*no* ¶] I am . . . June. (*MTL*) • [¶] He reports that he is . . . June. [*follows* 'I . . . night.' *(216.1–2)*] (*MTB*)
215.7 & • and [*also at 216.2*] (*MTB, MTL*)
215.7 shall • expects to (*MTB*)
215.7 east • East (*MTB, MTL*)
215.8 manuscript (*MTB*) • Manuscript, (*MTL*)
216.1 here . . . trip (*MTB*) • ~, . . . ~, (*MTL*)
216.1 night— (*MTL*) • ~; (*MTB*)
216.1–2 sixteen hundred dollars (*MTL*) • $1,600 (*MTB*)
216.2 house— (*MTL*) • ~; (*MTB*)
216.3–4 Yrs . . . Twain • [*not in*] (*MTB*); Yrs truly, | MARK TWAIN. (*MTL*)

▪ 12 May 1868 · To Mary Mason Fairbanks · San Francisco, Calif. · *UCCL* 02732

▪*Copy-text: MTMF*, 27 n. 1, copy #1 in CU-MARK. ▪*Previous publication:* none known except the copy-text. ▪*Provenance:* Wecter's text in *MTMF* was based on a typed transcript (now lost) owned by Fairbanks's grandson, Thomas Nast Fairbanks. Clemens's MS has not been found. ▪*Emendations and textual notes:*

216.5 San • "~
216.6 Dear • "~
216.7 [¶] I • [¶] "~
216.9 Kind • "~
216.10 Yours • "~"

▪ 12 May 1868 · To Frank Fuller · San Francisco, Calif. · *UCCL* 02782

▪*Copy-text:* None. The text is based on two transcripts, both of which derive independently from the lost MS:

P1	Transcript by Dixon Wecter, CU-MARK
P2	Parke-Bernet Galleries 1956, lot 90

As editor of the Mark Twain Papers, Dixon Wecter was actively engaged in collecting letters for publication, usually by carefully transcribing the MS. Lacking the MS in this case (P1), he transcribed the letter on a standard 3″× 5″ card, in pencil, from a (now lost) 1937 catalog entry of New York book and manuscript dealer James F. Drake. Wecter identified the letter as "SLC to Gov. Frank Fuller" and noted at the end of his copy: "1½ pp., sold by James F. Drake | March 11, 1937." The 1956 Parke-Bernet catalog (P2) might also have derived from the lost Drake catalog, but retranscription from the MS itself, which was then being resold by Parke-Bernet, seems at least as likely. On the one hand, P2 quoted no words from the letter which were not earlier quoted in P1, and all description of the MS in P2 had earlier appeared in P1, save only the notation "12mo." On the other hand, it seems unlikely that the 1956 Parke-Bernet cataloger would, contrary to modern usage, *add* commas to clarify the parentheses at 217.2–3. The appearance of commas together with parentheses in P2 seems more likely the result of retranscribing the MS, for in other letters from this period, Clemens sometimes used commas before closing and (less frequently) opening parentheses. But whether P2 transcribed the Drake catalog or retranscribed the MS, it derived from the MS independently of P1. Both texts have been judged to contain variants that reproduce the reading of the lost MS, and are therefore adopted here. ▪*Previous publication:* see *Copy-text*. ▪*Provenance:* This letter was sold by James F. Drake in March 1937, possibly to Alan N. Mendleson; the Mendleson collection, including this letter, was sold in December 1956. The present location of the MS is not known. ▪*Emendations, adopted readings, and textual notes:* Like many catalogs, P2 uses italic type for text quoted from MS, a convention silently normalized here.

216.11 May 12. • 12 May [1868]; (P1); May 12 [1868]. (P2)

216.12–13	[*editorial ellipsis*] | I • in part it reads: "I (P^1); ". . . . I (P^2)
216.13	States (P^1) • states (P^2) [*Compare MS* 'States' *at 223.12 in 17 June 68 to Fairbanks.*]
216.14	"Paris & Pompeii," (P^1) • '~ ~ ~,' (P^2)
217.1–2	& . . . July. (P^1) • [*not in*] (P^2)
217.2	book, (subscription, (P^2) • ~‸ (~‸ (P^1)
217.2	$4.50 ($P^1$) • $4,50 ($P^2$)
217.3	illustrated,) (P^2) • ~‸) (P^1)
217.3	December (P^1) • December . . ." (P^2)
217.3–6	& . . . friend, (P^1) • [*not in*] (P^2)
217.7–8	Mark Twain alias Sam | L. Clemens (P^1) • "~ ~ ~ ~ ‸ ~. ~" (P^2)

▪ 28 May 1868 · To Elisha Bliss, Jr. · San Francisco, Calif. · *UCCL* 02733

▪*Copy-text:* MS, Clifton Waller Barrett Library, University of Virginia, Charlottesville (ViU). ▪*Previous publication: MTLP*, 16. ▪*Provenance:* deposited at ViU on 17 December 1963. ▪*Emendations and textual notes:*

218.7	~~in~~ is • is‸~~n~~
218.10	~~∅~~ Mr. • ['M' *over partly formed* 'm' *or* 'n']
218.16	R.R.~~s~~ • [*deletion implied*]

▪ 7 June 1868 · To Jane Lampton Clemens and Family · San Francisco, Calif. · *UCCL* 02734

▪*Copy-text:* MS, Mark Twain Papers, The Bancroft Library, University of California, Berkeley (CU-MARK). ▪*Previous publication:* none known. ▪*Provenance:* see Moffett Collection, p. 516. ▪*Emendations and textual notes:* none.

▪ 17 June 1868 · To Mary Mason Fairbanks · San Francisco, Calif. · *UCCL* 02735

▪*Copy-text:* MS, Huntington Library, San Marino, Calif. (CSmH, call no. HM 14227). Clemens's actual enclosures do not survive, but they probably were: (1) Clemens's sketch "Important to Whom It May Concern," from the San Francisco *News Letter and California Advertiser*, 13 June 68, 8 (SLC 1868eee), reproduced in photographic facsimile from newsprint now in the San Francisco Public Library (CSf); and (2) a letter by Stephen C. Massett (Jeems Pipes) from the San Francisco *Morning Call*, 17 June 68, 1, which is reproduced in a line-for-line reprint because a fully legible photographic facsimile of the *Call* typesetting is not now feasible. ▪*Previous publication: MTMF*, 28–32, without the enclosures.

Of the two enclosures, SLC 1868eee was widely and frequently reprinted by contemporary newspapers (see *ET&S3*, no. 230); the Massett letter was not reprinted, as far as is known. ▪*Provenance:* see Huntington Library, p. 512. ▪*Emendations and textual notes:*

221.9	please, ~~;I~~ • ['I' *partly formed; semicolon mended to a comma*]
221.18	two [or] three • two | three
221.22	blast~~?~~. • [*Although the period physically precedes the canceled question mark in the MS, it was not inserted, but added, immediately after the question mark was wiped out.*]
222.4	~~josh~~ joking • jo~~sh~~king
222.17	‸But I am staunch & true.‸ • ‸~ ~ ~ ~ ‸~ ~.‸‸ ‖ [*The sentence was inserted following the last line on the MS page;* '& true.' *was interlined by Clemens only because he ran out of room.*]
222.18	~~1,843.~~ ‸2,343.‸ • ~~1,82,343.~~ ‸2,343.‸ [*Clemens inserted* '2,3' *over* '1,8' *to make* '2,343.'; *he then canceled* '2,343.' *and rewrote it by interlining, for clarity.*]
222.23	~~char-~~ • char-|
222.34	*them*, ~~in~~ ~~&~~ — ~~w~~ & would • [*Clemens canceled* 'in' *before dotting the* 'i' *by writing* '&' *over it, which he also canceled; he then began a* 'w', *which he canceled immediately by writing the second* '&' *over it; he then interlined the dash.*]
223.4	Magazines • [*possibly* 'Mag~~n~~azines']
223.10	man. Ross • ~.—|~
223.12	stateroom • state-|room
223.18	"re-union" • "re-|union"
223.24	permit. Write • ~.—|~
223.26	~~of~~ occasionally • o~~f~~ccasionally
223.29	your • your | your

▪ 23 June 1868 · To Elisha Bliss, Jr. · San Francisco, Calif. · *UCCL* 02736

▪*Copy-text:* MS, Special Collections Department, University of Pittsburgh Libraries (PPiU). ▪*Previous publication:* none known. ▪*Provenance:* This letter was tipped into a copy of *"My Début as a Literary Person" with Other Essays and Stories* (Hartford: American Publishing Company, 1903), volume 23 in set 163 of the Autograph edition of the Writings of Mark Twain. The Autograph edition, issued in 512 numbered sets, was one of four limited "editions" printed from the same plates and published by the American Publishing Company: the Autograph, Royal, De Luxe, and Japan editions. Volumes 1–21 of each edition were published in 1899, and subscribers had the option of purchasing subsequent volumes, bound uniformly with their own set, as they were issued: volume 22 in 1900, 23 in 1903, and 24 and 25 (published by Harper and Brothers) in 1907.

Each set of the Autograph edition included a leaf signed by Clemens bound into the first volume (*The Innocents Abroad*, Part 1) and one or more leaves of manuscript (sometimes a letter, sometimes leaves from a literary work) tipped into one or more volumes of the set. This letter to Bliss, who was president of the American Publishing Company until his death in 1880, was almost certainly tipped in by the publisher, before the volume was delivered to its first purchaser (a circumstance further evinced by the fact that the letter was not transcribed by Ayer; see Brownell Collection, pp. 509–11). Set 163 of the Autograph edition, which contains all twenty-five volumes, was donated to PPiU by Mrs. Pitt O. Heasley. ■ *Emendations and textual notes:* none.

■ 5 July 1868 · To Elisha Bliss, Jr. · San Francisco, Calif. · *UCCL* 02739

■ *Copy-text:* MS facsimile. The editors have not seen the MS, which is in the collection of Robert Daley. ■ *Previous publication:* none known. ■ *Provenance:* Robert Daley acquired the letter in 1974 along with eighteen other letters to Elisha Bliss, Jr. He provided CU-MARK with a photocopy of the MS in April 1974. An Ayer transcription of this letter is at WU; see Brownell Collection, pp. 509–11. ■ *Emendations and textual notes:* none.

■ 5 July 1868 · To Mary Mason Fairbanks · San Francisco, Calif. · *UCCL* 02738

■ *Copy-text:* MS, Huntington Library, San Marino, Calif. (CSmH, call no. HM 14229). ■ *Previous publication:* *MTMF*, 33–34. ■ *Provenance:* see Huntington Library, p. 512. ■ *Emendations and textual notes:*

234.21 H̸ • [*partly formed*]

■ 11 July 1868 · To Mathew B. Cox · SS *Montana* en route from San Francisco, Calif., to Panama City, Panama · *UCCL* 02741

■ *Copy-text:* MS facsimile. The editors have not seen the MS, which is in the Beaverbrook Collection, Harriet Irving Library, University of New Brunswick, Fredericton, Canada (CaNBFUA). ■ *Previous publication:* none known. ■ *Provenance:* unknown. ■ *Emendations and textual notes:*

235.9 ~~ever~~ a good • ['a go' *over* 'ever']

■ 3 August 1868 · To Mary Mason Fairbanks · New York, N.Y. · *UCCL* 02743

■ *Copy-text:* MS, *damage emended*, Huntington Library, San Marino, Calif. (CSmH, call no. HM 14230). A photographic facsimile of the MS is on pp. 463–

64. Clemens wrote this letter in black ink on both sides of a single unruled sheet of white wove Westminster Hotel stationery, measuring approximately 9 by $10\frac{7}{8}$ inches (22.8 by 27.5 cm), before folding it to make a single folder, approximately $5\frac{3}{8}$ by 9 inches. The closing and signature have been cut away, which in turn caused the loss of several words on the other side of the sheet, as well as all but the last line of the printed letterhead. The damage has been conjecturally repaired by emendation. The text of the printed letterhead has been supplied from Westminster Hotel stationery used in a dozen earlier letters in 1867, even though it is clear from the last three words of the copy-text letterhead, which are preserved, that the original was not necessarily identical with the earlier examples. The earlier examples all name "Roberts & Palmer" as proprietors, not "Roberts, Palmer & Ferrin," as the copy-text does. ▪*Previous publication: MTMF*, 34–35. ▪*Provenance:* see Huntington Library, p. 512. ▪*Emendations and textual notes:*

237.1–2	WESTMINSTER HOTEL, COR. OF . . . YORK • [*cut away*] | [COR. O] [*cut away*]
238.1	Capt. Duncan, or • Cap[◇◇ ◇◇◇◇◇◇◇] | or [*cut away*]
238.1–2	have Dan & • hav[◇ ◇◇◇] | & [*cut away*]
238.3	worked hard on an • worke[◇ ◇◇◇◇ ◇◇] | an [*cut away; possibly* 'long' *instead of* 'hard']
238.3	Tribune, concerning • Tri[b◇◇◇◇ ◇◇◇◇]|cerning [*cut away*]
238.4	Treaty, & I • [T◇◇◇◇y, ◇] | I [*cut away*]

▪ 15 August 1868 · To Frank Fuller · Hartford, Conn. · *UCCL* 02744

▪*Copy-text:* MS, The James S. Copley Library, La Jolla, Calif. (CLjC, call no. 2420). ▪*Previous publication:* none known. ▪*Provenance:* CLjC acquired this letter in July 1966, as part of a larger Fuller collection. At the time of acquisition, a note by Fuller, probably written in the 1890s or even later, accompanied the letter: "Probably I covered something here not adapted to general reading. I think the above was written to indicate the date of his speech on *The Weather* which I know much about. [*in ink:*] I walked with him through Union Square just before sunset 3 hours before that speech." Since Clemens gave his "weather" speech on 22 December 1876 to the New England Society of New York, at Delmonico's restaurant, Fuller's description is either mistaken, or intended for some other letter, now lost. ▪*Emendations and textual notes:*

240.5	Hartf[d] ooo ooo • [*This reading of the MS is doubtful because the meaning of the six characters represented here as zeroes is not known. Despite some appearance to the contrary, these "zeroes" are not superscript and in fact rest on horizontal rules present in the MS but not visible in the following illustration.*]

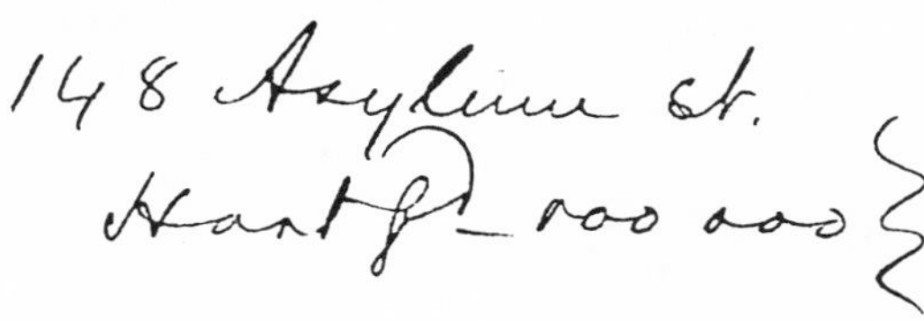

240.9 can. Or • ~.—|~

■ 17 August 1868 · To Mary Mason Fairbanks · Hartford, Conn. · *UCCL* 02745

■ *Copy-text:* MS, Huntington Library, San Marino, Calif. (CSmH, call no. HM 14231). ■ *Previous publication: MTMF*, 36. ■ *Provenance:* see Huntington Library, p. 512. ■ *Emendations and textual notes:*

241.4–5 right. [¶] It • ~.—| [¶] ~
241.9 M • [*partly formed*]

■ 21 August 1868 · To Charles J. Langdon *per* Telegraph Operator · En route from New York to Elmira, N.Y. · *UCCL* 02746

■ *Copy-text:* Jervis Langdon, 5. ■ *Previous publication:* none known except the copy-text. ■ *Provenance:* The actual document received has not been found; it was presumably owned by Jervis Langdon (Charles Langdon's son) when he published it in 1938. ■ *Emendations and textual notes:* none.

■ 24 and 25 August 1868 · To Jane Lampton Clemens and Family · Elmira, N.Y. · *UCCL* 02747

■ *Copy-text:* MS, Jean Webster McKinney Family Papers, Vassar College Library (NPV). The MS, which now consists of a single torn half-sheet, inscribed on both sides but unsigned, is almost certainly incomplete. ■ *Previous publication: MTL*, 1:154–55. ■ *Provenance:* see McKinney Family Papers, pp. 512–14. The missing part of the MS had been lost by 1917 at the latest, for *MTL*'s text is equally incomplete. ■ *Emendations and textual notes:* none.

■ 3 September 1868 · To Elisha Bliss, Jr. · Elmira, N.Y. · *UCCL* 02748

■ *Copy-text:* Transcript (handwritten in pencil) made by Dana S. Ayer of Clemens's now-lost MS, Rare Book Department, Memorial Library, University of Wisconsin, Madison (WU). The enclosure is separately treated below, pp. 590–91. ■ *Previous publication:* none known. ■ *Provenance:* see Brownell Collection, pp. 509–11. ■ *Emendations and textual notes:*

245.8 *Herald.*" • ~‸"

■ 3 September 1868 · To Henry M. Crane · Elmira, N.Y. · *UCCL* 02749

■ *Copy-text:* MS, Rare Book Department, Memorial Library, University of Wisconsin, Madison (WU). ■ *Previous publication:* none known. ■ *Provenance:* see Bassett Collection, p. 511. ■ *Emendations and textual notes:* none.

■ 7 and 8 September 1868 · To Olivia L. Langdon · Elmira, N.Y. · *UCCL* 02750

■ *Copy-text:* MS, Mark Twain Papers, The Bancroft Library, University of California, Berkeley (CU-MARK). This letter is the first of nineteen letters (only one of which—the third—is entirely lost) that Clemens wrote to Olivia Langdon during 1868. The envelope address ('Miss Olivia L. Langdon, | Present') indicates that he delivered it himself. Three of these letters (21 Sept, 18 Oct, 30 Oct) survive with envelopes that Clemens addressed and mailed directly to Olivia. Eleven later letters to her in 1868 (28 Nov, 4 Dec [twice], 5 and 7 Dec, 9 and 10 Dec, 12 Dec, 19 and 20 Dec, 21 and 23 Dec, 23 and 24 Dec, 25 Dec, and 30 Dec) survive with envelopes addressed like the one for the present letter, indicating they were hand delivered. They were delivered, however, by Olivia's brother, Charles Langdon, and must therefore have been mailed in outer envelopes, which do not survive, addressed to him (see p. 293 n. 5). Three letters survive with no envelopes of either kind: 4–5 Oct (presumably mailed directly to Olivia), and 27 Dec and 31 Dec (presumably mailed to her brother and then delivered by hand). ■ *Previous publication: LLMT*, 18–20. ■ *Provenance:* see Samossoud Collection, pp. 515–16. ■ *Emendations and textual notes:*

247.8	~~love you~~ have loved • ['have loved' *over wiped-out* 'love you']
247.17	~~is~~ it • it‸~~s~~
248.34	or~~, break~~ . . . ‸exhaust • [*comma deleted by caret for the insertion*]
249.4	~~B~~ • [*partly formed*]

■ 21 September 1868 · To Olivia L. Langdon · St. Louis, Mo. · *UCCL* 02751

■ *Copy-text:* MS, Mark Twain Papers, The Bancroft Library, University of California, Berkeley (CU-MARK). ■ *Previous publication: LLMT*, 20–22. ■ *Provenance:* see Samossoud Collection, pp. 515–16. ■ *Emendations and textual notes:*

250.9	did.—It • [*Clemens's dash does not fall at the end of a line here and is therefore not emended. He departed once more in this letter from his normal practice (of never following a period with a dash except at a line end) at 251.15 (see entry below).*]
251.1	~~time~~ to make • ['to make' *over* 'time']
251.7	~~[And you~~ ‸[You‸ • ~~[And y~~‸[Y‸ou

251.11 them. Mrs. • ~.—|~.
251.15 East.—Must • ~.|—~
251.15 ~~f~~ • [*partly formed*]

■ 24 September 1868 · To Mary Mason Fairbanks · St. Louis, Mo. · *UCCL* 02752

■ *Copy-text:* Transcript (handwritten in ink) made by Dixon Wecter of a TS copy of Clemens's MS (both now lost), Mark Twain Papers, The Bancroft Library, University of California, Berkeley (CU-MARK). Although Wecter wrote "(Fairbanks MS)" at the top of his transcript, he later referred to the document he copied as a "typescript" (see the emendation for 252.28 below). ■ *Previous publication: MTMF*, 37–38. ■ *Provenance:* Thomas Nast Fairbanks presumably owned the MS and supplied Wecter with the TS (see the textual commentary for 24 and 25 Dec 68 to Fairbanks, pp. 583–84, and *MTMF*, 55 n. 1, for discussions of another Wecter transcript made from a Thomas Nast Fairbanks TS). ■ *Emendations and textual notes:*

252.1 Sept. 24 • Sept. 24 [1868]
252.2 My Dear Mother— • [*Wecter inexplicably deleted these words, then marked them* 'STET'.]
252.19 something • something | (over) || [*Wecter's indication that his transcript continued on the recto.*]
252.28 night. • night. ‸[no complimentary close given]‸ | ~~[no signature or close is given in this typescript]~~ [*Wecter's description; he used the revised wording in* MTMF.]

■ 24 September 1868 · To Frank Fuller · St. Louis, Mo. · *UCCL* 02753

■ *Copy-text:* MS, The James S. Copley Library, La Jolla, Calif. (CLjC, call no. 2421). ■ *Previous publication:* none known. ■ *Provenance:* Many years after receiving this one-page letter, Fuller wrote in pencil on the back: "The 'Odorless Rubber Company' was started by me in Bridgeport to make certain India Rubber goods with little or no Sulpher in the rubber mixture. The products were beautiful but cost too much for the trade. I sold it to a Mr Post FF." CLjC acquired the letter in July 1966 as part of a Fuller collection. At that time, it was paired with the envelope for Clemens's 6 Sept 74 letter to Fuller (*UCCL* 01124), whose only surviving text is an Ayer transcript (WU). ■ *Emendations and textual notes:*

254.3–4 cundrum . . . cundrums . . . My aunt never uses them. • [*Someone other than Clemens heavily canceled these seven words sometime after the letter was received.*]

■ 4–5 October 1868 · To Olivia L. Langdon · Hartford, Conn. · *UCCL* 02770

■ *Copy-text:* MS, Mark Twain Papers, The Bancroft Library, University of California, Berkeley (CU-MARK). The surviving MS is a postscript only and consists of a single torn half-sheet of ruled paper, unnumbered and inscribed on one side. The page was folded up and sealed with glue, evidently after it had become separated from the body of the letter, which is lost. ■ *Previous publication:* none known. ■ *Provenance:* see Samossoud Collection, pp. 515–16. ■ *Emendations and textual notes:*

255.10 truth. Of • ~.—|~

■ 5 October 1868 · To Mary Mason Fairbanks · Hartford, Conn. · *UCCL* 02755

■ *Copy-text:* MS, Huntington Library, San Marino, Calif. (CSmH, call no. HM 14233). ■ *Previous publication:* Wecter, 34, excerpt; *LLMT*, 22, excerpt; *MTMF*, 39–40. ■ *Provenance:* see Huntington Library, p. 512. ■ *Emendations and textual notes:*

256.14 ~~& just~~ to leave • ['to lea' *over* '& just']
257.2 look~~in~~ • ['n' *partly formed*]
257.3 view—which • ~——|~

■ 5 October 1868 · To Abel W. Fairbanks · Hartford, Conn. · *UCCL* 02756

■ *Copy-text:* MS, Huntington Library, San Marino, Calif. (CSmH, call no. HM 14232). ■ *Previous publication:* *MTMF*, 41–42. ■ *Provenance:* see Huntington Library, p. 512. ■ *Emendations and textual notes:*

258.1 A~~y~~sylum • ['~~y~~' *partly formed*]
259.4 ~~wr~~ • ~~wri~~ ~~wr~~ ['wri' *miswritten*]
259.8 write • ~~wr~~ write ['wr' *miswritten*]
259.14 ~~M~~ • [*partly formed*]
259.16 ~~I~~ • [*partly formed*]
259.16 to-night. I • ~.—|~

■ 5–30 October 1868 · To Frank Fuller · Hartford, Conn. · *UCCL* 09079

■ *Copy-text:* MS, The James S. Copley Library, La Jolla, Calif. (CLjC, call no. 2422). The surviving fragment is the bottom half of a single leaf, inscribed on one side only, the top half of which has been cut away. Part of one (unidentified) character survives from the now-missing line just above the cut edge. The cut leaf has been glued to a heavy backing, which Fuller inscribed (see p. 260 n. 1). ▪*Previous publication:* see p. 260 n. 1. ▪*Provenance:* CLjC acquired the letter in July 1966 as part of a Fuller collection. ▪*Emendations and textual notes:* none.

▪ 7 October 1868 · To Edward L. Burlingame · Hartford, Conn. · *UCCL* 02757

▪*Copy-text:* Cyril Clemens, 18. ▪*Previous publication:* none known except the copy-text. ▪*Provenance:* In 1932, when Cyril Clemens published the letter, it belonged to Frederick A. Burlingame. The MS has not since been found. ▪*Emendations and textual notes:*

261.4 & • and [*twice; also at 261.5, 8*]
261.2 Mark Twain • MARK TWAIN

▪ 7 October 1868 · To Henry M. Crane · Hartford, Conn. · *UCCL* 02740

▪*Copy-text:* MS, Collection of Victor and Irene Murr Jacobs, Roesch Library, University of Dayton, Dayton, Ohio (ODaU). ▪*Previous publication:* possibly extracted in a 1968 issue of *The Collector: A Magazine for Autograph and Historical Collectors*, published by Walter R. Benjamin, Autographs, New York (now Hunter), N.Y., although its appearance there has not been verified. ▪*Provenance:* Victor Jacobs purchased the letter in December 1968 from Walter R. Benjamin, Autographs; Jacobs had begun transferring his collection to ODaU by 1984. ▪*Emendations and textual notes:*

262.2 Oct. • O[◇]t. [*blotted*]

▪ 12 October 1868 · To Mary Mason Fairbanks · Hartford, Conn. · *UCCL* 02758

▪*Copy-text:* MS, Huntington Library, San Marino, Calif. (CSmH, call no. HM 14234). ▪*Previous publication:* *MTMF*, 43–46. ▪*Provenance:* see Huntington Library, p. 512. ▪*Emendations and textual notes:*

263.4 bet~~ter~~ I • [‘I’ *over wiped-out* ‘ter’]
263.7 ~~bood~~ book • boo/dk
263.10 tittle • [*sic*]
263.15 lecture. I • ~.—‖~
263.29–30 ~~him~~ ‸them‸ • th/em
263.34 moonlight. Then • ~.—|~
264.2 glimpse • ~~glimps~~ | glimpse [*corrected miswriting*]
264.14 pickpockets. Only • ~.—|~
264.19 *over* • ~~*ov*~~ | *over* [*corrected miswriting*]

▪ 18 October 1868 · To Olivia L. Langdon · Hartford, Conn. · *UCCL* 02759

▪*Copy-text:* MS, Mark Twain Papers, The Bancroft Library, University of California, Berkeley (CU-MARK). ▪*Previous publication: LLMT*, 22–23, excerpts. ▪*Provenance:* see Samossoud Collection, pp. 515–16. ▪*Emendations and textual notes:*

266.4 hot-blooded • hot-|blooded
266.18 fault. I • ~.—|~
266.30 ~~som~~ sometimes • [*possibly corrected miswriting*]
267.8 man. ‸(And • ~.—‖ ‸(~
267.17 ~~y~~ • [*partly formed*]
267.32 ~~it~~ ‸&‸ • ['&' *over* 'it']
267.33 ~~keeps apologedizing~~ ‸apologized‸ • [*revision with a corrected miswriting:* 'ed' *mistakenly inserted following* 'g' *instead of* 'z']
267.37 indeed. This • ~.—|~
268.1 overtook • over-|took
268.2 ~~"Clem~~ "I have • "‸I have‸~~Clem~~
268.3 parish[i]oner • parish-|oner
268.12 it." You • ~."—|~
269.6 [HARTFOR]D • D [*first seven characters stamped off edge of envelope*]
269.7 OCT • [◇]CT [*badly inked*]

▪ 24?–27 October 1868 · To Jane Lampton Clemens and Family · Hartford, Conn. · *UCCL* 11442

▪*Copy-text:* Paraphrase in Orion Clemens to Mary E. (Mollie) Clemens, 30 Oct 68, Mark Twain Papers, The Bancroft Library, University of California, Berkeley (CU-MARK). ▪*Previous publication:* none known. ▪*Provenance:* Orion Clemens's letter survives as part of the Moffett Collection; see p. 516. Samuel Clemens's original letter may have been destroyed in 1904; see pp. 513–14. ▪*Emendations and textual notes:* none.

▪ 30 October 1868 · To Olivia L. Langdon · Hartford, Conn. · *UCCL* 02760

▪*Copy-text:* MS, Mark Twain Papers, The Bancroft Library, University of California, Berkeley (CU-MARK). ▪*Previous publication:* none known. ▪*Provenance:* see Samossoud Collection, pp. 515–16. ▪*Emendations and textual notes:*

272.4 Mrs. & Mrs. • [*sic*]
272.16 wierd • [*sic*]
273.12 Savior • [*possibly* 'Sa~~f~~vior']
273.21 XXV . . . XVII • [*small capitals simulated, not underscored*]
274.3 I • I|~~I~~

274.7–8	~~noth~~ notwithstanding • not~~h~~withstanding
274.25	again. I • ~.—|~
274.26	~~pretended~~ • ~~p[◇◇t◇n]d[◇]d~~ [*heavily canceled*]
274.28	~~love~~ like • lov~~ike~~
274.32	~~Good-bye~~ • ~~Good[◇]bye~~ [*heavily canceled*]
275.3	sieze • [*sic*]
275.4	~~bye—may~~ • ~~bye[◇◇◇y]~~ [*heavily canceled*]
275.7	~~Goo~~ • ~~G[◇◇]~~ [*heavily canceled*]

■ 31 October 1868 · To Mary Mason Fairbanks · New York, N.Y. · *UCCL* 02761

■ *Copy-text:* MS, Huntington Library, San Marino, Calif. (CSmH, call no. HM 14235). ■ *Previous publication: MTMF*, 47. ■ *Provenance:* see Huntington Library, p. 512. ■ *Emendations and textual notes:*

277.7	Cub • ~~Cub~~ Cub [*corrected miswriting*]
277.8	Mark • ~~M~~ Mark ['~~M~~' *partly formed; corrected miswriting*]

■ 4 November 1868 · To Jane Lampton Clemens · New York, N.Y. · *UCCL* 02762

■ *Copy-text:* MS, Jean Webster McKinney Family Papers, Vassar College Library (NPV). The surviving MS is a single torn half-sheet of ruled paper inscribed on both sides but unsigned, and almost certainly incomplete. ■ *Previous publication: MTBus*, 100–101. ■ *Provenance:* The missing MS page or pages may have been destroyed in 1904; see pp. 513–14. ■ *Emendations and textual notes:*

277.16	with • [w◇◇h] [*blotted*]
278.15	live. • [*This word ended the paragraph as well as the last line of the MS page.*]

■ 18 November 1868 · To Jane Lampton Clemens and Family · Cleveland, Ohio · *UCCL* 02763

■ *Copy-text:* MS, Jean Webster McKinney Family Papers, Vassar College Library (NPV). ■ *Previous publication: MTBus*, 102. ■ *Provenance:* see McKinney Family Papers, pp. 512–14. ■ *Emendations and textual notes:* none.

■ 18 November 1868 · To the President of the Scroll and Key Society, Yale College · Cleveland, Ohio · *UCCL* 02764

■ *Copy-text:* MS facsimile. The editors have not seen the MS, which is in a scrapbook in the Scroll and Key Society archives, Department of Manuscripts and

Archives, Yale University Library (CtY, call no. "Scrapbook: C.S.P. 1869. Vol. 2. Junior and Senior. 378.74 | YL 10 v. 2"). A photocopy of the MS was made available to the Mark Twain Papers through the kindness of Radley H. Daly and the Scroll and Key Society. ▪*Previous publication:* Maynard Mack, 214–15 n. 14. ▪*Provenance:* The MS has remained, since its receipt in 1868, in the possession of the Scroll and Key Society. ▪*Emendations and textual notes:* none.

▪ 18 November 1868 · To Joseph H. and Harmony C. Twichell · Cleveland, Ohio · *UCCL* 02765

▪*Copy-text:* MS, Joseph H. Twichell Collection, Beinecke Rare Book and Manuscript Library, Yale University (CtY-BR). ▪*Previous publication:* none known. ▪*Provenance:* It is not known when Twichell's papers were deposited at Yale, although it is likely that he bequeathed them to the university upon his death in 1918. He was a trustee of the Yale Corporation for thirty-nine years (1874–1913); Yale gave him an honorary M.A. in 1886, and made him an honorary Doctor of Divinity in 1913; and at least one of his sons (Joseph Hooker Twichell, who was on the football team) attended Yale (Strong, 162). ▪*Emendations and textual notes:*

282.2 J̸ T.‸'s.‸— • ['T' *over partly formed* 'J'; *possibly* 'T.—‸'s.‸']
282.6 the • [the] [*torn*]

▪ 20 November 1868 · To Jane Lampton Clemens and Family · Cleveland, Ohio · *UCCL* 02766

▪*Copy-text:* MS, Jean Webster McKinney Family Papers, Vassar College Library (NPV). ▪*Previous publication: MTL*, 1:155–56. ▪*Provenance:* see McKinney Family Papers, pp. 512–14. ▪*Emendations and textual notes:* none.

▪ 26 and 27 November 1868 · To Mary Mason Fairbanks · Elmira, N.Y. · *UCCL* 02767

▪*Copy-text:* MS, pages 1–5, Henry W. and Albert A. Berg Collection, The New York Public Library, Astor, Lenox and Tilden Foundations (NN-B), is copy-text for '**PRIVATE** . . . Slote's.' (283.1–285.2); MS, pages 6–[9], Huntington Library, San Marino, Calif. (CSmH, call no. HM 14243), is copy-text for 'P.S. . . . you?' (285.3–32). ▪*Previous publication:* Sotheby, lot 4, excerpt from the first five pages; *LLMT*, 23, brief excerpt from the first paragraph; *MTMF*, 48–52, the complete letter. ▪*Provenance:* The two parts of this letter have probably been separated since before 1918, when Henry Huntington acquired pages 6–9 among the Clemens letters he purchased from the Fairbanks family (see Huntington Library, p. 512). Pages 1–5 were owned by Mrs. E. A. Beardsley at the time of her death, and were sold by Sotheby of London on 27 June 1932. The Bergs probably purchased them then, or soon thereafter, depositing them at NN in 1940 along with the bulk of their collection. ▪*Emendations and textual notes:*

283.2 ~~Nov~~ • ['v' *partly formed*]
283.6 D̸ day • [*possibly* 'D̸day']
284.26 seeks̸ • ['s̸' *doubtful*]
284.31 beli[e]ves • be-|lives
285.9 must • ~~must~~ | must
285.23 Hip—hip • [*possibly* 'Hip-hip']
285.29 ~~Elmira~~ • [*deletion implied*]

■ 28 November 1868 · To Olivia L. Langdon · New York, N.Y. · *UCCL* 02768

■*Copy-text:* MS, Mark Twain Papers, The Bancroft Library, University of California, Berkeley (CU-MARK). ■*Previous publication: LLMT*, 23–27. ■*Provenance:* see Samossoud Collection, pp. 515–16. ■*Emendations and textual notes:*

289.12–13 ~~belive~~ believe • ~~believe~~ believe
289.21 out • out | ~~ou~~
290.6 ~~And I do~~ My whole • ['My whole' *over wiped-out* 'And I do']
290.13 ~~my~~ me • my̸e
290.14 ~~ther~~ their • ther̸ir
290.17 how • how how
290.24 underhanded • under-|handed
290.32–33 ~~prov~~ probed • prov̸bed
290.34 back;,— • [*semicolon mended to a comma by inserting the dash over the period of the semicolon*]
291.11 ~~bef~~ begin • bef̸gin
291.18–19 ~~full o~~ crowded • ['crowded' *over wiped-out* 'full o']
291.27 ~~I l~~ a • ['a' *over wiped-out* 'I l']
291.32 ~~Mark~~ Samuel • ['Samuel' *over wiped-out* 'Mark']
291.36 ~~or~~ picture • ['p' *over wiped-out* 'or']
292.4 *father*[.] • [*period written off edge of page or possibly torn away*]
292.7 LOVE • [*possibly* 'LOVE']
292.12 enough • ~~enough~~ | enough [*corrected miswriting*]

■ 28 November 1868 · To Joseph H. Twichell · New York, N.Y. · *UCCL* 02769

■*Copy-text:* MS, Clifton Waller Barrett Library, University of Virginia, Charlottesville (ViU). ■*Previous publication: MFMT*, 15–16; *LLMT*, 23, excerpt. ■*Provenance:* deposited at ViU on 17 December 1963. Twichell himself evidently returned to the Clemenses this and his 12 December 1868 letter, perhaps for sentimental reasons. Clara Clemens published it in 1931 (*MFMT*, 15–16); sometime between 1947 and 1949 she allowed Dixon Wecter to make a typescript of it (see Samossoud Collection, pp. 515–16); it was subsequently listed as "Mark

Twain, letter to his friend regarding his love" in the notorious "Mark Twain Library Auction" in April 1951 at Los Angeles, from which it was presumably purchased by Caroline Thomas Harnsberger. Harnsberger deposited a typed transcript of the letter in the Mark Twain Papers in 1954, at about the time she sold her several Mark Twain manuscripts. ▪*Emendations and textual notes:*

293.8	to your • to your to your
294.2	avoided • [*possibly* 'avo~~d~~ided']
294.3	NO • ['NO' *underscored twice*]
294.6	pass~~es~~ away • passe~~[◇~~ ◇]way [*blotted*]
294.9	*proud* she • *proud* ~~she~~ she [*corrected miswriting*]
294.12–13	‸There's . . . it.‸ • [*possibly added, rather than inserted*]
294.16	121 • ~~12~~ 121 [*corrected miswriting*]

▪ 29? November 1868 · To Pamela A. Moffett · New York, N.Y. · *UCCL* 02771

▪*Copy-text:* MS facsimile, *damage emended.* The editors have not seen the MS, but in 1982 a photocopy was provided to the Mark Twain Papers by its owner, Chester L. Davis (1903–87), then executive secretary of the Mark Twain Research Foundation (now Chester L. Davis, Jr.), in Perry, Mo. This four-page letter was written on both sides of two sheets of Slote, Woodman & Company letterhead. In compliance with the words 'Now—*Private*—Keep it to yourself, my sister' (295.5), and at the point where these words began a paragraph, two-thirds of the way down MS page 2, Moffett (presumably) cut apart the first sheet (pages 1–2). She preserved the bottom third of it and left the second sheet intact (pages 3–4), possibly even returning them to her brother for safekeeping (see *Provenance*). The top two-thirds of the first sheet were not preserved, however, resulting in the loss of some 150 words: only the bottom third of page 1, written on the other side of the preserved third of page 2, survives from the nonprivate portion of the letter. Despite this damage, the now-missing letterhead on page 1, including the dateline, has been conjecturally restored, on the assumption that the two sheets of paper originally carried identical letterheads. Clemens began the second sheet on its blank side (page 3), ignoring the letterhead at the top of what became page 4, which therefore preserves it, unused but intact. The inscribed date ('Nov. 29') is a less certain but necessary conjecture entailed by this restoration, since Clemens would not have left the dateline on page 1 blank. The inscribed date is thought to be one day later than, but otherwise identical to, the inscribed date on the previous letter, to Twichell, which this letter to Moffett resembles in many other ways (see pp. 295–96 n. 1). ▪*Previous publication: LLMT*, 28–29. ▪*Provenance:* At least this private part of the letter was returned to Clemens, presumably by Moffett, for it survived in the Samossoud Collection until 1947 or later: sometime between then and 1949 Dixon Wecter saw the MS there and made a typescript of it. Davis evidently acquired the MS, by gift or purchase, directly from Clara Clemens Samossoud sometime after 1947 (see Samossoud Collection, pp. 515–16). ▪*Emendations and textual notes:*

294.20–24 DANIEL . . . 1868. • [*not in; see* Copy-text *above*]

294.26 Rondout . . . other • [◇]on[d]ou[t & N]ewark & one [o◇ ◇◇◇] other [*partly cut away*]

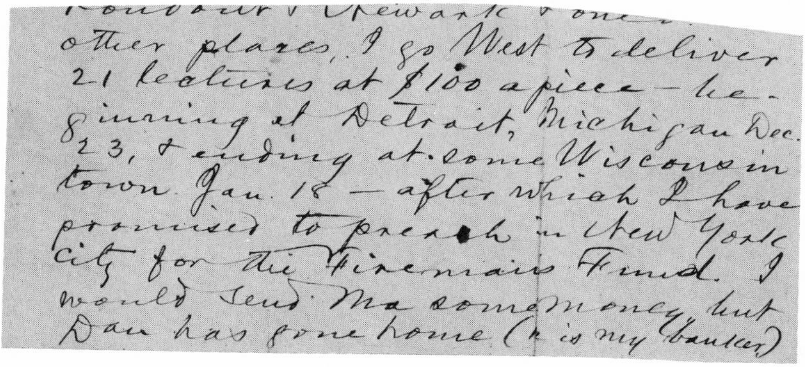
other places, I go West to deliver
21 lectures at $100 apiece—be-
ginning at Detroit, Michigan Dec.
23, & ending at some Wisconsin
town Jan. 18—after which I have
promised to preach in New York
city for the Fireman's Fund. I
would send Ma some money, but
Dan has gone home (he is my banker)

The bottom third of the first sheet (page 1) of the cut MS. Photocopy provided in 1982 by Davis reproduced at 54 percent of the actual size of the MS.

295.15 is • ~~is~~ is [*corrected miswriting*]

■ 2 December 1868 · To Jervis Langdon · New York, N.Y. · *UCCL* 02772

■ *Copy-text:* MS, Jervis Langdon Collection, Mark Twain Memorial, Hartford (CtHMTH). ■ *Previous publication: LLMT*, 29–31. ■ *Provenance:* donated to CtHMTH in October 1963 by Jervis Langdon's granddaughter Ida Langdon. ■ *Emendations and textual notes:*

297.3 ~~N~~ • [*partly formed*]

298.2 ~~Mr~~ Mrs. • M/rs.

298.18 ~~all~~ also • al/so

298.29–31 ~~delibera-~~ ‸but . . . paper.‸ [¶] Chase • ~~delibera-~~| but . . . paper. ‖ [¶] Chase [*Since* '~~delibera-~~' *originally ended the last line on MS page 6, the passage may have continued onto a subsequently discarded (now lost) MS page 7, and* 'but . . . paper.' *may then have been squeezed in below* '~~delibera-~~' *before the new paragraph beginning* 'Chase' *was begun on the present MS page 7. If so,* 'but . . . paper.' *was added, but not inserted.*]

299.5 me? But • ~?—|~

299.14 w • [*This character falls in the middle of a line; Clemens himself left his last sentence incomplete.*]

■ 4 December 1868 · (1st of 2) · To Olivia L. Langdon · New York, N.Y. · *UCCL* 02724

■ *Copy-text:* MS, Mark Twain Papers, The Bancroft Library, University of California, Berkeley (CU-MARK). ■ *Previous publication: MFMT*, 13, excerpts. ■ *Provenance:* see Samossoud Collection, pp. 515–16. ■ *Emendations and textual notes:*

301.3 ~~it~~ is • is~~t~~
301.5 ~~heat~~ heart • hea~~t~~rt
301.5 siezes • [*sic*]
301.8 ~~heat~~ heart • hea~~t~~rt
301.14 ~~It~~ I • ['I' *over wiped-out* 'It']
301.17 ~~exe~~ exacting • ex~~e~~acting
301.18 ~~b~~ • [*partly formed*]
301.18 ~~as~~ even • ['ev' *over* 'as']
301.24 already • ~~alr~~ already [*corrected miswriting*]
301.28–29 ~~looks~~ **naturally** • ['**naturally**' *over wiped-out* 'looks']
301.32–33 ~~wov~~ woke • wo~~v~~ke

■ 4 December 1868 · (2nd of 2) · To Olivia L. Langdon · New York, N.Y. · *UCCL* 02725

■ *Copy-text:* MS, Mark Twain Papers, The Bancroft Library, University of California, Berkeley (CU-MARK). ■ *Previous publication: LLMT*, 32–33, excerpt and paraphrase. ■ *Provenance:* see Samossoud Collection, pp. 515–16. ■ *Emendations and textual notes:*

303.5 ~~t~~ • [*partly formed*]
303.6 misgivings • [*possibly* 'mi~~v~~sgivings']
303.7 ~~I ◇~~ through • [~~I ◇~~ t]hrough [*torn and doubtful;* '◇' *partly formed*]
303.15 ~~ther~~ their • the~~r~~ir
303.20 ~~ded~~ devotee • de~~d~~votee ['~~d~~' *doubtful*]
303.21 ~~m~~ • [*partly formed*]
303.34 considere~~e~~ you • considere ~~y~~ you [*false start*]
304.1 ~~I~~ & • ['&' *over* 'I']
304.13 sunshine;) • [*no open parenthesis*]
304.19 with • with ~~with~~
304.32 ~~I~~ & • ['&' *over partly formed* 'I']
305.13–15 [◇◇◇pose] . . . el[◇◇] • [*The conjectured first and last lines of this suppressed passage (see p. 311 n. 6) are based on the following hypothetical reconstruction of the torn MS. Crucial evidence not entirely visible in the facsimile reproduction here is that Clemens wrote with some care on the faint, blue rules of the stationery, thereby limiting the characters possibly written even where the paper itself is entirely missing.*]

14

hour or two — but I am reas-
sured & comfortable now. If he
dares to ridicule me I shan't
inflict another letter on him for
three or four weeks! But do you
know, if I hadn't got your letter
to-day I would have arrived in
Elmira to-morrow night? In-
deed I would. You were saved
as by fire. I wouldn't have passed
another such a day as yesterday
for *any* thing. I suppose I ru-
ined one man's

Surviving portion of MS page 14, with part of the first line Clemens tore away from it editorially reconstructed; reproduced at 78 percent of actual size (CU-MARK).

keep nothing from you, else I
wouldn't have been betrayed into
this confession — & so I rely on
you not to take advantage of my
confidence to go & make your-
self sorry.

And now, being in a con-
fessing mood, I bow my expectant
head for your forgiveness, & pro-
ceed to reveal to you that I told
Dan — & have told the Twichell's
— & my sister — & Mrs. Fairbanks.
What a load is off my conscience
now! But observe, Livy, I know
who to tell. These several parties
are very, very dear to me — & each

Surviving portion of MS page 15, with the last line Clemens tore away from it editorially reconstructed; reproduced at 78 percent of actual size (CU-MARK).

306.22 down-hearted • down-|hearted
306.25 ~~worl~~ words • worl̸ds
307.3 ~~pole~~ • [*possibly* '~~pote~~' *with an uncrossed* 't']
307.10 letter. They • ~.—|~
307.16 ~~‸an individu‸ a man~~ • [*possibly* '~~‸an individu‸ a̸ man~~']
307.26 *yourself* • ['rself' *canceled before* 'you' *was underscored*]
307.33–34 I . . . destroyed. • [*Added, after the letter had been folded, to the otherwise blank verso of a preceding page (MS page 22). Clemens used the verso as if it were the lefthand margin of MS page 23, which is followed by two pages that he partly suppressed by tearing.*]
308.11 look. Why • ~.—|~
308.15 *twenty-nine . . . torn away* • [*The last four lines of MS page 25 were torn away, and all of MS page 26 was discarded.*]
308.19–20 ~~tr~~ terrible • tr̸errible
308.28–29 ~~do~~ shan't • ['shan't' *over wiped-out* 'do']
308.33 VI • [*small capitals simulated, not underscored*]
309.1 ‸will succeed‸— • ‸~ ~—‸—
309.21 ~~in your charac~~ • [*false ascenders and descenders used to discourage decipherment; see the illustration*]

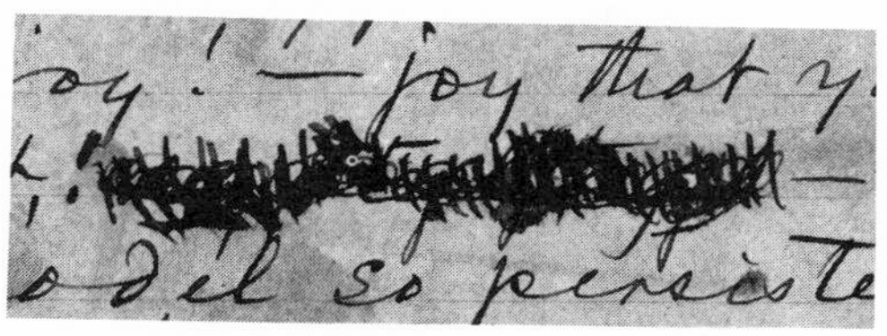

310.7 head • h[ead] [*torn*]
310.10 can. For • ~.—|~
310.18 might • ~~might~~ might [*corrected miswriting*]
310.21 ~~love~~ love • ~ | ~ [*possibly corrected dittography*]

■ 5 and 7 December 1868 · To Olivia L. Langdon · New York, N.Y. · *UCCL* 02726

■ *Copy-text:* MS, Mark Twain Papers, University of California, Berkeley (CU-MARK). ■ *Previous publication:* none known. ■ *Provenance:* see Samossoud Collection, pp. 515–16. ■ *Emendations and textual notes:*

312.16 ~~face of the~~ • [*false ascenders used to discourage decipherment*]
312.17 ~~feet~~ felt • fee̸lt
313.4 h̸ • [*partly formed*]
313.8 then, • ~[,] [*blotted and torn*]
313.19 ~~Oh,~~ • [*doubtful: very heavily canceled*]
313.24 ~~be~~ blessing • be̸lessing

313.28 coffined,/ • [*deletion implied*]
313.35 Thanksgiving • Thanǥksgiving ['ǥ' *partly formed*]
314.11 He will • Hew̸ will [*false start*]
315.16 20th/ • [*deletion implied*]
315.26 ~~wile~~ wild • wile̸d
315.33 your/ • ~|
316.20–21 ~~& long have~~ as good & • ['as good &' *over wiped-out* '& long have']
316.28 strangeness • strangenes[s] [*written off edge of page*]
316.32 ~~maj~~ magistrate • maj̸gistrate
316.32 ~~we~~—& • ['—&' *over* 'we']
316.36 time • ~~ti~~ time [*corrected miswriting*]
317.8 22d • 22[◇] [*torn*]
317.11 12/ • [*deletion implied*]
317.13 four • ~~four~~ four [*corrected miswriting*]
317.13 long. And • ~.—|~

■ 9 and 10 December 1868 · To Olivia L. Langdon with a note to Charles J. Langdon · New York, N.Y. · *UCCL* 02727

■ *Copy-text:* MS, Mark Twain Papers, The Bancroft Library, University of California, Berkeley (CU-MARK). ■ *Previous publication:* none known. ■ *Provenance:* see Samossoud Collection, pp. 515–16. ■ *Emendations and textual notes:*

318.7 train. We • ~.—|~
318.8–9 religion. I • ~.—|~
319.2 ~~sav~~ Savior • s̸Savior ['ior' *added after correction*]
319.4 give you • give y̸ you [*corrected miswriting*]
319.10 the • ~~the~~ ‖ the
319.13 ~~wa~~ • ['a' *partly formed*]
319.14 when? • ~?̸ ? [*corrected miswriting*]
319.17 obstacles. Then • ~.—|~
319.20 of • of ‖ ~~of~~
319.23 ~~do~~ dropped • do̸ropped
320.14 I must • [*possibly* 'm̸ I must'; 'm̸' *partly formed*]
320.16 ~~so~~ be • ['be' *over wiped-out* 'so']
320.25 ~~th~~ that • ~ | ~ [*possibly corrected false start*]
320.28 badly. I • ~.—|~
320.34 lecture. I • ~.—|~
321.11 ~~my self~~ myself • ['my self' *inscribed as two words, then the space between them marked for deletion*]
321.24 ~~no~~ • [*possibly* 'm̸']
321.25 ~~dare~~ *think* • ['*think*' *over wiped-out* 'dare']

321.29 contrary • contrayry
322.2 ~~the~~ nine-tenths • ['nine' *over wiped-out* 'the']
322.14 ~~litt~~ *literal* • *littleral* ['t' *partly formed*]
322.18 Innocence • Inno-‖nocence
322.29 ~~her~~ hear • herar
322.31 love. • ['e.' *blotted, possibly over illegible deletion*]
322.33 ~~had~~ have • hadve
322.35 m • [*partly formed*]
322.36 ~~"ja~~ "judgment" • "jaudgment"
322.37 interferes! Livy • ~!—|~
323.2 &— • [*dash over ampersand*]

■ 10 December 1868 · To Jane Lampton Clemens and Family · New York, N.Y. · *UCCL* 02728

■ *Copy-text:* MS, Jean Webster McKinney Family Papers, Vassar College Library (NPV). This letter is written on the three blank sides of the advertising folder shown in the illustration below. ■ *Previous publication: MTBus*, 102–3, with omissions. ■ *Provenance:* see McKinney Family Papers, pp. 512–14. ■ *Emendations and textual notes:* none.

■ 12 December 1868 · To Mary Mason Fairbanks · Norwich, N.Y. · *UCCL* 02730

■ *Copy-text:* MS, Huntington Library, San Marino, Calif. (CSmH, call no. HM 14257). ■ *Previous publication: MTMF*, 54–55. ■ *Provenance:* see Huntington Library, p. 512. ■ *Emendations and textual notes:*

326.24 was, • [*deletion implied*]

■ 12 December 1868 · To Olivia L. Langdon with a note to Charles J. Langdon · Norwich, N.Y. · *UCCL* 00205

■ *Copy-text:* MS, Mark Twain Papers, The Bancroft Library, University of California, Berkeley (CU-MARK). ■ *Previous publication:* none known. ■ *Provenance:* see Samossoud Collection, pp. 515–16. ■ *Emendations and textual notes:*

327.13 eastward • eastaward
327.15 No • [*possibly* 'NO']
328.19 "Lovingly • ~~"Lov~~ | "Lovingly [*corrected miswriting*]
328.23 ~~tw~~ too • twoo ['w' *partly formed*]
328.28 I • I I [*corrected miswriting*]
329.13 ~~Unil~~ Until • Uniltil

E. W. BURR, Jeweler,
Established 1832.

Office of HENRY H. LEEDS & MINER,

93 Liberty Street,

New York, November 20, 1868.

We respectfully announce that by order of

MR. E. W. BURR, Receiver & Trustee,

for the creditors of JOHN A. REED, we shall sell at Auction, without reserve, commencing on

MONDAY, DECEMBER 7th, at half-past 10 o'clock, A. M.,

and continuing until all is sold, the very large and valuable stock of superb, artistic &

Solid Gold Jewelry,

DIAMONDS, RUBIES, EMERALDS and other precious stones, now on exhibition at the store,

791 BROADWAY, opposite Grace Church, New York.

In this very valuable collection will be found the finest EMERALD and SAPPHIRE ever imported; also the finest first-class DIAMONDS of old and new mines; RUBIES, EMERALDS, PEARLS, OPALS, STONE CAMEOS of the great artists, mounted in the most artistic manner; Jewelry of all descriptions of the latest and most elegant styles, embracing a very large assortment of BRACELETS AND SETS in enamel and precious stones; a large and superb assortment of DIAMOND RINGS, EAR RINGS and SETS of new designs; also a speciality of SOLITAIRE RINGS and EAR RINGS of the finest water and cut; also ladies' CHATELAINES and LEONTINES, gents' and ladies' WATCHES of the best makers and finish. LOCKETS, SEAL RINGS, SCARF PINS, CHAINS, &c., of the best workmanship and finest gold, and other superb Jewelry incidental to a first-class Broadway Establishment.

Also, a number of FINE CABINET PAINTINGS and MOSAICS, GEMS by eminent masters. The GOOD-WILL AND LEASE OF THE PREMISES with the VALUABLE IMPROVEMENTS AND FIXTURES, viz.: SAFES by HERRING, AXMINSTER CARPETS, elegant carved and inlaid CASES and FURNITURE by HERTER, will be sold on last day of sale.

We assure the public that never before has so valuable a STOCK OF ARTISTIC WORK been offered at Auction in this country.

Very respectfully,

HENRY H. LEEDS & MINER.

Front of the advertising folder on whose three blank sides Clemens wrote his letter of 10 December 1868 to his family; reproduced at 75 percent of actual size. Courtesy, Vassar College Library (NPV).

329.17 until its • unt/il its
329.20–21 until patient • unt/il patient
329.23 until you • unt/il you
329.26 ETERNAL LIFE • [*block capitals, not underscored*]
330.4 again, • [*deletion implied*]
330.18 since." Livy • ~."—|~
330.28 ~~deg~~ decrees • deg/crees

■ 12 December 1868 · To Joseph H. Twichell · Norwich, N.Y. · *UCCL* 02729

■ *Copy-text:* MS facsimile. The editors have not seen the MS, but in 1982 a photocopy was provided to the Mark Twain Papers by its owner, Chester L. Davis (1903–87), then executive secretary of the Mark Twain Research Foundation (now Chester L. Davis, Jr.), in Perry, Mo. ■ *Previous publication: LLMT*, 33–34. ■ *Provenance:* Twichell himself evidently returned to the Clemenses this and his 28 November 1868 letter, perhaps for sentimental reasons. This letter survived in the Samossoud Collection until at least 1947: sometime between then and 1949 Dixon Wecter saw the MS there and made a typescript of it. Davis evidently acquired the MS, by gift or purchase, directly from Clara Clemens Samossoud sometime after 1947 (see Samossoud Collection, pp. 515–16). ■ *Emendations and textual notes:*

332.12–13 ~~in~~ on • i/on
332.13 flat-footed • flat-|footed
332.25 let • [*possibly* 'let/']
332.30 it, • [*deletion implied*]

■ 19 and 20 December 1868 · To Olivia L. Langdon · Fort Plain, N.Y. · *UCCL* 00206

■ *Copy-text:* MS, Mark Twain Papers, The Bancroft Library, University of California, Berkeley (CU-MARK). ■ *Previous publication: MFMT*, 22–23, excerpt. ■ *Provenance:* see Samossoud Collection, pp. 515–16. ■ *Emendations and textual notes:*

333.13 A/ • [*partly formed; possibly* 'N/']
333.13 teach • ~~teach~~ | teach [*corrected miswriting*]
333.18 book./] • [*bracket possibly inserted*]
333.24 choir." And • ~."—|~ [*period possibly a comma*]
334.1 ~~live~~ life • liovve
334.14 Kings • [*possibly* 'k/Kings']
334.18 consequence • conse-|~~quence~~ quence [*corrected miswriting*]

334.20 together. Scold • ~.—|~
334.21 there • ~~there~~ | there
334.28 eye • ~~eye~~ eye [*corrected miswriting*]
334.30 m̸ • [*partly formed*]
334.34 you. Already • ~.—|~
335.4 W̸ Mich. I • ~.—|~ [‘W’ *partly formed and doubtful*]
335.35 midnight • mid-|night
335.36 ~~rel~~ recollect • rel̸collect

■ 21 and 23 December 1868 · To Olivia L. Langdon with a note to Charles J. Langdon · Detroit, Mich. · *UCCL* 00207

■ *Copy-text:* MS, Mark Twain Papers, The Bancroft Library, University of California, Berkeley (CU-MARK). ■ *Previous publication:* none known. ■ *Provenance:* see Samossoud Collection, pp. 515–16. ■ *Emendations and textual notes:*

339.8 *won’t* • *w*[*o*]*n’t* [*torn*]
339.10 it! You • ~!—|~
339.16 knows • [‘s’ *possibly inserted*]
340.2 asleep. I • ~.—|~
340.3–4 ~~his~~ His • h̸‸His
340.4 22^{D} • [*numerals underscored twice*]
340.5 I̸ • [*partly formed*]
340.23 but I • [‘I’ *possibly over partly formed* ‘t’]
340.27 ~~to fo~~ • t̸‸fo
340.27 Mrs. • ~~Mrs~~ Mrs. [*corrected miswriting*]
340.29 then. Please • ~.—|~
340.33 ~~be~~ • ~ | [*doubtful*]
341.2–3 & night • [*sic*]
341.4 to-night • to-|night
341.19–20 love. [¶] *Do* • ~.—| [¶] ~
341.22 Sam.‸ • Sam[◇]‸ [*torn*]

■ 23 and 24 December 1868 · To Olivia L. Langdon with a note to Charles J. Langdon · Lansing, Mich. · *UCCL* 00208

■ *Copy-text:* MS, Mark Twain Papers, The Bancroft Library, University of California, Berkeley (CU-MARK). ■ *Previous publication: LLMT*, 34, brief excerpt. ■ *Provenance:* see Samossoud Collection, pp. 515–16. ■ *Emendations and textual notes:*

342.12 letters̸ • [‘s’ *partly formed*]

342.14 me. Now • ~.—|~
343.6 more • ~~more~~ | more [*corrected miswriting*]
343.9 ~~Mis~~ Mr. • Mr.~~is~~ [‘is’ *doubtful*]
343.14 measure! • [*possibly* ‘~,!’ *with the deletion implied*]
343.18 guess. And • ~.—|~
343.26 ~~Hor~~ Honoria • Ho/noria
343.38 you/ • [‘r’ *partly formed*]
344.3 finer • ~~finer~~ | finer [*corrected miswriting*]
344.7 ~~wa~~ what • w/hat
344.12 language. What • ~.—|~
344.15 ~~woul~~ wounded • woul/nded
344.28 again!” • [*Clemens tore away the remainder of MS page 9, which contained an apparently faulty quotation from Sterne; see the next entry.*]
344.31–36 ‸[*in . . . lines*]‸ • [*Clemens inserted this corrected quotation and explanation on an otherwise blank page that he numbered* ‘9½’; *before doing so, he had at least started his MS page 10, which begins* ‘Livy,’ *(345.1)*.]
345.3 when~~ever~~ everything • when~~ever~~ every-|thing [‘every-’ *over wiped-out* ‘ever’; *possibly corrected false start*]
345.9 anyhow/. • [*possibly* ‘~/.’]
345.21 ~~than~~ that • tha/t
345.22–23 ~~when~~ sometimes • [‘some’ *over wiped-out* ‘when’]
346.12 have • [*possibly* ‘ha/ve’; ‘r’ *mended to* ‘v’]
346.19 ~~& th~~ the • [‘the’ *over doubtful wiped-out* ‘& th’]
346.25 ~~real.~~ ‸in *reality*.‸ • ‸in‸ real/ity. [‘in’ *interlined with a caret;* ‘ity.’ *added to* ‘real/’ *and underscored once*]
346.31 ~~L. L~~ Livy • Livy~~. L~~

■ 24 December 1868 · To Pamela A. Moffett · Lansing, Mich. · *UCCL* 00209

■*Copy-text:* MS, Jean Webster McKinney Family Papers, Vassar College Library (NPV). ■*Previous publication: MTBus*, 106–7, with omissions, and misdated 1869. ■*Provenance:* see McKinney Family Papers, pp. 512–14. ■*Emendations and textual notes:*

347.10 Plain[,] Detroit • ~‸ | ~
348.5 ~~specious~~ species • spe-|~~cious~~ cies

■ 24 and 25 December 1868 · To Mary Mason Fairbanks · Lansing, Mich. · *UCCL* 02777

■*Copy-text:* A photofacsimile of MS page 4 published in Sotheby Parke Bernet 1976 (illustration for lot 42), ‘*at* . . . anywhere?’ (349.17–26), is copy-text for that portion of the letter. The remainder is based on one complete and three partial transcriptions, all deriving independently but at different removes from the original MS, which has not been found.

P^1	"Mark Twain," Cleveland *Herald*, 16 Jan 69, 4
P^2	Sotheby, lot 5
P^3	Sotheby Parke Bernet 1976, lot 42
P^4	Handwritten transcript (complete, CU-MARK) made by Dixon Wecter from a TS of the MS

Collation shows that they are in approximately the following relation to the MS:

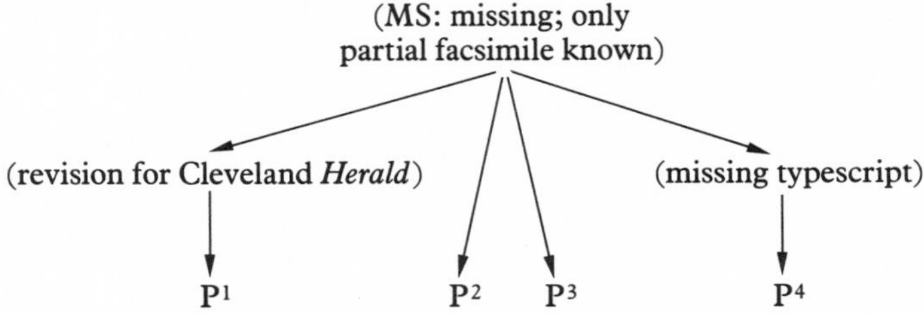

P^1 is a substantially accurate version of the letter's ninth paragraph ('About . . . heart.', 350.13–32) contained in a newspaper article promoting Clemens's second lecture appearance in Cleveland, on 22 January 1869. Clemens himself revised (and perhaps recopied) the passage for publication (see pp. 365–66, 367 n. 5).

P^2 and P^3, the 1932 Sotheby and the 1976 Sotheby Parke Bernet catalogs, indicate that the MS has probably survived intact to this day. The catalog description in P^3 reads:

> An important long early Autograph Letter Signed ("Mark"), 10 pp., 8vo, Lansing, Mich. Dec. 24 [1868] to "Dear Mother" (his close friend Mrs. Mary Mason Fairbanks) about his courtship of Olivia Langdon and closing with a poetical description of the Nativity. In a morocco-backed case.

The description in P^2 is briefer and makes no mention of the morocco case. Both catalogs publish extracts from the manuscript: P^2 publishes the dateline and the signature, 'Mark,' and quotes about six sentences from the body of the letter. P^3 provides longer excerpts from the letter, as well as the photofacsimile of MS page 4.

P^4, Wecter's transcription, was based on "a copy [probably a TS] of the original in the possession of Mr. Thomas Nast Fairbanks." Wecter further explained, "The manuscript was offered for sale by Sotheby's on June 27, 1932; its present whereabouts cannot be ascertained" (*MTMF*, 55 n. 1). P^4 is the only substantially complete transcript of the letter. ▪*Previous publication: MTMF*, 57–60; see also *Copy-text*. ▪*Provenance:* The MS was almost certainly owned by Thomas Nast Fairbanks, possibly until 1932; its subsequent and current owners are unknown. ▪*Emendations, adopted readings, and textual notes:* Like many catalogs, P3 used italic type for text quoted from MS (except for the dateline and signature), a convention silently normalized here.

348.12 Lansing, Mich., Dec. 24 • [*not in*] (P1); *Lansing, Mich., Dec.* 24 [1868] (P2); ~, ~.‸ ~. ~ [1868] (P3); ~, ~., ~. ~ [1868] (P4)
348.13 Dear Mother— (P4) • [*not in*] (P1); his Mother (P2); ~ ~‸ (P3)
348.14–16 [¶] I . . . present. (P2,4) • [*not in*] (P1,3)
348.14 & (P4) • and (P2)
348.14 2‸— • 2.— (P2); 2— (P4); [*not in*] (P1,3) [*The* P2 *reading has been partly adopted here because* P2 *was presumably copied directly from the MS, but cancellation of the period has been emended in to conform with Clemens's usual practice.*]
348.17–349.17 [¶] Don't . . . *that* (P4) • [*not in*] (P1–3)
348.17 & • and (P4)

[*MS facsimile is copy-text for* 'at . . . anywhere?' *(349.17–26)*]

349.17–24 *at* . . . threats." (MS facsimile, P4) • [*not in*] (P1–3)
349.18–19 MADE . . . ALWAYS (MS facsimile) • *made* . . . *always* (P4)
349.20–21 any one (MS facsimile) • anyone (P4)
349.21 along, (MS facsimile) • ~‸ (P4)
349.25–26 [¶] That . . . anywhere? (MS facsimile, P2–4) • [*not in*] (P1)
349.25 million. (MS facsimile, P3,4) • ~, (P2)
349.26 *you* (MS facsimile, P4) • *You* (P2); you (P3)
349.27–30 My . . . does—& (P4) • [*not in*] (P1–3)
349.30 do. And • ~.—~ (P4) [*It is likely that the Thomas Nast Fairbanks TS Wecter transcribed included an end-of-line dash here, which Wecter dutifully copied (see also the emendation below for 350.1). For the rationale for emending out these dashes, see Guide to Editorial Practice, p. 498.*]
349.30–33 it . . . you. (P3,4) • [*not in*] (P1,2)
349.33 *always* (P4) • always (P3)
349.33–37 And . . . perfect. (P4) • [*not in*] (P1–3)
349.37–350.2 Across . . . honest. (P3,4) • [*not in*] (P1,2)
350.1 Amen. And (P3) • ~.—~ (P4)
350.2 *that* (P4) • that (P3)
350.3–12 Write . . . you. (P4) • [*not in*] (P1–3)
350.7 & • and (P4)
350.8 & that • and that (P4)
350.13 [¶] About . . . so, (P3,4) • [*not in*] (P1,2)
350.13 time (P3) • ~, (P4)
350.13–18 Christmas . . . come. (P1,3,4) • [*not in*] (P2)
350.13 Christmas is here,) eighteen (P3) • ~ ~ ~‸) ~ (P4); [¶] "~ ~ ~—~ (P1)
350.14 & sixty nine (P3,4) • and sixty-nine (P1)

350.14	ago, ($P^{3,4}$) • $\sim_{\wedge}$ (P^{1})
350.15	Bethlehem—& ($P^{3,4}$) • Bethleham, and (P^{1})
350.16	Shepherds ($P^{3,4}$) • shepherds (P^{1})
350.17	flocks—& hovering (P^{3}) • flocks—& the hovering (P^{4}); flocks, and the hovering (P^{1})
350.17	singing Peace ($P^{3,4}$) • singing, peace (P^{1})
350.17–18	goodwill to men. For the Savior (P^{3}) • good will to men—for the Savior (P^{1}); good-will to men. For the Saviour (P^{4})
350.18–19	Don't . . . to ($P^{1,4}$) • [*not in*] ($P^{2,3}$)
350.18	turn, in fancy, now, (P^{4}) • $\sim_{\wedge}$ $\sim$ $\sim_{\wedge}$ $\sim_{\wedge}$ (P^{1})
350.19–20	that . . . turrets ($P^{1,2,4}$) • [*not in*] (P^{3})
350.19	wall ($P^{1,4}$) • walls (P^{2})
350.19	& its . . . & to ($P^{2,4}$) • and its . . . and to (P^{1})
350.19–20	& turrets (P^{4}) • and turrets (P^{1}); & turrets. (P^{2})
350.20–32	of . . . heart. ($P^{1,4}$) • [*not in*] ($P^{2,3}$)
350.20	Bethlehem (P^{4}) • Bethleham (P^{1})
350.22	& take (P^{4}) • and take (P^{1})
350.22	semblance (P^{4}) • resemblance (P^{1})
350.22	Poetry & (P^{4}) • poetry and (P^{1})
350.23	And (P^{4}) • [¶] $\sim$ (P^{1})
350.23	monks, & (P^{4}) • monks and (P^{1})
350.24	& the (P^{4}) • and the (P^{1})
350.24	& all (P^{4}) • and all (P^{1})
350.24	harsh, (P^{4}) • $\sim_{\wedge}$ (P^{1})
350.25	*real* (P^{4}) • real (P^{1})
350.25	& (P^{4}) • and (P^{1})
350.26	realize again, (P^{4}) • realize (P^{1})
350.27	there, & (P^{4}) • there, and (P^{1})
350.27	above, & (P^{4}) • above, and (P^{1})
350.28	Shepherds (P^{4}) • shepherds (P^{1})
350.28	& (P^{4}) • and (P^{1})
350.29	ever. And (P^{4}) • ever, and (P^{1})
350.31	& (P^{4}) • and (P^{1})
350.32	had (P^{4}) • had ever (P^{1})
350.32	& (P^{4}) • and (P^{1})
350.32	heart. (P^{4}) • $\sim$." (P^{1})
350.33–38	[¶] Please . . . scrub, (P^{4}) • [*not in*] (P^{1-3})
350.39	Mark. (P^{4}) • [*not in*] (P^{1}); $\sim$, (P^{2}); $\sim_{\wedge}$ (P^{3})

▪ 25 December 1868 · To Olivia L. Langdon · Lansing, Mich. · *UCCL* 00210

▪*Copy-text:* MS, Mark Twain Papers, The Bancroft Library, University of California, Berkeley (CU-MARK). ▪*Previous publication:* none known. ▪*Provenance:* see Samossoud Collection, pp. 515–16. ▪*Emendations and textual notes:*

352.9–10 to-morrow. I • ~.—|~
352.16 you be • you | y̸ be
352.18 humbug • hum-||bug
352.20 scribbling • scrib-|ling
352.26 overstep • over-|step

▪ 27 December 1868 · To Olivia L. Langdon · Tecumseh, Mich. · *UCCL* 00211

▪*Copy-text:* MS, Mark Twain Papers, The Bancroft Library, University of California, Berkeley (CU-MARK). ▪*Previous publication:* Wecter, 34–35, with omissions. ▪*Provenance:* see Samossoud Collection, pp. 515–16. ▪*Emendations and textual notes:*

353.18 inner • ~~inner~~ inner [*corrected miswriting*]
353.19 Chirstian • [*sic*]
353.26 p̸ • [*partly formed*]
353.30 notwithstanding • notwithstand‸ing‸ y̸ [‘ing’ *written over word space and partly formed* ‘y’]
354.12 p̸ • [*partly formed*]
354.26–27 letter. [¶] Livy • ~.—| [¶] ~
355.15 hurrah • hur-|rah
355.19–20 her? Just • ~?—|~

▪ 29 December 1868 · To Jervis Langdon · Cleveland, Ohio · *UCCL* 00212

▪*Copy-text:* MS facsimile. The editors have not seen the MS, but in 1982 a photocopy was provided to the Mark Twain Papers by the owner of the MS, Chester L. Davis (1903–87), then executive secretary of the Mark Twain Research Foundation (now Chester L. Davis, Jr.), in Perry, Mo. ▪*Previous publication:* Wecter, 35–37, with omissions; *MTMF*, 62, excerpt; *LLMT*, 36–40. ▪*Provenance:* This letter survived in the Samossoud Collection until at least 1947: sometime between then and 1949 Dixon Wecter saw the MS there and made a typescript of it. Davis evidently acquired the MS, by gift or purchase, directly from Clara Clemens Samossoud sometime after 1947 (see Samossoud Collection, pp. 515–16). ▪*Emendations and textual notes:*

357.12–13 ~~pefer~~ ‸prefer‸ • ~~pefer~~ || ~~fer~~ ‸prefer‸
357.13 incision • ~~incis~~ incision [*corrected miswriting*]
358.14 househ̸ • [‘h̸’ *partly formed*]
358.14 now-a-days • now-|a-days
358.36 staff, • [*deletion implied*]

359.3–4	Francisco. And • ~.—|~
359.15	mantelpiece • mantel-|piece
360.2	to-morrow • to-|morrow
360.7	$212,000 • [*possibly* '$22̸12,000'; '2̸' *partly formed*]
360.7	~~$22,000~~ ‸$42,000‸ • $2̸42,-|000
360.8	percentage • per-|centage
360.17	things. It • ~.—|~

■ 30 December 1868 · To Olivia L. Langdon · Cleveland, Ohio · *UCCL* 00213

■ *Copy-text:* MS, Mark Twain Papers, The Bancroft Library, University of California, Berkeley (CU-MARK). ■ *Previous publication:* none known. ■ *Provenance:* see Samossoud Collection, pp. 515–16. ■ *Emendations and textual notes:*

364.19	there. How • ~.—|~
364.22	h̸ • [*partly formed*]
364.27	Christ-like • [*possibly* 'Christlike', *if the hyphen is instead construed as the crossbar of the* 't']
364.37	~~ur~~ beg • ~~ur~~ ~~be~~ beg [*false start;* 'be' *over doubtful wiped-out* 'ur']
365.9	~~if your~~ if your • [*possibly corrected dittography*]
365.11	it. Please • ~.—|~
365.33	~~say,~~ says • says‸, ['s' *added over comma*]
366.6	Clevland • [*sic*]
366.11	street. But • ~.—|~
366.18	anywhere. She • ~.—|~
366.23	~~lovable~~ lovable • [*possibly corrected dittography*]

■ 31 December 1868 · To Olivia L. Langdon · Cleveland, Ohio · *UCCL* 00214

■ *Copy-text:* MS, Mark Twain Papers, The Bancroft Library, University of California, Berkeley (CU-MARK). ■ *Previous publication:* *LLMT*, 41, brief excerpt. ■ *Provenance:* see Samossoud Collection, pp. 515–16. ■ *Emendations and textual notes:*

368.13	an̸ • ['n' *partly formed*]
368.20	heart-aches • heart-|aches
368.25	Avenue • Ave-|~~nue~~ nue [*corrected miswriting*]
368.26	~~—you—~~ • —| ~~you~~—
368.33	s̸ • [*partly formed*]
368.36	them! And • ~!—|~
369.6	mark. I • ~.—|~

369.9 ~~its~~ to • ['to' *over* 'its'; 's' *partly formed*]
369.30 it.! • [*period mended to an exclamation point*]
369.31 then. So • ~.—|~
370.5 me. It • ~.+|~
370.12 ~~may~~ many • ma~~y~~ny
370.17 ~~nobe~~ noble • nob~~e~~le
370.22 hereafter • here-|after
370.22 other. It • ~.+|~
370.23 ~~me.~~ my • my~~e.~~ ['y' *over* 'e' *and the period wiped out*]
370.25 ~~die~~ dying • d~~ie~~ying
370.26 ~~pre~~ priceless • pr~~e~~iceless
370.28 Godspeed • God-|speed
371.6 Good-bye • [*hyphen possibly a stray mark*]

▪ Appendix E: Enclosure with 20 November 1867 · To Jane Lampton Clemens and Family (1st of 2) · New York, N.Y.

▪*Copy-text:* "The Quaker City Pilgrimage," New York *Herald*, 20 Nov 67, 7. Only the letter to the editor, entitled "The Cruise of the Quaker City," was written by Clemens (SLC 1867sss). ▪*Previous publication: TIA*, 313–19 (Clemens's letter only). ▪*Provenance:* The original clipping that Clemens enclosed is not known to survive. ▪*Emendations and textual notes:*

400.8 R. • [*period did not print*]
400.13 D. D. • [*second period did not print*]
401.1 sing a • sing a | a
401.16 blind-man's • blind-|man's
401.16 buff • [*sic*]
401.17 moonlight • moon-|light
402.4 dont't • [*sic*]
402.33 certainly • ['i' *did not print*]
404.12 slippers • ['l' *broken*]
404.12 Oh • [*possibly* 'On']
406.1 no malice • [*possibly* 'ne malice']

▪ Appendix E: Enclosure with 25 November 1867 · To Charles Henry Webb · Washington, D.C.

▪*Copy-text:* MS of *Quaker City* play, Josiah K. Lilly, Jr., Collection, Lilly Library, Indiana University, Bloomington (InU-Li). Clemens apparently completed only these twenty-eight MS pages (the first two acts) of his untitled play. Act 2 is probably unfinished. ▪*Previous publication:* SLC 1927 (private publication of 200 copies). ▪*Provenance:* donated to InU-Li in 1955. The MS is bound with its enclosing letter (David A. Randall, 43–44). ▪*Emendations and textual notes:*

406.22 the office • [◇]he office [*torn*]
406.22 Excursion • Excur-|[◇]ion [*torn*]
406.24 appearances, • [*deletion implied*]
407.27 b̸ • [*partly formed*]
408.3 ~~lop~~ lot • lot‸p̸ ['p' *partly formed*]
408.13 say.] • [*no open bracket*]
408.19 so. Where • ∼.—|∼
409.11 Humph! Twelve • ∼!—|∼
409.12 (ironically) • [*closing parenthesis runs off edge of page*]
409.35 body-servant servant • [*sic*]
410.2 c̸ • [*doubtful*]
410.9 Geore • [*sic*]
410.17 Credentials, • [*comma possibly inserted*]
410.27 ~~has~~ was • h̸‸was
410.30 state • stac̸te
410.33 grandfather • grand-|father
411.3 Steamer • Steam[◇◇] [*torn*]
411.16 ~~An abundance of~~ • ~~An abundance~~ | of [*deletion of* 'of' *implied*]
411.21 camp-meeting • camp-|meeting
411.25 ~~A◇~~ • [*possibly two words* '~~A p~~'; 'p' *partly formed*]
411.31 a̸ • [*doubtful*]
411.31 greenbacks • green-|backs
412.5 ~~Plains—~~ • [*deletion of dash implied*]
412.8 M. • [*possibly* 'M.~~-~~'; *deletion of partly formed dash implied*]
412.25 ~~pir~~ pilgrims • pi~~r~~il-|grims
412.27 seasick • sea-|sick
413.3 ~~tha~~ they • tha̸ey
413.10 would n't • ∼ | ∼
413.17 shortcomings • short-|comings
413.22 ~~is~~ it • it‸s̸
413.27 7-up • 7-|up
413.34 ~~aga~~ agin • aga̸in
414.6–7 fore-spanker-gaff-tops'l-jib-boom • fore-|spanker-gaff-tops'l-jib-|boom
414.10 blamd • blam[d] [*torn*]

▪ Appendix E: Enclosure with 3 September 1868 · To Elisha Bliss, Jr. · Elmira, N.Y.

▪*Copy-text:* "Eulogy on Woman," *Excelsior Monthly Magazine*, August 1868, 99–100, reproduced courtesy of the John Hay Library of Rare Books and Special

Collections, Brown University, Providence, Rhode Island (RPB-JH). The original folios and running heads have not been reproduced, and the border around each page has been editorially supplied. ■*Previous publication:* see the textual commentary for 14 Jan 68 to JLC and family. ■*Provenance:* The original clipping that Clemens enclosed is not known to survive. ■*Emendations and textual notes:* none.

■ Appendix E: Enclosure with 28 November 1868 · To Olivia L. Langdon · New York, N.Y.

■*Copy-text:* "Mark Twain as a Lecturer," New York *Tribune*, 11 May 67, 2. ■*Previous publication:* none known except the copy-text. ■*Provenance:* The original clipping that Clemens enclosed is not known to survive. ■*Emendations and textual notes:*

418.7 succceeded • [*sic*]

■ Appendix F: Contract for *The Innocents Abroad* · 16 October 1868 · Hartford, Conn.

■*Copy-text:* MS of Clemens's copy, drafted by Elisha Bliss, Jr., Mark Twain Papers, The Bancroft Library, University of California, Berkeley (CU-MARK). ■*Previous publication:* none known. ■*Provenance:* see Mark Twain Papers, pp. 514–15. ■*Emendations and textual notes:*

421.6 neccessary • [*sic*]
421.12 Compny • [*sic*]
422.1 neccessary • [*sic*]
422.2 correting • [*sic*]

■*Collation:* Variant readings from Elisha Bliss's copy of the contract, now housed in the Collection of American Literature, Beinecke Rare Book and Manuscript Library, Yale University (CtY-BR), are recorded below (entries on the right of the bullet). Both copies of the contract are in Bliss's hand.

421.1 1868. • $\sim_{\wedge}$
421.2 the • [*not in*]
421.3 City of New York • New York City
421.3 sd • said
421.4 Company • ~,
421.5 volume • Volume
421.6 neccessary, • $\sim_{\wedge}$
421.8 have the • have
421.8 Manuscript • ~,

421.10 manner, • ~∧

421.10 matter • ~.

421.11 City • ~"

421.12 publish • ~,

421.12 manuscript, • ~∧

421.12 form • ~,

421.14 same, the • same a

421.14 cent. • ~∧

421.14 every • each

421.15 them • ~,

421.16 book • said book

421.16 to • is to

421.17 Editors, • ~∧

421.17 to them • them

422.2 of • ‸of‸

422.2 correting the same if necessary • correcting them if neccessary

422.3 Book • ~,

422.7 spring • ~—

422.7 that they will use • will ‸that they‸ use [*insertion error*]

422.8 do. • ~.—

422.9–10 Elisha . . . Co • [*not in*]

422.11 Signed • ~ —

422.12–15 The . . . firm [*flourish*] • [*not in*]

422.16–19 [*on . . . Abroad* • [*not in; Bliss's copy bears the following docket by Bliss, which does not appear on Clemens's copy:*] Saml J. Clemens | Contract for | "Innocents Abroad"— | Oct 16th 1868. | no 1

References

THIS LIST defines the abbreviations used in this book and provides full bibliographic information for works cited by the author's name, by the author's name and publication date, or by a short title. The names of the passengers who wrote newspaper letters during the *Quaker City* voyage are marked with an asterisk (*); a complete list of the writing and publication dates of their letters (except Isham's) may be found in the Sources for Appendix D. Alphabetization is letter-by-letter; i.e., "Vandal" precedes "Van Deusen."

AAA.

1924. *The Renowned Collection of the Late William F. Gable of Altoona, Pennsylvania*. Part 5. Sale of 24 and 25 November. New York: American Art Association.

1926. *The Collections of Brandreth Symonds and Ralph E. Samuel*. Sale of 17 and 18 February. New York: American Art Association.

1927. *The Collection of Henry Goldsmith of New York City*. Sale of 28 February. New York: American Art Association.

AAA/Anderson Galleries.

1934. *First Editions and Manuscripts Collected by the Late Mr. and Mrs. William K. Bixby*. Sale no. 4098 (4 and 5 April). New York: American Art Association, Anderson Galleries.

1937. *The Collection of the Late Albert Bigelow Paine*. Sale no. 4346 (11 and 12 November). New York: American Art Association, Anderson Galleries.

AD Autobiographical Dictation.

Ajax [pseud.].

1867. "Letter from New York." Letter dated 7 May. Sacramento *Union*, 4 June, 1.

Alta California Bookstore.

1964. *Autograph Letters and Manuscripts*. Catalog 21. Berkeley: Alta California Bookstore (John Swingle, proprietor).

American Publishing Company.

1866–79. "Books received from the Binderies, Dec 1st *1866* to Dec 31. *1879*," the company's stock ledger, NN-B.

Anderson, Morris.

1943. "Red-Letter Books Relating to Missouri." Review of *The Adventures of Tom Sawyer*. *Missouri Historical Review* 38 (October): 85–93.

Andrews, Kenneth R.

1950. *Nook Farm: Mark Twain's Hartford Circle*. Cambridge: Harvard University Press.

Angel, Myron, ed.

1881. *History of Nevada*. Oakland, Calif.: Thompson and West.

Annual Cyclopaedia 1867

1870. "Indian War." *The American Annual Cyclopaedia and Register of Important Events of the Year 1867*. Vol. 7. New York: D. Appleton and Co.

Annual Cyclopaedia 1868

1871. "Rising, Rev. Franklin S." *The American Annual Cyclopaedia and Register of Important Events of the Year 1868*. Vol. 8. New York: D. Appleton and Co.

Baedeker, Karl.

1872. *Paris and Northern France. Handbook for Travellers*. 3d ed. Coblenz, Germany: Karl Baedeker.

1879. *Italy. Handbook for Travellers. First Part: Northern Italy*. 5th ed. Leipzig, Germany: Karl Baedeker.

1886. *Le midi de la France depuis la Loire et y compris la corse. Manuel du voyageur*. 2d ed. Leipzig, Germany: Karl Baedeker.

Baehr, Harry W., Jr.

1936. *"The New York Tribune" since the Civil War*. New York: Dodd, Mead and Co.

BAL

1957. *Bibliography of American Literature*. Compiled by Jacob Blanck. Vol. 2. New Haven: Yale University Press.

Barnum, Phineas T.

1869. *Struggles and Triumphs: or, Forty Years' Recollections of P. T. Barnum*. Hartford: J. B. Burr and Co.

Barrett, Don C.

1931. *The Greenbacks and Resumption of Specie Payments, 1862–1879*. Cambridge: Harvard University Press.

Bartlett, William C.

1881. "Samuel Williams, Journalist." *Californian* 4 (October): 323–30.

1898. "Overland Reminiscences." *Overland Monthly*, 2d ser., 32 (July): 41–46.

Bayles, James Copper.

1867. "Amusements." New York *Citizen*, 4 May, 8.

*Beach, Moses S.

1867a. "Mediterranean Bound—No. 1." Letter dated 8 June. New York *Sun*, 10 June, 2.

1867b. "Mediterranean Bound, No. 12." Letter dated 9 July. New York *Sun*, 13 August, 2.

1867c. "Mediterranean Bound—No. 36." Letter dated 21 October. New York *Sun*, 27 November, 2.

Beecher, Henry Ward.

1855. *Plymouth Collection of Hymns, for the Use of Christian Congregations*. New York: A. S. Barnes and Co.

1868. *Sermons by Henry Ward Beecher, Plymouth Church, Brooklyn*. 2 vols. New York: Harper and Brothers.

1869. *Plymouth Pulpit: The Sermons of Henry Ward Beecher, in Plymouth Church, Brooklyn. From Verbatim Reports by T. J. Ellinwood. First Series: September, 1868–March, 1869*. New York: J. B. Ford and Co.

[Beecher, Thomas K.]

1870. *Jervis Langdon*. [Elmira, N.Y.]: "Printed for use of friends, and not for sale."

Boase, Frederic.

1892–1921. *Modern English Biography*. 6 vols. Truro, England: Netherton and Worth.

Boatner, Mark Mayo, III.

1959. *The Civil War Dictionary*. New York: David McKay Company.

Bokum, Hermann.

1868. *The Tennessee Hand-Book and Immigrant's Guide: Giving a Description of the State of Tennessee; . . . with Special Reference to the Subject of Immigration*. Philadelphia: J. B. Lippincott and Co.

Booth, Bradford A.

1947. "Mark Twain's Friendship with Emeline Beach." *American Literature* 19 (November): 219–30.

Bower, Robert F.

1867. "Report of the Keokuk Library Association." Keokuk (Iowa) *Gate City*, 14 May, 4.

Boyd, Andrew, and W. Harry Boyd, comps.

1872. *Boyds' Elmira and Corning Directory: Containing the Names of the Citizens, a Compendium of the Government, and Public and Private Institutions . . . 1872–3*. Elmira: Andrew and W. Harry Boyd.

Boyd, William H., comp.

1857. *Boyd's Cleveland City Directory. Containing the Names of the Citizens, Business Directory, State and City Record . . . 1857*. New York: William H. Boyd.

Branch, Edgar Marquess, and Robert H. Hirst.

1985. *The Grangerford-Shepherdson Feud . . . with an Account of Mark Twain's Literary Use of the Bloody Encounters at Compromise, Kentucky*. Berkeley: The Friends of The Bancroft Library.

Broderick, John C.
1976. "John Russell Young: The Internationalist as Librarian." *Quarterly Journal of the Library of Congress* 33 (April): 117–49.

Brooks, Noah.
1898. "Mark Twain in California." *Century Illustrated Monthly Magazine*, n.s. 57 (November): 97–99.
1902. Letter to the editor dated 27 June. In "Reminiscences of Bret Harte," *Overland Monthly*, 2d ser., 40 (September): 220–39.

Brown, James Baldwin.
1867. *The Home Life: In the Light of Its Divine Idea*. New York: D. Appleton and Co.

Browne, Junius Henri.
1869. *The Great Metropolis; A Mirror of New York*. Hartford: American Publishing Company.

Brownell, George H.
1941. "Letters of Mark Twain, 1867–1909, Chiefly to Bliss of the American Publishing Company. Copies Made by Dana Ayer, Worcester, Massachusetts." PH in CU-MARK.
1943. "From 'Hospital Days.'" *Twainian* 2 (March): 1–5.
1945. Untitled item ("In an auction sale catalog . . ."). *Twainian* 4 (May): 4.

Browning, Elizabeth Barrett.
1857. *Aurora Leigh*. London: Chapman and Hall.

Bryan, Wilhelmus Bogart.
1916. *A History of the National Capital*. 2 vols. New York: Macmillan Company.

Bryan, William Alanson.
1915. *Natural History of Hawaii*. Honolulu: Hawaiian Gazette Co.

Budd, Louis J.
1972. "Did Mark Twain Write 'Impersonally' for the *New York Herald?*" *Library Notes* (Duke University, Durham, North Carolina), no. 43 (November): 5–9.

CaNBFUA Beaverbrook Collection, Harriet Irving Library, University of New Brunswick, Fredericton, New Brunswick, Canada.

CaQMMRB Department of Rare Books and Special Collections, McGill University, Montreal, Quebec, Canada.

Carlson, Helen S.
1974. *Nevada Place Names: A Geographical Dictionary*. Reno: University of Nevada Press.

Carmichael, Sarah E.
1866. *Poems*. San Francisco: Towne and Bacon.

Carnegie Book Shop.
[1963]. *Literary and Historical Autograph Letters. Documents and Manuscripts*. Catalog no. 272. New York: Carnegie Book Shop.

Carson City Census

[1870] 1965. "Inhabitants in . . . Carson City." *Population Schedules of the Ninth Census of the United States, 1870. Roll 834. Nevada: Church, Douglas, Elko, Esmeralda, Humboldt, Lander, Lincoln, Lyon, Nye, and Ormsby Counties*. National Archives Microfilm Publications, Microcopy no. 593. Washington, D.C.: General Services Administration.

CCamarSJ Estelle Doheny Collection, The Edward Laurence Doheny Memorial Library, Saint John's Seminary, Camarillo, California. See Christie.

Chester, Giraud.

1951. *Embattled Maiden: The Life of Anna Dickinson*. New York: G. P. Putnam's Sons.

Chommie, John C.

1970. *The Internal Revenue Service*. New York: Praeger Publishers.

Christie.

1988. *The Estelle Doheny Collection from The Edward Laurence Doheny Memorial Library, St. John's Seminary, Camarillo, California*. Sale of 17 and 18 October (Doheny IV). New York: Christie, Manson and Woods International.

City Book Auction.

1945. [*Catalog*]. Sale no. 305 (14 April). New York: City Book Auction.

Clark, Clifford E., Jr.

1978. *Henry Ward Beecher: Spokesman for a Middle-Class America*. Urbana: University of Illinois Press.

Clemens, Cyril.

1932. *Mark Twain the Letter Writer*. Boston: Meador Publishing Company.

Clemens, Orion. See OC.

Clemens, Samuel L. See SLC.

Clemens, Will M.

1900. "Mark Twain on the Lecture Platform." *Ainslee's Magazine* 6 (August): 25–32.

Cleveland Census

[1850] 1964. "Free Inhabitants in . . . Cleveland." *Population Schedules of the Seventh Census of the United States, 1850. Roll 672. Ohio: Cuyahoga County (pt.)*. National Archives Microfilm Publications, Microcopy no. 432. Washington, D.C.: General Services Administration.

[1860] 1967. "Free Inhabitants in . . . Cleveland." *Population Schedules of the Eighth Census of the United States, 1860. Rolls 952 and 953. Ohio: Cuyahoga County (pt.), City of Cleveland*. National Archives Microfilm Publications, Microcopy no. 653. Washington, D.C.: General Services Administration.

Cleveland Directory

1867. *Cleveland Leader Annual City Directory for 1867–68, Together with a General Business Directory*. Cleveland: Cleveland Leader Printing Company.

1868. *Cleveland Leader Annual City Directory for 1868–69, Together with a General Business Directory*. Cleveland: Cleveland Leader Printing Company.

CLjC The James S. Copley Library, La Jolla, California.

Coan, T. M.
1868. "The Greatest Volcano in the World." *Harper's New Monthly Magazine* 37 (September): 553–59.

CofC
1969. *Clemens of the "Call": Mark Twain in San Francisco*. Edited by Edgar M. Branch. Berkeley and Los Angeles: University of California Press.

Conard, Howard L., ed.
1901. *Encyclopedia of the History of Missouri*. 6 vols. New York: Southern History Company.

Congress.
1869. *Papers Relating to Foreign Affairs, Accompanying the Annual Message of the President, to the Third Session Fortieth Congress*. 2 parts. Washington, D.C.: Government Printing Office.

Coulter, E. Merton.
1937. *William G. Brownlow: Fighting Parson of the Southern Highlands*. Chapel Hill: University of North Carolina Press.

Crane, Ellery Bicknell.
1895–1900. *Genealogy of the Crane Family*. 2 vols. Worcester, Mass.: Charles Hamilton.

Crankshaw, Edward.
1981. *Bismarck*. London: Macmillan.

Craven Collection of Mrs. Robin Craven.

CSf San Francisco Public Library, San Francisco.

CSmH Henry E. Huntington Library, San Marino, California. The Huntington Library manuscript number (HM) is given in the textual commentaries for all Clemens letters owned by CSmH.

CtHMTH Mark Twain Memorial, Hartford, Connecticut.

CtHSD Stowe-Day Memorial Library and Historical Foundation, Hartford, Connecticut.

CtY Yale University Library, New Haven, Connecticut.

CtY-BR Collection of American Literature, Beinecke Rare Book and Manuscript Library, CtY.

CU-BANC The Bancroft Library, University of California, Berkeley.

Cullinan, Gerald.
1968. *The Post Office Department*. Foreword by James A. Farley. New York: Frederick A. Praeger, Publishers.

CU-MARK Mark Twain Papers, CU-BANC.

Cummings, Amos J.
1868a. "How Newspapers Are Made. The New York Tribune." *Packard's Monthly* 1 (October): 87–89.

1868b. "How Newspapers Are Made. The New York Tribune. [Second Article.]" *Packard's Monthly* 1 (November): 105–9.

CU-SB Department of Special Collections, University Library, University of California, Santa Barbara.

Cutter, Bloodgood H.
1886. *The Long Island Farmer's Poems. Lines Written on the "Quaker City" Excursion to Palestine, and Other Poems.* New York: N. Tibbals and Sons (published for the author).

DAB
1928–36. *Dictionary of American Biography.* Edited by Allen Johnson and Dumas Malone. 20 vols. New York: Charles Scribner's Sons.

Daley Collection of Robert Daley.

Davis Collection of Chester L. Davis, Mark Twain Research Foundation, Perry, Missouri.

Davis, Chester L.
1954. Untitled item ("In going over the correspondence . . ."). *Twainian* 13 (March–April): 4.

1956. "Letters from Frank Fuller." *Twainian* 15 (July–August): 1–3.

1967a. "Letters to Paine from Emma B. Thayer and S. L. Severance Concerning 'Quaker City.'" *Twainian* 26 (March–April): 2–3.

1967b. "Letter to Paine from John P. Vollmer." *Twainian* 26 (March–April): 3–4.

1979. "Mark Twain's Lectures to Benefit Public Libraries at Hannibal, Quincy and Keokuk." *Twainian* 38 (May–June): 1–4.

Dearmer, Percy, R. Vaughan Williams, and Martin Shaw.
1928. *The Oxford Book of Carols.* Oxford: Oxford University Press.

*Denny, William R.
1867. "*Quaker City* and Holy Land Journal." TS of 273 pages, Manuscripts Department, ViU, PH in CU-MARK.

Denslow, Ray V.
1924. "Mark Twain, a Missouri Mason." *Missouri Grand Lodge Bulletin* 1 (May): 53–60.

des Cognets, Anna Russell.
1884. *William Russell and His Descendants.* Lexington, Ky.: Samuel F. Wilson.

Diabolis [pseud.].
1898. Letter to the editors of the Fort Plain (N.Y.) *Standard* dated 14 February, reprinted in the Fort Plain *Mohawk Valley Register*, 18 February, no page, PH in CU-MARK.

Dickinson, Leon T.
1970. "*Mark Twain Abroad: The Cruise of the 'Quaker City.'* By Dewey Ganzel." *Modern Philology* 68 (August): 117–19.

DLC United States Library of Congress, Washington, D.C.

Dorson, Richard M.
1945. "Sam Patch, Jumping Hero." *New York Folklore Quarterly* 1 (August): 133–51.

Doten, Alfred.
1973. *The Journals of Alfred Doten, 1849–1903*. Edited by Walter Van Tilburg Clark. 3 vols. Reno: University of Nevada Press.

Duncan, Charles C.
1867a. "Excursion to the Holy Land, Egypt, the Crimea, Greece, and Intermediate Points of Interest." Excursion prospectus dated 1 February, CtHMTH. Reproduced in photofacsimile in Appendix B.

1867b. "'Quaker City' Journal." MS of 121 pages, Patton Free Library, Bath, Maine, PH in CU-MARK.

1868. "The Quaker City Excursion Again—Captain Duncan's Reply to 'Mark Twain.'" Letter to the editor dated 31 December 1867. Brooklyn *Eagle*, 2 January, 3.

*Duncan, Charles C., and Emily A. Severance.
1867. "The Cruise of the Quaker City." Extracts from letters dated 19 June and 4 July. New York *Independent*, 15 August, 2.

Duncan, John E.
1986. *The Sea Chain*. Scotia, N.Y.: Americana Review.

Edwards, Richard.
1866. *Edwards' Annual Director to the Inhabitants, Institutions, Incorporated Companies, Manufacturing Establishments, Business, Business Firms, etc., etc., in the City of St. Louis for 1866*. St. Louis: Edwards, Greenough and Deved.

1867. *Edwards' Annual Director to the Inhabitants, Institutions, Incorporated Companies, Manufacturing Establishments, Business, Business Firms, etc., etc., in the City of St. Louis, for 1867*. St. Louis: Edwards, Greenough and Deved.

Ellet, Elizabeth F.
1867. *The Queens of American Society*. New York: Charles Scribner and Co.

Elliott, George W.
1868. "Mark Twain Lecture." Fort Plain (N.Y.) *Mohawk Valley Register*, 25 December, 3.

Ellsworth, William Webster.
1919. *A Golden Age of Authors: A Publisher's Recollection*. Boston: Houghton Mifflin Company.

Elmira Census
[1860] 1967. "Free Inhabitants in Elmira." *Population Schedules of the Eighth Census of the United States, 1860. Roll 730. New York: Chemung County*. National Archives Microfilm Publications, Microcopy no. 653. Washington, D.C.: General Services Administration.

Emrich, Duncan.
1950. *Comstock Bonanza*. New York: Vanguard Press.

ET&S1
1979. *Early Tales & Sketches, Volume 1 (1851–1864)*. Edited by Edgar Marquess Branch and Robert H. Hirst, with the assistance of Harriet Elinor Smith. The Works of Mark Twain. Berkeley, Los Angeles, London: University of California Press.

ET&S2

1981. *Early Tales & Sketches, Volume 2 (1864–1865)*. Edited by Edgar Marquess Branch and Robert H. Hirst, with the assistance of Harriet Elinor Smith. The Works of Mark Twain. Berkeley, Los Angeles, London: University of California Press.

ET&S3

Forthcoming. *Early Tales & Sketches, Volume 3 (1866–1868)*. Edited by Edgar Marquess Branch and Robert H. Hirst, with the assistance of Harriet Elinor Smith. The Works of Mark Twain. Berkeley, Los Angeles, London: University of California Press.

ET&S4

Forthcoming. *Early Tales & Sketches, Volume 4 (1869–1870)*. Edited by Edgar Marquess Branch and Robert H. Hirst, with the assistance of Harriet Elinor Smith. The Works of Mark Twain. Berkeley, Los Angeles, London: University of California Press.

Eubank, Marjorie Harrell.

1968. *The Redpath Lyceum Bureau from 1868 to 1901*. Ph.D. diss., University of Michigan, Ann Arbor.

Exeter Census

[1860] 1967. "Free Inhabitants in Exeter." *Population Schedules of the Eighth Census of the United States, 1860. Roll 840. New York: Otsego County (pt.)*. National Archives Microfilm Publications, Microcopy no. 653. Washington, D.C.: General Services Administration.

Fairbanks, Lorenzo Sayles.

1897. *Genealogy of the Fairbanks Family in America, 1633–1897*. Boston: American Printing and Engraving Company.

*Fairbanks, Mary Mason.

1867a. "Pilgrimizing." Letter dated 9 June. Cleveland *Herald*, 13 June, 2.

1867b. "Pilgrimizing." Letter dated 28 August. Cleveland *Herald*, 8 October, 2.

1867c. "Pilgrimizing." Letter dated 12 September. Cleveland *Herald*, 20 November, 2.

1867d. "Pilgrimizing." Letter dated 14 November. Cleveland *Herald*, 14 December, 2.

1868. "Library Association—Lecture of 'Mark Twain.'" Cleveland *Herald*, 18 November, 1.

1892. "The Cruise of the 'Quaker City.'" *Chautauquan* 14 (January): 429–32.

1898. *Emma Willard and Her Pupils; or, Fifty Years of Troy Female Seminary, 1822–1872*. New York: Mrs. Russell Sage.

Fatout, Paul.

1960. *Mark Twain on the Lecture Circuit*. Bloomington: Indiana University Press.

Feldman Collection of John L. Feldman.

FM

1972. *Mark Twain's Fables of Man*. Edited with an introduction by John S. Tuckey. Text established by Kenneth M. Sanderson and Bernard L. Stein. Series editor, Frederick Anderson. The Mark Twain Papers. Berkeley, Los Angeles, London: University of California Press.

Ford, Richard.

1845. *A Hand-Book for Travellers in Spain, and Readers at Home*. 2 vols. London: John Murray.

1869. *A Handbook for Travellers in Spain*. 4th ed. 2 vols. London: John Murray.

Freeman and Co.

1936. [*Catalog*]. Sale of the Charles T. Jeffery Collection, part 1 (23 March). Philadelphia: Samuel T. Freeman and Co.

Fuld, James J.

1985. *The Book of World-Famous Music: Classical, Popular and Folk*. 3d ed., rev. and enl. New York: Dover Publications.

Fuller, Frank.

1911. "Utah's War Governor Talks of Many Famous Men." New York *Times*, 1 October, 5:10.

Ganzel, Dewey.

1964. "Samuel Clemens, Sub Rosa Correspondent." *English Language Notes* 1 (June): 270–73.

1968. *Mark Twain Abroad: The Cruise of the "Quaker City."* Chicago: University of Chicago Press.

Geer, Elihu, comp.

1879. *Geer's Hartford City Directory, for the Year Commencing July, 1879; and Hartford Illustrated: Containing a Classified Business Directory*. Hartford: Elihu Geer.

Gingrich, Arnold.

1968. "Cruise Centennial Addenda." *Esquire* 70 (August): 6.

Grant, Ulysses S.

1885. *Personal Memoirs of U. S. Grant*. 2 vols. New York: Charles L. Webster and Co.

Green, Floride.

1935. *Some Personal Recollections of Lillie Hitchcock Coit—5*. San Francisco: Grabhorn Press.

Greene, Nelson, ed.

1925. *History of the Mohawk Valley, Gateway to the West, 1614–1925*. 4 vols. Chicago: S. J. Clarke Publishing Company.

Gribben, Alan.

1980. *Mark Twain's Library: A Reconstruction*. 2 vols. Boston: G. K. Hall and Co.

Griswold, Louisa M. (Mrs. Stephen M. Griswold).

1871. *A Woman's Pilgrimage to the Holy Land*. Hartford: J. B. Burr and Hyde.

Griswold, Stephen M.
1907. *Sixty Years with Plymouth Church.* New York: Fleming H. Revell Company.

Gudde, Erwin G.
1960. *California Place Names: The Origin and Etymology of Current Geographical Names*. Rev. and enl. ed. Berkeley and Los Angeles: University of California Press.

Haas, Robert Bartlett.
1955–56. "William Herman Rulofson: Pioneer Daguerreotypist and Photographic Educator." Part 1, *California Historical Society Quarterly* 34 (December 1955): 289–300. Part 2, *California Historical Society Quarterly* 35 (March 1956): 47–57.

Hagood, J. Hurley, and Roberta (Roland) Hagood.
1986. *Hannibal, Too: Historic Sketches of Hannibal and Its Neighbors*. Marceline, Mo.: Walsworth Publishing Company.

Hamilton Galleries.
1981. [*Catalog*]. Sale no. 134 (22 January). New York: Charles Hamilton Galleries.

Hannibal Census
[1850] 1963. "Free Inhabitants in . . . Hannibal." *Population Schedules of the Seventh Census of the United States, 1850. Roll 406. Missouri: Marion, Mercer, Miller, and Mississippi Counties*. National Archives Microfilm Publications, Microcopy no. 432. Washington, D.C.: General Services Administration.

Harris, George Washington [Sut Lovingood, pseud.].
1867. *Sut Lovingood. "Yarns Spun by a Nat'ral Born Durn'd Fool."* New York: Dick and Fitzgerald.

Hart, James D.
1978. *A Companion to California*. New York: Oxford University Press.

Harte, Bret.
1865. "A Sheaf of Criticism." *Californian* 4 (23 December): 8.

Hazlitt, W. Carew.
1905. *Faiths and Folklore: A Dictionary of National Beliefs, Superstitions and Popular Customs, Past and Current, with Their Classical and Foreign Analogues, Described and Illustrated*. 2 vols. London: Reeves and Turner.

Heitman, Francis B.
1903. *Historical Register and Dictionary of the United States Army, from Its Organization, September 29, 1789, to March 2, 1903*. 2 vols. Washington, D.C.: Government Printing Office.

Herlihy, Patricia.
1986. *Odessa: A History, 1794–1914*. Harvard Ukrainian Research Institute Monograph Series. Cambridge: Distributed by Harvard University Press for the Harvard Ukrainian Research Institute.

Hesseltine, William B.
1932. "Tennessee's Invitation to Carpet-Baggers." *East Tennessee Historical Society's Publications*, no. 4 (January): 102–15.

1957. *Ulysses S. Grant: Politician*. 2d ed. New York: Frederick Ungar Publishing Company.

Heyl, Erik.
1953. *Early American Steamers*. Buffalo: n.p.

HF
1988. *Adventures of Huckleberry Finn*. Edited by Walter Blair and Victor Fischer, with the assistance of Dahlia Armon and Harriet Elinor Smith. The Works of Mark Twain. Berkeley, Los Angeles, London: University of California Press.

Higginson, Thomas Wentworth.
1868. "The American Lecture-System." *Macmillan's Magazine* 18 (May): 48–56.

Hill, Hamlin.
1964. *Mark Twain and Elisha Bliss*. Columbia: University of Missouri Press.

Hingston, Edward P.
1881. *The Genial Showman: Reminiscences of the Life of Artemus Ward*. London: Chatto and Windus.

Hirst, Robert H.
1975. "The Making of *The Innocents Abroad:* 1867–1872." Ph.D. diss., University of California, Berkeley.
1978. " 'He Trimmed & Trained & Schooled Me': How Bret Harte Edited *The Innocents Abroad*." TS in CU-MARK.

Hirst, Robert H., and Brandt Rowles.
1984. "William E. James's Stereoscopic Views of the *Quaker City* Excursion." *Mark Twain Journal* 22 (Spring): 15–33.

History of Lee County
1879. *The History of Lee County, Iowa*. Chicago: Western Historical Company.

Hittell, Theodore H.
1897. *History of California*. 4 vols. San Francisco: N. J. Stone and Co.

HM. See CSmH.

Hoeltje, Hubert H.
1927. "Notes on the History of Lecturing in Iowa 1855–1885." *Iowa Journal of History and Politics* 25 (January): 62–131.

Hogan, John C., and Ewald W. Schnitzer.
1957. "The Last Will and Testament of Stephen J. Field." *California Historical Society Quarterly* 36 (March): 41–55.

Holcombe, Return I.
1884. *History of Marion County, Missouri*. St. Louis: E. F. Perkins. Citations are to the 1979 reprint edition, Hannibal and Marceline: Marion County Historical Society and Walsworth Publishing Company.

Holdredge, Helen.
1967. *Firebelle Lillie*. New York: Meredith Press.

Hopkins, Caspar T.
1947. "The California Recollections of Caspar T. Hopkins." *California Historical Society Quarterly* 26 (June): 175–83.

[House, Edward H.]
1867. "Mark Twain as a Lecturer." New York *Tribune*, 11 May, 2. Transcribed in Appendix E.

Howard, John Raymond.
1925. *Remembrance of Things Past: A Familiar Chronicle of Kinsfolk and Friends Worth While*. New York: Thomas Y. Crowell Company.

Hughes, Josephine L., and Richard J. Wolfe.
1961. "The Tunes of 'The Bucket.'" *Bulletin of the New York Public Library* 65 (November): 555–69.

Hutchinson, Joseph.
1910. "Two Opinions of Twain." San Francisco *Call*, 24 April, 36.

IaK Keokuk Public Library, Keokuk, Iowa.

Inds
1989. *Huck Finn and Tom Sawyer among the Indians, and Other Unfinished Stories*. Foreword and notes by Dahlia Armon and Walter Blair. Texts established by Dahlia Armon, Paul Baender, Walter Blair, William M. Gibson, and Franklin R. Rogers. Mark Twain Library. Berkeley, Los Angeles, London: University of California Press.

Interior Department.
1868. *Register of Officers and Agents, Civil, Military, and Naval, in the Service of the United States, on the Thirtieth September, 1867*. Washington, D.C.: Government Printing Office.

InU-Li Lilly Library, Indiana University, Bloomington.

*Isham, John G.
1867. "Letter from Jerusalem." Letter dated 22 September. Cincinnati *Commercial*, 21 October, 1.

*Jackson, Abraham Reeves.
1867a. "Letter I. From the Mediterranean Excursion." Letter to the editor (A. O. Greenwald) dated 22 June. Clipping from the Monroe County (Pa.) *Democrat* preserved in a scrapbook owned by Horace Levy, PH in CU-MARK courtesy of Leon T. Dickinson.

1867b. ["Letter II. From the Mediterranean Excursion."] Letter dated 30 June; clipping in scrapbook described in Jackson 1867a.

1867c. "Letter IV. From the Mediterranean Excursion." Letter dated 5 July; clipping in scrapbook described in Jackson 1867a.

1867d. "Letter VI. From the Mediterranean Excursion." Letter dated 11 July; clipping in scrapbook described in Jackson 1867a.

1867e. "Letter VII. From the Mediterranean Excursion." Letter dated 16 July; clipping in scrapbook described in Jackson 1867a.

1867f. "Letter XIII. From the Mediterranean Excursion." Letter dated 11 August; clipping in scrapbook described in Jackson 1867a.

1867g. "The Quaker City Pilgrimage. A Malcontent Passenger's Story of the Excursion—The Serio-Comic Features of the Enterprise." Undated letter to the editor, signed "A Passenger." New York *Herald*, 21 November, 3.

Jackson, George Pullen.
1964. *Spiritual Folk-Songs of Early America.* New York: Dover Publications.

*James, William E.
1867. "The Mediterranean Excursion." Letter dated 30 August. Brooklyn *Eagle*, 20 September, 2.

"James Mason Family"
n.d. "James Mason Family." TS of records in a family Bible, Chenango County Historical Society, Norwich, N.Y., PH in CU-MARK.

Jensen, Mrs. Dana O.
1950. "Wo-Haw: Kiowa Warrior." *Bulletin of the Missouri Historical Society* 7 (October): 76–77.

Jerome, Robert D., and Herbert A. Wisbey, Jr.
1977. *Mark Twain in Elmira.* Elmira: Mark Twain Society.

JLC (Jane Lampton Clemens).
1861–70. Account records written in SLC's Notebook 3, CU-MARK.

Jones, Bernard E., ed.
1912. *Cassell's Cyclopaedia of Photography.* London: Cassell and Co.

Jorkins [pseud.].
1868a. "'Jorkins' at Washington." Letter dated 24 January. San Francisco *Evening Bulletin*, 14 February, 2.
1868b. "Jorkins at Washington." Letter dated 18 February. San Francisco *Evening Bulletin*, 14 March, 5.

Julian, John, ed.
1908. *A Dictionary of Hymnology Setting Forth the Origin and History of Christian Hymns of All Ages and Nations.* London: John Murray.

Kaplan, Justin.
1966. *Mr. Clemens and Mark Twain: A Biography.* New York: Simon and Schuster.

Kelly, J. Wells, comp.
1863. *Second Directory of Nevada Territory.* San Francisco: Valentine and Co.

Kemble, Edward C.
1962. *A History of California Newspapers, 1846–1858. Reprinted from the Supplement to the Sacramento "Union" of December 25, 1858.* Edited and with a foreword by Helen Harding Bretnor. Los Gatos, Calif.: Talisman Press.

Keokuk Census
[1860] 1967. "Free Inhabitants in . . . Keokuk." *Population Schedules of the Eighth Census of the United States, 1860. Roll 330. Iowa: Kossuth and Lee Counties.* National Archives Microfilm Publications, Microcopy no. 653. Washington, D.C.: General Services Administration.

King, Moses, ed.
1893. *King's Handbook of New York City: An Outline History and Description of the American Metropolis.* 2d ed. Boston: Moses King.

Knox, T. H., comp.
1854. *The St. Louis Directory, for the Years 1854–5.* St. Louis: Chambers and Knapp.

Knoxville Census

[1850] 1964. "Free Inhabitants in . . . Knoxville." *Population Schedules of the Seventh Census of the United States, 1850. Roll 886. Tennessee: Johnson, Knox, Lauderdale, and Lawrence Counties.* National Archives Microfilm Publications, Microcopy no. 432. Washington, D.C.: General Services Administration.

Kuykendall, Ralph S.

1926. *A History of Hawaii Prepared under the Direction of the Historical Commission of the Territory of Hawaii.* New York: Macmillan Company.

L1

1988. *Mark Twain's Letters, Volume 1: 1853–1866.* Edited by Edgar Marquess Branch, Michael B. Frank, Kenneth M. Sanderson, Harriet Elinor Smith, Lin Salamo, and Richard Bucci. Berkeley, Los Angeles, London: University of California Press.

Langdon, Charles Jervis.

1867. "*Quaker City* Journal of Charles J. Langdon, 11 July through 28 July 1867." TS in CU-MARK.

Langdon, Jervis.

[1938]. *Samuel Langhorne Clemens: Some Reminiscences and Some Excerpts from Letters and Unpublished Manuscripts.* [Elmira, N.Y.]: Privately printed.

"Langdon Guest Book"

1867–68. "Langdon Guest Book." Record of visitors to the Langdons' Elmira residence with entries dated October 1867 to September 1868. Catalogued as "Charles Langdon's autograph book," CtHSD.

Langley, Henry G., comp.

1858. *The San Francisco Directory for the Year 1858.* San Francisco: S. D. Valentine and Son.

1859. *The San Francisco Directory for the Year Commencing June, 1859.* San Francisco: Valentine and Co.

1860. *The San Francisco Directory for the Year Commencing July, 1860.* San Francisco: Valentine and Co.

1862. *The San Francisco Directory for the Year Commencing June, 1862.* San Francisco: Valentine and Co.

1865. *The San Francisco Directory for the Year Commencing December, 1865.* San Francisco: Towne and Bacon.

1867. *The San Francisco Directory for the Year Commencing September, 1867.* San Francisco: Henry G. Langley.

1868. *The San Francisco Directory for the Year Commencing October, 1868.* San Francisco: Henry G. Langley.

Larned, Augusta.

1868. "Parson Fielder's Christmas Visit." New York *Independent*, 24 December, 2.

Lauber, John.

1985. *The Making of Mark Twain: A Biography.* New York: American Heritage Press.

Leamington Book Shop.
1972. *Rare Books*. Catalog no. 40. Fredericksburg, Va.: Leamington Book Shop (Sidney Hamer, proprietor).

Leary, Lewis.
1970. "More Letters from the *Quaker City*." *American Literature* 42 (May): 197–202.

Lewis, Oscar.
1969. *The Big Four: The Story of Huntington, Stanford, Hopkins, and Crocker, and of the Building of the Central Pacific*. New York: Alfred A. Knopf.

Lex
1963. *A Mark Twain Lexicon*. By Robert L. Ramsey and Frances G. Emberson. New York: Russell and Russell.

Lindsay, Maurice.
1959. *The Burns Encyclopaedia*. London: Hutchinson and Co.

Lionberger, Isaac H., ed.
1935. "Scattered Letters of Mark Twain, Together with Eulogistic Contributions for His Centennial." *Glimpses of the Past* 2 (October): 123–32.

LLMT
1949. *The Love Letters of Mark Twain*. Edited by Dixon Wecter. New York: Harper and Brothers.

Lloyd, B. E.
1876. *Lights and Shades in San Francisco*. San Francisco: A. L. Bancroft and Co.

Lorch, Fred W.
1929. "Lecture Trips and Visits of Mark Twain in Iowa." *Iowa Journal of History and Politics* 27 (October): 507–47.

1952. "A Note on Mark Twain's Lecture on the Far West." *American Literature* 24 (November): 377–79.

1968. *The Trouble Begins at Eight: Mark Twain's Lecture Tours*. Ames: Iowa State University Press.

Lord, Eliot.
1883. *Comstock Mining and Miners*. Washington, D.C.: U.S. Government Printing Office. Citations are to the 1959 reprint edition, introduction by David F. Myrick, Berkeley: Howell-North.

Lorgnette [pseud.].
1868. "Newark Amusements." Newark *Courier*, 11–13 December, clipping in CU-MARK.

Lover, Samuel.
1842. *Handy Andy: A Tale of Irish Life*. London: Frederick Lover and Richard Groombridge.

Lutz, Alma.
1940. *Created Equal: A Biography of Elizabeth Cady Stanton, 1815–1902*. New York: John Day Company.

Lytle, William M., comp.
1952. *Merchant Steam Vessels of the United States, 1807–1868*. Mystic, Conn.: Steamship Historical Society of America.

McCaskey, J. P., comp.
1885. *Franklin Square Song Collection: Two Hundred Favorite Songs and Hymns for Schools and Homes, Nursery and Fireside*. 6 vols. New York: Harper and Brothers.

McCulloch, Hugh.
1868. "Letter from the Secretary of the Treasury, in Answer to a Resolution of the House of November 26 and 27, Relative to Special Agents Employed in That Department since June, 1866." In *Executive Documents Printed by Order of the House of Representatives during the Second Session of the Fortieth Congress, 1867–'68*. Washington, D.C.: Government Printing Office.

Mack, Effie Mona.
1964. "William Morris Stewart, 1827–1909." *Nevada Historical Society Quarterly* 7 (January–June): 11–110.

Mack, Maynard.
1978. *A History of Scroll and Key, 1842–1942*. [New Haven]: The Society.

Mahony, Roger.
1987. *Building a Foundation for the Future: The Development of The Edward Laurence and Carrie Estelle Doheny Seminary Foundation; Its Purposes and Goals*. New York: Arton Associates.

Mansfield, Lillian M.
1965. *The History of Asylum Hill Congregational Church, Hartford, Connecticut*. Hartford: Asylum Hill Congregational Church.

Marbut, F. B.
1971. *News from the Capital: The Story of Washington Reporting*. Foreword by Howard Rusk Long. Carbondale: Southern Illinois University Press.

Marsh, Andrew J.
1868. *Marsh's Manual of Reformed Phonetic Short-Hand: Being a Complete Guide to the Best System of Phonography and Verbatim Reporting*. San Francisco: H. H. Bancroft and Co.

1972. *Letters from Nevada Territory, 1861–62*. Edited by William C. Miller, Russell W. McDonald, and Ann Rollins. [Reno]: Legislative Counsel Bureau, State of Nevada.

Marsh, Andrew J., Samuel L. Clemens, and Amos Bowman.
1972. *Reports of the 1863 Constitutional Convention of the Territory of Nevada*. Edited by William C. Miller, Eleanore Bushnell, Russell W. McDonald, and Ann Rollins. [Reno]: Legislative Counsel Bureau, State of Nevada.

Mathews, Mitford M., ed.
1951. *A Dictionary of Americanisms on Historical Principles*. 2 vols. Chicago: University of Chicago Press.

MEC Mary E. (Mollie) Clemens.

Melendy, Howard Brett, and Benjamin Franklin Gilbert.
1965. *The Governors of California: Peter H. Burnett to Edmund G. Brown*. Georgetown, Calif.: Talisman Press.

Meltzer, Milton.
1960. *Mark Twain Himself*. New York: Thomas Y. Crowell Company.

MFMT
1931. *My Father, Mark Twain*. By Clara Clemens. New York: Harper and Brothers.

Miller, Bryce B.
1964. "A Rare Mark Twain Letter Found." New York *Journal American*, 29 November, 1L. Printed also in St. Louis *Post-Dispatch*, 29 November, 6H.

Miller, James, comp.
1866. *Miller's New York as It Is*. New York: J. Miller. Citations are to the 1975 reprint edition, *The 1866 Guide to New York City*. New York: Schocken Books.

Minden Census
[1860] 1967. "Free Inhabitants in . . . Minden." *Population Schedules of the Eighth Census of the United States, 1860. Roll 787. New York: Montgomery County*. National Archives Microfilm Publications, Microcopy no. 653. Washington, D.C.: General Services Administration.

Moffat, Alfred.
[1897]. *The Minstrelsy of Ireland: 200 Irish Songs, Adapted to Their Traditional Airs, Arranged for Voice with Pianoforte Accompaniment, and Supplemented with Historical Notes*. London: Augener and Co.

Moore, Thomas.
1843. *The Poetical Works of Thomas Moore*. London: Longman, Brown, Green, and Longmans.

Morris, Lloyd.
1951. *Incredible New York: High Life and Low Life of the Last Hundred Years*. New York: Random House.

Moss, Sidney P.
1984. *Charles Dickens' Quarrel with America*. Troy, N.Y.: Whitston Publishing Company.

Mott, Frank Luther.
1938. *A History of American Magazines, 1850–1865*. Cambridge: Harvard University Press.

1957. *A History of American Magazines, 1865–1885*. 2d printing [1st printing, 1938]. Cambridge: Belknap Press of Harvard University Press.

*Moulton, Julius.
1867a. "Holy Land Excursionists. Letter from a St. Louisian." Letter dated 23 July. St. Louis *Missouri Republican*, 19 August, 2.

1867b. "Holy Land Excursionists. Letter from a St. Louisian." Letter dated 30 August. St. Louis *Missouri Republican*, 14 October, 3.

MS Manuscript.

MTA
1924. *Mark Twain's Autobiography*. Edited by Albert Bigelow Paine. 2 vols. New York: Harper and Brothers.

MTB

1912. *Mark Twain: A Biography*. By Albert Bigelow Paine. 3 vols. New York: Harper and Brothers. [*Volume numbers in citations are to this edition; page numbers are the same in all editions.*]

MTBus

1946. *Mark Twain, Business Man*. Edited by Samuel Charles Webster. Boston: Little, Brown and Co.

MTE

1940. *Mark Twain in Eruption*. Edited by Bernard DeVoto. New York: Harper and Brothers.

MTHL

1960. *Mark Twain–Howells Letters*. Edited by Henry Nash Smith and William M. Gibson, with the assistance of Frederick Anderson. 2 vols. Cambridge: Belknap Press of Harvard University Press.

MTL

1917. *Mark Twain's Letters*. Edited by Albert Bigelow Paine. 2 vols. New York: Harper and Brothers.

MTLBowen

1941. *Mark Twain's Letters to Will Bowen*. Edited by Theodore Hornberger. Austin: University of Texas.

MTLP

1967. *Mark Twain's Letters to His Publishers, 1867–1894*. Edited by Hamlin Hill. The Mark Twain Papers. Berkeley and Los Angeles: University of California Press.

MTMF

1949. *Mark Twain to Mrs. Fairbanks*. Edited by Dixon Wecter. San Marino, Calif.: Huntington Library.

MTN

1935. *Mark Twain's Notebook*. Edited by Albert Bigelow Paine. New York: Harper and Brothers.

MTS

1910. *Mark Twain's Speeches*. With an introduction by William Dean Howells. New York: Harper and Brothers.

1923. *Mark Twain's Speeches*. With an introduction by Albert Bigelow Paine and an appreciation by William Dean Howells. New York: Harper and Brothers.

MTSpk

1976. *Mark Twain Speaking*. Edited by Paul Fatout. Iowa City: University of Iowa Press.

MTTB

1940. *Mark Twain's Travels with Mr. Brown*. Edited by Franklin Walker and G. Ezra Dane. New York: Alfred A. Knopf.

Murphy, Miriam B.

1975. "Sarah Elizabeth Carmichael: Poetic Genius of Pioneer Utah." *Utah Historical Quarterly* 43 (Winter): 52–66.

Murray, John.
1868. *A Handbook for Travellers in Syria and Palestine*. 2 vols. London: John Murray.

N&J1
1975. *Mark Twain's Notebooks & Journals, Volume I (1855–1873)*. Edited by Frederick Anderson, Michael B. Frank, and Kenneth M. Sanderson. The Mark Twain Papers. Berkeley, Los Angeles, London: University of California Press.

National Geographic Atlas
1981. *National Geographic Atlas of the World*. 5th ed. Washington, D.C.: National Geographic Society.

NCAB
1898–1984. *The National Cyclopedia of American Biography*. Volumes 1–62 and A–M plus index. New York: James T. White and Co.

Nesbit, Benjamin B.
1867. "Quaker City Journal." MS owned by Mary N. Shelnutt, Claremont, Calif., PH in CU-MARK courtesy of Leon T. Dickinson.

*Newell, Julia.
1867a. "From Janesville to the Holy Land." Letter dated 10 August. Janesville (Wis.) *Gazette*, 17 October, no page, PH in CU-MARK.

1867b. "From Janesville to the Holy Land." Letter dated 15 September. Janesville (Wis.) *Gazette*, 6 November, no page, PH in CU-MARK.

1867c. "From Janesville to the Holy Land." Letter dated October in Spain. Janesville (Wis.) *Gazette*, 14 December, no page, PH in CU-MARK.

New Madrid Census
[1860] 1967. "Free Inhabitants in . . . New Madrid." *Population Schedules of the Eighth Census of the United States, 1860. Roll 636. Missouri: Morgan, New Madrid, and Newton Counties*. National Archives Microfilm Publications, Microcopy no. 653. Washington, D.C.: General Services Administration.

New York Census
[1850] 1963. "Free Inhabitants in . . . New York City." *Population Schedules of the Seventh Census of the United States, 1850. Roll 553. New York City, Part of Ward 16*. National Archives Microfilm Publications, Microcopy no. 432. Washington, D.C.: General Services Administration.

[1860] 1967. "Free Inhabitants in . . . New York City." *Population Schedules of the Eighth Census of the United States, 1860. Roll 798. New York City, Ward 10*. National Archives Microfilm Publications, Microcopy no. 653. Washington, D.C.: General Services Administration.

NHi New York Historical Society, New York City.

NN The New York Public Library, Astor, Lenox, and Tilden Foundations, New York City.

NN-B Henry W. and Albert A. Berg Collection, NN.

"Nook Farm Genealogy"
1974. "Nook Farm Genealogy." TS by anonymous compiler, CtHSD.

NPV Jean Webster McKinney Family Papers, Francis Fitz Randolph Rare Book Room, Vassar College Library, Poughkeepsie, New York.

OC (Orion Clemens).

1857. *Keokuk Directory and Business Mirror for the Year 1857*. Keokuk: O. Clemens.

1862–63. "Abstract of Disbursements on Account of the Legislative Assembly of the Territory of Nevada from December 20th 1862 to June 30th 1863." Miscellaneous treasury account no. 147608. Record Group 217. National Archives, Washington, D.C.

1866a. "Letter from St. Louis." Letter dated 15 October, signed "Missouri." San Francisco *Times*, 10 November, 2, clipping in Scrapbook 4:37–38, CU-MARK.

1866b. "Letter from St. Louis." Letter dated 2 December, signed "C." San Francisco *Times*, 28 December, 1.

1867a. "Letter from St. Louis." Letter dated 15 December 1866, signed "Fentress." San Francisco *Times*, 12 January, 3.

1867b. "Letter from St. Louis." Letter dated 22 December 1866, signed "Fentress." San Francisco *Times*, 19 January, 1.

1867c. "Letter from Tennessee." Letter dated 28 December 1866, signed "Cumberland." San Francisco *Times*, 26 January, 2, clipping in Scrapbook 4:38, CU-MARK.

1867d. "Letter from Tennessee." Letter dated 4 January, signed "Cumberland." San Francisco *Times*, 2 February, 4, clipping in Scrapbook 4:38–39, CU-MARK.

1867e. "Letter from St. Louis." Unsigned letter dated 11 March. San Francisco *Times*, 13 April, 2.

1867f. "Letter from St. Louis." Letter dated 24 April, signed "Conrad Crozier." San Francisco *Times*, 22 May, 1.

1867g. "Letter from St. Louis." Letter dated 25 April, signed "Conrad Crazier." San Francisco *Times*, 23 May, 3.

OClWHi Western Reserve Historical Society, Cleveland, Ohio.

O'Connor, Richard.

1966. *Bret Harte: A Biography*. Boston: Little, Brown and Co.

ODaU Collection of Victor and Irene Murr Jacobs, Roesch Library, University of Dayton, Dayton, Ohio.

Odell, George C. D.

1927–49. *Annals of the New York Stage*. 15 vols. New York: Columbia University Press.

Ogilvie, Frank B., comp.

1896. *Two Hundred Old-Time Songs*. New York: J. S. Ogilvie Publishing Company. Clemens's annotated copy in CU-MARK.

OLC Olivia (Livy) Langdon Clemens.

OLL Olivia (Livy) Louise Langdon.

Paff, Harriet Lewis.

1897. "What I Know about Mark Twain." MS of twelve pages, CtY-BR.

Paine, Albert Bigelow.

1912. "Mark Twain: Some Chapters from an Extraordinary Life. Seventh Paper." *Harper's Monthly Magazine* 124 (May): 934–47.

PAM Pamela Ann Moffett.

Parke-Bernet Galleries.

1940. *The Entire Collection of the Late John Gribbel, Philadelphia. Part 1*. Sale no. 223 (30 October–1 November). New York: Parke-Bernet Galleries.

1941. *First Editions, Standard Sets, Autograph Letters & Manuscripts . . . Including . . . the Property of a New York Lady*. Sale no. 248 (15 and 16 January). New York: Parke-Bernet Galleries.

1956. *Books, Autographs and Mss of Samuel L. Clemens, Collection of Alan N. Mendleson*. Sale no. 1719 (11 and 12 December). New York: Parke-Bernet Galleries.

Parton, James.

1867. "Henry Ward Beecher's Church." *Atlantic Monthly* 19 (January): 38–51.

PBL Robert B. Honeyman Collection, Linderman Library, Lehigh University, Bethlehem, Pennsylvania.

PH Photocopy

Phelps, William Lyon.

1914. *Essays on Books*. New York: Macmillan Company.

1939. *Autobiography with Letters*. New York: Oxford University Press.

Pommer, Henry F.

1962. "Mark Twain's 'Commissioner of the United States.'" *American Literature* 34 (November): 385–92.

Poore, Benjamin Perley.

1868. *Congressional Directory for the Second Session of the Fortieth Congress of the United States of America; Compiled for the Use of Congress*. Washington, D.C.: Government Printing Office.

Pope, Alexander.

1745. *An Essay on Man*. Enlarged and improved by the author. London: John and Paul Knapton.

Portrait

1895. *Portrait and Biographical Record of Marion, Ralls and Pike Counties, Missouri*. Chicago: C. O. Owens and Co. Citations are to the 1982 1st rev. reprint edition, edited by Oliver and Goldena Howard, New London and Marceline: Ralls County Book Company and Walsworth Publishing Company.

Portsmouth Census

[1860] 1967. "Free Inhabitants in . . . Portsmouth." *Population Schedules of the Eighth Census of the United States, 1860. Roll 679. New Hampshire: Rockingham County (pt.)*. National Archives Microfilm Publications, Microcopy no. 653. Washington, D.C.: General Services Administration.

Pourquoi [pseud.].

1880a. "Notable Autographs." *Californian* 1 (April): 353–57.

1880b. "Notable Autographs." *Californian* 1 (June): 528–36.

PPiU Special Collections Department, University of Pittsburgh Libraries, Pittsburgh, Pennsylvania.

QC SS *Quaker City*.

Randall, Alexander W.
1868. "Report of the Postmaster General." In *Message of the President of the United States and Accompanying Documents, to the Two Houses of Congress at the Commencement of the Third Session of the Fortieth Congress*. Washington, D.C.: Government Printing Office.

Randall, David A.
1973. *An Exhibition of American Literature*. Bloomington: The Lilly Library, Indiana University.

Rasmussen, Louis J.
1965–70. *San Francisco Ship Passenger Lists*. 4 vols. Colma, Calif.: San Francisco Historic Records.

Regan, Robert.
1981. "Mark Twain, 'The Doctor' and a Guidebook by Dickens." *American Studies* 22 (Spring): 35–55.

Riley, John H.
1868a. "Letter from Washington. [From the Resident Correspondent of the Alta.]" Letter dated 15 December 1867. San Francisco *Alta California*, 16 January, 1.

1868b. "Letter from Washington. [From the Regular Correspondent of the Alta.]" Letter dated 26 January. San Francisco *Alta California*, 15 February, 1.

Rincon [pseud.].
1868a. "Letters from Washington." Letter dated 20 December 1867. San Francisco *Evening Bulletin*, 17 January, 1.

1868b. "Letter from Washington." Letter dated 21 February. San Francisco *Evening Bulletin*, 14 March, 1.

Robinson, Clarence C., et al.
1963. *A Century of Christian Witness: History of the First Congregational Church, Santa Cruz, California*. Santa Cruz: Sentinel Printers.

Rode, Charles R., comp.
1853. *The New-York City Directory, for 1853–1854*. New York: Charles R. Rode.

Rogers, Franklin R.
1961. *The Pattern for Mark Twain's Roughing It: Letters from Nevada by Samuel and Orion Clemens, 1861–62*. Berkeley and Los Angeles: University of California Press.

Rose, William Ganson.
1950. *Cleveland: The Making of a City*. Cleveland: World Publishing Company.

Rowell, George P.
1869. *Geo. P. Rowell & Co's American Newspaper Directory*. New York: George P. Rowell and Co.

RPB-JH John Hay Library of Rare Books and Special Collections, Brown University, Providence, Rhode Island.

Sabin, Edwin L.

1919. *Building the Pacific Railway*. Philadelphia: J. B. Lippincott Company.

St. Louis Census

[1860] 1967. "Free Inhabitants in . . . St. Louis." *Population Schedules of the Eighth Census of the United States, 1860. Roll 143. Missouri: St. Louis County (pt.), St. Louis City (pt.), Wards 1 (pt.), 2, 4, 9, 5, and 8 (pt.)*. National Archives Microfilm Publications, Microcopy no. 653. Washington, D.C.: General Services Administration.

[1870] 1965. "Inhabitants in . . . St. Louis." *Population Schedules of the Ninth Census of the United States, 1870. Roll 816. Missouri: St. Louis County (pt.), St. Louis City (pt.), Ward 6*. National Archives Microfilm Publications, Microcopy no. 593. Washington, D.C.: General Services Administration.

Salsbury, Edith Colgate.

1965. *Susy and Mark Twain*. New York: Harper and Row.

San Francisco City and County.

1867. *General List of Citizens of the United States, Resident in the City and County of San Francisco, and Registered in the Great Register of Said City and County. July, 1867*. San Francisco: Towne and Bacon.

1869. *Supplementary List of Citizens of the United States, Resident in the City and County of San Francisco, and Registered in the Great Register of Said City and County, Since the Making out of the Supplemental List in August, 1868. August, 1869*. San Francisco: M. D. Carr and Co.

Scharf, J. Thomas.

1883. *History of Saint Louis City and County, from the Earliest Periods to the Present Day*. 2 vols. Philadelphia: Louis H. Everts and Co.

Second Life Books.

1983. *Samuel L. Clemens (Mark Twain), 1835–1910: A Collection of His Works, 1852–1983, Gathered by Samuel N. Freedman*. Catalog printed in March. Lanesborough, Mass.: Second Life Books (Russell and Martha Freedman, proprietors).

Seitz, Don C.

1919. *Artemus Ward (Charles Farrar Browne): A Biography and Bibliography*. New York: Harper and Brothers.

Senate.

1868. "List of Committees of the Senate of the United States." In *Miscellaneous Documents of the Senate of the United States for the Second Session of the Fortieth Congress, 1867–'68*. Washington, D.C.: Government Printing Office.

1887. *Journal of the Executive Proceedings of the Senate of the United States of America*. Vol. 13, *From December 1, 1862, to July 4, 1864, Inclusive*. Vol. 14, Part 2, *From February 13, 1866, to July 28, 1866, Inclusive*. Vol. 15, Part 2, *From March 13, 1867, to November 29, 1867, Inclusive*. Vol. 16, *From December 2, 1867, to March 3, 1869, Inclusive*. Washington, D.C.: Government Printing Office.

1901. *Journal of the Executive Proceedings of the Senate of the United States of America*. Vol. 17, *From March 5, 1869, to March 3, 1871, Inclusive*. Vol. 20, *From March 5, 1875, to March 3, 1877, Inclusive*. Washington, D.C.: Government Printing Office.

Severance, Emily A.
1938. *Journal Letters of Emily A. Severance: "Quaker City" 1867*. Foreword by Julia Severance Millikin. Cleveland: Gates Press.

[Shillaber, Benjamin Penhallow.]
[1863?]. *Mrs. Partington's Carpet-Bag of Fun*. Engravings by Samuel P. Avery. [Reprint of 1854 edition, published by Garrett and Co.] New York: Dick and Fitzgerald.

Shufeldt, George A., Jr.
1867. "The Whiskey Frauds. Reasons Why the Tax Should Be Reduced. Outrages and Abuses of Special Agents of the Revenue Department." Letter to the editor dated 31 October. Chicago *Tribune*, 1 November, 2.

Siebert, Wilbur H.
1898. *The Underground Railroad from Slavery to Freedom*. New York: Russell and Russell.

Simpson, Alan.
1977. *Mark Twain Goes Back to Vassar: An Introduction to the Jean Webster McKinney Family Papers*. Poughkeepsie, N.Y.: Vassar College.

Sims, Henry Upson, ed.
1949. *150 Great Hymns in the English Language*. Richmond, Va.: Dietz Press.

SLC (Samuel Langhorne Clemens).
1866a. "Ministerial Change." Virginia City *Territorial Enterprise*, 8 or 9 February, no page. Reprinted in *ET&S3*, no. 174.

1866b. "An Open Letter to the American People." New York *Weekly Review*, 17 February, 1. Reprinted in *ET&S3*, no. 181.

1866c. "The Mysterious Bottle of Whiskey." *Saturday Press* 5 (3 March): 3. Reprinted in *ET&S3*, no. 186.

1866d. "A Strange Dream." *Saturday Press* 5 (2 June): 1–2. Reprinted in *ET&S3*, no. 189.

1866e. "The Moral Phenomenon." *Californian* 5 (25 August): 9. Reprinted in *ET&S3*, no. 191.

1866f. "Forty-three Days in an Open Boat." *Harper's New Monthly Magazine* 34 (December): 104–13.

1866g. "Depart, Ye Accursed!" New York *Weekly Review*, 15 December, 1. Reprinted in *ET&S3*, no. 199.

1867a. *The Celebrated Jumping Frog of Calaveras County, And other Sketches*. Edited by John Paul. New York: C. H. Webb.

1867b. "Cholera in Nicaragua." Telegram dated 12 January. San Francisco *Alta California*, 13 January, 1.

1867c. "Letter from 'Mark Twain.'" Letter dated 20 December 1866 on "Steamship 'America.'" San Francisco *Alta California*, 18 January, 1. Reprinted in *MTTB*, 11–19.

1867d. "Letter from 'Mark Twain.' Number 2." Letter dated 20 December 1866 on "Steamer 'Columbia.'" San Francisco *Alta California*, 22 February, 1. Reprinted in *MTTB*, 20–27.

1867e. "Letter from 'Mark Twain.' Number 3." Letter dated 23 December 1866. San Francisco *Alta California*, 24 February, 1. Reprinted in *MTTB*, 28–33.

1867f. "The Winner of the Medal." New York *Sunday Mercury*, 3 March, 3. Reprinted in *ET&S3*, no. 203.

1867g. "Barnum's First Speech in Congress." New York *Evening Express*, 5 March, 1.

1867h. "Letter from 'Mark Twain.' Number IV." Letter dated "Christmas Eve" 1866. San Francisco *Alta California*, 15 March, 1. Reprinted in *MTTB*, 34–45.

1867i. "Letter from 'Mark Twain.' Number V." Letter dated "New Year's Day." San Francisco *Alta California*, 16 March, 1. Reprinted in *MTTB*, 46–57.

1867j. "A Curtain Lecture Concerning Skating." New York *Sunday Mercury*, 17 March, 3. Reprinted in *ET&S3*, no. 204.

1867k. "Letter from 'Mark Twain.' Number VI." Letter dated 1 January. San Francisco *Alta California*, 17 March, 1. Reprinted in part in *MTTB*, 58–68.

1867*l*. "Letter from 'Mark Twain.' Number VII." Letter dated 6 January. San Francisco *Alta California*, 23 March, 1. Reprinted in *MTTB*, 69–81.

1867m. "Barbarous." New York *Sunday Mercury*, 24 March, 3. Reprinted in *ET&S3*, no. 207.

1867n. "'Mark Twain' in New York. Letter Number VIII." Letter dated 2 February. San Francisco *Alta California*, 28 March, 1. Reprinted in part in *MTTB*, 82–89.

1867o. "'Mark Twain' in New York. Letter Number IX." Letter dated 18 February. San Francisco *Alta California*, 30 March, 1. Reprinted in part in *MTTB*, 90–100.

1867p. "'Mark Twain' in New York. Letter Number X." Letter dated 23 February. San Francisco *Alta California*, 5 April, 1. Reprinted in part in *MTTB*, 101–10.

1867q. "Female Suffrage." New York *Sunday Mercury*, 7 April, 3.

1867r. "'Mark Twain' in New York. Letter Number XI." Letter dated 2 March. San Francisco *Alta California*, 9 April, 1. Reprinted in *MTTB*, 111–21.

1867s. "Official Physic." New York *Sunday Mercury*, 21 April, 3.

1867t. "'Mark Twain' in St. Louis. [No. XII.]" Letter dated 15 March. San Francisco *Alta California*, 13 May, 1. Reprinted in *MTTB*, 122–30.

1867u. "Letter from 'Mark Twain.' [No. XIII.]" Letter dated 25 March. San Francisco *Alta California*, 19 May, 1. Reprinted in *MTTB*, 131–40.

1867v. "Letter from 'Mark Twain.' [No. 14.]" Letter dated 16 April. San Francisco *Alta California*, 26 May, 1. Reprinted in *MTTB*, 141–48.

1867w. "Letter from 'Mark Twain.' [No. 15.]" Letter dated 19 April. San Francisco *Alta California*, 2 June, 1. Reprinted in part in *MTTB*, 149–58.

1867x. "Letter from 'Mark Twain.' [No. 16.]" Letter dated 30 April. San Francisco *Alta California*, 10 June, 1. Reprinted in *MTTB*, 159–66.

1867y. "Letter from 'Mark Twain.' [No. 17.]" Letter dated 17 May. San Francisco *Alta California*, 16 June, 1. Reprinted in *MTTB*, 167–79.

1867z. "Letter from 'Mark Twain.' [No. 18.]" Letter dated 18 May. San Francisco *Alta California*, 23 June, 1. Reprinted in part in *MTTB*, 180–91.

1867aa. "Letter from 'Mark Twain.' [No. 19.]" Letter dated 19 May. San Francisco *Alta California*, 30 June, 1. Reprinted in part in *MTTB*, 192–201.

1867bb. "Letter from 'Mark Twain.' [No. 20.]" Letter dated 20 May. San Francisco *Alta California*, 7 July, 1. Reprinted in *MTTB*, 202–13.

1867cc. "A Reminiscence of Artemus Ward." New York *Sunday Mercury*, 7 July, 3. Reprinted in *ET&S3*, no. 211.

1867dd. "Jim Wolf and the Tom-Cats." New York *Sunday Mercury*, 14 July, 3. Reprinted in *ET&S3*, no. 212.

1867ee. "Letter from 'Mark Twain.' [No. 21.]" Letter dated 23 May. San Francisco *Alta California*, 14 July, 1. Reprinted in *MTTB*, 214–25.

1867ff. "Letter from 'Mark Twain.' [No. 22.]" Letter dated 26 May. San Francisco *Alta California*, 21 July, 1. Reprinted in *MTTB*, 226–37.

1867gg. "Letter from 'Mark Twain.' [No. 23.]" Letter dated 28 May. San Francisco *Alta California*, 28 July, 1. Reprinted in *MTTB*, 238–48.

1867hh. "The Mediterranean Excursion." Letter dated 23 June. New York *Tribune*, 30 July, 2. Reprinted in *TIA*, 10–18.

1867ii. "Mark Twain in Quarantine." Letter dated 2 August. Naples *Observer*, 3 August, no page. Reprinted in the San Francisco *Alta California*, 16 September, 1, and in *TIA*, 74–76.

1867jj. "Letter from 'Mark Twain.' [No. 24.]" Letter dated 2 June. San Francisco *Alta California*, 4 August, 1. Reprinted in *MTTB*, 249–58.

1867kk. "Letter from 'Mark Twain.' [No. 25.]" Letter dated 5 June. San Francisco *Alta California*, 11 August, 1. Reprinted in *MTTB*, 259–69.

1867*ll*. "Letter from 'Mark Twain.' [Number 26.]" Letter dated 6 June. San Francisco *Alta California*, 18 August, 1. Reprinted in *MTTB*, 270–79.

1867mm. "The Holy Land Excursionists." Unsigned letter dated 1 August. New York *Herald*, 20 August, 1. Reprinted in Ganzel 1964, 271.

1867nn. "The Holy Land Excursionists." Unsigned letter dated 2 August. New York *Herald*, 22 August, 5. Reprinted in Ganzel 1964, 272.

1867oo. "The Holy Land Excursion. Letter from 'Mark Twain.' [Number One.]" Letter dated 19 June. San Francisco *Alta California*, 25 August, 1. Reprinted in *TIA*, 3–10.

1867pp. "The Holy Land Excursion. Letter from 'Mark Twain.' [Number Two.]" Letter dated 30 June. San Francisco *Alta California*, 27 August, 1. Reprinted in *TIA*, 18–25.

1867qq. "The Holy Land Excursion. Letter from 'Mark Twain.' [Number Three.]" Letter dated 1 July at "Tangier, Africa." San Francisco *Alta California*, 31 August, 1. Reprinted in *TIA*, 25–30.

1867rr. "The Holy Land Excursion. Letter from 'Mark Twain.' [Number

Four.]" Letter dated 1 July at "Tangier, Africa." San Francisco *Alta California*, 1 September, 1. Reprinted in *TIA*, 30–36.

1867ss. "The Holy Land Excursion. Letter from 'Mark Twain.' [Number Five.]" Letter dated 12 July. San Francisco *Alta California*, 5 September, 1. Reprinted in *TIA*, 36–41.

1867tt. "The Mediterranean Excursion." Letter dated July "At Large in Italy." New York *Tribune*, 6 September, 2. Reprinted in *TIA*, 72–74.

1867uu. "The Holy Land Excursion. Letter from 'Mark Twain.' [Number Six.]" Letter dated 16 July. San Francisco *Alta California*, 8 September, 1. Reprinted in *TIA*, 41–47.

1867vv. "The Holy Land Excursion. Letter from 'Mark Twain.' [Number Seven.]" Letter dated July at "Milan, Italy." San Francisco *Alta California*, 15 September, 1. Reprinted in *TIA*, 48–53.

1867ww. "The American Excursionists." Unsigned letter dated 27 August. New York *Herald*, 18 September, 7.

1867xx. "Americans on a Visit to the Emperor of Russia." Letter dated 26 August. New York *Tribune*, 19 September, 1. Reprinted in *TIA*, 142–50.

1867yy. "The Holy Land Excursion. Letter from 'Mark Twain.' [Number Eight.]" Letter dated July at "Lake of Como." San Francisco *Alta California*, 22 September, 1. Reprinted in *TIA*, 53–59.

1867zz. "The Holy Land Excursion. Letter from 'Mark Twain.' [Number Nine.]" Letter dated July "Abroad in Italy." San Francisco *Alta California*, 26 September, 1. Reprinted in *TIA*, 66–71.

1867aaa. "The Holy Land Excursion. Letter from 'Mark Twain.' [Number Ten.]" Letter dated August at "Naples, Italy." San Francisco *Alta California*, 29 September, 1. Reprinted in *TIA*, 76–83.

1867bbb. "The Holy Land Excursion. Letter from 'Mark Twain.' [Number Eleven.]" Letter dated August at "Naples." San Francisco *Alta California*, 1 October, 1. Reprinted in *TIA*, 83–89.

1867ccc. "The Holy Land Excursion. Letter from 'Mark Twain.' [Number Twelve.]" Letter dated August at "Naples." San Francisco *Alta California*, 6 October, 1. Reprinted in *TIA*, 89–94.

1867ddd. "The Holy Land Excursion. Letter from 'Mark Twain.' [Number Thirteen.]" Letter dated August at "Naples." San Francisco *Alta California*, 10 October, 1. Reprinted in *TIA*, 95–100.

1867eee. "The Holy Land Excursion. Letter from 'Mark Twain.' [Number Fourteen.]" Letter dated 29 July. San Francisco *Alta California*, 13 October, 1. Reprinted in *TIA*, 59–66.

1867fff. "The Holy Land Excursion. Letter from 'Mark Twain.' [Number Fifteen.]" Letter dated 15 August. San Francisco *Alta California*, 18 October, 1. Reprinted in *TIA*, 100–110.

1867ggg. "The Holy Land Excursion. Letter from 'Mark Twain.' [Number Sixteen.]" Letter dated 20 August. San Francisco *Alta California*, 20 October, 1. Reprinted in *TIA*, 110–15.

1867hhh. "The Holy Land Excursion. Letter from 'Mark Twain.' [Number Seventeen.]" Letter dated 23 August. San Francisco *Alta California*, 23 October, 1. Reprinted in *TIA*, 115–20.

1867iii. "A Yankee in the Orient." Letter dated 31 August. New York *Tribune*, 25 October, 2. Reprinted in *TIA*, 128–32.

1867jjj. "The Holy Land Excursion. Letter from 'Mark Twain.' [Number Eighteen.]" Letter dated August at "Constantinople." San Francisco *Alta California*, 27 October, 1. Reprinted in *TIA*, 120–23.

1867kkk. "The Holy Land Excursion. Letter from 'Mark Twain.' [Number Nineteen.]" Letter dated August at "Constantinople." San Francisco *Alta California*, 29 October, 1. Reprinted in *TIA*, 123–28.

1867*lll*. "The Holy Land Excursion. Letter from 'Mark Twain.' [Number Twenty.]" Letter dated 22 August at "Sebastopol." San Francisco *Alta California*, 1 November, 1. Reprinted in *TIA*, 132–37.

1867mmm. "The American Colony in Palestine." Letter dated 2 October. New York *Tribune*, 2 November, 2. Reprinted in *TIA*, 306–9.

1867nnn. "The Holy Land Excursion. Letter from 'Mark Twain.' [Number Twenty-one.]" Letter dated 22 August at "Odessa." San Francisco *Alta California*, 3 November, 1. Reprinted in *TIA*, 137–42.

1867ooo. "The Holy Land Excursion. Letter from 'Mark Twain.' [Number Twenty-two.]" Letter dated 27 August at "Yalta." San Francisco *Alta California*, 6 November, 1. Reprinted in *TIA*, 150–57.

1867ppp. "The Holy Land. First Day in Palestine." Letter dated September at "Baldwinsville, Galilee." New York *Tribune*, 9 November, 1. Reprinted in *TIA*, 209–13.

1867qqq. "The Holy Land Excursion. Letter from 'Mark Twain.' [Number Twenty-three.]" Letter dated 27 August at "Yalta, Russia." San Francisco *Alta California*, 10 November, 1. Reprinted in *TIA*, 157–63.

1867rrr. "The Holy Land Excursion. Letter from 'Mark Twain.' [Number Twenty-four.]" Letter dated 5 September. San Francisco *Alta California*, 17 November, 1. Reprinted in *TIA*, 163–68.

1867sss. "The Cruise of the Quaker City." Undated letter written 19 November. New York *Herald*, 20 November, 7. Reprinted in *TIA*, 313–19. Transcribed in Appendix E.

1867ttt. "The Holy Land Excursion. Letter from 'Mark Twain.' [Number Twenty-five.]" Letter dated 6 September. San Francisco *Alta California*, 21 November, 1. Reprinted in *TIA*, 168–72.

1867uuu. "The Holy Land Excursion. Letter from 'Mark Twain.' [Number Twenty-six.]" Letter dated 8 September. San Francisco *Alta California*, 24 November, 1. Reprinted in *TIA*, 173–78.

1867vvv. Untitled MS fragment of twenty-eight pages, written ca. 25 November, an unfinished play on the *Quaker City* excursion, InU-Li. Transcribed in Appendix E.

1867www. "The Holy Land Excursion. Letter from 'Mark Twain.' [Number Twenty-seven.]" Letter dated 11 September. San Francisco *Alta California*, 1 December, 1. Reprinted in *TIA*, 178–82.

1867xxx. "The Holy Land Excursion. Letter from 'Mark Twain.' [Number Twenty-eight.]" Letter dated 12 September. San Francisco *Alta California*, 4 December, 1. Reprinted in *TIA*, 183–88.

1867yyy. "The Holy Land Excursion. Letter from 'Mark Twain.' [Number Twenty-nine.]" Letter dated 17 September. San Francisco *Alta California*, 8 December, 1. Reprinted in *TIA*, 188–93.

1867zzz. "The Holy Land Excursion. Letter from 'Mark Twain.' [Number Thirty.]" Letter dated September at "Banias." San Francisco *Alta California*, 15 December, 1. Reprinted in *TIA*, 193–98.

1867aaaa. "A New Cabinet 'Regulator.'" Letter dated 14 December. Washington *Evening Star*, 16 December, 2. MS in Box 1, Crosby Noyes Boyd Papers, Manuscript Division, DLC.

1867bbbb. "Information Wanted." New York *Tribune*, 18 December, 2. Reprinted in *ET&S3*, no. 216.

1867cccc. "Letter from Mark Twain: The Facts in the Case of the Senate Doorkeeper." Letter dated 15 December. New York *Citizen*, 21 December, 1.

1867dddd. "The Holy Land Excursion. Letter from 'Mark Twain.' [Number Thirty-one.]" Letter dated September at "Banias." San Francisco *Alta California*, 22 December, 1. Reprinted in *TIA*, 198–204.

1867eeee. "Mark Twain's Letters from Washington. Number I." Letter dated 4 December. Virginia City *Territorial Enterprise*, 22 December, no page, PH in Willard S. Morse Collection, CtY-BR.

1867ffff. "The Facts Concerning the Recent Resignation." New York *Tribune*, 27 December, 2. Reprinted in *ET&S3*, no. 217.

1867gggg. "The Holy Land Excursion. Letter from 'Mark Twain.' [Number Thirty-two.]" Letter dated September at "Banias." San Francisco *Alta California*, 29 December, 1. Reprinted in *TIA*, 204–8.

1868a. "The Holy Land Excursion. Letter from 'Mark Twain.' [Number Thirty-three.]" Letter dated September 1867 at "Williamsburgh, Canaan." San Francisco *Alta California*, 5 January, 1. Reprinted in *TIA*, 213–19.

1868b. "Mark Twain's Letters from Washington. Number II." Letter dated 16 December 1867. Virginia City *Territorial Enterprise*, 7 January, no page, PH in Willard S. Morse Collection, CtY-BR.

1868c. "Letter from 'Mark Twain.' Home Again." Letter dated 20 November 1867 at "New York." San Francisco *Alta California*, 8 January, 1. Reprinted in *TIA*, 309–13.

1868d. Untitled MS fragments, totaling thirteen pages, written ca. 8–9 January as a draft for a lecture entitled "The Frozen Truth," catalogued as A13 (one page numbered 67) and A23 (three pages numbered 59–61 and nine pages numbered 71–79), NPV.

1868e. "Mark Twain's Letters from Washington. Number III." Letter dated 20 December 1867. Virginia City *Territorial Enterprise*, 11 January, 2.

1868f. "The Holy Land Excursion. Letter from 'Mark Twain.' [Number Thirty-four.]" Letter dated September 1867 at "Williamsburgh, Palestine." San Francisco *Alta California*, 12 January, 1. Reprinted in *TIA*, 219–25.

1868g. Untitled speech in response to the toast to "Woman," as reported in "Annual Banquet of the Corres[pon]dents' Club." Washington *Evening Star*, 13 January, 2. Reprinted in *ET&S3*, no. 218.

1868h. "Mark Twain in Washington. [Special Correspondence of the Alta California.]" Letter dated 10 December 1867. San Francisco *Alta California*, 15 January, 1.

1868i. "The Holy Land Excursion. Letter from 'Mark Twain.' [Number Thirty-five.]" Letter dated September 1867 at "Capernaum." San Francisco *Alta California*, 19 January, 1. Reprinted in *TIA*, 225–29.

1868j. ["Colloquy between a Slum Child and a Moral Mentor."] Untitled MS of fifteen pages, written ca. 20 January–March, catalogued as A15, NPV. Published in *FM*, 105–9, and *ET&S3*, no. 219.

1868k. "Letter from 'Mark Twain.' [Special Correspondent of the Alta California.]" Letter dated 14 December 1867. San Francisco *Alta California*, 21 January, 2.

1868*l*. "Information Wanted." Undated letter to the editor. New York *Tribune*, 22 January, 2.

1868m. "The Holy Land Excursion. Letter from 'Mark Twain.' [Number Thirty-six.]" Letter dated September 1867 at "Tiberias." San Francisco *Alta California*, 26 January, 1. Reprinted in *TIA*, 229–36.

1868n. "Mark Twain in Washington. [Special Correspondent of the Alta California.]" Letter dated 17 December 1867. San Francisco *Alta California*, 28 January, 2.

1868o. "Mark Twain's Letters from Washington. Number IV." Letter dated 10 January. Virginia City *Territorial Enterprise*, 30 January, 2.

1868p. "General Washington's Negro Body-Servant. A Biographical Sketch." *Galaxy* 5 (February): 154–56. Reprinted in *ET&S3*, no. 220.

1868q. "The Holy Land Excursion. Letter from 'Mark Twain.' [Number Thirty-seven.]" Letter dated September 1867 at "Nazareth." San Francisco *Alta California*, 2 February, 1. Reprinted in *TIA*, 236–42.

1868r. "Gossip at the National Capital. Special Correspondence of the Herald." Letter dated 1 February. New York *Herald*, 3 February, 5.

1868s. "Mark Twain in Washington. [Special Correspondent of the Alta California.]" Letter dated 11 January. San Francisco *Alta California*, 5 February, 2.

1868t. "Letter from Mark Twain." Letter dated 31 January. Chicago *Republican*, 8 February, 2.

1868u. "The Holy Land Excursion. Letter from 'Mark Twain.' [Number Thirty-eight.]" Letter dated September 1867 at "Nazareth." San Francisco *Alta California*, 9 February, 1. Reprinted in *TIA*, 242–48.

1868v. "Washington Gossip. Special Correspondence of the Herald." Letter dated 8 February. New York *Herald*, 10 February, 8.

1868w. "Mark Twain in Washington. [Delayed Letter.]" Letter dated 23 December 1867. San Francisco *Alta California*, 11 February, 1.

1868x. "The Facts Concerning the Recent Important Resignation." Letter dated 9 February. New York *Tribune*, 13 February, 2.

1868y. "Mark Twain in Washington. [Special Correspondent of the Alta California.]" Letter dated 16 January. San Francisco *Alta California*, 14 February, 2.

1868z. "The Holy Land Excursion. Letter from 'Mark Twain.' [Number

Thirty-nine.]" Letter dated September 1867 at "Nazareth." San Francisco *Alta California*, 16 February, 1. Reprinted in *TIA*, 248–54.

1868aa. "Mark Twain's Letters from Washington. Number V." Letter dated 11 January. Virginia City *Territorial Enterprise*, 18 February, 2.

1868bb. "Washington Gossip. Special Correspondence of the Herald." Letter dated 15 February. New York *Herald*, 18 February, 3.

1868cc. "Mark Twain in New York. [Special Correspondence of the Enterprise.]" Letter dated 20 January. Virginia City *Territorial Enterprise*, 19 February, 2.

1868dd. "Mark Twain in Washington. [Special Travelling Correspondent of the Alta.]" Letter dated 12 January. San Francisco *Alta California*, 19 February, 1.

1868ee. "Mark Twain's Letter." Letter dated 14 February. Chicago *Republican*, 19 February, 2.

1868ff. "The Holy Land Excursion. Letter from 'Mark Twain.' [Number Forty-three.]" Letter dated September 1867 "At Large in Palestine." San Francisco *Alta California*, 23 February, 1. Reprinted in *TIA*, 254–60.

1868gg. "Mark Twain's Letters from Washington. Number VII." Letter dated 30 January. Virginia City *Territorial Enterprise*, 27 February, 2.

1868hh. "The Holy Land Excursion. Letter from 'Mark Twain.' [Number Forty-four.]" Letter dated September 1867 at "Jerusalem." San Francisco *Alta California*, 1 March, 1. Reprinted in *TIA*, 260–66.

1868ii. "Mark Twain's Letter." Letter dated 21 February. Chicago *Republican*, 1 March, 2.

1868jj. "Mark Twain's Letters from Washington. Number VIII." Letter dated 5 February. Virginia City *Territorial Enterprise*, 1 March, 2.

1868kk. "Mark Twain on His Travels. [Special Correspondent of the Alta California.]" Letter dated 1 February. San Francisco *Alta California*, 3 March, 1.

1868*ll*. "Mark Twain's Letters from Washington. Number IX." Letter dated February. Virginia City *Territorial Enterprise*, 7 March, 1.

1868mm. "The Holy Land Excursion. Letter from 'Mark Twain.' [Number Forty-five.]" Letter dated September 1867 at "Jerusalem." San Francisco *Alta California*, 8 March, 1. Reprinted in *TIA*, 266–72.

1868nn. "The Chinese Mission." Undated letter to the editor. New York *Tribune*, 11 March, 2.

1868oo. "Mark Twain's Letters from Washington. Number X." Letter dated 22 February. Virginia City *Territorial Enterprise*, 13 March, 1.

1868pp. "The Holy Land Excursion. Letter from 'Mark Twain.' [Number Forty-six.]" Letter dated September 1867 at "Jerusalem." San Francisco *Alta California*, 15 March, 1. Reprinted in *TIA*, 272–77.

1868qq. "The Holy Land Excursion. Letter from 'Mark Twain.' [Number Forty-seven.]" Letter dated September 1867 at "Jerusalem." San Francisco *Alta California*, 22 March, 1. Reprinted in *TIA*, 277–81.

1868rr. "The Holy Land Excursion. Letter from 'Mark Twain.' [Number Forty-eight.]" Letter dated September 1867 at "Jerusalem." San Francisco *Alta California*, 29 March, 1. Reprinted in *TIA*, 281–87.

1868ss. "The Holy Land Excursion. Letter from 'Mark Twain.' [Number Fifty-two.]" Letter dated September 1867 at "Jerusalem." San Francisco *Alta California*, 5 April, 1. Reprinted in *TIA*, 302–6.

1868tt. "Mark Twain's Letters from Washington. Number XI." Letter dated 2 March. Virginia City *Territorial Enterprise*, 7 April, 1.

1868uu. "The Holy Land Excursion. Letter from 'Mark Twain.' [Number Fifty-three.]" Letter dated September 1867 at "Jerusalem." San Francisco *Alta California*, 12 April, 1. Reprinted in *TIA*, 287–91.

1868vv. "The Holy Land Excursion. Letter from 'Mark Twain.' [Number Fifty-four.]" Letter dated September 1867 at "Jerusalem." San Francisco *Alta California*, 26 April, 1. Reprinted in *TIA*, 291–96.

1868ww. "My Late Senatorial Secretaryship." *Galaxy* 5 (May): 633–36. Reprinted in *ET&S3*, no. 226.

1868xx. Untitled MS fragment of nineteen pages, written in early May, a discussion of Christian dogma, catalogued as A11, NPV.

1868yy. "The Holy Land Excursion. Letter from 'Mark Twain.' [Number Fifty-one.]" Letter dated September 1867 at "Jerusalem." San Francisco *Alta California*, 17 May, 1. Reprinted in *TIA*, 296–301.

1868zz. "I Rise to a Question of Privilege." MS of fifteen pages, written ca. 18–23 May for the San Francisco *News Letter and California Advertiser*, although left unpublished, a discussion of reverence versus ridicule, catalogued as A15, NPV. Published in *ET&S3*, no. 227.

1868aaa. "Letter from Mark Twain." Letter dated 1 May. Chicago *Republican*, 19 May, 2.

1868bbb. Untitled MS fragment of two pages, written 20 May, an obituary of Colonel J. Heron Foster drafted as a footnote for SLC 1869a, chapter 20, catalogued as A7, NPV.

1868ccc. "Letter from Mark Twain." Letter dated 2 May. Chicago *Republican*, 31 May, 2.

1868ddd. Untitled MS fragment, five pages numbered 959–63, written ca. 1–15 June as part of SLC 1869a, chapter 46, but not included in the published book, a discussion of the Bible, catalogued as A26, NPV.

1868eee. "Important to Whom It May Concern." San Francisco *News Letter and California Advertiser*, 13 June, 8, CSf. Reprinted in *ET&S3*, no. 230.

1868fff. Untitled MS fragment of twenty-seven pages, written ca. 15–30 June, a discussion of Christian dogma, catalogued as A20, NPV.

1868ggg. Untitled MS fragment, three pages numbered 1256–58, plus the versos of 1257 and 1258, written ca. 17 June as working notes and a draft of the passage published in SLC 1869a, chapter 58, 628–30, a description of the Sphinx, catalogued as A27, NPV.

1868hhh. Untitled MS fragment, forty-three pages numbered 1289–1331, written ca. 17–23 June as part of SLC 1869a, chapter 59, but not included in the published book, a description of the week in Spain, catalogued as A27, NPV.

1868iii. "The Public to Mark Twain." Handbill dated 30 June in San Francisco, PH in CU-MARK.

1868jjj. "By Rail through France." *Overland Monthly* 1 (July): 18–21.

1868kkk. "The Treaty with China." New York *Tribune*, 4 August, 1–2.

1868*lll*. "Letter from Mark Twain." Letter dated 17 August. Chicago *Republican*, 23 August, 2.

1868mmm. "Letter from 'Mark Twain.' Number One." Letter dated August at "Hartford, Conn." San Francisco *Alta California*, 6 September, 1.

1868nnn. Untitled MS fragment of forty-one pages: one page unnumbered, the rest numbered 7–8 and 20–57, written ca. 7 October, a draft of "The American Vandal Abroad" lecture, CU-MARK. Published in part, with variants, in *MTSpk*, 27–36.

1868ooo. "Letter from 'Mark Twain.'" Letter dated 22 October. San Francisco *Alta California*, 15 November, 1.

1868ppp. "A Mystery." Cleveland *Herald*, 16 November, 2. Reprinted in *ET&S3*, no. 233.

1868qqq. "Letter from 'Mark Twain.'" Letter dated 28 October. San Francisco *Alta California*, 22 November, 1.

1868rrr. "Concerning Gen. Grant's Intentions." New York *Tribune*, 12 December, 4.

1869a. *The Innocents Abroad; or, The New Pilgrims' Progress*. Hartford: American Publishing Company.

1869b. "Scenery." MS of eleven pages, written ca. July as part of a lecture to be called "Curiosities of California," catalogued as DV17, CU-MARK. Published in *ET&S4*, no. 236.

1870. "Riley—Newspaper Correspondent." *Galaxy* 10 (November): 726–27.

1872. *Roughing It*. Hartford: American Publishing Company.

1877. Letter to the editor dated 14 February. New York *World*, 18 February, 5.

1884. "Ye Equinoctial Storm." *Wasp* 12 (19 January): 2. Written ca. 19 March–2 April 1868, but first printed in 1884; the present location of the MS is unknown. Reprinted in *ET&S3*, no. 224.

1889."Mark Twain. An Interview with the Famous Humorist." New York *Herald*, 19 May, 19.

[1900]. "Scraps from My Autobiography." MS of forty-two pages, CU-MARK. Published in *MTA*, 1:125–43.

1903–4. Notebook 46, CU-MARK. Published in part in *MTN*, 383–90.

1904. "Notes on 'Innocents Abroad.'" Autobiographical Dictation, TS of thirteen pages numbered 68–80, written in April, CU-MARK. Published in *MTA*, 1:238–46.

1907. Marginalia on frontispiece of SLC's copy of Stephen M. Griswold, inscribed "S L. Clemens | 1907" on the front endpaper, CU-MARK.

1927. *The Quaker City Holy Land Excursion. An Unfinished Play by Mark Twain, 1867*. New York: Privately printed for M. Harzof.

1977. "Mark Twain's [1908] Speech for the Benefit of the Bermuda Hospital." *Bermuda Historical Quarterly* 34 (Autumn): 54–59.

Smiley, James Bethuel [Mrs. Julia M. Bradley, pseud.].

1889. *Modern Manners and Social Forms*. Chicago: James B. Smiley.

Smith, James H.
1880. *History of Chenango and Madison Counties, New York, with Illustrations and Biographical Sketches of Some of Its Prominent Men and Pioneers*. Syracuse: D. Mason and Co.

Sotheby.
1932. *The Property of the Late Mrs. E. A. Beardsley*. Sale of 27 June. London: Sotheby and Co.

Sotheby Parke Bernet.
1974. *The William E. Stockhausen Collection of English & American Literature, Part 1*. Sale no. 3694 (19 and 20 November). New York: Sotheby Parke Bernet.

1976. *The Katharine de B. Parsons Collection*. Sale no. 3901 (6 October). New York: Sotheby Parke Bernet.

Spaeth, Sigmund.
1948. *A History of Popular Music in America*. New York: Random House.

Startsev, A.
1942. "Sem'desiat piat' let tomu nazad" [Seventy-five years ago]. *Oktiabr'* 10 (July): 117–27.

State Department.
1869. *Register of the Department of State, for the Year 1869–'70*. Washington, D.C.: Government Printing Office.

Stern, Madeleine B., ed.
1980. *Publishers for Mass Entertainment in Nineteenth Century America*. Boston: G. K. Hall and Co.

Stewart, George R.
1941. "Bret Harte upon Mark Twain in 1866." *American Literature* 13 (November): 263–64.

Stewart, William M.
1908. *Reminiscences of Senator William M. Stewart*. Edited by George Rothwell Brown. New York: Neale Publishing Company.

Stoddard, Charles Warren.
1866. "My Friend." New York *Weekly Review*, 15 September, 1.

Stoddard, Henry Luther.
1946. *Horace Greeley: Printer, Editor, Crusader*. New York: G. P. Putnam's Sons.

Strong, Leah A.
1966. *Joseph Hopkins Twichell: Mark Twain's Friend and Pastor*. Athens: University of Georgia Press.

Tennyson, Alfred.
1847. *The Princess; A Medley*. London: Edward Moxon.

1862. *Poems*. London: Edward Moxon.

Thompson, Noyes L.
1873. *The History of Plymouth Church. (Henry Ward Beecher) 1847 to 1872*. New York: G. W. Carleton and Co.

Thomson, William McClure.
[1859]. *The Land and the Book; or, Biblical Illustrations Drawn from the Manners and Customs, the Scenes and Scenery of the Holy Land.* 2 vols. New York: Harper and Brothers.

Thorpe, T. B.
1871. "The New York Custom-House." *Harper's New Monthly Magazine* 43 (June): 11–26.

TIA
1958. *Traveling with the Innocents Abroad: Mark Twain's Original Reports from Europe and the Holy Land.* Edited by Daniel Morley McKeithan. Norman: University of Oklahoma Press.

Towner, Ausburn.
1892. *Our County and Its People: A History of the Valley and County of Chemung from the Closing Years of the Eighteenth Century.* Syracuse, N.Y.: D. Mason and Co.

Townsend, Malcolm, comp.
1895. *The Townsend's.* New York: Mooney and Co.

Trumbull, James Hammond, ed.
1886. *The Memorial History of Hartford County, Connecticut: 1633–1884.* 2 vols. Boston: Edward L. Osgood.

TS Typescript.

Tsai, Shih-Shan Henry.
1983. *China and the Overseas Chinese in the United States, 1868–1911.* Fayetteville: University of Arkansas Press.

TxU Harry Ransom Humanities Research Center, University of Texas, Austin.

UCCL
1986. *Union Catalog of Clemens Letters.* Edited by Paul Machlis. Berkeley, Los Angeles, London: University of California Press.

Upton, Matthias (Matthew) Gilbert.
1867a. "Letter from New York." Letter dated 1 January. San Francisco *Alta California*, 3 February, 1.

1867b. "Letter from Washington." Letter dated 12 January. San Francisco *Alta California*, 11 February, 1.

1867c. "The Way Home." Letter dated 28 August. San Francisco *Alta California*, 13 September, 2.

Vandal [pseud.].
1869. "Funny." Pittsburgh *Post*, 3 November, 1.

Van Deusen, Glyndon G.
1953. *Horace Greeley: Nineteenth-Century Crusader.* Philadelphia: University of Pennsylvania Press.

Van Tassel, David D., and John J. Grabowski, eds.
1987. *Encyclopedia of Cleveland History.* Bloomington: Indiana University Press.

Virginia City Census
[1880] 1969. "Inhabitants in . . . Virginia." *Population Schedules of the Tenth Census of the United States, 1880. Roll 759. Nevada: Nye, Ormsby, Roop, Storey, Washoe, and White Pine Counties.* National Archives Microfilm Publications, Microcopy no. T9. Washington, D.C.: General Services Administration.

ViU Clifton Waller Barrett Library, Alderman Library, University of Virginia, Charlottesville.

Walker, Franklin.
1969. *San Francisco's Literary Frontier.* Seattle: University of Washington Press.

Wallace, Lew, et al.
1889. *Living Leaders of the World: Comprising Graphic Biographies of the Men and Women of Greatest Eminence, Influence, Wealth, Power or Fame.* Chicago: Hubbard Bros.

Wallace, Robert D.
n.d. " 'A Gentleman of Some Notoriety': Mark Twain Speaks in Illinois." TS in CU-MARK.

Walpole Galleries.
1924. *A Collection . . . Relating to the Drama.* Sale no. 327 (22 May). New York: Walpole Galleries.

Way, Frederick, Jr.
1983. *Way's Packet Directory, 1848–1983.* Athens, Ohio: Ohio University.

Webb, Charles Henry [Inigo, pseud.].
1866. "Inigoings." Letter dated 30 May. *Californian* 5 (30 June): 9.
1867. "Letter from Twain's Publisher." Letter to the editor dated 9 May. Brooklyn *Eagle*, 11 May, 3.

Webster, Annie Moffett.
1949. "Recollections of the Clemens Family in St. Louis When Sam Was a River Pilot." *Twainian* 8 (March–April): 1–2.

Webster's New Geographical Dictionary
1988. *Webster's New Geographical Dictionary.* Springfield, Mass.: G. and C. Merriam Company.

Wecter, Dixon.
1947. "The Love Letters of Mark Twain." *Atlantic Monthly* 180 (November): 33–39.

Wentworth, Harold, and Stuart Berg Flexner, comps. and eds.
1960. *Dictionary of American Slang.* New York: Thomas Y. Crowell Company.

Whitfield Collection of Mrs. Theodore Whitfield, a descendant of William R. Denny.

Whitney, Orson F.
1893. *History of Utah.* 4 vols. Salt Lake City: George Q. Cannon and Sons.

Whitney, William Dwight, and Benjamin E. Smith, eds.
1889. *The Century Dictionary: An Encyclopedic Lexicon of the English Language.* 6 vols. New York: Century Company.

Who Was Who
1943. *Who Was Who in America. A Companion Volume to Who's Who in America. Vol. 1: 1897–1942.* Chicago: A. N. Marquis Company.

Wilkins, William Glyde.
1912. *Charles Dickens in America.* New York: Charles Scribner's Sons.

"William Mason Family"
n.d. "William Mason Family." TS of records in a family Bible, Chenango County Historical Society, Norwich, N.Y., PH in CU-MARK.

Williams, Frederick Wells.
1912. *Anson Burlingame and the First Chinese Mission to Foreign Powers.* New York: Charles Scribner's Sons.

Wilson, H., comp.
1855. *Wilson's Business Directory of New York City.* New York: John F. Trow.

1866. *Trow's New York City Directory, . . . Vol. LXXX. For the Year Ending May 1, 1867.* New York: John F. Trow.

1867. *Trow's New York City Directory, . . . Vol. LXXXI. For the Year Ending May 1, 1868.* New York: John F. Trow.

1868. *Trow's New York City Directory, . . . Vol. LXXXII. For the Year Ending May 1, 1869.* New York: John F. Trow.

Wilson, Rufus Rockwell, and Otilie Erickson Wilson.
1947. *New York in Literature.* Elmira, N.Y.: Primavera Press.

Wiltshire Collection of Timothy Wiltshire.

WIM
1973. *What Is Man? and Other Philosophical Writings.* Edited by Paul Baender. The Works of Mark Twain. Berkeley, Los Angeles, London: University of California Press.

Winter, William.
1909. *Old Friends: Being Literary Recollections of Other Days.* New York: Moffat, Yard and Co.

Winterich, John T.
1930. "The Life and Works of Bloodgood Haviland Cutter." *The Colophon: A Book Collectors' Quarterly.* Vol. 1, pt. 2 (May): no page numbers.

Woodworth, Samuel.
1831. *Melodies, Duets, Trios, Songs, and Ballads, Pastoral, Amatory, Sentimental, Patriotic, Religious, and Miscellaneous.* 3d ed. New York: Elliot and Palmer.

WU Memorial Library, University of Wisconsin, Madison.

WWD
1967. *Mark Twain's Which Was the Dream? and Other Symbolic Writings of the Later Years.* Edited by John S. Tuckey. The Mark Twain Papers. Berkeley and Los Angeles: University of California Press.

Young, James Harvey.
1952. "Anna Dickinson, Mark Twain, and Bret Harte." *Pennsylvania Magazine of History and Biography* 76 (January): 39–46.

Young, John Russell.
1868. "Illuminated Diary for 1868." Box 36, John Russell Young Papers, Manuscript Division, DLC, transcript in CU-MARK.

Index

THE FOLLOWING have not been indexed: citations and cross-references, fictional characters, Editorial Signs, Guide to Editorial Practice, and Textual Commentaries. Place names are included when they refer to locations that Clemens lived in, visited, or commented upon, but are excluded when mentioned only in passing.

Alphabetizing is *word-by-word*, except for the following. (1) When persons, places, and things share the same name, they are indexed in that order: thus "Ajax" the correspondent precedes "*Ajax*" the ship. (2) Formal titles (Mr., Mrs., Dr., and so forth) may be included with a name, but are ignored when alphabetizing. (3) When the subheading "letters to," "letters from," or "note to" appears, it *precedes* all other subheadings; when the subheading "mentioned" appears, it *follows* all other subheadings.

Recipients of Clemens's letters are listed in **boldface type;** boldface numbers (**146n5**) designate principal identifications. Numbers linked by an ampersand (343 & 347n6) indicate that the allusion in the letter text is not explicit, and can best be located by reading the note first. Works written by Mark Twain are indexed separately by title *and* under "Clemens, Samuel Langhorne: works," as well as, when appropriate, under the publishing journal. Works written by others are indexed both by title and by author's name. Newspapers are indexed by their location (city or town), other periodicals by title.

The text of this book is set in Mergenthaler Linotype Plantin. Headings are in Plantin Light. Plantin was originally designed for the Monotype Company by F. H. Pierpont in 1913. The paper is Perkins & Squier High Opaque Offset, acid free, manufactured by the P. H. Glatfelter Company. The book was composed by Wilsted & Taylor Publishing Services of Oakland, California, using Data General Nova 4c and Nova 4x computers, Penta software, and a Linotron 202 typesetter. It was printed and bound by Maple-Vail Book Manufacturing Group in Binghamton, New York.

MONTGOMERY COLLEGE LIBRARIES
0 0000 00482601 2

DATE DUE